MYTHOPOESIS

MYTHOPOESIS

Mythic Patterns in the Literary Classics

by **Harry Slochower**

Wayne State University Press   Detroit, 1970

To my daughter Joyce

Contents

Illustrations   8
Acknowledgments   9
Preface—Mythopoesis: The Tradition of Creativity   12
Introduction   19
Hebrew Memory of a Chosen God: The Book of Job   47
—Greek Mythopoesis: The Blessed Crime—
    Aeschylus, Sophocles, Euripides   67
The Catholic Vision of Divine Harmony: *The Divine Comedy*   103
The Golden Age of Chivalric Honor: *Don Quixote*   132
Renaissance Mythopoesis: *Hamlet*   154
Teutonic Inwardness: *Faust*   178
The Quest for an American Myth: *Moby Dick*   223
The Pan-Slavic Image of the Earth Mother:
    The Brothers Karamazov   246
The Marxist Homage to Creative Labor: *Pelle the Conqueror*   284
The French Myth of the Living Social Chain:
    André Gide's *Theseus*   290
Contemporary Myth of the Impersonal Antagonist: Franz Kafka   298
The Existentialist Myth: The Value of Homelessness—
    The Myth of Sisyphus and *The Flies*   302
Threat and Promise in Germanic Insulation:
    The Magic Mountain and *Doctor Faustus*   312
Conclusion   327
Appendices
   I. Primitive and Oriental Mythology   332
  II. A Note on the Prometheus of Shelley and Goethe   339
 III. A Note on Virgil's *Aeneid*   340
 IV. A Note on Eissler's *Goethe*   341
  V. A Note on Mark Twain and Walt Whitman   343
 VI. Freud's Analysis of a Katya Figure   345
VII. Appendix to the Conclusion—Related Philosophic
    Attitudes   349
Index   357

Illustrations

facing Page

1. *Book of Job*, Plate 17, "I have heard of thee with the hearing
   of the Ear but now my Eye seeth thee" by William Blake   96
2. *Oedipus Consulting the Sphinx* by J. A. Ingres   97
3. *Dante and Virgil* by Eugene Delacroix   112
4. *Faust, Marguerite and Mephistopheles in the Street*, lithograph illustration to Goethe's *Faust*   113
5. *Jonah*, by Albert Pinkham Ryder   192
6. *Don Quixote Crossing the Mountain*, by Honoré Daumier   193
7. *Assyrian Sun God Pursuing the Demon of Chaos*   208
8. *The Enigma of a Day* by Giorgio De Chirico   209

Acknowledgments

I AM INDEBTED to the Bollingen Foundation which helped further these studies.

Many of the ideas in this book were stimulated by discussions with my students at Brooklyn College, The New School, The William Alanson White Institute and Drew University.

I am grateful for permission to quote from articles of mine which appeared in the following publications:

American Quarterly II:3 (Fall, 1950): "*Moby Dick*: Myth of Democratic Expectancy." Copyright, 1950, Trustees of the University of Pennsylvania.

The Chicago Jewish Forum (Fall, 1951): "Hebrew Myth of a Chosen God."

Complex (Fall, 1950): "Freudian Motifs in Moby Dick"; (Spring, 1952), "Oedipus: Fromm or Freud."

Drew Gateway (Winter, 1954): "The Divine Comedy as Mythopoesis."

Grune & Stratton, Inc.: "Psychoanalysis and Literature," in *Progress in Clinical Psychology*, IV (1960).

International Record of Medicine, 171 (December, 1958): 761: "The Book of Job: Its Symbolism and Psychoanalytic Process."

Manas (August, 1961), "Man's Creative Potential."

Yale French Studies (Spring, 1948): "The Function of Myth in Existentialism"; (December, 1949), "André Gide's *Theseus* and the French Myth."

And I also wish to make acknowledgment to the following for permission to reprint:

Basic Books Inc., Publishers, New York: from Chapter 9, Volume IV; from Chapter 21, Volume V of *The Collected Papers of Sigmund Freud*, edited by Ernest Jones, M.D.

Gioia Bernheim and Edmund R. Brill: The material in note 3, Appendix VI is from *The Basic Writings of Sigmund Freud,* translated and edited by Dr. A. A. Brill, copyright 1938 by Random House, Inc. Copyright renewed 1965 by Gioia B. Bernheim and Edmund R. Brill.

The Clarendon Press, Oxford: Dante, *Convivio,* trans. W. W. Jackson (1947); Euripides, *Bacchae,* 2d ed., trans. E. R. Dodds (1960).

J. M. Dent & Sons Ltd.: Dante, *De Monarchia,* Temple Classics edition (1947).

The Dial Press, Inc.: *The Short Novels of Dostoevsky,* Introduction by Thomas Mann (1945).

Farrar, Straus & Giroux, Inc.: *The Golden Ass of Apuleius,* trans. and Introduction by Robert Graves. Copyright 1951 by Farrar, Straus & Young, Inc.; Theodore Reik, *Ritual: Four Psychoanalytic Studies.* Copyright 1946 by Grove Press, Inc.

Harcourt, Brace & World, Inc.: *Heinrich Heine: Paradox and Poet,* Vol. II: *The Poems,* ed. and trans. Louis Untermeyer (1937); Carl Sandburg, *The People, Yes* (1936).

The Hogarth Press Ltd.: Freud, *Collected Papers,* ed. James Strachey, Vol. V (1950).

The Hogarth Press Ltd., Sigmund Freud Copyrights Ltd., and The Institute of Psycho-Analysis: Freud, *Standard Edition,* rev. and ed. by James Strachey, Vol. IX: "Creative Writers and Day-Dreaming" (1959), Vol. XVIII: *Group Psychology and the Analysis of the Ego* (1955), Vol. XXI: "Dostoevsky and Parricide" (1961), Vol. XXII: *Moses and Monotheism* (1964).

Liveright Publishing Corp.: Freud, *Group Psychology and the Analysis of the Ego, Standard Edition,* Vol. XVIII (1955).

W. W. Norton & Co., Inc. and Routledge and Kegan Paul Ltd.: Freud, *Totem and Taboo, Standard Edition,* Vol. XIII (1955).

Philosophical Library: Jean-Paul Sartre, *Existentialism,* trans. Bernard Frechtman (1947).

Random House, Inc., Alfred A. Knopf, Inc.: Albert Camus, *The Myth of Sisyphus and Other Essays,* trans. Justin O'Brien (1959); *The Complete Greek Drama,* ed. W. J. Oates, and Eugene O'Neill, Jr. (1938 and renewed 1966); Dostoevsky, *The Brothers Karamazov,* trans. Constance Garnett (1950); Freud, *Moses and Monotheism, Standard Edition,* Vol. XXII (1964); André Gide, *Two Legends: Oedipus, Theseus,* trans. John Russell (1950); Goethe, *Faust,* trans. Bayard Taylor; Franz Kafka, *The Trial,* trans. Willa and Edwin Muir (1937); Thomas Mann, *Doctor Faustus,* trans. H. T. Lowe-

Porter (1948), *Joseph and His Brothers*, trans. H. T. Lowe-Porter (1948), *The Magic Mountain*, trans. H. T. Lowe-Porter (1927 and renewed 1955); Otto Rank, *The Myth of the Birth of the Hero* (1959); Jean-Paul Sartre, *No Exit and Three Other Plays*, trans. Stuart Gilbert.

The Society of Authors as the literary representative of the Estate of Laurence Binyon: Dante, *The Divine Comedy*, trans. Laurence Binyon (1947).

The Viking Press, Inc.: Cervantes, *The Ingenious Gentleman Don Quixote de la Mancha*, trans. Samuel Putnam. Copyright 1949 by The Viking Press, Inc.

Preface
Mythopoesis: The Tradition of Creativity

THIS BOOK IS based on the persuasion that, despite the agonizing conflicts and inhibiting forces of our day, man's creative impulse can be quickened by looking back towards the tradition of creativity embodied in mythopoesis from the Book of Job to *Joseph and His Brothers*.

Ours is an alienated and an alienating era. This condition is not only attributable to dislocations in our socio-economic relations. The hunger for bread is gradually being met by the development of technology which is liberating the energies of our natural resources. But there is a deeper hunger which is not being satisfied by these achievements. It is the hunger to be oneself, to be creative.

The present holds a special threat to individual autonomy. The fateful question today is this: How do I prevent my self from being flattened by the system, the machine, "integrated" with the party, the committee, the organization? How can I feel and say "*I* exist?" This burning question is opened up to Mitya Karamazov in his prison cell. "You wouldn't believe," he tells his brother Alexey,

> how I want to live now, what a thirst for existence and consciousness has sprung up in me within these peeling walls . . . . And I seem to have such strength in me now, that I think I could stand anything, any suffering, only to be able to say and to repeat to myself every moment, "I exist." In thousands of agonies—"I exist!" I'm tormented on the rack—but I exist! Though I sit alone in a pillar—"I exist!"

Today, the individual, particularly the creative artist, writer, and scientist, feels himself to be in a kind of prison, the prison of impersonal authorities. The problem of creativity is immense in our time because of the difficulty of identifying with creative models. The egalitarian fashion, supported by the standard of mechanical uniformity, discourages the emergence of "personalities" who kindle our enthusiasm by virtue of what they are.

"Identification," in our day, is molded by forces which make for a coordination in which the individual feels left out and alone. Our "communication media" foster an automatic response from the viewer. Radio and television inform, evaluate, and interpret, even supply us with ready-made imagery and feelings. Automation "integrates" to the point of wiping out indigenous folk-roots and folkways, stamping out personal insignia. It makes for little and hollow men, for Mr. and Mrs. Zeroes, for dead salesmen, for the naked and the dead. Over all rules the organization man who puts everything into a uniform.

The hope that technical power with its resultant increase of material goods and leisure would bring gladness of heart is withering away. Indeed, many feel that these very "goods" tend to increase spiritual and emotional tensions. Thermonuclear energy could turn deserts into gardens, but it can also turn gardens into deserts. Here, contemporary man faces an impersonal power of incalculable and universal dimension, a diabolical power that could be unleashed by a single individual pushing a gadget. Gadgets ride man today, conditioning the feverish rhythm and directionless pace of his life. They determine his "other-directed" needs and wants, distorting his personal needs and wants.

Some react to this situation by passive withdrawal, others by the rage of the angry young men and the defiant beatniks. Where the individual can find no organic attachments to the demands of the day, he tends to succumb to the devil's two major temptations: lethargy and dullness or violence and frenzy.

Are these the sole alternatives open to us? To become part of the "mass-cult," to merge with what Ernst Toller called the *Massemensch?* Or else vainly to seek the blessed isles which are surely becoming extinct? Both of these alternatives are at odds with the kind of life we hope for and dream about, are at odds with what ancient prophets, seers, artists, poets and mythmakers have envisioned.

The machine and leisure in themselves cannot be held responsible for our spiritual "malaise." It is true that the corruption of our economic-social-political relations contributes to the corroding of our motives, to the reigning attitude of "what's in it for me?" However, on a deeper level, the difficulty is nurtured by our obsession with the immediate present, the latest fashion, the *nunc et stans.* But, by itself, "news on the hour" can offer no direction, no purpose or goal. It produces what Thomas Mann once called "futurism without a future." It has no future because—and this anticipates the argument of the book—it lacks the vision of values created in the past by our living mythic tradition. Without such a basic platform, the satisfactions of technology are not humanly adequate. We remain restless, nervous, irritable.

This study points to an alternative identification that could counter-act this gloomy outlook, an identification with the symbolic values of our mythic heroes as fashioned in the outstanding literary classics. This mythic hero is not the average, nor the common denominator of human-ity. Neither is he the aristocratic individual disconnected from what is common to man. He is close to the *elemental* sources of life, but repre-sents them in their higher, wider and deeper phases. In the study and "imitation" of mythic heroes, of Job, Prometheus, Oedipus, Virgil and Dante, of Don Quixote, Hamlet, Faust, Mitya Karamazov, and Captain Ahab, yes, even of contemporary heroes, of Nexö's Pelle, Thomas Mann's Joseph and Gide's Theseus, lies the hope for the revival of creativity.

According to Greek legend, Memory was the Mother of the Muses. Mythology draws on our oldest memories, and it has always fascinated the common man, as well as the artist, writer and thinker. In the form of a picture, a story or a song, myth touches on man's basic relation to his world and fellow men, on his original roots, his future possibilities and destiny. Myth has cast a spell on the very ages which denied or opposed it. Like the severed head of Orpheus, it "goes on singing even in death and from afar."[1]

The perennial appeal and vitality of mythic thinking stem from the fact that it makes us feel that in all civilizations men face analogous sit-uations, undergo similar experiences. Myth draws on these underlying correspondences which inevitably make for One World. Men, writes William E. Hocking, "must loyally remember. . .if only to retain their identity. . .must be united in their sense of destiny to which their journey points." Myth supplies "a symbolic memory and a symbolic hope, and an allegorized account of the perils of the way."[2]

In sum: the myth unfolds the living chain which connects the re-current recognition scenes of the human drama. They assure us that we are not strangers and alone in the world.

MYTHOLOGY AND MYTHOPOESIS

The subject matter of this study is not the myth as such, nor the mythologies, such as we have in Ovid, Hesiod and others which relate the adventures of gods, titans and heroes, giving us multiple variations

14

of plots. This book deals with mythopoesis. It examines those myths which have seized the imagination of our classical writers who then transformed the various mythological accounts into a single, unfied work of art. Mytho-*poesis* (from the Greek *poiein*, meaning to make, to create) *re*-creates the ancient stories. And, while mythology presents its stories as if they actually took place, mythopoesis transposes them to a symbolic meaning. Indeed, *the mythopoeic works examined in this study arose when the literal account of the legend could no longer be accepted.* They arose *in periods of crisis, of cultural transition,* when faith in the authoritative structure was waning. It is at this juncture that our great prophets and artists would redeem the values of the past and present in their *symbolic* form, transposing their historic transitoriness into permanent promises.

The modern revival of the myth began in the nineteenth century, that is, at the very time when technology threatened to wipe out ancient folkways. In our own day, the theme has again fired the imagination of artists from Picasso to the surrealists, and of writers from Proust, Joyce and Thomas Mann to Kafka, Sartre, Cocteau and Faulkner. It penetrates our cultural areas, from anthropology, philosophy and religion to criticism and psychology in the work of Malinowski, Cassirer and Tillich, of Spengler and Toynbee, of I.A. Richards and T.S. Eliot, of Freud, Jung and Reik. The revival of myth in our time is an attempt to satisfy the human need for relatedness to fellow-travelers on our common journey.

The myth addresses itself to the problem of identity, asking "who am I?" And it proceeds to examine three questions that are organically related: "Where do I come from?", "Where am I bound?", and "What must I do now to get there?" In mythic language, the problems deal with Creation, with Destiny and with the Quest.

In his *Life of Reason*, George Santayana makes the pithy observation that those "who cannot remember the past are condemned to repeat it." The living myth would not restore the dead past, but would *redeem* its living heritage. The myth also contains *the tradition of re-creation.* Unrest, disquiet and revolt are as much part of man's history as is the tradition of idolatry. The culture hero in mythopoesis *chooses* his tradition, rejects the stultified in favor of the creative roots in the past. His choice of tradition is a recollection of man's native genius. By aligning himself with the high levels of the past, man gains the dignity of belonging without becoming depersonalized.

The myth is of particular import for the modern artist who feels himself estranged from the divisiveness and uniformity of our age.

Many have responded by removing themselves to a pure esthetics, to a no-man's land of abstract fancy. But this purist realm is itself an expression of the very specialization against which it is directed, and it addresses itself and communicates to a specialized audience. The myth offers the artist a theme which sounds a basic motif and thus makes it possible for him to return to his world-wide audience.

The myth is a power by which men live. And this power can be used for good or evil. Mythic symbols can represent an ideal or an ideology. The fateful import of the myth for our day stems from the fact that it is pivotal to the idea of One World. It can determine whether this world is to be one of unity and totality or one of uniformity and totalitarianism, whether the powers of man are to be freed or shackled.

The living, humanized myth is not given, but must be won:

> "What from your father's heritage is lent,
> Earn it anew, to really possess it!"
>
> (Goethe, *Faust I*)

This depends partly on historic pressures which can quicken or drain a myth. But it also depends on the vision and the will to realize it.

At this moment, we seem to be rushing towards an abyss. Yet, we can draw comfort from the story of mythopoesis, from its long-range perspective which enables us to see beneath and beyond the dust of the hour. It assures us of the never-extinguished genius of man which needs to be remembered and reactivated. Our own time records such memory in Nexö's *Pelle the Conqueror*, Malraux's *Man's Fate* and *Man's Hope*, Gide's *Theseus*, and Thomas Mann's *Joseph and His Brothers*. In each, the tradition of a rebellious quest is pitted against a paralyzing tradition.

This study centers in Western mythopoesis. It touches on Oriental mythology and presents the residue of the Eastern myth of the Earth-Mother in *The Brothers Karamazov*. The literary works selected are not equal in scope, artistic structure and resonance. *Oedipus* and *Hamlet* have more universal echo than *Moby Dick* and *The Trial*; *The Brothers Karamazov* and *The Magic Mountain* have a broader canvas than Gide's *Theseus* and Sartre's *The Flies*. *The Divine Comedy* is more structured than *Don Quixote*. What they all have in common is that each sounds the perennial motifs of human nature, its origin, quest and destiny. This is their universal relevance. But each speaks this universal language in its particular dialect. Every epoch has its own myth which provides the center of its life, gives the tone, manner and rhythm to its existence, permeates its institutions and thought, its art, science, religion, politics, its psychology and its folkways—that is, *the myth organizes the values of its epoch.* The literary form of the myth preserves its symbolic values which transcend the drossy historical surface. "The old myths," a writer states,

> the almost forgotten myths of antiquity were stories we can no longer believe, as stories, but we may still discover in these ancient intuitions the thread of an undying vision . . . in these days of crumbling institutional forms and beliefs, and in the agony of a desperation which finds no peace or promise of peace in the world we know, we may begin to hear our own voices as almost the cry of disembodied intelligence, demanding its spiritual rights. And then, perhaps, we shall begin to make a new sort of alliance with the world, on terms which acknowledge and declare, first of all, the humanity of the human race.[3]

NOTES

1. Carl Kerenyi in *Essays on a Science of Mythology* by C. G. Jung and C. Kerenyi (New York, 1949), p. 5.
2. *Goethe and the Modern Era* (Chicago, 1949), pp. 279-280.
3. "The Dynamics of Change," *Manas*, Vol. XIV, No. 8. The methodology of this study is indebted to Ernst Cassirer. His notion of "serial order" postulates the question "what are the conditions according to which one element is arranged and connected with another?" rather than pursuing the abstract philosophical quest for the characteristics which are common to various elements. What is sought are analogous correspondences. In this system, "each separate form gains its meaning purely from the position which it occupies, where its content and import are marked by the wealth and the individuality of relations and implications through which it is connected with the other human forces, and finally with their totality." The unity which is achieved thereby is not of materials, but "a functional unity" of the creative process. The productive promise in this method is that it permits us not only to establish the relationship between existing entities, but also to envisage the relationship between what exists and what is possible. For a discussion of Cassirer's functional approach, see my essay "Ernst Cassirer's Functional Approach to Art and Literature" in *The Philosophy of Ernst Cassirer*, The Library of Living Philosophers, VI (Evanston, Illinois, 1949), 631-661.

   Cassirer's functional unity is similar to Silberer's functional symbol-phenomena. In Silberer's psychoanalytic approach, the important element in images is not the content, but the form of the mind's functioning.

   Put another way, this study attempts to do justice both to the universal schema of the myth and to its temporal or story-sequence, with the literary form picturing its moving face. Stated in terms of the classical Four Causes, one might say that the mythic pattern provides the formal and the final cause, while the historical content operates as the material and efficient cause.

Introduction

MYTH AND REALITY

THE WORD *myth* is derived from the same root as *mystery* and *mystic*, and the Oxford dictionary defines it as a "purely fictitious narrative." The philologist Max Müller called myth a disease of language. He traced its origin to the circumstance that primitives used the same name for different objects and different names for the same object, and he concluded that mythology was the result of the ambiguous meaning of words. In *Das Leben Jesu* (Stuttgart, 1905), David Friedrich Strauss separated the truth of Jesus' teachings from the mythical accounts of his personality. Machiavelli supported his counsel that a prudent ruler has to be "a great feigner and dissembler" by referring to the myth of Achilles, who was educated by the centaur Chiron so that he might know his beastly as well as his human nature. While Machiavelli's intent was to destroy false myths about human nature, George Sorel's *Reflections on Violence* advocated the use of fictions to set loose primitive mass forces in a class war, arguing that, to dominate people, we must give up truth in favor of myths.[1]

On the other hand, writers from Wilhelm Wundt to Franz Boas have shown that myths are not freely "made," but represent a folk product expressing the collective labors, emotions and genius of peoples. They are either composite productions, such as the epics of the ancient Orient, or, where they have been molded into mythopoesis by an individual artist, they rest on a long tradition. (Even Blake's "private" myths grow out of Greek, Christian, and his own tradition.) The ancient stories are retold, rewritten, and transmitted as people find in them analogies to their own situation and destiny. In this sense, myth is not something invented or fancied. It is rather *a pictorial hypothesis* about the nature of man. While myths do not have existence, they enter the realm of *reality* in that they enable us to explain and predict events in the empirical world.[2]

19

Myth and Science

In popular usage, myth and science exclude each other. However many thinkers and scholars see them as closely related. Freud regarded the mythological view of the world as "nothing other than psychological processes projected into the other world." And, in a letter to Albert Einstein, he wrote:

> It may perhaps seem to you as though our theories are a kind of mythology. . . . But does not every science come in the end to a kind of mythology like this? Cannot the same be said today of your own Physics?[3]

Ernst Cassirer, a student of mathematical physics, states that science begins with mythic perception. His *Philosophy of Symbolic Forms* (New Haven, 1953-1957) also shows that the beginnings of science, as of art, language, writing, and philosophy lead us back to the stage when they are rooted in mythical images and expressions.

Following Cassirer, Susanne K. Langer's studies in symbolic logic emphasize that both science and myth deal with symbolic transformation (discursive in one and non-discursive in the other). She calls myth a primitive and indispensable forerunner of metaphysical thought. Langer further points out that modern science also deals with fictions—such as zero and infinity, square roots of negative numbers, incommensurable lengths, fourth dimensions, imaginary numbers—which have relevance to reality. In his eloquent essay "Science and Human Values" (*The Nation*, December 29, 1956), J. Bronislawski elaborates the point that such scientists as Copernicus, Kepler, and Newton felt their laws to be metaphors and symbols, which "are as necessary to science as to poetry." Science, he writes, "is the search for unity in hidden likenesses," and mass, time, magnetic moment are symbolic concepts. In sum, "thinking as we understand it is made possible only by the use of names or symbols."

Historically, myth and science often went hand in hand. Frazer (*The Golden Bough* [New York, 1929]) sees a form of science in the magical practices of early man, in that the primitive believed "in a certain established order of nature on which he can surely count, and which he can manipulate for his own ends." To be sure, primitive man errs in his notion of the nature of this order, and when he finds that his predictions do not come about, he "throws himself humbly on the mercy of certain great invisible beings . . . to whom he now ascribes all those far-reaching powers." At this point, religion supersedes magic.[4] And, when the religious belief in a variable and irregular succession of events proves unsatisfactory, man turns to the assumption that natural events operate

20

with constant regularity. This scientific stage is won by exact observation of the phenomena themselves and not, as in magic, by a false analogy of the order in which ideas present themselves to the mind. Yet, this newly won scientific ground does not drive out mythic thinking. The Greeks, for example, were firmly pledged to the scientific method; still, their literature and philosophy were filled with mythic imagery. Even as Plato rejected the myth in his political theory, he made extensive use of it in his Dialogues and created his own myth, the Demiurge of *The Timaeus*, in his natural philosophy.

The relationship between myth and science may also be seen in mythopoesis: Dante attempts to hold his realms together by an exact triadical scheme; Mark Schorer's analysis of Blake indicates the scientific aspects of his mythic symbolism, and Lewis Mumford has shown that *Moby Dick* blends science and mythic imagination; Thomas Mann's *Doctor Faustus* carries mathematical symbolism over into mythic musicology.

At the same time, there remain significant differences between the two realms. Science gets its universal laws by abstracting from particular phenomena, reducing them to precise univalent formulae. Mythic symbolism, on the other hand, is pictorial—the fire of Prometheus, the snakes of Orestes, the ketonet of Joseph—and is by nature inexact and ambivalent.[5] Furthermore, where science is neutral to human values, mythic thought views nature as friendly or hostile. Science and myth are further distinguished by their concepts of causation. In science, no theory can explain the final "why"; that is, scientific method precludes a final hypothesis which may not be questioned. But the myth assumes a basic "it is," to which there is no "why." Spinoza stated that a scientific definition consists in determining what a thing is not (*omnis determinatio est negatio*). The mythic vision, however, would enclose the whole.

Myth and Religion

Myth and religion jointly answer man's need for collective identification and the feeling of his intimate relation to the world. Mythic and religious motifs are nearly indistinguishable in primitive and Oriental mythology. They are also closely interconnected in the mythopoesis of Greece and Rome, in *The Divine Comedy* and *Don Quixote*. Religion also penetrates modern mythopoesis, such as Racine's *Phædre*, Rabelais' *Gargantua*, Goethe's *Faust*, Wagner's *Ring*, Melville's *Moby Dick*, the poetry of William Blake, Dostoyevsky's *The Brothers Karamazov*, the work of James Joyce, Franz Kafka and Thomas Mann.[6] Myth and religion are differentiated from other cultural forms by their anthropomorphic orientation and their normative approach. Their interest is, not the universe, but man, not pure objective data, but what contributes to man's welfare.

While myth and religion have never been completely divorced, Western mythopoesis, beginning with the Book of Job and Greek tragedy, separates itself from religion to the extent that it does not acknowledge a supernatural authority to which man must surrender. Even as the hero in mythopoesis must learn to curb his rebelliousness, he remains a hero only if he does *not* completely submit. This is connected with the *immanent* character of the myth, which distinguishes it from those religions which emphasize the transcendental nature of salvation. Because the mythic hero never fully surrenders or recants, he cannot achieve complete redemption and his problem cannot be resolved by heavenly grace.[7]

MYTHOPOESIS: A DRAMA IN THREE ACTS WITH AN EPILOGUE

This study interweaves two basic perspectives: the *historic* and the *recurrent*.

On the historic level, each mythopoeic work is viewed as the center which unifies the multiple cultural forms of its era, organizing its art, psychology, philosophy, religion and social currents.

Intertwined with the historic level—and this is the second major thesis—is a universal pattern. The Ariadne thread which runs through all mythopoesis is a *structural unity* that consists of *the analogous stages* in the development of the mythopoeic heroes from Job to Thomas Mann's Joseph and Sartre's Orestes. This unity takes on the form of *a drama* in three acts, followed by *an epilogue*. By implication, this pattern constitutes the nature of the human journey itself, is characteristic for the unheroic as well as for the heroic, obtains for the individual and for society.

The Drama begins with a *First Act* of communal harmony. In the *Second Act*, this harmony is disturbed by the emergence of the hero who sets out on his *Quest* which entails a challenge to his group. The *Quest* is pivotal for the mythopoeic drama. *For, it is through his challenge and revolt that the hero can become a creative agent of his community.* This creative impulse moves the hero towards the *Third Act*. This is a kind of "Homecoming" through which a new harmony is reached. However, the harmony attained carries within itself the earlier moments of dissidence and contains the seeds of a renewed conflict. This determines the *Epilogue* which makes for *the tragic residue* in the mythopoeic drama.

The functional unity in this dramatic structure constitutes the link in all-human development, even as its individual expressions vary in polar and dialectic rhythms. Throughout, the hero's quest aims at the recreation of the One Human World which presumably once existed and which might be approximated in the future. Thus, the mythopoeic journey could release the ageless springs of human creativity.

Act I: Creation or Eden

Mythology speaks of an initial state of blissfulness, called Eden or Paradise, Islands of the Blessed, Elysium or the Golden Age. Here man was at home, at one with nature and his group. In mythopoesis, however, this first act no longer exists, but is only a nostalgic "memory."

Act II: The Quest—Homeleaving or Expulsion of the Hero

Act II begins with the "birth" of the hero, who is set out or invites expulsion by his authoritative powers. In primitive mythology, the hero does not stand in opposition to his community, but carries out his task in conformity with its traditional symbols. However, almost from the beginning, the nature of the hero is ambiguous. Franz Boas has shown that in the role of the Transformer, American legends present him at once as a culture hero and as an irresponsible trickster, intent on gratifying his personal desires. In either case, he transgresses against what the group regards as a natural or sacred order, violates a taboo by peering into forbidden mysteries. He becomes "the dangerous child." In Nietzsche's language, the hero *must* commit a crime. The crime is usually one of commission: He steals the fire, becomes a parricide, commits incest. In the case of some heroes—Job, Hamlet—the crime is one of omission. In others—Kafka's Joseph K., Mann's Castorp—the character is arrested or arrests himself, not for what he has done or has deliberately planned to do, but for his unconscious wish to do something that is prohibited.

The consequence of the mythic crime is the hero's fall and his Journey.

The Journey is a central experience in all the great myths. It takes the form of a descent into Hell (in the myths of Krishna, Zoroaster, Osiris, Baldur, Adonis, Bacchus, Hercules, Mercury, Odysseus), or of

23

a symbolic entry into the "dark night of the soul" (Jesus, Aeneas, Dante, and every modern mythic hero). In pre-Renaissance mythopoesis, the journey has a definite, fixed goal, and we know—even if the hero does not—that the wanderer will be brought home at last. Homecoming is assured because, in his very rebellion, the hero represents the reigning symbols of his group. In the modern myth, where the individual would free himself more radically from his community, the journey takes on an indefinite character, and the homecoming is tenuous, as in *Don Quixote, Hamlet, Faust, Moby Dick*, and in the work of Kafka and Thomas Mann.

Act III: Destiny—Re-creation or Homecoming

The fall of the hero is not final. Jessie L. Weston (*From Ritual to Romance* [New York, 1957]) has shown that, even in the early vegetation cults, the important element is not the worship of the dead, but the restoration to life.

In primitive and Oriental mythology, rebirth generally constitutes return to the identical earlier form, an analogy to the never-varying order of the seasonal changes. In Western mythopoesis, rebirth depends on the extent to which the quest results in the hero's own questioning of his deviation. The furies which pursue Orestes, Oedipus and Dante, Don Quixote and Ahab are, in this sense, self-inflicted punishments. This self-questioning holds the promise of the hero's transformation.[8] Through it, he comes to recognize the *symbolic* values which are present in the very tradition he has violated. He is thereby moved to recast the function of his demon and realign himself with the wider interests of his group. In this way, he can become a *culture* hero. He now sees his supra-individual relation as complementing and fulfilling his individuality. Reintegration lies *beyond* individual autonomy. Return is not to the earlier starting point, for the hero's rebellion has re-created the authoritarian mode, has quickened and transformed its earlier sluggishness. In this sense, the culture hero acts for the others, becomes the instrument of social salvation, and his sacrifice makes him a blessed figure. Such sanctification comes to Oedipus in Colonus, Virgil in Latium, Don Quixote in La Mancha, Hamlet in Horatio's final prayer.

This has become possible through the hero's knowledge and consciousness. He now reaches a higher form of acceptance, one which follows from having made his *own* choice. This choice makes for responsibility and ethics. In sum, the victory of the mythopoeic hero is the victory of consciousness and of social morality.

Epilogue: Tragic Transcendance

In *The Myth of the Birth of the Hero* (New York, 1959), Otto Rank points out that all mythic heroes go through certain stages:[9]

> The hero is the child of most distinguished parents, usually the son of a king. His origin is preceded by difficulties, such as continence, or prolonged barrenness, or secret intercourse of the parents, due to external prohibition or obstacles. During the pregnancy, or antedating the same, there is a prophecy, in the form of a dream or oracle, cautioning against his birth, and usually threatening danger to the father, or his representative. As a rule, he is surrendered to the water, in a box. He is then saved by animals, or by lowly people (shepherds) and is suckled by a female animal or by a humble woman. After he has grown up, he finds his distinguished parents, in a highly versatile fashion takes his revenge on his father, on the one hand, is acknowledged on the other, and finally achieves rank and honors.

Rank's scheme may be transposed into naturalistic-psychological terms: The child's distinguished parents point to the hero's exceptional sources; the difficult conception suggests the obstacles in the way of the creative process. As a potential hero, the son is "the dangerous child" and a threat to the father. This is sensed by the father, or, in mythic language, is told him by an oracle, dream or prophecy. The father's natural love for his child prevents him from removing his son and he orders someone to expose him. But the child is saved by animals or humble people, that is, by "nature" or "the folk."

The Rankian scheme ends with the success of the hero. It applies to many primitive and Oriental myths, fairy tales and some religio-mystic systems in which all problems are resolved in a paradisiac finale.[10]

Mythopoesis, however, precludes such a resolution. Since its final reference is to the reality character of the human condition, it only unfolds the successful *tempering* of the conflicting relations. On the other hand, the tertiary phase of the hero's reintegration incorporates the critical approach in the quest; indeed, it is conditioned by his maintaining this critique: Job, who questions the ways of the Lord, is uplifted, not the Friends who urge submission; Oedipus, who retains his "tyrannical" personality becomes the Savior-figure, not the just and kindly Theseus; Hamlet, not Horatio, emerges as "a noble heart"; Thomas Mann's ravaged Judah, not his comfortable Joseph, receives Jacob's blessing in Egypt.

The living character of mythopoesis appears in the never-ending need of the dissident hero to galvanize his state towards reshaping its tradition. The heroic quest is not eliminated but *assimilated*.

Here lies the *revolutionary* leaven of mythopoesis. To be sure, the myth contains a conservative fibre which makes for idolatry of the past. However, it would also preserve another kind of tradition—*the tradition of freedom*—expressed in the myths of Dionysus and Prometheus where the hero is pledged to a *futuristic* tradition.

In this interplay between preservation and challenge, the mythic quest is inherited and passed on. Prometheus is carried forward by Hercules, Oedipus by Polyneices, Don Quixote by Sancho Panza, Hamlet by Fortinbras and Horatio, Ahab by Ishmael, Nexö's Pelle by Morton, Joyce's Earwicker by Shem-Shaun, Mann's Joseph by Judah. Mythic transcendence does not allow for a paradisiac ending, and reconciliation in the mythopoeic drama is on a tragic plane.

MYTHOPOESIS AND PSYCHOLOGY

"It had occurred to me long ago," Ferenczi writes, "that for any useful writings on individual psychology we have to go not to scientific literature, but to belles-lettres."[11]

In recent years, there has been a growing preoccupation on the part of writers with the depth implications of literature. At the same time, more and more psychoanalytic criticism has turned towards an examination of the arts. Following the pathfinding work of Freud, Rank, Hanns Sachs, Ferenczi, and Jung, we have had the contributions to this problem by Kris, Jones, Marie Bonaparte, Ella Sharpe, Reik, and, more recently, D. E. Schneider, Kubie, Kanzer, Phyllis Greenacre, Bergler, Eissler and others.

Concern with unconscious motivation in the arts is a relatively modern phenomenon. The impetus came with the Renaissance conception of the "free" individual whose inner self was regarded as the crucial factor determining his destiny. Whereas Orestes' Erinyes and Dante's Lucifer were external physical powers, the Renaissance interiorized such powers, as in Marlowe's Mephistophilis, Hamlet's Ghost, and Faust's Grey Women. More explicit recognition of unconscious conflicts appeared in Diderot's *Rameau's Nephew*, in the writings of the German Romanticists and in Wagner's music drama. For Dostoyevsky, Chekhov, Artzybashev, and Andreyev, the lacerated Russian personality became the central problem. Finally, the theme of psychological alienation may be said to be the leitmotif of twentieth century writing.[12] Structurally, the impact of psychoanalysis on literature produced styles that tend toward "free association."[13] In impressionistic, expressionistic and surrealistic art (Joyce is the most extreme example in literature), form was freed from the logic of syntax and grammar.

Manifold Motivation in Art

Ernst Kris stressed the point that in analyzing a creative work we need to consider not only the unconscious drives, but also the conscious and preconscious powers in the writer's personality, as well as his social conditioning. Some literary critics focus on the technical forms of a work. A rounded psychoanalytic interpretation needs to examine the interrelationships among these various aspects. Very little is revealed, for example, by noting that Shakespeare's Hamlet has an oedipal burden. For his Hamlet is not Sophocles' Oedipus. Furthermore, Shakespeare does not give us a living person, but a dramatic-poetic figure, produced by his particular language. To understand the specific motivations of *Shakespeare's* Hamlet, we need to analyze *his* idiom and imagery, and *his* historic framework. Neglect of the technical, esthetic and social categories can give us only an impoverished general psychological type, applicable at once to the Hamlet of a great writer and that of his imitators.

It is well known that Freud thought artistic attainment as "psychoanalytically inaccessible to us," that psychoanalysis has to lay down its arms before artistic genius and the problem of artistic technique. Indeed, Freud expressed envy of poets who, he said, "discovered the unconscious" before he did, and who "salvage from the whirlpool of their emotions the deepest truths to which we others have to force our way, ceaselessly groping among torturing uncertainties." And one may add that more can be learned about the concrete dynamics of psychological processes from *Hamlet, The Brothers Karamazov, The Magic Mountain* and *Joseph and His Brothers* than from many psychoanalytic texts.

In the dramatic style of his case presentations, Freud was himself something of an artistic "story-teller," and *The Interpretation of Dreams* has recourse to metaphoric analogies.[14] The basic affinity between literature and psychoanalysis is this: both are concerned with human motives and both deal with them as expressed in language and gesture. Psychoanalysis is a science to the extent that it can predict human behavior on the basis of primary principles. But it is also an art. The sensitive analyst may get his deepest insights not so much from the content of a patient's productions, as from his tone, the use of metaphors and imagery. The analyst can also sense the secret import of a

27

patient's communication from his "body-language," his gestures and other physical movements. In both psychoanalysis and literature, "style" is the final method of communication and is the clue to the underlying motif behind the multiple "voices." A psychoanalytic examination of art must therefore consider the formal aspects, must pay attention to the dramatic sequence—how, when, where and to whom a character speaks.[15]

The limitations of most psychoanalytic criticism arise from its failure to give due weight to these factors. It has been particularly deficient in evaluating the crucial relationship between form and "meaning" in art. It treats a poetic work and its characters as "a case study," thereby reducing the rich sensuousness and individuation of the dramatic process in the literary arts to a thin psychological category.[16] The style and form of a literary work—that which distinguishes it from a critical argument—has been virtually ignored.

Bergler on Literature as Pathology

Edmund Bergler's *The Writer and Psychoanalysis* (New York, 1950) may be taken as a representative example of the extremes to which the disregard of literary form may lead. Bergler argues that writers are *ipso facto* neurotic. He focuses on the pathological processes in a writer's *life* and projects them into his *work*. Bergler sees writing as the result of oral, anal-sadistic syndromes in the writer's personality and states flatly: "Normal people just don't feel impelled to write." This method commits the genetic fallacy in that it identifies the writer's biographic sources with his literary product. Furthermore, it does not distinguish between the writer (a *living* person) and his poetic characters (his *symbolic* figures). Moreover, two positive factors are left out in this analysis: The *creative* nature of literature and *the joy* it gives both the creator and his audience. Indeed, Bergler is not primarily concerned with the creative writer as such, stating that it is "immaterial, for psychological evaluation, whether he is a good or bad writer." And, where Freud speaks of "the pleasure of the writer in creation," Bergler states that "the man who suffers" and "the man which [!] creates are one and the same."[17]

The focus on genetic factors neglects the specific element which defines a work of art, namely, *the transformation* of these factors. Many psychoanalytic examinations reveal that an artist's work exhibits oral-anal-oedipal derivatives which have been repressed. But *repression does not explain art*. In the artistic process, such drives are transformed into something which is not orally wet, anally smelly, and not oedipally incestuous and murderous. Art and the artist cannot be understood solely by the method of analytical reduction. The artist embodies and expresses not only the genetic-pathological "background"; he also employs the "forward-" tendencies and intactness of his ego.

Symbolism and Distortion

Ernst Cassirer has developed the thesis that symbolism is central in human culture or, in his striking formulation: man is a symbolical animal.[18] Cassirer's notion that symbolism is the differentiating characteristic of human life is shared by such philosophers, psychologists and anthropologists as Russell, Piaget, Wertheimer, Köhler, Korzybski and Devereux. Symbolic transformation allows man to transcend the immediacy of experience, to convert memory of the past and vision of the future into present possession. In an essay on "The Distortion of the Symbolic Process in Neurosis and Psychosis," (*Journal of the American Psychoanalytic Association,* I [1953], 59-86), Lawrence S. Kubie writes of the symbolic capacity as "the unique hallmark of Man" and notes its function as "a bridge." Kubie confines himself to showing this function in the field of psychology. But it also pertains to art. The arts present the universal through the particular. Thereby they bridge or mediate between the concept and the precept, thought and sensuousness, the object and the subject, fact and fancy. The writer, in particular, acts as a mediator in establishing "communication"—communication among his multiple characters, as well as between them and his audience. Form itself expresses this bridging function: its sensuous imagery carries "unlawful" discharges, held in check by the grammar of language.[19]

Bergler makes a valid point in speaking of the criminal motivation in writing. Art deals with crime in that it presents a drama in which characters violate a convention, undergo conflict and crisis. He is also right in stating that a writer must present such crime as having a degree of legitimacy if the "villains" are not to be mechanical stereotypes. Now, such legitimacy is an expression of a writer's sensitivity to "the other side." Nietzsche called man *das kranke Tier*—the sick animal. And, in the work of Thomas Mann, this "sickness" constitutes "the honorable" in man, for it sensitizes him to the value-element in the opposition and, in the case of the artist, makes possible his attempt to mediate among his different characters. But, by its very nature, this is an unstable bridge and renders the symbolic process a borderline activ-

29

ity.[20] (In passing, it should be noted that the general psychoanalytic meaning of symbols—in distinction to the esthetic—is that in the former "one member of the equation is repressed into the unconscious," as Ferenczi puts it in his essay "The Ontogenesis of Symbols" [*Sex in Psychoanalysis*]. Rank and Sachs make the same distinction.) Thus, the symbolic process is subject to a greater degree of distortion and may, as Kubie pointed out, fixate the emotional disturbance. That is, man's sensitivity, expressed in his symbolic vision, can become the condition for neurosis and psychosis. Animals are less vulnerable because they do not respond to symbols but to signs (Pavlov's bell and food). And, whereas signs are fixed and unambiguous, symbols are variable and ambiguous in their meaning. In other words, precisely because man is a symbolical animal, he is especially vulnerable to neurotic distortions. Man, Kubie stated, would not develop a neurosis or psychosis "without those very symbolic potentialities which are essential to his highest psychological development."[21]

The symbolic view also introduces an element of the tragic. Unlike science, philosophy and religion, art does not pretend to offer final resolutions or precise answers. As noted, the symbolic vision reveals the legitimacy of alternate possibilities. But all action calls for *choice*, the selection of some particular way (as when we vote, we can choose only one candidate), thus forcing us to negate the validity of an alternate choice. Here is the inevitability of the tragic sense of life, of what Malraux once called *La Condition Humaine (Man's Fate)*.

Integrative Function of Art and Literature

Freud called myths "secular dreams," the day-dreams of young peoples. He saw a correlation between the mentality of early man and the unconscious mind, particularly of childhood. In this context, Freud saw the neurotic proclivities in the artist. In "Creative Writers and Day-Dreaming" (St. Ed., Vol. IX [London, 1959]) he indicates that day-dreaming gratifies the artist's archaic wishes in imaginary form. Artistic creation has its origin in a desire to discharge a private burden. The artist, like any other person who has unsatisfied longings, "turns away from reality and transfers all his interest, and all his Libido too, on to the creation of his wishes in the life of phantasy from which the way might readily lead to neurosis." The art of the dramatist, Freud also notes, consists in decomposing his inner self into the various characters of the play, embodying his self in each of the characters and his ontogenetic self through the phylogenetic forms of the myth. In "Relation of the Imposter to the Artist," Phyllis Greenacre speaks of the artist's "special disturbances in the sense of identity and reality." These follow from the heightened sensibility and imaginativeness with which the artist is endowed and perhaps even more from the fact that the writer splits his over-all identity into the multiple characters which he creates. This attests to the breadth and strength of his ego, but it also makes for a delicate balance among the elements in his ego.

This situation can lead to neurosis. However, Freud shows that, while the artist at first separates himself from his audience in his imagination, he finds his way back to reality through telling his story to and sharing it with others. What tends to counteract a neurosis in the case of the artist, Freud goes on to say, is probably that his constitution is endowed "with a powerful capacity for sublimation and with a certain flexibility (*Lockerheit*) in the repressions determining the conflict." In this manner, art provides "a path from phantasy back again to reality." This way back is available to the "true artist" who knows how to elaborate his daydreams, "so that they lose their personal note." For, the artist "possesses the mysterious ability to mould his particular material until it expresses the ideas of his phantasy faithfully." Because he can exercise "flexibility" of the repressions, the artist derives pleasure not only from the discharge, but also from the mastery of his emotions, achieved by employing the rules operative in technique, design and structure.

This aspect of literature and art contains a "curative" ingredient. There is a crucial distinction between a crime committed in fantasy and a crime committed in a literary work. Whereas the neurotic would gain his goal in imagination, the artist wins it by *embodying* his fantasy in particular concrete objects, thereby setting *limits* to the fantasy. (John Crowe Ransom calls art "the world's body" and Yeats speaks of "the thinking of the body.") The symbolism of art is *immanent*. An artist, Cassirer points out, does not merely "feel"; he externalizes what he feels and imagines in visible, audible, tangible modes. He works not simply "in a particular medium—in clay, bronze or marble—but in sensuous forms, in rhythms, in color patterns, in lines, in plastic shapes."[22] Shakespeare illustrated this aspect of the poetic imagination in *A Midsummer Night's Dream*:

> And, as imagination bodies forth
> The forms of things unknown, the poet's pen
> Turns them to shapes, and gives to airy nothing
> A local habitation and a name.

And Goethe summed it up in the opening scene of *Faust II*: "Am farbigen Abglanz haben wir das Leben."

Art is furthermore an act of construction: it organizes its material and thus expresses emotion in a disciplined way. At the same time, art contains an element of freedom. This factor is inherent to its symbolic functioning which presents life as a mobile, dynamic process, transforming our passions into "a free and active state."[23]

Writing as a Function of the Ego

In "Dream-Work" (*The Interpretation of Dreams*, St. Ed., Vols. IV and V [London, 1953]), Freud assigns "final significance" not to the importance of symbols, but "to the utterances of the dreamer," that is, to his associations. Now, there is a rough analogy between a dreamer's symbols and a writer's fantasy, and between a dreamer's associations and the writer's elaboration of his poetic or fictional creations. However, "associations" in the literary work are not "free." Insofar as the work has structure, design and form, the "associations" are *organized*.[24] This is dictated by the fact that the writer has an audience to whom he wants to communicate. That is, the writer is both the dreamer and the one who associates to and structures the associations to his dream. Form organizes the inchoate fantasy material and its elaboration into a coherent unity. And, it is precisely by structuring "the dream-work" of his characters that a writer produces a work of art. In a brief, but penetrating chapter on "Freud and Modern Philosophy" Abraham Kaplan writes that, for Freud,

> Not Narcissus but Pygmalion is the true artist. He is in love not with his own image, but with a creation having a form, movement, and substance—in a word, a life—of its own. . . . Art is the triumph of the pleasure principle and the reality principle acting in concert . . . Freud poses the challenge of providing an esthetics which does equal justice to both inspiration and skill, inner idea and outer expression, latent content and manifest form—in short, to both wish and reality . . . the unifying conception which binds together these two moments of the esthetic . . is the symbol.[25]

Herein lies the integrative function of literature and art. A character in literature becomes integrated to the extent that the writer develops him towards sensing the nature of his hidden motivations and the disintegrating effect of yielding to his immediate drives. As is the case in the psychoanalytic process, "catharsis" takes place by substituting the symbolic act for physical acting out. A few quick examples: Sophocles' Oedipus in Colonus repeats the violation of the Mother, but does it only symbolically; similarly, Dante on the Earthly Paradise with Beatrice, and Goethe's Faust with Helena. Form in art also helps to integrate the writer. Through his work, the writer at once discharges psychic tensions and controls the discharge by the ramparts of the formal design.[26]

The basic link between psychoanalysis and literature consists in the function of language. Sapir calls language primarily a vocal actualization of the tendency to see reality symbolically. Language has wrought the humanization of the primitive myth by the symbolic and evocative nature of the metaphor. In the pre-literary myth, the word was synonymous with the dreaded object and primitive man felt himself in the grip of vague, undefined mythic demons. Mythopoesis *names* these demons. Thereby it *externalizes* them, thus converting them into the partly known. The amorphous, indeterminate and undefined becomes formed, determined and defined. This element constitutes a degree of freedom by which, as Ernst Cassirer puts it, mythic fate and guilt become natural necessity and moral guilt. In Aeschylus' Oresteia, Athena states that the function of speech is "to free man from the bondage of irrational fears." In the words of Theodor Reik, such reactivating has "a freeing and cathartic, a 'telling' effect."

To be sure, art is sublimation, and sublimation begins with a narcissistic libido. Yet, in *The Ego and the Id* (St. Ed., Vol. XIX [London, 1961]), Freud suggests the possibility of widening this libido towards "another aim."[27] The writer is also in contact with the wholesome aspects of his own ego and with those of his characters. In this sense, we can say that there cannot be a totally unhealthy artist or art-work.[28]

In his *Neurotic Distortion of the Creative Process* (Lawrence, 1958), Lawrence Kubie, like Kris, places major stress on the creative role of preconscious processes. But, in his attempt to counter the position that the unconscious is the source of creativity, Kubie calls it "our straitjacket" and assigns it a warping and destructive function: "Where unconscious influences play a dominant role the creative process in science or art becomes almost identical with the neurotic process." Kubie's over-all argument is that normality and creativity depend on whether the conscious-preconscious alliance is dominant over the unconscious.

The thesis presented here is that normality and creativity are endangered where there is a preponderence of any *one* of these three powers, and that their functioning is conditioned by the harmonious interplay among them. Seen as a whole, the creative process entails three stages: It begins with "prelogical experience," or the primary process of the fantasy or inspiration. It becomes a formal work through the secondary process in which the fantasy is elaborated and organized.

In this phase, writing is a function of the ego in its preconscious-conscious alliance. However, in the final creative product, the original fantasy is not totally repressed or destroyed, but continues to exert a nutritive pressure, even as it is held in check by the controlling forces of the ego.

Psychoanalytic Differentiation Between Myth and Mythopoesis

Psychoanalytic theory has dealt with myth and mythology, but has not clearly differentiated them from mythopoesis. Writers on the subject[29] hold that the function of the myth is to *adapt* the individual to the group. The myth is seen as binding repressed instinctual impulses, thereby warding off feelings of guilt and anxiety. Referring to the myth of Prometheus, Arlow writes that it represents the stage of

> the overwhelming impact of the fear of retaliation . . . pointing to the desir-
> ability of establishing internal prohibition and condemnation in order to ward
> off punishment and castration.[30]

Mythopoesis develops from mythology, never wholly loosens itself from the genetic base, and it does "warn" against a rebellion, which does not "remember" its social sources and keep in mind its societal needs. Indeed, structure and form—the ego element in mythopoesis—check the wish for immediate gratification. Art is a social and socializing force and a character in mythopoesis becomes *a culture hero* precisely by assuming a sense of responsibility towards the *living* and *creative* forces in his society. To this extent, mythopoesis also exercises an adaptive function.

However, this function is primarily characteristic for those historic scenes where the ruling powers are in a position to impose acquiescence to and "identification" with their own special interests. This holds for some primitive societies, Oriental kingdoms, and for subsequent varitions of totalitarian regimes.

Now, the argument of this book is that the adaptive function is nearly *reversed* in mythopoesis, beginning with the Gilgamesh epic and the Persian myth,[31] and more markedly in Western mythopoesis from the Book of Job to Mann's Jacob and Joseph. In the *re*-creation of the myth by outstanding individual artists, the hero's quest becomes *a critique* of the existing social norms and points to a futuristic order which is envisaged as integrating the valuable residues of the past and present. And the argument of this study is that it is precisely this rebellious function which renders the hero *redeemable*—shown most pointedly in *Oedipus in Colonus.*

34

Moreover, if one centers the adaptive approach in terms of the audience, the author of the art work should be included as part of this audience. Indeed, our artists and mythmakers represent the high level of their society. Now, their "point of view" does not lie only in the manifest "what," that is, the content of the plot. More crucial is the "how," their imagery, metaphor and symbolism which determine the richness and stature of the characters. And, it is the relative power and fullness of the writer's delineation which give us his *artistic sympathy* and *identification*. Marlowe, for example, condemns his Doctor Faustus to hell fire for his social infractions. Yet, even as Marlowe's historic scene did not permit his Faustus to be saved, the art of the drama unmistakably reveals that Marlowe bleeds for his hero. Similarly, while Dostoyevsky calls Alyosha his "hero" or his "future hero," it is the rebels—Mitya, Ivan and even Smerdyakov—who are drawn with greater power. Such artistic identification is illustrated in all mythopoeic works, beginning with the Book of Job.

The phenomenologic and metapsychological distinction between myth and mythopoesis hinges on the historical development from tribalism to hierarchic class societies which is accompanied by the evolution towards greater consciousness, individuation and the emergence of the rebel as hero. In many instances, the author may feel himself to be a violator, as in the case of Dante, Dostoyevsky and others. At any rate, such "violation" is a necessary quality of the hero. And, it is his rebellious acts which constitute the necessary condition for the emergence of creative values. Our mythopoeic authors do not merely "explain" the world to which their heroes are to "adapt." Their function is not to "support" their society. In indirect and oblique ways, that is, through their art form, they would transform it by identifying with the hero who would change the world.

The distinction between myth and mythopoesis can also be seen by noting the varying import of mythic powers in each. In the primitive myth and Oriental mythologies, the elements *are* divine powers; in mythopoesis, they become *verbalized symbols* of these powers. The myth which was primarily ritual did "adjust" the individual to the existing authority—the chieftain, Pharaoh, King etc. It also served as a defense against his chaotic drives and narcissistic tendencies. But, it is precisely this form of adaptedness that was used to place the individual in the service of established mores, ideologies and institutions, that is to say, what Francis Bacon called "the idols of the tribe," a function which is today filled by our mass media as Jacob Arlow suggests.[32]

Still, intrapsychic conflicts and conflicts with the world of reality persist. That is, these powers succeed only in keeping the conflict from bursting all bounds. At most, one gets used "to not getting used", as Thomas Mann's Hans Castorp puts it in *The Magic Mountain.*

The concept of "adaptation," as applied to the myth is undistributed. It transposes the function of the ritualistic and religious myth to all types of myth, including mythopoesis. It neglects to note the progression from primitive and Oriental mythology to Western mythopoesis in which history enacts a transformative function through which the old myths are re-created by our great artists. Here, the decisive role of the hero is to counter that identification and "adaptation" which acquiesces in and supports the status quo.[33] The mythopoeic hero would cleanse the stables of the state in which "there is something rotten" and would awaken and quicken the creative powers in his society. In mythopoesis, identification with the hero, who is engaged in the transvaluation of old values, works counter to idolatry and to identification with the stagnant society. His labors hold forth a futuristic promise in which "adaptation" to and "identification" with also refer to the rebellious act.[34]

Freud foreshadows the argument presented here. His brief formulations on the myth include the notion that the myth enables the individual to emerge from the group. (*Group Psychology and the Analysis of Ego*, pp. 69-143.)

Freud's Dramatic Structure

In the Freudian drama, Eden has but a shadowy existence, limited to the child's security in the mother's womb. Man's actual history begins with the domination of the father, followed by his murder. Now, whether this is understood as an actual historic event or as an hypothetical human paradigm, the crucial relevance of this theory to mythopoesis is the transformation of this murder into a *symbolic* act. According to Freud, this transformation takes place in totemism where the totem is killed and eaten, and revered as the protecting ancestral spirit of the clan. This substitution of the symbol for the act makes possible the control of the libidinal urges.

Here lies the futuristic horizon in Freud's schema. In his essay on "Freud and the Future," (*Essays of Three Decades* [New York, 1947]) Thomas Mann writes that the work of the founder of psychoanalysis contains "hidden seeds and elements of a new and coming sense of our humanity . . . of a wiser and freer humanity," and makes him "the pathfinder towards a humanism of the future" which may one day lead to "the resolution of our great fear and our great hate." Mann reminds us that Freud once called his theory of dreams "a bit of scientific new-found land won from superstition and mysticism," and likened his labor to a "reclamation work like the dredging of the Zuyder Zee." Writing to Einstein, Freud himself expressed this hope in the statement that "within a measurable time," and depending on "the growth of culture," there may be an end to the waging of war.

While Freudianism labors toward humanizing and controlling the dark powers in man's archaic heritage, it regards the irrational unconscious as "the larger circle . . . the true psychic reality," whose *"daemonic power"* is immortal.[35] For Freud, "the Devil" is ever-present, personified in the "repressed unconscious instinctual life" (*Interpretation of Dreams*).

As we have seen, mythopoesis also has its tragic residue. But, since it envisages a first act of harmony, peace and unity, it can have a third act in which these are restored on a higher, more complex level. This re-creation of an approximate Golden Age in which the bad authority is converted into a good authority appears in every mythopoeic work from the Book of Job, Aeschylus' *Eumenides* and Sophocles' *Oedipus in Colonus* to Goethe's *Faust*, Dostoyevsky's *The Brothers Karamazov*. Nexö's *Pelle the Conqueror*, Gide's *Theseus* and Thomas Mann's *Joseph and His Brothers*.

Archaic Heritage and the Individual

Mythopoesis pictures the recurrent phases of human action and passion in their variant historic and individual forms. A similar dynamic relationship between the recurrent and the unique is also characteristic of Freudian strategy.

Freud's theory of the primal horde has been interpreted by some critics to mean that for Freud, man is doomed to repeat a pattern which has its prototype at the beginning of his history. But a close reading of Freud's clinical observations and presentation of specific case material makes it clear that he considers the archaic heritage as a kind of poetic picture which indicates *a general inherited tendency* that can be modified and varied according to particular family and individual experiences. The unconscious memory that "once upon a time" men had a mother they desired, a father they killed, brothers with whom they quarreled, does not predetermine the recurrence of such relationships.

To my mind, the import of Freud's theory in *Totem and Taboo* (St.

37

Ed., Vol. XIII [London, 1955]) is that of a symbol, rather than as a statement of pre-historical precedent.[36] Freud calls it "only a *hypothesis*" which postulates that the emotional life of human beings shows the same essential characteristics and stages. And in psychoanalytic treatment of individuals, we find this same *predisposition* to reenact the primal crime. This predisposition exists today as it did at "the beginning":

> since all human beings go through the same experiences, at least in their earliest years, they also react to them in the same way.

And, while these reactions need not be "re-acquired," they do need, as Freud states in *Moses and Monotheism* (St. Ed., Vol. XXII [London, 1964]), to be "awakened" by some traumatic experience to become operative in the life of the individual.

Similarly, Freud's thesis that the development of the individual is "an abridged repetition" of racial evolution ("ontogeny recapitulates phylogeny") is modified by his *historical and social* perspective. To begin with, the memory of "psychical antiquities" is received by the individual in the form of his *specific family mores* which differ with varying historical cultures and particular social settings. The social drive, Freud notes, may have "the beginnings of its development in a narrower circle, such as the family."[37] It is sometimes overlooked that the libido contains a social drive which Freud likens to Plato's Eros:

> Libido is the energy which keeps the members of the group together . . . the energy . . . which can be composed under "love" to people, parents, ideas, humanity, objects.

Freudian individual psychology is also social psychology:

> In the individual's mental life someone else is invariably involved, as a model, as an object, as a helper, as an opponent, and so from the very first Individual Psychology is, at the same time, Social Psychology as well—in this extended but entirely justifiable sense of the word.[38]

One of the most neglected strains in Freudian doctrine is its historical outlook which modifies its substantive thought. Herbert Marcuse's *Eros and Civilization* is the first major study which indicates the hidden role which historical change plays in Freud's metapsychology. In "Why War" (St. Ed., Vol. XXII [London, 1964]) Freud states that "for incalculable ages, mankind has been passing through a process of evolution and culture," and in his preface to Theodor Reik's *Ritual* (New York, 1949), he suggests that the Oedipus complex too may have had stages of development, and that the study of prehistory may enable us to trace them out. Investigation suggests that life in the human family took a quite different form in those remote days from that with which we are now familiar. (pp. 3, ff.)

Central to psychoanalytic theory, writes Abraham Kaplan, is the plasticity of impulse and the range of its socially conditioned expressions. . . . Psychoanalysis postulates constancy, not fixity—a regularity of pattern, not recurrence of the elements composing the pattern from case to case. . . . What is insisted upon is only that the variability is not endless. It occurs within limits, and it is these, rather than a fixed 'essence,' that make for discernable regularities. (*The New World of Philosophy*, pp. 136-137)

The criticism that Freud failed to see the impact of social forces loses its point when we bear in mind that, for Freud, repression is not self-imposed by the individual, but is generated by society, primarily through the family. Hence, the individual cannot be understood apart from an analysis of social pressures. As Kaplan puts it: where Kant focused on the superego, Nietzsche on the id, Dewey on the ego, Freud would show their interrelation and the effect of culture which provides the setting and significance of moral action.

HISTORY AND THE TIME-TABLE OF MYTHOPOESIS

In *Essays on a Science of Mythology*, Carl Kerenyi distinguishes between two levels of mythology. There are the *archai*, or first principles, "to which everything individual and particular goes back and out of which it is made, whilst they remain ageless, inexhaustible, invincible in timeless primordiality." However, man can experience the *archai* only through a historic prism, in the form of a definite culture and tradition which speak in the manner of a certain people. In the "Prelude" to his Joseph cycle, Thomas Mann makes a similar distinction between the "bottomless . . . well of the past" and "provisional origins." The latter are man's "conditional beginnings." They

form the first beginnings of the particular tradition held by a given community, folk or communion of faith; and memory, though sufficiently instructed that the depths have not actually been plumbed, yet nationally may find reassurance in some primitive point of time and, personally and historically speaking, come to rest there. (*Joseph and His Brothers* [New York, 1948], p. 3)

39

Mythology may be said to present a picture of reality through a story, painting, etc. Commenting on proposition No. 2 of his *Tractatus-Logico Philosophicus* (London, 1961), Ludwig Wittgenstein states that, in order to discover whether the picture is true or false, we must compare it with reality.

If we view the myth as a picture, then the reality behind it is the concrete social-historic life which conditions each of the culture-myths. For each age shapes the old myths in accordance with the needs and character of its climate. The story of mythopoesis receives its vitality from history, from the mark of time, place and atmosphere. Attention to the historic roots of mythology and mythopoesis can rescue its living relevance from the romantic view in which mythology is an ineffable universal.

The myth would present the complete man. But historic fissures have limited or warped this total view. Aristotle had warned against this function of the myth. In the 11th book of his *Metaphysics*, he stated that myths (such as that the heavens are gods and that the Divinity encompasses the whole of nature) have been brought forward by legislators "for the purpose of winning the assent of the multitude, and enforcing the utility that is urged in favour of the laws, and of general expediency." The mythic pattern thus shows a rhythmic swing between such historic ideology and the universal archetype. Its uses are benign and malign; they appear in the dual forms of Zeus-Nimrod, Jacob-Cronos, Rebecca-Rhea, Abel-Cain.

There is a need to de-romanticize the myth, to rescue its living relevance from the oceanic night of the romantic conception which views it as an eternal fixed substance, unaffected by empirical forces and the clash of interests. This study will attempt to show the extent to which the historic scene and social hierarchical divisions define each of the poetic myths and give expression to their partisan "ideology." Indeed, such pressures tend to distort the mythic import, moving it towards mysticism or a parody of the myth.

However, historic ideologies never completely eliminate the universal vision. Every age has its prophets and artists who transcend the boundaries of their era towards the all-human. Their symbolic creations at once give central focus to the culture of their time and connect them with what Goethe called "the truth, the old truth" present in all our culture myths.

The dramatic structure which characterizes the literary myth also appears in the historic development of mythopoesis itself. Here, primitive and Oriental mythology serves as a kind of an idealized Edenic first act. Mythopoesis proper begins with the Hebrew Book of Job and Greek tragedy, which center in the second act—the emergence of the rebellious hero, his expulsion and quest. In *The Divine Comedy*, we reach a third act of homecoming in a divine kingdom, followed by the epilogue in *Don Quixote* which questions the reality of the hero's reintegration.

The major emphasis in Renaissance mythopoesis—*Hamlet, Faust, Moby Dick*—is the renewal of the quest. This quest differs from the Hebrew and Grecian in that the modern hero is more alienated from his group. In *The Brothers Karamazov*, the quest assumes an Eastern quality. Here, there is greater belief in the possibility of homecoming, for its hero has the memory of the Pan-Slavic Mother Goddess who incorporates the values of communality and of equality.

In the contemporary era, we move towards the third act of reintegration in the notion of One World. But here the question arises whether this world is to be a living organic unity or a deadening uniformity alternating with a desolate loneliness. The hope is expressed by Thomas Mann's Joseph story and, in a narrower compass, by Nexö's *Pelle the Conqueror* and Gide's *Theseus*. More characteristic of our immediate present are the doubts over this promise. We find them again in the representative work of Thomas Mann, in the figures of Joseph and Judah, and more explicitly in *The Magic Mountain* and *Doctor Faustus*, as well as in the work of Franz Kafka and the existentialists. Here is the epilogue to the historic unfolding of mythopoesis.

NOTES

1. Here, Sorel reversed Plato who sought to free politics from the conservatism of mythic tradition. At the same time, Plato feared the wild and unrestrained in the Dionysian element of the myth.

2. Freud, Rank and Ricklin have indicated that wish-fulfillment occupies a dominant place in the happy ending of the fairy tale. We are not disturbed by these tales because we know that the hero will triumph in the end. Myth, on the other hand, takes account of the obstacles and recalcitrances in the objective world which introduce a tragic element. Where the fairy tale presents the hero in pure opposition *to* the world, the myth sees him involved *within* the world with which he attempts to be reconciled.

    Yet, fairy tales and utopias are also rooted in social history. In his study of Utopias, Ernst Bloch shows that they bear the stamp of their historic epochs. This is more apparent in the case of legends and folk tales where the hero has a definite geographic locus and has more limited powers, and where he is shown as a carrier of tribal tradition. But, in contrast to the myth, his affiliation and import are national, rather than universal, as seen in the legends of Charlemagne, King Arthur, William Tell, Frederick Barbarossa, Napoleon. According to Franz Boas, folk tales, legends and myths sometimes blend into one another, for example in the Northwest coast of America. See Franz Ricklin, *Wishfulfillment and Symbolism in Fairy Tales.* Nervous and Mental Disease Monograph Series No. 21 (New York, 1915).

3. *Psychopathology of Everyday Life,* St. Ed., Vol. VI (London, 1960); *Group Psychology and the Analysis of the Ego,* St. Ed., XVIII (London, 1955), 114-115; *Collected Papers,* V (London, 1950), 283.

4. R. R. Marrett and others hold that religion does not follow magic, but that both are aspects of the same pattern. Frazer and Taylor tend to blur the difference between the primitive and the civilized mind, underestimating their varying historical levels. On the other hand, theories such as those of Levy-Brühl, which regard them as completely opposed, wipe out their historical continuity.

5. Such ambivalence may be seen in the meaning of some words: the Greek *eschatos* means both highest and lowest, the Latin *altus* both deep and high.

6. See my essay, "The Use of Myth in Kafka and Mann," in *Spiritual Problems in Contemporary Literature* (New York, 1957).

7. The religious symbol is moral and sacred, specific and undeviating; in mythopoesis, the symbolic meaning is multivalent.

8. The psychological process involved here is well suggested by Henri Bergson in *The Two Sources of Religion and Morals* (New York, 1954). He writes of "the disturbance which is the passage from the static to the dynamic," and of the image which rises to the surface in the course of this agitation. Where the agitation is futile, the image will be only hallucination. But, in the case of artistic and psychical transcendence, the disturbance will contain "a systematic rearrangement looking toward a higher unity: the image is then symbolic of what is being prepared, and the emotion is a concentration of the soul in the expectation of a transformation." Here, transcendence becomes possible because the agitation is not indulged in, yielded to and "enjoyed." (Translation by Francis Fergusson.)

9. Lord Raglan's *The Hero* (London, 1936) restates Rank's thesis. For Raglan, the most striking features are the attempt on the hero's life at birth. Neither Rank nor Raglan place the erotic relation with the mother in the foreground. However, in *Das Inzest-Motif in Dichtung und Sage* (2d ed.; Leipzig und Wien, 1926), Rank draws on numerous literary works to illustrate incest-motifs in mother-son, father-daughter, sister-brother relations.

10. Thus, the final stage of the mystic way, as outlined by Evelyn Underhill (*The Essentials of Mysticism* [London, 1920]) is absolute attainment of Truth. In Blake, it is "Innocence," with the added wisdom of "Experience."

11. *Sex in Psychoanalysis* (New York, 1956), p. 15.

12. In modern art, the organic connection which art once had with work, politics and ethics has been loosened, and art is regarded as an autonomous, specialized activity. In Thomas Mann, the artist becomes a white or black magician, divorced from reality. However, as Phyllis Greenacre ("The Relation of the Im-

postor to the Artist," *Psychoanalytic Study of the Child*, XIII [New York, 1958], 521-541) points out, the artist is distinguished from the counterfeiter in that the former knows that he counterfeits and why.

13. In Ernst Kris' formulation: "Creative artists of our day are wont to use free association as a training ground for creative thinking or as an independent mode of expression, and some among the surrealists have assigned to their work the function of thus making explicit what had previously been implicit." *Psychoanalytic Explorations in Art* (New York, 1952), pp. 25, 30.

14. E. S. Tauber and M. R. Greene, *Prelogical Experience* (New York, 1959).

15. Schneider makes this point. However, his analytic categories are not clear and, in his analysis of writers and painters, Schneider does not apply his own principle. Daniel E. Schneider, *The Psychoanalyst and the Artist* (2d ed.; New York, 1954).

16. Irving Howe argues that such impoverishment is inherent to the use of the psychoanalytic method. The case is quite the reverse. Psychoanalysis is peculiarly concerned with the individual manifestations of a psychological law, and not simply with "archetypes." Howe's point is valid with respect to the sociological approach to literature. It is in the nature of sociology to view processes in "large curves." Irving Howe, *Modern Literary Criticism* (New York, 1959).

17. According to Bergler, writers concern themselves "exclusively with abnormal human reactions." They do not depict reality, but unconsciously select those segments which are needed for their defensive efforts. The writer is "the most anti-social human being conceivable," does not want to communicate, but writes "solely to solve an inner conflict." To be able to produce, the writer must think that he gives to himself out of himself, that he is the autarchic personality, combining mother and child. It would seem to follow that to cure a writer's "block," the analyst must try and get the writer to regress towards the infantile delusion of omnipotence.

18. Cassirer's Kantian attachment sometimes leads him to suggest that the human mind *creates* reality and that man is "in a sense constantly conversing with himself."

19. Kant's *Critique of Judgment* argues for this function of art which mediates by the "third faculty," Imagination.

20. In Mark Kanzer's formulation:

> ". . . the essential ingredients of art take their origin in the psychological sphere that has as its purpose not the perpetuation of sleep, nor yet the achievement of reality testing, but rather the fascinating and all-important area of choice between both tendencies. Art draws part of its sustenance from a dream, but only part; the remainder comes from a portrayal or reality that keeps attention riveted to the waking world. In this sense, the mental state of the artist is close to that of the neurotic, and also to the analysand under the influence of transference."
>
> "Contemporary Psychoanalytic Views of Aesthetics," *Journal of the American Psychoanalytic Association*, III (1957), 514-524.

21. In a subsequent paper, "The Fundamental Nature of the Distinction Between

Normality and Neurosis," Kubie modifies this position, stating that the symbolic process makes possible our great cultural achievement, and he sees the evolvement of neurosis only "through a distortion of the symbolic process." *Psychoanalytic Quarterly*, XXXIII (1954), 167-204.

22. Truth in art is what Heidegger calls "apophantic," in that it *shows* its truth, rather than proves it.

23. Ernst Cassirer, *An Essay on Man* (New Haven, 1944), pp. 23-26.

24. See G. Kepes' *Language and Vision* (Chicago, 1951) and H. Read's *The Nature of Literature* (New York, 1956). In non-objective art, there is the trend toward retransposing the object into the fantasy.

25. Kaplan, *The New World of Philosophy* (New York, 1961), pp. 136-137. Cf. Harry Slochower, "Symbolism and the Creative Process of Art," *American Imago*, Vol. XXII (Spring-Summer, 1965).

26. In terms of Ernst Kris' application of ego psychology to art:
    "We are no longer satisfied with the notion that repressed emotions lose their hold over our mental life when an outlet for them has been found. We believe rather that what Aristotle describes as purging enables the ego to re-establish the control which is threatened by dammed-up instinctual demands. The search for outlets acts as an aid to assuring or re-establishing this control, and the pleasure is a double one, in both discharge and control." *Psychoanalytic Explorations in Art*, pp. 25-30.
    For a modification of this position, see Ernest G. Schachtel's *Metamorphosis* (New York, 1959), pp. 237-448.

27. See Herbert Marcuse's brilliant study, *Eros and Civilization* (Boston, 1955), which argues that Freud's metapsychology allows for the possibility of a non-repressive sublimation.

28. Edward Glover has well formulated this point:
    "Whatever its original unconscious aim, the work of art represents a *forward* urge of the libido seeking to maintain its hold on the world of objects. Its instinctual compromises are not the result of a pathological breakdown of the repressive system. Rather it acts as an auxiliary device to maintain the efficiency of repression. It is in the truest sense a sublimation, and consequently obviates the need for self-punishment." *Freud or Jung* (New York, 1950), p. 185.

29. *The Psychoanalytic Study of Society*, Vol. III, ed. Warner Muensterberger and Sidney Axelrad (New York, 1964).

30. J. A. Arlow: "Ego Psychology and the Study of Mythology," *Journal of the American Psychoanalytic Association*, IX (1961), 383.

31. See Appendix I, "Primitive and Oriental Mythology."

32. Cf. Erich Kahler, "The Persistence of Myth" in *Out of the Labyrinth* (New York, 1967), pp. 41-51.

33. In *Ego Psychology and the Problem of Adaptation* (New York, 1958), Heinz Hartmann uses "adaptation" to cover both social compliance and attempts to change the social environment. He distinguishes between a passive "*state of*

adaptedness," which may be regressive and *"the process of adaptation"* which may be progressive involving the individual's changing and adapting the environment to "human functions." In this discriminatory use of "adaptation," Hartmann leaves some room for the function of mythopoesis, especially when he notes that individual adaptation "may clash with the adaptation of the species." (pp. 12-32)

34. Tarachow (in *The Psychoanalytic Study of Society*, III, 11) also notes that myths may be "maladaptive and rebellious," but this point is not developed.

35. However, Marcuse's *Eros and Civilization* interprets Freud's metapsychology as offering a basis for a free culture and society.

36. Ernest Jones states that it is "a gross misunderstanding" to say that Freud dated "the whole genesis of culture from a single event." He points out that some of our eminent anthropologists support Freud's theory. He cites Clyde Kluckhohn, among others, who wrote him: "I am convinced that the essential universality of the Oedipus complex and of sibling rivalry are now established by the anthropological record." *The Life and Work of Sigmund Freud*, III (New York, 1957), 328 f. For a recent evaluation of Freud's theory, see Derek Freeman: "Totem and Taboo. A Reappraisal," *The Psychoanalytic Study of Society*, IV (New York, 1967), 9-34. While Freeman argues that for Freud the killing of the father was an actual historic event, he supports Freud's psychic hypothesis. That Freud at least wavered on whether he regarded the killing as an actual event, appears in his calling it "only a hypothesis . . . a 'Just-So-Story,' as it was amusingly called by a not unkind English critic [the anthropologist R. R. Marrett]; but I think it is creditable to such a hypothesis if it proves able to bring coherence and understanding into more and more new regions." (*Group Psychology and the Analysis of the Ego*, p. 122.)

37. *Group Psychology and the Analysis of the Ego*, pp. 1-3 and chapter 4.

38. *Collected Papers*, V, 96, 74, 286. In this emphasis, Freud approaches Marx. In *Neue Folge*, he states that the strength of Marxism lies not in its conception of history, but in its perceptive indication of the influence which economic relations have on man's intellectual, ethical and artistic attitudes. See the chapter "Clash and Congruence Between Marx and Freud" in my *No Voice Is Wholly Lost* (New York, 1945; paperback edition: *Literature and Philosophy Between Two World Wars* [New York, 1964]).

Erich Fromm and others have charged that Freud's androcentric theory (the domination by the father) is refuted by the research of Bachofen and his followers on the existence of societies ruled by "mother-right." Now, to begin with, the term "mother-right" is misleading since (as Engels observed) in many matrilineal societies there are no rulers or ruled, but each sex contributes its share, with leadership held by the most able.

More telling are the findings of Bronislaw Malinowski. Malinowski showed that among the Trobriands, the wish was not to kill the father and to sleep with the mother, but to kill the maternal uncle and to sleep with the sister. He sets forth a number of important variables, not considered by Freud: the distribution of power within the family, the pattern of descent, inheritance and succession, the residence of parents and children, and the transmission of skills. Yet, despite these modifications, he found that Freud's essential thesis was valid, concluding that "Freud's theories not only roughly correspond to human psychology . . . they follow closely the modifications in human nature brought about by various constitutions of society." (*Sex and Repression in Savage Society* [London, 1949], p. 81.)

A. L. Kroeber also accepts Freud's account to the degree that the incest drive and incest repression are operative in the psychic process. See A. L. Kroeber, "Totem and Taboo: An Ethnological Psychoanalysis," *American Anthropologist*, XXII, 48-55 and his "Totem and Taboo in Retrospect," *American Journal of Sociology*, XLV, 446-451.

Freud's more basic methodological strategy refers to *the symbol of authority*. This point is made by Ralph Linton. Oedipal attitudes, he notes, are directed at any figure—father or mother's brother—who assumes this function (*Culture and Mental Disorders* [Springfield, Illinois, 1956]). In any case, even if Freud's theory is not altogether valid for early history, it is clearly relevant to Western societies in which the father is the dominating figure.

The Hebrew Memory of a Chosen God
The Book of Job

Why did the Holy One, blessed be He, choose Israel? Because . . . Israel chose the Holy One, blessed be He, and His Torah.

—Midrash
Numbers Rabba

MYTHOLOGY OCCUPIES a minor place in the Hebrew pantheon.[1] Myths did not take root in the popular mind of the Jews partly because their history did not favor the formation of a settled folk-tradition and because the Hebraic injunction against the making of "graven images" of God worked against the representation of mythic powers in pictures and stories. To be sure, the figure of Job was an old folk memory.[2] Still, the specific *Hebraic* quality of Job, as presented in the Book of Job, is shaped by the very absence of a cohesive folk-life and by the admonition against the portrayal of God through imagery.

The only Biblical theme which has been molded into a mythopoeic work is the story of Job. Like the Oriental legends, the *Iliad*, *Odyssey* and the Germanic *Niebelungenlied*, it is a folk product, the work of multiple authors. It is also a folk memory reaching back into a distant past. Job is mentioned by Ezekiel as a man of piety. He appears in the Epistle of James, in Arabic and other literature. There is an earlier Babylonian poem (*Ludlul bel nimequi*) dealing with the suffering of a pious king which has been called the "Babylonian Job." However, it is not the specific story of Job, but the *question* he propounds that has become an organic part of the universal myth. We find it among the psalmists (37, 49, 73) and the prophets, notably Jeremiah:

Wherefore doth the way of the wicked prosper?
Why are they at ease that deal treacherously?

47

The question is asked by later mythic heroes, from Prometheus, Oedipus and Hamlet to Ivan Karamazov, Kafka's Joseph K. and Mann's Jacob.

Traditional Exegeses

Commentators generally treat the Book of Job as a religious poem. Job is seen as a man whose righteousness is tested by suffering. When he demands to know the reason for his punishment, he is told that man cannot know the ways of God. He is finally redeemed through humble acceptance of God's mystery. In this view, Job's affliction becomes a "false arrest," of the type experienced by Kafka's characters. It implies that man is originally or natively guilty, that he can be delivered only by divine grace.[3]

This religious interpretation aligns the book with the Oriental and Christian myth, but fails to bring out its *Hebrew* character, specifically that of the post-exilic, post-prophetic era.[4] In the religious myth, man's suffering on earth may be compensated for by a physical or spiritual after-life, and the suffering of innocents becomes a condition for the eventual happiness of all mankind. But, as Father Kissane points out, these interpretations do not fit the Hebrew poem.[5] Job does not believe in a paradisiacal after-life—a notion developed only later in the Book of Wisdom—holding that "man dieth . . . and riseth not."[6] Sheol is but a shadowy domain where all souls, guilty and innocent, survive without distinction. Nor can Job find solace in the idea that he is punished for the sins of his ancestors. Indeed, the notion of tribal guilt had been shattered by the prophets. "Everyone," Jeremiah writes, "shall die for his own iniquity." Ezekiel states: "The son shall not bear the iniquity of the father, neither shall the father bear the iniquity of the son." The only "Hebraic" theme which remains in this approach is that of the Jew who suffers simply because he is a Jew.

This interpretation runs into a number of difficulties. To begin with, *it ignores Job's revolutionary indictment* which comprises the body of the book, and implies that Job's position at the end is the same one he held at the beginning. Furthermore, if Job is uplifted because he accepts God as an unfathomable mystery, then the Friends should have been rewarded even more, for this is their persistent argument. Yet Yahweh condemns the Friends.

The difficulties of the religious exegesis, which comes to a *credo quia ignorabimus*, have led to a second line of interpretation, represented by Morris Jastrow. His main thesis is that the book is not a unity, but a composite production and one of gradual growth. The older book contained a protest against the prophets' assurance that the world is governed by a just and merciful power. Later additions and amplifications attempted to controvert the older book in the interests of Jewish orthodoxy. According to Jastrow, the protesting Job of the discussions and the pious Job of the Prologue and Epilogue cannot be reconciled.[7]

The argument of this study is that the Book of Job, despite its composite character, contains a unified statement of the Hebrew myth, if approached as a drama in which Job and his God are developing characters. It will attempt to show that the Book breaks the long chain of the Oriental religious myth in that it introduces the category of *choice* which renders the character both heroic and guilty, and he is *redeemed because of his guilt*. It takes the step from collective to individual responsibility while maintaining supra-personal standards. However, even as it moves away from Eastern impersonality and mystic identification, it does not quite affirm the Greek and Western notions of personality, freedom and the rebellious quest.

Folk-Memory

The universal character of the Book has its roots in the post-exilic period of Jewish life. This historic base conditions the nature of its hero, his mythic crime and rehabilitation.

The decisive experience of the Hebrews was their forty years of desert life. The "waste-howling wilderness" (Deuteronomy) formed their conception of a nomadic or transcendent God and their notion of freedom.[8]

> In the stark solitude of the desert where nothing changes, nothing moves (except man at his own free will), where features in the landscape are only pointers, landmarks, without significance in themselves—there we may expect the image of God to transcend concrete phenomena altogether. Man confronting God will not contemplate him but will hear his voice and command, as Moses did, and the prophets, and Mohammed. (Frankfort *et al.*, *Ancient Man*, p. 372.)

However, the development of urban life and the formation of the kingdom introduced a luxurious court-life, the employment of Hebrew slaves and a life of ease for the wealthier classes.

It was against such life of adulation and self-indulgence that the prophets levelled their scorn, excoriating social injustice and inequality of wealth. Some, such as Hosea, held up the past as an ideal, the time when Israel lived in tents. They spoke out against pagan rituals of lustration, insisting that only the personal moral act and "thoughts of the heart" could bring purification. God, according to Jeremiah, will put His law in men's "inward parts, and will write it upon their heart." He wanted no ritual sacrifices, writes the psalmist:

> Thou hast no pleasure in burnt offering . . . A broken and contrite heart, O God, thou wilt not despise.

The Hebrews developed their concept of the deity while journeying through the desert. Thus, Yahweh became a wandering, restless God.[9] Later, under the influence of Moses and the prophets, the tribal conception of Yahweh is transformed into a single God ruling over the whole world. He was not a local Baal, but a universal God who could not find corporeal representation in graven images. Totemism therefore never became part of Hebrew ritual. Yahweh is now conceived as a Father-God. Where the Oriental and Graeco-Roman myth regarded the God incomplete without the Goddess (who is generally his mother—or sister-wife), the Hebrews stressed the all-sufficiency and sternness of the patriarchal God. This may account for one of the distinctive features of the Hebrew myth—the absence of the incest theme.[10]

Hebrew monotheism stood for one humanistic, moral world. In Egypt, monotheism meant "imperialism in religion"(Breasted), whereas in Israel it was a morality of freedom. It answered the condition of a people whose freedom was constantly restricted, whose country was, in Heine's phrase, a "portable fatherland." It was this spirituality and universalism, coupled with the idea of individual responsibility, which made "the Jew" the center of attack by "Blood and Soil" Nazism.[11]

Throughout, Yahweh retained the characteristics of disquiet and unrest. In Thomas Mann's formulation, Abraham chose to serve "The Highest," that is, one God for all, one of "Geist" who could not be confined or limited.[12] In terms of the mythic vocabulary, the Hebrew God was one whose creation required constant re-creation, that is, He was a God of the Quest. The Messianic idea does not envisage a finished paradise, but calls on man to continue "the act of creation." This is the critical meaning of the term "the chosen people." God chose to protect those who would not bow down to anything less than the highest. This means, as Willa Cather put it, that the Jews were the chosen people in that they were *the people who chose*. In this sense, the Hebrew myth becomes the myth of the chosen God.

Job as a Mythic Hero

The crucial phase of the mythic hero begins when he is "set out" without apparent cause. This question recurs in mythopoesis. We find it in Oedipus, who insists that "in nature" he was not evil; in Hamlet, who states that his is "unpregnant" of the cause for his "bad dreams," in Ahab, who does not understand why the whale bit off his leg; in Ivan Karamazov's question, why do the innocent suffer; in Kafka's Joseph K. who is arrested "without having done anything wrong."

Early in the Book, Job asks: "Why is light given to man whose way is hid, and whom God hath hedged in?" Here, Job sounds the protest against God for having infused man with infinite desires and imposed numberless obligations upon him, but has not given him the powers to carry them out. "What is man," Job asks, "that thou shouldest magnify him, and . . . try him every moment?"—a cry echoed by Goethe's Faust.

And Job goes beyond this general indictment: He wants to know wherein *he* erred as an individual, and the main body of the Book consists of Job's insistent demand to be told wherein he transgressed. In this question and in Yahweh's final response, we have the nature of both Job's mythic crime and his redemption. To understand the dialectic complex of this problem, we need to analyze the work as *a drama*.

The Book of Job is a ballad, that is, a story in dramatic form. As such, the various characters—Elohim, the Satan, Job, the Friends, Elihu and Yahweh—are externalizations of the development *within* Job.

Act I: Tribal Harmony

The exact date of the Book is uncertain, but scholars agree that it belongs to the post-prophetic era. It is therefore relevant to ask: Was Job of the Prologue "perfect and upright" in the light of the values stressed by the prophets?

The Book begins with a picture of tribal harmony. Job lives in peace with his family and his community, fears God and avoids evil. Yet, Job's piety appears primarily in that he does not violate the laws set down in "the books"; he performs the required rituals, offering sacrifices for his sons on the possibility that they may have sinned. The author speaks of Job's "great household," of his exceptional "substance"—sheep, camels, oxen—which makes him "the greatest of all the men of the east." He gives to the poor, but has enough left to wash his "steps with butter." And Job *gloried* in his favored position. In chapter 29, he recalls the days

When I washed my steps with butter,[13] and the rock poured me out rivers of oil . . .
The young saw me, and hid themselves: and the aged arose, and stood up.
The princes refrained talking, and laid their hand on their mouth.
The nobles held their peace. . . .

51

This was the time when he "sat chief, and dwelt as a king in the army," enjoyed ease, "safety," "rest" and "quiet." What is even more telling, Job appears indifferent when his animals, servants and children are killed. Is this the attitude of a "perfect and upright" man? Does it not rather suggest that there is something rotten in the land of Uz belying its outer harmony?

Job's crime is not in the nature of an active violation, such as that of Prometheus. His is the passive crime of contentment and self-satisfaction with his superior status. His failing lies not in his wealth, but in his *attitude*—that wealth is his due, and that it is proper to indulge in pompous enjoyment of the power it gives him. In Elihu's later formulation, Job enjoyed the comforts of the table.

Now, sluggishness of the soul is a crime in the eyes of the God envisioned by the prophets. This God calls for a hero who does not rest comfortably in the present, but who peers back towards the mysteries of creation and carries the burden of future re-creation, one who has knowledge of the abyss, experiences homelessness and nomadic wandering, one who is aware of man's infinite obligations. The Job of the Prologue knows little of these things. Paul Weiss speaks of Job's psychological, moral and social suffering ("Job, God and Evil," *Commentary*, VI, No. 2 [August, 1948], 144-151.) One must add that his suffering is related to his crime of psychic lassitude, moral smugness and social insensitivity to existing disparities. Not until he is personally afflicted does he begin to lament, insisting on *his* rights and his righteousness.

But, it is urged, does not Elohim of the Prologue Himself speak of Job as "a perfect and upright man, one that feareth God and escheweth evil?" However, we must examine the nature of the Lord in the Prologue. Paul Weiss calls attention to His callousness in permitting the Satan to kill Job's flocks, servants and children, that is, to destroy those who, unlike Job, are not involved in the trial at all, but are innocent bystanders. Is not Elohim here as insensitive and complacent in the use of His power as Job is? Now, Elohim to whom Job appears perfect and upright must be differentiated from the Voice of Yahweh which addresses Job at the end.[14] As will be shown, the latter does not "judge" Job with the same standards by which he is declared upright at the beginning. That is, *the God of the Book, like its hero, also undergoes dramatic development.*

Traditional Guides: The Friends

Job's moral state in the Prologue may be gathered from the fact that his position is apparently the same as that of the Friends.[15] The three

Friends represent the approach of the average man who is guided by the stock answers contained in "the books." They argue *ad hoc* that Job is guilty since he is being punished—a striking analogy to the case of Kafka's Joseph K. whose "friends" (Fräulein Bürstner, the advocate, his uncle) take it for granted that the very questioning by officials indicates that Joseph K. must have done something wrong. The Friends constitute the "chorus," reduced from the discriminating Greek voice to a crowd-attitude. They are "cabalists," uncritical followers of traditional theology, holding fast to that "which wise men have told from their fathers," and advising Job to heed their teachings (7,15). They are calculators who believe that by unquestioning surrender, man will be rewarded. Thus, their stand amounts to a *quid pro quo* business theology. Essentially, they de-dignify the Hebrew God viewing Him in terms of mystery, miracle and authority. And, as in the case of Dostoyevsky's Grand Inquisitor, they have no faith in moral freedom. Man, they believe, is impure by nature and is but a "worm" before God. Their "secret," like the Inquisitor's, is that they do not believe in God, setting themselves up as the final judges of Job's guilt. Their passive acceptance amounts to an irreligious repudiation of the dynamic nature of Yahweh. Indeed, it is not clear whether they are Hebrews.[16]

Yet, the author does allow dramatic justification for some of their arguments. Eliphaz charges that Job did not give water to the weary, withheld bread from the hungry, and respected the rich. Bildad indirectly suggests Job's sinful state when he refers to the iniquities of his children. Above all, since their stand is one which Job once shared, they represent the dramatic hurdle he must overcome before he can be uplifted.

Act II: Expulsion and Rebellion

The punishment heaped upon Job may be likened to the expulsion of the Hebrews from the fleshpots of Egypt into a barren wilderness. Job loses his possessions, is stripped of his status, and is driven out into the dark night of his soul. He is set out from his Eden-like state of security and comfort, separated from his fellowmen by the Cain-mark of physical wounds, social loss and spiritual anguish. His life becomes a psychic journey through a desert-existence, in quest of an answer to the question which Jews have asked throughout the ages: *Eli, Eli, lama sabachtani?* As in the case of Aeschylus' Prometheus—who likewise remains in one spot throughout the drama—the journey is one of the mind and the emotions. In both, the dramatic "action" consists in the change of tone in the lament and argument, in the speeches of the various characters. This makes for a fluctuating rhythm and pace, at times quiet, at times whirling and torrential like the elements.

Job's trial is his "experience" which galvanizes him into "revolution." Not until he is reduced to the elemental level of human existence, placed on an equal footing with the lowest, is Job awakened to consciousness. His false security which had blunted his critical and imaginative faculties is shattered, and he is catapulted out of his settled and sated condition towards a dynamic challenging attitude. Job's suffering is not only a punishment; it is also, and first of all, *a guide* to his higher self. It prods and harries him into his integrity. His refusal to accept the Friends' conception of God as a mysterious and miraculous authority defines the assertion of this self.

Job's new character emerges through his debate with the Friends.[17] His opening words strike a despairing, self-denying note, voicing the temptation to regress towards pre-natal security. He curses the day on which he was born, even wishes he had not been conceived. Job proceeds to argue in the causal, legalistic manner characteristic of the Friends. He wants his grief "weighed" and his calamity balanced. Yet, almost at once, he insists on his right to question: "Therefore I will not refrain my mouth; I will speak in the anguish of my spirit; I will complain in the bitterness of my soul" (7). He turns from the Friends to God and asks to "see" and "reason" with Him, "as a man pleadeth for his neighbour," that he might know his transgressions. He passes from the theme of the injustice done him to the general proposition that God's world is one where the wicked prosper and the just are a laughing stock. As to the Friends, their uncritical belief in God's ultimate justice stamps them as "miserable comforters . . . forgers of lies . . . physicians of no value," and their "wisdom" will die with them (10-16).

Job's *impatience marks the birth of his ego*. It appears in *his own* realization that he had *not* been perfect and upright. Job recalls the iniquities of his youth. He now sees that his righteousness was "put on . . . and it clothed me," that he had only scorn for those who suffered from "want and famine" (13,29,30). He now indicts those who, through greed and violence "turn the needy out of the way," and the condition in which they who tread the winepresses suffer thirst. Job admits that he may have hidden "mine iniquity in my bosom," in fear of "the great multitude" and "the contempt of families" (24,31). To be sure, these are admissions not to wilful or conscious acts, but to what Job may have done in his ignorance.[18]

The most direct statement of Job's rebirth appears in chapters 13 and 27. They contain Job's declaration of moral independence in which he insists on holding his "own ways," though he may burn for it:

Though he slay me, yet will I trust in him:[19] but I will maintain mine own ways before him.

He shall also be my salvation: for a hypocrite shall not come before him . . .

Behold now, I have ordered my cause; I know I shall be justified.

Who is he that will plead with me? for now, if I hold my tongue, I shall give up the ghost.

And later, in his reply to Bildad:

God forbid that I should justify you: till I die I will not remove mine integrity from me.

My righteousness I hold fast, and will not let it go: my heart shall not reproach me so long as I live . . .

For what is the hope of the hypocrite though he hath gained, when God taketh away his soul. . . .

Job's "patience," as Gersonides points out, lies in his steady belief that when God had tried him, he would "come forth as gold" (23). Indeed, Job affirms God more passionately in his state of affliction than he had in his state of complacency.[20]

The Herald: Elihu

Like Dante, Job feels himself lost in a dark forest. God "hath fenced up my way that I cannot pass, and He hath set darkness in my paths." The Friends are the "rational" guides whose traditional wisdom helps Job only in making him aware that he must go beyond it. They are followed by Elihu and by Yahweh.

It is generally held that Elihu merely recapitulates the arguments of the Friends.[21] However, this contention is not borne out by the text. To begin with, Elihu's wrath is kindled not only against Job, but also against the Friends "because they had found no answer, and yet had condemned Job." Furthermore, where they excoriated Job for voicing his grievance, Elihu calls on him to "speak, for I desire to justify thee." He is a younger man who claims to be speaking "in God's stead." (His name means "My God is he.") God, he says, communicates to man by dreams and illness, through which He "openeth the ears of men, and sealeth their instruction." In this manner, God warns man, and thereby gives him an opportunity to provide against what may be forthcoming, that is, allows *human choice*. (Prometheus similarly says that man can anticipate the future through dreams.) Job himself spoke earlier of the dreams through which God terrifies him at night (7). But, Elihu charges, Job did not realize his social shortcomings, did not come to the aid of the oppressed who "cry out by reason of the arm of the mighty." Instead, he indulged in a life of ease and luxury, enjoyed the comforts of the table.[22]

Elihu's role as herald or messenger of the Lord appears in that he offers the definition of God which Yahweh gives of Himself at the close: The union of wisdom and power, manifested in His creation and purposeful manipulation of the elements. He speaks of God's voice which "roareth" and "thundereth," foreshadowing Yahweh's speeches "out of the whirlwind."

Act III: Recognition Scene—Yahweh

Nearly all critics are of the opinion that the speeches of the Lord do not answer Job's question. Kissane's view is representative of this position:

> The implication in the First Speech is that the suffering of the just, like all the phenomena of the universe, enters into the scheme of Divine Providence; but the motive of God's action in an individual case remains a mystery. The aim of the Speeches is not to penetrate this mystery, but to show that man is to accept God's will with humility and resignation, without questioning the propriety of God's action . . . the writer teaches that suffering is not always the result of sin (Dialogue), and . . . that it is not due to God's want of knowledge of the just man's distress, nor want of power to intervene on his behalf. But in neither case does the writer give any *positive* solution of the problem. (*Book of Job*, p. xxix)

This view raises several questions. If man must accept God's will with humility and resignation, why does not the Lord continue to punish a recalcitrant Job? Why does He bother to appear and challenge him to "answer?"

Yahweh speaks of Himself as encompassing the whole universe. This has led Horace Kallen to see in him a "God of indifference," akin to the Greek Moira, and in the Book "a Greek tragedy."[23] But, unlike the Aristotelian *Nous*, Yahweh is not an "unmoved mover," and does not view physical and human nature as belonging to the same order of things. On the contrary, this is a patriarchal deity of will and purpose. His rule is not one of cosmic neutrality, but of *choice*. Yahweh is concerned about man's welfare, singles out Job, comes and speaks to him with dramatic passion and in *human* terms, as he did to Adam, Eve, Noah. In the end, he *discriminates* between Job and the Friends.

In his first speeches, Yahweh emphasizes His power and wisdom, and it is to be noted that Job reacts to them with *a sullen response*. Called upon to answer, he states:

> Once have I spoken, but I will not answer again;
> Yea, twice, but I will proceed no further.

Yahweh then introduces a new motif. He now adds that *Job can save himself*:

> Then will I also confess unto thee
> That thine own right hand can save thee.

Job remains silent and answers only after Yahweh proceeds to speak of Behemoth and the Leviathan.

Yahweh first speaks of Behemoth, the land animal, as having been created at "the beginning," together "with thee." He dwells at greater length on Leviathan, the sea monster, emphasizing the fact that he will not allow himself to be subdued: One cannot "play with him as with a bird;" he does not supplicate or "speak soft words;" one cannot "press down his tongue with a cord," lead him by the nose, for he will not permit himself to be made into "a servant for ever."

These passages have been interpreted as arguing that if the Lord rules such mighty creatures, then how can a man stand up to him? However, I would suggest a supplementary meaning: If an animal such as the Leviathan, won't let himself become enslaved, how much less should man submit, he who is made in God's image? Yahweh states that the skin of these animals cannot be penetrated by arrows. Now, the human skin *is* penetrable, and its "openness" is associated with man's greater sensitivity—the very quality that makes him receptive to the spiritual nature of the Hebrew God and renders him creative.[24] For, Yahweh speaks of Himself not only as the archer, but also as *the rain which fructifies the land* to the extent that its "skin" is penetrable:

> Who hath cleft a channel for the waterflood,
> Or a way for the lightning of the thunder;
> To cause it to rain on a land where no man is . . .
> To satisfy the desolate and waste ground,
> And to cause the bud of the tender herb to spring forth.

In this sense as well, Yahweh should be distinguished from Elohim of the Prologue. Where the latter appears indifferent to the fate of Job's animals, servants and children, Yahweh speaks of His animal creations, particularly the war-horse, with something of an artist's pride in his creations. And, he has faith in Job's human powers, calling on him to gird himself like a man, assuring him that he can be saved by his "own right hand."[25]

One of the crucial features of the mythic hero is his acting as a scapegoat for society. Prometheus endures for mankind, Oedipus and Orestes suffer for the Greek *polis*, the trials of Hamlet, Goethe's Faust, Gide's Theseus and Thomas Mann's Joseph are finally in the interests of social welfare. Job, on the other hand, appears to be concerned only about himself.

To be sure, the Book does not reach the degree of socialization voiced by Deutero-Isaiah. Still, in the course of his psychic journey, Job moves towards a powerful indictment of social wrong and exploitation. In chapter 24, he speaks of those who carry the sheaves and go about hungry, who work the winepresses, yet suffer thirst:

> There are that pluck the fatherless from the breast,
> And take a pledge of the poor;
> So that they go about naked without clothing,
> And being hungry they carry the sheaves;
> They make oil within the rows of these men;
> They tread their winepresses, and suffer thirst. . . .

In chapter 30, he talks of men

> . . . gaunt with want and famine;
> They gnaw the dry ground, in the gloom of wasteness and desolation. . . .
> In the clefts of the valleys they must dwell,
> In holes of the earth and of the rocks.

In the following chapter, Job champions the human rights of the slave:

> Did not He that made me in the womb make him?
> And did not One fashion us in the womb?

Commenting on such passages in the Book, Isaac Mendelssohn writes that Job is the first in the ancient Near East who "raised his voice in a sweeping condemnation of slavery as a cruel and inhuman institution, irrespective of nationality and race."[26] At the end, Job forgives the Friends who had calumniated him, and gives his daughters inheritance along with his sons, thereby going beyond the old patrilineal law.

The Psychic Process of Job's Redemption

This chapter argues that Job's "redemption" comes about through a change in his personality. And, I want to suggest that this change is analogous to a psychoanalytic process if we view the Friends, Elihu and Yahweh as developing aspects of his ego. This process is dramatized in Job's debates with these characters in the course of which he relives the intellectual and emotional experience of his "guilty" past.

58

At the beginning, we find Job at home, amidst family and friends, enjoying his material possessions and social status. Following his "breakdown," we see him lying or sitting. He then begins to "talk."[27]

The crucial stage in Job's growing awareness is reached in the speeches of Elihu which follow his debate with the Friends.

In his final answer to the Friends, Job casts a last nostalgic glance back to "the days of my youth," when young and old, the poor and wealthy paid him homage. In the next chapter, Job admits that he *may* have committed many sins.

> If I have walked with vanity . . .
> If my heart have been enticed unto a woman . . .
> If I did despise the cause of my man-servant . . .
> If I have withheld aught that the poor desired . . .
> If I have made gold my hope
> If after the manner of men I covered my transgressions,
> By hiding mine iniquity in my bosom—
> Because I feared the great multitude. . . .

At this point, Job becomes ready for Elihu's revelations to which he makes no rejoinder.

Elihu begins by rebuking the Friends for not meeting Job's argument. He then states that God also communicates with man by dreams, "though man perceiveth it not." Elihu then points to Job's central sin: his life of ease amidst the comforts of the table. In a vague way, Job had known what Elihu makes explicit. He spoke earlier (7) of God scaring him "with dreams," terrifying him "through visions," and of the iniquities he may have hidden in his bosom. Finally, Elihu prepares Job for the revelation imparted by Yahweh.

Yahweh is the all-sufficient, unfathomable "giant," whom Job had been asking for an answer and who at last tells him what his "talk" comes to. He is at first a threatening disturbing father figure to Job. Job feels himself condemned by Yahweh, proved "perverse," although he thinks himself innocent. Job likens Yahweh to the archer who shoots his arrows into him, breaches and cleaves his reins, gnashes him with his teeth:[28]

> I was at ease, and He broke me asunder;
> Yea, He hath taken me by the neck, and dashed me to pieces;
> He hath also set me up for His mark.
> His archers compass me round about,
> He cleaveth my reins asunder, and doth not spare;
> He poureth out my gall upon the ground,

> He breaketh me with breach upon breach;
> He runneth upon me like a giant.

Towards the end, Yahweh also appears as creator and nourisher, as the power that brought Job out of the womb, poured him out "as milk," clothed him "with skin and flesh" (10). And Job's attitude toward God is correspondingly ambivalent. Like Ivan Karamazov, he rejects God's world as unjust, and like him, he accepts God himself. Ahab too addresses his "fiery father" with ringing defiance, yet begs him to "come in thy lowest form of love, and I will kneel and kiss thee."

Job is rewarded for his critical examination and the God who had been a total mystery, reveals Himself and talks to Job. Before, Job had only "heard" of God through the precepts handed down by tradition. But what Job wanted was to "see" him: "Lo, He goeth by me, and I see Him not;" After Job has gone through his ordeal, the wish is granted, and he says to Yahweh:

> I had heard of Thee by the hearing of the ear;
> But now mine eye seeth Thee.

The speeches of Elihu and Yahweh are a dramatization of what Job has come to "see" in the course of his psychic development. In this process, Job is shocked into life, that is, to a critical attitude towards his God and himself. At the end, he accepts Yahweh. But, unlike the Friends, he does so only after he has passed through the revolt by reason and the stages of emotional understanding. With Prometheus, Job rebels only against the father who seems to act arbitrarily and tyrannically, but affirms Him when His power is directed by wisdom. Above all, Job can accept the God who reproves the uncritical Friends, just as Job had hoped:

> He shall surely reprove you,
> If ye do secretly show favor.

Stated summarily, *Job is redeemed precisely because he has refused to accept an irrational authority*, because he has insisted on maintaining his own ways without losing faith in a substantive principle. Job persists in making his own choice and, to this extent, is his own instrument for salvation. In these several ways, the Book of Job redeems the ancient prophetic temper by symbolic representation.

Epilogue

The value placed on the critical approach precludes a paradisiac Third Act in the Hebrew Myth—Moses too was not to enter the Promised Land. Even as the Hebrew God developed from the tribal to the cosmic deity, he retained the restless features of the desert- and volcano-God. He *is* the whirlwind who dislocates Job. In turn, Job is rehabilitated because he exhibits the qualities of the God of the whirlwind. In this connection, history takes on a new function. Mircea Eliade points out that while time is a factor in Greek mythopoesis, it is only with the Hebrews that *historical time* plays a vital role, that they were the first "to discover the meaning of history as the epiphany of God. . . ."[29]

This note introduces an element of mystery into the Book of Job. The poem belongs to a time when the myth had not yet emancipated itself from its magic-religious layers. The Hebrew God is *a will*, that is, a force which cannot be grasped by logic. Yahweh's appearance has an apocalyptic character, his language has a tone of sublimity, is more incantatory than reasoned. Job had demanded complete justice. But, Yahweh asks him:

> Where wast thou when I laid the foundations of the earth?
> Hast thou commanded the morning since thy days began. . . .

The individual comes into a world "given" to him in order and sequence so that, already at birth, he owes an infinitude of debts. Man cannot know the bottomless well of the past, the ultimate why and how of creation, but only some of its implications.

However, this is less an anticipation of the doctrine of grace than a statement of the quest proper to those who have chosen to follow a God who is not content with creation and preservation, but insists on dynamic recreation.[30] This makes for tragic heroism. The Book does close with Job restored to his former greatness. Yet, his restitution is not without its tragic residue—his servants and children are dead, and cannot be replaced by those given him. Moreover, this reward is out of rhythm with the tone of the Book, and with the story of "The Wandering Jew," of a people whose history, as Erich Kahler puts it, *begins* with exile, given over to the loneliness of the quest. In the words of H. and H. A. Frankfort:

> Nowhere in the literature of Egypt or Babylonia, do we meet the loneliness
> of the Biblical figures . . . Saul . . . David . . . men in terrible isolation facing
> a transcendent God: Abraham trudging to the place of sacrifice with his son,
> Jacob in his struggle, and Moses and the prophets. (*Ancient Man*, p. 371.)

This loneliness appears in the characters of Franz Kafka and Sholem Asch, in Joyce's Bloom, Mann's Naphta and Jacob, makes itself felt in Proust's Swann.

Yet, this alienation is also the promise of a creative future. Thorstein Veblen speaks of the Jew as "a disturber of the intellectual peace . . . a wanderer in the intellectual no man's land, seeking another place to rest, further along the road, somewhere over the horizon. . . . never complacent nor contented." Similarly, for Jacques Maritain, Judaism "bars slumber, it teaches the world to be discontented and restless as long as the world has not God; it stimulates the movement of history."[31] It is in this sense that the Book of Job is a *statement of the symbolic value of exile*, that is, the value of spiritual rebellion, which is a concomitant of the exiled condition. In a basic sense, the *Book of Job is a dramatic statement of the religious attitude.*

Jewish characters in modern literature, far removed from Job's memory of his origins, have become too "civilized" to insist on their own ways, or too "sensitive" to challenge the hidden or open accusations of their alleged guilt. The historic fate which has deprived the Jew of a folk base hangs over these characters—Lessing's Nathan, Proust's Swann, Kafka's Joseph K., Mann's Naphta.

However, Thomas Mann's later epic of Jacob and Joseph is a contemporary reaffirmation of the Hebrew myth and its universal import. This work was conceived and executed even as Hitlerism attempted to reduce the Jew to dust and ashes. This very attempt served as a shock which roused in many the memory of their tradition, making possible the heroic resistance by the Warsaw ghetto and the Israeli war of liberation.

There remains the perennial mythic import of the Book—its homily on the living value of the critical conscience. Historic circumstances have produced perhaps an over-accentuation of this faculty in the Jew. Yet, criticism is a function of the spirit itself. "Spiritually," Maritain writes, "we are all Semites." Transposed into human affairs, the Book is a warning against the self-sufficiency of folk interests. For the prophets, Amos in particular, the Jew was nearly synonymous with mankind in its higher strivings. The author of the Book speaks of Job, not as a Hebrew, but as "a man." And Job becomes truly human and alive through his quest and questioning, for the God he chose to follow is a God of The Quest. In this sense, the Book is a link in the mythic tradition of freedom from Aeschylus' Prometheus to Thomas Mann's Jacob.

NOTES

1.　See Angelo S. Rappoport, *Myth and Legend of Ancient Israel* (London, 1928), Vol. I; H. and H. A. Frankfort *et al.*, *The Intellectual Adventure of Ancient Man* (Chicago, 1946). S. H. Langdon (*The Mythology of All Races*, Vol. V

[Boston, 1931]) considers the following stories specifically Jewish: The Tables of the Law, Sodom and Gomorrha, the Egyptian Plagues, Balaam and the Ass, Jonah and the Whale, Samson and Delilah. But none of them has become the subject of a major mythopoeic work.

2. Morris Jastrow states that "from an early age, Job has become a popular figure among the Hebrews." (*The Book of Job* [Philadelphia and London, 1920], p. 46). According to William F. Albright (*From the Stone Age to Christianity* [Baltimore, 1940]), the name of Job first appears in an Egyptian list of Palestinian chieftains (about 2000 B.C.). See Shalom Spiegel's article, "Noah, Daniel and Job" in *Louis Ginsberg's Jubilee Volume* (New York, 1945), pp. 305-355.

3. According to the Talmudic view (quoted in Dr. Victor E. Reichert's *Job* [The Soncino Press, 1946], p. 223), Job shows "the virtue of resignation." Moses Buttenwieser (*The Book of Job* [New York, 1925]) sees the Book as teaching that finite man "cannot fathom the infinite wisdom of God, or comprehend the mystery of his Rule."

Carl Jung (*Answer to Job* [London, 1954]) follows the traditional view that Job is guiltless. But he makes two startlingly new points: Job finally recognizes that Yahweh is an amoral, antinomical God who is impervious to moral considerations. However, Jung argues that, in the end, Yahweh becomes conscious that the victim, Job, stands morally higher than God, his victimizer. To catch up with man, Yahweh has to become human and regenerate himself. This intention, according to Jung, is fulfilled in Christ's life and sufferings. The basis for Jung's diatribe against Yahweh is his disparagement of the Father Imago, primarily representing Power, in favor of the compassionate Mother Imago.

4. The "Babylonian Job" accepts God's ways as unfathomable, asking "How can mortals learn the way of a God?"

5. *Book of Job* (New York, 1946).

6. All quotations follow the King James version.

7. Jastrow (*The Book of Job*) not only denies any connection between the defiant and the resigned Job, but sees none between the sympathetic Friends and their later harsh judgments of Job, and none between the God of the Prologue and the God in the discussions. Yahweh's speeches are said to be independent compositions which have no bearing on the central theme.

8. For an elaboration of this historical element, see William Irwin and H. and H. A. Frankfort in *The Intellectual Adventure of Ancient Man*.

9. Sinai, where the law was given, is encircled by the desert. From here, the Jews wandered to Kadesh, in the wilderness of Zin. (See Jack Finegan, *Light from the Ancient East* [Princeton, 1946].) W. F. Albright denies a fixed nomadic tradition in early Israel, arguing that mass nomadic movements were not possible because the desert would not sustain them. (*Archaelogy and the Religion of Israel* [Baltimore, 1942]). On the other hand, Th. H. Robinson argues for their nomadic ancestry and W. O. E. Oesterley holds that the Feast of Passover

was originally a nomadic Moon-festival. (See S. H. Hooke, *Myth and Ritual* [London, 1933].) Theodor Gaster (*Thespis* [New York, 1950]) refers to frequent allusions in the Old Testament to the seasonal ritual and to the detailed description in the Mishnah of an elaborate rain-making ceremony. Yet, fertility rites found no central place since the uncertain life of an exiled people offered no basis for feeling a bond between nature and man. Indeed, there are no nature myths in the Hebrew tradition. "Those who served Yahweh must forego the richness, the fulfilment, and the consolation of a life which moves in tune with the great rhythms of earth and sky." H. and H. A. Frankfort, *Ancient Man*, pp. 343 ff.

10. Prior to the time of Job, Hebrew theology was laden with elements of Babylonic mythology where the Earth-Mother is the creatress of mankind. Even later, when the Semitic myth identifies Yahweh with the Rain-and Thunder-God, Adad, he is still associated with the Canaanitish Mother-Goddess Ashtart-Anat. (See S. H. Langdon, *The Mythology of All Races*). Isolated instances of the incest theme remain: the cabalistic story of the Messiah as issuing from incest; Noah and his daughters; Judah and Tamar. What may be the reasons for the minor role of incest in the Hebrew myth? Was the taboo "naturally" adhered to because of the need to keep intact the unity of a people which was threatened in many other ways? Is the God-Father self-sufficient because all-containing? Does his spirituality forbid his mingling with an "earth-"mother? Is this why woman is pictured as the temptress (Lillith, Delilah, Job's wife)? To be sure, the "female" element of love is not altogether absent in the Hebrew Father-God. Hosea (11) writes of God's "tenderness." The Psalmist speaks of his "tender mercies" (103, 145). The element of comfort is more prominent in modern Jewish writers, notably Franz Werfel and Sholem Asch.

11. This point is developed by Ernst Cassirer in his essay "Judaism and the Modern Political Myths," *Contemporary Jewish Record* (April, 1944).

12. Cf. my study, *Thomas Mann's Joseph Story. An Interpretation* (New York, 1938).

13. Jastrow translates: "When my guests washed in cream."

14. The point is strengthened by the fact that the text uses various terms for the Lord. According to Kissane (*Book of Job*): "In the Prologue, Job, his wife, the messenger and Satan use the name *Elohim* for God; in the Dialogue the names used are *El* (55), *Eloah* (41), *Shaddai* (31), and *Elohim* (6), all of which were employed in the patriarchal age. The writer himself, in the narrative passages, uses the name Yahweh, which indicates that he is an Israelite." *Elohim* (Job's term) is used at times in the sense of "Judge," a name not reserved for the Lord, as when God tells Moses to speak to Aaron in his office as *Elohim*. One should also note the Lord's active role in Job's affliction. In Goethe's *Faust*, the Lord mentions Faust only after Mephisto (who is differentiated from "the true sons" of God) speaks derogatorily of man. In the Book, the Satan (who is included among the sons of God) does not censure man,

but speaks of "going to and fro in the earth." Thereupon, the Lord challengingly brings up the case of Job, stating that he is perfect and upright. Thus, it is the Lord who provokes the Satan towards proposing that Job be tried, and sets up the situation which leads to the massacre of his household and to his plight.

15. Kissane cites various authorities for holding that the lines "I will teach you by the hand of God. . . . This is the portion of a wicked man with God" are spoken by Bildad in his third speech where he is "quoting Job's words spoken to those who, in former days, were perplexed by the prosperity of the wicked. Job's earlier views coincided with those of his Friends, which he now so vehemently rejects." *Book of Job*, pp. 166, 163.

16. Gersonides and Jastrow say flatly that they are not Hebrews.

17. Job does not begin his lament until the Friends appear. Their unspoken acceptance of his punishment seems to rouse Job against them.

18. In chapter 10, Job distinguishes between "wickedness," which is deliberate flouting of God's will, and "sin," which is due to ignorance. Kissane calls attention to a similar distinction made in Numbers, the Psalms, Leviticus and elsewhere between "sins of ignorance," "errors," or "hidden sins" and "sins committed with a high hand." In the Prologue, Job speaks of the possibility that his sons may have cursed God "in their hearts."

19. Jastrow states that this line must be translated as: "Though he slay me, I tremble not." This makes Job's challenge even stronger.

20. In chapters 36 and 37, Job characterizes the nature of God in the way in which Yahweh defines himself at the end.

21. According to Kissane, only a few critics, Budde and Cornill in particular, maintain that Elihu's chief contribution is "that suffering is an effective instrument in God's hands, leading man to the knowledge of himself, of the evil propensities within him." *Book of Job*, p. xxxix.

22. The text is somewhat corrupt here, but according to Kissane, a literal translation reads: "And He hath enticed thee from . . . the comfort of the table full of fatness." It also suggests that Job has been partial to the wealthy and powerful. *Book of Job*, pp. 247, 248.

23. *The Book of Job* (New York, 1918). Kallen interprets Yahweh as analogous to the *deus ex machina* of Euripides and argues that only "moral indifference can be genuine justice" and that Job is comforted by Yahweh's very indifference. Kallen's view of Yahweh fits the earlier conception of the Hebrew God as a nature power, that is, neutral to moral issues. A different analogy to Euripides could be drawn in that he too presented revolutionary characters who insist on their personal choice. However, whereas his *deus ex machina* device was meant to disparage the Greek god, the author of the Book treats Yahweh with unreserved awe.

24. Cf. Northrup Frye, *Fearful Symmetry, A Study of William Blake* (Boston, 1962).

25. In the Greek version, Yahweh says to Job:

"Despise not my chastisement!
Dost thou think I would have revealed myself
Were it not that thou mightest be proven righteous!"
(Quoted by Moses Buttenwieser, *The Book of Job*, p. 62.) Albright suggests that the Hebrew God is both "jealous" over his sovereignty, as well as "zealous" for the well-being of his people. The dual meaning is also present in the German word *Eifer-sucht*.

26. *Slavery in the Ancient Near East* (New York, 1949).
27. It is to be noted that the main "action" of the Book consists of "talking." These talks are between Job and only one character at a time— one of the Friends, or Elihu or Yahweh. When he is not responding to the arguments of the Friends, Job lapses into ruminations about his past.
28. Dr. Reichert points out that the word "reins" is "metaphorical for the most sensitive and vital part of the body." Job also speaks of God's "rod" (9) which terrifies him, of God, the "lion" who hunts him.
29. *The Myth of the Eternal Return* (New York, 1954), p. 104.
30. According to S. R. Driver (*An Introduction to the Literature of the Old Testament* [New York, 1903], p. 418), "Redeemer" is used to denote "a deliverer, not from sin, but from affliction and wrong not due to him."
31. *True Humanism* (2d ed.; New York, 1954); *Freedom in the Modern World* (London, 1935).

Greek Mythopoesis
The Blessed Crime
Aeschylus, Sophocles, Euripides

ACCORDING TO HESIOD'S version of the first or Golden Age of Man, men lived "without cares or labor . . . never growing old, dancing and laughing much; death to them was no more terrible than sleep. They are all gone now, but their spirits survive as happy genii" (Transliteration by Robert Graves). And in Plato's *Timaeus*, Critias states that when Solon was in Egypt, one of its priests told him:

> You do not know that there formerly dwelt in your land the fairest and noblest race of men which ever lived, and that you and your whole city are descended from a small seed or remnant of them which survived. . . . For there was a time, Solon, before the great deluge of all, when the city which now is Athens was first in war and in every way the best governed of all cities, and is said to have performed the noblest deeds and to have had the fairest constitution of any of which tradition tells, under the face of heaven . . . excelled all mankind in all virtue . . . preserved from slavery those who were not yet subjugated, and generously liberated all the rest of us.

Freud speculates (*Moses and Monotheism*) that Greek mythology drew on the memory of an ancient glory, possibly that of Minoan and Mycenean culture.[1] With the development of a mercantile and monetary economy, based on a growing slave market, the memory of this splendor was growing dim. It is at this point that the idea of Greece's golden age is redeemed symbolically in its mythopoesis.

The mythic view was native to the Greeks. They viewed nearly everything on a mythic plane—from flies and asses to men and gods, from the seasonal cycle to human birth and death, from the idea of number, space and time to religion, philosophy and the arts. Poetry, in particular, was mytho-poesis to them (Werner Jaeger points out that the Greeks had no word which exactly corresponds to "literature.") The poet was a "maker," combining the functions of teacher, prophet and interpreter. His art was part of *Paideia*, and *Paideia* encompassed the whole of man in his varied relations. The unitary quality of the myth fitted the compact Greek world which was then the anchor of civilization. And, it fitted in with the *polis* which embraced the citizen's entire activity, integrating his politics, art, science, philosophy and religion.

The Greek myth, like all myths, had a historic-social function. George Thomson and Henri Frankfort have shown that it was used to further social-political interests and for that reason the tyrant Peisistratos gave the mythic rituals official sanction, instituting them as part of the Dionysian festival. In George Thomson's formulation, the Achean Olympus "was the mythical mirror of social reality."[2] His *Studies in Ancient Greek Society* presents interesting material on the social genesis of the Moirai. These supreme powers (they also rule over Zeus) represented social authority in everything except their immortality. Thomson traces the original meaning of the Moirai to "portion" of wealth, or "division" of labor, representing man's "share" and "lot" or fate. In Plato, they are associated with the "spinners" of destiny— Clotho, Atropos, Lachesis—who spin man's lot at the moment of his birth.

Like the spinners of destiny, the Moirai are female powers, and probably connected with mother-right in Indo-European pre-history. As such, they have a democratic, egalitarian function and the "lot" used to guarantee equal, impartial distribution. The Moirai, Thomson writes

> stood for the authority of ancestral custom, which determined each man's birthright . . . . [They] originated as symbols of the economic and social functions of primitive communism—the sharing of game, the sharing of booty, the sharing of land, the sharing of labour between the clans; that is to say, they grew out of the neolithic mother-goddesses, who, emanating from the female elders of the matriarchal clan, symbolized the collective authority of countless generations of ancestresses. (*Ancient Greek Society*, pp. 337, 339.)

When Greece passed from tribalism to the city state and its slave system, the Moirai were displaced or joined by Ananke (Necessity) which was to reconcile men with slavery.[3]

The period of the merchant princes also witnessed the emergence of political democracy.[4] Its effect appears in Aeschylus where the tyrant Zeus of *Prometheus Bound* becomes a just ruler in the fragments of *Prometheus Unbound* and the stern Erinyes of the Oresteia are transformed into the kindly Eumenides. Summary vengeance is abandoned for trial by jury, which considers not the act alone, but the individual's motive and his subsequent change of heart. Orestes tells the Furies:

> . . . Look, how the stain of blood
> Is dull upon mine hand and wastes away,
> And laved and lost therewith is the deep curse
> Of matricide . . .
> How oft since then among my fellow-men
> I stood and brought no curse. Time cleanses all—
> Time, the coeval of all things that are.[5]

Apollo and Dionysus

Winckelmann characterized Hellenic art as exhibiting "noble simplicity and quiet grandeur" (*edle Einfalt und stille Grösse*). Erwin Rohde and Friedrich Nietzsche saw this as the "Apollonian" face of Greece, standing for restraint and reason, for equilibrium and order.[6] This aspect has been stressed in our own day by Edith Hamilton who identifies it with the Western temper.

In *The Greeks and the Irrational*, E.R. Dodds has modified and corrected this sharp contrast between the "rational" religion of Apollo and the "irrational" religion of Dionysus. According to Dodds, there is evidence in the *Iliad* that Apollo was originally an Asiatic and that there were shamanistic elements in the cult of Apollo.[7] In his *Dionysus, Myth and Cult*, Walter F. Otto states that the worship of Dionysus was older than that of Apollo but adds that their two worlds coexisted and were interdependent.[8] Dodds tends to support this approach, pointing out that Apollo was simultaneously the patron of scientific medicine and of healing by prayer and incantation. Each, he writes, ministered "in his own way to the anxieties characterized by a guilt culture. Apollo promised security . . . Dionysus offered freedom. . . ." (*The Greeks and the Irrational*, p. 76).

While it is therefore inaccurate to use "Apollo" and "Dionysus" as representing clearly demarcated historic stages or as sharply divided categories, they might be employed as *symbolic* representations in the relative weight traditionally accorded to Western "Apollonian" light and reason in contrast to Eastern "Dionysian" unrestraint and ecstasy.

In any case, the Hellenic period did attempt to cleanse the myth of primitive magic and Oriental religious mystery, to naturalize it by science and humanize it by ethics. For Protagoras, *man*, not God, was the measure of things. The authority of the priesthood was replaced by the authority of a critical dialectic.[9] With the pre-Socratic philosophers, Moira and Nemesis became Substance and Causality which were subject to scientific analysis. Socrates' basic assumption was that truth and justice can be found by critical examination. Ernst Cassirer has shown that for Greek philosophy, the same laws govern nature (Kosmos), logic (Logos) and morals (Dike). Its substantive thinking converted chronological beginnings into philosophic priorities, the mythic "once upon a time" into first principles. Where the Hindu Brahma saw only the ephemeralness of existence, Greek substance emphasized *the law* in change. And the Greek thinkers sought to find this law in philosophy, physics and art.[10]

This principle is applied in Aristotle's *Poetics*. Poetry, it states, is more philosophical than history in that the poet "imitates" an action which is not unique, but has archetypal representation. Similarly, art effects a "catharsis" by revealing that the outcome was not an accident of history, but has the character of universal necessity: the hero's fall is not due to "vice or depravity," but to "frailty" (*hamartia* or faulty insight), that is, to inadequate knowledge of the order of things. Thus, we may interpret Aristotle as saying that knowledge of necesssity purges man of pity (which comes from feeling that the unfortunate event was avoidable) and of fear (which comes from not knowing the nature and source of the threat).

The principle was also applied in the Greek theatre, which fused all the arts—drama, acting, dancing, poetry, designing, song. It presented myths, that is, stories which were universally known, performed in an open amphitheatre large enough to hold the entire Athenian citizenry. The actors wore masks indicating their representation of generic characters ("the King," "Priest," etc.) and the chorus summed up the inevitability of the action in a "doxology." Inevitability was further indicated by the use of the "analytical technique," or what Schiller called "tragic analysis," in which the tragic ending was determined by events preceding the opening of the dramatic action.

However, the necessity of the action did not preclude individual choice and responsibility. As *an art*, Greek tragedy presented the law of Moira through particular individuals and events. In Gerhard Nebel's formulation, the infinite was given finite form and the tragic process became "the definition of the indefinite." Aeschylus, Sophocles and Euripides dealt more or less with the same mythic stories involving Oedipus, Electra, Antigone, Orestes, etc. Yet, each dramatist gave the various figures differentiating characteristics, which provided the basis for the shift from tribal to individual guilt, and from "Fate" to human choice. And, as we shall see in discussing Aeschylus' *Prometheia*, the hero was not only fated to accept; he was also fated to rebel.

The union of necessity and freedom brought a reorientation in the function of the oracle. The mythic curse and blessing still operated; but to be effective, they had to be renewed by *an individual act* of *hybris* or *arete*. The oracle did not simply pronounce an inevitable happening. It became *a warning voice*, calling attention to *the tendencies* of an individual or a family to perform certain acts. The fate of Odysseus and his companions is not sealed in the *Odyssey*. They are warned by the oracle that *if* they slay the cattle of Helios, they will perish. This "if" corresponds to the hypothesis in science, pointing to elements in a character which predispose him to act in a certain way. And, *knowledge of his predisposition* gives the individual an opportunity to provide against such acting out.[11]

The Greeks were the first to see the dialectic relationship between necessity and freedom. It is clearly stated in Plato's myth of Er at the end of *The Republic* (Book X): The distaff of Necessity spins around with uniform velocity, accompanied by the song of sirens producing a single harmony. The Fates chant to their music—Lachesis sounds the events of the past, Clotho of the present, Atropos of the future. And Lachesis, the daughter of Necessity, declares that man's destiny is not allotted, but shall be *chosen* by him: "The responsibility lies with the chooser. Heaven is guiltless." And Socrates continues:

> and for this reason, above all others, it is the duty of each of us diligently to investigate and study . . . that science which may haply enable a man to learn and discover . . . as to be able to discriminate between a good and an evil life, and according to his means to choose, always and everywhere, that better life, by carefully calculating the influence which the things just mentioned, in combination or in separation, have upon real excellence of life.

This means that *man can choose his fate*, or as Heraclitus put it: "Man's character is his fate." When Clytemnestra tries to shift the blame for the murder of Agamemnon "to the old Avenger," the Chorus indignantly exclaims:

> Thou guiltless of this murder, thou!
> Who dares such thought avow?

Dionysus

Greek culture had emerged from primitive and Eastern civilizations which left their mark. The traditional picture of Greek serenity ignores the fact that, except for the relative tranquility in the brief cultural flowering between the Persian and Peloponnesian wars, Greek history is filled with war and civil war. These historic incidences help explain why the Greeks also felt the power of an older, primitive god, Dionysus.

In *The Birth of Tragedy*, Nietzsche stressed the Dionysian *Rausch* or ecstasy in Greek drama. In our own time, Jane Harrison has analyzed Greek tragedy in terms of the primitive ritual, and George Thomson has found remnants of totemism in Greek history. This suggests that the Greeks *needed* Apollonian form to control the rage of their Dionysianism, that their stress on law was to meet the threat of disorder and unrestraint.

Greek tragedy arose, not out of the Apollonian, but out of the ancient Dionysian cult. Where Apollo was associated with light and with the aristocratic patriarchal Olympus, Dionysus derived from the dark Chthonic underground and from the democratic matriarchy.[12]

The worship of Dionysus had the character of rapture, associated with his companions, the raging maenads.[13] To be sure, the function of the ritual was to promote fertility of the soil.[14] However, its temper was one of rebellious defiance. In Euripides' *The Bacchae*, Dionysianism is the underground storm which breaks up the stratified intellectual civilization of Pentheus.[15]

Jane Harrison (*Ancient Art and Ritual* [London, 1913]) argues that the art of tragedy has its origin in the ritual vestiges of tribal initiation and is connected with the seasonal ritual. Applied to mythopoesis, this approach can be helpful in directing attention to the *literary* ritual, that is, to the dramatic language, form and structure through which the myth is humanized. However, the limitation of the seasonal approach lies in its failure to consider the distinction between the year-god and the human personality. For primitives, almost wholly at the mercy of natural powers, the seasonal rhythm was the pattern for life of man as well. Mythopoesis breaks with this static rhythm. It connotes that by the use of knowledge and the tool, man can control the forces of nature and thus become a *culture* hero. Just as Hellenic art moved from rigid archaic figures towards the human body, so it reshaped the seasonal rhythm of the old myth into the human act. To give two brief examples: The Oresteia begins with the death of the king and queen and the mangling of Orestes. It ends with a "higher" replacement of the old king and queen (by Apollo and Athena) and the rebirth of Orestes. This process is foretold by the Chorus in *Agamemnon*:

> List! on my soul breathes yet a harmony,
> From realms of ageless powers, and strong to save!

and by Clytemnestra:

> As saith the adage, *From the womb of Night*
> *Spring forth, with promise fair, the young child Light.*

Similarly, Sophocles' Oedipus tragedy begins with the winter scourge of Thebes and closes with the promise of peace and security.

The development of the chorus also indicates the emergence of this element. Through music and the dance, the chorus expressed that which was hidden, was supra-individual and supra-rational. In Greek tragedy, the chorus generally (though not always) consists of the most distinguished members of the community, but is not the sole spokesman, as it may have been in its beginnings. For, now we get "the second actor," the leader of the chorus. With the introduction of the mythic hero, we get the condition for conflict, or *drama* proper.

The Dionysian myth unleashed the savagery of primitive subterranean forces. At the same time, its very frenzy served, as Dodds points out, to bring psychological release: "it purged the individual of those infectious irrational impulses . . . it relieved them by providing them with a ritual outlet." Thus, in Euripides' *The Bacchae*, Dionysus is "the cause of madness and the liberator from madness." The Apollonian attempted to control these powers by form and order. In Greek mythopoesis as a whole, "Dionysus" and "Apollo" interacted in a dialectic rhythm.

In his study of the Doric Temple, Max Raphael shows that the equilibrium of the Doric column is not achieved by the "compromise" of the Roman arch, but by tension and stress, producing a delicate balance between the horizontal and the vertical.[16] In Greek mythopoesis, harmony is likewise won by strain and strife. Greek cosmogony is crowded with patricide and incest. With the help of his mother, Gaia, Kronos castrates his father, Uranus, and later swallows his own children; Zeus who is saved by Rhea's ruse, dethrones his father, Kronos, and is in turn challenged by Prometheus; Oedipus kills his father, and Orestes, his mother. Equally pervasive is the theme of incest between mother-sister and son-brother, as between Orthos and Echidna, Oedipus and Jocasta, Gaia-Rhea and Uranus-Cronos. Fratricide and infanticide appear in the stories of Atreus, who slays his brother's children and serves them to their father at a banquet; Medea kills her sons; Agamemnon sacrifices his daughter; Oedipus is exposed on the mountain by his parents. It is to be noted that in the mythological stories such acts are committed with full knowledge, whereas in mythopoesis, they are covered and take on a more symbolic character. As noted, here *a*

73

character becomes heroic only after he has violated some primary taboo. Nietzsche refers to the Persian belief that a wise man is born of incest, and the same idea is found in the Hebrew legend of the Messiah. Thomas Mann's *The Holy Sinner* treats the medieval story of Gregory, who is born of the union between a brother and sister, later marries his mother, and subsequently is elected Pope. Infringement of established rules is a condition for the development of the heroic in mythopoesis.

Greek mythic thought exhibits the same dialectic principle with respect to the relation between the aristocratic and democratic forms and between the matriarchic and patriarchic values. Historically, Greece was developing towards the patriarchy; yet, its memory of the matriarchy was never wholly submerged.[17] The most dramatic example of this principle of conservation is Athena: In Homer, she is Odysseus' guiding hand and counters the wrath of Poseidon. And, while she argues for the greater importance of the father in *The Eumenides*, it is *her* vote which is decisive in acquitting Orestes.[18] The crucial role of the mother-goddess is later revived in Christianity and Greek orthodoxy.

The entrance to Apollo's temple at Delphi bore the inscriptions: "Nothing too much" and "Know thyself." The first summed up the ideal of moderation (*sophrosyne*), echoing the argument of Plato's *Republic* that justice is the harmonious interplay among the various powers in the individual and society. The second inscription, "Know thyself," pointed to man's need to recognize the tendency of one or the other of his powers to overreach itself. For the Greeks, beauty also lay in the harmonious proportions of the *human* body, in contrast to the rigid forms of animals, griffins, demons of the archaic period. Its keynote of *flexibility* was connected with the political aim of the *polis*. The Oresteia ends with Athena's chant that

> . . . gracious powers on earth
> Henceforth be seen to bless the life of men.

This prayer was briefly voiced during the Periclean period. But soon, the slave system and the imperialism of the city state brought conflict of authorities. "The middle way" which is "dearest unto God," of which the Chorus sings in *The Eumenides*, was being disturbed. By the time of Euripides the "Apollonian" was defied and the "Dionysian" came to the fore.

AESCHYLUS' PROMETHEIA

The legend of the fire-bringer belongs to the earliest folk-traditions. In primitive stories, fire is brought by an animal or wrested by a giant. In Greek mythology, it is stolen by a titan.

According to Hesiod, Uranus named those who tended to "overreach" themselves "titans." Fire has been connected with the titanic because of its elemental savagery and because it too "overreaches" itself.[19] In Greek thought, fire was considered an ambivalent force. Heraclitus called it the Logos or basic Substance whose "life" depended on the very material it destroyed.[20] Pliny saw it as an active agent in the work of human ingenuity:

> Fire takes in sand and gives back, now glass, now silver, now minium, now various kinds of lead, now pigments, now medicines. By fire stones are melted into bronze, by fire iron is made and mastered, by fire gold is produced, by fire that stone is calcined which, in the form of cement, holds our houses over our heads. (*Natural History*, xxxvi)

Pliny concluded by calling fire a "measureless and implacable portion of nature," asking whether it should rightly be called "destroyer or creator."

According to legend, Aeschylus was involved in the Eleusian and Dionysian mystery rites. Of the Greek tragedians, he stood closest to the primitive and religious mode and his style shows greatest restlessness. The action of *The Persians* is dominated by mythic powers in whose hands man is an object of their passion and will.

The central character of *Prometheus Bound* is a titan, surrounded by figures who are either allegorical, such as Power and Force, or divine missionaries, such as Hephaesthus, Oceanus and Hermes. (Io is a human character; but her story is secondary to the main theme.) The *Oresteia* is dominated by the Tantalus curse of ancestral guilt and retribution.

Despite these features, it is misleading to interpret Aeschylus as a religious mythicist. For, as we shall see, his Prometheia relies less on supernatural than on human power.

Aeschylus' Prometheus is the first culture hero in mythopoesis. He develops from an intransigent rebel to a hero who is mindful of the powers above (Zeus), the powers below (Themis, his Earth-Mother), and of his ties with man. In the older versions, Prometheus was doomed to defeat.[21] Hesiod saw in Prometheus' rebellious action the cause of human toil. In other accounts, it brought evil into the world, such as the box of Pandora which let sorrow, sickness and labor loose in the world. Aeschylus recast these ancient legends in naturalistic, human terms, transforming Moira into a character to whom Zeus too is subject (even he will be dethroned "by his own folly").[22]

In *The Birth of Tragedy*, Nietzsche stated that the core of the Prometheus myth is the necessity of the titanic individual to commit a crime. But only in the Greek version is the crime directed against a god. And, where Job is punished for what he neglected to do and Oedipus for what he did without conscious knowledge, Prometheus suffers from an active crime, committed with full awareness. He tells the Leader of the Chorus: "With open eyes, with willing mind, I erred." He knows what he did and is ready to face the consequences. In Oriental mythology, the past determines the future. In Aeschylus' Prometheia, knowledge of the future determines the present.

Act I: Harmony with Parental Authority

The Prometheia refers to an initial and to a final state of harmony between Prometheus and Zeus:

> Often to me my mother Themis (or call her Earth, for many names she hath, being one) had foretold in oracles what was to be, with warning that not by might or brutal force should victory come, but by guile alone.

When the titans tried to make themselves "lords by force," Prometheus supported Zeus in his struggle with them. But later Zeus became a tyrant who, as the Chorus proclaims, "unlawfully rules," wanting to blot out the whole human race.

"Prometheus" means "fore-knowledge." From his mother, he knows the future, knows the secret which conditions Zeus' fate—that if Zeus marries Thetis, he will be dethroned. It is this "if" which constitutes the dramatic conflict of Aeschylus' poetic version. The gloom of the opening setting in which Prometheus is bound to the rocks in a winter-bitten gorge where no human voice can reach him, where he is to waste his strength in ceaseless lamentations, is lightened by Prometheus' foreknowledge of ultimate reconciliation.

The drama opens with the hero set out, bound "in never-yielding fetters." Yet, from the beginning, there is promise of rescue by natural and human powers. In his opening chant, Prometheus invokes, not magical forces, but the elements: the "air divine," the "swift-winged winds," the "river-fountains," the "ocean waves," his "mother earth" and the "all-discerning orb o' the sun." Moreover, he has the sympathy of all the characters in the drama, with the exception of Zeus' lackeys: Power, Force, and Hermes. Even Hephaesthus, who uses his art of fire to bind Prometheus, does this against his will and he groans for the titan's pangs.

Act II: The Crime—Freedom from Fear

Prometheus displayed extraordinary courage in stealing fire from Zeus. Yet, as he is riveted to the rocks, he is gripped by fear "in whatever approaches." But, as he *speaks* of his act and becomes aware of its character, he regains courage. Aeschylus transposes the gift of fire into the psychic power of consciousness that removes the old fear of dark authorities.

Before he gave mankind "understanding and a portion of reason," Prometheus tells the Leader of the Chorus, the people were in a womb-like state:

> like children . . . seeing they saw not, and hearing they understood not, but like as shapes in a dream they wrought all the days of their life in confusion . . . like the little ants they dwelt underground in the sunless depth of caverns.

"Understanding" and "a portion of reason" are more than reflective thought. By *sophia* or "wisdom," the Greeks understood *practical application* of knowledge. Prometheus taught man "to discern the seasons by the rising and the obscure setting of the stars." He gave them understanding of their rituals, "of the altar-flames that before were meaningless." No longer would they need to propitiate a capricious "seasonal god," but could predict and provide for the workings of the natural phenomena. He revealed the technique for coping with disease, taught the use of "the secret treasures of the earth . . . copper, iron, silver, gold." In this context, fire becomes a technical-social lever for freeing human power, *a tool* which raises man from the animal towards the human stage.

Prometheus' "reason" went beyond the rational meaning of language; he "found the subtle interpretation of words half heard or heard by chance, and of meetings by the way." He even penetrated into the realm of the unconscious as revealed in dreams:

> From dreams I first taught them to judge what should befall in waking state.

At the same time, Prometheus stressed the value of tradition: "I taught them the grouping of letters, to be a memorial and record of the past, the mistress of the arts and mother of the muses." Prometheus thus combined bold re-creation of the human heritage with piety towards its valuable residue. In sum, "all human arts are from Prometheus."

The Journey

Prometheus attempted to free man from "the disease of tyranny." Now, he himself is a titan who had once been Zeus' ally; hence, the dramatic need for introducing the story of Io, a human victim. Unlike Prometheus, Io is an innocent sacrifice, and her fate presents the case for Prometheus in more human terms than his own story.

77

Io had been Hera's priestess in Argos and she became the double target of Zeus' desire and of Hera's jealousy. Stung by the gadfly, pursued by the spectre of Argus, she is driven "weary and famished," over land and water. The physical journey of "the wandering virgin of sorrows" is the counterpart of Prometheus' psychic journey.

Prometheus is punished for having committed a deliberate act; Io is punished although she seems to have done no wrong. Yet, she too is not free from guilt. Aeschylus recreates the legend to suggest that Io "wished" Zeus' passion for her. Before the God's desire is made manifest, Io is stirred by "Wild, perturbing wonders," and dreams that she is being exhorted to satisfy Zeus' yearning for her:

> For always in the drowsy hours of night
> I, sleeping in my virgin chambers, saw
> Strange visitations pass, and as they passed
> Each smiled and whispered: O sweet-favored girl,
> Why cherish long thy maiden loneliness,
> When love celestial calleth? Fair art thou,
> And thronèd Zeus, heart-smitten with desire,
> Yearns from his heaven to woo thee. Nay, sweet child,
> Disdain him not.

This is Io's "oracle," a warning of her desires. Here, again punishment fits the crime. As the fire-bringer is fettered by the fire-god Hephaesthus, so the passion of Io's dreams results in the "madness" which smites her brain "as a fire," and her animal desires are requited by her transformation into a heifer.[23]

The case for Prometheus is also made by the contrasting figure of Hermes who attempts to persuade Prometheus to divulge the secret knowledge of the conditions under which Zeus might be dethroned. He argues that there is no "profit" in his stand, and threatens that his body will be encased in the fiery rock and that Zeus' ravening eagle will feast on his liver. But Prometheus declares: "There is no fear in me," and that there is

> no torment or contrivance in the power of Zeus to wring this utterance from me, except these bonds are loosened.

He will not grow "woman-hearted . . . It is not in my nature." He tells Hermes: "I will not barter my hard lot for your menial service."

In Aeschylus' poetic version, Prometheus is punished not merely because he gave fire to man. (Conceivably, Zeus might recover, or mankind might lose the material substance of fire.) What Prometheus bequeathed is the fire of revolt, the spirit of defiance, that is, man's freedom from fear. Once set free, this power can never be lost, and with it ultimate victory over tyrannical authority is certain. In the magnificent lines of Prometheus' final chant, he sings of freedom as self-determination:

> Ay, let the lightning be launched
> With curled and forked flame
> On my head; let the air confounded
> Shudder with thunderous peals
> And convulsion of raging winds;
> Let tempests beat on the earth
> Till her rooted foundations tremble;
> The boisterous surge of the sea
> Leap up to mingle its crest
> With the stars eclipsed in their orbs;
> Let the whirling blasts of Necessity
> Seize on my body and hurl it
> Down to the darkness of Tartarus,—
> Yet all he shall not destroy me!

Here, Job's implicit insistence on self-determination is made explicit by Prometheus.

The Chorus approximates the people who shelter the hero. "Fear nothing" are the first words of the Chorus, and it goes on to assure Prometheus that the peoples of East and West are with him:

> Lo, all the land groans aloud;
> And the people that dwell in the West
> Lament for thy time-honored reign
> And the sway of thy kindred, Prometheus;
> And they who have builded their homes
> In holy Asia to the wail
> Of thine anguish lament.

The sympathy of the Chorus is for the plight of Prometheus, but his defiance frightens it. The Leader of the Chorus even advises him to "Abandon vaunting pride and seek wise counsel." Still, after he and Io have stated their case, the Chorus identifies itself with his stand:

> Better I deem it to suffer
> Whate'er he endures; for traitors
> My soul abhorreth, their shame
> I spew from my heart as a pest.

When, at the close of the drama, Prometheus is hurled down, the Chorus sinks with him, chooses to share his fate.

Hybris

Emerson called Prometheus the Jesus of Greek mythology, in that he freely chose to sacrifice himself because of his love for man. (An ancient vase painting shows Prometheus with pillars piercing his chest.) Yet, like all mythopoeic heroes, Prometheus is guilty. His mythic guilt lies in the titan's tendency to overreach himself. Above all, it lies in his uncompromising attitude, in being as intransigent as his adversary, Zeus. A more subtle aspect of overreaching consists in the fact that Prometheus never asks himself whether mankind is ready to use fire for its own good. The point is made by the Chorus:

> Their weakness hast thou not discovered,
> Their feeble blindness wherein
> Like dreaming shadows they move?

The Erinyes similarly accuse Apollo in *The Eumenides*:

> For thou too heinous a respect didst hold
> Of man, too little heed of powers divine

As a whole, the work of Aeschylus celebrates freedom of will. The Leader of the Chorus urges Electra and Orestes in *The Choephori*: "Take fortune by the hand and work thy will." And, in *The Eumenides*, Apollo encourages Orestes:

> Have thou too heed, nor let thy fear prevail
> Above thy will.

But the Chorus also sees the threat in its misuse. It declares in *The Choephori* that of all the things to fear the greatest is "the aweless soul" in man. That is, Aeschylus' drama sees the need to control the rebellious temper. Io's fire spends itself in her wanderings, Prometheus becomes a culture hero by curbing his fiery demon. Aeschylus affirms freedom of will, and at the same time points to its limiting determinants.

The mother of Prometheus seems to bear no relation to his stealing the fire. But it is through her that he finds the strength to confront Zeus' wrath. From her, he knows the secret by which Zeus can lose honor and throne, and that, in the end, Zeus will implore him for his friendship.

In his essay on the Prometheus legend, "The Acquisition of Power over Fire," Freud points out that primitive man

> could not but regard fire as something analogous to the passion of love. . . .
> The warmth radiated by fire evokes the same kind of glow as accompanies
> the state of sexual excitation, and the form and motion of the flame suggest
> the phallus in action.

In stealing Zeus' fire, Prometheus took the secret of his power. (In one version, Prometheus secretly made his way to the Olympian hearth and hid the flame in a hollowed-out stalk.)[24]

In mythology, the gratification of sensual desires is a special privilege of the gods, in particular of Zeus, who possesses unlimited sexual power. Zeus punished Prometheus by binding him to a rock where a vulture fed on his liver. Freud states that in ancient times the liver was regarded as the seat of all the passions and desires. Prometheus' punishment thus fits his crime: he is reduced to infantile helplessness and his organ of desire is eaten away.

By assigning a *cultural* use for fire, Prometheus urged renunciation of instinctual desires. This aroused resentment in instinct-ridden humanity, which could therefore welcome Zeus' retaliatory action. However, Prometheus did not keep the fire to himself, but passed it on to man. He is rewarded for this by the daily renewal of his liver. This, Freud writes, is the second reaction of primitive man to the blow struck at its instinctual life. Following the punishment of the criminal, "comes the assurance that, after all, he has done nothing irreparable."

Act III: Reconciliation

From fragments (available in Latin translation by Cicero and Accius) it may be assumed that *Prometheus Bound* was followed by *Prometheus Unbound* and *Prometheus the Fire-Bringer*. After thousands of years, Prometheus is readmitted to Olympus and he reveals his secret that Zeus can avoid his downfall by wedding Hera instead of Thetis. The two antagonists have abandoned their inflexible positions and are reconciled. As in the Book of Job, the Prometheia rejects the narrow tribal god, but reaches an understanding with a god who approximates a universal deity. The agency of change is time which "teaches all things." Prometheus is delivered after many thousands of years and Io is restored after wanderings over Europe and Asia. Here, Zeus also plays a role. In foreswearing Thetis and delivering Io from torment, Zeus contributes to Prometheus' ultimate deliverance.

Epilogue

Prometheus is rescued by Hercules, the son of Zeus' union with a mortal woman, Alcmene. That is, he is rehabilitated, not by a god, but by a god-man.[25] In turn, the deliverer must engage in his "Twelve Labors" and serve as woman-man to Omphale. Once again, the hero has the task of cleansing the stables of the rotten state.[26]

THE NUCLEUS OF MYTHOPOEIC DRAMA:
SOPHOCLES' OEDIPUS

Become who you are after you have learned it.

—Pindar

In Greek mythology, Oedipus is subject to an inexorable Moira or "Fate" which completely predetermines his acts. This approach has been carried over into the interpretation of Sophocles' Oedipus dramas. Gerhard Nebel's *Weltangst und Götterzorn* is a religious formulation of this view. Sophocles' *Oedipus* is seen as expressing the inscrutable decree of "the angry God" before whom Oedipus incurs guilt no matter what he does. His very attempts to circumvent fate only hasten its fulfilment.

A more analytical approach is that of the Cambridge School, which examines the myth in terms of its ritual. Here, the fortune of Oedipus is viewed as the ritual of the seasonal god whose dismemberment is "the winter" preceding the rejuvenation of the city he represents. In *The Idea of a Theater* (Princeton, 1949), Francis Fergusson achieves perceptive results by applying this method to Sophocles' text. Yet, Oedipus' individual choice is not shown as affecting this ritual, and his character is reduced to an "analogue" in a general tragic rhythm.

Erich Fromm's interpretation (*The Forgotten Language* [New York, 1951]) explains the Oedipus myth as marking the transition from democratic matriarchy to authoritarian patriarchy. Fromm makes a much needed contribution towards de-romanticizing the myth by suggesting its social-historic basis. But here, too, the character of Sophocles' Oedipus itself is not considered.

Now, general categories, such as the legendary curse, the seasonal rhythm and the historic scene are necessary but not sufficient conditions for explaining a character in an art-work. This chapter proposes to indicate that Sophocles' work, like all mythopoesis, shows the interplay between "the gods" (or Moira) and the individual personality.[27] A careful reading of the text bears out the Freudian thesis, at least to the extent that it reveals Oedipus' *tendencies* towards incest and patricide; finally, that Oedipus' heroic and prophetic qualities are bound up with his guilt.[28]

Like Shakesleare's *Hamlet*, Sophocles' Oedipus drama begins by focusing on the social disease. Indeed, in Sophocles, it is more than the underlying situation in the drama. As a representative and king of the state, Oedipus identifies himself with its plight and concentrates his entire effort to rid it of the burden no matter what the cost be to himself.

In this respect, the ancient Oedipus is much less concerned with his personal welfare; he feels himself more a part of his Greek *polis* than Hamlet of his Danish state.[29]

At the same time, Sophocles presents Oedipus not as an average man or as an anonymous "King," but as a personality who measures up to the Greek notion of an eminent character. The Priest of Zeus calls him "the first of men" and Oedipus refers to himself as "renowned of all." And we learn that he has *earned* his exceptional stature. Like Prometheus, Oedipus is not a speculative thinker. He is a philosopher-king whose concern is with the city and its people. In solving the riddle of the sphinx, he showed himself to be wiser than the seer Teiresias. Furthermore, he exhibited bravery at the Crossroads and in confronting the sphinx. Finally he has shown himself a successful ruler. As he had once saved the city, he is now ready to do so again regardless of the consequences to himself. Unlike Hamlet, Oedipus has already proved himself, has succeeded in replacing his predecessor as king, husband and father. He expresses no doubts as to his ability to set things right. In all this Oedipus appears as a strong individual. As such, his character is necessarily a function of his "fate."

Oedipus' Mythic Crime

From Oedipus' own account of what transpired before the plague strikes the city, we learn the following:

During a banquet at Polybus' court, Oedipus was taunted by a man "full of wine"[30] with not being the son of Polybus and Merope. The attempts of the king and queen to reassure Oedipus fail to dispel the doubts raised in his mind, especially as the story "still crept abroad with strong rumor." Thereupon, he sought clarification from the oracle. The latter did not answer his question. Instead, it "set forth other things, full of sorrow and terror and woe; even that I was fated to defile my mother's bed . . . and that I should be the slayer of the sire who begat me." Although he was still uncertain, Oedipus fled from Corinth so as to avoid contact with Polybus and Merope.

On his flight, Oedipus met a man, old enough to be his father. Although the oracle had foretold that he would kill his father, Oedipus did not stop to ask who this man was, but killed him. To be sure, Oedipus was first assaulted by the old man; still, he was able to kill not only his assailant, but "every man of them."

Oedipus next faced the sphinx. Presumably, he knew that the one who could answer its riddle would become king and be rewarded with the queen as a wife. One may then say that when Oedipus confronted the sphinx, he was offering himself as a candidate for both. And, in the queen, he met a woman who was old enough to be his mother. Yet, though the oracle had also spoken of his marrying his mother, Oedipus accepted Jocasta as his wife without inquiring into her past. Nor did he reveal anything of his own past to her or anyone else. Oedipus admits that he had heard of how the king met his death. Yet, he never mentioned to anyone the adventure in which he killed an old man (who presumably was dressed as a king).

Oedipus Brings His Birth to Light

Oedipus' patricide and incest precede the opening of the drama. The work itself unfolds the process by which Oedipus becomes aware of these acts. He gets to know himself, or, in his own words, brings "his birth to light."

When the play begins, the Eden-like peace and well-being which Oedipus brought to the city and which he himself enjoyed are gravely disturbed by drought and pestilence. There is something rotten in the state of Thebes, and its people have come to ask their ruler to rid them of their plight. Now, Oedipus knows all this. "Oh my piteous children, known, well known to me are the desires wherewith ye have come . . . So that ye rouse me not, truly, as one sunk in sleep." Indeed, he tells the Priest that he identifies himself with the disease which has seized the city: ". . . my soul mourns at once for the city, and for myself, and for thee." Oedipus has anticipated the cry for help and sent Creon to ask Phoebus by what deed or by what "word" he might deliver the town. Creon reports that Phoebus bids them banish the man who slew Laios. However, nothing is said about where the murderer is to be found, and Oedipus sets himself the task to unravel "the dim track of this old crime," in order "once more to make dark things plain." He calls on the people to help him find the slayer of Laios. In the end, however, Oedipus accomplishes the task mainly by his own efforts and questionings.

Early in the drama, Oedipus' choice of words hints at his own entanglement, of which he is as yet unaware. He declares that he will uphold Laios' cause, "even as the cause of mine own sire." He tells Creon that his effort to "dispel this taint" is not in behalf of some "far-off friend, no, but in mine own cause." Oedipus speaks of the slayer's "hidden guilt," and without any apparent reason suggests the possibility that the murderer might be "an inmate" of his own house, adding that in such a case, "I may suffer the same things which even now I called down upon others."

Further indirect confessions of Oedipus' "hidden guilt" appear in the precipitate manner he adopts as he accuses others of the crime. When Teiresias at first refuses to divulge the secret, Oedipus calls him "basest of the base . . . a scheming juggler . . . a tricky quack" and declares that he helped plot the murder. Following the blind seer's revelation, Oedipus at once turns the charge against him and Creon. Before Creon has a chance to utter a word, Oedipus calls him "the proved assassin" and demands his death. The deep irony in this situation is that Oedipus' discernment as a social seer and his ability to govern the city are at the price of blindness to his own involvements. Like Hamlet and Ahab, Oedipus shifts the guilt to the world and to others.[31]

The method by which Oedipus discovers the secret of his birth is analogous to the psychoanalytic process if we may regard Teiresias, the Herdsman, Jocasta, Creon and Theseus as aspects of Oedipus' self.

The first act in Oedipus' drama of personal unfolding is his summoning of Teiresias. The ancient blind seer knows the past and future and is said to be "most like our lord Phoebus." Teiresias was present at Oedipus' birth, and it is he who prophesies to him: "This day shall show thy birth . . ." He and the old Herdsman hold the secret of Oedipus' past and both at first resist his efforts to unravel it. When Oedipus continues to press him, Teiresias finally tells him:

> . . . *thou* art the accursed defiler of this land . . . I say that thou hast been living in unguessed shame with thy nearest kin . . .

To this, Oedipus reacts with an anger that seems irrelevant to the accusation. He merely warns Teiresias: "Dost thou think that thou shalt always speak thus without smarting?" It is as though Oedipus had not been listening. Only later, and not until Teiresias speaks of "the parents who begat thee," is Oedipus ready to *hear*. As though struck for the first time by the possibility of his involvement, he asks: "What parents? Stay . . . and who of men is my sire?" But Oedipus is not yet altogether prepared to accept the revelation of his past. He dismisses the seer in the hope that "when thou hast vanished, thou wilt vex me no more." But the past cannot be banished. Teiresias replies: "I will go when I have done mine errand, fearless of thy frown: for thou canst never destroy me!"

Jocasta is the second act in Oedipus' drama of self-recognition. If Teiresias knows the past and future, Jocasta would ignore the past as having no bearing on the future. Ferenczi calls her the pleasure principle within Oedipus. Jocasta knew, of course, about her son's ankles and should have been struck by her husband's swollen feet. And, although she noticed that Oedipus' "form was not greatly unlike" Laios', she married him without making any inquiries. (Oedipus and Jocasta seem to have entered into a kind of mutual "conspiracy" of not questioning each other about themselves). Now as the past begins to intrude upon and disturb the present, she urges Oedipus to ignore it all:

'Tis best to live at random, as one may . . .

And, as the Messenger is about to reveal Oedipus' relation to Polybus, she cries out desperately:

Regard it not . . . waste not a thought on what he said . . . 'twere idle . . . forbear this search . . . Mayst thou never come to know who thou art.

Above all, she would have him disregard the oracle's incest prophecy. It is the voice of his mother who became his wife, that is, the voice of her who carries his past over into the present, which stirs Oedipus' memory. When she mentions that Laios was killed "at a place where three highways meet," he calls out:

What restlessness of soul, lady, what tumult of the mind hath just come upon me since I heard thee speak.

At this point, he recalls his past and tells the story of his life from the time when he was taunted at the house of Polybus to his encounter at the meeting of the three highways.[32]

From this point on, the process of Oedipus' self-revelation assumes less hidden form. Attention has been called to his harsh treatment of Teiresias. Oedipus shows the same temper towards the old Herdsman who saved his life as an infant. In his attitude towards these father-figures, Oedipus is committing symbolic patricide. This "oedipal" tendency in his character is furthermore made plain in his reaction to the news that Polybus is dead. At this stage, Oedipus still regards himself as his son. He is aware of the love Polybus had for him, even suggesting that possibly the king "was killed by longing for me." We can understand that Oedipus should be relieved at the Messenger's news, for now he cannot become Polybus' slayer. But what is astounding is that Oedipus shows *only relief*. He does not utter a single word of sorrow. In his exchange with the Messenger, Oedipus merely expresses curiosity as to the cause of Polybus' death. (In passing, it should be noted that Oedipus interprets Polybus' death as possibly a fulfillment of the oracle, saying that if he was killed by longing for Oedipus, then "indeed, I should be the cause of his death.")

Following the revelation of the Messenger (another old memory), Oedipus announces: "The hour hath come that these things should be finally revealed." He brushes aside Jocasta's pleading to disregard it all as "idle." This time, Oedipus turns his character as "Tyrannos" towards bringing his "birth to light," regardless of the consequences. Following the Herdsman's disclosures, Oedipus at last beholds "the whole truth." He now realizes that he had acted blindly, that his eyes had looked without seeing.

The most dramatic instance showing that Jocasta and Oedipus are not mere objects of "Fate" or of an "angry God" are their acts of *self-punishment*. Whereas in Homer guilt is determined by the gods and even Aeschylus' Prometheus, Io and Orestes suffer mainly at the hands of heavenly or underground powers, Sophocles' Jocasta and Oedipus punish themselves. Oedipus acknowledges his guilt in words as well. This curse, he cried earlier, "was laid on me by no mouth but mine own!" To be sure, within the framework of Greek mythology, this curse is sent by some power above man:

> Apollo, friends, Apollo was he that brought my woes to pass, these my sore, sore woes.

But Oedipus adds:

> The hand that struck the eyes was none save mine, wretched that I am!

The Chorus agrees:

> These things were even as thou sayest.

Earlier, the Second Messenger declared that the ills of the house of Labdacus were "wrought not unwittingly, but of purpose. And those griefs smart most which are seen to be of our own choice." Later, he reports that as Oedipus smote his eyeballs, he uttered the following:

> No more shall ye behold such horrors as I was suffering and working! Long enough have ye looked on those whom ye ought never to have seen, failed in knowledge of those whom I yearned to know—henceforth ye shall be dark!

In these lines Oedipus recognizes that his act was at once one of *fate* and *character*, or in his words, of "suffering and working." Not only does Oedipus condemn himself; he also determines what his punishment is to be—exile from the *polis*—perhaps the severest penalty for a Greek citizen and king:

> . . . hide me somewhere beyond the land, or slay me, or cast me into the sea, where ye shall never behold me more!

Oedipus' Incest Guilt

The theme of incest is particularly prominent in Oriental legends, with patricide in the background. Sophocles' Oedipus drama is the first major literary myth in which the two themes are directly interwoven although here too incest appears as the greater crime.

In his essay on the Oedipus myth, (*The Forgotten Language*) Erich Fromm would counter Freud's interpretation by showing that the attitude toward authority, not sexual desires, is the central theme of the myth. Like Voltaire, though for different reasons, Fromm would relegate the incest-motif to a minor place. He argues that

> the myth can be understood as a symbol not of the incestuous love between mother and son but of the rebellion of the son against the authority of the father in the patriarchal family; that the marriage of Oedipus and Jocasta is only a secondary element, only one of the symbols of the victory of the son, who takes his father's place and with it all his privileges.

Fromm also stresses that "there is no indication whatsoever in the myth that Oedipus is attracted by or falls in love with Jocasta." As to this, it should be noted that generally Greek tragedy did not treat the theme of "falling in love" as a specialized activity. Love, together with beauty, goodness and truth were parts of an organic cluster making up the whole man. Furthermore, as Freud indicates, we are dealing here— more so than in *Hamlet* and *The Brothers Karamazov*—with a more suppressed and covered drive. And, as pointed out before, in attempting to answer the sphinx Oedipus applies for the queen as well, knowing that she "goes with the throne" (to use Fromm's formulation). Fromm does not explain Oedipus' unquestioning acceptance of Jocasta as his wife, despite her age, despite the prophecy of the oracle, and despite his uncertainty whether Merope was his mother. Nor does he consider the lines spoken by Jocasta to Oedipus which Freud calls "the key to the tragedy and the complement to the dream of the death of the father":

> But fear not thou touching wedlock with thy mother. Many men have so fared in dreams also: but he to whom these things are as naught bears his life most easily.[33]

Fromm would strengthen his interpretation of *Oedipus the King* by arguing that the father-son conflict is also present in *Oedipus in Colonus* (between Oedipus and his sons) and in *Antigone* (between Creon and Haemon). This conflict is present in these dramas, although it may be questioned whether the father-son opposition in *Antigone* is as much in the foreground as is the devotion Antigone exhibits towards her brother's memory. However, towards the end of the essay, Fromm modifies his thesis. Here, he states that it may be "doubtful" whether patricide or incest is dominant in *Oedipus the King*, though he still insists that the former is central in *Antigone*. He also qualifies his hypoth-

88

esis that *Oedipus the King* exemplifies the victory of the patriarchal system over the matriarchal by saying that it is a "blend" of the two. But he maintains his thesis that the incest motif is secondary.

Now, the passages cited make it evident that Oedipus feels at least as guilty in having married his mother as in having killed his father. Teiresias, Creon and the others also refer to both acts as constituting Oedipus' crime. And, it is significant that Oedipus punishes only that organ with which he had beheld (as he puts it) "such horrors as I was suffering and working," with which he had "looked on those whom ye ought never to have seen . . ."—clearly pointing to his incest guilt. It is the marriage-rites that wrought "the foulest shame among men" which Oedipus bewails first and foremost:

> O marriage-rites, ye gave me birth, and when ye had brought me forth, again
> ye bore children to your child, ye created an incestuous kinship of fathers,
> brothers, sons,—brides, wives, mothers,—yea, all the foulest shame that is
> wrought among men!

The difficulty of Fromm's position is that it cannot explain the guilt Oedipus feels over having married his mother, a guilt which is at least as great as that over having slain his father.

Towards the end of the chapter, Fromm writes of the all-important place occupied by the Eumenides, the earth-goddesses, in the Oedipus myth. He argues that Oedipus' patricide expresses his connection with the mother-goddesses through whom he is redeemed. At the end, Oedipus finds rest in the grove of the Eumenides, that is, he is "brought back to the place he belonged, to the mothers." To reinforce his point regarding the mother-aspect of the Eumenides, Fromm draws a suggestive parallel between them and the Mothers in Goethe's *Faust*, underscoring the "dread" and "awful" aspect which is ascribed to them in both works.[34]

Fromm, however, does not consider why the sight of the Eumenides should produce dread, nor does he attempt to integrate this aspect of the Mothers with his thesis as a whole. As a matter of fact, it would seem, ironically enough, that the point Fromm makes here provides additional support for the central importance of the incest element in Sophocles' Oedipus myth. For, Oedipus' relation to the Eumenides renews—on another level—his contact with Jocasta. Indeed, the horror expressed at his daring to approach their forbidden grove is similar to that voiced at his earlier violation. That is, Oedipus' attempt to penetrate the hidden abode of the Earth-Mothers *repeats his incest* with his biologic mother. To be sure, Oedipus is now more aware of what he is doing, and readily heeds the call of the Chorus to respect "the customs of the land" and withdraw. Above all, there is this crucial difference: His "return to the mother" now takes place, not on a literal, but on *a symbolical level.*[35] And there is this further difference: where actual incest was coupled with patricide, symbolic incest is followed by cooperation with a surrogate father, Theseus.

Otto Rank sees the symbolic import of the Oedipus legend as the attempt of the individual "to be neither father nor son, but simply Self." In the primitive myth, Oedipus was "a phallic vegetation spirit, an offspring of the earth-mother whose son was also her husband." Incest is the means whereby the individual tries once more to be reborn through his own mother. As a whole, the Oedipus legend would solve

> the mysterious question of the origin and destiny of man . . . not intellectually, but actually returning into the mother's womb.

However, Rank apparently does not mean an actual return, for he goes on to state:

> This happens entirely in a symbolic form, for his blindness in the deepest sense represents a return into the darkness of the mother's womb, and his final disappearance through a cleft rock into the Underworld expresses once again the same wish tendency to return into the mother earth.[36]

The supreme import of the incest-patricide theme in Sophocles' dramas lies in its symbolic transformation through which Oedipus becomes a sanctified figure. His final resting place serves as a blessing to the community, a defense, "better than many shields, better than the succouring spear of neighbours." His very acts of *hybris* express a heroic temerity to gain knowledge of his sources, to wrest from nature the secret of human creation. But, the criminal violator is turned into "a prophet" only after *he repeats these acts symbolically.*[37] Like other heroes in mythopoesis, Oedipus enacts his journey into the underworld twice, once in physical indulgence, the second time, in symbolic recreation. In this transformation, physical blindness (as later in Goethe's Faust, Melville's Ahab and Mann's Joseph in the pit) becomes prophetic vision. The man who committed patricide and incest comes to Colonus "as one sacred, and pious, and fraught with comfort for this people."

From this perspective, Oedipus' *hybris* does not lie, as many critics hold, in his rashness, impatience, or even in the excesses of his wrath, with which Creon charges him. For we note that Oedipus retains this intemperance in Colonus, in his treatment of Polyneices and Creon. The Greek character remains the same in both phases. What has changed is the direction and the plane in which his energy is expended. In Colonus,

Oedipus turns his "Tyrannos" character against filial ingratitude and Creon's tyrannical rule.

Act III: Rehabilitation

Sophocles' Oedipus makes a complete revolution from a blessedness given him by nature to one earned by him through his journey to the underworld. He begins as a royal son, that is, one blessed in social status. He is next blessed with an extraordinary rescue as an infant, is endowed with the blessed knowledge to solve the riddle of the sphinx, becomes king and experiences the highest blessing of all (at least according to Freud)—union with the mother. At this point, he is roused by a social disease which turns out to be interwoven with his own crime. Oedipus becomes aware that he had lived in self-indulgence, which is equated with blindness to the societal aspects of the self. He learns the need to tame Dionysian excess, learns that "patience is the lesson of suffering" as "of a noble mind." Oedipus gets to know himself in his generic alignment and names himself as belonging to "the race of Labdacidae." As Jocasta is replaced by the Eumenides, the kindly Earth-Mothers, so is Laios replaced by Theseus, the kindly surrogate father. The king offers Oedipus shelter and establishes him as a citizen in the land. He too has known exile and wrestled with dangers in foreign lands. "Never, then," he tells Oedipus, "would I turn aside from a stranger, such as thou art, . . . for well know I that I am a man, and that in the morrow my portion is no greater than thine." Likewise, Oedipus' own collective representation has been widened. The Theban Oedipus becomes the benefactor of Athens, then embodying the democratic state. Sophocles was born in Colonus. *Oedipus in Colonus*, presumably Sophocles' last drama, is a kind of "homecoming" for the poet as well.

The passing of Oedipus, characterized as "above mortals wonderful," has something of that mystery and sublimity suggested in Yahweh's appearance before Job. Here, too, there is an uproar of the elements, followed by the hero's rehabilitation. For the death of Oedipus is in the nature of an epiphany. Summoned by the god, the blind man becomes guide to others, "beckoning the others onward." Like Jacob and Aeneas, Oedipus ends his days "on foreign ground, the ground of his choice." Like Moses, he is buried in a secret place.

Oedipus' transformation is not a change in his basic character, but only of its function. The acts of slaying Laios and marrying Jocasta were done without examining the realities of the situation. Oedipus continues to exhibit intemperance in his treatment of Teiresias, Creon, the

Herdsman and his son. But in these instances, his acts are directed by the passion for the truth and in the interests of the community. To be sure, the redemption appears in part as a mysterious event, as it does in the Book of Job. Yet, in both, it is conditioned by the knowledge the characters gain about themselves. Oedipus now realizes that "in knowledge is the safeguard of our course."

Epilogue: Reaffirmation of Revolt

In Colonus, Oedipus seems to reverse himself in the matter of admitting his guilt. Although, in replying to Creon's attacks, he speaks of "myself-wrought woes," he tells the Chorus that his acts, at least, "have been suffering rather than doing." He demands to know how "in *nature*" was he evil?

> I, who was but requiting a wrong, so that, had I been acting with knowledge, even then I could not be accounted wicked; but, as it was, all unknowing went I—whither I went—while they who wronged me knowingly sought my ruin.

And reiterating the point later:

> I have suffered misery, strangers,—suffered it through unwitting deeds, and of those acts—be Heaven my witness!—no part was of mine own choice . . . they whom I slew would have taken mine own life: stainless before the law, void of malice, have I come unto this pass!

Yet, even as Oedipus is protesting his innocence, he is at the same time giving a *hypothetical justification* of his acts, disregarding the fact that he did not know that he was "but requiting a wrong."

These passages again indicate that Oedipus retains his rebellious character in Colonus. The point is supported by the opening setting of which we are told that it contains not only the grove of the conciliatory Eumenides, but also that of Prometheus, "the fire-fraught god." The view that Sophocles accepts the law of the Moirai and that such acceptance brings Apollonian calm not only underrates the *Dionysian process* through which harmony is reached, but ignores the fact that Oedipus *earns his sanctification partly by his violations.*

The *hybris* element in Oedipus' character carries over into Colonus, as shown in his bearing towards Polyneices. Here, Oedipus nearly reenacts the way of Cronos who, having emasculated his father Uranos, in turn swallows his own sons. Even in Thebes, Oedipus is strangely indifferent to his sons' welfare. While he begs Creon to watch over his daughters, he adds: "Take no care on thee for my sons; they are men."

To be sure, when Oedipus was later banished, the sons took no steps to prevent it. Yet their father's wrath is out of all proportion to this crime of omission. When Polyneices appears in Colonus as a wretched suppliant, Oedipus calls him "a murderer," invokes curses that he die by "a kindred hand," and prays that the strife between the brothers may never end: "I call the paternal darkness of dread Tartarus . . . I call the Destroying God, who hath set the dreadful hatred in you twain."

Oedipus, like other heroes in mythopoesis, is redeemed *because* of his questioning. But, whereas Job's crime is mainly one of omission and Aeschylus' Orestes acts more at the behest of the god than his own nature, remaining a passive sufferer, Oedipus' failing is shown to be a function of his character. (Oedipus' sons, too, are said to have been "moved by some god and by a sinful mind.") Sophocles breaks with the older notions of an impenetrable Moira and of tribal guilt by introducing individual choice and responsibility to the point where *fate* and *character* are in dynamic balance.

THE EPILOGUE OF GREEK MYTHOPOESIS: EURIPIDES

The tragedies of Sophocles approximate the third act of the Greek mythopoeic process. Despite its reactivization of strife among Oedipus and his sons, Sophocles' last work ends on an epiphanic note of resurrection and peace, with the "Apollonian" gaining mastery over the "Dionysian."

Writers from Aristophanes to August Wilhelm Schlegel and Friedrich Nietzsche have charged that Euripides undermined the aristocratic Apollonian myth. Aristophanes specifically took Euripides to task for attempting to destroy the ancient religious beliefs and for presenting the ignoble passions of common people. Likewise, Nietzsche criticized Euripides for bringing the "mass" on the stage and replacing the dignified demi-god by "bourgeois mediocrity." In our own time, A. W. Verrall has written of *Euripides the Rationalist*, (Cambridge, England, 1895) who "stood up to answer the Sphinx." Euripides subjected the Gods and the Moirai to a scathing critique, showing that they use their power immorally or blindly, that they act arbitrarily—*ex machina*—using hocus-pocus trickery.

To appreciate Euripides' position towards the Greek myth, we must examine the social changes which were taking place in the Greece of his time. The age of Euripides saw the disintegration of the city-state

93

through civil strife and war. It was a period of territorial expansion, of increased slave labor and what Aristotle called the "limited slavery" of the poorer aliens, and of the lowered position of women. Law and justice were displaced by discord, poverty, and the violation of individual rights.

Euripides was an opponent of Athenian imperialism and, with the Sophists, a critic of the state. His work pictures the eclipse of the aristocratic Apollonian myth which had become a class ideology, and in which the individual had become a puppet in the hands of the "gods." Hence, the characters of Euripides act less as individuals than as products of social pressures. In the end, he shows them rebelling against being pushed around by external forces, a rebellion that is expressed in Dionysian frenzy. That is, Euripides revives the worship of Dionysus, the primitive Eastern god, to counteract the Western Apollo who had become hollow and unscrupulous. We see this most directly expressed in *Medea* and *The Bacchae*.

Jason, a traditional Greek hero, had once exhibited daring and valor, had wrested the Golden Fleece from the monster and won Medea, who was descended from the sun-God. In Euripides, Jason has become careful and calculating. He would banish Medea, who is now a "barbarian" to him, and marry Creusa, daughter of the king of Corinth. He does this not out of changed feelings towards Medea nor out of passion for Creusa, but because he has become "prudent," desires comfort and security. He admits to Medea:

> 'Tis not because I loathe thee for my wife . . . 'tis not because I am smitten with desire for a new bride . . . Nay, 'tis that we—and this is most important —may dwell in comfort . . . and that I might rear my sons as doth befit my house.[38]

In *Antigone* and elsewhere, Sophocles had decried the "excessive" pursuit of money, and the Chorus in *Medea* laments that "Order and the universe are being reversed . . . honor is found no more." The Greek hero who had once engaged in the quest of the Golden Fleece has become a slave of gold. Greece is turning towards an ingrown nationalistic endogamy. Jason tells Medea:

> Thou received more than ever thou gavest. . . . First thou dwellest in Hellas, instead of thy barbarian land, and hast learnt what justice means and how to live by law.

Euripides displays his subtlety in showing the dialectic relationship between the two forces. Out of her love for Jason, Medea had deceived her father and slain her brother. By her union with the Greek hero, she had gained something of a new ego. But, when Jason himself betrays his Grecian values, Medea turns her newly found ego against his false state, in which women are poor relations. Her resurrected Circean frenzy is the answer to a Moira which had become a static formula.

In *The Bacchae*, such calculating prudence turns Pentheus against another Eastern figure, Dionysus, who has come to waken "all that faint and stray." Pentheus' rationalistic temper rejects the Dionysian mystery, calling the story of his second birth "blasphemies," mocking the new God as a "girl-faced stranger," an "Eastern knave," a "trickster . . . praying on our maids and wives." He suspects that the Dionysian gathering of the Theban women "to wild and secret rites" is for the purpose of making love. Dionysus must be met with "an iron hand," and he would quell his "music" by interning the god within walls.

The transformation of the stratified Apollonian into a raging Dionysianism also appears in *The Bacchae*, where Pentheus himself becomes a participant of the new worship. Pentheus becomes vulnerable to the irrational forces precisely because he had overstressed reason. He, who had jeered at Dionysus' female figure, dresses as a Bacchanal, eager to witness his rites. The words he suddenly hears himself speak are the voices he had attempted to still.[39] His rationalistic self is "blinded" so that he can witness the forbidden, "holy and fearful" rites of his mother which he had characterized as "love" rites:

> They lie there now, methinks—the wild birds caught,
> By love among the leaves, and fluttering not!

The incest motif is sounded when Pentheus declares that

> I am their king,
> Aye, their one Man, seeing I dare this thing!

Euripides, who is charged with having destroyed the myth, actually reintroduced its more primitive ritual in diction and style.[40] His criticism of the gods is never applied to Dionysus or Eros. In *The Bacchae*, Dionysus appears as the conglomerate God who fuses the qualities of Zeus and Prometheus. He is called the "Lord of Many Voices" who unites music and laughter, prophecy, dance and prayer, the aristocratic and democratic, the "immaculate" and the "Living Fountain," the sacrificer and the sacrifice:

> Yea, being God, the blood of him is set
> Before the Gods in sacrifice, that we for his sake may be blest.

The womanly figure of Dionysus, worshipped by the band of Eastern maidens wearing fawn-skins, brings back "the soul of that dead life of old."

The age of Euripides marks the breakdown of an old culture. War-frenzy is replaced by nature-frenzy, the *ex machina* deities by a wild divinity. Its effect has an "underground" character and people are moved to join Dionysus without knowing why. With Dionysus,

> God's child hath come, and all is overthrown! . . .
> . . . with a great wind . . .
> Blowing to beautiful things,
> On, amid dark and light,
> Till Life, through the trammelings
> Of Laws that are not the Right,
> Breaks, clean and pure, and sings
> Glorying to God in the height!

Yet, the epilogue in the work of Euripides is not a simple return to the pre-Aeschylean period. Medea and Agave are extreme *Western* re-actions to an inflexible and deteriorated Apollonianism. Here, as in Franz Werfel's "The Goatsong" (*Bocksgesang*), the primitive under-ground explodes into "tragedy" (*tragos oidos*). Euripides saw the pro-ductive possibilities of Dionysian frenzy, especially the cathartic value of its ritual. But he also feared the destructiveness which it set loose. If Jason's self is sterile and smug, Medea's is threateningly alive, caring for nothing except its blind feelings of limitless revenge. Hers, too, is de-structive of the self. Medea kills her innocent sons, the only possessions which tie her to life. She punishes Jason according to the primitive no-tion of ancestral guilt—she kills his offspring. The "revolution" devours its own children. Except for the chorus, Euripides' Bacchic women deny their womanliness and contradict their motherly and familial ties: Medea kills her children and Agave tears off the head of her son. Euripi-des indicates his reservations over resurrecting Dionysianism by making Pentheus the dismembered god and sacrifice who evokes our pity and fear. Like Aeschylus and Sophocles—though with different emphasis —Euripides saw the need to curb Dionysian passion with Apollonian reason.

NOTES

1. M. P. Nilsson's *History of Greek Religion* (2d ed.; New York, 1949, p. 42) likewise shows that the great cycles of Greek myths belong to the main centres of Mycenean culture, that "their richness and fame are in direct correspond-ence with the importance of the towns in Mycenean times."

2. Nilsson writes that religious festivals served to weld the citizen to the "mar-ket." He points out that "panegyrics" means both "festival" and "market," and that festivals were popular in part because they offered the only opportunity

Book of Job, Plate 17, "I have heard of thee with the hearing of the Ear
but now my Eye seeth thee" by William Blake
(facsimile edition, Detroit Institute of Arts)

Oedipus Consulting the Sphinx
by J. A. Ingres (Louvre, Paris)

for many men to eat roast beef. According to Thomson, the Delphic priesthood became the religious stronghold of the aristocracy, and the priestly clan of the Branchidae at Miletus owed their power to the skillful manipulation of oracles. Cf. George Thomson's *Studies in Ancient Greek Society* (New York, 1949), pp. 163, 637.

3. Aristotle noted that under the oligarchy, "the poor were enslaved by the rich, they and their wives and children. . . . All land was in the hands of a few men." Thomson states that Ananke, is connected with Douleia or slavery. He refers to a painting of the Orphic underworld in which Sisyphus is watched over by Ananke, a slave driver. Under Orphism (which developed with the urban revolution), the older hylozoism, in which the body was an organic part of the soul, is replaced by a dualism with hope lying in separation from the evil world. Yet, the Orphic doctrines of love and unrestraint were a rebellion against *sophrosyne* or contentment in the mean, and against Ananke.

4. The rule of the merchant prince towards the end of the seventh century B.C. encouraged science, but also emphasized the importance of money, giving rise to the new "money-mad" kings who were called tyrants. This provided the basis for the story of the Phrygian king Midas, who turned all he touched into gold, and for the old legend of Gyges, whose gold ring made him invisible and gave him the power to penerate everywhere. Cf. George Thomson, *Aeschylus and Athens* (New York, 1950), pp. 85 ff., 215 ff.

5. *The Complete Greek Drama*, ed., Whitney J. Oates and Eugene O'Neill, Jr. (New York, 1938). Subsequent quotations are from this edition.

6. Johann J. Winckelmann, *Kunsttheoretische Schriften* (Baden-Baden, 1962-66); Erwin Rohde, *Psyche* (1891-94, English translation, 1925); Friedrich Nietzsche, *Birth of Tragedy* in *The Philosophy of Nietzsche* (New York, 1927).

7. E. R. Dodds, *The Greeks and the Irrational* (Berkeley and Los Angeles, 1966), pp. 68-76.

8. Walter F. Otto, *Dionysus, Myth and Cult* (Bloomington and London, 1965), pp. 53, 65, 142, 203. Otto states:

   "Apollo shared the Delphic festival year with Dionysus. . . . The pediments of the temple of Apollo portray on one side Apollo with Leto, Artemis, and the Muses, and on the other side Dionysus and the thyiads, in short, the raging God. . . . A vase painting of about 400 B.C. shows Apollo and Dionysus in Delphi holding out their hands to one another." (p. 203)

9. The Greek gods were not transcendental powers, but mixed in human affairs, often in sordid ways. Aside from their immortality, they were superior to humans only in the range of power and the intensity of passion. The democratization of the myth appears in the institution of the Council of the Four Hundred by the side of the Council of the Areopagus. In Aeschylus' *Eumenides,* it is this court, with Athena (rather than Zeus, Apollo or the Erinyes) casting the deciding vote, which acquits Orestes. For a development of this point, see G. Thomson's *Aeschylus and Athens*, pp. 89 ff.

97

10. Pre-Socratic philosophy and science were not pure theory. Philosophy was "love of wisdom," and the Milesian school, as well as Heraclitus, engaged in natural research. They attempted to give a naturalistic explanation of man and his world by reducing substance to one or several of the elements. In poetry and drama, the earth is generally singled out. A Homeric hymn sings to "the Earth Mother":

> "O Universal Mother, who dost keep
> From everlasting thy foundations deep
> Eldest of things, Great Earth, I sing of thee!"

Aeschylus paid tribute to the earth, the mother of Prometheus. In his *Eumenides*, the Pythian Priestess names "the prophet-mother Earth" as the first of the Gods.

11. Where, as in the Oresteia, the tribal curse is the main reference, the character is more a passive victim than a hero. Orestes is saved by the intervention of Apollo and Athena.

12. According to Thomson, the cult of Dionysus developed from the totemic clan during the later phases of tribal society. This suggests that the cult goes back to *group* worship connected with the mother deity. Dionysus is shown almost everywhere surrounded by a chorus of women. Dionysus himself (at least after the fourth century B.C.) appeared with long hair and flesh-tints. His drapery had a soft texture and he wore the *kothornos*, the high boot, used principally by women; also the *krokotos*, a woman's over-mantle and the *mitra*, a woman's head band. Cf. *Mythology of All Races*, Vol. I (Boston, 1916); G. Thomson's *Aeschylus and Athens*, p. 442.

13. In this guise, Dionysus is more than the bull of the dithyrambic contests. He is the pupil of Silenus, and the god whose last gift was the grape. As the center of a chorus dressed as goats, he is a satyr figure with phallic associations.

14. The Dionysian ritual was connected with the Chorus which accompanied the God. Hence, Nietzsche rejected Schlegel's view that the Greek chorus was an "ideal spectator," a passive Apollonian observer, as well as the notion that it represented the viewpoint of "the people" against that of the ruling class. Tragedy, Nietzsche argued, arose out of the Dionysian chorus and was at one time nothing else but this chorus. Hence, it could not be an ideal spectator, even as Greek tragedy struggled towards an Apollonian world.

15. Dionysus is connected with the underground. In one version, he is the son of Persephone and receives the surname of Chthonios; in another, he is the son of Semele, the name given to Chthonia by the Phrygians. Cf. Carl Kerenyi's *The Gods of the Greeks* (London and New York, 1951). For a detailed, scholarly discussion of Dionysianism, its nature, religion, especially as it appears in the *Bacchae* of Euripides, see E. R. Dodds, *Euripides: Bacchae* (2d ed.; New York, 1960).

16. *Der Dorische Tempel* (Augsburg, 1930). Cf. Helene Deutsch, *Apollo and Dionysus* (New York, 1969).

17. Olympus is dominated by the father-god, not admitting the chthonic mother

deities or Dionysus. When Odysseus meets Agamemnon in Hades, he observes that the counsel of women has brought ruin to the house of Atreus. Odysseus himself is held captive by Calypso, tempted by Circe and the Sirens, threatened by Scylla and Charybdis. Yet, at the end, his rehabilitation depends on the faithfulness of his wife Penelope.

18. To be sure, Athena herself has no mother, and in the patriarchal state, she becomes a valorous masculine figure. The use of the snake symbol in connection with Athena is a further illustration of the principle that the heroic depends on violation: From ancient times, the snake has been regarded as immortal, owing to its ability to renew itself by casting off its slough. In the figures of Demeter and Athena, the snake first appears as the protector of the house. However, in the Oresteia snake-worship takes on an ambivalent meaning. On the one hand, it is associated with the tradition of tribal revenge—the Erinyes take the form of snakes and Orestes along with his mother are likened to snakes. Now, the avenging Erinyes are not eliminated, but are *converted* into the merciful Eumenides (the Greek term "Eumenides" is sometimes used to designate both the dark and the light powers), and Orestes has a change of heart and is acquitted. The Erinyes yield to the persuasive plea of Athena who is herself a snake-goddess (Phidias' statue of Athena in the Parthenon shows a little snake curled at the goddess' feet).

19. The association of the titanic with fire was extended to the sun, conceived as a male god. In the case of the Minotaur, to whom seven boys and seven girls were periodically sacrificed, the sun assumed the character of a cruel father.

20. Theophrastus' treatise *On Fire* makes this idea explicit:

   "Fire can not only generate itself but extinguish itself. . . . The other elements are self-subsistent, they do not require a substratum. Fire does. . . . Speaking generally fire is always coming into being. . . . It perishes as it comes into being. As it leaves its substratum it perishes itself. That is what the ancients meant when they said that fire is always in search of nutriment. They saw that it could not subsist of itself without its material." (Quoted in B. Farrington's *Greek Science*, II (Pelican edition), 25-26.

21. Other rebellious titans are also unredeemed: Atlas has to bear the heavens on his head and hands; Minoitios is struck by lightning.

22. He omits Hesiod's version—Prometheus' creation of man and how he tricked Zeus into choosing the bones wrapped in gleaming fat. All translations are by Paul Elmer More as revised by Oates and O'Neill in *The Complete Greek Drama*.

23. Io also plays the role of Prometheus' future "mother." As Themis' prophetic powers gave Prometheus assurance of his ultimate delivery, so Io's union with Zeus results in the birth of Hercules, who is to free Prometheus.

24. Sigmund Freud, *Collected Papers*, Vol. V (London, 1950). In his *Trauma of Birth* (New York, 1950), Otto Rank interprets the fire of the hearth as mother warmth.

25. Freud points out that it is Hercules who extinguishes the fire which Prometheus set loose. Hercules subdues the water-serpent (the hydra of Lerna) by fire, burning off its immortal head. Freud sees in the myth "the reaction of a later epoch of civilization to the circumstances in which power over fire was acquired." Hercules, nearer to man than the titan Prometheus, practices the control of fire.

26. For a note on the Prometheus of Shelley and of Goethe, see Appendix II.

27. Sophocles does not refer to the legendary curse according to which Pelops cursed Laios with childlessness or with death at his child's hands in retaliation for Laios' having carried off Pelops' son. This is confirmed by the Delphic oracle which pronounces that Laios is doomed to be killed by his son.

   On the other hand, Sophocles introduces several features which he uses to re-create the ancient legend: the plague in Thebes, Creon's report of the oracle pointing to the murderer of Laios as the cause of the city's plight, and the Messenger who brings the news of Polybus' death.

28. Cf. Mark Kanzer's "The Oedipus Trilogy," *The Psychoanalytic Quarterly*, Vol. XIX, No. 4 (October, 1950), also his "On Interpreting the Oedipus Plays" in *The Psychoanalytic Study of Society*, ed.; Muensterberger and Axelrad (New York, 1967).

29. By the time of Strindberg's *The Father*, the personal issue occupies the center. The Captain's discontent is pictured as his own with only the barest hints of its social determinants.

30. Translations of *Oedipus the King* and *Oedipus in Colonus* by R. C. Jebb in Oates and O'Neill, *The Complete Greek Drama*.

31. As in the case of Ahab, Oedipus' public stature is contradicted by his personal defeat. Both are "marked" men, Ahab with his maimed leg, Oedipus with his swollen foot. Exposure was common practice among the Greeks. On this basis, A. J. Levin has argued that Oedipus' "Fate" was "a life of wrath and vengeance" for what was done to him as an infant ("The Oedipus Myth in History and Psychiatry," *Psychiatry*, XI, [1948]). Levin's point is well taken with regard to the initial wrong done Oedipus and to its historic condition. But in Sophocles there is no reference whatsoever to Oedipus' knowledge that Laios had ordered his ankles pierced. The theme of the diseased foot and its blessed function also appears in *Philoctetes*, with Neoptolemus approximating the role of the Herdsman. And, as Oedipus becomes the surety for peace in Athens, so Troy cannot be conquered and harmony reestablished without Philoctetes.

32. The number three is a pervading motif in the play (we also find it in *The Divine Comedy, Don Quixote, The Brothers Karamazov*). According to Jocasta, Oedipus was three days old when he was exposed on the mountain; the sphinx's riddle refers to three stages in man's life; the plot revolves about the relationship among the two parents and their son; Oedipus calls on his "three-fold help against death" (Athena, Artemis, Phoebus); he speaks of himself as "accursed in birth, accursed in wedlock, accursed in the shedding of blood!," as "thrice wretched" through marriage-rites which "created an incestuous kinship of fathers, brothers, sons—brides, wives, mothers."

Similarly, in Aeschylus' Oresteia: Zeus, the Deliverer, is called the Third; Orestes speaks of three motives for carrying out his task and of a "deep third draught of rich unmingled blood" which shall drain the house; the Erinyes ask Orestes three questions (whether, how and why he killed); Clytemnestra deals Agamemnon three blows.

The number three is indeed central to Greek mythology as a whole. According to it, the world is divided into three parts, ruled by a three-fold goddess or by three mother goddesses (the sea, the night and the earth). There are three main goddesses—Hera, Demeter, Hestia. Rhea produces three great son-gods—Zeus with his lightning, Poseidon with his trident, Hades with his head turned back to front. There are three Moirae (Clotho, Lachesis, Atropos), three Gorgons and (whenever their number is mentioned) three Erinyes. The number is, of course, pivotal in the ritual process of the year-god (Birth, Mangling, Rebirth).

33. In terms of the "manifest" content, Oedipus first killed his father and then married his mother. Yet, in Oedipus' own account of the oracle's portent and in nearly all of his later references, he *mentions the incest ahead of the patricide*. This reversal corresponds to the psychological sequence in the Freudian scheme.

34. The Eumenides are called "the dread goddesses . . . the daughters of Earth and Darkness." The Chorus trembles to speak their names and passes them by "with eyes turned away." When it discovers that Oedipus has entered their "untrodden grove," it warns him: "too far thou goest—too far! . . . retire—withdraw! . . . leave forbidden ground. . . ." When Thesus witnesses Oedipus' disappearance at the end, he is seen "holding his hand before his face to screen his eyes, as if some dread sight had been seen, and such as none might endure to behold. And then after a short space, we saw him salute the earth and the home of the gods above, both at once, in one prayer."

35. The symbolical transformation also appears in that the Eumenides are called "maidens" and their number is plural. Oedipus' relation to his daughters may have some bearing on this point. At the close of the first drama, he says that his one wish is not to be parted from Antigone and Ismene, begotten "at the sources of his own being!" He begs Creon: "Ah, could I but once touch them with my hands, I should think that they were with me, even as when I had sight. . . ." He predicts, as well as bewails, that they wiill remain unwed: "The man lives not, no, it cannot be, my children, but ye must wither in barren maidenhood." Oedipus' last words, addressed to his daughters, speak of the love they had from him, "as from none beside." We know that, in the myth, Antigone's most intense devotion is for her brother Polyneices.

For textual support of this interpretation, and a critique of Fromm's position, see Helen H. Bacon's "Woman's Two Faces: Sophocles' View of the Tragedy of Oedipus and His Family" in *Science and Psychoanalysis*, Vol. X (New York, 1966); see also her "The Shield of Eteocles" in *Arion* (Autumn, 1964).

36. Rank's view (as summarized in Theodor Reik's *Dogma and Compulsion* [New York, 1951]) is that the sphinx and the mother were once one. Later, the orig-

inal *violation* of the mother was replaced by a *conflict* with the sphinx and still later into an *intellectual* contest. For Rank, the sphinx episode represents a "doubling" of the rape of Jocasta, introduced in the course of repression and mythic stratification.

For Theodor Reik, "the slaying of the Sphinx is originally the killing of the totem." Later, it became the rape of the mother. Hence the duplication of the father-image and the mother-image in the figure of the Sphinx. Thus, the legend as we now have it is a condensation in which the slaying of the father and the violation of the mother are compressed into a single act of which the sphinx is the victim.

37. For an analogy in the Christian myth, cf. *John* 3.5.3. To Nicodemus' question, can a man "enter a second time into his mother's womb, and be born"! Jesus answered: "Verily, verily, I say unto thee, Except a man be born of water and Spirit, he cannot enter into the Kingdom of God."

While Oedipus has a human "flaw" (*hamartia*), there is a religious element in his epiphany: he receives "grace" in a divine form, is accorded immortality —perhaps because his suffering was supra-human. Antigone, by contrast, is drawn more as representing human suffering and human love (for her father and brother). She voices no self-pity and does not ask for nor does she get any "reward."

38. Translation of *Medea* by E. P. Coleridge in *The Complete Greek Drama*, ed., Oates and O'Neill.

39, E. R. Dodds (*Euripides: Bacchae*, p. 172) calls it "a psychic invasion. . . . The god wins because he has an ally in the enemy's camp: the persecutor is betrayed by what he would persecute—the Dionysiac longing in himself."

40. Dodds, *Bacchae*, p. xxxvii.

The Catholic Vision of
Divine Harmony
The Divine Comedy

THE MEDIEVAL ERA provided favorable ground for mythic thought in that Catholicism and feudalism offered a unifying reference for the religious, cultural and social life of man. Christianity had systematized the Hebrew idea of a universal God and the Stoic principle of world citizenship. Its theology taught that all men belonged to one human race, having a single origin, ruled by one God and church, subject to one truth and love through which "Everyman" could find salvation. Philosophically, this doctrine was expressed in "realism" (the reality of universals); ritualistically, in group worship, enacted in the communal love feast (*agape*); socially and economically, in the international perspective of feudalism.

Christianity was a response to the disintegration of Graeco-Roman civilization. Disillusionment with secular authority led to hope in a divine Prince who would establish the City of God in which justice and harmony would abide. Nor was this ideal simply otherworldly. Christian thought attempted to correct Platonism by connecting the ideal with the real, ethics with existence. Christ was conceived as both real and transcendental, and the church as the incarnation of the Christian idea. Transposed into social-economic thought, this meant that all men were to be treated as children of God and were to enjoy what Karl Kautsky called "communism of consumption."

In actual practice, however, one social-economic group dominated and exploited another. This disparity between the ideal and the real brought forth a protest which based itself on the gospels. It pointed to the Christ who drove the money changers from the temple, who rejected the three temptations of property, wealth and the political church, and who opposed the Pharisee's notion of law as the final authority. St. Luke expressed the class hatred of the downtrodden. This note was continued by St. Augustine, who held that there must always be an unbridgeable gulf between church and state, and by later figures, such as Joachim di Fiore, who complained that "they adorn the altars and the poor suffer hunger." It appeared in Christian chiliasm and mysticism. These continuous, if sporadic, movements of social protest indicate that the Middle Ages did not enjoy the unity which Henry Adams and T. S. Eliot have ascribed to this period. In its feudal system, all possessions were held as imperial fiefs and the power of the ruling hierarchy was declared to be derived from God. St. Paul had stated in Romans:

> Let every soul be subject to the higher authorities. There is no authority that
> is not from God, and the existing authorities are appointed by God . . .
> Wherefore he that opposeth the authorities resisteth the ordinance of God . . .
> ye shall pay them taxes; for they are the functionaries of God.

This directive was systematized some twelve centuries later by Thomas Aquinas. To be sure, Aquinas argued that divine creation made for fundamental equality, unity and order in the world where God's love "works good to all things." Yet, his *Summa* was a grand argument for mediation and compromise. It attempted to join Aristotle and Christian thought, reason and faith, natural and divine law, state and church. It taught that inner security depended on acceptance of one's assigned place in the religious and social order. It sanctioned the social inequality in feudalism by pointing to its counterpart in the divine hierarchy of the theologic scheme. Aquinas even found casuistic grounds for defending "just" usury. Thus, the church attempted to combine two seemingly contradictory positions: it held that this world was essentially sinful and that it was good, since it was created by God. St. Augustine made a distinction between evil enacted by man and as used by God for good. In his *Confessions*, evil is an "eclipse" of the good.[1]

THE DIVINE COMEDY AS MYTHOPOESIS

The approach to *The Divine Comedy* as mythopoesis conceives Dante's epic as a fusion of religious doctrine and esthetic imagery, both centering in the Catholic vision of divine harmony. This notion deviates from the view of Croce, who would separate Dante's teaching from his poetry. More generally, it runs up against the thesis—vigorously argued by Joseph Haroutunian—that Christian theology and the mythic perspective are incompatible.[2]

Haroutunian rejects the position of Ernst Cassirer which couples mythical and religious feeling, and he criticizes Reinhold Niebuhr along with other thinkers who hold that "religion seeks mythically to grasp life in its unity and wholeness." Referring to Athanasius' statement in *Contra Gentes*, "such then is their mythology,—far be it for us to call it religion," Haroutunian flatly asserts that "according to the church, mythology and Christian theology exclude one the other."

The basis of Haroutunian's position is the doctrine that Christianity rests on a particular historic event: the life of Christ. In his brilliant study, *The Crisis of Faith*, (New York, Nashville, 1944) Stanley Romaine Hopper calls the historic Incarnation of Jesus Christ the "Archimedian point" with which it proposes "to lift the whole world." He adds that "conceding to an event in history a character of eternal significance is indeed paradoxical—at least to the reason." For Arnold Toynbee, too, Christianity attains its deepest spiritual meaning from

> the interpretation of the future coming of the Saviour or Messiah as the future return to Earth of an historical figure who had already lived on Earth as a human being.[3]

(This motif was later adopted in the legends of the Second Coming of King Arthur and of Emperor Frederick Barbarossa.)

Now, Haroutunian argues that this belief gives Christianity a unique temporal mission which is obscured or swallowed by the concept of mythic universality. For the myth speaks not of historic existence but of symbolic reality in which figures and events are only analogous to one other. It follows that in the mythic schema, Christ is *like* other heroes who precede and follow him. Here, the mythopoeic faculty emphasizes human imagination. The Church, on the other hand, "has made a radical distinction between the revelation of God in Jesus Christ and the products of human imagination embodied in ethnic mythologies." Its truth, revealed once and for all, at a particular time, teaches that man was made in God's image, not God in man's image. This means that God the Father "is not an imaginary person after the likeness of a human father." To see Christianity merely as one historical function of a universal process is therefore "a source of weakness rather than strength." Niebuhr and Tillich, who interpret Christian doctrine as particular myths, give us the deepest symbolism, but they confuse Christian faith and revelation with religious and mythopoeic vision. The doctrine of *imago dei* is not a variation of a theme common to mythical anthropologists, but "constitutes a unique understanding of man, in and through Jesus Christ." The belief that God created the world *ex nihilo*, that not until Jesus Christ appeared was God's truth proclaimed, has its

105

authority in the Bible and the Church and depends not on vision but on faith. "The Church says, *credo*, not *video, ut intelligam*." Summing up, Haroutunian states:

> If myths are products of man's common imagination under the influence of a dimension of the empirical world . . . if they embody timeless truths about man and surroundings; if they are illustrations of a common religious principle such as sympathy . . . then Christian doctrines are not myths.[4]

Indeed, Haroutunian's thesis implies other disparities between the Christian and mythic outlook, particularly on the question of guilt.

The myth does not speak of sin, but of crime. And mythic crime is "original" only in that the hero, by his very nature of being a hero, *must* commit a crime. And what he violates is not a heavenly decree, but a taboo set up by what Cassirer calls "the society of life." Moreover, his revolt is beneficent to the extent that it overthrows a tyrannical or recharges a lethargic authority. The mythic hero thus becomes a blessed figure *by virtue* of his rebellion. In mythopoesis, the basic task of the hero is to uncover his original sources, *to discover who he is*. In Catholic doctrine, this attempt to find the First Cause is an attempt to be akin to God, and is therefore sinful. Here, the heroic way lies not in expression and fulfillment of the self, but in self-denial, obedience, and faith, with man gaining will and knowledge to the extent that he participates in God's love. And man's love for God should take precedence over social, familial and fleshly attachments. Whereas in mythopoesis the hero's rebellion is an element in his ultimate rehabilitation, redemption in the Catholic scheme is possible only by a *complete* change in the hero's sinful nature. And he earns his redemption, not so much by what he has learned, as by the rite of communion, by revelation and grace. Finally, where Catholic doctrine offers the possibility of a paradise, the myth disallows such a happy ending.

Of mythopoesis since the Book of Job, *The Divine Comedy* is closer to religious doctrine than to literature. Not that its poetic scope is narrow.[5] In his monumental study of Dante, Karl Vossler calls his epic "an international folk song," the only poem, besides *Faust*, in which "all culture and the entire world" are absorbed and re-created in a single work of art. Indeed, the epic sums up some thirteen centuries of Christianity, the history of Italy and Florence, dramatized through the author's personal experiences in love and politics.

However, by Dante's time, the firm medieval-Catholic tradition which had provided unifying reference for the cultural and practical life of men was being challenged by Protestantism in religion, by nominalism and individualism in philosophy, by nationalism in politics, and by commercial capitalism in economics. In Dante, Jacques Maritain states, "age-old Christendom was singing its last song." Precisely at this point, a great writer summons up his poetic genius and religious persuasion to present the supra-historical or symbolic reality of the Catholic idea. Like other mythopoesis, *The Divine Comedy* is the poetic re-creation of a glorious past.

Now, as noted, symbolic transformation is a deflection from belief in literal existence. Hence, it can be said that *Dante saves the mythic reality of the Catholic idea precisely by such deviation from and transposition of historic dogma.* In doing this, the poet, to be sure, blunts its uniqueness. But he also enriches its import by indicating its affinity with other mythopoeic works. In *Myth and Ritual in Christianity*, Alan W. Watts argues that Christianity acquires the dignity of myth to the extent that it is not restricted to its historical uniqueness. That Christ is *man*, not *a* man, Watts writes, means "that the Incarnation of God is not something which comes to pass in a single particular individual alone," and his release of pre-Christians in Hell "particularly suggests the timeless and mythological character of Christianity." Indeed, Watts thinks that "Christianity began to die in the moment when theologians began to treat the divine story as history." Yet, there is much evidence that nearly every Christian ritual has a precedent in pre-Christian mythology and legend.[6]

Even as Arnold Toynbee highlights Christ's historic existence, he sees Christ as part of a universal pattern (a kind of Rankian hero):

> Jesus is the babe born to a royal heritage—a scion of David or a son of God Himself—who is cast away in infancy . . . finds no room in the inn and has to be laid in a manger, like Moses in his ark or Perseus in his chest. In the stable He is watched over by a wolf and Cyrus by a hound; he also receives the ministrations of shepherds, and is reared by a foster-father of humble birth, like Romulus and Cyrus and Oedipus. Thereafter He is saved from Herod's murderous design by being taken away privily to Egypt, as Moses is saved from Pharaoh's murderous design by being hidden in the bulrushes, and as Jason is placed beyond the reach of King Pelias by being hidden in the fastness of Mount Helio. (*A Study of History*, p. 222.)

We also have the recurrent motif of the Journey: Jesus' withdrawing into the wilderness for forty days, following his baptism by John, his later withdrawal into "the high mountain apart," and his subsequent descent.

Dante's Deviations in Theology

Dante is generally thought of as a faithful disciple of traditional Christian doctrine, although there is a dispute as to whether he is a follower of St. Augustine or of Aquinas. Dante consistently follows the Thomistic doctrine that there are transitional spatial stages between the world of nature and the hereafter, and that sin and hell are part of the divine scheme. Yet, Dante deviates from Catholic doctrine.[7] His heretical temper manifests itself in his attitude towards the temporal claims of the papacy and the relation between church and state.

Dante regarded ideal politics as emanating from ideal ethics (an implication of his method which deduces the higher from the lower). Now, Dante follows the Roman-medieval tradition which viewed politics as a natural activity of all citizens. And, whereas Aquinas declared theology to be the queen over the empire, Dante wrote that it was only "the dove," and that *state* rule was the remedy "against the malady of sin" (*De Monarchia*, II,12;III,4). Hence, he extolled Virgil for upholding a supra-national world organization, centered in Rome, and Henry VII for working towards a polyphonic world state.

To be sure, Dante saw that man, in his helplessness, needed the authority of "two suns," both the state and the church, to regulate his terrestrial and his spiritual life.[8] But unlike Aquinas, who taught that the state must be subordinated to the church, Dante saw them as independent entities. This is the evangelical idea when Rome

> Was used to have two suns, by which were clear
> Both roads, that of the world and that of God.
>
> (*Purgatorio*, XVI)[9]

At that time, the church did not engage in worldly political affairs, its property was then held in common and used not "for one's kin, nor yet some viler soul," whereas today

> Walls that were once an abbey now conceal
> A den of thieves. (*Paradiso*, XXII)

The "two suns" now intrude on each other's orbits and the papacy has become a "shameless harlot" mating with political despotism (*Purgatorio*, XXXII).[10]

Dante's most dramatic deviation is *his assumption of a God-role* in the epic. The author places himself in the center of the divine process, as the prototype of mankind's fate. He—not Christ—descends to hell. He and he alone makes the complete journey and is accorded the unique grace of being allowed to enter Paradise while still alive.[11] Dante sets himself up as the supreme judge, determining who is guilty, who is to be in hell, who is to pass on to purgatory and heaven. And these decisions rest, not on revelation, but on Dante's *personal preferences.*

In his role of supreme arbiter, Dante celebrates pagan philosophers and poets as noble and divine, despite the fact that they had not been baptized. Virgil, in particular, becomes "Guide, master, lord." He is accorded equal status with Jesus and Mary in that Dante gives him a similar existential reality, and makes him as indispensable to the success of his journey as are St. Bernard and Mary.[12] Dante pays tribute to Aristotle as the master "of them that know," and to Homer as *poeta sovrano*. The *Convivio* states that following Beatrice's death, Dante sought consolation in Boethius and Tully who directed him "to the love, that is to the study, of this most gentle lady, Philosophy." Cato is declared to be more worthy "to symbolize God" than any man on earth—this although Cato committed the sin of suicide. In *Purgatorio* (XXVIII), Matilda suggests that the Earthly Paradise is like the Golden Age of which the ancients sang:

> They who in old time dreaming poetized
> Of the felicity of the Age of Gold
> On Helicon perchance this place organized.

The "memory" which Dante invokes in the second canto of the *Inferno* goes beyond Biblical revelation, when he calls on the "Muses" and "high Genius" for the power to reveal "memory, that errs not." Finally, Dante admits into Paradise heathens of both pre-and post-Christian eras: the Trojan Ripheus, Emperor Trajan, and the declared enemy of Christianity, Siger of Brabant. Indeed, the Symbolic Eagle declares that some non-Christians shall be nearer to Christ on the day of judgment than many who cry out his name.

Even more telling is the place the poet chooses to accord Beatrice. As Maritain puts it: Dante has the "brazen audacity" to exalt a certain girl "as the incarnation of theological knowledge, in whose eyes the humanity and the divinity of Christ are mirrored," simply because in his life, Dante's "flesh burned for her."[13] We should add that in the *Commedia*, Dante "forgets" that Beatrice was a married woman and transfers to her the religious imagery of the Virgin.[14] This unorthodox "chivalric" treatment of Beatrice has implications for Dante's attitude towards art, his conception of sin in the *Inferno* and of salvation in the *Paradiso*.

Dante's Deviations in His Conception of Art

Christian doctrine before Dante allows but peripheral value to poetry. Augustine accepted only the "non-material" art of music as a Christian form. In the Middle Ages, poetry was generally regarded as a pagan heritage. Scholasticism denied that it had a cogitive function and Aquinas held it to be below reason. He characterized metaphors as a defection from truth, quoting the Greek saying that poets are liars. The Middle Ages and Aquinas believed in a literal hell and heaven.

Dante is the first great Catholic writer to break with this tradition in that he distinguishes between existence and its symbol. The *Commedia* presents demons and angels as *likenesses*. The *Inferno* associates Greek mythic furies with Christian devils and demons. In *Purgatorio* (VI), Christ is addressed as "O highest Jove," and the *Paradiso* begins by invoking the "good Apollo" as an aid in describing the heavenly realm.

Dante's deviation also appears in his "four-fold" interpretation—literal, allegorical, tropological, anagogical.[15] His work would not only teach the fixed meaning of church doctrine, would not only give its moral and spiritual teaching, but would also be allegorical. And, allegory, he explains, as derived from the Greek and Latin, means diverse, varying. Its form of treatment is "poetic, fictive, descriptive, digressive, transumptive . . . by way of example." The *Convivio* (II,i) admits that theologians, "to be sure, take this sense otherwise than poets," and that he is using the allegorical "as the poets use it." (In the *Paradiso* we are told that to speak of things which are beyond the bonds of human sense, we must be satisfied with using "the example.") Dante's endorsement of the method "by way of example" makes his work translatable. In sum, Catholicism becomes mythopoesis in *The Divine Comedy* through Dante's deviation from orthodox theology and orthodox esthetic doctrine. These deviations are embodied in the art of the epic.

In his *Mimesis*, Erich Auerbach illustrates the realism of Dante's beyond: The eternal realms contain earthly frenzy, anger, action and passion. In Georg Lukacs' formulation (*Theorie des Romans*), Dante makes the transcendent immanent. Even the *Paradiso* is studded with metaphorical likenesses of the invisible and intangible, employing musical and planetary images to suggest the immateriality of the vision. His work as a whole presents man's problems in a highly personal form.

Charles Williams (*The Figure of Beatrice* [London, 1943].) distinguishes between the use of imagery ("the Way of Affirmation") and the renunciation of all images ("the Way of Rejection"). He shows that the two ways are intertwined in Dante and that the meaning of his work is gathered into what the *Convivio* terms "one simple substance." Dante does not stop at philosophic and religious sublimation of the passions. He *redirects* their frustrations into the sensuous sphere of his art. His poem thus *reasserts* the adventure of sensuous living and expresses the symbolic fulfillment of his self. This approach can help us see that *Dante's three realms coexist in each one*: Elements of paradise are foreshadowed in hell and the heavenly realm affirms the beauty of the body. His work receives its *dramatic* quality from the tension between the inchoateness of human existence and the peace of divine reality. This tension is present everywhere. It is at its greatest in the first and third realms, least in the middle kingdom where the poet gives freer expression to mythic analogies and to Italian legend and folktale.

As noted, for Christianity, redemption is possible only if the sinner undergoes absolute repentance. Dante follows this precept to the extent that the people in his *Inferno* are doomed to eternal punishment because they remain uncontrite. But Dante's *poetic attitude* tells a different story: The poet evinces sympathy, even admiration for some of his sinners. They know the consequences of their action (they suffer for it), yet insist on their ways. Farinata, Capaneus, Odysseus, Ugolino, above all, Francesca and Paolo, do not ask to be taken out of hell. They *accept* the result of their character, and one might say that Dante views them *as sacrifices to a doctrine*.

Dante argues against pride, excessive love and power. Yet, even doctrinally, he regards them as distortions of divine love. A strong will is superior to a good will. (Those with a good will are placed in the lowest Paradise.) But the crucial test, I repeat, is Dante's esthetic attitude. The poet pours more of his sensuous passion into the love which moves the rebellious sinners than into the love which moves the sun and other stars. As artist, Dante allows more "grace" to Francesca than to Beatrice. Indeed, as Charles Williams points out, the love which Dante finally affirms is itself a *restless* power: it *moves* man.

Beatrice and the City

Dante's epic contains the first extended love story in Western mythopoesis. Vossler remarks that Dante is among the first to counteract the depreciation of women, taught by the Greeks, Ovid and the church. But the new element in Dante is his linking woman with the city, state and God. The poet relates the fate of Beatrice to the fate of the community, likening her death to the scourge which descends on the city: "How doth the city sit solitary, that was full of people! how is she become a widow." When the *Convivio* (I, III) states that its author is

> a vessel without sail and without rudder, driven about upon different ports
> and shores by the dry wind that springs out of dolorous poverty,

the tone and some of the imagery are similar to those used in complaining that Italy has no government, no peace, is without a pilot in a storm, denuded by priests, growing fat from filth and gain.

Dante's work is the first to raise sex-love to the existential plane of politics and religion. In Graeco-Roman mythopoesis, women are important primarily in their relation to the *polis*. (In Aeschylus, Zeus' passion for Io and Aegisthus' for Clytemnestra are a sub-theme.) Oedipus wins Jocasta as a reward for ridding the city of its blight; Medea is outraged because she is rejected as coming from a barbarian land; the love of Virgil's Dido for Aeneas is intertwined with her social role of founding a city. In traditional Christianity, the Virgin remains inaccessible as a woman and sex love is a hindrance to the pure love of God. Dante is the first major writer to celebrate love for a particular woman and to see in it the kernel of social and religious love, the first whose hero is redeemed through the intercession of a woman. In the manner of the Orpheus legend where the beloved is resurrected by word and song, and of Novalis' "Hymns to the Night" in which the poet apotheosized his dead beloved, Dante resolved to write of his departed Beatrice "what hath not before been written of any woman."[16] Beatrice's passing produced what Vossler characterizes as "the germ of a poetic world of Christian mythology."

Act I: Eden

For Dante, the Golden Age of universal peace and love of truth is at the root of man (*l'umana radice*), the source of his innocent beginnings. In the life of mankind, it is the memory of our communal mother (*commune madre*); in the life of the individual, it is the nursery stage, the time of "our true first speech"; historically, it was ancient Rome and Florence, the age of the "two suns," when property was held in common and there was concord, simplicity, chastity.[17] And, the poet invokes these memories to counteract the schism and corruption of his day.

In his letter to Can Grande (*The Letters of Dante* [Oxford, 1920], p. 202), Dante states that the *Commedia* was undertaken, not for the sake of speculation, but "for a practical purpose." The work, with its demons, minotaurs and angels, its hell, purgatory and heaven, has been called a "vision." But medieval man believed such visions to have physical existence, and Dante's art makes them visible, audible and tangible. Unlike the allegorical figures in Bunyan or the thin shadows in Kafka,

112

Dante and Virgil by Eugene Delacroix (The Bettmann Archives)

Faust, Marguerite and Mephistopheles in the Street,
lithograph illustration to Goethe's *Faust*
(Dept. of Graphic Arts, Harvard College Library)

Dante's characters are sensuous people and his journey into the realm
of the dead becomes an experience in the realm of the living. *The Divine Comedy* deals with man in nature. We know the lament of Francesca and Farinata, the storms and flames which lash and scorch the
sinners, know their anguish and restlessness, the torment of their loneliness. We also know the hope of the repenting sinners in purgatory and
get a sense of the overwhelming gladness of those who are in paradise.
The author who writes about the other world is alive and can view it
only in its likeness to the living world. If *The Divine Comedy* is to be
taken seriously, then its other life must be relevant to our life, the only
kind we know.

Act II: The Mythic Crime

The starting point of *The Divine Comedy* is the same as that in other
mythopoesis: There is something rotten in the state. The point is restated in the *Paradiso* (XI), where sin consists in being insensitive (*in-
sensata cura dei mortali*) to abiding values:

> Distracted mortals! of what paltry worth
> Are the arguments whereby ye are so prone
> Senselessly to beat down your wings to earth!
> One wooed the Law, one the Aphorisms, one
> Coveted the priesthood, and another pressed
> Through force or fraud to acquire dominion;
> One plunder, and one business, quite possessed;
> One in the pleasures of the carnal sty
> Grew weary; another in his own ease caressed . . .

Dante's charge is directed to Everyman, but his examples are historic
and contemporary. Sin is so recent in the poem, Mark Van Doren remarks, that the author can name the sinners, locating them in Italian-
Florentine politics.

Now, the world of sinners includes Dante, who has gone astray. And
this happened, not "originally," but "midway the journey of this life,"
when he *became aware* of being lost (*mi ritrovai*—"came to myself").[18]
The *selva oscura* where he is lost is at once the general situation of
man, of Italy and Florence, and the darkness in Dante's own life. But
what was Dante's personal sin?

Beatrice's specific charge is that Dante neglected her for some little
girl (*pargoletta*):

> Thou oughtest not to have stooped thy pinions downward
> To wait for further blows, or little girl,
> Or other vanity of such brief use. (Longfellow's translation).

Nowhere does Dante summon up as much pity and sympathy as he does for the carnal sinners with whom Hell proper begins.

Dante's sensuous burden is foreshadowed in the very first canto where the Leopard, the Lion and the She-Wolf bar his path. These animals are interpreted as having political meaning or as representing Incontinence, Violence and Fraud. I would suggest that two of them also refer to Dante's own carnal demon.

The poet mentions the Lion briefly and concentrates on the Leopard and the She-Wolf. They are described in imagery which alludes to quick, unsteady movements and alluring seductiveness. The Leopard, "light and swift of limb," is the animal with the gay skin (*gaietta pelle*), the She-Wolf is "That restless beast," lean and full of cravings (*tutte brame*). Dante is finally stopped by the She-Wolf, which drives him back "To where the Sun is silent." Virgil says of this female animal that "Her craving maw never is satisfied," that after feeding, she is hungrier than before. Again, in *Purgatorio* (XX), Dante curses the "she-wolf of old" that preys more than all the other beasts, whose hunger is unappeasable. The quality of restlessness, of insatiability also appears in the wind and tempest metaphors of the carnal sinners in Canto V. Through such figures, *the author relives their sins symbolically*. His very intemperate denunciations point to his affinity with the sinners. And, in depicting their punishment, Dante also experiences symbolical atonement for his own sins. Dante's vicarious acceptance of punishment, meted out to others, is a well-known device for displacement of personal guilt.[19]

Dante's elevation of sin as a moral condition for redemption appears obliquely in his attitude towards those who were neither virtuous nor immoral. They live in Ante-Hell, for even "deep Hell refuses them." Virgil comments that besides such, "the sinner would be proud," for he at least made a choice, although a bad choice. In contrast to their realm, Hell is made part of the divine order, the inscription on its door reading

> Me did Divine Authority Uprear;
> Me Supreme Wisdom and Primal Love Sustain.

Those in Hell are better off than the forlorn spirits in Ante-Hell who "never were alive," who acted "without infamy and without praise." Virgil and Dante pass them by in contempt.

The poet's identification with those assigned to the Inferno begins in that part of Limbo which he reserves for his favorite non-Christians. Although they have not been baptized and hence have no faith, they suffer no pain, but are placed in what Zimmer calls a "sort of idyllic,

Elysian lobby." Among them are the "four great shades," Homer, Horace, Ovid and Lucan. Dante is proud to join them and feels exalted when he sees other "great spirits," such as Hector, Aeneas, Caesar, Brutus, Aristotle and Plato.

The Pattern of the Inferno: Paolo and Francesca

It is generally acknowledged that Dante imparts the greatest intensity, vividness and dramatic realism to the *Inferno*. Where Aquinas says very little about hell, Dante devotes a third of his epic to it.

The distinguishing character of suffering in hell is that here man has no hope of ever emerging from it. And there is no hope because there is no love. In the formulation given by Dostoyevsky's Father Zossima, hell is the suffering of loneliness which comes from the inability to love.

The Canto dealing with the carnal sinners Paolo and Francesca is deservedly renowned for its poetic quality and it is pivotal for establishing Dante's principle of *contrapasso,*—that a man shall be punished wherewith he sins.

In life, the two lovers allowed the storm of their passion full sway and their punishment consists in having to experience this passion, and this passion alone, forever:

> To and fro, down, up . . . in helpless flight,
> Comforted by no hope ever to lie
> At rest, nor even to bear a pain more light.

Forever, they are to be whirled by "The abysmal tempest that never can sleep," smitten and driven by the warring wind and the billowing sea.

From a strict view, the punishment meted out to the lovers exceeds their crime. For a few hours of unpermitted passion, Paolo and Francesca are given over to an eternity of torment. Yet, what Dante intends to show is that *their act is a way of living which carries over into the life pattern as a whole.* Dante's moral-esthetic strategy consists in *essentializing* both the good and the evil act. For all its realism, his art does not aim at the three-dimensional fullness that we find, say in Tolstoy, but goes out for the essence—in medieval language, the "quiddity"—for the pure "reality" which underlies the appearance of actuality. In *Purgatorio* (XXI), Dante tells us:

> The live appeared living and dead the dead.
> Not better he who saw the actual deed
> Saw than I, stooping, all beneath my tread.

115

His characters are at once sensuous beings in time and space, and lead what Hegel called a "changeless existence." We are, Auerbach observes, "in an eternal place, and yet we encounter appearance and concrete occurrence there." He formulates Dante's method by calling it "the absolute realization of a particular earthly personality in the place definitely assigned to it," which "constitutes the Divine Judgment." The individual, concrete appearance of passion is viewed in its intrinsic substance.

This approach appears in Dante's treatment of Paolo and Francesca. Dante reduces the hours of their specific indulgence to *the principle of indulgence,* and they are made to experience their passion *to the exclusion of everything else.* This is specialization, and specialization is hell for man who wants to be a complete human being. By being endlessly repeated, the love of Paolo and Francesca becomes at once agonizing restlessness and monotonous sameness. Hell is the monotony and futility in changeless repetition, its "law and quality" ever remaining the same (*Inferno* VI).

This, then, is the "practical" import of the poem: It warns us that once we have established a certain way of life—of indulging, falsifying, betraying—we are driven to repeat it. Once we have established our character, it becomes our fate. Capaneus cries out: "What I was alive, that I am dead" (XV). According to this pattern, the punishment of the sinners consists in their having to repeat their transgressions forever: The heretics are divided, the avaricious assail one another, the flatterers are immersed in filth, the envious have their eyelids sewn, etc.

Charles Williams indicates the relation of the Paolo-Francesca scene to the larger theme of communality in the *Commedia.* The deeper meaning of their adultery is that it shuts out the public, communal aspect of the self. In *Purgatorio* (XIV), Guy del Duca bewails the fact that man sets his heart there where he must separate himself from his consorts:

> O gente umana, perchè poni il core
> là v' è mestier di consorto divieto?[20]

In self-indulgence, man deprives himself of fulfilling his whole being, and this, Williams notes, is "possible to all lovers, married or unmarried, adulterous or marital." The evil of mutual indulgence lies in that it is "bound too soon to become two separate single indulgences." This holds for Dante's lovers as well as for Tolstoy's Vronsky and Anna Karenina. They too begin with a concealed kiss; they too shut themselves off and are shut off from their city; in time, they develop hatred of each other's indulgence, are in hell while they are alive. The supreme achievement of hell, writes Williams, "is to make interchange impossible." All the sinners in Hell are "without regard for the City. Farinata is the pride of the citizen in his house or his party held more passionately close than the City . . . the usurers make private profit out of the City. . . ."

Yet, to repeat the point made earlier, while Dante the religious thinker condemns such sinners, Dante the artist makes the most renowned of them—Francesca, Farinata, Cavalcante, Ulysses, Ugolino—attractive, even heroic. Again, his treatment of the Paolo-Francesca story may serve as a prototype. When Dante hears their wailings, he begs Virgil that he might speak with them. Their transgression rouses him, not to indignation, but to tears, as he considers

> How many sweet thoughts and what longings fain
> Led them into the lamentable pass![21]

His identification is such that—like the lovers who that day read no further in their book—Dante too goes no further in his book, but swoons, "like a body falling dead."

It is noteworthy that Dante does not dwell on the sinful acts of his major figures. In his *Life of Dante*, Michele Barbi points out that the poet reevokes that which has nothing to do with their being in hell. This is especially the case with Ugolino: " . . . not the act of betrayal performed and suffered by Count Ugolino, but the cruel mode of his death," is what Dante places in the foreground. And, we are wrung with grief by Dante's account of how the father stood helplessly while his little sons vainly begged for food and then saw them starve to death.

Dante evinces a similar attitude towards Farinata, whom he calls *magnanimo*, and Capaneus, whom he calls "that great spirit." Farinata lies in a burning coffin, scorched by flames, and Capaneus is charred by a fiery rain. Yet, both are undaunted and unbent. Farinata rises up in front of Dante "As if of Hell he had a great disdain." The poet grants them something of the stature of Aeschylus' Prometheus and Milton's Satan. Likewise, Dante's account of Cavalcante fills us with deep pity, as we hear him sorrowing in the belief that his son is dead. "We cannot," writes Erich Auerbach,

> but admire Farinata and weep with Cavalcante. What actually moves us is not that God has damned them, but that the one is unbroken and the other mourns so heart-rendingly for his son and the sweetness of the light. (*Mimesis*, p. 200.)

And, in the story of Ulysses, Dante pays homage to the adventure of earthly experience. Even in hell, Ulysses insists that nothing

> Could conquer the inward hunger that I had
> To master earth's experience, and to attain
> Knowledge of man's mind, both the good and the bad.

The *Inferno* can thus be viewed as both an expression of and a check on Dante's own drives. The check is felt in his anger at the sinners and expressed formally in the severe, mathematical architecture of the poem. As Karl Vossler puts it, these are the ramparts with which Dante would dam up the raging tides within himself.[22] Yet, the very rigidity of the design points to the power of the emotional storms within.

In *Purgatorio* (X), we are told "Think of the sequel." The sequel of establishing a sinful pattern is to repeat it eternally. Yet, Dante seems to be saying that to learn what sin is, we must experience it. In this connection, it is relevant to note that Virgil and Dante are helped by Antaeus and Satan in their journey through hell. (They are taken by Antaeus into the deep of the Ninth Circle and are enabled to leave the inferno by clinging to Lucifer's fell). Nearly as much as in Goethe's *Faust,* the devil helps man to achieve the realm of clarity. Dante had first attempted to reach the mountain of purgatory by a direct short route. But, stopped by the She-Wolf, he was forced to take a round-about passage, had to traverse the hellish terrain to find his way to the earthly and divine paradise.

Purgatory: Visual Recognition

Purgatory is still the world of sinners. But in the inferno they were *made* to suffer, whereas here they *desire* to suffer: The proud want to be humbled, the gluttons to be famished, the slothful to be in restless motion. One extreme is to be purged by its *converso*, by another extreme. Yet—and here again the attractiveness of sin is obliquely acknowledged—to prove themselves capable of withstanding its seductiveness, *they must expose themselves to the temptation of sinning*: the unchaste practice chastity amidst the fire and heat of glowing flames; the gluttons sing as they weep from hunger:

> That appetite they followed with such heat,
> Holy again through hunger and thirst shall be.
> The scent that from the apple comes so sweet
> And from the sprinkling of the leaves with spray
> Fires us with craving both to drink and eat.

That is, in purgatory, *man becomes aware of sin by re-experiencing it symbolically.*

In the inferno, awareness was obscured by hell's murky grey. But purgatory is lit up by the sun, objects are shown in soft colors (*dolce color*), and *sin becomes visible*. It is here that the angel inscribes the letter P on Dante's forehead; only here do the seven deadly sins become

visible. Suffering in purgatory does not have the stark physical character
of the inferno and is more suggestive of mental suffering.[23] What had
been lived through physically is now lived through symbolically.

In *Purgatorio* (XXVII), Dante calls sleep a state

> ... which often will apprize
> Of things to come, and ere the event foreknow.

Charles Williams calls attention to the fact that only in purgatory does
Dante sleep and that only here does he cast a shadow. Hell is too disturbing for sleep and too murky to allow for a shadow. It is in the midway realm of purgatory that sleep and dream enable Dante to achieve
awareness, what Dante calls *amore d'animo*. The psychological process is also suggested by the circumstance that here Dante *journeys backwards*. By moving *against* the stream (Lethe), memory of guilt is
washed away. Dante advises those guilty of Envy that their bad conscience may be removed by "The stream of memory down-flowing ..."
(*per essa scenda della mente il fiume*). By alternate sleep and wake-
fulness, Dante moves backwards towards remembering and reordering
his past.

From Virgil, Dante learned that love is

> ... the seed of virtue pure
> And of all works deserving chastisement.

and that "natural" love, which is always free from error, is to be distinguished from love "of the mind," which may become excessive or distorted love (*Purgatorio*, XVII, XVIII). Dante is also told that he can
master sinful desires "of the mind" by proper exercise of the free will.
With the removal of guilt, there is left only the memory of the better
self which Dante recovers by drinking from the waters of Eunoë. Having been purified, Dante becomes freed of the memory of original sin
and achieves the highest form of freedom of the will. Virgil declares
that Dante is now his own master and can be left to go the rest of the
way without him.

Act III: Return to Origins

One of the supreme ironies of *The Divine Comedy* is that precisely
at this point, Dante becomes a "child" again. When he beholds Beatrice,
Dante turns to Virgil for help

> With such trust as a child that is afraid
> Or hurt, runs to his mother with his pains.

119

But the father-guide is gone and Dante faces Beatrice alone, like "a child" confronted by "a mother." Whatever self-knowledge and self-esteem Dante had gained vanish, as he stands before Beatrice in fear and confusion, "letting gush the sighs and tears." He confesses his basic sin, which he calls enslavement to momentary pleasures—*le presenti cose:*

> Weeping I said: "Things of the passing day,
> Soon as your face no longer on me shone,
> With their false pleasure turned my steps away."

Dante's *le presenti cose* correspond to the Mephistophelian bed of sloth or the denial of the quest. But neither Faust nor any other hero in mythopoesis renounces his crime as completely as Dante does. When Beatrice continues to upbraid him, charging that he paid attention to girls, Dante accepts the rebuke in the manner of children (*fanciulli*):

> As boys that dumb with shamefastness remain,
> Eyes to ground, listening to their faults rehearsed,
> Knowing themselves in penitence and pain,
> So stood I . . .

Beatrice, who had been his wished-for beloved now becomes his *mamma.*

In the *Convivio*, Dante writes that

> the supreme desire of everything, and that first given by nature, is to return
> to its source; and since God is the source of our souls . . . to him this soul
> chiefly desireth to return (IV, 12).

And, when Dante is asked in *Purgatorio* (II) why he is taking the journey, he replies that he may thereby achieve a return:

> . . . per tornare altra volta
> La dove son, fo io questo viaggio.[24]

Unlike Job, Prometheus and Oedipus, Dante makes no decisions of his own, but follows his trusted guides from Virgil, Statius and St. Bernard to Lucy, Leah, Matelda, Beatrice and the Virgin Mary.

When Dante reaches the Earthly Paradise on Purgatory, his purification is completed. Why, then, it has been asked, is it necessary for him to go on to Paradise? Adam had to forsake Eden because he desired knowledge of good and evil before he was ready for it. But Dante had already learned the consequences of false choice, had become his own master. What need then for further instruction and purification? Vossler calls Paradise "the heavenly reflection of the peaceful and visionary piety" of Dante's childhood. But if it is no more than that, then Dante has learned nothing from his journey.

However, Dante has passed through the plane of knowledge which the *Convivio* calls "the ultimate perfection of our soul, in which consists our ultimate felicity."[25] And Dante himself suggests that return to infancy is neither possible nor desirable. His *De Vulgari Eloquentia* begins with an attempt to justify the replacement of Latin by Italian as a literary medium. At first, Dante defends "vulgar" speech as the natural "mother-tongue" which infants imitate from their nurses. But he goes on to argue in behalf of *ideal* speech, one that is "illustrious, cardinal, courtly, and curial."

Gertrude Leigh thinks that Dante succeeded in transforming his sensual desires into spiritual channels. In his *Goliath* (New York, 1938), Borgese also argues that Dante sublimated the failures in his personal life by projecting a religious and universal realm. Indeed, Dante's life as a whole shows a series of basic deprivations and estrangements: He lost his mother when he was only a small child; his father became a usurer; his wife, Gemma Donati, was chosen for him by his father (Dante never mentions her in his work); he felt himself rejected by Beatrice; he was frustrated in his political efforts as a Florentine and Italian, and he died in exile.

Dante himself lends support to the thesis that his work is a symbolic compensation for his wordly failures. He tells us in the *Convivio* that the loss of Beatrice led him first to philosophic, then to religious love. However, I would suggest that we need to examine elements of Dante's carnal passion *within* his invocation of heavenly love. Dante's temperament did not allow for peace in sublimations. He remained proud, arrogant and rebellious to the end. And both the *Vita* and the *Commedia* offer clues that Dante did not succeed in curbing his sensual nature.

Sex and Love

Dante's *Vita Nuova* (Rosetti translation) states that his love for Beatrice sprang from ideal boyhood feelings and that it retained this quality nine years later when he was eighteen. When he was nine years old, "the glorious Lady" of his "mind" seemed to him a heavenly figure,—

> so noble and praiseworthy that certainly of her might have been said the words of the poet Homer, "She seemed not to be the daughter of a mortal man, but of God."

When he saw her again nine years later, he had a dream about this "daughter . . . of God," in which Dante's "master" appears, "a lord of

terrible aspect," enveloped by "a mist of the colour of fire." He has the
sleeping lady in his arm, and holds Dante's heart, "burning in flames."
The master bids the lady eat Dante's heart and then "it seemed to me
that he went with her up towards heaven." Whereupon, "such a great
anguish came upon me that my light slumber could not endure through
it, but was suddenly broken."

The implicit rivalry between Dante and his "master" over the lady,
as well as the inevitability of Dante's renunciation ("When Love was
shown me with such terrors fraught") are made explicit in a sonnet,
written after Beatrice's death. Here, "the Eternal Sire" is seized by
"a sweet desire" for Beatrice's "lovely excellence" and thence bids her
"to Himself aspire":

> Beatrice is gone up into high Heaven,
> The kingdom where the angels are at peace ; . . .
> For from the lamp of her meek lowlihead
> Such an exceeding glory went up hence
> That it woke wonder in the Eternal Sire,
> Until a sweet desire
> Enter'd Him for that lovely excellence,
> So that he bade her to Himself aspire:
> Counting this weary and most evil place
> Unworthy of a thing so full of grace.

> (Rosetti translation)

From that night on, the natural functions of his body began "to be vexed
and impeded." There follows a second dream in which the master bids
him "compose certain things in rhyme . . . And thus she shall be made
to know thy desire."[26] Having written the sonnet, Dante begins to be
harassed by doubts whether his master is good or evil and concludes
that he can only commend himself to Pity. But Dante's ambivalent
feeling towards him becomes clear when he calls Pity "mine enemy."[27]

In the meantime, other "Beatrices" came his way. One with whom

> . . . dwells the counterpart
> of the same Love who holds me weeping now.

There was another, called Pietra (addressed in the poem "To the Dim
Light"), who "stone-like" refused his love. Dante would have it that
these other women were "a screen for so much love" he felt for Beatrice;
but it is also possible that the love for the Lady of his "mind" was a
screen for so much passion he felt for more accessible women. (In the
Commedia, Dante admits shamefacedly to having paid attention to
such, and in the *Vita*, he speaks of "the unsteadfastness of mine eyes.")

Dante did not regard asceticism as an ideal. In *Paradiso* (XIV), Solomon hopes for the resurrection of the body:

> When flesh is glorified and sainted state
> Shall be re-clothed, our persons in esteem
> Shall be more pleasing, being then complete . . .
> For the organs of the body shall acquire
> Strength to support all that may most delight.

Dante's three dreams in *Purgatorio* (IX, XIX, XXVII), contain a similar erotic-esthetic configuration.

Stirred by "something of Adam," Dante first dreams that an eagle snatches him up into the fiery sphere.

> We approached and were arriving at a spot
> Whence, there where first to me a gap appeared
> Like in a wall some crack that it hath got,
> I saw a gate . . .

Here stands "a guardian," with a countenance "such as I could not sustain," who bids them halt and declare their will, after which Dante "mounts" the three steps towards the gate. Next, Dante dreams of the sweet Siren who leads mariners astray with her wiles. She is promptly confounded by another figure, "a lady in whom was holiness."

Dante has the third dream when he is about to behold Beatrice on the Earthly Paradise. Virgil tells him that first he will have to pass through a "womb of flames," which is the "wall" between him and Beatrice. Dante is terrified and troubled like a child until he is reassured. Dante then dreams of Leah, who sings while she gathers flowers, and of Rachel, who sits before the mirror which reflects her beautiful eyes. As Dante beholds Beatrice at the topmost step, he feels the mighty power of ancient love (*d' antico amor senti la gran potenza*). Beatrice accuses him of seeking girls and forgetting the great "pleasure" her own "fair limbs" presented to him. As he is drawn into the dance of the star-nymphs and led up to the Gryphon's breast, he sees Christ reflected in Beatrice's eyes. At this point, he is stirred by "thousand desires, hotter than flame":

> Thousand desires, hotter than flame, constrained
> The gaze of mine eyes to the shining eyes
> Which on the Gryphon only fixed remained.

In the midst of Dante's recognition scene with Beatrice, the harlot turns her wanton eyes on him, as she is about to mate with a towering giant. Dante's meeting with Beatrice amidst "the living green of the divine forest" (XXVIII) is in the mythic tradition of the union between the mother-sister-goddess and the son-brother-hero, here clothed in Christian imagery.

The term "ancient" recurs in these Cantos (*antico amor, antica fiamma, selva antica, l'antica madre*; Beatrice's self is called *se stessa antica*.) But the ancient love which Dante feels in the ancient forest for Beatrice's ancient self cannot be Eden, for it is experienced by one who knows the temptations of sin. This dialectic carries over into the *Paradiso* where Beatrice has to reprove Dante for continuing to find the "sacred flame" solely in her eyes:

> She spoke to me: "turn now and listen anew!
> Not only in my eyes is Paradise."

Here again, Dante mixes religious and sexual allusions: Led by Beatrice, Dante sees a ladder standing erect (*eretto*), reaching up towards the Heavenly Rose, where he is to resolve his passionate desires (*Solvi il tuo caldo disio*). The Saints reach up to touch the Virgin, with their flame, in the manner of a child stretching his arms when he has milked the mother's breasts; the angels descend into and reascend the divine Rose, like bees "which deep into the flowers retreat" (XXIII, XXXI). The emotions of the Sixth Beatitude are expressed in terms of the May breeze which stirs the sweet winds, impregnate with grass and flowers. Beatrice appears "amid a cloud of flowers . . . Clothed in the colour of a living flame." Charles Williams and Allen Tate have helped correct the view that Beatrice "represents theology" by pointing out that the love which Dante expresses for her in *Purgatorio* includes the passion he felt for the bodily charms of the girl he saw in the streets of Florence.

The fiery wall which stands between Dante and Beatrice is roughly analogous to the pestilential fire which Oedipus is called upon to put out before he can gain Jocasta, and to the ring of fire which Siegfried must penetrate to reach Brunhilde. Dante's meeting with the mother-figure takes place only after Virgil, his father-mentor, has left. In *The Magic Mountain*, Castorp approaches his Beatrice on Walpurgisnight only after he has dismissed Settembrini, his Virgilian guide.

The three realms suggest three psychic powers in varying proportions: In the *Inferno*, primitive, anti-social acts predominate; in *Purgatorio*, the ego, or the operation of the will gains mastery; in the *Paradiso*, the psyche is integrated.

Here again, the function of the ego appears in Dante's art which molds the underlying erotic fantasies into their symbolic forms.

Epilogue

Dante's epic ends with the light-simile *stelle,* in contrast to the sombre *umbras* of Virgil's *Aeneid,* and the author called his work a *Commedia,* to indicate its happy resolution. As noted, the doctrine of grace precludes final tragedy in the Christian religion.

Yet, *The Divine Comedy* does contain the tragic residue of mythopoesis. In his essay, "The Symbolic Imagination" (*Kenyon Review* [Spring, 1952]), Allen Tate has noted this element by distinguishing between the hero and the author. He points out that after Dante has ended the poem, he still faces the *human* task and fails "in the sense that he will have to start over again when he steps out of the poem." Tate also questions that we are to suppose the hero actually attains the Beatific Vision. The vision in the poem, he writes, "is imagined, it is *imaged;* its essence is not possessed. . . . Perhaps the symbolic imagination is tragic in sentiment, if not always in form, in the degree of its development." In *De Vulgari Eloquentia,* Dante himself states that "the style which we call tragic appears to be the highest style."

The disparity between existence and reality appears in the social order of Dante's *Paradiso* itself. In early Christian doctrine, God's love is equally distributed to everyone at all times. In Dante's paradise, God, "the Prime Equality" (XV), distributes his love *unequally.* The first Canto announces this theme by declaring that the glow of God's glory penetrates more in some regions and less in others. There is "disparity" (XV) in heaven: Some souls are placed in lower, others in higher heavens. (Even new-born infants, saved by baptism, are placed in varying orders.) Apart from the spaceless and timeless Empyrean, where all are united in one heavenly rose, Paradise consists of hierarchical orders. *Dante's Heaven thus reconstructs the medieval feudal system where everyone was to accept his assigned station.* That is, Dante's poem spiritualizes the very historic system which was the basis for his political dissidence.

Yet, here too, Dante evinces his criticism of this structure. This is manifested directly in his inclusion of heathens and declared enemies of Christianity in his Catholic Heaven, and more subtly in the Canto dealing with Piccarda and Constanza. Piccarda had been forced by her brother to leave the cloister and accept a political marriage. Yet, Santayana points out, she is placed in the lowest Paradise of the Inconstant Moon although she had broken her vows *unwillingly.* When Dante asks her whether she wishes for a higher sphere, she replies that such desire is impossible, for our peace lies in His will. The hierarchical order is itself an expression of the diversity of God's grace (XXXII).[28] The case of Piccarda shows that divine justice is exacting. Love is administered, not by the tender Mother-Goddess, as in Eastern Orthodoxy, but by God the Father and the Son. Dante retains the hierarchy of the patriarchal scheme. (Even Beatrice is, for the most part, a "masculine sage," as Vossler calls her, an "angelic creature under the hood of a doctor of theology.")

Peace on Earth

From Virgil, Dante learned that social-political peace was a condition for spiritual harmony. A terrestial paradise must precede the heavenly peace which Dante finds in Paradise.[29] How deeply Dante felt about this emerges from the prayerful lines in *De Monarchia* (Book I):

> Whence it is manifest that universal peace is the best of all those things which are ordained for our blessedness. And that is why there rang out to the shepherds from on high, not riches, not pleasures, not honors, not length of life, not health, not strength, not beauty, but peace. For the celestial soldiery proclaims, 'Glory to God in the highest; and, on earth, peace to men of good will.' Hence, also, 'Peace be with you' was the salutation of him who was the salvation of man.[30]

In *Purgatorio* (XV), Virgil told Dante that sharing increases the things shared and later he heard Beatrice's "We are" (*Ben sem*) countering the Siren's song, "I am." Dante saw Florence and Rome, the city and the church, corrupted by self-indulgence, torn by strife and treachery. His Paradise is a prayer that earthly divisiveness might be supplanted by universal communality. The heart of his idea was the union of an ethical politics with a practical morality, aiming at a supra-national world. Perhaps Friedrich Engels had this in mind when he characterized Dante as the first international mind of our modern era. Dante seems to be saying, as Santayana puts it, that what mankind was once, that it must become again: "What in his day seemed a dream—that mankind should be one commonwealth, is now obvious to the idealist, the socialist, the merchant." This idea may be one of the reasons for the appeal which Dante has in our day.

Yet *The Divine Comedy* shows the marks of the coming Renaissance in that the main focus is on the hero, Dante, for whose sake the journey takes place (the word "I" is on nearly every page of the poem). His mission is to save himself, rather than the others, who remain where they are.[31] However, this individual emphasis is also expressed in Dante's rebellious spirit. In life, Dante was a dissident, suffering exile from

country, friends and family, rather than recant his beliefs. In the famous
lines written to a friend:

> Far be it from the preacher of justice, when he hath suffered a wrong, to
> pay his coin to them that inflicted it as though they had deserved well of
> him. . . . What then? May I not gaze upon the mirror of the sun and stars
> wherever I may be? Can I not ponder on the sweetest truths wherever I may
> be beneath the heaven, but I must first make me inglorious, nay infamous,
> before the people and the state of Florence? Nor shall I lack bread. (*Letters
> of Dante*, p. 659.)

The epilogue in *The Divine Comedy* is connected with its transcendent concept of God. In contrast to Job's Yahweh and the Greek deities
who can be seen, addressed, and who manifest themselves in the dynamics of natural phenomena, Dante's God transcends the sphere of
nature. To be sure, there is grace. But the nature of human desires is
such that man is forever tempted by earthly illusions. This precludes a
paradisiac finale in Dante's Catholic myth as well. Charles Williams
points out that the very last lines of the epic emphasize will, desire and
movement:

> Already on my desire and will prevailed
> The Love that moves the sun and the other stars.

In the final analysis, the epilogue follows from the mystery of primary causation. Man, we are told, can know only the effects of the divine plan, but not its cause (in theologic terminology, only the *quia*,
not the *propter quid*). In connection with the mystery of the Trinity,
Dante is instructed:

> He is mad who hopes that reason in its sweep
> The infinite way can traverse back and forth
> Which the Three Persons in one substance keep.
> With the quia stay content, children of the earth!

While this may also discourage inquiry into temporal maladjustments,
it can serve as the basis for the inspiration of the quest. In the beautiful
lines from the final Canto, Dante sings of the sweet effect which lasts in
memory, even as the cause remains a mystery:

> As he who dreams sees, and when disappears
> The dream, the passion of its print remains,
> And naught else to the memory adheres,
> Even such am I; for almost wholly wanes
> My vision now, yet still the drops I feel
> Of sweetness it distilled into my veins.[32]

NOTES

1. Arthur Lovejoy's *The Great Chain of Being* (Cambridge, Mass., 1936) summarizes the ways this problem was handled. The Scotists argued that whatever God willed was good because he willed it and Abelard held that the goodness of the world followed from the fact that it was created by a good and rational deity. Aquinas rejected such necessitarian optimism since it disallowed free will and made the distinction between absolute and hypothetical necessity. At the same time, he stated that "a universe in which there was no evil would not be so good as the actual universe." According to Lovejoy, Aquinas evaded the consequence of the two premises when they led towards admitting the complete correspondence of the possible and the actual.

2. The quotations from Mr. Haroutunian are taken from an unpublished paper he read before the Duodecim Society in November, 1948.

3. Arnold Toynbee, *A Study of History* (New York and London, 1947), p. 223.

4. The historic existence of a figure, by itself, does not prevent its becoming the subject of mythopoesis. The crucial question is whether such a figure is *translatable* into other frameworks. In an essay on "Typological Symbolism in Medieval Literature" (*Yale French Studies*, No. 9), Erich Auerbach argues that "figurative interpretation" in Christian literature attributes a common meaning to causal and chronological events. Thus, an event which preceded Christ is revealed "as a prefiguration of a fulfillment or perhaps as an imitation of other events." Hence, Dante can include the Roman empire of Augustus as a "figure of God's eternal empire." The figurative interpretation derives from the eternal wisdom of God in whose sight "what happens here and now, has happened from the very beginning, and may recur at any moment in the flow of time." In Auerbach's interpretation, the difference between Christian and mythic doctrine is mainly terminological, the Christian God corresponding to the mythic eternal "It is." However, whereas in medieval thought God alone is both the eternal and temporal first cause, in the mythic perspective any figure or period can be "first." In mythopoesis, the imaginative power of man brings forth a reinterpretation, and in that sense, a re-creation of the world.

5. Erich Auerbach's *Mimesis* (Princeton, 1953) points to Dante's range of technical levels, from the elevated antique style to the vernacular realism and the "comic" mood. To Eliot, no poet of similar stature "has been a more attentive student of the *art* of poetry, or a more scrupulous, painstaking and *conscious* practitioner of the *craft*," no poet has the same "width of emotional range." Dante himself recognized the importance of technical skill and style. In *De Vulgari Eloquentia*, he wrote that the tragic style "can never be attained to without strenuous efforts of genius, constant practice in the art and the habit of the sciences." (All quotations from Dante are from *The Portable Dante* [New York, 1947].)

6. Alan Watts, *Myth and Ritual in Christianity* (New York, 1953). Cf. J. M. Robertson, *Christianity and Mythology* (London, 1936), Homer W. Smith, *Man and his Gods* (Boston, 1952), C. O. James, *Christian Myth and Ritual* (London, 1933).

7. Gertrude Leigh's *The Passing of Beatrice: A Study of Heterodoxy* (London, 1932) discusses some of these aspects. In his own time, Dante was neglected or abused by Catholic circles and his *De Monarchia* was burned by an inquisitor. See Ernest Curtius' essay, "The Medieval Basis of Western Thought" in *Goethe and the Modern Age* (Chicago, 1949).

8. Even St. Augustine, for whom the state was the work of the devil, wrote that the earthly city is "its own obvious presence," and the "symbolic presentation of the heavenly city." *Confessions*, Book XV, ch. 2, and *The City of God*.

9. Translations of *The Divine Comedy* are by L. Binyon.

10. Dante is especially scornful of Boniface VIII, whom he calls "the prince of the new Pharisees," consigning him to hell while he was still alive (*Inferno*, XI, XIX, XXVII).

11. This line of thought was suggested to me by Prof. M. J. Benardete. In the *Inferno* (II), Dante raises the question why he is selected to traverse the three realms, though he is "not Aeneas, no, nor Paul," is deemed by himself and others "too weak . . . for this thing." The question is not raised again and is never answered.

12. In *Purgatorio*, Statius declares that he became both a poet and a Christian through Virgil.

13. "Dante's Innocence and Luck," *The Kenyon Review*, XIV, No. 2, 303.

14. Maritain argues that Dante could diverge from Catholic tenets *because* he was "so perfectly sure of his faith," that his very heresies confirm belief, and sees Dante's elevation of Beatrice as due to the poet's naivete which "believes all things." This approach minimizes the implication of the fact, mentioned by Maritain himself, that Dante lived in a time when the old faith was being disputed.

15. For Dante, the literal sense "must come first, being the one which compriseth the others in its significance, and without which the study of the others would be impossible and irrational." Here, Dante shares Aquinas' position that all knowledge has its origin in the senses. For Aquinas, "the phantasm" is "the foundation of intellectual operation" (*On the Trinity*, VI). The "*quiddity* or nature existing in corporeal matter" is "the proper object of the human intellect, which is united to a body" (*Summa*, I, 87). However, Aquinas distinguishes between Theology (or metaphysics) and physics, holding that in the former the intellect frees being from its material trappings and from the imagination: "Therefore although the imagination is necessary for any consideration of divine things according to our status as wayfarer, yet it is never necessary to effect verification in the imagination in the case of divine things" (*On the Trinity*, VI, 2 *ad* 5). See William M. Walton, "Being, Essence and Existence for St. Thomas Aquinas," *The Review of Metaphysics*, III (1950), No. 3.

16. See Kurt Leonhard, *Der gegenwärtige Dante* (Stuttgart, 1950).

17. *De Monarchia*, Bk. I, ch. 4; *Purgatorio* XXVIII; *De Vulgari Eloquentia*, Bk. I, ch. 2.

18. There is a question whether *The Divine Comedy* fully accepts the doctrine of original sin. In *Purgatorio* (XVI), Mark Lombardo tells Dante that the root

cause of all evil is not human nature, but corrupt leadership (*mala condotta*) in the state and church:

> "The evil guidance whereto 'tis enslaved
> Thou seest is that which doth the word corrode,
> Not nature, that in you may be depraved."

And Omberto says that what made him insolent was his family's blood. Gertrude Leigh's *The Passing of Beatrice* argues that Dante denied original sin and held with Aristotle that the seed of nobility is instilled in all men before birth. This made it possible for Dante "to proclaim the divinity of the Roman people, the glory of the Greeks, to declare Aristotle to be divine and Cato to be a symbol of God the Father, to admit pagans, such as Ripheus, into the realm of the blessed."

19. Attention has been called to the wrath which begins with Canto VIII, where Dante wants to see Argenti plunged into the muddy broth and where he enjoys the sight of his being mangled. In Canto XXX, Virgil reproves him for listening "All ears" to the squabbles of perjurers and civic criminals.

20.
> "O human people, why the heart confide
> There where fruition ousteth partnership?"

21. In *Purgatorio* (XXIV), Dante repeats the lines he had once written:
> ". . . I am one who hearkens when
> Love prompteth, and I put thought into word
> After the mode which he dictates within."

Dante appears to justify any form of love, so long as it is dictated from "within."

22. *Medieval Culture: An Introduction to Dante* (New York, 1958).

23. Cf. P. H. Wicksteed, *Dante and Aquinas* (New York, 1913). Vossler slurs over the conscious element which is operative in purgatory when he writes that here the sinners "are contending unconsciously against a part of their own ego."

24.
> ". . . 'that this place I may see
> Hereafter,' I said, "have I this journey made.' "

Even Vossler notes the infantile nature of Dante's final stage (Santayana suspects that the mystical transformation of Dante's love for Beatrice to philosophy and theology was made possible by some lack of natural manliness in that love). In *Paradiso* (XXI), Beatrice likens Dante to a woman-figure (Semele) and herself to a male god (Zeus). She warns Dante that, were she to smile,

> "Thou would'st be as Semele, when her eyes' desire
> She had, and straightway was to ashes burned."

In *Dante's Drama of the Mind* (Princeton, 1953), Francis Fergusson holds that Purgatory and Paradise are new beginnings for Dante. One should add that he begins each new life as though he had learned almost nothing from the previous one.

25. In *Purgatorio* (XXI), knowledge is called "the natural thirst," and the opening of the *Convivio* repeats Aristotle's dictum that "All men by their very nature yearn for knowledge." Although authority and love are the supreme principles, knowledge is the condition of Love (*Paradiso*, XXVIII).

26. The master now appears as a youth, yet addresses Dante as "My son."

27. There is a remarkable analogy between Dante's dreams and the primitive ritual of sexual initiation. In *Sex and Religion* (New York, 1919), Pierre Gordon writes that among primitive people, ritual defloration is performed by a holy deflowerer. "Obviously, the ritual had to be accomplished by a qualified being endowed with supernatural force . . . Owing to this fact, her entire future sexual activity bore the stamp of divinity." He adds that by a gradual transition, "sexual sanctification had been transformed into sacrificial killing." Dante's dream of Beatrice's death is followed by her actual death.

28. Here, Dante is instructed on the distinction between the free will of man which is relative (though the "most precious" gift God made to man) and the absolute will of God. Aquinas argued that man is free to the extent that his acts are determined not by past but by future life and that he can be regenerated by knowing the consequences of sinning. Yet, since human choices are known to God beforehand and he alone can directly act upon the will, human acts are, in this sense, predestined. Free choice would seem to depend upon grace—it happens to man ("Seizes the soul," as Dante learns in *Purgatorio* [XXI]). In Catholic doctrine, knowledge, bliss and love follow from grace, which is the first principle. Man can only resist "sufficient," but not sanctifying or "efficient" grace, administered by the church. From this, it would appear that guilt and grace—not character—are "fate." It is doubtful how much of this was congenial to Dante's temperament. As noted, there is a question whether *The Divine Comedy* fully accepts original sin. Despite all the instructions Dante receives, he declares that the problem of freedom is incomprehensible (*Paradiso*, XIX).

29. This point was suggested to me by Dr. Roderick Marshall.

30. Peace is the leading motif of the poem: In the *Inferno*, Francesca greets Dante with prayers for the peace denied to her and Paolo; in *Purgatorio* (XXVI), we hear of the angel who came down with the decree of peace, "for ages prayed and wept for." Earlier (V, X), Dante says that he is pursuing peace "From world to world," and is buoyed by the knowledge that he will finally reach a peaceful state. And, as noted, Piccarda speaks the celebrated line "In Sua voluntade e nostra pace" (*Paradiso*, III).

31. Dante's "heroism consists primarily in the fact that he suffers from seeing the plight of others. His own salvation depends on the heavenly, not the social community.

32. See Appendix III for "A Note on Virgil's *Aeneid*."

The Golden Age of
Chivalric Honor
Don Quixote

IN THE THREE CENTURIES which separate *The Divine Comedy* from *Don Quixote*, faith in tradition begins to give way to individual exploration. Dante's way is rigorously fixed by venerable theological law and revelation. In contrast, Quixote does not rely on religious guidance, but draws on his own resources. The Don is the first hero who would prove himself by his personal exploits, who himself chooses to engage in a quest and whose journey has no assigned designation. *Don Quixote* marks the transition from medieval to Renaissance mythopoesis.

For this kind of journey, the novel—and *Don Quixote* is the first major work of this genre—is a particularly fitting form. In contrast to the strict conventions of the Greek drama and the rigid structure of Dante's epic, the novel has a loose organization, permitting a "wandering" journey. The novel arose concurrently with the beginnings of the middle class and pictures its commonplace life in the language of prose. The Prologue to *Don Quixote* suggests this change. A friend advises the author that the grave tone of classical writing and the fantasies of chivalric romances are to be replaced by a colloquial realism and comic overtones:

> . . . there is no reason why you should go begging maxims of the philosophers, counsels of Holy Writ, fables of the poets, orations of the rhetoricians, or miracles of the saints; see to it, rather, that your style flows along smoothly, pleasingly, and sonorously, and that your words are the proper ones . . . without any intricacy or obscurity.[1]

Chivalry

The idea of chivalry was adventure for the sake of adventure.[2] Honor consisted in "pure" service for the Lady who was not present, and the knight's only purpose was to prove *himself* brave, constant and courteous. Ideally, he expected no reward, did not fight for country, profit or God. The Crusades linked the two main chivalric strains—love and war—into a religious pattern. (Earlier, Mohammedanism had joined religion and war in the slogan of "the Holy War.") The chivalric myth was to counteract the knight's merciless cruelty to the enemy and his sexual promiscuity. Service to the feudal lord and to the Lady was transposed into service to God and the Virgin Mary. The knight's courage and courtship were assimilated into Christian chivalry which was to help the needy, weak and oppressed, "the downtrodden, the widow and the orphan" (the Council of Clermont).

However, in his actual historic function, the knight was a member of a highly selected group, did not serve mankind, but the upper hierarchy, for which he was remunerated by grants of land and protection of his castle. Chivalry contributed to the rise of militant feudalism and supported it, as in the case of the Frankish *commendatores* and *caballeri*, and the Teutonic *commutatus*. The knight helped the Frankish rulers resist the invasion of the Vikings, Magyars and Slavs, and helped the Christian kings overthrow the Moorish rule in Spain. Likewise, ideal service to the Lady deteriorated into bigamy and adultery. (The knight was supposed to direct his love towards a married lady.) Knight-errantry became errant passion even as Troubadours and Minnesingers continued to sing of the one true love.

By the time of the Renaissance, chivalry and its international feudal base were no longer a living force in Western Europe and were being supplanted by the national state and middle class commercialism. Artillery fire had made the knight's armor and his personal valor useless. Spain, however, ignored the Western Renaissance. Economically backward and geographically insulated, it had developed no dynamic middle class. Hence, it held fast to its older values, to the memory of its resplendent *conquistadores* and to its Catholic faith. And it clung to the myth of chivalry. The phenomenon was embodied in the *hidalgo* who keeps up the appearance of nobility by shunning work (except sheep industry) as below his dignity. He is represented in the picture of a hungry man who would create the impression that he has dined well by ostentatiously picking his teeth.

Still, by 1600—when *Don Quixote* was being written—even Spain could no longer believe in this medieval myth. The barbers, merchants, the new university students, and the soldiers equipped with modern weapons made the *hidalgo* look foolish. The chivalric idea took on a pseudo-form and became a parody of itself. At this point, Cervantes attempts to save the mythic reality of the chivalric idea by creating the *poetic* figure of Don Quixote.[3] His novel attempts to picture *the knight-errant as a complete man* who transcends the specialized qualities of chivalry. Knight-errantry, the author states, is a discipline "that comprises within itself all or most of the others in existence." The knight must be skilled in jurisprudence, astronomy, mathematics, must be a theologian and physician. Unlike the medieval knight, the Don both argues and fights for his idea, is at once a dreamer, philosopher, soldier and god-man.

Cervantes and Don Quixote

Unamuno argues that the greatness of Cervantes' personality is not to be found in his own biography but in the hero of his novel. Yet, the facts of Cervantes' life show both a direct and an ironic relation between the author and his work.

Cervantes and his Don are both poor noblemen whose decline parallels that of Spain; they leave their small villages to become far-wanderers, Cervantes travelling to Italy, Portugal, the Azores and Algiers, Quixote throughout the Spanish peninsula. Neither is successful in meeting practical problems: in his life, Cervantes failed to establish himself as a soldier and public official. (Only in the battle at Lepanto, he is supposed to have shown unusual bravery or perhaps desperation; there is also a story that he refused to name those who tried to help him escape from captivity.) We have an analogy between Quxote's youthful Lady whom he never sees and Cervante's wife, half his age, whom he left shortly after marriage, returning to her only in his old age. Finally, in their last years, both resort to symbolic values: Quixote becomes a visionary knight; Cervantes becomes the poetic creator of the knight.

On the other hand, *Cervantes over-compensates for his personal practical deficiencies by absolutizing Quixote's spiritual assets*: Quixote is poor in material possessions, but rich in generosity; he is physically emaciated, but the bravest of men, never suffering serious disability from his frequent falls; he is an old man, but youthful in his love; he is an unknown *hidalgo*, but becomes famous, the written account of his exploits appearing during his own life. The most prominent over-compensation appears in Quixote's asceticism. Where Cervantes is rumored to have had many love affairs (there are also accounts of his bastard daughter's sordid sexual involvements), the Don's relation to women is one of rigid abstinence. He remains loyal to the Lady he never sees, expending on her his entire love-energy. And he derives his spiritual powers from this asceticism. The novel itself contains an ironic comment on this phenomenon. When the Don returns home, his niece says to him:

> And yet, to think that you could be so blind and foolish as to try and make out that you are a hero when you are really an old man, that you are strong when you are sick, that you are able to straighten out the wrongs of the world when you yourself are bent with age, and, above all, that you are a knight; for, while the real gentry many become knights, the poor never can.

Act I: The Mythic Golden Age

Cervantes' *Don Quixote* transcends historic chivalry, its allusions pointing not so much to actual chivalric figures as to heroes in classical mythology. Its very ideal of the Golden Age is taken from Ovid.[4]

The Don and his squire are in the company of six goatherds who graciously invite them to share their meal, spread on sheepskins. Quixote asks Sancho to seat himself by his side "to see the good that there is in knight-errantry . . . that you may be even as I who am your master and natural lord, and eat from my plate and drink from where I drink; for of knight-errantry one may say the same as of love: that it makes all things equal." After he has stilled his hunger, Quixote begins his celebrated soliloquy:

> Happy the age and happy those centuries to which the ancients gave the name of golden, and not because gold, which is so esteemed in this iron age of ours, was then to be had without toil, but because those who lived in that time did not know the meaning of the words 'thine' and 'mine.' In that blessed era all things were held in common. . . . All then was peace, all was concord and friendship. . . . Thoughts of love, also, in those days were set forth as simply as the simple hearts that conceived them, without any roundabout and artificial play of words by way of ornament. Fraud, deceit, and malice had not yet come to mingle with truth and plain-speaking. . . . Maidens in all their modesty . . . went where they would and unattended; whereas in this hateful age of ours none is safe. . . . It was for the safety of such as these, as time went on and depravity increased, that the order of knights-errant was instituted, for the protection of damsels, the aid of widows and orphans, and the succoring of the needy.

Quixote's picture of primitive rustic communality stands in contrast to the sophisticated institution of knighthood and to the chivalric forms in the court epics of *Tristan* and *Parsifal*, of *Orlando Furioso*, the *Nibelungenlied*, and the Spanish *Cid*. The Don does invoke medieval knights—especially Amadis—to teach him how to imitate their deeds, but he does so with occasional irony, as when he refers to their robberies and thefts. He calls attention to the difference between the romantic style of the chivalric books and the "thoughts of love" in his Golden Age which were set forth "as simply as the simple hearts that conceived them, without any roundabout and artificial play of words by way of ornament." Here, life had no "orders," was not organized by rigid ordinances and rituals.[5]

To be sure, this pagan age is welded to a religious function. The novel comes out of a Catholic country, and Cervantes assures the reader that he and his hero are devout Christians. Yet, the memory which Quixote summons up is not of institutionalized Christianity, but *the idea of religion* which can be enacted by men of various faiths. His service calls for no recompense, and reminds one of Spinoza's saying that he who loves God does not expect that God love him in return. Sancho even thinks that his master is "better fitted to be a preacher than a knight-errant," and later suggests that they ought to become "saints." Quixote's reply is that "Chivalry is a religion in itself, and there are many sainted knights in glory."

Act II: The Journey

At the opening, we find Quixote living in harmony with himself and his fellowmen, to whom he is known as Alonzo the Good. It is a womb-like harmony, confined to the tight enclosure of his room which his chivalric books have transformed into a fairy realm, so that he almost wholly forgets "the administration of his estate."

But this Eden, gained by fancy, stands in contrast to the rotten state of the world which Quixote later calls an "iron age," ruled by indolence, arrogance and expediency, by injustice, dishonor, poverty and false pride. As the Don is about to go out on his third sally, he declares to his household:

> Today, sloth triumphs over diligence, idleness and ease over exertion, vice over virtue, arrogance over valor, and theory over practice of the warrior's art.

The novel illustrates the truth of Quixote's indictment from the Andres episode at the beginning to the picture of Sancho's "kingdom," Baratria. That both the ideal knights in the cave of Montesinos and Dulcinea, the peerless lady, should be in need of money, and that Don Quixote, the honored knight, should discover holes in his silk stockings, illustrates what Madariaga calls "the melancholy of poverty" in the knight's world. In these "calamitous times," Quixote sees his task

> to devote himself to the hardships and exercises of knight-errantry and go about righting wrongs, succoring widows, and protecting damsels . . . favor

and aid the weak and needy . . . spare the humble and trample the proud under foot.

His calling, Quixote says, does not permit "easy pace, pleasure and repose—those things were invented for delicate courtiers; but toil, anxiety, and arms." Quixote reasserts the Quest which calls for repudiating Dante's *le presenti cose* and Faust's *Faulbett*.

This infernal state sends Alonzo the Good out from the security of his book-encrusted room to set things right. But, where the medieval knight took a specific direction and for a specific purpose, Quixote wanders anywhere and on principle. And, where the function of the former was restricted to saving a particular king, chieftain or Lady, the Don would liberate the entire Christian world, inspired by love for a Lady he never meets.

Quixote's journey takes him through a realm which he later characterizes as purgatory and in which he *invites punishment* as do the sinners in Dante's middle kingdom. Later, he reaches a kind of earthly paradise in the Cave of Montesinos where he meets his Beatrice, Dulcinea, as well as in the duke's court where he is treated as though he were a real knight and where he again meets Dulcinea in an enchanted shape. Dante goes on from here into the heavenly paradise. In Cervantes' post-medieval setting, Quixote's paradise turns out to be an illusion and the hero returns home to recognize that swine are swine. Still, as we shall see, his journey is not in vain and Alonzo the Good is symbolically saved in the myth of Don Quixote.[6]

Windmills Are Lawless Giants

In his first sally, Quixote continues the fanciful temper he showed at the beginning. He insists that the inn is a castle and that the district prostitutes are ladyships. He is treated like an infant (the girls feed him through a reed) and his behavior (such as his beating the muleteer) is carried out in a kind of somnambulistic state. Upon his return home, he asks Sancho to join him. This is his first realization that he lacks self-sufficiency and that he needs a realistic guide.[7]

Like Shakespeare's Hamlet, who announces in the first act that he plans to put on an antic disposition, Don Quixote states at the beginning of his journey: "I mean to imitate Amadis by playing the part of a desperate and raving madman. . . ." The Don too *knows that he is playing the madman*. Sancho recognizes this when he says that the Don is "a madman with good sense." Quixote himself becomes aware that his attack on the windmills is a moral and social attack on "lawless giants." He tells Sancho:

137

In confronting giants, it is the sin of pride that we slay, even as we combat
envy with generosity and goodness of heart; anger, with equanimity and a
calm bearing; gluttony and an overfondness of sleep, by eating little when
we do eat and by keeping long vigils; lust and lewdness, with the loyalty we
show those whom we have made the mistresses of our affections; and sloth,
by going everywhere in the world in search of opportunities that may and
do make of us famous knights as well as better Christians.

Those very windmills, observes Salvador de Madariaga, "have grown
what his wild imagination fancied and seems to have guessed—giants
of industry whose hundred powerful arms encircle the world, awe-
inspiring powers which work in the night."[8] Quixote's windmills reap-
pear in Faust's Mephistophelian giants who work in the night, in Wagner's dark Nibelungen, and in the myriads of "arms" in the "fallout" of
the Hydrogen Bomb.[9] It is mad or foolish to fight windmills, but the
temerity to brave dangers is not. The Don is fully aware that "the
readiness is all," as Hamlet declares. In the adventure of the fulling
hammers, he tells Sancho:

Supposing that, in place of fulling hammers, this had really been another
dangerous adventure, did I not display the requisite courage for undertaking and carrying it through?

The Mythic Crime

In the earliest myths, such as Tammuz-Osiris, to play God means to
be God. Beginning with the Grecian myth, the hero only pretends that
he is enacting a God-role, realizing that to fulfill his task, he needs the
aid of others. Prometheus leans on his mother's foreknowledge and the
Chorus, Orestes on Apollo and Athena, Oedipus on Theseus.

Don Quixote would be completely self-sufficient. In Dante, redemption is unthinkable without the church. The Don never seeks its help,
placing reliance on himself. He assumes that he alone knows what
truth and goodness are—in other words, that he is God and—that he
alone knows how they are to be brought about—in other words, that he
is also God's minister.[10] Like Spinoza's Substance, he would be his own
cause and develop out of his own assumptions. He insists that all must
act in accordance with his standards and must do so *without compromise*. Quixote's "crime" lies in his arrogant attempt to replace both God
and society. He tells a group of the Holy Brotherhood:

Who is so ignorant as not to know that knights-errant are beyond all juris-
diction, their only law their swords, while their charter is their mettle and
their will is their decrees?

This attitude is criminal or mad in an age when chivalric-religious honor is no longer useful. The Don is not careful or calculating; he insists on justice without regard for practical consequences. A knight-errant, he says, "must uphold the truth though it cost him his life to defend it." Indeed, the Don's "madness" is a deliberate strategy to counteract the "reason" of his time and to remind men of the Golden Age, and its anti-pragmatic values of honor, justice, equality and freedom.

Guides

To become a culture hero, the mythic figure must work not only for, but also with elements of his group. Despite his pretended godlike self-containment, Quixote too relies on guidance—Rocinante, Dulcinea, Sancho, Sansón and Roque.

Rocinante and Dulcinea

As noted, one of the stages of the mythic hero is his rescue by animals or people of humble origin. Among the former is the motif of the horse, found in many myths, from the Oriental novel to Thomas Mann's Joseph.[11]

On the physical level, Rocinante and Dapple provide Quixote and Sancho with the "stature" of a knight and squire on horseback. Sancho is nearly helpless without his Dapple, and Rocinante selects the direction of Quixote's planless journey, the Don letting the horse "take whatever path it chose, for he believed that therein lay the very essence of adventure." Quixote names his humble steed "Rocinante," that is, one that comes "before" all others.

If Rocinante is Quixote's animal guide or "first cause" on the lowest level, Dulcinea is his Platonic guide or entelechy. Like Rocinante, she "accompanies" Quixote throughout, is his silent steady pilot. "God knows," he tells the duchess, "whether or not there is a Dulcinea in this world or if she is a fanciful creation," like the Phyllises, Dianas, Galateas. What matters most is that she is the conception of what

> needs must be, seeing that she is a damsel who possesses all those qualities that may render her famous in all parts of the world, such as: a flawless beauty; dignity without haughtiness; a tenderness that is never immodest; a graciousness due to courtesy and a courtesy that comes from good breeding . . . in short, the ideal of all that is worth while, honorable, and delectable in this world!

Although Dulcinea is of humble origin, she is more to the Don than Helen and Lucretia were to their lovers, her beauty being the realiza-

139

tion of "all the impossible and chimerical attributes the poets are accustomed to give to their fair ones." As is the case with Dante's Beatrice, Dulcinea's existence lies in her essence—with this difference: Where Beatrice is a heavenly ideal, Dulcinea is as she "needs must be" on earth. Cervantes transposes Dante's theologic values into the esthetics and morals of chivalry. Since he has become a knight-errant, the Don tells the canon,

> I am brave, polite, liberal, well-bred, generous, courteous, bold, gentle, patient, and long-suffering when it comes to enduring hardships, imprisonment and enchantments.

Here, Cervantes points to the living relevance of his chivalric idea. When Sancho questions his master's service to Dulcinea, the Don replies:

> Do you not know, clodhopper, drudge, scoundrel, that if it were not for the valor she infuses into my arm, I should not have the strength to kill a flea? . . . She fights and conquers in my person, and I live and breathe and have my life in her.

Dulcinea is the poem of the book. And when Quixote speaks of poetry, his metaphors are similar to those he applies to Dulcinea. Poetry, he says, is "a young and tender maid of surpassing beauty." Yet, art by itself does not make a poet, but only art combined with nature. Hence, knight-errantry requires more than imagination, must put its art into practice.

But Quixote's "practice" shuns the sexual sphere. Apart from the episodes of the muleteer and Maritornes—and even here the sex act is not consummated—Cervantes keeps male-female involvements in a courtly, decorous key. This motif of chastity is absolutized in Quixote, the Prologue announcing that he is "the most chaste lover and the most valiant knight." The Don never deviates from his abstinence, and his hand, which "no other woman has ever touched," remains pure. ("Quixote," in Spanish, means the piece of armor that protects the thigh.)

Quixote begins like Goethe's Faust. He too is middle aged, unmarried, leading a contemplative life in a room stuffed with books, and he also goes out for a life of experience. Yet, where Faust does allow himself the realistic experience with Gretchen, Quixote remains chaste, and successfully withstands the amorous advances of Altisidora and others.

Sancho: The Folk-Guide

Sancho Panza is the realistic Virgilian guide in Quixote's inferno, his practical sense for compromise balancing the knight's unconditional demands. In Sancho, Cervantes pays homage to the common earthy

140

man, to his steadfastness, loyalty and folk-wisdom. Sancho is fond of using proverbs which the author tells us are "concise maxims drawn from the wisdom and experience of our elders." Sancho's peasant roots also give him a feeling of security and self-respect. When the Don reproves him for refusing to lash himself, Sancho retorts that he is "simply standing up for myself, for I am my own lord." He has no reservations about being able to govern the island, "for I have a soul like anybody else and a body like the rest of them."

The novelist needs Sancho as *the witness* who can verify and lend some creditability to Quixote's visions. Sancho is the bodily corrective of Quixote's spirituality.[12] His earthy and watery personality sustains the airy and fiery knight and prevents his brittle figure from breaking apart. Sancho is a kind of mother-wife to Quixote. Bickerman has noted Sancho's "womanly" aspects: He is soft-hearted, cries readily, is gossipy and noisy, docile, and earthy. His job, Sancho tells Sansón, is "to look after (Quixote's) person and see to keeping him clean and comfortable. . . ." He compares himself to "a piece of land that of itself is dry and barren, but if you scatter manure over it and cultivate it, it will bear good fruit." And he hopes that his master's conversation will bring forth "blessed fruits" in him. Quixote himself says that it is his burden to support Sancho as one "who hath served him faithfully in fertility and abundance." He draws an analogy between the choice of one's wife and the selection of a dependable companion on a journey, one who "must ever be with him, in the bed, at table, wherever he may go."[13]

Sancho has been interpreted as the the reverse of Quixote. But this ignores Sancho's own latent idealism and imaginativeness. While he is sceptical about Quixote's stories of what he saw in the Cave of Montesinos, he is ready to challenge anyone who dares say that his master is a madman. Indeed, Sancho's fantasy is at times even less grounded in fact than his master's. Although he himself has thought up the scheme of Dulcinea's enchantment, he becomes persuaded that the enchantment actually came to pass. When he feels himself borne towards heaven in the duke's mock pageant, his imagination is as rich as was Quixote's in the Cave of Montesinos. For all his sobriety, scepticism and sense for the concrete, Sancho has something of the fiery restlessness of his countrymen who once traversed oceans to found an empire.

Above all, Sancho is loyal. He may think his master stark mad, yet cannot help following him:

> We're from the same village, I've eaten his bread, I like him very much, he's generous to me, he gave me his ass-colts, and, above all, I'm loyal.

He follows the Don not because he really expects to be rewarded with an island, but because he loves him.[14] Like Ahab's Starbuck, he senses his master's "humanities." At the end, he is the one to recognize that in his recantation, Quixote had returned "a victor over himself . . . the greatest victory that could be desired." At the beginning, Sancho exhibits the peasant's psychology of skeptical caution and prejudice, as well as the tendency to believe everything. Through his contact with the Don, Sancho develops an appreciation of Quixote's Golden Age. He learns to depreciate the value of money and property. He tells his wife that while he has brought her no pearls, he has something "of greater value and importance," adding that "there is nothing in the world that is more pleasant than being a respected man, squire to a knight-errant who goes in search of adventures." As for the island, if he does not get it, "my bread will taste as good, and it may be even better, without a governship than if I was a governor."

Towards the end, Sancho approaches Quixote's own anti-pragmatic attitude. His central motivation is also loyalty rather than expediency. Yet, even when he acts without "reason," he rarely leaves solid ground. On the island, he rules "with Solomonic wisdom rather than Quixotic genius," as Entwistle puts it. Sancho cuts through the formalism of the island's feudal bureaucracy and nearly enacts the kind of justice Quixote calls for.

THE SOCIAL MACROCOSM

In the second part of the novel, Quixote learns that Cid Hamete Benengeli has already written a history of his exploits which romanticizes his adventures and makes him appear absurd. *The Don can now see himself as history and society see him.* By this device, Cervantes prepares us for the modification of Quixote's private realm through the entry of *a public witness* which is more inclusive than Sancho. In Part II, Quixote and Sancho enter the social macrocosm, represented by the duke's castle and Sancho's "state" of which he becomes governor. This socialization corresponds to that of Orestes and Oedipus in Athens and Thebes, of Aeneas in Latium, Dante in Paradise, Hamlet and Faust at their courts, Siegfried at Gunther's castle, Mitya Karamazov in court, Mann's Joseph in Egypt.

Act III: The Cave of Montesinos: Eden Regained

At the very point when Quixote's vision has been exposed to public view, the Don undertakes *his most private adventure,* the only one in

142

which *there is no witness* who can either corroborate or refute him. Quixote proposes to enter the Cave of Montesinos to verify the marvelous tales told about its knights. He will penetrate to its bottom, "even it was as deep as Hell . . . an undertaking that is reserved for me . . . that the world may know that there is nothing, however impossible it may seem, that I will not undertake and accomplish." This adventure is analogous to Faust's descent to the realm of "The Mothers."

Quixote is lowered by a rope "into the depths of the horrendous cavern," and upon his return, tells of wonderful experiences: He fell into a profound sleep, and when he awoke, found himself "in the midst of the most beautiful, pleasant, and delightful meadow that nature could create or the most fertile imagination could conceive." His eyes next fell on a sumptuous royal palace where he saw his Dulcinea and Montesinos. Montesinos told him that he and the other knights have waited for him a long time that he "might go back and inform the world of what lies locked and concealed in the depths of this cave." He further learned that Merlin held many of the knights and ladies under a spell. However, Merlin also prophesied that Quixote would come to revive the profession of knight-errantry and that by his favor and mediation, they themselves may be disenchanted. In this adventure, Quixote has his deepest dream, gains the absolute fulfillment of his wishes. He sees his Lady and meets his model forerunners, who accept him as a knight and extol his mission.

Quixote's cave adventure into "those remote regions that are hidden from our sight" is a journey to gain knowledge of his sources, a return to the womb for his "parental" origin. The hero has to delve into these enchanted solitudes alone, only the rope connecting him with the outside human world. As Quixote is lowered, his voice grows fainter and fainter. He returns with his eyes closed, apparently "sound asleep." When he awakens, he gazes about with a bewildered look and asks for something to eat. And his first words are about the Eden-like state he had experienced:

> You have taken me away from the most delightful existence mortal ever knew and the pleasantest sight human eyes ever rested upon.

In this earthly paradise, Quixote saw Montesinos, his "father-model" and Dulcinea, the "mother" of his idea. Here, his mission to free Dulcinea and the world from its present enchantment is sanctioned.

In the cave adventure, Quixote allows his fantasy fullest sway, unimpeded by any audience. Here, he goes *through* the last phase of self-indulgence and thus completes the narcissistic aspect of his self. The "three whole days" spent in the cave prepare his rebirth towards social maturity.[15]

But Quixote's rebirth becomes possible because the reality principle invades his wish. To begin with, his heroes are *historic* prototypes, taken from Carolingian and Arthurian sources. And Quixote sees them not as they were once, but in the state to which they have been reduced in Quixote's own time—in want and in exile. Their sorry state is underscored by the fact that the peerless Dulcinea is obliged to ask for a loan of half a dozen reales.

Disenchantment

In Quixote's next adventure, the Montesinos setting is transposed into the existing social world, the ducal castle, where the Don permits himself to be honored as though he were a real knight. Here, as in the cave, he reaches an earthly paradise, again "sees" his Dulcinea in an enchanted form.

But, this time he realizes that the chivalric idea has degenerated into mock-ritual and pageantry, and active knight-errantry into a theatrical game and hocus-pocus. Quixote enters into this game half-heartedly, ceases to to be a knight and plays the court-fool. He allows himself to become part of an idle world, "leisurely enjoying all the comforts and luxuries." Here, he accepts precisely the kind of ease which he had earlier condemned as invented "for delicate courtiers," embraces the kind of life which threatens the quest of the mythic hero. Quixote's adventures deteriorate to frivolous pranks, such as removing beards from allegedly enchanted ladies, defending the simulated dishonor of the duenna's daughter, battling with cats (here he suffers more serious wounds than when he fought against "giants"). Without Sancho, who has left to assume rule of his island, Quixote is a sad and lonely figure; he has neither a historic nor poetic function. *For the first time, the Don appears in an undignified role.*

His adventures in the cave and at the duchy are the peripety of his journey and the point at which his disenchantment begins. His reversal is foreshadowed in his doubts whether the stories about knights are true, and the Don now questions his cave-adventure. For the first time, Don Quixote exhibits fear. In the braying episode, he flees, without thinking of the danger in which he left Sancho. His confidence is shaken and he speaks of his ultimate defeat.

The change in Don Quixote is further revealed in the advice he gives Sancho on how to rule his island. He, who had been against any compromise, now writes his squire: "Be not always strict, nor always lenient but observe a middle course between these two extremes, for therein lies wisdom." He urges Sancho to lean towards mercy rather than justice and advises him to "consider slowly and deliberately" petitions from beautiful women. And he, who had never doubted who he was, tells Sancho: "You are to bear in mind who you are and seek to know yourself, which is the most difficult knowledge to acquire that can be imagined."

The episode with Sansón Carrasco is a further stage in Quixote's disenchantment. More than any other character in the story, Carrasco seems to make it his life's mission to refute Quixote. While Sansón writes poetry, Quixote's notion of *applying* the claims of poetry strikes him at first as ludicrous, then fills him with envy, especially when Quixote's exploits are written down by Cid Hamete. He does not laugh the knight away, is not amused by him as are the duke and duchess, but grimly proceeds against him. When Quixote insists on sallying forth a third time, despite repeated mishaps, Carrasco hits on the strategy of defeating the Don by entering his realm, becoming a "knight," and forcing Quixote to admit that Dulcinea is not the most beautiful lady. That is, Sansón *would refute the reality of Quixote's vision.* And he would do this, not in the interests of restoring his wits, but out of a bitter "thirst for vengeance."

The passing of chivalry is brought to Quixote's attention by a new type of "knight," Roque Guinart. Roque is a highwayman and his life is also full of strange and dangerous adventures. He, too, is courteous and generous, "better suited to be a friar than a highwayman." Originally, he engaged in this activity to exact personal revenge, but later took up the task to right all kinds of wrongs. Now Roque identifies himself with Quixote, not as a matter of faith, but because he regards him as the most "sensible man in all the world."

But Roque is a Quixote with real enemies and real adventures, and he does not attempt to do everything by himself, but works with his group. He is more merciful than exacting, and he meets injustice by expedient measures, such as providing people with money and safe-conducts. He has little to say about ultimate goals, but works for immediate practical results. Don Quixote's silent acceptance of Roque's way constitutes a silent critique of his own functionless knight-errantry.

Swine Are Swine

The meeting with Roque prepares us for the defeat Quixote suffers in the encounter with Sansón. As he lies on the ground, the Don acknowledges that his sorry end was brought about by "presumptuous-

145

ness." His subsequent plan for a pastoral Arcadia is a weak echo of his original quest. In this effort to achieve an imitation-Eden, he is trampled by bulls. With that, he and Sancho push on "with more of shame than pleasure in their mien." Quixote ceases to idealize his obstacles, calling the bulls "a herd of filthy animals." At this point, the author steps into the story to tell the reader that from now on Quixote calls an inn an inn and not a castle. In his final adventure, he and Sancho are trampled by grunting and snorting pigs. This time, Quixote recognizes that swine are swine, and makes the melancholy observation that Heaven has decreed that a vanquished knight be "eaten by jackals, stung by wasps, and trampled by swine." Unlike Shakespeare's Prospero, who preserves his magic framework, Quixote is shocked back into reality.

On his last return home, Quixote admits the defeat of his historical mission, renouncing the idea that the Golden Age can be brought back into his own time. "In last year's nests," he states, "there are no birds this year." These words express his new insight that a past model cannot be literally transposed to serve different cultural-social foundations. His words take the form of a proverb. They are his final acknowledgment of folk-wisdom.

Parody

From one perspective, Cervantes presents Don Quixote as a parody of a human being. Insisting on a fixed principle, his thrusts, in Thomas Mann's phrase, are "into empty space." Cervantes, who could create a full-dimensioned Sancho, made Quixote a one-dimensional character. Here is Cervantes' own implied reservation over his hero—analogous to Virgil's drawing of Aeneas.

Cervantes' reservation also appears in the fact that Quixote's idealistic attempt to enact justice results in the opposite. He frees dangerous convicts, wrecks funerals and inns, beats innocent servants, smashes Pedro's sole possessions. In the incident with Andres, Quixote makes the lad's master promise to pay Andres what is due him, and then leaves, satisfied that the promised word is sufficient. Not only does Andres' master not pay him, but after Quixote's departure, he mishandles the boy for having complained. When they meet again, Andres begs the knight:

> For the love of God, Sir Knight-errant, if ever you meet me, even though they are hacking me to bits, do not aid or succor me but let me bear it, for no misfortune could be so great as that which comes of being helped by you.

146

Don Quixote belongs to the mythic tradition of the "Fool" who disregards or is unaware of worldly demands and conditions. Such is the foolishness of Buddha, Parsifal, Emanuel Quint, Prince Myshkin and Alyosha Karamazov.[16] These Fool-Figures act without "reason," ignoring practical considerations. Especially in the first half of the book, Quixote approximates the "pure" foolishness of the child which assumes that its imaginative projection is equivalent to the nature of things and that it can remove what it does not like by its magical wish. In these instances, Quixote is a humorous figure.[17] As in the case of Dostoyevsky's Prince Myshkin, Quixote would do away with unjust consequences without inquiring into social causes and without considering the consequences of his own acts.[18]

Reality and Existence

At the beginning, Quixote impresses us as a subjective idealist who would create the world out of his personal idea, or as a Cartesian might argue, "I think, therefore it is." Quixote himself is aware that he is postulating a poetic model and not material existence, that he is not imitating things "as they were but as they ought to have been." Now, Cervantes' hero suffers defeat at the hands of things as they are, but emerges with dignity in refusing to give up the ideal image of things as they ought to be. In a similar way, Faust's inner light is dignified by Goethe, Prospero's magic world by Shakespeare, Wotan's Valhalla by Wagner, Peer Gynt's dreamings by Ibsen, the musical values of Hanno Buddenbrook, Hans Castorp and Andreas Leverkühn by Thomas Mann.[19]

However, *Don Quixote* must be approached from what Americo Castro calls a double perspective. W. H. Auden calls the Don the greatest representation of the Religious Hero in literature in that he is committed to his idea "with absolute passion," pursuing the absolute truth by himself. But Auden slights the other perspective in the novel when he adds that such a religious hero is, in a sense, "not related to others at all."[20] For, alongside his insistence on absolute commitment, Quixote is thoroughly related to others. Where Dante postulates an unbridgeable gulf between existence and essence (the inferno and paradise), Cervantes would join and reconcile them through human effort.

The motif of reconciliation also appears in the introduction of the comic. Cervantes *invites us to laugh at Don Quixote* by presenting the incongruity between his godlike pretentiousness and his human limitations. Yet, this very comic element *socializes and humanizes* his hero. In Dante's "Comedy," there is no laughter, except possibly on the part

147

of God, as he views man's futile effort to extend himself beyond human power. In Cervantes' work, we have *human* laughter. And laughter in turn humanizes. While *The Divine Comedy* dwells on divine love, *Don Quixote* shifts towards man's compassion for man. Dante's Catholic "Comedy" precludes tragedy, postulating a transcendental harmony. Cervantes' novel introduces tragedy into man's earthly function and destiny. At the same time, he softens and socializes man's tragic lot by the comic mode.

In this spirit, Cervantes also democratizes the traditional aristocratic hero. For Quixote, the mark of excellence is character, not station. "They alone impress us as being great and illustrious," the Don tells his niece and housekeeper, "that show themselves to be virtuous, rich and generous." Indeed, the point of the novel is that all can be "knights." It elevates a poor old man into a knight-errant, a peasant into a squire. Rocinante is said to be equal or even superior to Alexander's Bucephalus; the village wench Dulcinea is endowed with the virtues and gifts of the Helens and Didos. Where the picaresque novel regarded the commonplace as something uninteresting, Cervantes' work treats it as containing the elements of excellence.

Waldo Frank holds that Quixote does not convert a single person. This is true in the sense that poetry is not completely translatable into existence. Yet, we have *approximations of conversion*. To begin with, nearly all enter into Quixote's realm of discourse and action, are transformed "into madmen and fools." All the characters derive their legitimacy through the Don—without him, they would cease to have any function in the novel.

In the course of the story, nearly all the characters and the reader develop respect, sympathy and love for the Don. What impresses them most is not so much his courage, nor that he is ready to fight against impossible odds, but that he is *a good man*. "For," the author interpolates at the end,

> as has been stated more than once, whether Don Quixote was plain Alonso Quijano the Good or Don Quixote de la Mancha, he was always of a kindly and pleasant disposition and for this reason was beloved not only by the members of his household but by all who knew him.

And, even as they ridicule his methods, *nobody laughs at the idea* behind them.

Quixote's mission is to free the noble resources which he believes are present in all. And, by acting *as if* goodness, justice and honor are inherent in all, he encourages them to come alive. And here are the practical effects of Quixote's idea: His courteous treatment of the inn-keeper, the prostitutes and others results in their acting in a courteous manner. All sense that his idea is the reservoir of inspiration and hope, of kindness, courage and loyalty, that without it, their life would be a drudge. The students look upon him "with admiration and respect", and as Quixote lies on his death-bed, Sancho begs him:

> Ah, master, don't die, your Grace, but take my advice and go on living for many years to come; for the greatest madness that a man can be guilty of in this life is to die without good reason, without anyone's killing him, slain only by the hands of melancholy. Look you, don't be lazy but get up from this bed and let us go out into the fields clad as shepherds as we agreed to do. Who knows but behind some bush we may come upon the lady Dulcinea, as disenchanted as you wish.

The conversion of Sansón is even more impressive. He, who had gone to such extremes to refute the Don's idea, now reverses himself, saying that "the worthy Sancho speaks the truth." At Quixote's death, he is anxious to keep his "madness" alive, and his verses praise the Don as "a gentleman bold." Earlier, he had commented on Cid Hamete's history of Don Quixote: "Little children leaf through it, young people read it, adults appreciate it, and the aged sing its praise."

Towards the end of his life, Quixote declares that he has been "too daring." In this admission, he realizes that no one, however brave, can go it alone. Like Faust, Quixote renounces his superhuman claims and accepts the fact that man must eat dust. But, whereas Faust and other Renaissance heroes fight primarily for themselves, Quixote would be the sacrifice for others. This motive "to live dying," as he puts it, distinguishes him—as Turgenev and Waldo Frank point out—from other mythic heroes, such as Hamlet and Ahab. Quixote's sacrifice has for its aim freedom, justice and peace on earth. Freedom, he tells Sancho

> is one of the most precious gifts that the heavens have bestowed on man . . . for the sake of freedom, as for the sake of honor, one may and should risk one's life.

And, in a speech delivered "in such manner and couched in such excellent terms that it was quite impossible for the moment for any of those who heard him to take him for a madman," Quixote states that the end of letters is

> human knowledge, whose object is to administer distributive justice and give to each that which is his and see that good laws are observed . . . the objective is peace, which is the greatest blessing that men can wish for in this

life. . . . For the first good news that mankind and the world received was that which the angels brought on the night that was our day: "Glory to God in the highest, and on earth peace, good will toward men."

Here, Cervantes continues Dante's political philosophy, his hope for one world of church and state. For the achievement of this goal, Cervantes saw the need of uniting Quixote's idealism with Sancho's realism. Yet, the two are not united but run parallel to each other. In Spinozistic language, the order and connection of ideas in the one is the same as the order and connection of things in the other. *Don Quixote* was published about the same time as *Hamlet*. Here, the perspectives are no longer parallel, but conflict with each other.

NOTES

1. The translations are from Samuel Putnam's *Don Quixote* (2 vols.; New York, 1949).
2. The chivalric idea has a long history, from the Bushio in Japan and the ancient Beduins of North Arabia to the Teutonic and Frankish orders. The English printer William Caxton gives chivalry a mythic heritage, tracing it back to Adam and Eve. He identifies the archangel Michael as the first knight and claims that chivalry was the earliest divine device for the recovery of the human race from the ruin of the fall. See Hearnshaw's article, "Chivalry," in *The Encyclopedia of the Social Sciences*.
3. Byron's oft-quoted statement that *Don Quixote* laughed chivalry away is therefore misleading. Quixote is not a knight and must "burnish up some old pieces of armor," fashion a half-helmet out of cardboard and a barber's basin. Quixote himself knows that his horse is a homebred steed, that Sancho is a peasant and Dulcinea a farm-girl of his neighborhood. The figure of an *hidalgo*, ridiculed and beaten, could neither disparage nor glorify the traditional picture of chivalry. This point is developed by Joseph Bickerman, *Don Quixote und Faust* (Berlin, 1929).
4. Quixote's tasks are likened to the labors of Hercules and Jason, his trials to those of Aeneas, his wanderings to those of Ulysses. Analogies are drawn between Quixote and Tantalus, Sisyphus, Ixion; between his demise and the fall of Troy; between his relation to Sancho and that between Castor and Pollux, Orestes and Pylades. The Don's journey through perilous regions is described as a descent into the Orphic shade. References to other legends include Tityus, Silenus, Helen, Pyramus and Thisbe, Zeus and Danae, Actaeon and Diana, Daphne, Perseus, Merlin, Nisus.
5. The irony is that Quixote's soliloquy is delivered after he has fed, not on honey, fruit and water, but on meat and wine. While the herdsmen-theme recurs in the book (Quixote feasts and fights with herdsmen and wants to become one himself at the end), the novel dwells but little on the role of nature and,

with the exception of the episode of the fulling hammers, is strikingly devoid of nature-descriptions.

6. Cervantes himself suggests that his novel has the character of a seasonal ritual. In the chapter dealing with the end of Sancho's government on the island, he writes that "everything moves in a circle, that is to say, around and around: spring follows summer, summer the harvest season, harvest autumn, autumn winter, and winter spring." Quixote's journey begins in spring-like fancy, followed by a period of "probation" during which he descends into the labyrinth of the Montesinos, "traversing deserts and solitudes." He enjoys a "summer" when he is feted as an honored knight at the ducal palace. His journey culminates in his "fall" in the encounter with the swine, followed by the "winter" of his death. But his death is not final in that his idea is carried forward by Sancho and Sansón Carrasco.

7. The Don retains faith in his idea even after the barber and the curate burn his chivalric books (except for the books of Amadis which are his principal inspiration). The burning of books has as little effect here as it did in Hitlerite Germany. Quixote does *not* need the books as Madame Bovary does to keep her romanticism alive. Hence, she ends as a suicide, none the wiser for her fancies.

8. *Don Quixote* (London, 1940), pp. 2-3.

9. By such transposition, we can also grasp the sense in which Quixote sees a flock of sheep as an army in disguise. And, when we bear in mind the Don's attitude towards the clergy of his day, we can understand why he calls the Benedictine friars a lying rabble and sees in the priests travelling at night "something evil . . . phantoms and monsters from the other world."

10. The religious, Quixote tells Vivaldo,

    "in all peace and tranquillity, pray to Heaven for earth's good, but we soldiers and knights put their prayers into execution by defending with the might of our good arms and the edge of the sword those things for which they pray. . . . Thus we become ministers of God on earth, and our arms the means by which he executes His decrees."

    He has praise for those saints who were valiant and men of arms, such as St. James, the patron saint of Spain; St. Paul, who was "a knight-errant in life"; St. George, who was "a protector of damsels" (he slew the dragon to save the King's daughter) and hence was "one of the best knight-errants that the heavenly militia ever had"; St. Martin, who was even more charitable in giving to the poor than he was valiant.

11. We find it in the Satapatha Brahmana where "the Gods, ascending, knew not the way to the heavenly world, but the horse knew it." It appears in Lucian and in Apuleius' *The Golden Ass*. In the Irish legend of Conn-Eda, the knight lets the animal lead him, and Owain of King Arthur's Round Table is guided by the lion. In the Greek novel, the donkey attains a heroic quality by the quiet patience with which he endures beatings. (See Carl Kerenyi's *Die Griechisch-Orientalische Romanliteratur* [Tübingen, 1927] and Heinrich Zimmer's *The King and the Corpse* [New York, 1948]). In Apuleius, Lucius' transformation

into an ass constitutes punishment. But Robert Graves reminds us that the ass was sacred to the God Set-Typhon:

"The ass had been so holy a beast that its ears, conventionalized as twin feathers sprouting from the end of a sceptre, became the mark of sovereignty in the hand of every Egyptian deity: and the existence of an early Italian ass-cult is proved by the cognomens Asina and Asellus in the distinguished Scipionian, Claudian and Annian families at Rome. . . . Asses are connected in Western European folklore, especially French, with the mid-winter Saturnalia at the conclusion of which the ass-eared god, later the Christmas Fool with his ass-eared cap, was killed by his rival, the Spirit of the New Year—the child Horus, or Harpocrates, or the infant Zeus . . . there was an eastern European tradition identifying Saturn's counterpart Cronos with the ass. . . . This explains the otherwise unaccountable popular connection between asses and fools." (Introduction to *The Golden Ass of Apuleius* [New York, 1951].)

Thomas Mann's Joseph experiences a rebirth in the pit by the mishap to his donkey Hulda, and it is a donkey which leads him through part of the Egyptian desert. In general, the donkey embodies the wisdom of the lower instincts; in Thomas Mann, there is also a suggestion of the donkey as phallic guidance.

12. Their relation is similar to that of Orestes and Pylades, Leander and Naukleros, Hamlet and Horatio-Fortinbras, Faust and Mephisto, Ahab and Starbuck, Castorp and Joachim, Joseph and his brothers. In particular, the analogy to Mann's *Transposed Heads* suggests itself where Nanda is the body, Schridemann the head. In both, a transposition takes place in which their roles are interchanged.

13. When Quixote insists that Sancho lash himself on his bare back and seat himself on the bare board of the magic horse, Sancho complains that his master wants him to be both pregnant and a virgin.

14. Sancho's faithfulness to Quixote is matched by his devotion to Dapple. Upon giving up his governorship, all he asks for is "a little barley for his gray and half a cheese and half a loaf of bread for himself."

15. As in other mythopoesis (Oedipus, Dante, Faust, Karamazov, Mann's Castorp, Joseph, Grigors) the number three is a recurrent figure: Quixote makes three sallies in all, and leaves for his third sally after spending three days at home; Quixote feasts three days before he goes down into the cave, stays three days with Roque and dies three days after he has made his will; there are three peasant lasses, one of whom Sancho would have him believe is Dulcinea.

16. Variants of this role appear in the simulated foolishness of David, Moses, Cyros, William Tell, and the Hamlet figures of Saxo and Shakespeare. Cf. Otto Rank's *Inzest Motif in Sage and Dichtung*, pp. 264-265.

17. Freud calls humor "the triumph of narcissism." It "refuses to be hurt by the arrows of reality," insisting that "it is impervious to wounds dealt by the outside world." Humor is "rebellious," asserting itself "in the face of the adverse

152

real circumstances." It "asseverates the invincibility of one's ego against the real world and victoriously upholds the pleasure principle." The humorist plays the part of a superior adult, identifying himself to some extent with the father, "while he reduces the other people to the position of children." *Collected Papers*, V, 217-218.

18. Prince Myshkin also attempts the impossible, knowing that it is impossible, enacting the myth of the sacrifice and atonement for others. Myshkin is the selfless "idiot" who exposes himself and passively accepts suffering; Quixote is the wilful hero who brings about his suffering and insists on being the sacrifice. And, where Dostoyevsky's character would achieve the good by being good, Quixote would change conditions by individual "revolutionary" acts.

19. In the stories of Grisóstomo and Anselmo, Cervantes seems to be saying that one should *not* attempt a literal implementation of the idea. Grisóstomo would also be a knight. But his desire to possess Marcela (his Dulcinea) in flesh and blood results in her death. Similarly, in the story of "One Who Was Too Curious For His Own Good," Anselmo's error is to try and prove the virtue of his lady by presenting her with *real* temptations.

20. W. H. Auden, *The Enchafed Flood* (New York, 1950), pp. 97 ff.

Renaissance Mythopoesis

Hamlet

THE MYTHIC VIEW undergoes an eclipse in the Renaissance. A more critical temper arises and piety for communal standards shifts towards reliance on individual and "private" experience. This shift appears in the varieties of cultural experience: in Cartesian doubt, in portrait painting and the closet drama, in the private economic market and in Lockian empiricism. Personality, or what the Italian Renaissance called the *uomo singolare*, was something new and exciting in the age of Erasmus, Leonardo and Michelangelo, of the Borgias and the Medici.

In the earlier mythopoesis, the revolt of the heroic character takes place *within* the framework of tradition. The Renaissance hero does not have such ties with his community, family, state, church or God. He does not have the guiding voice of Yahweh, Moira or God, the counsel of a Chorus or the intercession of a Virgil and Beatrice. The new hero stands alone. He becomes the exploratory "journey"-man, and must seek the sanctions of belief within himself. Absolute truths and values are replaced by unlimited possibilities, the unified vision by "perspectivism." In the religious realm, this takes form in the split of the universal Catholic Church into varieties of Protestant churches.

In *The Great Chain of Being* (pp. 242 ff., 315) A. E. Lovejoy characterizes this trend as "the temporalizing of the Chain of Being." Previously, the conception of the Chain of Being rested on the principle of plenitude which precluded belief in progress or in any significant change in the world as a whole. It was based on the Solomonic dictum that there is nothing new under the sun. This principle with its reference in the past or in an eternal present broke down in the Renaissance which placed the golden age in a future consisting of endless ascending stages. The Platonic notion that the highest good lay in cessation of desire and the Dantesque vision of an eternal celestial paradise were supplanted by the principle of man's natural insatiable desires in the sensuous world. And God was interpreted as himself desiring that man should be insatiable. The new conception of God was not of a self-sufficient, timeless Absolute, but (in Lovejoy's formulation) one "whose prime attribute was generativeness, whose manifestation was to be found in the diversity of creatures and therefore in the temporal order and the manifold spectacle of nature's processes."

The new perspective was an ambiguous gift to those in the Renaissance who were sensitive to the dangers of such unlimited freedom. They welcomed the opening up of the universe, but felt bewildered by the multiple winds of doctrine; they were buoyed by the new freedom and its futuristic possibilities, but were disquieted in seeking a future which could never be present; they hailed the new science which took its reference from the cosmic scheme, but missed the older approach which centered in specifically human norms and values; they felt dignified by the stress on individual responsibility, but missed the firm guidance which had provided a steady platform in society, ethics and religion. In sum, individual freedom brought expansion and enrichment, as well as perplexity and confusion. For, as the term re-naissance indicated, the new age did not completely repudiate tradition: Rabelais' Gargantua is reared on classical models; Corneille and Racine revived ancient themes and characters; Shakespeare tried to save his kings and princes, and Goethe contrasts the idyllic life of the old couple Philemon and Baucis with Faust's "Sorge." That is, these mythmakers tried to integrate individual expression with "the great chain of being."

They pictured the emerging dislocations through the broken structure of the family—in Hamlet, Faust, Siegfried, Ahab, Mitya Karamazov, Hans Castrop and other modern figures.

THE RESIDUE OF SENSIBILITY:
SHAKESPEARE'S HAMLET

The Hamlet story does not have the same ancient background which we find in earlier mythopoesis. Still, its roots reach back to the heroic age of Scandinavia, and it has a rich legendary background—Icelandic, Celtic, French, possibly Roman and Persian.[1]

Even as Hamlet appears as a strange and unique individual, we feel a deep kinship with him. Indeed, a "Hamlet-problem" and a "Hamlet-character" have become something like figures of speech. And Hamlet's mission is the same as in all mythopoesis: to rid the body politic of its diseased state. Furthermore, the play's specific motifs connect it with traditional myths. The theme of fratricide (here called "the first murder") is found in the Egyptian saga of *The Two Brothers* and in the Bible; the conflict of son and mother has its prototype in the Babylonian myth of Marduk and Tiamat; revenge on the usurping uncle in the Hindu myth of Kans-Krishna.

Shakespeare's *Hamlet* is also replete with mythic allusions. These are not a matter of decoration (as is the case with much of Renaissance literature), but are evocative of Hamlet's own situation. To Hamlet, his father was a Herculean hero with the qualities of "every god." In the closet-scene, he tells Gertrude:

> See what a grace was seated on this brow;
> Hyperion's curls, the front of Jove himself,
> An eye like Mars to threaten and command,
> A station like the herald Mercury
> New-lighted on a heaven-kissing hill;
> A combination and a form indeed,
> Where every god did seem to set his seal,
> To give the world assurance of a man.

(All quotations are from *The Tragedies of Shakespeare* [London, 1939]).

The union of Hamlet's father with an ordinary woman reenacts the mythic union of the god with a mortal woman (Zeus-Jupiter with Alcmene-Semele-Danae), giving birth to the hero-son (Hercules-Dionysus-Perseus). In Shakespeare's play, the god is also dismembered and reappears on earth to shape the destiny of the family-world.

"Remember Me"

The mythic character of *Hamlet* is established by the Ghost. He corresponds to the Greek Chthonic deity whose voice carries over into the present and the future. The Ghost's call to Hamlet, "Remember me," is the *Grundbass*-motif of the play and defines Hamlet's social and psychological burden. For the audience, the Ghost is an accepted convention; for Horatio, he may be an illusion or an evil omen. For Hamlet, he is a personal voice whose words "Remember me" echo in his mind throughout the play. The voice from the past is a portentous reality for Hamlet. He is the only one both to see and talk to the Ghost.

The Ghost is the sphinx of the play. And its function, as that of the sphinx, is to bring the hero's attention to his origins and to set his future task. In mythic vocabulary: The Ghost reaches back to Creation and forward to Re-creation, with the Quest as the necessary mediate labor toward the fulfillment of this task.

Now, the Ghost speaks an ambiguous language. In this Renaissance work, the voice of authority is no longer clear. Hamlet himself *begins* by questioning tradition. He has been to Wittenberg, Luther's university, where he may have received an intellectual framework for "protesting." Yet, Hamlet's Protestantism is dialectically limited. For, he is the son of a Catholic father who dwells in Purgatory ("Till the foul crimes done in my days of nature/Are burnt and purg'd away"). Thus, Hamlet is pressed from two sides, finds arguments for being and nonbeing, for acting and not acting, for self-esteem and self-depreciation. The ancestral voice has a "questionable shape," and Hamlet cannot carry out its command although it calls on him "by heaven and hell." Hamlet's over-all dilemma lies in that he can live neither with nor without this tradition. The present is gross and sensual, its mirth "heavy-headed revel." The King is a satyr, the Queen a "pernicious woman," Polonius a fish-monger, the people a "distracted multitude," the state "rotten."

Still, Hamlet will not "be bounded in a nut-shell." He is no Pyrrhic skeptic and makes a heroic effort to resolve his dilemma by thought, passion and action. The result is a pendular swing between action and inaction, between faith and doubt. He believes that there *are* objective norms of right and wrong but does not know which action corresponds to these norms. All action is in a specific direction and Hamlet's difficulty consists in *his inability to be a specialist* in an age of developing specializations. Hence, when he does act, he questions the wisdom of his decision; and when he does not act, he condemns himself for letting "all sleep." Hamlet incorporates the legacy of doubt. He doubts himself and he doubts others (unable to confide his plans even to Horatio); he doubts the "idols of the tribe," demanding adherence to the old, the "idols of the cave," inviting detachment, and the "idols of the market-place," clamoring for attention to the demands of the hour. His cosmic vision paralyzes his arm and his realistic sense prods him into action.

Such ambiguities haunt Hamlet throughout the play. He thinks that the apparition may be "an honest ghost," or that he may be a "fiend." This dialectic carries over into Hamlet's attitude towards his mother, Ophelia, even to Claudius. In sum, this Renaissance hero remains in the midway stage. He is *the first hero in mythopoesis who questions himself from the beginning, the first who fails to carry out his mission, until it no longer really matters to him.*

Act II: The Journey

Preceding the action of the play, Hamlet was presumably united in love with his family. His father had the attributes of a god, the mother of a saint, and Ophelia of a "heavenly child."[2] There follows the second stage in which the hero leaves home. Now, Hamlet is not set out as were Job, Prometheus, Oedipus and Orestes, nor deserted as was Mitya Karamazov. Yet, for Hamlet, his mother's remarriage, closely following his father's death, spells a world that is "out of joint."

When Hamlet returned from the university, he found that experience was at odds with the theory he and Horatio had learned at Wittenberg. After he has spoken with the Ghost, he tells his friend that there are more things in heaven and on earth than are dreamt of in his philosophy. His father's death estranges him from Gertrude, Ophelia, Claudius and the court. He has been expelled from Eden and must begin the tortuous journey through life's inferno.

Before Hamlet meets the Ghost, he is in relative equilibrium. His mother's remarriage shocks him into a *settled* state of melancholy. The world as a whole becomes an unweeded garden, its uses "weary, stale, flat and unprofitable." The world has rejected him, and Hamlet in turn rejects it as well as himself.

It is at this point that the Ghost appears. Hamlet feels himself "call'd," his "fate cries out," and he descends to meet the Ghost on the underground-platform, like Gilgamesh, Aeneas and Dante. Here, he undergoes the rites of initiation and is given the task of cleansing the rotten stables of the state.[3] The Ghost's command that Hamlet revenge the murder is issued at the beginning of the play, but Claudius is not killed until the end of the five-act drama. What accounts for the delay?

Ernest Jones points out that in the earlier versions, both the motive and the delay are traced to external and political factors. The murder of Feng (Claudius) is a public act, and only physical difficulties delay Amleth's revenge and triumph. In Shakespeare, not the political, but the family-situation, is in the foreground, and the external difficulties in carrying out the mission are minimized.[4]

Coleridge and the Romanticists have popularized the "inner" approach, arguing that Hamlet is too much of a speculative thinker to be a practical doer. This interpretation ascribes "Hamlet-" traits to dreamy and idling characters, such as Goethe's Werther, Jacobsen's Niels Lhynne, Ibsen's Hjalmar Ekdal, and the *nichevo* figures in Russian literature. But Shakespeare's hero is no such "Hamlet." He is a philosopher, to be sure; but he is also a soldier and a skilled fencer. Indeed, at the risk of over-statement, it can be said that *Hamlet is the most active character in the play*. Only where Claudius is involved, does Hamlet show hesitancy.

Some criticism centers Hamlet's problem in the social-political condition. For example, Smirnov's Marxist study argues that Hamlet is "caught between the corruption of the court, the vulgarity of the growing bourgeoisie, and the masses in whom he has no belief."[5]

Claudius' regime is corrupt. But, is it as corrupt as Hamlet says? The King is shown eager to make amends, and promises Hamlet the succession. His rule is no worse than that of other kings in the Tudor era. Only after Hamlet discloses his threatening designs in the playlet does Claudius move against him. Hamlet overstates the case against Claudius, as well as against Gertrude and Ophelia. And he overstates the case against himself as well. The social situation in the court is a necessary, but not a sufficient, condition for unravelling what Hamlet calls his "mystery." The analysis of *Hamlet* as the tragedy of a noble character in an ignoble society makes a sharp separation between him and his society and thereby lifts him out of his Renaissance setting. Hamlet himself says that his own "thinking" makes Denmark a prison for him, tells Rosenkrantz that "there is nothing either good or bad, but thinking makes it so." He confesses that he has "bad dreams," and is "unpregnant" of their cause.

THE PSYCHIC BURDEN

Shakespeare's *Hamlet* cannot be viewed as a Renaissance work in the same sense in which we speak of the Oedipus dramas and *The Divine Comedy* as Greek and Catholic. The problem of Oedipus and Dante is nearly identical with that of their culture. This is not the case with Hamlet. The Renaissance hero feels himself alone. There is no clear-cut voice of tradition, no existing symbols of authority with which he can identify. To know himself, Hamlet cannot engage in a social dialogue, but must try to analyze his burden by himself. This gives the play the character of *interiorization* and invites a psychoanalytic approach.

T. S. Eliot (*The Sacred Wood* [London, 1945]) observes that Hamlet's emotions are excessive without attempting to explain why they are so or why Hamlet vacillates. The most extended and brilliant exposition of this problem (suggested by Freud and somewhat developed by Otto Rank) is contained in Ernest Jones' *Hamlet and Oedipus*.

Jones argues that Hamlet's vacillation is not due to his general incapacity for action, nor to the unusual difficulty of the task, but to the fact that at heart he does not want to carry out the task. He is held back because unconsciously he identifies himself with Claudius who is the realization of his own repressed infantile wishes: sexual union with the mother and death of the father. When Claudius usurps his place, the repressed desire for the mother is stimulated. Hamlet can cover up this love by attention to Ophelia because she least reminds him of his mother. Hamlet detests Claudius, but "it is a jealous detestation of one evil-doer towards his successful fellow. . . . In reality his uncle incorporates the deepest and most buried part of his own personality, so that he cannot kill him without also killing himself." Hamlet's attitude towards Claudius is a complex projection of his attitude towards himself: disgust with his infantile wishes to take his father's place by the side of his mother, mixed with admiration for Claudius' success. The repressed energy seeks outlets in many secondary acts which wear Hamlet out. Only when the possibility of incest is removed—when his mother is dead —and Hamlet knows that he is going to die, is he free to kill Claudius. Hamlet's cosmic and social vision is disturbed by his private involvements.[6]

Although Hamlet does not actually commit incest or patricide, he is tortured by guilt-feelings from the outset

> That I, the son of a dear father murder'd,
> Prompted to my revenge by heaven and hell,
> Must like a whore unpack my heart with words.

Whether or not Hamlet does procrastinate is not as crucial as that *he himself thinks* that he is procrastinating and feels guilty. He confesses to Ophelia that he could accuse himself of such things

> that it were better my mother had not borne me . . . with more offences at my beck than I have thoughts to put them in, imagination to give them shape, or time to act them in.

And to Horatio, he speaks of his imagination which may be "as foul as Vulcan's stithy."

Hamlet's self-depreciation is his secret which cannot be accounted for by anything he has done. Indeed, the play as a whole has a tone of secrecy: It opens with a secret message, imparted to Hamlet at a secret place; when he returns, he solemnly pledges his friends to secrecy; the Ghost's appearance in the closet-scene is a secret known only to Hamlet. His over-all secret is the motive for his delay in executing the Ghost's commission, despite the fact, as Hamlet admits, that he has "cause, and will, and strength, and means" to do so.

What Hamlet does know is that he has bad dreams. The theme of bad dreams is also central in the soliloquy "To be, or not to be." Hamlet states that he is held back from suicide by "the dread of something after death." But what is the dread? Hamlet first says that it is simply the fear of the unknown ("that we know not of"). In the next lines, he twice associates death and sleep:

> . . . . .To die; to sleep,
> . . . . 'tis a consummation
> Devoutly to be wish'd, to die, to sleep;

He then proceeds to link sleep with dream—and here is "the rub."

> To sleep; perchance to dream; ay, there's the rub;
> For in that sleep of death what dreams may come,
> When we have shuffled off this mortal coil,
> Must give us pause;

Hamlet feels guilty not over something he has done, but only of what he *thought* of doing. He is the precursor of our modern characters for whom a symbolic crime, one committed in fantasy, is a real crime. The reason for this lies partly in the new historic climate.

Oedipus was able to shift part of his burden to public powers—the oracle, Apollo, "the pleasure of the gods," with whom he could identify. As he tells the Priest of Zeus at the opening of the action: "my soul mourns at once for the city, and for myself, and for thee." And, for the sake of the city, he insists on uncovering the truth, regardless of the consequences to himself. With the increase of personal freedom in the Renaissance, there came an increase of solitude and loneliness.

Aristotle declared that all men of genius are melancholy men. Isolation, or what Nietzsche called the "pathos of distance," may be a source of inspiration and is necessary for the organization of one's creative powers. Examples of such productive solitude may be seen among the Hindu sages and Christian Eremites, in figures such as Spinoza and Santayana. But, not all solitude bespeaks of genius, not where withdrawal stems from fear or guilt. In that case, one *suffers* from isolation.

Hamlet's melancholy is connected with his being apart from others and hence he has a deep need for association. In the last lines of the first act, he twice begs his friends to stand with him:

> . . . . let us go in together,
> . . . .
> Nay, come, let's go together.

His melancholy does not arise merely from a pessimistic evaluation of man and the world. He tells Guildenstern:

> What piece of work is a man! how noble in reason! how infinite in faculties!
> in form and moving how express and admirable! in action how like an angel,

in apprehension how like a god! the beauty of the world! the paragon of animals!

It is characteristic of Hamlet's broken dialectic that he goes on to say
that to him man is but the "quintessence of dust."

Hamlet's relation to Ophelia is an enigma to critics who ignore his
psychological conflict. What is the nature of this "love" that Hamlet
does not even allude to in his monologues or in his talks with Horatio?
What kind of love is it that can kill the beloved's father without a twitch
of remorse or thought of its effect on her, that (as Dover Wilson remarks) feels less distressed about her death than about the remains of
a jester dead long ago? What has Ophelia done to justify Hamlet's in-
sulting language?

From the psychoanalytic perspective, Hamlet's behavior to Ophelia
can be explained as a displacement of the prohibited love for the
mother. He transfers his affection from the one to the other, veiling the
identification by choosing a woman who "should least remind him of
his mother" (Jones). But it is a *displaced* love, and Hamlet devotes
himself but little to Ophelia. Actually, he tells her, "I never gave you
aught." What he did give was to the "idol" of his "soul," to an Ophelia
"beautified" in his projection. But because of his confusion between the
two, he treats Ophelia with the same mixture of insult, bitterness and
love which he expresses to Gertrude in the closet-scene.[7] Because Gertrude has proved sensual and deceptive, Ophelia (and all women) are
charged with "frailty." Indeed, Hamlet shows more affection for Horatio, even for Laertes than for Ophelia.[8]

The Strategy of Displacement

Ernest Jones points out that in the early version, Amleth feigns
madness to disguise his intention to revenge the murder which was a
matter of public knowledge. In Shakespeare, Claudius does not know
that Hamlet has learned of the murder. Here, the external situation does
not dictate Hamlet's simulated madness.

Hamlet's need "to put an antic disposition on" is his method of insu-
lating himself against the disturbing emotions which the Ghost's voice
set loose. Hamlet knows that he is "passion's slave" and might betray
the nature of his passion. He has as great a fear of exposing it to himself
as to others. In appearing to be aroused over Claudius' incest, he
screens his own unpermitted desire; in appearing to be concerned with
revenge for the murder, he conceals his concern over his feeling about
Gertrude. The strategy of displacement is the core of "play" in the

drama. For Hamlet, the "poet," the play *is* the thing,—the method by which he shifts attention away from his personal burden. Similarly, Hamlet substitutes preparations to carry out the action for the deed itself. A lightning verbal dialectic and rapid succession of movements are substituted for decisive steps, the play-murder and "bloody" thoughts for the murder itself.[9] Hamlet, the philosopher, the playwright, the actor, exhausts himself in continuously devising means, thereby continuously postponing the end.

Hamlet's strategy of displacement points to the coexistence of powerful forces within him which cross each other. The one calls for the murder of Claudius; the other inhibits him from carrying it out. Hamlet makes continuous preparations for both: He not only plans the killing of Claudius; he also frames these plans in a manner which prevent their success. For, as Jones points out, Hamlet's multiple devices are such as to *arouse suspicion against himself*: His antic disposition makes Polonius and Claudius wary; the playlet increases their suspicion; in the closet-scene, he nearly makes a full confession. This ambivalence appears in Hamlet's behavior as a whole: He tells Ophelia that he did and did not love her; his attitude to Gertrude bespeaks love and contempt. Even the King is not simply a Nimrod-Herod figure to Hamlet. When he sees Claudius at prayer, Hamlet reflects that only heaven knows "how his audit stands." Claudius' desire to pray shows that " 'Tis heavy with him," and that he may even be fit for "the purging of his soul."

Hamlet's strategy of displacement is further substantiated by analysis of the opening soliloquy, the platform scene, the playlet, and the closet-scene.

The Trappings of Woe

The extraordinary feature of the first soliloquy consists in what it *omits*: It contains not one word of *regret* over the death of his father. Even the clothes of mourning—Hamlet tells Gertrude—do not "denote" him truly, are "but the trappings and the suits of woe." In this soliloquy, Hamlet confines himself to condemning his mother: that she remarried, that she did so shortly after the King's death, that she married a man who is "a satyr" compared to his father, an "Hyperion." In the midst of these complaints, Hamlet reluctantly recalls the intimacy between his father and mother:

> Must I remember? why, she should hang on him,
> As if increase of appetite had grown
> By what it fed on. . . .

163

Next, he contrasts his father with *both Claudius and himself*. His mother, Hamlet complains, married his father's brother,

> . . . but no more than my father
> Than I to Hercules. . . .[10]

To be sure, Hamlet loved his father. But this love was disturbed by his mother's remarriage. The new pattern is a slightly distorted re-enactment of the young boy's oedipal conflict, stimulates this earlier hostility and partly submerges the love. As noted, Hamlet speaks of his father as god-like, likening his eye to that of "Mars, to threaten and command." And the Ghost speaks to him as a commander to his subject.[11] In the midst of calling on Hamlet to revenge him, the Ghost issues a strange and seemingly uncalled for warning:

> But, howsoever thou pursuest this act,
> Taint not thy mind, nor let thy soul contrive
> Against thy mother aught; leave her to heaven.

When the Ghost leaves, Hamlet dwells on his commandment, then interrupts this theme with the exclamation: "O most pernicious woman!" Why "pernicious," when the Ghost had only called her "my most-seeming, virtuous queen"?

Following the Ghost's departure, there takes place a remarkable change in Hamlet's mood: His melancholy is gone, and he speaks to Horatio and Marcellus in a spry, lighthearted tone, telling them that he has heard "wonderful" news, and addresses the Ghost playfully as "boy," "true-penny," and refers to him as "this fellow" and "old mole."

What is the reason for this change? Why does the news of the murder and the commandment to exact revenge lift his depression? Again, Hamlet's use of displacement offers a clue. He can now cover up the source of his personal anxiety by assuming a public mission, can put on his "antic disposition" and act out his secret burden in an acceptable form. The Ghost's command converts Hamlet's "bad dreams" into respectability by substituting a justifiable motive (a son's duty) for a guilty motive. It quickens him into life.

The Ghost's appearance is the catalyst for the subsequent action of the drama. The Voice from Purgatory *organizes* Hamlet by providing him with a mission. This vision does not express his death-wish; on the contrary, it makes for his *living, active* role. The Ghost propels Hamlet from a settled hellish melancholy towards dynamic restless activity.

However, Hamlet's high spirits do not last. While he does not revert to his earlier dejection, he begins to doubt his ability to carry through his "play." Will he be able to carry out his filial duty while

weighed down by his private burden? *Can he take over and be King?*
He, who feels himself to be no more like his father than is Claudius?
Hamlet questions his adequacy and laments the "cursed spite" which
commissions him to "set it right." The time is out of joint. But so is Hamlet. The final lines of the first act summarize the dual motif of the play:
the disjointedness and schism in the social and in the individual body.

When the Ghost leaves, Hamlet vows to "remember" only that which
the Ghost has charged him with, and to forget all those thoughts and
fantasies, associated with his father and mother, which might hinder
the execution of the assignment:

> Yea, from the table of my memory
> I'll wipe away all trivial fond records,
> All saws of books, all forms, all pressures past
> That youth and observation copied there,
> And thy commandment all alone shall live
> Within the book and volume of my brain,
> Unmix'd with baser matter: yes, by heaven!

But, for all his conscious resolve, this "baser matter" does mix with the
commandment, and gives him bad dreams.[12] Not "thought" or "reflection" as such, but memory of "pressures past" sap him of the energy
needed for resolute decision.

The Conscience of the Nephew

In "The Murder of Gonzago," Hamlet has found a ready-made play
in which a king is murdered by his brother who then marries the king's
wife. Dover Wilson has called attention to the fact that Hamlet *changes*
the play by inserting 12-16 lines of his own. It is not clear which lines
are Hamlet's. But the all-important consideration is that the playlet, as
presented, is *not* analogous to the situation as described by the Ghost.
Hamlet replaces Claudius by "one Lucianus, nephew to the king."
Dover Wilson concludes that in this substitution, Hamlet deliberately
indicates his intention to kill Claudius. The "nephew" points to Hamlet.
But who is "the king"? Is the reference to Claudius or to Hamlet's
father?[13] On either reading, Hamlet makes a central admission: that he
plans to kill Caudius, or that, concealed as the "nephew," he desired
the death of his father. In other words, the play which was to "catch the
conscience of the king," reveals instead the conscience of Hamlet, "the
nephew" who does the killing and then "gets the love of the king's wife."
The substitution is Hamlet's own poetic contribution and confession.

The scene gives other hints of Hamlet's personal involvement by the way in which he plays off Ophelia against his mother. (It is the only scene in which Hamlet confronts both women at once). When his mother asks him to sit by her, Hamlet replies that Ophelia is "metal more attractive." He lies down at Ophelia's feet and indulges in sexual word-play within his mother's hearing—"Shall I lie in your lap . . . I mean my head upon your lap . . . That's a fair thought to lie between maid's legs." To Ophelia's remark that Hamlet is "keen," he replies: "It would cost you a groaning to take off mine edge."

Confession in the Closet

Hamlet had complained bitterly that he must hold his tongue even though his heart should break. But once he stands in his mother's room, he pours forth in unrestraint. From the moment when Hamlet is told that his mother wishes to speak with him "in her closet ere you go to bed," we feel that everything else is crowded out of his mind. When Hamlet is left alone, he speaks in metaphors which suggest that he is about to enter a hellish terrain where he is to "drink hot blood" and "speak daggers":[14]

> "By and by" is easily said.
> 'Tis now the very witching time of night,
> When churchyards yawn, and hell itself breaks out
> Contagion to this world: now could I drink hot blood,
> And do such bitter business as the day
> Would quake to look on. Soft! now to my mother.
> O heart, lose not thy nature, let not ever
> The soul of Nero enter this firm bosom;
> Let me be cruel, not unnatural:
> I will speak daggers to her, but use none;[15]

In the closet-scene, he uses related metaphors:

> Let me wring your heart, for so I shall,
> If it be made of penetrable stuff,
> If damned custom have not braz'd it so,
> That it be proof and bulwark against sense.

As soon as he enters, Hamlet assumes a commanding tone: "Come, come, and sit you down; you shall not budge." It is as though he wanted to assume his father's role who had "An eye like Mars, to threaten and command. . . ." Gertrude is frightened by her son's threatening manner and when the concealed Polonius calls for help, Hamlet stabs the "rat."[16]

Hamlet is not the least disturbed by his "bloody deed," and at once reverts to his earlier tone, ordering his mother to sit down and let him "wring" her heart, hoping that despite "damned custom," it is made of "penetrable stuff." Following the Ghost's disappearance, Hamlet harps on a single theme: He begs his mother not to go to bed with Claudius:

> . . . go not to my uncle's bed;
> . . . Refrain tonight,
> And that shall lend a kind of easiness
> To the next abstinence; the next more easy.[17]

In this scene, Hamlet catches his own conscience even more than he did in the playlet. Here, his antic disposition is discarded, exposing his innermost obsession. Hamlet outdoes himself in apotheosizing the father, but does not even allude to the mission with which the Ghost has entrusted him. He seems to have completely forgotten this "memory," harping only on Claudius' unworthiness of his mother's caresses. This provides the context for the entrance of the Ghost.

Hamlet alone knows (the Queen neither sees nor hears the Ghost) the reason for his father's appearance. Before the Ghost has spoken, Hamlet anticipates him:

> Do you not come your tardy son to chide,
> That laps'd in time and passion, lets go by
> The important acting of your dread command?

The Ghost appears in his wife's closet, dressed "in his habit as he liv'd" (the first Quarto has him appear in his bedroom attire) and, in effect tells Hamlet: What are you doing in my wife's bedroom? Your business is outside with Claudius. The Ghost is the censorious voice directed against the forbidden fantasies of the son.[18] The scene is Hamlet's distorted and frantic attempt to gain the gratification of his infantile and boyhood wish, a reenactment of the meeting between the mythic Mother-Goddess and the husband-son.[19]

Act III: The Sea-Journey and Home-Coming

Harold Rosenberg suggests that Hamlet's sea-voyage to England is a turning point and crisis of the drama.[20] In speaking of it, Hamlet says to Horatio:

> Sir, in my heart there was a kind of fighting,
> That would not let me sleep. . . .

On this journey, Hamlet again faces death, escapes both execution in England and murder by the pirates, and he himself kills Rosenkrantz and Guildensterm.

167

When Hamlet returns from England, his first meeting is once more with death in the grave-yard scene. At this point, we notice a marked change. Hamlet has become relatively serene, no longer swerves between melancholy and spryness, between concern with himself and cosmic speculations. It has been noted that the fifth act contains no soliloquies. Hamlet's orientation has shifted towards the We and he is now ripe for social identification. As he leaps into Ophelia's grave, he names himself generically (as Oedipus does in Colonus):

> . . . . This is I,
> Hamlet the Dane.

Hamlet's last words show concern, not for himself, but for his friend Horatio, for the state and the succession. Hamlet now realizes that his personal destiny is part of a general order, that "heaven ordinant" is operative in all that happens:

> There's a divinity that shapes our ends,
> Rough-hew them how we will.

Hamlet's sensibility has gone through the Protestant quest and he appears ready for Catholic acceptance. As he handles skeletons in the grave, he becomes aware of the democracy of death.

Hamlet tells Horatio that "providence" is operative even in the fall of a sparrow, but in his own case, it was a "special" providence. And, indeed, there is more accident than necessity in his discovery of Claudius' letter, his victory over the pirates, the exchange of the swords. Where the pre-Renaissance hero could regard his fate as a function of nature or of God, Hamlet is aware that what happened to him might have been averted or modified. He has gained the deep insight which he sums up in the words "the readiness is all" (in *King Lear*, it is "Ripeness is all"). But Hamlet's "readiness" is tinged with wistful sadness. "Thou wouldst not think," he tells Horatio, "how ill all's here about my heart, but it is no matter." His readiness is not for life but for death. In this mood, Hamlet does not believe that any traveller can return from the "undiscover'd country." He has lost all zest for carrying out his task and his killing the king is more a weary gesture than an act of revenge.[21]

Homecoming presupposes a home. If there is to be a third act of re-creation, we must have a first act of creation, or in Paul Claudel's line, "To know the end, one must know the beginning." The relative absence of tradition in Hebrew and American history results in a hesitant third act in the Book of Job and in *Moby Dick*. The complete rejection of tradition in existentialism precludes its heroes from meaningful engagement and rehabilitation. In *Hamlet*, the third mythic act is as questionable as is the nature of the ghostly father.[22]

168

Epilogue: Fortinbras-Horatio

Fortinbras and Horatio are the Ariadne-characters who link Hamlet's entrance into and exit from the labyrinth to which he is summoned by the Ghost.

Fortinbras is mentioned at the very beginning (his threat to the state is the reason for the midnight watch), and it is he who speaks the final line of the play. Unlike Hamlet, Fortinbras can act resolutely, lacking "the pale cast of thought" and "conscience" which makes "cowards." Moral considerations do not sway him, and he has "shark'd up a list of lawless resolutes" to recover "by strong hand" the lands his father has lost. On his journey to England, Hamlet learns that Fortinbras is on his way to Poland, ready to sacrifice twenty thousand men for "a little patch of land." Yet, here is Hamlet

> That have a father kill'd, a mother stain'd,
> Excitements of my reason and my blood,
> And let all sleep. . . .

Fortinbras has also had a father killed. But he does not think "too precisely on the event," and instead of seeking revenge, adopts a practical approach, demanding return of the land taken from his father. Moreover, he readily follows the decision of his uncle, his surrogate father-king, not to make war against Denmark.

But the extremes touch. Fortinbras, too, is intent on the game, not the gain, when he sets off to win "an egg-shell," finds "quarrel in a straw when honour's at the stake." Hamlet senses their affinity when he prophesies "the election lights on Fortinbras." As Hamlet dies, Fortinbras appears and bids "the soldiers shoot" in honor of Hamlet. Once again, Fortinbras acts in the interests of a cause as such. If Hamlet is an artist of play, Fortinbras is an artist of action.

Hamlet was born on the day when his father slew King Fortinbras. Ophelia's death marks the burial of Hamlet's ambiguous love and initiates his rebirth to "readiness." The rebirth ritual closes with his death and Fortinbras' succession.

Horatio is Hamlet's other replacement. If Fortinbras is the "strong arm," Horatio is the sensitive artist-observer. Like Ahab's Ishmael he has viewed the drama, and it is to him that Hamlet finally turns and asks

> If thou didst ever hold me in thy heart,
> Absent thee from felicity awhile,
> And in this harsh world draw thy breath in pain,
> To tell my story.

Despite the eclipse of the traditional mythic temper, Shakespeare's *Hamlet* reasserts certain mythic values which are connected with the very Renaissance sensibility which condition Hamlet's hesitations.

In a passage from the second scene of the last act, Osric is sent to ask Hamlet whether he will fence with Laertes. Osric is a kind of impersonal delegate, an example of what Riesman calls the attitude of other-directedness, of mouthing that which he thinks others expect or want him to say. Thus, when Hamlet says to him that it is hot, then that it is very cold, then that it is very sultry, Osric readily agrees, as had Polonius in Act III, when Hamlet played similarly on the theme of the shape of a cloud. After Osric, the "water-fly" leaves, Hamlet sums up the emerging temper of the new "drossy age":

> He did comply with his dug before he sucked it. Thus has he—and many more of the same breed that I know the drossy age dotes on—only got the tune of the time and outward habit of encounter; a kind of yeasty collection, which carries them through and through the most fond and winnowed opinions; and do but blow them to their trial, the bubbles are out.

As against such selling of one's beliefs (or "soul"), *Hamlet* would save the remnants of two traditions: feudal honor expressed in the Ghost's command to revenge his name, and the Renaissance value of individual conscience and sensibility. This sensibility is also exhibited by other characters: Laertes confesses his "foul practice" to Hamlet; the Queen reacts to her son's reproaches with "O Hamlet, thou hast cleft my heart in twain"; even Claudius feels a "heavy burden," is "full of discord and dismay."

Of the principal characters, only two remain to carry on Hamlet's legacy: Fortinbras and Horatio. Both are vital to the plot. Yet Shakespeare preserves their honor by involving them only peripherally in the action and passion of the court drama. We accept Fortinbras, not so much for what he actually does, but mainly because Hamlet calls him "a delicate and tender prince." And we accept Horatio primarily because Hamlet has faith in him. Horatio himself is not distinguished by what he says or does. Neither Fortinbras nor Horatio is *tested* on Shakespeare's stage. Hamlet gives his "dying voice" to a man he never meets, and asks his friend to "report" his cause which he himself did not get to know "aright."

THE ART OF THE DIALECTIC PARADOX

In *Shakespeare's Use of the Arts of Language* (New York, 1947). Sister Miriam Joseph notes that Shakespeare is "especially fond of negative terms which are the contradictories of the corresponding positive terms." She cites a study by Alfred Hart which shows that words beginning with the prefix *un* amount to nearly four per cent of Shakespeare's vocabulary and that a fourth of these belong to his own coinage; that he uses synoeciosis, a composition of contraries (such as "I must be cruel, only to be kind").

The art of Shakespeare's *Hamlet* receives its unique rhythm from the use of a paradoxical dialectic which shapes the dramatic structure, situation, language and dialogue of the play. Amidst it all, we feel that Hamlet is essentially alone. For all his verbal exchanges, Hamlet has no one to talk to, and must try to understand himself by debates between the conflicting elements within himself. Hamlet speaks and acts much like Nietzsche's lonely Cosmic Dancer. This produces a language which turns and leaps, rises and ebbs, swerves between poetry and prose, set in a changing atmosphere between shadows and light.

Hamlet would approximate the Renaissance ideal of the complete man. In Ophelia's words, he possesses "the courtier's, the soldier's, the scholar's eye, tongue, sword." He can do what the others can, and do it better: he knows more about acting than the players, fences better than Laertes, can plot and counterplot with Claudius and Polonius. He would heed the Ghost's "Remember me" and also the new humanism calling for individual responsibility. In sum, Hamlet would encompass the Whole. But the new age is on the threshold of specialized labor, and, specialization is hell for Hamlet as it was for Dante. Hamlet would resolve this dilemma by absolutizing each specialty. Put differently, he would "play" with each possibility, be the political actor and the artist actor, be both Sancho and Don Quixote.

The Seasonal Ritual

The play begins and concludes with motifs which suggest the ritual of the seasonal god. It opens with the theme of winter and death, and closes with the death of Hamlet and the promise of his rebirth in the figures of Horatio-Fortinbras. The platform scene presents the seasonal ritual in a mock-form. As Hamlet waits for the Ghost, he hears in the distance the sounds of Claudius' carousal, drinking his Rhenish wines. The Ghost reveals that the new king and his spring-like marriage celebration were false assumptions. At the end of the play, the death-duel takes on the character of a similar mock-celebration ("the queen carouses to thy fortune, Hamlet"), with the hope in the succession of Fortinbras.[23]

The elements of water, fire, earth and air are interwoven with the life and destiny of the characters and appear in a state of transition. At the beginning, they hold nature and man in an icy and eery grip. The Ghost emerges from "sulphurous and tormenting flames" and summons Hamlet towards his duty on earth. At the end, the elements are loosened and dissolved: Ophelia is drowned and brought to her earthy rest, the fire of the duel is followed by the drinking of the wine, and the play ends with Horatio's prayer that "flights of angels" accompany Hamlet on his way to heaven while Fortinbras bids the soldiers "shoot."

In Hamlet, the over-all character, the elements rage as in a tempest. He begins in a sluggish state, wishing that the "solid (or sullied) flesh" would "melt." The Ghost's message instils him with the fire of revenge which unfolds itself in wild and whirling movements, in passions which would "drink hot blood," in an airy dialectic of "words." At the end, he contemplates man's earthy origin and destiny, leaps into Ophelia's grave, is wounded by the fiery poison of Laertes' sword, and is led off to the accompaniment of Horatio's heavenly invocation and the "music" of Fortinbras' soldiers.

If the opening midnight scene suggests a terrain somewhere between hell and heaven, and the ending invokes "flights of angels," the drama proper is enacted on earth.[24] This earth is weedy or "rotten." Claudius is the master of this earthly kingdom with his adviser Polonius "feeding" him maggots and carrion (the metaphors associated with his character). Gertrude is the vegetative, earthy element, fluid in her unresisting acceptance and surrender, finally "drowning" in the poisoned wine.[25] The references to Ophelia are in terms of a "sweet spring-flower," until she is awakened to sensuality in her mad songs. She is watery in her soft and submissive nature (Hamlet calls her a "nymph"), giving in to the slighest pressure of her father and brother. In the play as a whole, the elements appear as a human tempest. In Shakespeare's last work, the nature-elements are liberated from their distortions in the human-wordly frame and return to their native "tempest."

Shakespeare's *Hamlet* is the richest expression of English Renaissance mythopoesis. The work is the high center of Shakespeare's own dramatic art. The Hamlet-problem begins with Brutus ("poor Brutus, with himself at war") who does not belong in "the world." Neither do Macbeth, Othello and King Lear, all of whom are touched by what Friedrich Gumdolf calls "strange powers." In *The Tempest*, the problem is resolved by magic. Ferdinand is a Hamlet whose father's ghost is an unquestionable spirit, and who returns to become king. This Hamlet marries his Ophelia, undisturbed by personal discords. But the happy ending becomes possible only by being set in a fairy world in which life is "such stuff as dreams are made on." Where Claudius and Polonius appear as potent forces in Hamlet's fate, Gonzalo and Antonius are not given serious roles and are nearly irrelevant to the central action. *The Tempest* reverses the order of reality. Here, practical political strategy is illusion, and magic becomes reality; here, "the play is the thing" and the whole thing. Shakespeare has moved from the human-political tempest of Brutus-Hamlet-Macbeth-Lear-Othello to the nature-tempest of the elements for which man is an object of play. Prospero gladly abdicates in favor of worldly forces which seem to him trivial compared to the power of his poetic magic. The tragic myth of *Hamlet* is resolved in the magic fairy tale of *The Tempest*.

NOTES

1. Ernest Jones' *Hamlet and Oedipus* (New York, 1949) cites studies showing that "the Norse and Irish variants . . . are descended from the ancient Iranian legend of Kaikhosrav . . . some members of which can be traced back to the beginning of history." There were Hamlet Ballad-Cycles in Iceland and there is an allusion to Hamlet as a nature myth in the Edda. Although the story is originally a Scandinavian saga, the name of the hero, Amlothi, has no discoverable Germanic etymology. One scholar suggests that the first part of the name, Aml, means "labor without much progress," and that the whole compound may be rendered as "annoyingly mad." Cf. Sir Israel Gollancz, *The Sources of Hamlet* (London, 1926); Th. M. Parrott and H. Craig, *The Tragedy of Hamlet* (Princeton, 1936); Kemp Malone, *The Literary History of Hamlet* (Heidelberg, 1923).

2. The Ghost ascribes Claudius' success in winning over Gertrude to "witchcraft of his wits," by which he gained "the will of my most seeming-virtuous queen." We may reasonably identify the Ghost's view with Hamlet's own "prophetic voice." In any case, the mother as saint is normal for the boyhood state. In her case, as in that of Ophelia, we can surmise Hamlet's earlier view by his later extreme reaction, when the mother becomes a prostitute, and "celestial" Ophelia fit for a "nunnery," or a house of ill fame.

3. The Ghost is the summoner or "herald" (in the third act, Hamlet refers to his father as "the herald Mercury"). Here, Hamlet reveals unhesitating courage, is ready to follow the Ghost though it "tempt" him "toward the flood," the "dreadful summit of a cliff," or draw him "into madness." The opening scene marvelously creates the mood of *foreboding* and of *transition*: The change from night to day, the irregular challenge in the change of guards, foreboding some "strange eruption." In the next scene, we hear that the funeral of Hamlet's father, followed by the Queen's remarriage produced "mirth in funeral . . . dirge in marriage . . . delight and dole," and learn of the peace-war situation created by the demands of Fortinbras. This disjointed dialectic dominates the play as a whole, its mood and metaphors, its action and philosophic expression.

4. Some critics ascribe Hamlet's delay to external factors. Since the murder was not an open act, it is argued, Hamlet must make certain that Claudius is the murderer; furthermore, he must prove publicly that it was Claudius, lest he himself be judged a murderer; finally, that Hamlet simply lacked the opportunity to kill Claudius until the end.

A. C. Bradley (*Shakespearean Tragedy* [London, 1949]), has effectively disposed of this theory. He points out: 1) Hamlet himself never refers to external difficulties. 2) Hamlet assumes that he *can* obey the Ghost. 3) Hamlet need have no fear of reprisal, as shown by the ease with which Laertes rouses the people against Claudius.

In Belleforest, Hamlet's difficulties are mainly external. Moreover, his Hamlet wants more than revenge; he seeks the crown, and to gain it, he must conquer not only Claudius, but his supporters as well. In Shapespeare, Hamlet has no such problem. He *can* be king. He has Claudius' public promise, and he is loved by the "distracted multitude."

Bradley also refutes the view that Hamlet is held back by ethical considerations. He indicates that Hamlet is not restrained by moral scruples. He stabs Polonius; he readily sends Rosenkrantz and Guildenstern to their deaths (although he is not certain of their guilt), telling Horatio that "they are not near my conscience."

On the question of Hamlet's making sure that the king is the murderer: Hamlet does not have absolute certainty, but he clearly has the strongest suspicion from the beginning. The King's reaction to the Gonzago play provides a public manifestation of guilt before the whole court.

A word on the argument that Hamlet needs to convince the court of Claudius' guilt: Hamlet, it is said, is a Renaissance man who loves life, and will not endanger it lightly. To ascribe Hamlet's central dilemma to fear of reprisal is to trivialize his character. He shows no fear in following the Ghost, in striking through the curtain to stab Polonius. Hamlet is not afraid to die. He tells Horatio:

> "Why, what should be the fear?
> I do not set my life at a pin's fee. . . ."

5. A. A. Smirnov, *Shakespeare. A Marxist Interpretation*, The Critics Group, No. 2 (New York, 1936). Similarly, Roy Walker's *The Time Is Out of Joint. A Study of Hamlet* (London, 1948) sees the play as the tragedy of a noble man, limited by a "body politic . . . poisoned at the ear, accepting fair appearances for fair reality." He holds that Hamlet is separated from his group by an impassable gulf and has "no real communication with the creatures of this world."

6. In the section on the mythic mechanism of "decomposition," Jones shows how the father-son conflict recurs in the interrelationships among Hamlet, Laertes, Polonius and Ophelia.

The psychoanalytic approach is validated only if the esthetic and the historic are considered in its context. Indeed, one could maintain that literary analysis, if it penetrates deeply enough, should come to much the same conclusion. A. C. Bradley's study is an early example. Bradley holds that the key to Hamlet's inactivity, hesitancy and procrastination lies in his "profound melancholy," where "melancholy" is used in the Elizabethan sense of nervous instability and moral sensibility. Bradley does not propose to inquire into the factors which make for Hamlet's state, saying that Shakespeare simply meant to portray "a pathological condition." Yet, in his actual analysis, Bradley is on the edges of psychoanalytic formulation. He writes of Hamlet's "unconscious self-excuses, [his] unconscious weaving of pretexts for inactivity" which he is unable to understand. He hesitatingly suggests that the kind of melancholy from which Hamlet suffers can be symptomatically expressed in paralysis or even perversion of love. He notes that the Hamlet who must hold his tongue suddenly becomes most eloquent in his mother's chamber "beside his father's marriage-bed." As to Hamlet's relation to Ophelia, Bradley says he does not understand it, but adds the suggestive footnote that "there are signs that Hamlet was haunted by the horrible idea that he had been deceived in Ophelia as he had been in his mother."

J. Dover Wilson (*What Happens in Hamlet* [London, 1935]) also speaks of Hamlet's emotional instability, notes his personal inadequacy, and that Hamlet loved Ophelia before his mother took off the rose "from the fair forehead of an innocent love." As Jones observes, Wilson is sometimes close to noting Hamlet's incestuous tendencies; but Wilson himself has argued against Jones' interpretation.

7. Jones adds that the identification may also be seen in Hamlet's killing the men (Polonius and Claudius) who stand between him and his mother.

8. Upon her death, Hamlet leaps into the grave, announcing "I lov'd Ophelia," more than forty thousand "brothers." But the love of "brothers," even of forty thousand, is not what is called for. In the primitive plot, as reconstructed by Kemp Malone, Amleth rapes his sister or foster sister, and reveals his animal sexuality.

9. Hamlet's announced intention was to use the Murder of Gonzago to catch the conscience of the king. But he becomes more interested in the effectiveness and skill of the performance, as art and drama, than in its effect on Claudius. When the King has risen, Hamlet asks Horatio whether his skill could not get him "a fellowship in a cry of players." For the most comprehensive study to date of the psychoanalytic literature on Shakespeare, see Norman H. Holland, *Psychoanalysis and Shakespeare* (New York, Toronto, London, 1964).

10. Hamlet's identification with Claudius is also indicated by the similar terms both use in condemning themselves. Hamlet calls himself "a whore" (III,2) and Claudius calls himself a harlot (III,1).

11. Hamlet addresses the Ghost first as King, then as Father; the Ghost's first words to Hamlet are "Mark me," and his last "Remember me!". Ernest Jones remarks that where hostility towards the father is repressed, it is often accompanied "by the development of the opposite sentiment, namely of an exaggerated regard and respect for him."

175

12. Bradley notes that Hamlet is so afraid that he will forget his father's command that he writes it down in black and white "to force him to remember and to believe."

13. Another ambiguity is the reference to *the duke* Gonzago whose actual murder in Vienna is supposedly imaged in Hamlet's playlet.

14. Before Hamlet goes, he temporizes, as one might before entering on a vital mission. He admonishes Guildenstern for trying to "pluck out the heart of my mystery," at the very moment when he is about to reveal his mystery to his mother. In his word-play with Polonius, Hamlet indulges in child-like trans-formations of objects (cloud-camel-weasel-whale). When Polonius' agrees that the cloud looks like a whale, Hamlet breaks off with the words: "Then I will come to my mother by and by." (In mythology, the whale, or its belly, repre-sents the World Womb or the Earthly Paradise.) There follow the lullaby words "By and by" repeated three times.

15. J. Dover Wilson thinks that the "bitter business" refers to Claudius. Yet, com-menting on Hamlet's very next words ("Soft! now to my mother"), he writes that Hamlet "has forgotten the King altogether."

   Hamlet's first words are spoken outside her room. He calls out "Mother, mother, mother!" as though he were warning her or himself that it is his "mother" he is about to see. At the same time, he wishes, as he later tells her, "it were not so."

16. Hamlet asks: "Is it the king," and later says that he took Polonius for his "bet-ter." But does Hamlet really believe that he has killed the king? He had just left Claudius in a mood of prayer—hardly a prelude to eavesdropping. More-over, Hamlet heard Polonius cry out. He knows this voice well, has heard it more frequently than any other and could hardly confuse it with the king's voice.

17. Hamlet embroiders Gertrude's sexual relations with Claudius, speaking of "the rank sweat of an enseamed bed," of the king "paddling" her neck "with his damn'd fingers." It is a kind of vicarious sex-indulgence on Hamlet's part.

18. Hamlet had left his surrogate-father at prayer, on the way to "heaven," where he cannot obstruct Hamlet's "business" with his mother. But "the father" does appear, and precisely as Hamlet goes all out depreciating Claudius in favor of the dead father. Does Hamlet's reference to "A king of shreds and patches—" (at which point the Ghost enters) express an ambiguity as to which "king" he has in mind?

   Roy Walker notes that in his second appearance the Ghost does not em-phasize the revenge, but calls on Hamlet to be gentle and merciful with his mother. Is Hamlet's "mind's eye" now more open to seeing that the revenge-motive could no longer be accepted as a respectable explanation for his bad dreams?

19. In the first Quarto, the Queen condemns Claudius and agrees to assist Hamlet in "what strategem soe're thou shalt devise."

   Frederic Wertham has advanced the theory that Hamlet wants to kill his mother, not his father ("The Matricidal Impulse. Critique of Freud's Interpretation of Hamlet," *Journal of Criminal Psychopathology*, Vol. II, No. 4 [April, 1941]). Wertham grants that "the basis of Hamlet's hostility against his mother is his over-attachment to her," but argues that "this over-attachment to the mother need not necessarily lead to hatred against the father." He cites passages to show that Hamlet expresses no direct hatred against the father and no direct love for his mother and concludes that the analogy between Oedipus and Hamlet does not hold. Freud pointed out that in a more sophisticated era, Hamlet represses the wish fantasy, and that we discover it "only through the inhibitory effects which proceed from it."

20. In myths (as in dreams), rescue from water is connected with birth. In mythopoesis, this is approximated in Aeneas' sea-journey; Dante passes into Hell through the river Styx, into Purgatory by way of the frozen waters of Cocytus which receives all the rivers of the Inferno, and finally into Paradise after having drunk from the waters of Lethe and Eunoë. Other examples are Siegfried's Rhine-journey, Ahab's roamings in the Pacific, Aschenbach's crossing into Venice, the wandering of Thomas Mann's Joseph along the Nile and the water-journey of Grigors in Mann's *Holy Sinner*.

21. Even here, he needs to be reminded of his duty by Laertes who calls out to him: "the king, the king's to blame." In Laurence Olivier's film, Hamlet kills Claudius in the manner of a Western hero who finally gets his enemy. This mars Olivier's otherwise sensitive and consistent production.

22. Hamlet returns from England "naked" and "alone," as he writes Claudius. His rebirth into naked aloneness is followed by his death.

23. An old study (A. Zinzow, 1877) cited by Ernest Jones in *Hamlet and Oedipus*, examines *Hamlet* as a nature-myth, and modern scholarship (Gollancz) holds that the story may have borrowed from the Northern myth of the struggle between spring and winter.

24. The scheme is analogous to Goethe's *Faust* whose Prologue brings the Lord, the Angels and Mephistopheles on a common platform and whose final scene tells of Faust's Assumption.

25. It has been suggested that Gertrude is connected with the vegetation goddess Nerthus and with Groa, the Mother-Earth giant in the Orwendel myth of the Edda.

Teutonic Inwardness

Faust

OSWALD SPENGLER characterized Western culture as "Faustian" in its restless striving towards an ever-receding goal. In our own time, F. S. C. Northrop restated Spengler's designation of Western man in terms of time-metaphors, the arrow in flight and the river in motion:

> The Westerner represents time either with an arrow or as a moving river which comes out of a distant place and past which are not here and now, and which goes into an equally distant place and future which are also not here and now. (*The Meeting of East and West* [New York, 1946.])

Similarly, Wyndham Lewis argued in *Time and Western Man* that the West is pledged to the homage of time. This category is central to the Faustian folktale in which Faustus is granted a period of twenty-four years in which to indulge himself at will, after which he is to suffer hell-fire for all time. In this sense, Faustianism may be viewed as an insatiable appetite for limitless experience.

This salute to time—to Father Chronos—began with Western mythopoesis. Aeschylus' Prometheus is confident that time will deliver him from bondage; his Orestes is freed by the passage of time. The Renaissance period raised time to "a gift of God" (as Goethe puts it in *Wilhelm Meister*). This gift served individual and social expansionism, and culminated in the theories of progress by Renan, Turgot, Condorcet and Spencer. In the nineteenth century, Schopenhauer countered this trend by arguing that striving was an expression of the Satanic will. For Marx, history brought class societies with the promise of classless societies. Similarly, Melville saw both good and evil in Ahab's chase of Moby Dick and Nietzsche affirmed both the progressive transvaluations of the Superman and the theory of Eternal Recurrence. In our day, Spengler, and to a degree, Toynbee, question the equating of time with progress.

Teutonic Mythology

Teutonic mythology has three central features which are best expressed by their German terms: *Gemeinschaft* (collective solidarity), *Innerlichkeit* (inner directedness), and *Werden* (ceaseless development). They appear metaphorically in Goethe's *Faust*—his forest and cave ("Wald und Höhle") and his restless wandering.

Common to these features is German *Maasslosigkeit* or unrestraint. This temper tends to convert *Gemeinschaft* into totalitarianism, *Innerlichkeit* into isolative retreat, *Werden* into imperialist expansion for *Lebensraum*. Here, solidarity may coexist with individualism, spirituality with materialism, ceaseless striving with stasis or *Ruh*. The swing between extremes appears in another feature of Teutonic mythology: the connection between song and war. Odin or Wotan is the God of both, with war used as a sanction for song. Happiness in Valhalla consists in living as a warrior; even the goddesses, the Valkyries, are fierce and strong, rather than beautiful. And war is conceived as necessary and universal, leading to the *Götterdämmerung*, (*ragnarök*), as foretold to Odin by the "Wise Woman" in the Poetic Edda:

> Brothers shall fight and fell each other,
> And sisters' sons shall kinship stain;
> Hard is it on earth, with mighty whoredom;
> Ax-time, sword-time, shields are sundered,
> Win-time, wolf-time, ere the world falls;
> Nor ever shall men each other spare.
> (*Voluspa*, Bellows translation [New York, 1923]).

Finally, what happens to the Teutonic world is extended to the fate of the world as a whole. With the twilight of their gods, the entire universe comes to an end—a foreshadowing of Spengler's thesis that the defeat of Germany in the First World War was synonymous with the decline of the West.

Yet, this mythology also has reference to an initial and final harmony. The Edda speaks of an original Golden Age of peace which is to be reinstated following the destruction of the world, when Baldur will come back and a new green earth will arise.

Germanic Kultur-Freedom

These characteristic of Teutonic mythology are manifested in later German history. They are expressed in the rampant voluntarism of Schopenhauer's and Nietzsche's thought, in the dynamic pace of German industrialism which sought to outdistance its rivals, if necessary,

179

by warlike means. From its semi-nomadic beginnings to the Prussian *Herrenvolk*, Germany was dominated by arrogant leaders ruling over a submissive *Gefolgschaft*.

Germany remained feudal long after other leading European countries had had their Renaissance. The German Reformation offered a chance for a break with this tradition. Goethe called it a "turning point of German history," for the age of Luther, Erasmus, Melanchthon seemed to him—as to Thomas Mann—to have held the greatest promise for establishing a humanistic German tradition. His Faust and Goetz, conceived simultaneously, are both German figures and are connected with the Protestant rebellion. Goetz is defeated in his Robin Hood adventures and Faust is condemned to hell-fire in the chapbooks. Their fate is bound up with a crucial event in German history: the Peasant Rebellion.

The Peasant Rebellion in 1529 was the first realistic German effort towards social-economic emancipation, similar to that which the French gained in 1789. Alexander von Humboldt called its failure pivotal for German history and Georg Lukacs argues in *Goethe und seine Zeit* (Bern, 1947) that the entire development of Germany was determined by this event. As a result of the Peasants' defeat, Germany continued in semi-feudalism under its Junker ideology, in contrast to the national bourgeois culture which France and England developed.

To compensate for its economic-social bondage, German thinkers developed the concept of Kultur-freedom, where the greatness of German thought was seen in its *not* having any connection with material reality. It evolved systems of "pure" metaphysics, music, mysticism and mythology from Kant's invocation of the moral law within and the starry heavens above, to Max Weber's notion of science as a vocation (*Wissenschaft als Beruf*) and Karl Mannheim's position that the intellectual viewpoint is non-partisan. This *Innerlichkeit* also makes itself felt in the absence of a realistic and critical tradition, such as the French have from Montaigne, Moliere, Diderot and Voltaire to Balzac, Flaubert, Zola, Barbusse and Aragon, or the English from Defoe to Dickens and Shaw, or the Russians from Gogol to Gorky. In place of realistic revolutions, such as the Puritan, the French and the American, the Germans produced theoretic rebellions: Kant's Copernican Revolution, Schiller's call for *Gedankenfreiheit* and for moral-esthetic education, the "Blue Flower" and "Magic Idealism" of its Romantic schools. Above all, it manifested itself in the German penchant for music—music as a specifically German affair ("eine deutsche Angelegenheit"), as it reappears in Mann's *Magic Mountain* and *Doctor Faustus*.

In practice, this airy rebellion turned into a servile bowing to *Ordnung*. Luther assailed subservience in theology, yet condemned the German peasants when they attempted to translate the theory into economic practice. Kant's Copernican Revolution went hand in hand with his appeal to the "good will" and with his submission to changing forms of authority in Prussia. The German Romantic poets readily descended from their sidereal heights to become passionate adherents of the Junker war against Napoleon, and Wagner's revolutionary conception of Siegfried was followed by his "Kaisermarsch." In our own day, most of the advocates of un-political *Kultur* became Hitler's professors, poets, scientists and philosophers. The whole presents the complex of spiritual freedom and political sycophancy, of arrogance and flunkeyism, or as Troeltsch formulates it, of mysticism and brutality.

To be sure, Germany's idealistic version of freedom contained an element of internationalism. But, divorced from political realities, it lent itself to becoming the tool of an universal expansionism. It allowed the translation of Siegfried into Bismarck and Hitler. In Goethe's work, this association appears in the partnership between Faust and Mephistopheles.

GOETHE'S SOCIAL AND PERSONAL BURDEN

No other mythopoeic work is so closely bound up with its author's life as *Faust* on which Goethe spent about sixty years, from his late adolescence to a few months before his death.

Biographers have generally presented Goethe as a serene "Olympian." This view has been corrected, in Barker Fairley's study and most extensively in K. R. Eissler's psychoanalytic examination of Goethe. A reading of Ludwig Lewisohn's selections from the letters, diaries and works reveals Goethe as driven and harried, from the storm and stress of his youth to the seventy-three year old man who fell violently in love with a seventeen year old girl.[1] Goethe's restlessness also expresses itself in continuous "travels": from one locality to another, from one literary and scientific effort to another, and from one love object to another.

Goethe, like Shakespeare, spanned the transition from the medieval to the bourgeois era, and like him, attempted to unite the residual value of each. For Goethe, these forces were embodied in three geographic centers—Frankfort, where he was born, Weimar, where he spent the greater part of his life and Italy, where he sought to find a symbolic home. Frankfort represented the new bourgeois civilization, Weimar the passing feudal scene, with Italy envisaged as transcending both.

Frankfort offered "life." But this life consisted primarily of commercial and banking activity. Goethe called it "a rotten hole," complaining of its bad taste, "the discrepancy between the narrowness and slow tempo of middle class existence and the wideness and swiftness" of his character. Goethe was buoyed by its energy, but repelled by its insensitivity to poetic values.

In Frankfort, Goethe met Lili Schoenemann (she came from a Catholic family of brokers) towards whom he exhibited a similar ambivalence. Goethe told Sorel towards the end of his life that he loved Lili profoundly and had never been so close to happiness as he was with her. Yet, Goethe was "not able to marry her," for she was "an alien new existence," to whom he had "nothing to say." He felt a stranger in her "carnival" circle.[2] Goethe welcomed the call to Weimar partly because it offered him the chance to escape this girl who seemed to paralyze his will.

Although Weimar was a tiny principality, Goethe preferred it because its very feudal tradition offered the artist more encouragement than he could find in the banking city of Frankfort. But he soon realized that little Weimar was another form of "the business of the world." Here, he felt himself "a poor slave," bound to the Duke in whom "again and again the child and the donkey peep out." He had fled from Frankfort to Weimar, and now had to flee from Weimar to Italy. On his return, he removed himself even more from Weimar society, as well as from "the formlessness of Germany," where "no one understands my language," where there is "nothing left but the Philistine," and injustice is the order of the day. Goethe withdrew more and more from its political and social life, stood aloof from the nationalistic fervor of the Wars of Liberation. At the age of seventy-four, he told Müller that he wished to emigrate, if only he knew where.

While Goethe felt that he had no German public to whom he could communicate his deepest feelings, the problem was complicated by the fact that he felt himself part of this very public. He realized, as he wrote Schiller, that one cannot "separate his ship from the very waves that bear it."[3] And Goethe was no revolutionary.

Parents and Lovers

Goethe's attitude towards his father and mother was roughly analogous to that towards the business town of Frankfort and the duchy of Weimar.

The father, Goethe said, gave him "stature." But it was the stature

of a stern didactic commander, a man of "iron strictness . . . unbeliev-
able consistency . . . uninterrupted determination," with whom the
son could not establish "any kind of agreeable relationship." Instead
of studying law in Strassburg, where his father had sent him, Goethe
spent his time courting Friederike Brion and writing poetry.[4]

Goethe contrasted the exactitude of his father with his mother from
whom he got his gayety and imaginativeness ("die Frohnatur" and "die
Lust zum Fabulieren"). She was nearer in years to her son than to her
husband and Goethe called her "almost a child herself." In his Supplement to *Poetry and Truth* (Lewisohn, *Goethe*, I,7), Goethe wrote that
she "had not lived only for her son's sake but her son had lived for her
sake." The only girl to whom he became engaged—Lili Schoenemann—
was the one whom his mother favored. Goethe's attachment to his
mother appears to have had a secret, guilty element manifesting itself
by the strange distance he maintained towards her. More than once,
she delicately reminded her son of his rare visits—"It is now five years
since you've been here, and that is no joke." She complained to Lavater
that her son compensated her occasionally with "a magnificent letter,"
and begged Fritz von Stein to keep a diary of Goethe's doings, so that
she might know more about him, adding that if she were an actress,
she might do "the part of Hamlet's mother not ill."[5]

In his autobiography *Poetry and Truth*, Goethe frankly wrote of his
sensual relation to his sister Cornelia: ". . . she had accompanied me
through my whole conscious existence and therefore we were most
profoundly united." Together, they shared "the awakening of sensual
instincts," and Cornelia's only desire was to live "in the harmony of her
sisterly relation to me . . . it never seemed to me either natural or pleas-
ing to think of her as a wife; rather should she have been an abbess or
the head of some distinguished order." When Goethe heard that Schlosser was wooing her, he felt somewhat "dismayed," adding that "it was
only now that I confessed to myself that I was really jealous of my
sister." About the same time, the two "had drawn closer to each other
than ever." In turn, she was upset when Goethe became engaged to
Lili Schoenemann, and "begged" him, indeed "commanded" him "to
break with Lili."

Nearly all the women whom Goethe courted have some underground connection with his mother and sister. In his essay on "Goethe's
Romance with Friederike" in *Fragment of a Great Confession* (New
York, 1949), Theodor Reik points out that there is a repetitive pattern
in Goethe's relation to women: Violent falling in love, a period of torment and vacillation, followed by flight."[6] In his early poem to Friede-

rike Brion "Welcome and Departure," Goethe prophetically foreshadowed this pattern: He either ran away from those who were available—Friederike, Lili—or wooed those who were unavailable—Charlotte Buff, Charlotte von Stein, Marianne von Willemer, Ulrike von Levetzow—who were either engaged or married, too old or too young for him.[7] This is especially clear in Goethe's extraordinary love for Charlotte von Stein who was seven years older than Goethe and a mother of seven children.

Charlotte von Stein came into Goethe's life following his sister's marriage, and a poem of his would have it that long, long ago, she had been his sister or wife:

> Ach du warst in abgelebten Zeiten
> Meine Schwester oder meine Frau.

After he became attached to Charlotte, the thought of visiting his mother "doesn't even skim the surface of my mind. You have so absorbed me that I have no sensibility left for the other duties of my heart." She became, as he wrote Lavater, not only "the heir of my mother, my sister," but also "a sweetheart."

Goethe's need for Charlotte von Stein was intertwined with his need for Weimar where he met her. Weimar was the feudal-nature retreat to which Goethe fled from the bustle of Frankfort. Likewise, Goethe sought in Charlotte a curb on his stormy adolescence which had been unloosened in his relation to Friederike Brion and Charlotte Buff. She soothed the angry racing of his blood and, in her angelic arms, his breast found rest ("Tropfest Mässigung dem heissen Blute, richtetest den wilden, irren Lauf, und in deinen Engelsarmen ruhte die zerstörte Brust sich wieder auf."). He called his relationship to her "the purest, loveliest, truest that ever I had with a woman, except my sister." She became the Iphigenia who controlled the wild impulses of his Orestes. But, once again, Goethe fled. He felt the need to "wean" himself from Charlotte and wrote from Rome that the chief purpose of his Italian journey "was to cure myself of those physical and moral ills which plagued me in Germany."[8]

From now on, Goethe gave up the quest for a full union with a woman. Christiane Vulpius whom he brought into his house following his return from Italy, had worked in a flower factory and was thirteen years younger than Goethe. Christiane showed little interest in Goethe's writings, indeed, could not spell correctly. But she brought Goethe gayety and, above all, physical comfort, without making any social demands on him. This was, of course, no real marriage, even though Goethe legalized the union in 1806 (after Christiane saved his life from

a threatened attack by French soldiers during the Wars of Liberation).
Christiane was little more than a housekeeper and *Bettschatz*, rarely
addressed him with the familiar *du*, calling him "dear, kind Privy Councillor" even after their marriage.[9]

Goethe had "an unhappy nervous fear of marriage," as Schiller put
it. According to Müller's Diary (September 14, 1823), Goethe stated
that love "belongs in the realm of the ideal, marriage in that of the real,
and never are these two realms united with impunity." Goethe never
really married, in line with the pledge which the legendary Faustus
made to the devil. What he missed in life, he tried to create in symbolic forms. In another connection, he told Heinrich Luden (December
13, 1813) that he was trying to "transcend" the "wretched" German
people through science and art, adding that "I have found the wings
to bear me beyond these griefs."

But no degree of symbolic transformation can take the place of
missed experience. A deep and tragic dichotomy remained in Goethe's
life and "two souls" penetrate his symbolic world. They appear in the
contrasted characters of Goetz and Werther, Prometheus and Gany-
med, Prometheus and Epimetheus, Iphigenia and Orestes, Antonio and
Tasso, Mephisto and Faust.[10]

THE FAUST LEGEND

E. M. Butler's *Myth of the Magus* (New York, 1948) shows that the
Faustian theme belongs in the tradition of the pre-Christian magus and
derives from seasonal and kingship rites. Indeed, the attempt to gain
superhuman power by magic is an ancient motif, found in Persian
legends, the Hebrew Kabbalah, Arabic mysticism, neo-Platonism and
in St. Augustine.

In the sixteenth century German chapbooks by Spiess and Widman,
Faustus is damned. His defiance of church dogma, his use of magic to
gain pleasure and power are treated from the medieval perspective as
unforgivable sins. When his twenty-four years are up, Faustus is dismembered and sent into Hell-Fire. Faustus' willingness to give up eternal bliss for a few years of pleasure appears as a foolish act, "a warning and example to all good Christians, so that they shall not . . . injure
their souls and bodies like Doctor Faustus did."[11]

Although Faustus is damned, he represents the emerging Renaissance values of pleasure, wealth, widening experience and individual
power. And Renaissance writers in the age of Don Juan, the Borgias,

185

Luther, Erasmus, Melanchthon, Leonardo and Columbus depict Faustus not merely as a pursuer of ignoble lust, but also as a proud titan with a thirst for knowledge. Paracelsus calls the devil his friend and companion, and the Lord in Goethe's *Faust* declares that Mephisto can "create as devil."[12]

This new view is apparent in Marlowe's *Doctor Faustus*, although it appeared in the era of the German chapbooks. Writing in a land where middle class values had found firmer roots than they did in Germany, the English dramatist can treat Faustus' aspirations with a greater degree of sympathy. Marlowe's hero is a tragic figure whose eternal damnation is out of proportion to his twenty-four years of sinning. The miserable weakling of the *Volksbuch* becomes a "sound magician" and "demi-god" in Marlowe's drama. He wants more than wordly pleasure; he desires boundless power and honor, to be on earth "as Jove is in the sky." The opening chorus tells of his Icarus nature and foreshadows his Icarus fate. Faustus excels

> In heavenly matters of theology;
> Till swollen with cunning and self-conceit
> His waxen wings did mount above his reach,
> And, melting, Heavens conspired his overthrow.

Marlowe is the first to *interiorize* the myth by suggesting that Faustus' good and evil angels are within himself. This is indicated in Mephistophilis' definition of Hell as the absence of Heaven:

> Why this Hell, nor am I out of it:
> Think'st thou that I who saw the face of God,
> And tasted the eternal joys of Heaven,
> Am not tormented with ten thousand Hells
> In being deprived of everlasting bliss?

This Faustus is in "hell" *before* he is delivered into its fire. As soon as he signs the pact, he begins to waver, uncertain whether honor and wealth are worth the sacrifice of heaven. At the end, his remorse amounts to a renunciation of the pact.

Although Marlowe's Faustus is damned, he emerges as the titanic scapegoat to medieval and church authority, to its denigration of experience, knowledge and beauty. Particularly beauty. In the *Volksbuch*, Helen is a devilish figure who involves Faustus in a "swinish and epicurean life." In Marlowe, love of beauty helps Faustus alleviate his despair. And Butler observes, that this "gave a tragic significance to Helen which she had not had before." Marlowe's Faustus is damned primarily because his quest is for *individual* personal gain, to be "great emperor of the world." He rejects his society completely and in turn is rejected by it.

The German dramatist Lessing is the first writer to indicate that Faust is to be saved. In his dramatic sketch, *D. Faust,* Faust is exposed to the devil precisely because of his thirst for science and knowledge, a thirst which according to the top devil, makes certain that Faust will be his.[13] But, when the hellish tribe believes that it has succeeded, their triumph is interrupted by the voice of an angel: "You have not won over humanity and science. The Godhead did not give man the most noble urge in order to render him eternally unhappy. What you saw and believed to possess was nothing more than a phantom." Lessing did not develop this theme in his sketch, but it is implicit in his life-long struggle for intellectual and social freedom, in his *Education of the Human Race* and *Nathan the Wise.*

Goethe's Mythic Thinking

George Santayana's *Three Philosophical Poets* interprets Goethe's *Faust* as the philosophy of German romanticism. It is a matter of record, however, that Goethe rejected the romantic in favor of the classic and vigorously opposed the Romanticists' esteem of the old Germanic Edda, and the Middle Ages. He found the Norse legends bizarre, rigid and gloomy, the Nibelungen fable extravagant and monstrous, the gods of Friedrich Schlegel's Vedic India formless.[14] His *Faust* draws but little on Germanic mythology, and instead incorporates multiple mythic themes, from the Oriental, the Hebrew and Graeco-Roman to the Italian and English Renaissance. Goethe traced his cultural heritage primarily to non-Germanic sources—the Greeks, the French, Shakespeare. He paid homage to Kalidasa's Sakuntala and the Persian poet Hafis, to Slavic, Lithuanian and world poetry in general. He aimed to speak "above the nations," telling Eckermann (March 15, 1829) that one should regard "the weal and woe of a neighboring people as though it were one's own."

Goethe's interests were indeed nearly universal and he leaned towards those thinkers who stressed unity and universality. He was attracted to philosophy to the extent that "it unites," to Spinoza for strengthening his belief that he "who wills the highest must will the whole."[15] Long before Fechner and Whitehead, Goethe opposed what Hocking calls "the bifurcation of nature." His "symphronistic method" aimed to find the recurrent phase, the primal phenomenon or *Urphäno-*

187

men; in botany, the *Urpflanze*, in the animal world, the *Urtier*. The key-words in his vocabulary are "world" and "unity." Wilhelm Meister's "pedagogic province" is dominated by the concepts of world-view, world-community, world-piety. Finally, Goethe was among the first to advocate the promotion of "World Literature."

The great Dante scholar, Karl Vossler, regards *The Divine Comedy* and *Faust* as the only instances in which a writer "grasps and draws to itself all culture and the entire world, absorbs them, recreates them lifelike in a single work of art." Yet, while Dante's epic is organically knit and the product of a few years' concentrated effort, Goethe's poem was produced over a period of some sixty years. Dante's work summarizes some thirteen centuries of Christianity; Goethe's embraces nearly all of Western culture and is perhaps the most inclusive culture myth. Goethe remarked that his story spans 3000 years of Western history, from Homer and the fall of Troy (Helena) to the Greek wars of liberation (Euphorion-Byron). It encompasses European history from the feudal era to the Revolution of 1830 and Utopian Socialism, European thought from Bruno and Spinoza to Hume's skepticism, Schopenhauer's voluntarism and Hegel's panlogism.[16]

Still, for all its universal character, *Faust* deals with a German figure and is primarily a German expression. It is invoked by German Protestants and Catholics, individualists and socialists, realists and romanticists as containing the wisest and deepest thought and the greatest art.[17]

But, *Faust* is most uniquely German in the hero's unrestraint. This German Icarus wants to fly.[18] But he has no Dedalus counseling him to stay at a moderate height and so keep close to the father. He does not know the Greek sense of limit and his rebellion takes the form of *rage* aimed at absolute knowledge, power and gratification.

Ferdinand Freiligrath's poem "Hamlet" declares that "Germany is Hamlet . . . He muses and dreams, not knowing what to do . . . That comes from too much reading in bed . . . His finest action consists in thinking. As a result, he lacks resoluteness." But, the poem might have read that "Germany is Faust." For the action in Germany's most representative work is primarily poetic and visionary. *Faust* is a poet's poem and its hero is a genius without wings.

Faust succeeds in his venture, while Hamlet fails. Yet, his is the victory of German theory. Hamlet, on the other hand, confronts a real court world; hence his failure has greater functional import than Faust's symbolic successes. Hamlet is more active in his irresolutions than Faust is in his titanic pronouncements.

FAUST I: THE INDIVIDUAL JOURNEY

Unto God the Orient!
Unto God the Occident!
Northern lands and Southern lands
Rest in the peace of His great hands.

—Goethe (Lewisohn translation)

Das Wahre war schon längst gefunden,
Hat edle Geisterschaft verbunden:
Das alte Wahre, fass es an!

—Goethe

Dedication

The drama opens with a "Dedication," in which the poet laments
that he has no public to whom he can communicate his theme:

I bring the unknown multitude my treasures;
Their very plaudits give my heart a pang.

Similarly, the Poet tells the Manager in the Prelude:

Speak not to me of yonder motley masses.
Whom but to see, puts out the fire of Song!

Goethe therefore turns to a mythic audience. The historic present recedes into the background, as the poet is seized by a yearning for the
serene and solemn realm of the eternal present:

Und mich ergreift ein längst entwöhntes Sehnen
Nach jenem stillen, ernsten Geisterreich . . .
Was ich besitze, seh' ich wie im Weiten,
Und was verschwand, wird mir zu Wirklichkeiten.[19]

The living Faust who had become a legend in the sixteenth century is
to be transformed into a myth.

Act I: Creation—Illusion and Reality

"Prelude on the Stage" and "Prologue in Heaven" are the two gates
of the Faustian world, within which the drama of man is enacted. Both
the stage, representing the realm of illusion, and Heaven, standing for
the world of Reality, create. The first is interested in a theatrical product—the Manager (the Lord of the theatrical world) wants a play that
will attract a paying public; the Lord of Heaven aims at creation of
the whole man. And the Manager's Poet and Jester have their correspondence in Faust and Mephisto.[20]

189

The stately lines chanted by the archangel Raphael, with which "Prologue in Heaven" opens, bring Goethe's favorite sun-metaphor, sounding the motif of a harmonious and ordered world.

> Die Sonne tönt nach alter Weise
> In Brudersphären Wettgesang,
> Und ihre vorgeschriebene Reise
> Vollendet sie mit Donnergang . . .
> Die unbegreiflich hohen Werke
> Sind herrlich wie am ersten Tag.

Gabriel's song then introduces the imagery of the earth, the night and the raging sea, and the third, Archangel Michael, views these polar forces as interconnected parts of creation.

Birth-Stirrings

Faust comprises variations on the theme of creation and birth. Goethe's poetic-philosophical drama unfolds a titanic effort to give birth to a culture hero. The effort is "German" in its recourse to magic and romantic vision. All births fail: Gretchen drowns her child; Helen is a symbolic mother and her offspring is a "song" which fades into the air; Homunculus is a mechanical artifice which sinks into the ocean. Faust's final project to create virgin land, with the ocean as the mother-source, is a Utopian vision.

The celebrated soliloquy with which the drama proper begins breathes a feverish restlessness. It expresses Germany's *Sturm und Drang*, Goethe's own Promethean rebelliousness and desire to taste every possible experience:

> Und was der ganzen Menschheit zugeteilt ist,
> Will ich in meinem innern Selbst geniessen . . .

But insatiableness spells unfulfillment, and Faust cannot be satisfied with what he has. Here, as in the Hegelian dialectic, continuous transcendence lacks a logical scheme for its own determination. The anxiety of which Sorge makes Faust aware at the end is due to the nature of his passion which can never be requited. "All business," Goethe wrote Schiller (July 5, 1802),

> resembles marriage. You imagine you've done a great thing when one's copulation is accomplished, and it's exactly then that hell breaks loose . . . everything effectual must be regarded not as an end but as a beginning.

Shakespeare's Hamlet sees his task as limited to revenging his father's murder, and he is constantly beset with doubts as to his mission.

190

The German hero wants nothing less than to wrest the innermost secret of the world ("was die Welt im Innersten zusammenhält"), yet is not bothered by any doubts or scruples. Hamlet never forgets his father's admonition "Remember me," even though he appears in "questionable shape." Faust, on the other hand, would repudiate his parental tradition completely, declaring that it offers "nothing." The four medieval faculties to which he had devoted his life, amount only to an abstract unity, to a theory with which one can neither live alone nor with others.

Faust's opening soliloquy is a rejection of his heritage and an attempt of the German hero to emerge from the medieval womb. But the German scene did not offer the normal conditions for birth and Faust must turn to magic: "Drum hab' ich mich der Magie ergeben." Yet, the magical powers which Faust invokes are aspects of the very ancestral guidance he would spurn. The Macrocosm holds out a serene vision of an unchangeable substance. But, where Dante finds peace in such a vision, Goethe's Renaissance hero sees in it only a grand "pageant," an abstract universal which he can "contemplate," but not affect. Faust next turns to the magical sign of the Earth-Spirit which is a concrete universal, manifesting itself in dynamic living forms, suggesting the nature-spirit of Renaissance activism. It defines itself as

> A fluctuant wave,
> A shuttle free,
> Birth and the Grave,
> An eternal sea,
> A weaving, flowing
> Life, all-glowing . . .[21]

The appearance of the Earth-Spirit imbues Faust with "strength and heart to meet the world." But the German hero has only an intellectual grasp of its living unity and he is told by the Earth-Spirit that he measures up only to that spirit which he is able to "understand" (Germany had had no real Renaissance). He who had "expanded" himself to be its peer now realizes that he is but an infant (*Wurm*). Like an infant, he had been eager to "seize" the "breasts" of nature:

> Wo fass' ich dich, unendliche Natur?
> Euch Brüste, wo? Ihr Quellen alles Lebens, . . .
> Ihr quellt, ihr tränkt, und schmacht' ich so vergebens?

That Faust is not ready for creative activity is further seen in Wagner, his intellectual product. Wagner is an arrested Faust who still believes that human problems can be solved in the study and laboratory, that one can grasp the substance of things by examining their genesis and development. Historically, Wagner embodies the dried up form of German Humanism and Enlightenment, expressed in rhetoric and pedantic scholarship. He is the sexless product of his master's pure knowledge. Yet, he is loyal to Faust and tempers Faust's despair over the unattainableness of the absolute. Like Mephisto, he tends to debunk Faust's romantic strivings.

Death and Resurrection

Although the Earth-Spirit denies Faust's claim to be his peer, the German hero would still prove that he is god-like through an act of suicide. This final step is not accompanied by despair, but by "godlike rapture."[22]

As Faust lifts the cup of poison to his lips, the chimes of Easter bells and the song of angels break in. They tell of Christ's resurrection, reminding him of one who became God, not by the "heroism" of suicide, but by the passion of love. The Easter bells also bring memories of youth and of spring festivals, celebrating the eternal rebirth of man and nature. These multiple associations move Faust to tears, draw the cup away from his lips, and win him back to life—"Die Träne quillt, die Erde hat mich wieder":

> And Memory holds me now, with childish feeling,
> Back from the last, the solemn way.
> Sound on, ye hymns of Heaven, so sweet and mild!
> My tears gush forth; the Earth takes back her child![23]

Faust's tears are the first sign of a break in his arrogant self-sufficiency and prepares us for the next scene ("Before the City Gate"), where he comes down from his Gothic tower to mingle with the townspeople and the peasant-folk, who are also celebrating their day of resurrection—Easter Sunday. Where Dante begins with experience in Hell and ends with contemplation in Heaven, the Renaissance man begins with the contemplative life and descends to the valley of experience.

For a moment, Faust feels that among the folk, he can dare be a human being. But he soon realizes that a wide gap separates him from their gossipy and self-satisfied life. At this point, Faust speaks the famous lines of the "two souls" struggling within him:

> Two souls, alas! reside within my breast,
> And each withdraws from, and repels, its brother.
> One with tenacious organs holds in love
> And clinging lust the world in its embraces;

192

Jonah, by Albert Pinkham Ryder (ca 1890)
(National Collection of Fine Arts, Smithsonian Institution)

Don Quixote Crossing the Mountain, by Honoré Daumier
(The Bettmann Archives)

> The other strongly sweeps, this dust above,
> Into the high ancestral spaces.

Faust attempts to bridge or at least to narrow this gap by his pact with Mephistopheles.

Mephistopheles: The Pleasure Principle

> Also muss die Feuerquelle
> Sich im Abgrund erst entzünden,
> Und die Niederfahrt zur Hölle
> Soll die Himmelfahrt verkünden.

We know that what first attracted Goethe to the legend was the condition that Faust may not marry. To gain power and pleasure, he has to renounce unity and harmony, and this renunciation constitutes the pact with the devil.

Goethe's Mephistopheles is no Dantean Lucifer from whom "all streams of sorrow roll," does not hold the terror of Milton's Satan or of Marlowe's Mephistophilis. Indeed, he has few physical marks of the traditional devil. He appears in various forms—poodle, traveling scholar, squire, professor—and answers to various names—snake, animal, strange son of chaos, spirit of contradiction. He defines himself as the spirit who denies, as sin and destruction, as part of the primal Darkness or "Mother Night." The most novel feature of Goethe's devil is *his human and creative nature*. The Lord talks to him in a friendly tone and the author pictures him as quite likeable. Indeed, aside from Gretchen, he is the most human, if all-too-human, figure in the drama. His productive function is indicated by the Lord when he states that he has deliberately made the devil man's companion to counteract man's tendency towards lethargy. The devil, he says, rouses, excites, and thereby "must create," as devil. Mephisto too admits that he works the Good, even as he wills the Bad.

Goethe himself suggested that Mephisto's positive function emanates from his elemental nature. In *Poetry and Truth* (Book 8), he calls Mephisto the representative of all that "which we recognize as the form of matter, what we picture as heavy, firm and dark." In the drama, he is the earthy volcanic cobold who brings Faust in contact with sensuous life and fans his passion. Faust recognizes this earthy-fiery aspect when he calls Mephisto a mock-product of filth and fire ("Spottgeburt von Dreck und Feuer").[24]

In a highly suggestive essay, Hermann Reich has called attention to the relation between Mephistopheles and the demonic nature spirits

193

connected with fertility rites, tracing his connection with the ancient followers of Dionysus, the satyrs and sileni. The sign of their nature power is the immense phallus (the only suggestion of this in *Faust* is Mephisto's "indecent" gesture in "The Witches' Kitchen" and in "Forest and Cave") which again points to their fertilizing nature.[25]

Faust calls Mephisto the son of chaos. Here, Faust touches on the devil's work as the Trickster who would dissolve order by abolishing all lines of demarcation, including the boundary of sex. And when Mephisto names himself "the Spirit that denies," he is referring to his denial of abiding principles and the worth of creative effort—in mythic language—Creation and the Quest. He tells the Lord that man uses reason only as a screen to become "far beastlier than any beast."

From one perspective, *Mephisto is also the spirit who affirms.* To begin with, he affirms his dark underground sources in "Mother Night," or chaos, which was "once All," calling himself an expert on "The Under-World" (Act I, Part II). And he affirms sexual indulgence in its disguised "incognito" forms. As a relative of the snake, Mephisto belongs to the species of mankind's first seducers. In the role of Merry-Andrew ("Prelude on the Stage"), he urges the Poet to use his gifts "As in a love-adventure," and following the pact, he advises Faust:

> Take hold, then! let reflection rest,
> And plunge into the world with zest!
> I say to thee, a speculative wight
> Is like a beast on moorlands lean,
> That round and round some fiend misleads to evil plight,
> While all about lie pastures fresh and green.

He stimulates the sensuality of the student, rouses Faust's animal desires in "The Witches' Kitchen," leads him to Gretchen, and through the wild, dissolute Walpurgis-Night, where Faust sees Lillith, Adam's first wife, who lures young men with her beautiful hair.

Mephisto's confidence that he can call forth Faust's erotic desires rests on the fact that Faust had repressed them, minimizing "earthly meat and drink," guided solely by reason and "gray" theory. Thomas Mann's *Doctor Faustus* shows that such denial of the senses exposes one all the more to them, shows that the German *Denker und Dichter* have yielded to the material and bestial precisely because they had long restricted themselves to living in a *Luftreich des Traumes.* Faust acknowledges to Mephisto:

> I have myself inflated too high;
> My proper place is thy estate.

Faust's philosophical, juridical and theological rationalizations had not taken care of his deepest desires. And, when he finds no gratification in the four faculties, nor in his vision of the forbidding Macrocosm and the Earth-Spirit, Faust turns to Mephisto. The modern devil is a product of the repression enforced by the Nordic-Christian world.[26]

In the Faust legend, the devil is sent by Satan, whereas in Goethe's drama, as in the Book of Job, he is assigned by the Lord. But only in *Faust*, does *the hero himself invite the devil and suggest the terms of the pact.* In "Walpurgis-Night," Faust states that the devil may help him find the answer to the human riddle:

> They seek the Evil One in wild confusion:
> Many enigmas there might find solution.

Faust's readiness for the devil's temptations also stems from his appetite for infinite experience.[27] In sum, *Mephisto represents Faust's secret wishes.* (The devil's secretive office is indicated by his traveling "incognito," his proficiency in spying, overhearing and "prompting.")

Now, the distinctive character of Goethe's devil consists in that his creative effect is connected with his role as tempter. When the Lord states that man errs as long as he strives, he implies that if man is to find the right way, he must err, that is, yield to temptation.[28] The Lord agrees with Mephisto that the idealistic, ascetic Faust we meet at the beginning is "confused," but promises that he will ultimately gain "clarity." And the Lord chooses Mephisto as the means by which this is to be accomplished. Goethe's devil is the corrective of Faust's aspirations to be a superman. Moreover, the Mephistophelian temptations offer Faust a genuine choice, one based on a *knowledge of* alternatives, which can thus lend his choice a moral character. In this sense, Goethe's devil becomes an instrument of Faust's salvation.[29]

Pact and Wager

Mephisto's diabolical substance consists in the excess of his sensuous correction. On the one hand, Faust is to eat dust and like it; on the other hand, he is to leap restlessly from one object to another:

> That, to his hot, insatiate sense,
> The dream of drink shall mock, but never lave him . . .
> Refreshment shall his lips in vain implore.

Mephisto nearly succeeds. In "Forest and Cavern," Faust cries out:

> Thus in desire I hasten to enjoyment,
> And in enjoyment pine to feel desire.[30]

195

In the legend, the devil promises to be Faust's servant on earth, if he can possess Faust's soul after death. However, Goethe's Renaissance hero is not concerned with the beyond, but with the joys and sorrows of earthly life:

> Aus dieser Erde quillen meine Freuden,
> Und diese Sonne scheinet meine Leiden;

and he demands that Mephisto lead him "through the wildest life":

> Let us the sensual deeps explore,
> To quench the fervors of glowing passion!

At the same time, *he vows*—and this is the heart of the wager—*that he will never succumb to the pleasure principle*. Should he yield to it, then and only then would Faust lose his "soul," that is, become a slave of the devil. This Faustian wager is summed up in the crucial lines spoken by Faust (misleadingly translated by Bayard Taylor):

> Wie ich beharre, bin ich Knecht,
> Ob dein, was frag' ich, or wessen.

Here, loss of soul is equated with stagnation and inertia, seen as states of human enslavement. This point is made earlier in metaphorical language:

> When on an idler's bed I stretch myself in quiet,
> There let, at once, my record end!
> Canst thou with lying flattery rule me,
> Let that day be the last for me! . . .
> When thus I hail the Moment flying:
> "Ah, still delay—thou art so fair!"
> Then bind me in thy bonds undying,
> My final ruin then declare!

In this wager, Faust pledges himself to the perpetual quest, to critical questioning, persuaded that man's creative forces can lead towards "highest life" (Act I, Part II). Mephisto had wagered that if the Lord allowed him to fan Faust's sensuousness, he could get him to "eat dust."[31] And what Faust wagers is that the enjoyment of "the moment" would never gain dominance over him, reminding Mephisto that it "is not of joy we're talking." For Faust, the soul connotes activity grounded in basic principles. And, he would lose his soul either if he became satisfied with a life of ease or with pointless moving from one activity to another.[32]

196

Act II: The Journey

Like Don Quixote, Hamlet and other Renaissance heroes, Faust has no guide and no attachment to the folk, family or church. He, too, goes forth on a journey without a plan. To his question "Then how shall we begin?" Mephisto replies: We'll just go ahead ("Wir gehen eben fort."). Faust's journey is unconfined, limited primarily by his poetic will, in search of adventures with the arch-adventurer, Mephistopheles.

In the middle of his life's journey, Faust realizes that he had not lived. His bond with the devil is a desperate attempt to experience a "re-nascence." However, the historic basis for such rejuvenation was absent in Goethe's Germany whose Renaissance was an esthetic-literary awakening, stimulated by the study of classical culture. To regain his youth, Faust has recourse to a magic potion prepared by Mephisto's Witch. But the potion produces only a mock-rebirth—it only brings *his wish* for youthful living to the surface.[33]

Gretchen

The Gretchen scenes are an outgrowth of Goethe's deep personal experience and are the most realistic and effective executions in the drama. Goethe assigns Gretchen the role of providing Faust with an Ariadne-thread in his labyrinthine passage. Gretchen is at first a harlot figure to Faust who demands that Mephisto get him the girl he saw on the street. Next, he sees in her the Madonna who moves him to prayer in the "hallowed shrine" of her room. He then hears her speak of performing the duties of a mother to her little sister. At the end of the drama, she intercedes for Faust before the Mother of God and leads him towards Heaven. Gretchen is at once the object of Faust's major temptation and the instrument of his redemption.

Thomas Mann calls Gretchen a German folk-song.[34] She strikes us at first as the prototype of a German *Natur-Kind*—good, wholesome, genuine, spontaneous. But love transforms this simple girl into a rebel, like Faust. As a Catholic, living in a Protestant Germany, she too would leave the "Gothic" prison of her narrow "den." If Faust is hemmed in by his scholastic heritage, Gretchen is imprisoned by the German tradition that woman's world is limited to the three K's: *Küche, Kinder, Kirche*. As a woman, she faces more severe condemnation than Faust does and becomes a homeless fugitive:

> Meine Ruh' ist hin,
> Mein Herz ist schwer;

> Ich finde sie nimmer
> Und nimmermehr.

Gretchen knows that she is leaping into the abyss, but her love is "demonic", that is, anti-pragmatic, and she surrenders to it unhesitatingly:

> Mein Busen drängt
> Sich nach ihm hin.
> Ach dürft' ich fassen
> Und halten ihn,
>
> Und küssen ihn,
> So wie ich wollt',
> An seinen Küssen
> Vergehen sollt'![35]

The love of Dante's Francesca is limited to sensuous passion; Ophelia's love for Hamlet is passive and pitiful, that of Racine's Phèdre is veiled and furtive. Gretchen's love goes out for Faust's whole person. Even as the world is about to crumble and bury her, Gretchen still affirms her love which was good and sweet:

> Doch—alles, was dazu mich trieb,
> Gott! war so gut! ach, war so lieb!

Dante makes a sharp division between the carnal passion of Paolo and Francesca and the spiritual love of Dante and Beatrice. Croce points out that although Dante has deep compassion for the fate of the lovers, the Catholic poet never questions the necessity for their being in hell. Goethe, on the other hand, likens Gretchen to the Virgin Mother who knows her agony. The drama closes with her exaltation, as she leads Faust towards Heaven in the train of the Mater Dolorosa.

Faust develops a deep love for Gretchen, yet never considers marrying her. Goethe only hints at the social barrier in characterizing the German Walpurgis-Night as "monarchic," exhibiting "bourgeois limitation, moral confusion, superstitious belief."[36] It imprisons Gretchen in her den and later in the dungeon. Faust sees her on Walpurgis-Night as

> She falters on, her way scarce knowing,
> As if with fettered feet that stay her going.

In contrast to Faust, Gretchen would gladly accept a permanent union with Faust. Her affirmation of such a "moment" is expressed in the tender lyrical lines she speaks to Faust in the dungeon:

> O weile!
> Weil' ich doch so gern, wo du weilest.

But for the German "doctor," Gretchen is only a passing "moment" on his way to new conquests.

FAUST II: THE SOCIAL QUEST

In the first part of the drama, Faust yields to the Teutonic temptations of *Innerlichkeit* and *Werden* to the degree of *Maasslosigkeit*, resorting to magic and necromancy. In his unrestrained self-indulgence, Faust commits symbolic parricide: He declares that his ancestral tradition is "nothing," derogates his father, and is instrumental in the death of Gretchen, her child, brother and mother. At the end of Part I, Faust leaves Gretchen in the dungeon. However, Goethe indicates that his hero is redeemable. For Faust is not a Don Juan adventurer, but feels remorse, calls himself a "monster without aim or rest," wishing that he had "ne'er been born."

In the second part, Faust enters the supra-individual world in which he becomes aware of social powers and their pressures on the individual. He comes to realize what he had sensed earlier when he said that when one thinks that he is doing the pushing, one is actually being pushed.

Prologue on Earth

The opening scene of Part II (it contains some of the most lyrical and philosophical lines of the drama) is a kind of Prologue in an Earthly Paradise. Lying in a pleasant valley, a restless Faust, presumably troubled over Gretchen's fate, is vainly seeking sleep. A chorus of Nature-Spirits, led by Ariel, attempt to compose him. Like Dante, Faust is to drink from Lethe and Eunoë to forget the bad dreams of his past, regain his youthful hope, and be restored "to the holy light." The Chorus sings of the eternal recurrence of spring and calls on Faust to "Trust the new, the rising Day." Faust awakens refreshed and pledges to strive for "highest life." In Part II, Faust's spring-like awakening is followed by his "summer"—marriage to Helena, his "harvest"—the project that is to produce free land for a free people. The drama ends with Faust's "winter"—his death, with a promise of his redemption.

In Part I, Faust expressed the wish to travel with the sun. In the opening scene of the second part, he attempts to look at the sun, but blinded by its rays, he turns his eyes earthwards. He is now content with looking at the refraction of the sun-rays, the colors of the rainbow formed by the spray from the mountain-falls.[37] He transposes the mean-

199

ing of this phenomenon into the idea that man can experience only the symbolic manifestations of life: "Am farbigen Abglanz haben wir das Leben,"—an insight which is also voiced in the final verse of the drama:

Alles Vergängliche	All things transitory
Ist nur ein Gleichnis.	But as symbols are sent

It has been said that in Part II Mephisto recedes into the background. It is true that Goethe's devil is here less prominent as a character, but this is so only because *the terrain as a whole is more Mephistophelian.* If, in Part I, the devil's temptations appear in the form of individual aggrandizement where the self would swallow the world, in Part II the temptation lies in the self allowing itself to be swallowed by currents of the world.

In Part I, the social forces behind Gretchen's tragedy are veiled. By the time Goethe wrote the second part, he had gotten to know the court of Weimar and the shadowy figures of "Walpurgis-Night" are clearly recognizable as the disintegrating feudal order. In the court-scenes, it attempts to create the illusion of active life by pomp and pageantry by mummery and masquerade, with Mephisto, the devilish jester, as master of its ceremonies.[38]

The Mothers

One of the ironies of the drama is that the court-world of shallow amusements leads to the most basic quest—Faust's descent to The Mothers. The young emperor wants to see Helena and Paris, "The model forms of Man and Woman." Since Mephisto, the Northern devil, has no contact with the "old heathen race," Faust is entrusted with the mission to produce them by seeking out The Mothers.

Upon hearing this word, Faust is "terrified." His dread is similar to Dante's as he is about to undertake his journey into the hellish chasms. Homunculus, who later descends to the ocean-mother—speaks of the terminal nature of this ordeal:

Who to the Mothers found his way
Has nothing more to undergo.

Even Mephisto is moved to eloquent earnestness in mentioning The Mothers:

Unwilling, I reveal a loftier mystery.—
In solitude are throned the Goddesses,
No Space around them, Place and Time still less;

200

> Only to speak of them embarrasses.
> They are THE MOTHERS!

To Faust's question "Where is the way," Mephisto replies:

> No way!—To the Unreachable,
> Ne'er to be trodden! A way to the Unbeseechable,
> Never to be besought! Art thou prepared?
> There are no locks, no latches to be lifted;
> Through endless solitudes shalt thou be drifted.

Faust will have to "delve in the deepest depths,"

> Naught shalt thou see in endless Void afar,—
> Not hear thy footstep fall, nor meet
> A stable spot to rest thy feet.

In *The King and the Corpse*, Heinrich Zimmer calls The Mothers "that domain (which) has been for milleniums the holy goal of all the questing heroes," from Gilgamesh onwards. The journey is nearly always accompanied by dread in mythology and mythopoesis, and no other scene in *Faust* has the same mystery, terror and promise. Faust's journey to The Mothers is an attempt by the mythic hero to wrest the secret of nature by retracing his way to the origins of creation.[39]

In Part I, Faust is nearly damned for his destructive invasion of Gretchen's life. In Part II, Faust repeats the act with The Mothers, *but this time, his action is symbolic.* And, as in the case of Sophocles' Oedipus, Faust's symbolic reenactment brings him "heavenly gain," first Helena and at the end the Mater Dolorosa.[40]

Faust succeeds in bringing up the images of Helena and Paris, and in a spectral play "The Rape of Helena," he would use the key to rescue Helena for himself:

> What! Rape? Am I for nothing here? To stead me,
> Is not this key still shining in my hand?
> I'll rescue her, and make her doubly mine.
> Ye Mothers! Mothers! crown this wild endeavor!
> Who knows her once must hold her, and forever!

In this attempt, Faust is as violently impatient as when he challenged the Earth-Spirit. He is not ready for this task either, and is knocked unconscious by an explosion.[41]

Homunculus and the Classical Mother

While Faust lies unconscious in his study, his former student Wagner, who has since become a famous scholar, is busy trying to make a human being. His method of creation does not entail a descent to The Mothers, nor any sexual contact, but only a mixture of chemical elements.[42] The resulting synthesis, Homunculus, lives in a sealed glass-vial. Born with a mature mind, he knows at once that Faust is dreaming of Leda and the swan and wants to reenact Zeus' union with Helena's mother. He advises that Faust be taken to the Classical Walpurgis-Night where the spirits of classicism are gathered to celebrate their Hellenic legends. Faust must come in contact with the naturalistic spirit of Greece if he is to regain consciousness. Homunculus himself must make the same journey, but for the opposite reason—this cerebral product must acquire a body to become human. As he nears Galatea's chariot, longing for her beauty expands his light-body so that his glass-vial breaks and Homunculus sinks into the amorphous ocean to begin his gradual, organic development towards the human.[43]

Faust's wanderings through the classical terrain in quest of Helena are connected with Goethe's Italian travels. Italy, the home of humanistic art, was to Goethe a welcome alternative to the feudal-burgher commercialism of his homeland.[44] Faust's journey takes him from the archaic period to Hellenism where beauty is incorporated in the human figure of Helena.[45]

In classical and medieval mythology, Helena is a temptress and the Faust legend makes her an object for pleasure only. In Goethe, she becomes a wife and a mother. Faust's wedding with Helena is meant to symbolize the union of Northern unrestraint with Southern calm, the Gothic quest for the boundless and the infinite with the Grecian sense for the limited and finite, Germanic dynamism with Apollonian equilibrium.[46]

Ironically enough, this union results in combining only the extremes of Graeco-German culture. On the one hand, Faust and Helena disappear from the action and, watched over by Mephisto-Phorkyas, enjoy a bliss "Arcadian and free," that comes close to lying on "an idler's bed." On the other hand, their son Euphorion exhibits only his father's Germanic *Maasslosigkeit* and none of his mother's Hellenic *sophrosyne*:[47]

> I must clamber ever higher,
> Ever further must I see . . .
> Dream ye the peaceful day?
> Dream, then, who may!
> War! is the countersign:
> Victory—word divine!

However, Euphorion ("the lightly borne") is a *German* Hermes and Icarus, a "genius" without wings. Like Homunculus, he is the artificial product of German theory. Whereas Homunculus takes the downward journey to the ocean to become human, Euphorion takes the "German" way upwards: He throws himself into the air, leaving his garments and lyre on the ground, and calls out to Helena:

> Leave me here, in the gloomy Void,
> Mother, not thus alone!

Helena heeds his call, embraces Faust, saying to him that an "old word" becomes true: "That Bliss and Beauty ne'er enduringly unite."[48]

Before Phorkyas reverts to the form of the German devil, he advises Faust to preserve the garment and veil which Helena left in his hands:

> Hold fast what now alone remains to thee!
> The garment let not go! . . .
> It is no more the Goddess thou hast lost,
> But godlike is it. For thy use employ
> The grand and priceless gift, and soar aloft!
> 'Twill bear thee swift from all things mean and low
> To ether high, so long thou canst endure.

The point Goethe is making is that the usable heritage of Greece cannot lie in its historical material, no longer available, but in its mythic residue. It alone can save him "from all things mean and low," that is, from being engulfed by the pressures of the historic present. The value of the Greek way is not in its what, but in its how.

Now, Faust returns to his Northern "high mountains." To be productive, Faust must work with his native material and on his native ground. Faust's esthetic experience prepares him for his first moral act.

The Mighty Plan

While Faust was being transported home, his eye was drawn to the ocean:

> There endless waves hold sway, in strength erected
> And then withdrawn,—and nothing is effected.

The spectacle of this unfruitful effort roused "excited passion of the blood," and gives rise to Faust's "mighty plan" to create land by forcing the waters to recede.

Faust's plan to fertilize the "watery waste" and gain virgin land is a continuation of his effort to be a God-man. He would repeat the act of

Genesis and create a world out of watery chaos. Yet, a significant change has taken place. In the beginning, Faust sought first causes by invoking the Macrocosm and the Earth-Spirit. This absolutism is modified in the opening scene of Part II where he expresses the thought that man must be content with their symbolic reflection. Now, Faust takes a further step: In planning to set limits to and make use of the oceanic waters, *Faust turns from the substantive to the functional.* He is no longer concerned with first and final causes: "I ask not, Whence? and ask not, Why? . . .", satisfied that "Nature in herself her being founded." Where the rainbow was a spectacle used for philosophic reflection, Faust's new vision calls for work, for making natural power socially productive. It is Faust who suggests this task and in this sense, he moves towards *self-determination.*

The new scheme is announced to Mephisto on the "High Mountain." This setting and Faust's declaration that the new-won land would give him power and property ("Herrschaft gewinn' ich, Eigentum!") recall the temptation which Satan dangled before Christ on the High Mountain—power over the earthly kingdom. Christ rejected the temptation, even though he was assured that such power could bring universal peace and freedom. Faust yields to the temptation and it involves him in war. To receive title to the under-water land, Faust must help the Emperor in a battle against his rival.[49]

While Mephisto's sober realism serves to correct Faust's romantic idealism, his practical orientation knows no substance, but only process. In the social sphere, he stands for the fetishism of things and of money, believes that Gretchen can be bought with jewels, that the tottering feudal regime can be saved with paper money. His values are property, power and exploitation with which he tempts the Emperor. As the "foreman" of Faust's project to win land back from the sea, he would convert Faust's ideal of a free people on a free soil into the trinity of "War, Trade and Piracy," aiming at surplus accumulation:

> We sailed away with vessels twain,
> With twenty come to port again.

For this modern devil, a man is evaluated not by what he is, but by what he has:

> If I've six stallions in my stall,
> Are not their forces also lent me?
> I speed along, completest man of all,
> As though my legs were four-and-twenty.

and might makes right:

> You have the Power, and thus the Right.
> You count the *What*, and not the *How*.

Faust-Mephisto points to the polarity in German history: Idealistic theory and *Real-Politik*.[50] At the end of the drama, Faust is dead and Mephistopheles remains to "implement" Faust's idea. In German history, this implementation became Bismarck and Hitler.

Act III: Homecoming

> Lass den Anfang mit dem Ende
> Sich in Eins zusammenziehn.

The last act of *Faust*, completed shortly before Goethe's death, is the poet's testament, the precipitate of his long and rich life. The language is resonant, lapidary, with runic undertones. And the characters—Philemon and Baucis, the Wanderer, Lynceus, the Four Grey Women, the Angels and the Mater Dolorosa—derive from Classical and Christian mythology.

We have reached the last stage of the hero's journey. And, it is precisely now that Goethe expresses his reservations over Faust's "progress" by having recourse to overtly mythic themes. Part I had shown that Faust's titanic way wrecked Gretchen and her family. In Part II, Faust's social project entails a social sacrifice. Goethe dramatizes his reservation by drawing a contrast between his hero and Philemon.

In Ovid's *Metamorphosis*, Philemon and his wife Baucis save Zeus and Mercury from shipwreck. The sole reward they ask is that, at their death, they be converted into trees near their temple so that they might never be parted. In Goethe's drama, we see them living contentedly on their little hill, their only wish to end life in their old home, praying to the "old God" in their chapel.

In the opening scene, the old couple tell the Wanderer (Goethe's composite figure for Zeus and Mercury) of Faust's aspiration to become master over the ocean, complaining that his venture is claiming human lives:

> Nightly rose the sounds of sorrow,
> Human victims there must bleed.

Faust has become the leader of a vast colonizing enterprise which uses "serfs," and he has ordered Mephistopheles, his "Overseer," to use *any* means to accomplish the task:

> However possible,
> Collect a crowd of men with vigor,

> Spur by indulgence, praise, or rigor,—
> Reward, allure, conscript, compel!

Still, Faust is not satisfied and in addition demands that Philemon and Baucis surrender their little hut and chapel. Baucis tells the Wanderer:

> Since he lords it as our neighbor,
> We to him must subject be.

Philemon had engaged in a task, similar to Faust's, when he rescued the Wanderer from shipwreck. But, in contrast to Faust, who employs technical-devilish devices, Philemon labored alone, using only his hands, and solely in the interest of another.

To be sure, Faust offers to compensate the old couple with a strip of the land which he is winning back from the sea. But Baucis warns her husband that this new ground rests on quicksand:

> Trust not the watery foundation!
> Keep upon the hill thy stand!

They are self-sufficient, do not want any of Faust's "modern improvements." He, on the other hand, despite (or because of) his spectacular acquisitions, is dissatisfied.

Faust's explanation why he needs their small holding is that the linden trees and hut spoil his desire for world-possession ("Verderben mir den Weltbesitz"):

> No sorer plague can us attack,
> Than rich to be and something lack!

Faust feels that, without the lindens, his grand estate is not "pure." He would use them to recuperate from his feverish activities ("Und wünscht' ich dort mich zu erholen. . . ."), would erect a scaffold on the hill from where he can view the whole:

> Till for my gaze a look be won
> O'er everything that I have done.

It would seem then that Faust needs the quiet rhythm of their agrarian life to offset the hustle and bustle of his technological activities. In his "Night-Song," Goethe wrote of the "sweet peace" which the Wanderer yearns for:

> Ach, ich bin des Treibens müde!
> Was soll all der Schmerz und Lust?
> Süsser Friede,
> Komm, ach komm in meine Brust![51]

But, it is the tragic dilemma of the Faustian way that to gain peace, it must use terror. Philemon and Baucis refuse the exchange, (the old pair is shown to be "unprogressive" and unproductive—they have no children), their home goes up in flames and they are burned to death. The conservative principle is purged by the "revolutionary" process and the Moloch of industrialism steamrollers over the agrarian idyll. As Faustian titanism had destroyed Gretchen's peace, so now it uproots ancient values, what Goethe called "das alte Wahre."

> What erstwhile the eye enchanted
> With the centuries is gone.

Sorge

At this point, Sorge enters Faust's preconscious. (Bayard Taylor renders Sorge as Care. In the context of Faust's dilemma at this point, the word suggests anxiety or worry.)

Previously, Faust had not questioned the limitations of activity as such. To be sure, Goethe recognized that industrialization made the violence inherent in continuous technological innovations inevitable. He also knew the blood sacrifice they entailed, knew that its fire could be used to destroy, as it consumes Philemon and Baucis in the drama.

Immediately following the death of Philemon and Baucis, four grey women enter Faust's palace. Three of them—Want, Debt[52] and Need—leave almost at once, but the fourth, Sorge stays. An eerie, mystic colloquy takes place between Sorge and Faust. In the setting of a timeless "Midnight," she asks Faust whether he has ever known Sorge. Faust replies:

> I only through the world have flown:
> Each appetite I seized as by the hair;
> What not sufficed me, forth I let it fare,
> And what escaped me, I let go.
> I've only craved, accomplished my delight,
> Then wished a second time, and thus with might
> Stormed through my life . . .
> In marching onwards, bliss and torment find,
> Though, every moment, with unsated mind.

The overt import of Faust's reply is to deny that he has ever known anxiety or worry, that he found "bliss" as well as "torment" in his "incessant rolling." Sorge retorts that his kind of life spells perpetual postponement of joy:

Whom I once possess, shall never
Find the world worth his endeavor: . . .
Perfect in external senses,
Inwardly his darkness dense is; . . .
Luck and Ill become caprices;
Still he starves in all increases;
Be it happiness or sorrow,
He postpones it till the morrow;
To the Future only cleaveth:
Nothing, therefore, he achieveth.

From a broader perspective, Sorge is the concomitant of the Western apotheosis of time and progress, particularly of Germanic *Werden*. The breathless pursuit of an ever-receding tomorrow makes for an "unsated mind."[53] While Faust had gotten to realize the limitation of a contemplative life, he has remained insensitive to the limitation of restless activity. Hence Sorge can say to him:

Throughout their whole existence men are blind;
So, Faust, be thou like them at last.

Sorge's blinding of Faust is the peripety of the drama. As the blinded Faust steps out of his palace, he hears a clattering of spades and is happy in the belief that the sound is made by laborers digging moats for his project. Actually, Lemures (spectres of the night) are digging his grave. (The original plays on the words *Graben*, moat and *Grab*, grave). In Goethe's own time, "progress" brought the era of Metternich which is digging the grave of Faust's social idealism. Only by blinding Faust to this historical terror can Goethe have Faust "see" his Utopian plan. He would save its idea in a Platonic heaven, with the hope that it might be enacted in a more favorable historic moment.

The Utopian Vision

Lasst alle Völker unter gleichem Himmel
Sich gleicher Gabe wohlgemut erfreun.

According to Greek legends, Tiresias' prophetic power was greater when he became blind. Similarly, Sophocles' Oedipus began to understand his past after he put out his eyes and Thomas Mann's Joseph recognized his self-centredness when thrown into the dark pit by his brothers.

Goethe's blind hero repeats this pattern with deeper Germanic *Innerlichkeit*. As the night presses around him, Faust feels that a bright light shines within him:

208

Assyrian Sun God Pursuing the Demon of Chaos
(The British Museum)

The Enigma of a Day by Giorgio De Chirico (1914)
(Private Collection, New Canaan, Conn.)

> Die Nacht scheint tiefer tief hereinzudringen,
> Allein im Innern leuchtet helles Licht . . .

With this inner light, he visualizes a social Utopia:[54]

> And such a throng I fain would see,—
> Stand on free soil among a people free!
> Then dared I hail the Moment fleeing:
> "Ah, still delay—thou art so fair!"
> The traces cannot, of mine earthly being,
> In aeons perish,—they are there!—
> In proud fore-feeling of such lofty bliss,
> I now enjoy the highest Moment,—this!

With this hope for the promised land, Faust dies.
Mephisto now claims that in uttering the words

> Then I hail the Moment fleeting:,

Faust has accepted the immediate present and has therefore lost the wager. However, examined in the context of Faust's pronouncement *the words salute a continuous task in which the "Moment" is forever renewed.* His free soil is "not secure," and must ceaselessly be fought for. Ultimate wisdom ("der Weisheit letzter Schluss"), Faust states, is the realization that

> He only earns his freedom and existence,
> Who daily conquers them anew.

Mephisto had vowed that Faust would eat dust and like it ("Staub soll er fressen, und mit Lust"). Faust was made to eat dust, but he did *not* like it. That he did not yield to the pleasure principle is admitted by Mephisto himself in the line he speaks following Faust's death: "No joy could sate him, and suffice no bliss." Faust withstood the devil's temptation to lie down on an idler's bed, and the angels proclaim that Faust can be redeemed because he labored "eternally:"

> The noble Spirit now is free,
> And saved from evil scheming:
> Who'er aspires unweariedly
> Is not beyond redeeming.

According to Eckermann, Goethe saw the key to the poem in the last two lines which make Faust's activism the ground for his salvation. Thus, Goethe's hero is presumably saved by "The Act" which Faust had declared to be at "the beginning." The act is indeed a key-term in the German Renaissance—in Lessing's *Laocoon, The Hamburg Drama-*

turgy and *Nathan the Wise,* in Kant's *Critique of Practical Reason* and in Schiller's *William Tell.*

Now, this line of interpretation loses sight of the fact that the devil's temptation lies not only in man accepting a stagnant existence but also in his *directionless activity.* So the question of Faust's redemption hinges on whether Faust avoided the other threat as well. And, the point I would make is that *Faust is not saved by the act alone.*

Examination of Goethe's work makes it clear that he did not absolutize striving as such. One of Goethe's *Maxims and Reflections* states that "unconditioned activity, whatever it might be, makes for bankruptcy in the end." Goethe reflected with bitterness on his own activistic life which he likened to that of Sisyphus: "At bottom," he told Eckermann, "I have had nothing but trouble and toil. . . . Eternally I rolled a stone up the mountain; eternally it had to be done anew."[55] And Faust's activity comes close to having been "unconditioned." Also, when we consider his indifferent attitude towards Gretchen's mother, his own child and his behavior towards Philemon and Baucis, we are hardly prepared for his pronounced social idealism. Even as Faust speaks of freeing "many millions," he remains something of a charismatic leader, thinks of the project as *his* idea ("One mind suffices for a thousand hands"), and as assuring *his* immortality.[56] Indeed, some Faust criticism (Wilhelm Böhm, Reinhold Schneider) condemns Faust as an incorrigible and unscrupulous criminal who has made "history in the last hundred years" (Schneider). In Karl Viëtor's formulation, Faust remains

> one of the modern titans of will who knows only one need, one law: the own hybrid Ego. The cultures of the East do not know the Superman, and classical culture did not know him. . . . What the Greeks regarded as a cardinal crime and called hybris . . . that is for the modern European the real possibility to fulfill oneself and at the same time to further humanity. . . . What the colonizer Faust does to the patriarchal pair, Philemon and Baucis, that has always and everywhere happened, where the 'pioneering-spirit' of the European has come in contact with the so-called primitive peoples. When Goethe wrote these scenes, he stood under the impact made by the newest phase of the conquest by the white people of the North American continent. He admired this as a gigantic feat, but he also knew what blood-letting accompanied it. (*Goethe, the Poet* [Cambridge, 1949])

To the extent, then, that the would-be superman continues his unconditioned activity, the devil "wins" his wager." Yet, as Goethe remarked to Schubarth (November 3, 1820), Mephisto "may win the wager only by half." For, in Part II, Faust begins to reconcile himself to human limitation, realizes that the basis of creation and the conditions for self-development lie outside of himself: Act I shows these conditions in society, Act II ("Classical Walpurgis-Night") in the phenomenology of the race, Act III in Hellenic culture, Act IV in the forces of nature, Act V in the Mother of God. At the end, he would subordinate personal aggrandizement to a supra-individual goal, would stand *"among"* a free people. That is, Faust is redeemable to the extent that he renounces his super-human quest, and develops from an adventurer to a culture-hero.[57]

Goethe at once feared and hailed the Faustian man. His march brought Metternich and imperialism as well as Beethoven and Utopian Socialism. The German idea of social freedom was primarily "theory," and remains such in *Faust*. Goethe, who battled against German romanticism is forced to reintroduce it in his drama.[58] Faust admits to Sorge that he was unable to do without black magic:

> If I could banish Magic's fell creations,
> And totally unlearn the incantations,—
> Stood I, O Nature! Man, alone in thee,
> Then were it worth one's while a man to be.

But the scientific-natural means to bring about social and human freedom were unavailable in Goethe's Germany and his Faust must cling to Mephisto. The last act was written in the period of Metternich which Goethe characterized as barbarous, a time in which "confused doctrine [is] leading to confused action" (To Eckermann and von Humboldt). In his drama, the devil becomes the "Overseer" of Faust's venture. Historically, the Mephistos were digging a grave for the Fausts and Goethe blinds his hero so that he might "see" the possibilities in the future.[59]

As in Shakespeare, "inner-directedness" is brought into focus precisely at the time when it is threatened to be overrun by "other-directedness." Amidst the Wars of Liberation, Goethe wrote (to Knebel, November 24, 1813) that his task was

> to preserve, to create order and to lay the foundations in contradiction to the age . . . to preserve the sacred fire, which the coming generations will need so sorely, were it only beneath the ashes. . . .

In *Faust*, Goethe would rescue this imperishable kernel in German idealism itself. In "Forest and Cavern," Mephisto satirizes Faust for living in caves like an owl, adding ironically: "The Doctor's in thy body still." Faust replies that his isolated life is the fount of a blessed vitality:

> What fresh and vital forces, canst thou guess,
> Spring from my commerce with the wilderness?

But, if thou hadst the power of guessing,
Thou wouldst be devil enough to grudge my soul the blessing.

Goethe would save this German "idea," save it supra-historically or mythically.

Matriarchal Grace

Faust never mentions his mother, yet it is to mothers that he turns in his greatest need. He feverishly demands "the breasts of nature," is drawn to the earthy mother-figure of Gretchen and descends to the Earth-Mothers. The poem begins with a patriarchal God of justice and ends with maternal figures dispensing grace, with the final lines of the poem honoring the Eternal-Feminine:

Das Ewig-Weibliche
Zieht uns hinan.

That man cannot be saved by the act alone is suggested by the Lord himself when he declares in the "Prologue in Heaven" that man errs as long as he strives. Put another way: Man must err because any act entails means, and means are in their very nature imperfect. Hence, man cannot be saved by his works, but only by grace. On June 6, 1831, while Goethe was putting the finishing touches on *Faust*, he told Eckermann: "We are not saved through our own efforts but through the addition of Divine Grace." The poet makes this also explicit in the drama. Following the lines

Whoe'er aspires unweariedly
Is not beyond redeeming,

the angels add:

And if he feels the grace of Love
That from on high is given,
The Blessed Hosts, that wait above,
Shall welcome him to Heaven!

Faust had declared that in the beginning was The Act, but learns that in the beginning was Love.

The drama begins with an individual personal God and ends with collective guides. Faust's Ascension is prepared by the group of Blessed Boys (they can free Faust from his bodily remains because having died at birth, they have no trace of "earthly" ways), by the angels who declare: Him *we* can redeem,[60] and by the Chorus of Women Penitents. The final plea is made by Gretchen and Doctor Marianus.[61]

Epilogue

In the last summer of his life, Goethe composed "The Song of Lynceus" which he inserted in the Fifth Act of *Faust*. In the Dead of Night, Lynceus the Warder, who has a sharp and over-all view of both "the Distant" and "the Near," sings on the watch-tower of the Palace. He begins by affirming the human journey, "Whatever it might be":

Zum Sehen geboren,	For seeing intended,
Zum Schauen bestellt,	Employed for my sight,
Dem Turme geschworen,	The tower's my dwelling,
Gefällt mir die Welt.	The world my delight.
Ich blick' in die Ferne,	I gaze on the Distant,
Ich seh' in der Näh'	I look on the Near,—
Den Mond und die Sterne,	The moon and the planets,
Den Wald und das Reh.	The forest and deer.
So seh' ich in allen	So see I in all things
Die ewige Zier,	The grace without end,
Und wie mir's gefallen,	And even as they please me,
Gefall' ich auch mir.	Myself I commend.
Ihr glücklichen Augen,	Thou fortunate Vision,
Was je ihr gesehn,	Of all thou wast 'ware,
Es sei, wie es wolle,	Whatever it might be,
Es war doch so schön!	Yet still it was fair!

This mood is abruptly disturbed by a dissonant note, as Lynceus witnesses the horror which befalls Philemon and Baucis. The song of harmony is jarred by the blood sacrifice which issues "from some darksome world below!" Goethe himself found no harmony in his life. What he called the Demoniacal forever prevented resolution between thought and action, the self and society, providence and chance.

The Catholic setting of Faust's Heaven has led some critics to argue that Goethe saves Faust by repudiating his paganism and the Protestant nature of his personality. But this ignores Goethe's own statement to Eckermann that he used this device to give pictorial, sensuous form to Faust's Ascension. It is a matter of record that Goethe rejected ascetic religions, calling himself "a non-Christian" and "an old pagan."[62] Faust's social vision is an earthly paradise and the Mater Gloriosa, as Rickert points out, appears not as the Virgin of Immaculate Conception, but as the guardian of love between man and woman. More telling is the marked non-Catholic note which permeates the scenes themselves. Faust's Heaven is not a divinely ordered Dantean Paradise.[63] Its "Mountain-Gorges, Forest, Rock, Desert," ravines and foaming waves have more the character of a hellish terrain, and its ascending "higher spheres" do not culminate in rest and peace. Pater Ecstaticus hovers in "endless ecstatic fire," suffers boiling breast pains, invites "arrows . . . lances . . . bludgeons . . . lightnings" to pierce and shatter him, and for Father Profundus, love is heralded in the phenomenon of rocks heaving and swaying in savage roaring.

Goethe denied Kant's radical evil and the unknowability of "das Ding an sich." But, his hope was *optative*. Faust states that *if* he could see a free people on free soil, then he *might* hail that moment ("Zum Augenblicke dürft' ich sagen. . . ."). And he is shown not as reaching, but only as being led *towards* Heaven, with "das Ewig-Weibliche" remaining unreachable. These "Protestant" notes are the basis for the Epilogue in the Faustian mythopoesis.[64] *Faust* is called a tragedy and the hero dies before his task is completed. Like Moses, Oedipus, Virgil, and Don Quixote, Faust can see, but not enter the Promised Land. Still, Faust's personal tragedy contributes towards the draining of the social swamps and he becomes a kind of scapegoat for humanity.[65] In this way, Goethe's *Faust* transcends its Teutonic roots, linking itself into the great chain of mythopoesis.

NOTES

1. In his storm and stress period, Goethe spoke of "constant inner conflict and rebellion," of "sudden gusts of temper and . . . self-will." He speaks of his "inner restlessness," leaving him "no repose anywhere." (Letters of December 23, 1774, October, 1777, December 9, 1777. These and subsequent quotations from Goethe's letters, diaries, memoirs etc. are taken from Ludwig Lewisohn's *Goethe. The Story of a Man* [2 vols.; New York, 1949].

   Cf. Barker Fairley, *A Study of Goethe* (London, 1947); K. R. Eissler, *Goethe: A Psychoanalytic Study*, 1775-1786 (2 vols.; Detroit, 1963).

2. Letters of November 28, 1771, August 11, 1781, March 5, 1830, February 13, 1775, April 10, 1776.

3. Letters, Diaries etc. of August 7, 1799, November 21, 1782, October, 7, 1777, May 12, 1782, March 3, 1784, March 10, 1781, March 12, 1828, January 16, 1818, December 31, 1808, December 23, 1797.

4. In *Faust*, the father is called a *dunkler Ehrenmann*. Taylor translates the words to mean "a sombre, brooding brain," but they also suggest a man of ambiguous honor.

5. Letters of May 3, 1802, August 20, 1781, September 9, 1784.

6. Reik believes that Goethe was largely abstinent until about the forties, and that he probably suffered from psychic impotence until his Italian journey when he was cured by a "nature-" girl, Faustina.

7. Goethe was attracted to mother figures, such as Charlotte von Stein, as well as to young girl figures, such as Christiane Vulpius and Ulrike von Levetzow. The mother was his secret, and one of the most secret scenes in *Faust* is the

hero's descent to *The Mothers*. In the poem, all the mother-figures are killed off: Gretchen's mother, Gretchen and Baucis; Helena vanishes, after she gives birth.

8. After Goethe fled from Charlotte, he asked her to let his mother share in all he wrote her. Later, Charlotte expressed the wish that Goethe were "a child" to her. In time, the relationship levelled off to a respectful friendship and Charlotte reverted to addressing Goethe as "dearest Councillor." See Letters of June 11, 1784, October 28, 1784, December 13, 1812, September 20, 1780, March 10, 1782, May 24, 1776, January 15, 1776, May 12, 1776, January 25, 1788.

9. The recurrent motif in Goethe's letters to Christiane is his request that she be a good housekeeper: "Keep the house nicely in order. . . . Be a good domestic treasure . . . prepare yourself to become a dear little cook. . . . I look forward with pleasure to our well-ordered house." See Letter of July 15, 1795. Following his break with Charlotte and his union with Christiane, Goethe was able to accept his mother—he now invited her to live with him.

10. See Appendix IV.

11. These words of an English folk-book by P. F. are quoted in E. M. Butler's *The Fortunes of Faust* (Cambridge, 1952). This work discusses the treatments of the Faust theme from the Spiess version to Thomas Mann's *Doctor Faustus*. It should be noted that in the Catholic tradition, black magicians, such as Cyprian, Theophilus, Pope Sylvester II are not damned, but receive grace.

12. Even the medieval devil is part of God's world and his power is controlled by the deity. St. Augustine admits the existence of *good* magic. Cf. *Civitas Dei,* XII, 4.

13. Faust meets with seven spirits each of whom claims to be the quickest spirit of Hell. Faust accepts only the claim of the seventh devil who is "no more and no less quick than is the transition from good and evil." Lessing suggests here the ambivalent nature of the devilish, a notion developed by Goethe and Thomas Mann.

14. Fritz Strich's *Goethe und die Weltliteratur* (Bern, 1946) points out that Goethe expressed his antipathy against the Hindu gods precisely in his *West-Östlicher Divan* which calls for a union of East and West. Goethe's strong sense for historic-genetic development made the metaphysical absolute of Eastern thought distasteful to him. See *Recollections of Riemer*, August 28, 1808; Letters, etc. of October 22, 1826, to Jacobi, 1801, 1786, to Eckermann, January 31, 1827.

15. See my essay "Goethe and the Philosophic Quest," *The Germanic Review* (New York), III, No. 3 (July, 1933).

16. Its wide range is expressed in the most varied poetic forms, from the folk-song, the doggerel, free rhythms and blanc verse to the Alexandrine, Greek metres and Dantesque triple rhymes.

17. Yet, outside of Germany, *Faust* has found less appreciation than any other literary classic. Thus far, it has proved itself intractable to translation into English. Except for Shelley (who confined himself to a few short scenes), none of the many versions has recaptured its lyric-philosophic rhythms.

18. There are numerous allusions to flying: Lines 1074, 1091, 6984, 7034 ff., 9897, 10041.

19. The translations are by Bayard Taylor, available in the Modern Library edition. I quote the original to give the English reader a sense of Goethe's lyrical rhythms.

20. The organic connection between the two scenes has generally been missed. In particular, "Prelude on the Stage" is regarded as irrelevant and is omitted from some translations. Even though Goethe worked on *Faust* in various stages of his life, its final version has structure and dramatic sequence, as I will try try to show in passing.

21. Goethe likened the Earth-Spirit to Jupiter. In *Faust, Erd-Geist* is both masculine and feminine (he defines himself in terms of earth and water metaphors— tides, wave, storm, sea). Faust is lacking in the harmonious interaction of these principles. He speaks later of his "Two souls," the one clinging with crude passion to the earthy, the other lifting itself from the dust "into the high ancestral spaces."

22. The celebration of "free death" (*Freitod*) is a recurrent motif in the Germanic tradition, beginning with the *Götterdämmerung* in the old Edda. Other examples are the ecstatic letters of Heinrich von Kleist written before his suicide and the "Liebestod" duet of Wagner's Tristan and Isolde. The most recent instance was the glee with which the Nazis greeted the news that Hitler, Goebbels and Goering cheated the Allies by their self-inflicted deaths.

23. Faust's attempted suicide sums up the social mood of Goethe's time. Where the French middle class prepared for social and political revolution, the weak German bourgeoisie indulged in philosophic-esthetic revolutions or in suicidal attitudes.

    A note on the psychological import of Faust's attempted suicide: The death wish may express frustrated love for an object with whom the suicide hopes to "unite" through his act. Prior to the suicide scene, Faust yearns for "the breasts of life," and in the scene expresses the hope that death may show him the way to the "high seas."

24. Following a suggestion by G. W. Groddeck (*The World of Man* [London, 1934]), Mephisto may be considered the anal-phallic principle in the drama: He is lord of the vermin and of fire; in Auerbach's Cellar, he calls the flame "friendly element," and in The Witches' Kitchen, he is master of the witches who "fart and stink" and who watch over the flaming cauldron. Mephisto's anal function is manifested in his connection with money and gold: It is he who brings the Emperor "money" that lies "buried in the earth," and Mammon glows on his Walpurgis-Night. (In Milton's *Paradise Lost*, Mammon builds a palace for Satan in which the cells are crossed by veins of fluid fire.) Mephisto appears as Avarice in the scene "Spacious Hall"; provides the gold-casket by which Faust is to gain Gretchen's favors; Mephisto's companions in the "Classical Walpurgis-Night" are griffins, ants, arimaspians which (according to Herodotus) are connected with gold.

216

25. In the court-scenes (Act I, Part II), the medieval chancellor rejects Mephisto as a nature-spirit. Here, Mephisto appears in the company of satyrs, silenes and the Great Pan. In "The Classical Walpurgis-Night," his primary contact is with nymphs, lamiae and phallic cobolds. Mephistopheles also claims kinship with the snake-family. In *Myths and Symbols in Indian Art and Civilization* (New York, 1946), Heinrich Zimmer states that the representation of serpent genii occurs "in association with a variety of other divine patrons of fertility, prosperity, and are earthly health."

26. Faust invokes Mephisto partly by recourse to Christian symbols. The devil's medieval-Nordic sources are made explicit by Homunculus (Act II, Part II):

> ". . . Thou, from the North,
> And of the age of mist brought forth,
> In knighthood's and witchcraft's murky den."

Mephisto feels at home in the German Walpurgis-Night, but not in the Classical Walpurgis-Night.

27. Faust's desire to emulate the sun has erotic undertones. He would enter the sun's "portals of fulfillment" ("the sun" is feminine in German), which open up in wings (*"flügeloffen"*). Similarly, in the suicide scene, he hopes that the poison in the long-necked bottle will lead him out to the "high sea," enable him to "pierce" the ether, tear open the "gates." He will be able to show that "male" dignity (*Manneswürde*) does not tremble before that "dark cave" by forcing that passageway (*Durchgang*) around whose narrow mouth are the flames of all the fires of Hell. By the opening Part II, Faust is reconciled to the fact that he lacks the power to enter the "portals of fulfillment," and he renounces "the flood of flame" which issues from it.

28. This is also Mephisto's judgment! He tells Homunculus in Part II: "Unless thou errest, thou wilt ne'er have sense."

29. The irony is that Mephisto's function is *to serve* without the hope that he will succeed in his mission. He tells Faust that despite his eternal destructive work, there ever circulates new, fresh blood. In serving without asking or expecting any reward, the devil is akin to the artist and saint. At the close of the drama, Mephistopheles likens himself to Job:

> "How is't with me—Like Job, the boils have cleft me
> From head to foot, so that myself I shun;"

Moreover, he cannot even appeal to God, as Job could:

> "But unto whom shall I appeal for justice?
> Who would secure to me my well-earned right?"

In this light, Mephisto is the sacrifice to Faust's development.

30. These lines indicate that, contrary to general interpretation, "Forest and Cavern" does not show that Goethe achieved complete serenity during his Italian journey.

31. The *Paralipomena to Faust* makes clear that Mephisto is after more than Faust's flesh and blood ("Allein die Seel' ist unsre rechte Speise").

32. To the extent that Goethe's stress is on action and limitless development, his

conception of the soul has Western character. The Eastern notion is expressed in Tolstoy's *Anna Karenina* where Levin says that "living for one's soul" consists in spiritual equilibrium—a conception more attuned to the agrarian East.

33. The theme of the male climacteric is also present in the middle-aged figures of Dante, Don Quixote, Ibsen's Rubek and Thomas Mann's Gustav Aschenbach. Goethe himself sought repeated "cures" in Carlsbad and also by courting young girls.

34. In the dungeon scene, Goethe sounds folk-motifs of the step-mother: Gretchen sings a plaintive song of the mother who has put her to death and of the father who has eaten her. Gretchen's mother behaves in a stepmotherly way—leaves the chores of the household and the upbringing of her other daughter to Gretchen. In this context, Faust becomes "the father" who "eats" her in that the older man becomes the indirect cause for her pitiable end.

35. This Faustian rebel has her Mephisto in the wordly and cynical Marthe whom Mephisto calls fit "To ply the pimp and gypsy trade." She encourages and guides Gretchen towards fulfilment of her secret wishes for the casket and for Faust.

36. "Aufsätze zur Literatur," March or April 1827.

37. In this connection, it is relevant to note that Goethe wrote a book on the theory of *color,* not of light.

38. Neither Shakespeare in *The Tempest* nor Goethe in *Faust II* can summon up enough poetic enthusiasm to depict this social system with artistic effectiveness. As noted, while Goethe was attracted by the glamour of Weimar, he was depressed by its pettiness and historic anachronism. In the drama, as in Weimar, poetry (the Boy Charioteer) is entertainment, dependent on the state (Plutus), as Goethe was dependent on the good will of the duke.

39. The scene is charged with phallic-vaginal imagery: Mephisto gives Faust a "key" which he calls "That little thing." After he has taken hold of the key, it "grows" (*waechst*) in his hand. With it, Faust is to "mount" gradually to "happiness" ("Gelassen steigst du, dich erhebt das Glück"). The key leads Faust "Through realms of terror, wastes and waves," and brings him to "a blazing tripod" in whose glow and "immense mist" Faust will find The Mothers residing in "the utterly deepest bottom." However, he will not be able to open the realm of The Mothers with the key, but only "scent" the "true place." If his mission is to succeed, Faust must bring the tripod back. Theodor Reik calls attention to the sexual symbolism in the line (spoken by Mephisto): "Descend, then! I could also say: Ascend!" See also chapters 7 and 8 of Reik's *The Secret Self* (New York, 1952).

40. Goethe's conception of The Mothers well illustrates his manner of concretizing universal concepts. In *Goethe's Faust* (Tübingen, 1932), Heinrich Rickert effectively refutes the theory that The Mothers represent Platonic Ideas. The Mothers do not have the Reality of Plato's Ideas, but are shadowy, schematic forms. The Platonic way of deriving universals by the method of abstraction is opposed to Goethe's *gegenständliches Denken* which would present concepts

by concrete objectification. Thus, Goethe would replace Newton's mathematical theory of light by a theory of color (*das trübe Mittel*). And, when Schiller called Goethe's *Urpflanze* an "idea" he retorted that he can "see" his idea. Goethe's *Pandora* comes closest to expressing a Platonic universal. Yet, as Ernst Cassirer has shown, even this figure descends and particularizes itself. Goethe had nothing to say about the Absolute "in the theoretic sense." He argued for a philosophy which presented its concepts phenomenologically.

41. Faust's attempted short-cut to get Helena corresponds to the German effort to acquire a Renaissance through study of Hellenic art and culture. But Hellenism could not be acquired in feudal Weimar as it could not in the Emperor's court.

42. Even here, two people cooperate—Wagner and Mephisto. The latter is only an interested, if sensuous witness, but his female aspect becomes evident when he later appears as Helena's female attendant. Proteus calls Homunculus "a genuine virgin's-son."

43. No sooner is Homunculus born than he is eager to act. Goethe personifies in him the mechanistic and the romantic expressions of German theoretic activism. Both are formulae which can "live" only within a hermetically sealed system. Referring to himself, Homunculus says that "What's artificial, needs restricted space." Goethe's preference for the evolutionary process over revolutionary German *Schrecklichkeit* is shown in Homunculus' following the advice of Thales, the "Neptunist," who is contrasted with Anaxagoras, the "Volcanist."

44. Goethe called the Italian journey his "great leap. . . . If I perish, I perish! Without this experience, I was of no use any more." (Letters of December 13, 1786, January 20, 1787.) This journey takes on a "German" character in that Goethe confessed to Karl August that his longing for Italy assumed "the form of a sickness." (Letter of November 3, 1786.)

45. Goethe planned—but never wrote—a scene in which Faust propitiates Persephone to give up Helena. This would have been in the mythic tradition in which the hero wins the bridal bed by descending to the underworld.

46. Goethe invents the following plot: On her return from Troy, Helena has been sent ahead by her husband Menelaus to prepare a sacrifice. Mephisto-Phorkyas tells her that Menelaus intends *her* to be the sacrifice and suggests that Faust, a medieval knight in Pelepponesia, can save her. The entire episode is poetically flat. Not only does Faust win Helena by a ruse, but the marriage is contrived and gone through without the slightest manifestation of affection on either side. Its form is a "literal" ritual: Faust teaches the Greek woman to speak in German rhymes!

47. Euphorion is an allegorical figure (foreshadowed by the Boy Charioteer in Act I), representing Romantic poetry and action. Goethe had Byron in mind—his "unsatisfied temperament and his war-like tendency." Euphorion suggests two aspects of German nineteenth century Romanticism: its musical estheticism and its call for political freedom in the Wars of Liberation. Yet, whereas Byron

219

intended to fight for Greek independence, the younger German Romanticists supported the German princes against Napoleon and his democratic code.

48. Goethe attempted to bridge such Kantian *Kultur*-division between the beautiful and the useful, but could see only the possibility of a *symbolic* union, such as he projects here. While Gretchen was created out of Goethe's deepest personal experience, Helena is a culture-vision and esthetic compensation for Faust's loss of Gretchen.

49. Mephisto's paper-money scheme for solving the Emperor's economic problems brought false prosperity. A rival emperor, aided by papal power, challenges the legitimate ruler. The scene echoes the Wars of the Holy Alliance against Napoleon in which the German poets and thinkers also sought "liberation" by supporting the authoritative powers. Goethe's critical attitude towards such wars of liberation appears in his picture of the frivolous Emperor and of the Mephistophelian bullies who are used to win the battle. A more direct satire on the "Holy" Alliance is presented through the Archbishop who demands "Tithes, levies, tax,—the total income of the land,/Forever." He also demands the estate which Faust has not yet wrested from the ocean! Only if the Emperor will grant all this, can he be forgiven for having made a "covenant with Satan." The Archbishop's insistence on a "formal document" is similar to Mephisto's formal request that Faust sign his pact with a drop of his blood.

50. Mephisto's violent methods express his volcanic nature. His creation legend in Act V suggests an analogy between geologic, social and political revolution.

Goethe planned a scene ("Disputationsaktus"), presenting a debate between Faust, arguing for idealism, and Mephisto, upholding realism. Goethe may have decided to omit this scene, realizing that the drama as a whole consists of such debate.

51. Goethe told Eckermann: "Had I refrained from public business and lived in greater solitariness, I would have been happier and more productive," and wrote to Zelter (June 6, 1825): ". . . what everyone strives after are wealth and speed. Even educated people rival each other and try to surpass each other in order to establish railroads . . . and all kinds of facilities for communication."

52. Bayard Taylor translates the word *Schuld* as Guilt. However, *Schuld* also means Debt, and that it is used in this sense here becomes clear when this grey woman says that she has no place in a rich man's house.

53. Sorge makes her entry following Faust's destructive action against the old couple. She appears to him as darkness and mist and is Faust's dim recognition of his Mephistophelian involvements. The connection between Sorge and conscience is developed in H. Jaeger's penetrating essay "The Problem of Faust's Salvation" (*Goethe Bicentennial Studies* [Bloomington 1950]), Jaeger cites Goethe's paralipomena to the Midnight scene in which Sorge tells Faust: "Grad im Befehlen wird die Sorge gross." He argues further that Faust's love is one of the conditions for his salvation, referring to his love for Gretchen, and his "unselfish" and "self-surrendering" love for Helena. However, Faust's love for Gretchen is not great enough for him to consider marrying her or giving

any thought to their child. Nor does Faust surrender to Helena—she is placed at his disposal through Mephisto's trickery.

Jaeger also contends that Faust's guilt-feeling at the end is due to "self-deception, not . . . lust for unlimited power," and that Sorge makes him conscious of this and thereby *frees* him of his guilt. As to this point, we should note that, unlike other mythic heroes, *Faust never repents.* He curses Mephisto's "impatient" deed which results in the death of the old couple, and he gives their land to the robbers. But that is all. Following the scene with Sorge, Faust orders that Mephisto "Reward, allure, conscript, compel" to assure the success of his project. Faust's subsequent humanistic pronouncement is a *salto mortale.*

54. The idea is also suggested in the *Weltbund* of *Wilhelm Meister's Travels.* Goethe thought that America, which has no "useless memories," might realize this vision.

55. Goethe did affirm, what he called, "pure activity," by which he meant action which mediates between experience and an idea. On this point, see Georg Simmel's *Goethe* (Leipzig, 1923), pp. 136 ff.

56. The only indication in the drama of Faust's identification with the people appears in "Before the City Gate," where he says that among the common folk, he dare be a human being. In his letter from Goslar to Charlotte von Stein (December 4, 1777), Goethe writes of having "again fallen in love with that class of people which is called the lower class, but which may be the highest in God's sight. It seems to combine all virtues—a limitation of desire, contentment in frugality, straight thinking, loyalty, delight in merely tolerable possessions, harmlessness, long-suffering, steadfastness. . . ." To be sure, Goethe's emphasis here is on the ability of the lower classes to accept their limited life.

57. Lunacharsky's drama *Faust and the City* develops this theme. One of Goethe's *Maxims and Reflections* states: "All that which frees our spirit without giving us self-control, is ruinous." Elsewhere, the insight is summed up in the celebrated line: "In der Beschränkung zeigt sich erst der Meister." In Goethe's *Pandora*, written during the Napoleonic wars, Prometheus is no longer the absolute rebel of Goethe's storm and stress poem. He limits himself to the sphere of the attainable and has learned *to put out the fire.* On this, see Arnold Bergstraesser's *Goethe's Image of Man and Society* (Chicago, 1949), chapter 9.

58. The utopian nature of Faust's idea also appears in the fact that his projected commonwealth is agrarian, "a land like Paradise." Faust ignores the circumstance that the basis for his project is technics.

59. In the *Recollections of Henrich Luden* (December 13, 1813), wherein Goethe speaks of the German people as "wretched," and of his attempt "in every way to transcend them," he adds: "The only thing that can console me is the faith in Germany's future."

60. "Den können wir erlösen." The point is lost in Taylor's translation: "Is not beyond redeeming."

61. Marianus is the "father" who asks the mother that the son be allowed to ap-

proach her, pleading that Faust's breast, now purified from its earthly element, is filled with serious and tender emotions of holy love.

62. Goethe also regarded miraculous revelation a blasphemy against God, and wrote: "I cling more or less to the teachings of Lucretius and confine myself and all my hopes to this life." (Letters of January 11, 1808, August 9, 1782, February 2, 1789.) The historical Faust was a Protestant and one of Goethe's *Maxims and Reflections* calls for constant "protesting." He expressed strong aversion against the German Romanticists who became converts to Catholicism. Ecclesiastical history was to him "a union of error and brute force" and the doctrine of Christ's Divinity "had always tended to promote despotism" (Müller's Diary, October 20, 1823). After completing the scene of Faust's Assumption, Goethe turned to the fourth Act which ends with a sharp satire of the Archbishop.

63. Goethe's judgment of Dante was unusually harsh, calling the Inferno "loathsome," Purgatory "ambiguous," Paradise "boring." Dante's greatness, he said (1821) was "disagreeable," often "detestable."

64. The divine, Goethe told Eckermann, consists not in the motionless and finished, but in that which develops and is transmuted. Goethe's final category is no finished absolute, but what he calls *Steigerung*, connoting a process of intensification. He confessed to Kanzler von Müller that he would not know what to do with heavenly joy, if it did not offer him new problems. The play, according to the Manager in "Prelude on the Stage," is to move "From Heaven, across the World, to Hell!" and Goethe's notes indicate that the drama was to end with an epilogue.

65. Georg Lukacs sees here an analogy to the argument in Hegel's Phenomenology that the progress of the species is accomplished by the "List der Vernunft," which exacts the sacrifice of the individual.

The Quest for an American Myth
Moby Dick

AMERICA'S HISTORY has not provided the conditions which are necessary for the development of a rooted mythic tradition. Henry James complained that America had no state, no personal loyalty, no museums and no political society. And, in our own day, George Santayana found America still raw and juvenile.

The lack of tradition is partly based on the circumstances that *Amercan history begins with an act of secession* from its "Old World" parentage. Where Hamlet and Faust are haunted by the ghosts of their past, the American mythic hero is more concerned with the future.[1] Some Europeans have envied us for this. America, Goethe sang, is better off than the old continent—it has no decayed castles and no burdening heritage. Similarly Heine:

> This is America!
> This is the new world! . . .
> This is no graveyard of Romance; . . .
> Of fossilized wigs and symbols
> Of stale and musty Tradition!

(Louis Untermeyer, *Heinrich Heine: Paradox and Poet.* Vol. II: *The Poems* [New York, 1937], p. 338)

To be sure, we did find the Indians; but they became a curious movie vestige. The Negro brought with him a native tradition, but we have used his "service" more than his "spirituals." And, while the Negro is being emancipated, he is also being "freed" from his mythic heritage.

Yet, despite our relatively short history, we still cling to an indigenous lore. We have our legends of the Indians, of pioneers and goldseekers, our Kit Carsons, Paul Bunyans and Mike Finns. And, due to the accelerated changes in American life under the pressure of rapid

223

technological development, the era of the Indian, of the adventurous pioneer, and the daring Western Robin Hood seems to belong to an ancient past.

The myth imbedded in these pictures of earliest American life is that of a land offering a surfeit of opportunities, "a golden land," as it has been known to countless immigrants. The myth of America is that of a new, open, expanding world where "the sky is the limit," and *anybody* can go from rags to riches.[2] This success story is supplemented by the idea (portrayed in the earlier Chaplin pictures) that here the little man can maneuver amidst the big and powerful, and even outwit them. In place of fixed ancestral norms, we have the open future of limitless possibilities. The traditional myth of Creation becomes the Quest for the newest and latest.[3] This characteristic American temper is embodied in two of our major intellectual movements: transcendentalism and pragmatic operationalism.

Our legendary figures are "outdoor" heroes, wandering like Paul Bunyan and Davy Crockett through woods and forests, like Mike Finn and Huck Finn down the rivers, with Captain Ahab and Wolf Larsen in the Pacific, with Walt Whitman throughout our continent. They are American in their direct, empirical approach and in the practical nature of their pursuits — gold, whales or seals. These symbolic journeys draw on the feverish migrations in our earlier history. The task faced by our pioneers was not to re-create a Golden Age, not to redeem an old heritage, but to create a new community by gaining control of forest, land and river.

The ebb and flow of migratory living did not allow the hardening of a traditional core or the formation of a steady mythic reference. Instead, they encouraged unlimited play of "free enterprise," of an independence and adventurism, unchecked by feudal memories.

But there were those who saw a threat in this unrestricted freedom, individualism and futurism. And, indeed, they contained the basis for a Nietzschean "I will, therefore I am," leading to the ethics of the sea- and land-wolves. For the Puritans and for Jonathan Edwards, the myth of expansionism appears ambiguous, if not evil. By the time of Theodore Dreiser, William Faulkner and Robinson Jeffers, it has lost most of its legitimacy. The success story of Dreiser's "Titan" becomes suspect and the efforts of the little man to hit it rich provide the foundation for an "American Tragedy." The magic short cut to the happy ending receives more acid treatment in Faulkner and Jeffers. Among our contemporary writers, the myth of expectancy appears frozen (O'Neill's *The Iceman Cometh*), cornered (Tennessee Williams' *Streetcar Named*

Desire), dead (Arthur Miller's *Death of a Salesman*), and self-destructive (Clifford Odets' *The Big Knife*).

However, the celebration of rugged, self-reliant individualism was tempered by the enormous task of exploring a new world. The pioneer had to lean on the "good neighbor policy." Moreover, America is the expression of a *common* effort. Many races, religions and customs found themselves on one boat. The individualism of the American hero is modified by his fraternal affiliations—with the good neighbor, buddy and friend. Fraternity and Freedom are the American replacements for European Paternity and Order.

But what constitutes the core of this fraternity? Who is the "American?" Is it Melville's New Englander who yearns for the South Seas? Is it Mark Twain's Southerner with his chivalry and slave-plantations or his Huck and Jim who strike out for freedom? Is it the Western rancher? Is it the Indian, Negro and foreigner? Is it Dreiser's Quaker, Willa Cather's Bishop, Mike Gold's Jew? Is America the "melting pot" of its multiple elements?

Herman Melville stands at the watershed moment of a historic cycle. In his time, American was still tied to its European parent. But it is also the hour of Emerson's American Scholar and of America's growing economic independence and dynamism. And Melville is among those who question the ethic of expansionism. His *Moby Dick* at once continues the American Myth of unlimited possibilities and expresses disenchantment with it. Herein, Melville meets with Goethe whose Faust likewise at once affirms and questions the myth of modern expansionism.

The need for a native myth begins to be voiced as America develops towards economic and cultural autonomy. Emerson's Journal speaks of our need for "a theory of interpretation or Mythology." Alcott, Margaret Fuller and the Brook Farm Utopians sought to live it. In our own time, Thomas Wolfe called it the quest for a father. Wolfe became a "Far Wanderer" seeking the equivalent of a home and paternity. Faulkner and Hemingway labored to find replacement values, as did writers such as John Steinbeck, Benjamin Appel, and Alfred Kreymborg. The earliest and possibly the most passionate expression of the American quest for its common sources and resources is Melville's *Moby Dick*.[4] In American literature, Ahab stands closest to the classic, mythic prototypes of Job, Prometheus, Hamlet, and Faust. Melville is the first outstanding American writer to express the need for an American myth of creation.

In the past, *Moby Dick* has not been viewed as characteristically

American. Its labored symbolism and metaphysics seemed nearer to the European than to the American manner. Recent years have brought an unprecedented Melville interest. His vogue coincides with that of Franz Kafka and the existentialists. Both Melville and Kafka present the antagonist as a baffling "secret"—the feeling many have today that we are confronted by an ineffable, elusive opponent. Both are modern in making science an instrument in the quest. Still their heroes are almost at the complete mercy of ubiquitous and apparently indestructible forces.

The Borrowed Myth

In Melville's earlier conception, *Moby Dick* was to be simply an adventure story of a whaling expedition, and it can still be enjoyed as such. But the final version is clearly more than that. Melville interlaces the narrative with mythic, moral, social, metaphysical and allegorical allusions.

However, many of these are borrowed. The language of *Moby Dick* is an amorphous mixture of Biblical, Elizabethan and tough American speech; its form has elements of the epic, dramatic and lyric. These ingredients remain uncoordinated, as uncoordinated as is the Pequod crew and the congregation in Father Mapple's chapel. Melville attempts to give Ahab's quest an Oriental, Greek and Biblical geneology. The glory of whaling is shown to have a rich mythic ancestry in Perseus, St. George, Hercules, Jonah, and Vishnoo.

The Biblical analogies predominate: Elijah, the warning prophet, Jonah in Father Mapple's sermon, Captain Bildad whose "utilitarian character" suggests the Bildad from the Book of Job. Ishmael recalls the son of Abraham and Agar who was driven from home by Sarah's jealousy, became an "orphan," a wanderer and rover. It is he who, at the close of the novel, quotes the words from Job: "I only am escaped alone to tell thee."[5] Ahab bears the name of the Hebrew king who, misled by false prophets, worshipped Baal, thereby provoking the Lord more than any other of the Israelite kings. When tested by Elijah and challenged to invoke a fire under Baal's altar, King Ahab failed. He was then thrown to the dogs who licked his blood.

Moby Dick is the myth of what the novel calls an "unfathered birth."[6] The novel begins and ends with Ishmael, "another orphan." Miraculously saved from the grave of the sea, he may have learned "the secret of our paternity."[7]

The Savage Elements

"Long exile from Christendom and civilization," we read in *Moby Dick*, "inevitably restores a man to that condition in which God placed

226

him, i.e. what is called savagery. Your true whale-hunter is as much a savage as an Iroquois. I myself am a savage."

Melville's most persuasive references are to primitive and elemental powers. Having but an indirect kinship with the old legends, the American mythmaker invokes the earliest and most common memory of all, that of man and the universe in their primordial state.

On this level, the world seems to be governed by magical forces. The novel begins with animistic fantasies suggested by the Spouter Inn and by Elijah's warning. They are consistently associated with the Pequod and the White Squid. There is a magic about Ahab's personality, his strange power over the crew, and about the White Whale. Melville draws analogies between the chase of Moby Dick and the Western legends of the Jet-Black Stallion, the White Deer and the Big Bear of Arkansas.

The characters in *Moby Dick* are in a societal stage roughly approximating what Morgan called "savagery." Here, man is almost completely dependent on the elements which assume anthropomorphic character and divine power. Water and sea, fire, storm and lightning, air, wind and mist are leading "characters" in Melville's drama, are addressed, challenged or propitiated. As in the primitive myth and in Wagner's Siegfried cycle, the elements are sexualized and appear as parental and familial powers. The sun is spoken of as a king, the sea as a man, the air as bride, the fire as father.

Water and fire, or their interaction in storm, are in the foreground. The sea is the all-encompassing terrain of the story. For the crew on the Pequod, it is the "earth" on which they live and to which they return. It appears as an "underground-" reservoir, unplumbed, unknown, and unlimited, suggestive of an archetypal unconscious. Here, we are told, "millions of mixed shades and shadows, drowned dreams, somnambulisms, reveries; all that we call lives and souls, lie dreaming, dreaming still; tossing like slumberers in their beds."

Water (along with the other elements) has an ambivalent character of birth or rebirth (nourishment) and of death (drowning). For Starbuck, the sea induces a soothing, contemplative mood. Even Ahab is not immune to this peaceful aspect of the Pacific. In "The Symphony," he yields for a moment to the spell of the gentle day and drops a tear into the sea. But the stormy sea is also demonic, swallowing and devouring its victim.[8]

Addressing the fire, Ahab declares: "Thy right worship is defiance." Fire is most ominous when, combined with air and water, it produces thunder and lightning. Ahab's meeting with the White Whale is foreshadowed by a storm in which the waters are churned and the air is rented by fiery darts.

AHAB: THE MAIMED SATANIC HERO

Ahab was condemned by his own mother. In naming him "Ahab," she assigned him the fate of the king who was killed and whose blood was licked by dogs. Before his voyage on the Pequod, Ahab loses a leg to the White Whale.[9] We are also told of an event which suggests a kind of self-castration: Ahab was found unconscious in the street "by some unknown, and seemingly inexplicable, unimaginable casualty, his ivory limb having been so violently displaced that it had stake-wise smitten, and all but pierced his groin." Ahab stands before his crew "with a crucifixion in his face; in all the nameless regal overbearing dignity of some mighty woe." The Christ analogy is also suggested by Ahab's subsequent withdrawal, as a man apart, and his later return. However, he returns, in Satanic hatred, not in Christian love.

In forging the harpoon for the "white fiend," Ahab enacts the ritual of the bond with the devil. The ceremony is performed in a state of near-delirium, Ahab drawing "the baptismal blood" from the three pagan harpooners, howling "Ego no baptizo te in nomine patris, sed in nomine diaboli." Ahab's ritual is a pact with the Evil one, and an expression of his death wish.[10]

Ahab is the Satanic hero growing out of the Protestant tradition, and belongs to the lineage of Iago, Hagen and the Norse Loki. He spurns mediators and guides, would be his own Virgil, Beatrice and St. Bernard. In his "fixed and fearless, forward dedication," Ahab's revolt takes on a diabolic character which would destroy everything, including himself. Ahab is Satan, as *the maimed hero.*

Ahab's Satanism follows the old form: the attempt to be more than a man. And the price is the same: Thou must not love. And not to love means to be consumed by restlessness, doomed to ceaseless wandering. Goethe's Protestant Faust can be redeemed in that, at the end, he desires to be a man among men, and enjoys the futuristic vision of a free people on free soil. Ahab is closer to the guilty wanderers, to Cain, to the Flying Dutchman and the Wandering Jew. Like Cain, his crime is against fellow crew brethren; like the Wandering Jew, he repudiates the God in man.

Ahab is the focus for most of Melville's mythic parallels. He is Job who demands to know why he has been mutilated, calling on his ad-

versary to appear and confront him; but he is a Job who does not submit
to the Lord. He is Prometheus who challenges his enemy, but without
Prometheus' tool and love for mankind. He is Oedipus attempting to
bring his sources to light; but he is one who does not attain the redemption of Oedipus in Colonus. He is Don Quixote in his rigid consistency,
without the Don's lovable humanity. He is the Flying Dutchman, determined to chase his object "round the world." He calls himself
"Shem," referring to the son who uncovered his father's nakedness.
Finally, in the end, he is Homunculus who descends into the waters to
acquire a body.

The Pequod is a kind of Noah's Ark, harboring elements from the
savage and civilized world. Its hero would catch the great Fish Leviathan, but unlike the Messiah, his intent is not to divide it among the
faithful. He is not a preserver, but a destroyer of his group. The devil's
price is exacted to its fullest on the social level as well. It appears in
Ahab's relation to the crew.[11] Ahab is the ruler over his social universe.
All must submit to his will and do his bidding to the point of jeopardiz-
ing their collective existence. But what is the legitimacy of Ahab's rule?
What is the cause in which they are sacrificed?

In the classical myth, the "cause" has a public, all-human reference
—to bring peace to Thebes and Athens, to build the city of Rome, to
revive the Golden Age of Chivalry, to rid the state of Denmark of its
rottenness, to build a Faustian free city. To be sure, in all instances, a
personal need is interwoven with the public task; but in the end, the
individual need is a function of the public good.

The exclusive stake in the chase of *Moby Dick* is the righting of a
personal wrong suffered by Ahab. It is Ahab's leg which the White
Whale bit off. It is his and only his person which was violated. To the
crew, whaling is a practical business, a form of employment. They
have no special interest in Moby Dick. Yet, Ahab succeeds in per-
suading the crew that his objective is identical with their own. They are
somehow hypnotized by their leader's demon and they act as if they
were all a collective Ahab. The transformation is achieved by something akin to black magic.

Ahab succeeds in imposing his "sultanism" because at this stage
of American development, there is as yet no cohesive social grouping.
The crew belongs in the category of "Loose-Fish," which Melville defines as "fair game for anybody who can soonest catch it."[12] It is unable
to act jointly in its common interests. They are the raw, eclectic form
of the American lower depths towards the middle of the nineteenth
century. Artistically, Melville shows this by making them all (with the

exception of Queequeg) more or less stereotypes. Hence, Ahab can silence their rebellious murmurings, can melt their will down to the point where it serves his purpose.

Ahab's relation to the crew is the hero pitted *against* his community. He curses the "mortal inter-debtedness" of man and frets that he, who would be "a sovereign being in nature," must depend on the carpenter for a bone to stand on. In Schopenhauer, the wilful ego merges with the nothingness of Nirvana, what Freud later called the death-wish. In both, the individual is at the end "socialized" in a cosmic unity. Modern existentialism—which claims Melville as one of its forerunners —contains a variant of this dialectic. Its individual would also be "as free as air." It begins with "nothing," and by a series of "leaps," reaches death or shipwreck. Similarly Ahab. His commanding voice ends in helpless voicelessness and his dictatorial ego is communalized in the womb of the sea.[13]

Transposed into American social history, Ahab foreshadows the way of the Robber Barons.[14] If Ahab stands for an unbridled individualism, the crew stands for a loose, unorganized fraternity. In the novel, the will of the one and the willessness of the other produce their common catastrophe.

The Psychic Burden

Moby Dick also contains Melville's secret psychological burden. The author repeatedly states that the White Whale is a secret which remains hidden to him. Hamlet freely admits that he has "bad dreams," condemns and depreciates himself for his hesitancy in avenging his father's murder. Ahab has "nightmares" but they do not paralyze his will for revenge. Although his eye is "troubled," he remains arrogant and defiant.

Now, the novel suggests that it was Ahab's own "thoughts" which produced the vulture that "feeds upon the heart forever" ("The Chart"). Following this clue, it would appear that Ahab *invites* punishment to relieve deep-seated guilt-feelings.

The novel tells us almost nothing about Ahab's past, as though that too must remain a secret. But, early in the story, we learn that Ahab married when he was past fifty, and that he has a son. Towards the end of the novel, Ahab tells Starbuck in a confessional moment, that the very day after his marriage, he sailed for Cape Horn, "leaving but one dent in my marriage pillow." A "mild, mild wind, and a mild looking sky" wring the admission from Ahab that he half suspects why he has exposed himself to "forty years of privation and peril, and storm-time! forty years on the pitiless sea!" There follows his reference to "that young girl-wife" whom he wedded late in life and left the succeeding day. "Aye, I widowed that poor girl when I married her," he tells Starbuck. The next sentences return to the theme of his frenzied life:

> And then, the madness, the frenzy, the boiling blood and the smoking brow, with which, for a thousand lowerings old Ahab has furiously, foamingly chased his prey—more a demon than a man!—aye, aye! what a forty years' fool—fool—old fool, has old Ahab been! Why this strife of the chase? why weary, and palsy the arm at the oar, and the iron, and the lance? how the richer or better is Ahab now?

This passage indicates an association in Ahab's mind between his having left "but one dent" in his marriage pillow and the "frenzy" with which he chased his prey—"furiously, foamingly . . . more a demon than a man."

Is there a connection between the "troubled" look in Ahab's eye and his marriage late in life to a "young girl-wife"? Was Ahab's mutilation by the White Whale but an intensification of an already existing feeling of personal inadequacy? Is Ahab's pursuit of whales an attempt to prove himself? To prove himself *master at sea* to cover up his not being *master on land*? Would his conquest of Moby Dick give him the illusion that he can be a man, just as his ivory leg makes him feel that he possesses a sound limb?

Homoeroticism and Isolation

Attention has been called to Melville's fixation on his mother. The theme of incest which breaks out openly in *Pierre*, remains underground in *Moby Dick*. However, the homoerotic motif which is connected with it, is pervasive in the novel.

A striking feature of the book is the almost complete absence of reference to sex, even though the crew is composed of rough primitive men who spend months at sea. The men allow themselves but dreamy erotic snatches when, in "Midnight, Forecastle," they dance and sing together. And only when the Pequod, bound for the waters of the White Whale crosses the Bachelor returning home with its jubilant crew dancing with their Polynesian brides, do we have mention of sex-joy. The "love-" element in *Moby Dick* is confined to the world of men.

A revealing passage in the chapter "A Squeeze of the Hand" describes the way in which the lumps of the sperm are converted into fluid. The process entails "squeezing":

231

> It was our business to squeeze these lumps back into fluid. A sweet and unc-
> tuous duty! No wonder that in old times sperm was such a favourite cosmetic.
> Such a clearer! such a sweetener; such a softener; such a delicious mollifier!
> After having my hands in it for only a few minutes, my fingers felt like eels,
> and began, as it were, to serpentine and spiralize.

As Ishmael continues to squeeze, he is filled with a strange sort of good will, almost a kind of "insanity," an "affectionate, friendly, loving feeling," especially when he finds himself

> unwittingly squeezing my co-laborers' hands in it, mistaking their hands for
> the gentle globules. Such an abounding, affectionate, friendly, loving feeling
> did this avocation beget; that at last I was continually squeezing their hands,
> and looking up into their eyes sentimentally; as much as to say. . . . Come;
> let us squeeze hands all round; nay, let us squeeze ourselves into each other;
> let us squeeze ourselves universally into the very milk and sperm of kind-
> ness. . . . In thoughts of the visions of the night, I saw long rows of angels in
> paradise, each with his hands in a jar of spermaceti.[15]

A more overt homoerotic note is manifested in the relationship be-tween Ishmael and Queequeg. On the morning of the night in which they sleep together at the Spouter Inn, Ishmael finds Queequeg's arm thrown over him in a most loving manner—"you had almost thought I had been his wife." And, by the savage's side slept the tomohawk, "as if it were a hatchet-faced baby."[16]

Ahab, who was socially "inaccessible," and whose concern is only with himself, embodies the most extreme form of the Narcissus-motif which is sounded at the beginning of the novel. The crew, too, are what Melville calls "Isolatoes." As Ishmael enters the chapel he finds

> a small scattered congregation of sailors and sailors' wives and widows. . . .
> Each silent worshipper seemed purposely sitting apart from the other, as if
> each silent grief were insular and incommunicable . . . silent islands of men
> and women . . . each *Isolato* living on a separate continent of his own.

There is isolation in Ahab's lonely monologues, in Pip's mad self-absorption and, at the close, in the isolated rescue of Ishmael.

THE WHITE WHALE: THE PARENTAL SEX-MYSTERY

It was suggested that Ahab's pursuit of whales is a mask for covering and relieving his private burden. Yet, Ahab is also a representative figure, and we must ask ourselves not only what Moby Dick means to Ahab, the "old" man, but also to Ahab, as an American mythic hero.

The White Whale is an individualized animal, who has earned his name "Moby Dick." At the same time, the story endows this whale with magical powers, and even with a degree of sanctity. Here, Melville's Moby Dick assumes some of the characteristics which are associated with the Rhine Gold, the Golden Fleece and the Holy Grail.[17]

Moby Dick is called a "god," indestructible, eternally elusive and "unknowable." His brow reveals no distinct features, no face, nothing but a forehead, "pleated with riddles." Watching him in his elements, he seemed heavenly: "Not Jove, not that great majesty Supreme! did surpass the glorified White Whale as he so divinely swam."

Melville-criticism has popularized the notion that to Ahab the White Whale is the personification of Evil. This view is supported only by what Ahab says about Moby Dick. The problem becomes more complex when we analyze Ahab's *attitude* and *behavior* towards the Whale.

Ahab fears Moby Dick. But he is also hypnotized by him. He is both repelled by the White Whale and drawn to him. The reader is expressly told that Moby Dick is a "magnet" to Ahab. It is Ahab, not Moby Dick, who is the pursuer. On the third day of the chase, Moby Dick is seen swimming away from the ship, pursuing his own straight path in the sea. At this point, Starbuck pleads with the Captain: "Oh! Ahab, not too late is it, even now, the third day, to desist. See! Moby Dick seeks thee not. It is thou, thou, that madly seekest him!"

Moby Dick is a "secret" to Melville and to Ahab precisely in that he is *not* an unambigous incarnation of evil. Describing the Whale as he is about to plunge into the deep, Melville remarks that if one is in the Dantean mood, "the devils will occur to you; if in that of Isaiah, the archangels." Even on the third day of the chase, in the very midst of the Whale's ferocious attacks, we read that Moby Dick then seemed possessed "by all the angels that fell from heaven."

The awe with which Melville surrounds Moby Dick is connected with the hero's attempt to plumb the origins of his being. *Moby Dick* is replete with parental references and with allusions to the sex-act. One of the more revealing chapters is "The Gilder."

Towards the close of this chapter, Melville-Ahab asks despairingly:

Where is the foundling's father hidden? Our souls are like those orphans whose unwedded mothers die in bearing them: the secret of our paternity lies in their grave, and we must there to learn it.

This passage is preceded by references to the sea as a field of "long-drawn virgin vales." The ship is compared to horses who show only their "erected ears, while their hidden bodies widely wade through the

233

'amazing verdure." "The Symphony" speaks of the sun as "a royal czar and king . . . giving this gentle air to this bold and rolling sea; even as bride to groom," and of "the loving alarms, with which the poor bride gave the bosom away."

Sex-allusions are particularly crowded in the descriptions of the White Whale. They point to Moby Dick as a male-female, father-mother figure.

Male-Female Dialectic

The chapter on "The Tail" is crowded with phallic and coitus-imagery. It is a hymn to the vast power of the tail:

> The broad palms of his tail are flirted high into the air! then smiting the surface, the thunderous concussion resounds for miles. You would think a great gun had been discharged; and if you noticed the light wreath of vapor from the spiracle at his other extremity, you would think that that was the smoke from the touch-hole.

When he is about

> to plunge into the deeps, his entire flukes . . . are tossed erect in the air, and so remain vibrating a moment, till they downward shoot out of view. Excepting the sublime *breach*—somewhere else to be described—this peaking of the whale's flukes is perhaps the grandest sight to be seen in all animated nature.

The gigantic organ seems to emerge

> out of bottomless profundities. . . . spasmodically snatching at the highest heaven. So in dreams have I seen majestic Satan thrusting forth his tormented colossal claw from the flame Baltic of Hell.[18]

As Moby Dick appears,

> his whole marbleized body formed a high arch, like Virginia's Natural Bridge, and warningly waving his bannered flukes in the air, he reveals himself as the grand god.[19]

Moby Dick is not only a god-king-father figure. The male is joined to the female. We get an allusion to Aphrodite, as the White Whale emerges from the waters, like "some plumed and glittering god uprising from the sea." And, we have more direct indication of Moby Dick's bisexuality in the metaphors Melville uses to describe the whale. The head is said to be both a "battering ram" and "a dead blind wall," enveloped by a boneless toughness. It has "the rare virtue of thick walls," and "the rare virtue of interior spaciousness." The tail possesses terrifying power; yet, the immense flukes sweep "with a certain slow softness" the surface of "the masculine sea," and the tail moves with "maidenly gentleness" and "delicacy." On the first day of the chase, Moby Dick appears with a tall shattered pole projecting from his back. The sight recalls to Melville the myth of Jupiter carrying Europa:

> . . . the white bull Jupiter swimming away with ravished Europa clinging to his graceful horns; his lovely leering eyes sideways intent upon the maid; with smooth bewitching fleetness, rippling straight for the nuptial bower in Crete.

The White Whale is the disguised form of the hermaphroditical mystery.[20] Ahab invades the "man-like sea," challenging it to give up its primal secret. His attitude is a mixture of defiance and fear, of hatred and love. In "The Candles," Ahab addresses the lightning as "my fiery father." Even as he owns that the father is "omnipotent," and "an incommunicable riddle," he would dispute his "speechless place-less power" and "unconditional, unintegral mastery." Yet, amidst this Promethean harangue, Ahab confesses that his deeper desire is to "worship," to "burn" and to be "welded" with him. A suppliant note steals into Ahab's defiance, a womanly submissive tone, as he speaks of "the queenly personality" in himself which demands "her royal rights." He would rather not make war, and he pleads: "Come in thy lowest form of love, and I will kneel and kiss thee."

A still deeper secret envelops the "foundling sire:" the Mother. Ahab cries out: "My sweet mother, I know not. Oh, cruel! what hast thou done with her? There lies my puzzle." Wagner's Siegfried also wonders what his mother was like. Siegfried, in his fearless "innocence," finds a surrogate mother in Brunhilde. Ahab, in his unacknowledged guilt finds one in final "attachment" to Moby Dick.[21]

Did Melville become somewhat aware of this? In a letter to Hawthorne, he stated that he had written a "wicked book," and now felt "spotless as the lamb." *Moby Dick* is followed by *Pierre* in which the parents' attitude stands in the way of Pierre's becoming a mature man.[22] And Billy Budd readily accepts the death-judgment of Captain Vere, his father-figure. Billy Budd is primarily "body" as Ahab is primarily "spirit." Billy has the innocent physical power, Ahab the guilty fiery passion with which they dominate and kill. Both revert to speechless infancy. Ahab returns to it with desperate defiance, Billy in serene passivity.

From the psychoanalytic perspective, *Moby Dick* and *Pierre* present the interlocking pattern of the oedipal and incest drives. In *Moby Dick* the oedipal predominates (modified by Ahab first "getting" his woman, abandoning her and his son later). And here, the oedipal is linked to the homosexual—Ahab's attitude towards the father-element in the White Whale is also a wooing. Ahab would cover up this impermissible desire and projects it on to the Whale, insisting that it is Moby Dick who pursues him—a paranoid manuever, characteristic in latent homosexuality. In *Pierre*, incest (distributed between mother and sister) and matricide predominate. And again, these impulses are used to mask the homosexual drive. But the artistic thinness of *Pierre* is an esthetic confession that this defense has failed.

However, we need to bear in mind that Melville's works are *novels*, not psychological tracts, and that his sexual symbolism is an aspect of his aesthetic symbolism. His art gives us the *resistance* against the primitive urges. In all-over terms, his work contains various levels of attempted integration of the ego with the id.

The Quest for Creation

The passages cited indicate that the White Whale stands for the feared and desired object harboring the secret of the sexes and of parental creation. It is a fearful thing, Melville tells us, "to have one's hands among the unspeakable foundations, ribs, and very pelvis of the world." Ahab's journey represents a maximum effort to face and solve the riddle. But this hero is maimed, and his very efforts expose his impotence: His leg had been torn off; on the first day of the chase, the whale's jaw comes within inches of his head, and Ahab falls flat-faced on the water; on the second day, his ivory stump is snapped; on the third day, he is strangled. Crippled Ahab lacks the power to penetrate Moby Dick's "thick walls." The hunter feels "impotent" before this prey: "The severest pointed harpoon, the sharpest lance darted by the strongest human arm, impotently rebounds from it." The wall remains "impregnable," and Ahab never reaches its most "buoyant thing within." Melville draws an analogy between the fate awaiting him who would conquer Moby Dick and that which befell "the weakling youth" who desired to lift "the dread goddess' veil at Sais."

Despite these terrors, Ahab does hurl his spear at the White Whale. As Ahab sees Moby Dick successfully breaching the thick walls of the Pequod, he makes his final supreme effort "to give up the spear." The gesture is performed in an orgiastic frenzy and exaltation, Ahab feeling "like a billow that's all one crested comb." At the end he is "united" at last to the whale by his line. The umbilical cord is retied, and Ahab sinks like an infant, "voicelessly" into the ocean by the side of the mystery he has been unable to fathom.

The novel calls the whale "king of creation" and "the incarnation of Vishnu." What Brahma, Moira and God were to earlier mythmakers, that Moby Dick is to Ahab. Ahab's voyage is the American journey to bring its birth to light.[23]

Whiteness: Demonic Ambiguity

Melville attaches special importance to his chapter on "The Whiteness of the Whale," remarking that he must try to explain what it was to Ishmael, "else all these chapters might be naught."

Traditionally, he notes, the color white represented the white man's "mastership over every dusky tribe." In *Typee* and *Oomoo*, Melville had questioned the idea of white superiority. *Moby Dick* goes beyond the social towards the legendary and mythic.

The apparent intent is to explain why the whiteness of the whale "appalled" Ishmael, filling him with a "vague, nameless horror." Melville cites examples of white objects which instill terror: The white bear and white shark, the albatross, the white steed of the prairies in the Indian tradition, the whiteness of ghosts, and of the shroud.

Yet, Melville begins the chapter by enumerating examples which have benign, even reverent associations. Whiteness stands for virginal bridal purity and the benignity of old age. He speaks of white as the sign of divine spotlessness and power, as "the very veil of the Christian deity."

What emerges from the dual set of illustrations is not the malign character of whiteness but its *ambiguity*. Like Melville's "Whiteness," Moby Dick is a mixture of good and evil, the angelic and the satanic, which may appear to human understanding as indifference.[24] All this makes life seem like a High Comedy and death as "only sly, goodnatured hits . . . bestowed by the unseen and unaccountable old joker."[25]

The Reflexive Metaphor

Ahab is the leader without or against the group. The crew is a community lacking in social cohesion. The two extremes meet in a reflexive arc.

The reflexive is the leading metaphor of the story. The geometric sign is the circle:

> There is no steady unretracing progress in this life; we do not advance through fixed gradations. . . . But once gone through, we trace the round again.

Whales are marvels. Yet, like all marvels, they are

> mere repetitions of the ages; so that for the millionth time we say amen with Solomon—Verily there is nothing new under the sun.

Melville pays tribute to the idea of metempsychosis:

> Oh! Pythagoras . . . I sailed with thee along the Peruvian coast last voyage —and foolish as I am, taught thee, a green simple boy, how to slice a rope.

Ahab's journey is called a "round the world voyage," which takes one back "to the very point whence we started." Ahab sees himself as "the image of the rounder globe, which like a magician's glass, to each and every man in turn but mirrors his own mysterious self." Here, Ahab has a fleeting recognition that his journey is a circular narcissistic quest.[26] Childlike, he challenges the elements, dashes the quadrant to the deck, sails against the wind. Childlike, he sinks into the deep.

The elemental nature of Melville's writing makes itself felt in those passages in which his imagination draws on his personal experiences at sea. Here, his prose swells and undulates in lyrical wave-rhythms. But the art of the book is uneven. Passages vibrating with genuine passion are broken up by vague, mystico-religious dissertations and expressionistic monologues. *Moby Dick* is primarily the story of the self obsessed with itself. The book is largely a drawn out soliloquy. This gives Melville's prose an "ejaculatory" character to use Matthiessen's term.[27] Only in the last chapters, does the novel approach a high level of drama.

Epilogue

Ishmael is the only member of the crew who completes the journey and returns home. Ishmael is Ahab's Horatio, left to "tell" his story. He represents the principle of maximum consciousness and interdependence in the novel, bridging the religious and cultural distance between himself and the rest. As the spectator of the drama, he has "full sight of the ensuing scene." As the narrator, he is the esthetic mediator among the various perspectives in the book. The Journey is his ritual of initiation from which he learns—what Ahab does not—the price exacted for dictatorial wilfulness, as well as for automatic obedience.

Yet, Ishmael does not earn heroic stature. As a character in the novel, he is colorless, almost anonymous. Ishmael is the only one who has no relationship to Ahab, nor does he communicate his thoughts and feelings to anyone on the ship. Ishmael has been likened to the Greek Chorus. But, unlike the Greek Chorus, he does not take part in or suffer from the action (except at the end). His knowledge of the whole issues in a kind of cosmic sympathy approaching an ironic indifference, an indifference akin to that of the Carpenter. Ishmael does not show Starbuck's human receptiveness to Ahab's agony; he does not possess the quality of spontaneous sharing and self-sacrifice of Queequeg.[28]

Ishmael is saved, not by his works, but by miracle and grace: the miracle of Queequeg's "coffin" floating by his side and the gracious action of the Rachel's captain. Ahab, obsessed by his private grievance, had refused to help the Captain find his son. The Captain reverses Ahab's temper, "adopting" the Pequod's orphan as a replacement for his own son. Following the three-day chase and his descent into the watery pit, Ishmael is saved.[29]

Through the character of Ahab, Melville gives us both the threat and the promise in the American quest. Ahab is more intent on conquest than on comradeship. In *Moby Dick* the Quest is restricted to its egocentric or demonic quality and is not transmuted into a communal blessing. Ahab's *hybris* is closer to religious sin than to mythic error or crime. He lacks the communal bond which rehabilitates the hero in mythopoesis. While Ahab's ruthless egotism is not for material gain and ownership, his "irresistible dictatorship" foreshadows the individual enterprise which Jack London pictures in *The Sea Wolf*.[30]

Still, *Moby Dick* is not altogether lacking in a social ethos. To be sure, the crew is not an Athenian chorus, not the noble citizen of the Roman state, not even Hamlet's "distracted multitude," but is "chiefly made up of mongrel renegades and castaways, and cannibals." Yet, Melville writes in praise of the "democratic God" who selects champions "from the kingly commons," who gave power to "the swart convict Bunyan," to "the pampered arm of old Cervantes," and who picked up Andrew Jackson "from the pebbles." He would celebrate "that democratic dignity which, on all hands, radiates without end from God." Ahab himself is a "democratic" hero, one who does not possess "the dignity of kings and robes." But Melville's paean is first of all to Ahab's mates, the "Knights and Squires," to the harpooners, to the arm "that wields a pick or drives a spoke." They all belong to the "same ancient Catholic Church . . . the great and everlasting First Congregation." Melville translates the transcendental democracy of Emerson and the idyllic internationalism of Thoreau into a communal idea.

In a sense, it is the crew which compose the tragic note in *Moby Dick*. They are placed in a situation with which they cannot cope; yet, they face it with courage. The crew accepts Ahab, sensing his "humanities." Their acceptance is an element of grace which contributes towards his redemption. Starbuck suffers with Ahab in "The Symphony." All witness his human relationship to little Pip. They see suffering written on his face, as he stood there "in all the nameless regal overbearing dignity of some mighty woe." In such moments, the Satanic hero almost becomes the sacrificial scapegoat.

In this phase, Ahab has affinity to the figure of the Fisher King, connected with the legend of the Holy Grail. As developed by Jessie L. Weston's *From Ritual to Romance*, the Fisher King is incapacitated by the effects of a wound and becomes known as the Maimed King. In the Grail Legend, the wound of the King is a punishment for his sinful passion towards a pagan princess, and the nature of the wound suggests injury to the reproductive energy. The Fisher King, who is either in middle life or an aged man, is healed by his successor, a youthful figure.

Ahab would be at once the middle-aged Fisher King and the young hero who saves him, would be both Satan and the Messiah.[31] He fights the colossus although he knows he will be defeated, and emerges with the dignity of the tragic which arises from his very flaw. This flaw and the redemption are foreshadowed in "The Sermon" which states the two main motifs of the book.

The text of Father Mapple's sermon is "And God had prepared a great fish to swallow up Jonah." Jonah's sin lay "in his wilful disobedience of the command of God." Now, Jonah finally makes his confession and accepts his punishment as just, and the sermon declares him to be "a model of repentance." However, Father Mapple poses the dilemma which comes with the Judaic-Christian, and specifically, the Protestant epoch: "if we obey God, we must disobey ourselves." And his sermon is partly in praise of being true to one's "own inexorable self." He concludes: "Delight is to God, a far, far upward and inward delight—who against the proud gods and commodores of this earth, ever stands forth his inexorable self."

To this self, Ahab has been true, and to that extent, he is a tragic and redeemable figure.[32] Like Job, he insists on maintaining his own ways before God. However, in the end, Ahab reverses Job, as well as the Greek and Christian mythic heroes.[33] Only in his relation to Pip, and when he urges Starbuck to stay on the boat and be saved, does Ahab reveal a measure of social sympathy.

Melville's *Moby Dick* is the first major American mythopoeic work which sounds the motifs of Creation and Quest. Its distinctive American quality lies in its uncertain attitude towards Creation. Dante and the mythmakers before him accepted Creation as their natural and communal heritage, and were concerned with its how, not its what or why. Even Hamlet feels himself bound to origins, although his father appears in "such a questionable shape," and at the close, he gives his dying voice to a new king. The American mythic hero is still in search of his creative sources and in doubt as to the possibility of their transformation and succession.[34]

The American Renaissance, as Matthiessen's study shows, was not a re-birth, but America's first maturity. Melville's *Moby Dick* shares some of the features of the other Renaissance myths, has some of the breadth, sense of varied experience and expansiveness of Hamlet, Faust and Siegfried. But its hero does not reach the tertiary phase of reintegration because he questions or cannot find his primary sources. *Moby Dick* comes at the point when industrialism begins its forward movement. Ahab and Ishmael leave the solid land, where men are "nailed to benches." But on the ocean, Ahab continues the way of the landsmen, driving others and himself towards conquest. Yet, he knows that his way is circular and, in this sense, *Moby Dick* questions a "progress" which does not know its original base and therefore has no conception of its destiny.

Still, *Moby Dick* carries the insight that if America is to know its destiny, it must recollect and transmute its creative beginnings. In figures such as Paul Bunyan we have a hero who combines Ahab and the crew, the exceptional and the democratic, perseverance and kindness. Paul Bunyan moves mountains, tames rivers, slays beasts, all in the interests of his loggers. America began as an interracial grouping with the desire to be free. Technics and automation threaten to reduce our unity to streamlined conformity, compensated by a capricious freedom. Theodore Dreiser's *The Bulwark* warns that the American tradition of brotherly linkage ("religion") was being supplanted by a religion of gadgets and of a gambling freedom. Yet, Melville saw great promise in the harmonious interplay between fraternity and freedom which constitute America's unique original values. He thought that Americans were "the peculiar, chosen people—the Israel of our time; we bear the ark of the liberties of the world."[35]

NOTES

1. The philosophy of John Dewey is the systematized expression of this temper. See the section "Philosophy of the Possible: John Dewey" in my *No Voice Is Wholly Lost*, pp. 43-56.

2. In Franz Kafka's *Amerika*, for example, Karl Rossman leaves Europe to find

employment in the free nature-theatre of Oklahoma. Here, *everybody* is welcome and no one is asked about his qualifications.

3. One thinks of our New Year celebrations with their unreserved impiety towards the old and their unbounded expectancy of the new year. Twelve months later, we treat the new as hopelessly old.

4. References throughout this chapter are to the Modern Library edition (New York, 1926).

5. An indirect reference to the Book of Job is Melville's correlation between the White Whale and the Leviathan of whom Job's Lord says:
    "None is so fierce that dare stir him up
    . . . he is a king over all the children of pride."

6. Whaling is compared to "that Egyptian mother, who bore off-springs themselves pregnant from her womb."

7. All mythic heroes are "orphans" in the sense that they are set out. It is a particular characteristic of Renaissance mythopoesis in which the hero repudiates his heritage (Hamlet, Faust, Siegfried).

8. In mythology, the earth-mother destroys her son Adonis, after giving birth to him. The effigy of the dead god Adonis is not buried, but thrown into the water —a part of the fertility ritual. Cf. Jessie L. Weston's *From Ritual to Romance* (New York, 1941), p. 48.

9. We are reminded of Oedipus whose club-foot is due to his parents having set him out, of Hephaesthus who was lamed by being hurled down from a height by the Goddess Hera, of the Scandinavian Smith-God Wieland who was lamed by a woman. In Greek mythology, laming and emasculation were equivalents.

10. The whole suggests the analogy to initiation ceremonies in primitive hunting communities. The White Whale is the totem of the tribe and the basis of its cohesion. Ahab is "the novice" who is tested by the amputation of his leg. He undergoes a further period of probation by living among men on the Pequod ("the Men's House" in the primitive rite). The supreme test is his quest of the White Whale.

11. I am indebted here to suggestions made by Benjamin Appel.

12. In "Fast-Fish and Loose-Fish," Melville carries the social analogy further:
    "What was America in 1492 but a Loose-Fish, in which Columbus struck the Spanish standard by way of waifing it for his royal master and mistress? What was Poland to the Czar? What Greece to the Turk? What India to England? What at last will Mexico be to the United States? All Loose-Fish. What are the Rights of Man and the Liberties of the World but Loose-Fish?"

13. The fate which overtakes Ahab is similar to that of the hunter Actaeon who invades the privacy of the virgin goddess Diana, of Pentheus who sought to view the secret ritual of his mother Agave, of Oedipus who is blinded by recognition of his incestuous life. When, at the end, Ahab beholds Moby Dick, about to pierce the hull of the Pequod, he staggers, smites his forehead, and cries out: "I grow blind; hands! stretch out before me that I may yet grope my way. Is 't night?"

14. All officers of whaling ships were Americans. Ahab is the captain ruling over a motley colonial group. We know of Melville's stand against exploitation of the colored people, against slavery and economic imperialism.

15. Ahab's ivory leg is referred to as his "man," and Ahab calls the carpenter who fashions it "man-maker." The carpenter thinks that in the ivory leg, Ahab has "a stick of whale's bone-jaw for a wife."

   There are indications of Melville's attraction for male strength and power in *Oomoo* and *Typee*. *Billy Budd* is dedicated to Jack Chase, the handsome sailor under whom Melville worked in the Pacific.

16. The theme of love between a white man and a colored outcast also appears in Fenimore Cooper's *Leatherstocking Tales* and is prominent in Mark Twain's *Huckleberry Finn*. I came across an unpublished manuscript in which the term "Ishmael Complex" is suggested, to designate such relationships, and which the authors think is characteristic of the American scene. Here, homoeroticism is not overt, but has the character of juvenile innocence. It is acted out in social isolation, on the high seas, rivers, or in forests, remote from conventional mores. The colored character acts as the parent to the white man. In Mark Twain's novel, Jim reenacts the role of Queequeg. He is the mother of Huck (in his gentle, tender and sensual care of the boy) as well as a father (tall, strong).

17. In many mystery cults, the fish is a holy food, and the myth often identifies him with the primal Creator, connected with the God Vishnu, the Goddess Astarte and others. Cf. Jessie L. Weston, *From Ritual to Romance*, pp. 119 ff.

18. In "The Cassock," Melville describes the huge male organ of the whale. The passage would invoke an attitude of Biblical piety towards this "Grandissimus." It follows the chapter, "A Squeeze of the Hand."

19. The White Whale is the "herald" of Ahab's adventure. Like Hamlet's father, he announces himself in "midnight-spouts."

20. In discussing the tail, Melville refers to the hermaphroditical Italian paintings of the Son of God.

21. For the mythic imports of the Whale's Belly, see Joseph Campbell's *The Hero with a Thousand Faces* (New York, 1949), pp. 90 ff. Ahab is *jealous* of anyone who might first sight or touch Moby Dick.

22. Melville's mother apparently had little love for him, was cold and hard. The imagery used in describing the mother's face in *Pierre* ("too familiar, yet inexplicable") is similar to that used for Moby Dick. Melville's work knows no gracious figures, such as Beatrice, Dulcinea, Gretchen or Grushenka.

23. William E. Sedgwick hinted at this when he wrote that the White Whale "stands for the inscrutable mystery of creation" (*Herman Melville* [New York, 1962]).

24. Moby Dick gained the name "white" from the "milky-way wake of creamy foam" which he leaves as he glides through the sea. Melville's seminal metaphors further suggest the erotic element in Ahab's quest.

25. This unintegrated dialectic is also suggested by the fact that each of the whale's eyes focuses on a different object. Ahab's own vision is "one-eyed" and

makes for his fixed and distant relation to the others. In Moby Dick, the two eyes do not meet. This dual perspective first appears in Don Quixote-Sancho Panza. There, the two eyes are "harmonized" by remaining parallel to each other. They come in conflict in Hamlet's and Faust's two souls.

26. The biologic image is cannibalism—the cannibalism of the sea, with sharks snapping at each other's disembowelments. Ahab calls himself "old cannibal me." In his *The Great Mother* (New York, 1955), Erich Neumann examines the uroboros, "the circular snake biting its tail," as the symbol of the original situation, the "Great Round," in which male and female, consciousness and unconsciousness, are intermingled, a totality of the united primordial parents.

27. Melville writes that the subject makes him "expand to its bulk." In his effort to do it justice, his "arms" tire, and he calls out: "Friends, hold my arms."

28. Queequeg, the "soothing savage" in a "wolfish world," is "the mother" who delivers both Tashtego and Ishmael into life. But he is primarily a fairy-tale figure in comparison with the rest.

29. The number three occurs in other contexts: Ahab married three voyages prior to setting out on his hunt for the White Whale; there are three mates and three harpooners. As in other mythopoeic works, the number three suggests ambivalent values: The White Whale is God-Devil; the Pequod is at once the Ship of the Dead and "the mother" of the boat in which Ishmael is saved.

30. In F. O. Matthiessen's formulation (*American Renaissance* [New York, 1941]). Ahab anticipates much of America's development:

"The strong-willed individuals who seized the land and gutted the forests and built the railroads were no longer troubled with Ahab's obsessive sense of evil, since theology had receded. . . . They tended to be . . . as blind to everything but their one pursuit, as unmoved by fear or sympathy, as confident in assuming an identification of their wills with immutable plan or manifest destiny, as liable to regard other men as merely arms and legs for the fulfilment of their purposes . . . [Melville] also provided an ominous glimpse of what was to result when the Emersonian will to virtue became in less innocent natures the will to power and conquest."

Jack London's Wolf Larsen approximates the combined features of Ahab and Moby Dick. He is fascinating and terrifying, unites intellect with "savage instincts." Like Ahab, Larsen is only outwardly formidable. Actually, he is a very sick man, goes blind, and dies in a helpless state. In Larsen's own terminology, he moves from a living "to do" towards a deathly "to be," an existence without movement.

31. W. H. Auden, "The Christian Tragic Hero," *The New York Times Book Review* (December 16, 1945). Miss Weston notes that in Christian art and tradition, "the Lance or Spear, as an instrument of the Passion, is found in conjunction with the Cross, nails, sponge, and Crown of Thorns." We find this conjunction in Ahab's spear and his mark of crucifixion which is "completed" as he gives up the spear and is strangled.

32. For this reason, I cannot go along with Matthiessen who holds that Ahab suffers, but remains damned. But Auden overstates the case in calling Ahab a "saint" who wills one thing for which he gives up everything.

33. Fedallah is not Ahab's evil spirit, as some maintain. His death only intensifies Ahab's demoniac drive. More is made of Fedallah than the story itself justifies. Melville's *intention* was to make Fedallah's speechless impersonality the Eastern counterpart to Ahab's Western rhetorical and wilful individualism. But this is not executed. Fedallah remains a "shadow" as a literary character as well.

34. Melville "tacks on" a hopeful portent: The sky-hawk is nailed to the Pequod by Tashtego's hammer. The bird goes down with the ship which, "like Satan would not sink to hell till she had dragged a living part of heaven with her, and helmeted herself with it." Joseph Campbell's *The Hero With A Thousand Faces* notes that in many myths, the birds rescue the hero from the Whale by pecking open the side of the Whale's belly.

35. See Appendix V for note on Mark Twain and Walt Whitman.

The Pan-Slavic Image of the Earth Mother

The Brothers Karamazov

OF THE MYTHOPOEIC WORKS considered in this study, only the Russian does not stem from a patriarchate civilization.[1] The core of the Pan-Slavic myth is connected with the matriarchy, and the most cherished values are presented in terms of the Mother image: The country is Mother Russia, the church Mother Church, Kiev, is regarded as "the mother of Russian Cities." In contrast to the Western Father, the Russian Mother stands for mercy and equality, and her image merges with that of the fertile Earth. For Maria Timofevna in Dostoyevsky's *The Possessed*, "the Mother of God is the great Mother Earth, and she offers great joy to man." And F. Fedotov writes:

> In Mother Earth, converge the most secret . . . religious feeling of the folk. . . . The source of all fertilizing powers, the nourishing breast of nature, and their own last resting place. The very epithet of the earth in the folk-songs, "Mother Earth, the Hermit," known also in Iranian mythology, alludes to the womb rather than to the face of the Earth. It means not beauty but fertility is the supreme virtue of the earth . . . Earth is the Russian "Eternal Womanhood," not the celestial image of it; mother, not virgin; fertile, not pure: and black, for the best Russian soil is black.
>
> (*The Russian Religious Mind*, pp. 12, 13)

Fedotov further indicates that there is no Russian parallel to Athena or other virgin goddess, and that the Slavic myth lacks the erotic features found in the Oriental-Greek accounts of marriages between Earth and Heaven. (There is no Russian word for "sexy" in the Anglo-American usage, although, of course, there is a word for sexual in the anatomical sense.) Demeter, the fruit-bearing goddess, not Aphrodite, is in the center of the Russian pantheon.[2]

246

The social analogue of the earthy Mother-Goddess is the common folk. Salvation—this is the theme of many Russian writers—lies in return to the people who are conceived as the all-nourishing source of the nation. From the people, writes Dostoyevsky, "everything will come to us: our thoughts and our images." And, just as in Russian legends, the earth does not have the character of "blood and soil" nationalism, so the people are thought of as all-human rather than as exclusively Russian,—an idea which may be connected with the fact that Russia comprises a vast variety of ethnic groups.

Here is the context for the emphasis on *sobornost*, the principle of communality, which permeates the mythology and legends of the Slavs.[3]

Bylini and Skazky

The *Bylini* and *Skazky* (ballads and folktales) of early Russian literature likewise express the Slavic values of communality. *The Slavic myth has no God of war and its literature has no hero cult.* Like the American Paul Bunyan, the hero in the Russian ballads and folktales uses his super-human strength in the interests of the people. Mikúla Selyáninovich, along with Ilyá Múrom (the chief and most popular figure in the ballad cycles) champion the poor and widows, defend the peasants and their native soil. The emphasis is on strength which stems from the earth (Ilyá can use his strength because the earth *can* bear it) and from the mothers, who are represented as wise and practical.

Many of these features are combined in the legend dealing with Igor's campaign. The tale is based on the struggle of the Russian princes against the nomads of the southern steppes, and relates Prince Igor's imprisonment and his escape. A characteristic note is the defensive nature of Igor's campaign and his obvious dislike of bloodshed. As is the case in early Slavic mythology, the most striking imagery is the identification of man with nature and the anthropomorphic function of the elements: the sun bars the way, the grass droops in pity, the tree bows down in grief, the night groans. Similarly, the Russian people and folk singers are spoken of as descended directly from nature-gods: They are the grandchildren of Dazhbog, the god of prosperity, of Volos, the god of cattle, of Stribog, the god of winds.[4] Igor's escape is effected by the three laments of his wife, addressed to Wind, the River and the Sun. Written when Kievan culture was in decline, the poem invokes the older values of Slavic unity.[5]

This temper took historic form in the *mir* which approximated a type of primitive communism despite its patriarchal structure.[6]

The Earthy Mother Church

Russia adopted Byzantine Christianity without its Hellenic culture. And the earthy element in Slavic mythology was akin to Greek orthodoxy which put stress on man's opportunity on earth. Discussing the character of religious Byzantism, Fedotov points out that whereas Western Christology adopted Pope Leo's distinction between the divine and the human, Byzantism taught with Cyril of Alexandria that Christ was God in human flesh:

> In this sacramental religion, the Deity ceases to be transcendent. It takes its abode in the temple. The Church becomes "heaven on earth," according to classical Orthodox saying. The Divinity is accessible through matter, that of sacraments and sacred objects: it can be not only seen, but even smelled, tasted, kissed. . . . Practically the whole of Byzantine religion could have been built without the historical Christ of the Gospels, upon a simple myth of the heavenly saviour similar to Hellenistic saviour myths. . . . The Eastern pathos is: heaven on earth, God's presence here in His temple in His mysteries, icons, relics, in sacred matter. . . . The dome of the Byzantine temple is large and round, a living symbol of heaven descending upon earth.[7]

And Maynard remarks that perhaps Dostoyevsky thought of this when he said that he belonged to a people capable of making a religion of materialism.

The earthiness of the church is an aspect of its democratic motherliness. God, says Dostoyevsky's Prince Myshkin, finds gladness in man's gladness, like a mother who sees her baby smile. In *The Brothers Karamazov*, the Orthodox Church is "a tender, loving mother." While the Grand Inquisitor prophesies that "we shall triumph and shall be Caesars," Father Paissy declares:

> The Church is not to be transformed into the State. That is Rome and its dream. That is the third temptation of the devil. On the contrary, the State is transformed into the Church.[8]

While the official church was despotic, the Russian monk, nearly as poor as the peasants among whom he worked, leaned towards a kind of primitive socialism, represented by "underground" movements, such as the Khlysty. The chapter on "The Russian Monk" in *The Brothers Karamazov* is a panegyric on one of its orders, projected in the figure of Father Zossima. Why, asks this Elder

> should not my servant be like my own kindred? . . . Even now this can be done, but it will lead to the grand unity of men in the future, when a man will not seek servants for himself, or desire to turn his fellow creatures into

248

servants as he does now, but on the contrary, will long with his whole heart to be the servant of all, as the Gospel teaches.

On such grounds, Berdyaev thinks that socialism "is deeply rooted in the Russian nature," for which man is a higher principle than property. While Berdyaev opposed communism, he argued that it must be transcended, not destroyed:

> Communism is the Russian destiny. . . . The Russian Revolution awakened and unfettered the enormous powers of the Russian people. The Soviet constitution of the year 1936 has established the best legislation on property in the world; personal property is recognized, but in a form which does not allow of exploitation.[9]

These primitive components stem from Russia's retarded development. Its geographical remoteness from the West, the long, devastating invasions of the Mongols, did not allow the rise of a strong, independent middle class, precluded a Renaissance, Reformation or revolutions, such as the American and the French. (The emancipation of the serfs in 1861 only burdened the impoverished peasantry by forcing redemption payments upon them). In sum, Russian undevelopment did not favor Western notions of free enterprise, of social, political and intellectual emancipation. In Berdyaev's words—Russia has never been bourgeois and its mentality was averse towards taking a "middle" position. By the time of Dostoyevsky, the ancient matriarchate and its strong family tie had given way to a tyrannical patriarchate.[10] Apart from the *mir*, the only equality which the Russian people knew in the Tsarist era was that of equal oppression and exploitation by the princes, the large landowners and the church. This situation produced the *nichevo* attitude—passive acceptance and resignation—or wild explosions, expressed in sporadic "Dionysian" acts of nihilism. Berdyaev speaks of this when he quotes a Pole during the Soviet Revolution as saying that "Dionysus is abroad in the Russian land."[11]

The Slavophiles And The Intellegentsia

Peter and Catherine the Great attempted to westernize Russia. This trend was opposed by the Slavophiles in the nineteenth century who, Herzen said, loved Russia as a Mother. They idealized the plain folk or the *narod* and saw in the very backwardness of the peasant commune the basis for a *Russian* socialism.[12] The Westerners drew their adherents from the ranks of repentant nobles and theoretic social revolutionaries. This Russian "intellegentsia"—Turgenev, calls them Don Quixotes and Hamlets—had roots neither in the established Tsarist rule nor in the oppressed masses. They were what the Russians call "superfluous people," men and women who had no function in their society and spent their energy in passionate discussion.[13] The social radicals among them felt that Russia was threatened by both Western and Russian exploitation. In its desperate and futile attack on both the Slavophiles and the Russian regime, the Intellegentsia approached an anarchist mood of what Toynbee terms "pure futurism."

Yet, the two opposing groups were at one in that both opposed the existing state. They decried the emptiness and ugliness of middle class commercialism, repudiated the bourgeois conception of private property and hoped that Russia would escape the evils of capitalism.[14]

Dostoyevsky transcended both camps. He was severely critical of Western freedom and extolled Russia.[15] Yet, as his speech on Pushkin makes clear, what he meant by being "truly national" is the ability of the Russian to identify with and to understand other peoples. To a Russian, he stated, Europe is also dear, precisely because it is Russia's vocation to realize all-human unity: "Our future lies in universality, not won by violence, but from the strength derived from our great ideal —the reuniting of all mankind." Russia's mission is "to lead the common interests of entire humanity." To be a Russian is to have

> the gift of world-wide sympathy . . . means being a brother to all men . . . to be a true Russian means nothing but to reconcile European contradictions within oneself, to give European longings an outlet in the all-uniting Russian soul, to receive all into this soul of brotherly love, and so, perhaps, to say the last word of universal harmony, and of the understanding and peace among all peoples according to the Evangelical law of Christ.[16]

DOSTOYEVSKY'S ODE TO LIFE

"The most important thing in life," says Hippolyte, the doomed consumptive in *The Idiot*, is "life and nothing else." And, amidst his torturous ordeal, the heart of Mitya Karamazov beats to the rhythm of Schiller's "Ode to Joy."

The life which Dostoyevsky and his characters celebrate is wild, uninhibited or anti-bourgeois. His Underground Man disputes the theory that man's interests, "include only prosperity, riches, freedom, tranquillity," and holds that there may indeed be

> some supreme interest of interests . . . for which man . . . is ready to contravene every law, and to lose sight alike of common sense, honour, prosperity, and ease.

Man may wilfully choose what is foolish, and

such folly may also be the best thing in the world for him, even though it work him harm. . . . This is because it is possible for his folly to preserve to him, under all circumstances, the chief, the most valuable, of all his possessions—namely, his personality, his individuality.[17]

Dostoyevsky's own life is characterized by such underground tremors. During his adolescence, Dostoyevsky lost his mother and father within the space of two years. The father was a stern patriarch, and Dostoyevsky later told his wife Anna that when he would dream of his father or brother Michael, he knew that a misfortune was about to descend upon him.

In his essay "Dostoevsky and Parricide" (*Collected Papers, V*), Freud passes over Dostoyevsky's mother and gives central place to the murder of his father. If we assume that Dostoyevsky secretly wished this murder, then we are tempted, Freud writes, "to see in that event the severest trauma and to regard Dostoyevsky's reaction to it as the turning point of his neurosis," as having released his epileptic seizures. Prior to the murder, Dostoyevsky suffered from a groundless melancholy, accompanied by a feeling that he was going to die on the spot. Freud sees this melancholy as a self-inflicted punishment: "One has wished another person dead, and now one *is* this other person and is dead oneself . . . the attack . . . is thus a self-punishment for a death-wish against a hated father." And when the fantasy became reality, the attacks assumed an epileptic character.

In letters to Strakhov and Soloviev, Dostoyevsky expressed himself freely about his epileptic fits. According to Myshkin's account in *The Idiot*, the fit was preceded by supreme rapture and ecstasy, so sweet "that one is ready to exchange ten years of life or even life itself for the bliss of these few seconds." Then came the "fall" which brought extreme depression, accompanied by the feeling "of being a criminal" who has committed some unknown awful deed. The account suggests the analogy between the epileptic and sexual discharge. Freud calls attention to the fact that physicians once described copulation as a little epilepsy.

Dostoyevsky's characters also seem fearful of sexual consummation. Mitya Karamazov solemnly asserts that his Grusha is holy and that he had never been her lover. Dostoyevsky's own life was ruled by sexual irregularities. To begin with, there was the prolonged abstinence of his youth and the enforced continence during the four years of his Siberian imprisonment. Moreover, we have indications of pedophelia, hinted in "Starvrogin's Confessions," and in Dostoyevsky's talk with Turgenev.[18]

In his book, Marc Slonim treats the three women in Dostoyevsky's life as approximating the triad of mother-mistress-child. Maria, his first wife, was the mother of a seven year old son. Like Dostoyevsky's own mother, she was consumptive and her solicitude for Dostoyevsky had a maternal character.[19] Although Maria was bed-ridden in the latter part of her life, Dostoyevsky felt that his bonds to her were unbreakable. A year after her death, he wrote to Wrangel that she "was the most honest, the most noble and magnanimous woman of all those whom I have known in all my life." If Maria was a mother figure, Polina was the harlot. Twenty years his junior, Dostoyevsky thought of her primarily as a sex object, although she apparently never surrendered to him.

In Anna, his second wife, Dostoyevsky found a woman who combined the child, mother and mistress. Anna was his adoring youthful secretary, completely submissive and concerned only with making him physically comfortable. Above all, she accepted the abnormal expressions of his eroticism. With her, he could do as he wished. As Slonim puts it:

> He may have felt embarrassed with others but with her everything was permissible. . . . With her he could play the husband, the lover, the father, the child. . . . Her role was a liberating and cathartic one; therefore she released him of his burden of guilt, and he ceased to feel like a sinner or a voluptuary. (*Three Loves of Dostoyevsky*, p. 241)

She also accepted his gambling mania. Relieved of shame in this area as well, Dostoyevsky was soon able to give up gambling and perhaps also his masturbatory practice. Of all his women, she alone does not appear in a recognizable form in his writings. Perhaps he had no need to create her symbolically since she fulfilled him in reality.

However, only in his last years did Dostoyevsky enjoy relative contentment. His life as a whole was filled with, what Gide calls, a "perfect mania for assuming burdens": His first marriage was to a consumptive widow whose son he adopted and cared for; later, he undertook to support his brother Michael and, after his brother's death, his family. Aside from his compulsive gambling, the most telling example appears in Dostoyevsky's attitude towards his Siberian imprisonment.

According to Simmons, there is evidence that the Petrashevsky circle to which Dostoyevsky belonged did not confine itself to reading and discussing the Utopian socialists, and that Dostoyevsky was among those in the group who planned even violent action to overthrow the despotic Tsarist regime. Yet, Dostoyevsky was accused only of having associated with the group and its reading of Belinsky's famous letter to

Gogol in which the critic attacked Gogol's apology for the social conditions in Russia. For this "crime," Dostoyevsky and others were sen-
tenced to be shot. At the very last moment, the Tsar theatrically com-
muted the sentence to imprisonment and Dostoyevsky was sent out
into the Siberian winter in an open sledge, weighed down by ten-pound
chains. In prison, he suffered from terrible cold in the winter and from
stifling heat in the summer. Yet—Dostoyevsky calmly accepted this dis-
proportionate punishment: "I do not complain," he wrote, "this is my
cross and I have deserved it." And, far from feeling resentment, he
added that he "venerates" the Tsar, who is "infinitely generous and
kind."

Freud believes that Dostoyevsky accepted punishment from the
Tsar (whom Russians called the Little Father) "as a substitute for the
punishment he deserved for his sin against his real father." From this
viewpoint he could regard the commutation of the sentence by the
all-powerful authority as an act of grace.[20] Freud further sees in Dostoyevsky's gambling mania—he gambled until he lost everything—"another method of self-punishment" which he connects with his long-
buried compulsion to masturbate, that his burden of guilt took shape
"as a burden of debt."

These dramatic events made for a feeling that precipitate disasters
were impending, that there was a disparity between cause and effect.
And this feeling carries over into Dostoyevsky's art. Its structure, form
and organization are loose, chance predominates and anything seems
possible. His characters are unpredictable, leap in emotional extremes
from one abyss to another. They have no organic development and
seem fully grown from the start. Their creator too could find no middle
course. His death, as well as his life, was explosive. Dostoyevsky died
by bursting a blood vessel.

THE BROTHERS KARAMAZOV

Dostoyevsky was deeply affected by a Claude Lorraine painting
which he renamed "The Golden Age." In *The Possessed*, this age is
called the first act of mythology:

> Here was mankind's earthly paradise, gods descended from heaven and
> united with mortals, here occurred the first scenes of mythology. Here lived
> beautiful men and women! They rose, they went to sleep, happy and inno-
> cent; the groves rang with their merry songs, the great overflow of unspent
> energies poured itself into love and simple-hearted joys. . . . The most im-

probable of all visions, to which mankind throughout its existence has given
its best energies, for which it has sacrificed everything, for which it has
pined and been tormented, for which its prophets were crucified and killed,
without which nations will not desire to live, and without which they cannot even die! (Modern Library edition, p. 715)

But Dostoyevsky recognized that his Russia was not an earthy paradise, but an inferno, where "money-lenders and devourers of the commune were rising up . . . I've seen in the factories children of nine years
old, frail, rickety, bent and already depraved."[21] *The Brothers Kara-*
mazov echoes such social criticism through Rakitin and Zossima,
through Ivan's stories of tortured children and Mitya's dream in the
court-room. At the trial, the attorney receives the most "irrepressible
and almost frantic applause" by at least "a good half" of the audience,
including "persons of high position," when he declares that the Mityas
are a product of the Russian social situation, of the unreasonable acts
of their fathers.

In Dostoyevsky's era, memory of the Pan-Slavic Earth Mother was
fading. At this point, two outstanding writers attempted to re-create
her mythic values in symbolic form: Tolstoy counterposed the "motherly" Pierre, Platon Karatayev, Levin and the Russian peasant to
the Western and Eastern Napoleons; Dostoyevsky countered Sonia,
Myshkin, Marie, Zossima and Alyosha to the would-be Caesars, the
Raskolnikovs, Stavrogins and Grand Inquisitors. In *The Brothers Ka-*
ramazov, Dostoyevsky's summary and terminal novel, we have the most
dramatic mythopoeic expression of Pan-Slavism in its historic nineteenth
century dress: In Zossima and Alyosha, it presents holy Mother Russia;
in Ivan and Smerdyakov its modern rationalistic and "epileptic" forms;
in Mitya, Russia "*as she is* . . . our mother Russia, the very scent and
sound of her . . . a marvellous mingling of good and evil." The Karamazov family as a whole is the *selva oscura* of the Russian inferno, a
distortion of the ancient Slavic "Big Family."

Act I: Adam

The Father (Dostoyevsky gives him his own name, Fyodor), is the
"Adam" of the Karamazov family. A prominent feature is his Adam's
apple:

I have mentioned already that he looked bloated. . . . Besides the long fleshy
bags under his little, always insolent, suspicious, and ironical eyes; besides
the multitude of deep wrinkles in his little fat face, the Adam's apple hung
below his sharp chin like a great, fleshy goitre, which gave him a peculiar,
repulsive, sensual appearance; add to that a long rapacious mouth with full

lips, between which could be seen little stumps of black decayed teeth. He slobbered every time he began to speak.

Fyodor used his energies to look after his "wordly affairs" and after nothing else. In the words of the prosecuting attorney at the trial,

> his vitality was excessive. He saw nothing in life but sensual pleasure, and he brought his children up to be the same. He had no feelings for his duties as a father. He was an example of everything that is opposed to civic duty, of the most complete and malignant individualism.

Yet, Fyodor's "primitive . . . and . . . unbridled" zest for life is also fertile.[22]

Even as Dostoyevsky depicts Fyodor as the devouring parent, he also suggests hidden creative elements in him. To begin with, he is said to be "of noble birth." Alyosha thinks that his father is "not ill-natured, but distorted," and the author points to the environmental pressures which drove Fyodor to play the buffoon. Fyodor himself explains it as "revenge for my youth, for all the humiliation I endured," says that his buffoonery has the object "of amusing people and making myself agreeable."

That Fyodor's nature is not exhausted by his sensualism is obliquely shown by the women he married. The outstanding characteristics of his first wife, Adelaida, were her beauty and proud independence, of his second wife, Sofya, her meekness and innocence (this greedy man married her although she came to him penniless). The first became the mother of the rebellious Mitya, the other gave birth to the Christ-like Alyosha and the Judas-like Ivan.

Now, according to rumor, Fyodor had another son, Smerdyakov, whose mother is Lizaveta, described as a "dwarfish creature," with "a look of blank idiocy," more of an earth-animal than a woman:

> Her coarse, almost black hair curled like lamb's wool. . . . It was always crusted with mud, and had leaves, bits of stick, and shavings clinging to it, as she always slept on the ground and in the dirt . . . She could hardly speak, and only from time to time uttered an inarticulate grunt.

Yet, to Fyodor, her very sub-earthy appearance lent her a certain piquancy and he is quoted as having said that it was by no means impossible to look upon her as a woman. Shortly afterwards, she is found in Fyodor's garden bathhouse, having given birth to Smerdyakov.

In his choice of the three women, Fyodor did not exhibit sensuality, but a desire for beauty and rebelliousness, for saintliness and innocence, and even an appreciation of the amorphously earthy.[23] We should also note that the author shows Fyodor to be somewhat cultured (he quotes Diderot), critical of social evils in the Russian church (living "at other people's expense"). He is said to have moments of "spiritual terror," is troubled over the question as to whether there is a God and whether there is immortality.

Every one of Fyodor's sons partakes of his sensualism and drunken rebelliousness. They are all intoxicated: Alyosha with God, Ivan with theory, Mitya and Smerdyakov with justice. They are all "Karamazovs," —Alyosha too calls himself one. And, to be a Karamazov, Alyosha says, is to war against father and brother:

> My brothers are destroying themselves, my father, too. And they are destroying others with them. It's the primitive force of the Karamazovs, as Father Paissy said the other day, a crude, unbridled, earthly force. Does the spirit of God move above that force? Even that I don't know. I only know that I too, am a Karamazov. . . . And perhaps I don't even believe in God.

This primitive restlessness breaks through Alyosha's religious and Ivan's rationalistic censor. In Smerdyakov, it expresses itself first in "orgiastic" fits, and later in murder. In Mitya, the pleasure principle is wild and inchoate.

Act II: The Four-Fold Quest

If Fyodor may be regarded as the principle of Creation in the story, his four sons approximate the four-fold Quest taking form in rebellion against the father who exploits the Russian mother and her sons: Smerdyakov explodes in the underground, Mitya rages with every nerve in his body, Ivan rebels with cold dialectic, and Alyosha with religious fervor.[24]

Ivan

Ivan's problem is perhaps closest to the author's, in that his Westernism, grafted on to his Russian character, was Dostoyevsky's own most troublesome problem. He is the deepest secret of the book and some of the most secret chapters—the poem about the Grand Inquisitor, the interviews with Smerdyakov and with the Devil—deal with Ivan.[25]

Ivan is the most alienated of the four brothers. His "Euclidian" mind keeps him from a "living life," and he is unable to express or to accept love. He has contempt for his father and for Smerdyakov, hates Mitya, and even Alyosha appears to him as a "fanatic." Yet, he is unable to find rest in his negativism, not so much because he has a Hamlet-like sensibility, but because he too is a Karamazov. In his confessional scene with Alyosha in "Pro and Contra," Ivan tells Alyosha that he too has a "frantic . . . thirst for life . . . that thirst for life regardless of everything," and "in spite of logic." He adds that even if he did not believe in life and lost faith in the order of things, he would still want to taste of the cup and not turn away till he had drained it.

> I have a longing for life . . . I love the sticky leaves as they open in spring. I love the blue sky . . . without knowing why. . . . It's not a matter of intellect or logic, it's loving with one's inside, with one's stomach.

Ivan's Westernism is only loosely attached to his Karamazovism. In contrast to Miusov and Rakitin (the Western liberals), Ivan uses reason to find grounds for proving contradictions. He argues "Pro and Contra," for and against the domination by the church over the state, for and against freedom and security. And, precisely because he would give exclusive priority to his rational motives, Ivan is helpless in coping with his underground forces. He expects that Mitya will kill his father, that "one reptile will devour another," and that he himself was ready to bring this about. But his unconscious wish is that Smerdyakov commit the act. At a decisive stage in the plot, Smerdyakov hints that by leaving, Ivan would be granting him permission to kill Fyodor. Ivan means to tell Smerdyakov that he is a miserable idiot. But, "to his profound astonishment, he heard himself say, 'Is my father still asleep, or has he waked?' He asked the question softly and meekly, to his own surprise. . . ." In the end, Ivan's airy rationalism undermines his reason and drives him to the ultimate antinomy of madness.

Ivan's Russian character, his deep skepticism over reason and logic, are exposed in his colloquy with Alyosha in "Pro and Contra." Ivan begins his confession "as stupidly as I could on purpose." When Alyosha asks him why he did this, Ivan answers:

> To begin with, for the sake of being Russian. . . . And secondly, the stupider one is, the closer one is to reality. The stupider one is, the clearer one is. Stupidity is brief and artless, while intelligence wriggles and hides itself. Intelligence is a knave, but stupidity is honest and straightforward.

On the philosophical level, Ivan raises here the "eternal question" about the dilemma between freedom and happiness. But this question arises out of his personal dilemma. Ivan has just broken off with Katya, despite the fact that they love each other. This is his private "Pro and Contra." Ivan wants to celebrate his "freedom" from Katya and he tells Alyosha that his heart is now light. Actually, his heart is heavy, and he has a great need to speak with Alyosha. His Western logic cannot cope with the irrational situation in which two people have decided to part despite the fact that they love each other. And, in this scene, the anti-Euclidian aspect of Ivan breaks through: He speaks in soft, pleading tones of his need for faith. His cold exterior opens up to expose his wounds, and he tells Alyosha that perhaps he wishes to be "healed" by him. The problem he poses—the theologic-metaphysical antinomy between freedom and happiness, between innocence and suffering—is an extrapolation of his personal burden: He is free from Katya, yet unhappy; he has done no wrong, yet suffers.

Ivan begins by confessing his Karamazovism. He would drain the cup at least until he is thirty, and then dash it to the ground. While he does not allow himself Fyodor's dissipations, Ivan's "Everything is lawful," sanctions his father's unbridled sensualism. In this sense, we can understand Fyodor calling Ivan "the dearest of my flesh," and Smerdyakov's saying: "If there is one of the sons that is like Fyodor Pavlovitch in character, it is Ivan Fyodorovitch."

Ivan's Jobian Poem

The Book of Job was one of Dostoyevsky's favorite poems. While Ivan himself does not mention the Book, it is the Jobian question of why the innocent suffer that preoccupies him here.

Ivan narrows the problem to the sufferings of children. He refers to accounts of children tortured or torn to pieces before their mothers' eyes for some trifling act. He proceeds to the theologic-metaphysical implications and sums up by his poem of the Grand Inquisitor.

Like Job, Ivan cannot accept the argument that children suffer because of their parent's sins. Nor is he consoled by the promise that other-worldly happiness will compensate for their suffering. Ivan wants justice "here on earth." This "rationalist" is at bottom "a believer," as he tells his brother. But, he says, "there are the children." Why should these innocent ones too "furnish material to enrich the soil for the harmony of the future?" If such harmony is at the expense of a child's suffering, then "From love for humanity I don't want it." Ivan grants the existence of God, that is, of an order incomprehensible to man, yet he cannot accept his world. He admits that this is rebellion, and that one cannot live in rebellion, adding somewhat pathetically, "and I want to live."

The heart of Ivan's argument is reached in his poem of the Grand Inquisitor. He, who would appear as a cold logician, finds it necessary to clinch his point by recourse to analogy, metaphor and dramatic fiction. His "Poem" is a closet drama which takes place during the Inquisition in the sixteenth century, in which a Spanish cardinal confronts the Christ of the Gospels who has come down to earth. The Grand Inquisitor has him seized and imprisoned. The next night, the cardinal appears in the cell and there takes place a "dialogue" in which Christ remains silent throughout.

The cardinal begins by stating that Christ has come "to hinder us" and that he will be burned at the stake "as the worst of heretics." He harangues Christ for having refused the three temptations — turning stones into bread, accepting earthly domination, and assuming authoritative power — and having exalted freedom instead. Yet, while nothing is more seductive for man than his freedom of conscience, "nothing is a greater cause of suffering." Freedom entails choice, and most men are weak, and having to make a choice brings confusion and suffering into their lives. Freedom makes them rebellious, but they are "impotent rebels," hence the lot of mankind has become "unrest, confusion and unhappiness." What the many desire above all is bread and "some one to worship, some one to keep his conscience, and some means of uniting all in one unanimous and harmonious ant-heap."

The Inquisitor recognizes that there is an even more powerful appeal to man than bread, namely his conscience. He admits that

> if some one else gains possession of his conscience—oh! then he will cast away Thy bread and follow after him who has ensnared his conscience. In that Thou wast right. For the secret of man's being is not only to live but to have something to live for.

But he insists that Christ's mistake lay in making men's freedom greater than ever instead of taking it away from them. Christ rejected the miracle and called for faith and love given freely. The Church has "corrected" Christ's work and founded it upon miracle, mystery and authority. In this way, the Inquisitor proclaims

> we shall triumph and shall be Caesars, and then we shall plan the universal happiness of man. . . . The most painful secrets of their conscience, all, all they will bring to us, and we shall have an answer for all. And they will be glad to believe our answer, for it will save them from the great anxiety and terrible agony they endure at present in making a free decision for themselves.

Now, Ivan and Alyosha agree that the secret of the Inquisitor is that he "does not believe in God" in that he does not believe in man. (This is the basis for Dostoyevsky's saying that the West has lost Christianity through "the error of Catholicism".) The Inquisitor is the Western father-authority who would keep his son in perpetual childish dependence.

Yet, the scene is more than an intellectual-theologic disquisition. It is a drama. To be sure, Christ remains silent, although challenged by the cardinal to "speak" and to "be angry." Still, there is a kind of speech in the listener's soft, mild eyes and demeanor. Indeed, the Inquisitor changes his tone and argument *as though he were being answered*. Furthermore, the cardinal voices his own reservations on his position in admitting that man's secret "is not only to live but to have something to live for." He is uneasy in his position and would show that what the church has done stems from its *love of man*. It has imposed mystery, miracle and authority because otherwise man, faced with a terrible choice, would have been unhappy. Indeed, this same love of man has led the church's leading representatives to take the burden of freedom upon themselves, "lovingly lightening their burden, and permitting their weak nature even sin with our sanction. . . ." Thus, there is a conflict within the cardinal owing to the co-existence of Christ's gospel of freedom and the church's assumption of authority. And Christ recognizes the anguish of the cardinal when he approaches him at the end, and softly kisses his bloodless aged lips. "That was all his answer," Ivan adds.[26] The kiss is given in the spirit in which Zossima bowed down before Mitya, and it is reenacted when Alyosha kisses Ivan at the close of his story. Here, Alyosha acknowledges the agony within Ivan, the conflict between his rationalistic "everything is lawful" and his Russian concept that all human life is sacred. Ivan cannot argue himself into killing Fyodor. He can act only unconsciously, through Smerdyakov.

Father Zossima

In the chapter on "The Russian Monk" which follows Ivan's Poem, Dostoyevsky would counter the Western Caesaristic Father, in the form of the temporal Catholic Church, with the Eastern Mother Goddess, as embodied in the teachings of the *Russian monk* and the institution of the elders.

The Inquisitor argues that if people are to be happy, they must be led to accept mystery, miracle and authority. In contrast, Father Zossima would shun mysteries, specifically the mystery that hell-fire is material, and underplays miracles (denying Fyodor's story about the saint who carried his head in his hands). Above all, his stand is a repudiation of the cardinal's central thesis that people are weak and vile and cannot be allowed freedom of choice. Father Zossima teaches, on the other hand, that he who believes in God will believe in God's people. And, where the cardinal held that salvation rests in the ruling church, Zossima states: "The salvation of Russia comes from the people. And the Russian monk has always been on the side of the people," getting his image of Christ, not from the organized church, but "fair and undefiled . . . from the times of the Fathers of old, the Apostles and the martyrs."

Here is the basis of the monk's Russian "socialism" which opposes the new individuality and freedom of the West which result, not in fullness of life and self-realization, but in self-destruction and complete solitude. Western freedom, Zossima teaches, leads men to "distort their own nature."

Zossima's theology is based not on law but on what he calls, "active love." And, he applies it in a way which has startling analogies to modern psychological therapy. He calls hell "the suffering of being unable to love." And, in speaking of self-deception, he admonishes Fyodor:

Above all, don't lie to yourself. The man who lies to himself and listens to his own lie . . . loses all respect for himself and for others. And having no respect he ceases to love, and . . . gives way to passions and coarse pleasures. . . . The man who lies to himself can be more easily offended than any one.

Similarly to Madame Hohlakov:

Above all, avoid falsehood, every kind of falsehood, especially falseness to yourself. . . . What seems to be bad within you will grow purer from the very fact of your observing it within yourself. . . . Love in dreams is greedy for immediate action, rapidly performed in the sight of all. . . . But active love is labour and fortitude.

Zossima speaks of the earthliness of the monk's religion, its exultant celebration of life. He relates how his dying brother begged his mother not to cry, for "life is paradise."

Zossima's social critique and his notion of freedom nearly justify rebellion. But, he shrinks from violence and hopes that "salvation will come from the people, from their faith and meekness." This attitude becomes focally relevant to his role in Mitya's ordeal. Zossima can only bow down to but not help Mitya. And, Dostoyevsky obliquely exposes Zossima's impotence here by removing him early in the story, before Mitya's problem becomes acute. In this way, the author spares himself the embarrassment of revealing the Elder's helplessness in Mitya's trial.

Dostoyevsky's complex view of Zossima is also manifested in the style and structure of the section "The Russian Monk." Dostoyevsky spent more time and labor on this section than on any other, planning to make it the "culminating point of the novel," the answer to Ivan's Inquisitor. "For its sake," he wrote to Liubimov, "the whole novel is being written." Yet, only the account of Zossima's sinful youth and the pages on his brother are executed with artistic power. The rest, dealing with Zossima's teachings, is in the form of a lawyer's brief. Dostoyevsky himself felt that he had not succeeded in his attempted refutation of Ivan's stand.[27] The artist invokes more fervor in picturing the skepticism of Ivan, the passion of Mitya, even the nihilistic act of Smerdyakov. Such esthetic consideration tells us more about Dostoyevsky's position than his forensic statements.[28]

Alyosha: "The Man of God."

The determining force in Alyosha's life is the memory of his mother and the treatment she received from his father. Although Alyosha lost his mother in his fourth year, he remembered her all his life. He recalled one particular fragment in which his mother prayed for him to the Mother of God:

> one still summer evening, an open window, the slanting rays of the setting sun (that he recalled most vividly of all); in a corner of the room the holy image, before it a lighted lamp, and on her knees before the image his mother, sobbing hysterically with cries and moans, snatching him up in both arms, squeezing him close till it hurt, and praying for him to the Mother of God, holding him out in both arms to the image as though to put him under the Mother's protection. . . . And suddenly a nurse runs in and snatches him from her in terror. That was the picture! and Alyosha remembered his mother's face at that minute. He used to say that it was frenzied but beautiful as he remembered.

And one might say that Alyosha dedicates himself *to redeem the life of his mother*. He carries forward not only her meekness, passivity and submission, but also something of her "crazy" character, as when he shakes in hysterical paroxysm of weeping when Fyodor mentions his mother.

Dostoyevsky tells us that Alyosha's love had to be "active," that he had to help the one he loved. Now, "to do so he must know what he was aiming at; he must know for certain what was best for each." But Alyosha's love could not discern a clear way through the distortions of his day. Not only did this "early lover of humanity" not know "for certain what was best for each," but the very character of his religious outlook to accept everything "without the least condemnation," precluded his acting on the basis of a choice. Hence, Alyosha's absolute acceptance meets with Ivan's absolute skepticism (the two brothers are the only ones who have the same father and mother). To Ivan, all is lawful, to Alyosha, all is lovable; that is, in both cases, all is "acceptable,"—for Ivan in the light of pure reason, for Alyosha in the eyes of a loving God. The pragmatic consequences are that *neither can act* on the basis of a clear-cut resolution—Ivan cannot because for him every pro has its contra; Alyosha cannot because for him every contra has its pro. Hence, Ivan can only talk and argue; Alyosha can only feel and weep. Both can be only passive, suffering spectators. Although the author expressly refers to Alyosha as "the young hero I love so much," he cannot be a heroic character in the plot because accepting everything, *he cannot be the guide* they all look to. Towards the end of the novel, Mitya needs Alyosha's consent before he will agree with Ivan's plan for his escape; but Alyosha is unable to lend his active support. While the others are busy planning for Mitya's rescue, Alyosha devotes himself to the boys and to Ilusha's funeral.

Alyosha is at most Dostoyevsky's "future hero," as he calls him in another place. In the planned sequel, Alyosha was to marry Lisa (his moral opposite) and "sin his way to Jesus." But, in *The Brothers Karamazov*, he does not sin, is as sexless as Prince Myshkin. In his Foreword to the novel, Dostoyevsky admits that he did not succeed in molding Alyosha to heroic proportions:

> . . . although I call Alyosha my hero, I myself know that he is by no means a great man, and hence I foresee such unavoidable questions as these: "What is so remarkable about your Alyosha Fyodorovitch that you have chosen him as your hero? What has he accomplished?" . . . For me he is remarkable, but I doubt strongly whether I shall succeed in proving this to the reader. The fact is, if you please, that he is a protagonist, but a protagonist vague and undefined.

Dostoyevsky draws Alyosha with less literary power, pours less of his artistic blood into him than he does in the case of his criminal brothers. And this has esthetic "justice." For, Alyosha does little to affect the central problem. He is a hero only in Tolstoy's sense—in being nonheroic. Alyosha, and Father Zossima are the novel's moral censors. But neither can or do help Mitya. Zossima is removed from the story before the trial opens and Alyosha is on the sidelines during Mitya's ordeal.

In his essay on Dostoyevsky, Freud sees the patricidal guilt distributed among Mitya, Ivan and Smerdyakov, but exempts "the contrasted figure of Alyosha." However, it may be said that Alyosha is both one of the four "elements" and one of the four "causes" in the Karamazov murder, perhaps even the "final" cause. To begin with, Alyosha confesses to being a Karamazov, full of low desires. He admits to Lisa that there is some truth in her saying that "every one loves having killed his father." Alyosha had been strongly admonished by Father Zossima to keep an eye on Mitya, having in mind the latter's threat to kill his father. But Alyosha "forgets" this and instead busies himself with the boys.

A crucial psychological motif for Alyosha's feeling of guilt appears in the fact that, like Father Zossima, Alyosha *invites punishment and begs forgiveness.* Now, unlike Father Zossima, Alyosha is not shown to have sinned. Does he feel guilty only because of his impotence in relation to the problem of the Karamazovs?

Alyosha's actions following the death of Father Zossima suggest clues of more latent guilt-feelings.

When Father Zossima dies, Alyosha expected, in his naive faith, that the elder's body would not decompose. But, when the smell of decay becomes evident, Alyosha is shaken to the core. He talks, like Ivan, about rejecting God's world, and readily accepts Rakitin's invitation to visit Grushenka. In a perceptive essay, Dr. Mark Kanzer sees in Alyosha's encounter with this temptress the psychological pivot of the novel. With the death of the father-figure, Alyosha's repressed erotic drives erupt and he goes to Grushenka who is a mother-sister figure to him. At this point, Grushenka's former lover appears and Alyosha returns to the bier of Father Zossima. This "critical moment" in Alyosha's life is followed by a dream-like scene in which Alyosha beholds Christ reenacting the first of his miracles—the conversion of water into wine.[29] There follows the passage in which Alyosha embraces, kisses and wets the earth, "vowed passionately to love it, to love it for ever and ever." Gazing on the coffin of the elder, Alyosha "longed to forgive every one and for everything, and to beg forgiveness. . . ."

Still, Alyosha's personality has a productive function. He is the steady, ever-present listener, a liquid vessel in which passions tend to be softened. He is a catalyst, not only for the rage, but also for the love latent in the others.

Smerdyakov: The Underground

Smerdyakov is the Russian Underground Man whose surface calm hides a diabolic abyss. If Fyodor embodies the pleasure principle that leads to its own destruction, Smerdyakov embodies the principle of destruction itself, receiving its sanction from Ivan's conceptual dialectic.[30] His resentment is stored up in his mental underground:

> A physiognomist, studying his face would have said that there was no thought in it, no reflection, but only a sort of contemplation.

The author compares him to a painting by Kramskoy in which a peasant stands lost in thought:

> Yet he is not thinking; he is "contemplating" . . . . if he were asked what he had been thinking about, he would remember nothing. Yet probably he has hidden within himself, the impression which had dominated him during the period of contemplation. Those impressions are dear to him and no doubt he hoards them imperceptibly, and unconsciously.

Fyodor refers to him as "a Balaam's ass . . . that thinks and thinks, and the devil knows where he gets to."

Dostoyevsky endows Smerdyakov's mother with mysterious subearthy features. His account of her delivery suggests that it had a supranatural character—in her pregnant condition, Lisaveta climbed a high fence to reach Fyodor's bath-house where she gave birth. In Grigory's words, she comes "from the devil's son and a holy innocent," and so is a "child of God," and the author remarks that she is regarded as an "idiot," which means, one "specially dear to God."

In Smerdyakov's own mind, he is "descended from a filthy beggar" with no father. (He is the only character in the novel who has no surname and is called by the nickname given to his mother—a kind of fatherless son of the Russian earth-mother).

Smerdyakov is the Slavic Alberich with a fierce resentment against his father-authorities who despise him and, like Alberich, he steals the gold. To Ivan, he is "raw material for revolution. . . . His kind will come first, and better ones after." He is the harbinger of the revolutionary underground which was to explode in Russian history.

Dostoyevsky assigned his personal epileptic burden to Myshkin, one of his noble characters, and to Smerdyakov, one of his base characters. In Dostoyevsky's dialectic, the two are interrelated: their idiocy has a malevolent and a cathartic function. Dostoyevsky suggests this aspect in Smerdyakov by assigning him—along with Mitya—the stages of the Rankian hero: A "difficult" conception and delivery, abandonment (in a "stable"), rescue by a servant (Grigory), and subsequent revenge for his humiliation.

Smerdyakov is not simply "a parody of Ivan," as Simmons calls him. While he lets himself be guided by Ivan, Smerdyakov has personal grounds for hating Fyodor and, at the end, he rejects Ivan. In the course of his three interviews with his brother, Smerdyakov's former awe of Ivan is turned to contempt. He discovers that his "God almighty" was unsure of himself and refused to take responsibility for his maxim that "everything was lawful." He now defies Ivan to kill him: "You won't dare to do anything, you who used to be so bold."

Commenting on Smerdyakov's face, Dostoyevsky writes that a man, such as he

> may suddenly, after hoarding impressions for many years, abandon everything and go off to Jerusalem on a pilgrimage for his soul's salvation, or perhaps he will suddenly set fire to his native village, or perhaps do both.

After the murder, Smerdyakov undergoes a remarkable change. He, who was said not to have "the Russian faith at all," attempts to find consolation by reading The Sayings of the Holy Father Isaac the Syrian. (It should be mentioned that Smerdyakov developed epilepsy after he expressed doubt over God, for which Grigory slapped him violently.) And, he who had been thought to have bourgeois ambitions, refuses to take Fyodor's money. In the end, he repudiates Ivan, unable to live by his brother's values after all. To be sure, he does not confess and clear Mitya, and his suicide is an act of despair, not of penance. Yet, it is an indirect confession of his share in the guilt and his self-destruction is a distorted self-sacrifice.

The Devil

Smerdyakov is the Mephistopheles of the book, and, like Goethe's devil, has "some kind of compact, some secret" with Ivan, the would-be man-God. He, too, is the "Overseer," helps to implement the thoughts and desires of his Russian Faust.

The devil appears to Ivan at about the hour when Smerdyakov hangs himself. His death deprives Ivan of "the raw material" for his theory and he is now left with "pure reason" which involves him in antinomies. The bodily, irrational element which he attempted to deny rises to the surface of his mind and he can now recognize the devil in himself.

Ivan's devil lacks the terrifying aspect of the classical or medieval adversary. He is reduced to a poor relation who would give all "simply to be transformed into the soul of a merchant's wife. . . ." This devil is a vulgar accommodator, "ready to assume any amiable expression as occasion might arise," a bureaucrat for whom hell is mechanical routine. He is the modern devil, tempting men with commercialism and "adaptation." This form of evil also appears in Raskolnikov's vision of microbes threatening to destroy man and in the mechanistic socialism of *The Possessed*. Such denial of God, the devil tells Ivan, can destroy mankind.

Ivan is unable to exorcize the devil because he is an aspect of his own self. He admits to the devil:

> You are the incarnation of myself, but only of one side of me . . . of my thoughts and feelings, but only the nastiest and stupidest of them.

The appearance of the devil is Ivan's partial awareness of the unconscious role which Smerdyakov played in his life, the ideas which came to Ivan "when he was asleep" and did not "want to believe."[31]

Dostoyevsky gives even his devil a "Russian" character by having him repudiate his destructive function. Although he is predestined "to deny," Ivan's devil is "not at all inclined to negation," and to evil. He calls himself "perhaps the one man in all creation who loves the truth and genuinely desires good," would use his critical powers to make men disbelieve in him and thereby sow "a tiny grain of faith." Likewise, the Ivans are "secretly longing" to save their souls. At the end, it is Ivan who makes the most persistent efforts to rescue Mitya, would even sacrifice himself for his brother. Neither he nor Raskolnikov have the persuasion that justice is the interest of the stronger. In Alyosha's words, Ivan's illness is "the anguish of . . . an earnest conscience," in which God and the devil were battling and where "God, in whom he disbelieved, and His truth were gaining mastery over his heart, which still refused to submit."

Katya: The Incest Figure in the Brothers Karamazov

Dostoyevsky criticism has accepted Grushenka as the incest figure in the novel, since Mitya publicly competes with his father for her favors. However, Mitya's major dilemma centers, not in Grushenka, but in Katya who, as this section will show, is the deeper of Mitya's incest burdens.

Freud names *The Brothers Karamazov*, *Hamlet* and *Oedipus Rex* three literary masterpieces, dealing with patricide, motivated by sexual rivalry.[32] Now, *The Brothers Karamazov* is a later, more complex form of the oedipal situation. In Sophocles, Oedipus actually commits patricide and incest. Shakespeare's modern, sophisticated scene, as we have noted, presents more tangled relations.

In Dostoyevsky, the pattern is still more intricate. We have three father figures: Fyodor, Grigory (who brings up Mitya and Smerdyakov) and Father Zossima; three or four sons: Mitya, Ivan, Alyosha and Smerdyakov, who divide the patricidal guilt. Grushenka is the manifest object of Mitya's desire. The hidden and latent incest-figure is Katya.

Katya is the source of Mitya's obsessive feeling of his "debt" to her. His inability to return the money he took from her is the chief ground of his emotional disturbance. This is the reason, Mitya says, "why I fought in the tavern, that is why I attacked my father." Here, Mitya associates his patricidal impulse with his "debt" to Katya. What tortures him when he is arrested is not the false charge that he murdered his father, nor so much the thought that he killed Grigory, but "the damned consciousness" that he had not repaid Katya and had become "a downright thief." (In passing, we might note that Mitya recalls that as a boy he stole some kopecks from his mother which he returned "three days later.") Why does Mitya feel that this is "the most shameful act of my whole life," that his very *"life"* depends on his returning the 3000 rubles to Katya?

Dostoyevsky gives Katya features which are similar to those he assigns to Mitya's mother, Adelaida. Both belong to fairly rich and distinguished families and become heiresses. Both possess an imperious beauty and are described as strong, vigorous and intelligent. Mitya's mother was "a hot-tempered, bold, dark-browed, impatient woman," and according to rumor used to beat her husband. She left Fyodor, running away with a divinity student. Katya strikes Mitya as proud, reckless, defiant, self-willed. She too defies convention: She comes to Mitya alone, impulsively offers to become his wife.

From the outset, Katya appears to Mitya as a kind of goddess. At the meeting in Father Zossima's cell, he is particularly outraged by his father's aspersions of Katya's good and honorable name for whom Mitya feels "such reverence that I dare not take her name in vain." And just as the question is raised how Adelaida could have married "such a worthless puny weakling" as Fyodor, so Mitya cannot understand that Katya should choose "a bug" like himself.

Mitya comes to Katya's attention by his wild exploits which set the whole town talking. He felt that this made him "a hero." But, he complains, Katya "didn't seem to feel it." When she first saw him, she "scarcely looked at me, and compressed her lips scornfully." Thereupon, Mitya plans revenge on Katya by humiliating her. The opportunity comes when Katya, desperately trying to save her father from dishonor, gets word from Mitya that he will give her the money if she comes to him alone, Mitya promising "to keep the secret religiously."

When Katya came to him, Mitya's first thought "was a—Karamazov one," to treat this "beauty" as a prostitute. But, she also appeared to him beautiful "in another way . . . because she was noble
. . . in all the grandeur of her generosity and sacrifice for her father." In
contrast, Mitya thought of himself as a little animal, "a bug . . . a venomous spider." His feelings towards her comprised a mixture of hatred
and love. His hatred for Katya, he tells Alyosha, was such as he never
felt for any other woman. But, it is the kind "which is only a hair's-
breath from love, the maddest love."

Katya's visit roused a powerful sexual desire in Mitya. He was so
excited by the "venomous thought" of possessing her that he nearly
swooned "with suspense." Although Mitya gained mastery over his
demon, his deep guilt begins at this point. It is as though by offering
herself to him, Katya divined his hidden wish to enter into an impermissible relation with her. But Mitya curbed his desire, gave Katya the
money (we should bear in mind that it is the money left him by his
mother). After she left, Mitya drew his sword, nearly stabbing himself—"why, I don't know," he adds. Mitya's ability to control his Karamazov sensualism in this scene is a major test of his manhood and *foreshadows that he will resist the other temptation, that of killing his
father.* He was held back from taking Katya by—perhaps also despite
—the thought that she was ready to surrender herself for the sake of
her father.

However, soon afterwards, Mitya yielded to another enticement. He
took the 3000 rubles which Katya asked him to post and spent half
of the sum on his mistress-figure, Grushenka (repeating his father's act
in which Fyodor attempted to keep the dowry of Mitya's mother). At
about the same time, he agreed to Katya's proposal or demand that
they become engaged. (How this comes about, Dostoyevsky-Mitya
does not make clear.)[33] For some unexplained reason, Mitya sends his
brother Ivan to her who thereupon falls in love with Katya. This "one
stupid thing," he says later to Alyosha, "may be the saving of us all
now."[34]

Katya as the Possessive Mother

The identification of Katya with Mitya's mother lies above all in
their attempt to dominate their men. Katya's authoritative character
is suggested first by her outward appearance. Alyosha is struck "by
the imperiousness, proud ease, and self-confidence of the haughty girl."
Her love for Mitya is that of a commanding or pitying mother for a
wayward son. She would be Mitya's "God," as she says:

Let him feel ashamed of himself, let him be ashamed of other people's knowing (that he had not returned the money he owed her), but not of my knowing. He can tell God everything without shame. . . . I want to save him for
ever. Let him forget me as his betrothed.

The Pan-Slavic Mother Goddess is worshipped for her fruit-bearing
and yielding qualities, not for her beauty. She is generally identified
with the good Russian earth and its earthy peasant folk. Katya, with
her aristocratic pride, stern virtue and possessiveness is a distortion of
this Eastern Mother Goddess. She cannot produce because she cannot
yield.[35]

Katya offers to sacrifice herself for Mitya. But she would *impose*
her sacrifice on him, *would be his Mother-Saviour by command.*[36]
Mitya senses that her love for him is "more like revenge." It is the
threat of the mother engulfing the son by her all-possessive love.

Mitya keeps speaking of his "debt" to Katya and of his "disgrace,"
referring to the fact that he had squandered 1500 of Katya's 3000
rubles on a spree with Grushenka. Mitya makes desperate efforts to
free himself from the "debt" to his "God"-mother. This, although Katya
herself does not press him for the money, indeed, acts as if she did not
care what he did with it. Furthermore, Mitya *could* get the money:
Alyosha offers him 2000 rubles and says that Ivan would give him another 1000. Moreover, he could borrow from Grusha. But no! Mitya is
obsessed with the feeling that *he can pay his "debt" to Katya only by
giving her the money which he has inherited from his mother and
which his father is withholding from him.* (Mitya's attempts to get the
money from Samsonov, Lyagavy, Madame Hohlakov are a wild goose
chase which invites failure.) And he wants no more than 3000 rubles,
although by his reckoning, his mother left him 28,000 rubles. If his
father would give him 3000 rubles, Mitya tells Alyosha, he would draw
his soul "out of hell:"

Let him give me back only three out of the twenty-eight thousand. . . . For
that three thousand—I give you my solemn word—I'll make an end of everything, and he shall hear nothing more of me. For the last time, I give him the
chance to be a father.[37]

Grushenka: The Hetaira-Magdalene

From this perspective, Grushenka is the lesser of Mitya's burdens.
The conflict with his father over her is open and somewhat literal.[38]
Mitya is ready to accept all his rivals, except Fyodor. It is of some sig-
nificance that Mitya's attitude towards Grushenka is a transference of
Katya's towards him. As Katya was willing to accept any conditions if
Mitya would agree to be her husband, so he declares:

I'll be her (Grusha's) husband if she deigns to have me, and when lovers come, I'll go into the next room. I'll clean her friends' goloshes, blow up their samovar, run their errands.

However, Mitya does not want to force his love on Grusha. And, it is his hope that she may be the means by which he can free himself from Katya. Her soft, voluptuous, noiseless movements contrast with Katya's bold and vigorous step, her simple "childlike good nature" with Katya's complex ironic consciousness.

Mitya speaks of Grusha's "infernal curves." Yet, the story does not have a single erotic scene between them. Even at his "wedding" with Grusha at Mokroe, Mitya does not go beyond kissing his beloved. Dostoyesvky himself remarks that Grusha is Russian in that her beauty is only of the moment. Russian literature, as Berdyaev notes, does not know the erotic motifs of the West. It has no stories comparable to Tristan and Isolde or Romeo and Juliet. The attraction of Russian women (as of the Russian Mother Goddess) lies not in their seductiveness but in their earthy productivity.

Mitya's meeting with Grushenka at Mokroe is the poem of *The Brothers Karamazov*, the lovers' Dionysian song to life. For the first and only time, the two are united, at one with "the people," the Russian peasants, over whom they reign as King and Queen. It is their Eden where all is love, kindness, forgiveness and generosity. To the rhythm of children's songs, Mitya and his bride themselves act like children. Everything—down to the language and mood—is simple, elemental and earthy. Here, all are equal (except for the "foreigners," the Poles, who leave before the high point of the revel is reached).

But it is a Karamazov-Eden, and the celebration takes on the character of a delirious orgy. Mokroe is the scene of Mitya's and Grushenka's "wedding." It takes place at about the same time when the father is murdered and after Mitya thought he may have killed his surrogate-father Grigory. At this point, "society" steps in and arrests Mitya.

Like many of Dostoyevsky's women, Grushenka turns from the hetaira to the Madonna. Her transformation begins during Alyosha's visit when his kindness acts as a catalyst freeing her for a generous, overflowing love of the "soul," becoming "more loving than we," as Alyosha puts it. The change takes on a stable form after Mitya's arrest. Now, there were

> signs of a spiritual transformation in her, and a steadfast, fine and humble determination that nothing could shake. . . . There was scarcely a trace of her former frivolity.

Through Grusha's love, Mitya declares, he has "become a man himself."

Mitya's Need of the Two Women

Although Mitya states that Grusha has made "a man" of him, it appears that she does not completely fulfill his needs. *She accepts Mitya as he is.* But Mitya also needs the censorious conscience, especially since his father lacks this quality altogether. Fyodor is a Satyr-figure, embodies an amorphous, chaotic sensualism intent solely on the pursuit of pleasure. And Mitya has only a distant relation to Father Zossima, Alyosha and Ivan, the religious and rational super-egos in the novel.

This may explain why Mitya cannot and does not want to free himself from Katya, why he kneels and prays "to Katya's image" in Grusha's presence. When she produces the letter which virtually condemns him, Mitya cries out:

> We've hated each other for many things, Katya, but I swear, I swear I loved you even while I hated you, and you didn't love me![39]

When, at the trial, Katya tells of her visit to Mitya and her bow to him, Mitya sobs: "Katya, why have you ruined me? . . . Now, I am condemned!" Does her recital reactivate his incestuous desire for her? Does her attempt to save him again put him in her "debt?"[40]

Even as Mitya turns towards Grushenka, he remains bound to Katya. Following the trial, he seems concerned only about seeing Katya. Alyosha tells her:

> He needs you particularly just now . . . he keeps asking for you. . . . He realizes that he has injured you beyond reckoning. . . . He said, if she refuses to come, I shall be unhappy all my life.

When Katya appears in the doorway of his prison cell,

> a scared look came into his face. He turned pale, but a timid, pleading smile appeared on his lips at once, and with an irresistible impulse he held out both hands to Katya.

And now, the two confess their mutual tie. Katya tells him:

> Love is over, Mitya! but the past is painfully dear to me. . . . I shall love you for ever, and you will love me; do you know that? Do you hear? Love me, love me all your life! she cried, with a quiver almost of menace in her voice.

Mitya replies: "I shall love you . . . all my life! So it will be, so it will always be. . . ." He pleads with her that she forgive him for having wanted to humiliate her, for his desire to have "the proud aristocratic girl" appear as "the hetaira." His plea is granted in Katya's final resignation, in her words to the rival Grushenka: "Forgive me. . . . Don't be anxious, I'll save him for you."

Dostoyevsky-Mitya divide the mother-figure into Katya and Grushenka. Mitya moves from attachment to the commanding goddess-mother to the yielding mistress-mother. In the end, he needs both: "the proud aristocratic girl and the 'hetaira.'" Grusha can only follow, but not guide. He needs both, moreover, for the mixture of elements in each. Grusha is submissive. Yet, in the scene with Katya, Mitya recognizes in her "the queen of all she-devils." Katya is defiant, haughty and domineering. Yet, Alyosha notes that her face can beam "with spontaneous good-natured kindliness, and direct warm-hearted sincerity." In the end, the two women-figures tend to merge.

Mitya almost marries Katya and nearly kills Fyodor. Like Hamlet, he wrestles with the demon driving him to violate the primary taboos. Mitya, too, shows no hesitation to "act"; except where it concerns Katya and Fyodor. His promise lies in a gradual awareness of the nature of his "debt" and guilt, awareness that his involvement with Katya was injurious to her and himself.[41]

Act III: Mitya—"Our Mother Russia"

While his brothers seem to stand for 'Europeanism' and 'the principles of the people,' he seems to represent Russia *as she is*. Oh, not all Russia, not all! God preserve us, if it were! Yet, here we have her, our mother Russia, the very scent and sound of her. Oh, he is spontaneous, he is a marvellous mingling of good and evil, he is a lover of culture and Schiller, yet brawls in taverns and plucks out the beards of his boon companions.

This characterization by the prosecutor at the trial points to Mitya as embodying the central problem of Russia. The plot of the novel has its pivot in his dilemma, and we are told that his trial has all Russia excited.

Mitya incorporates the most inclusive traits of the Karamazov character, combining the elements of the others: his father's primitive lust, Ivan's culture, Smerdyakov's resentment, and Alyosha's conscience (his "guardian angel" which holds him back from killing Fyodor). Yet, basic in Mitya's Karamazovism is his zest for life, his feeling that "There's no living without joy." Where Ivan's pro-contra logic paralyzes his action and passion, where Alyosha's all-embracing acceptance bars him from an active choice, and where Smerdyakov's passion can discharge itself only in his fits, Mitya dares live out his intoxication with life in a sensuous "Russian" manner. If one wants to become a man (Mitya quotes from Schiller's *Eleusinian Festival*):

He must turn and cling forever
To his ancient Mother Earth.

Mitya's earthiness is a promise that his passion may become productive.

In his talk with the Mysterious Visitor, Zossima makes the point that the real revolution must be psychological, must involve the heart of man. Mitya expresses a similar idea in discussing the problem of God's existence with Rakitin. He is greatly upset by Rakitin's theory that one is not to be blamed for murdering his father, that it all has to do with having been corrupted by the environment. But Mitya argues that if a man's actions are a resultant of social forces, then there is no standard for human conduct, man has no clear moral choice, and this means that God does not exist. It is this which worries Mitya:

> It's God that's worrying me. That's the only thing that's worrying me. What if He doesn't exist? What if Rakitin's right—that it's an idea made up by men? Then, if He doesn't exist, man is the chief of the earth, of the universe. Magnificent! Only how is he going to be good without God? . . . For whom is man going to love then? . . . Rakitin says . . . "You'd better think about the extension of civic rights, or of even keeping down the price of meat. You will show your love for humanity more simply and directly by that, than by philosophy." I answered him, "Well, but you, without a God, are more likely to raise the price of meat, if it suits you, and make a rouble on every kopeck." He lost his temper.

To Mitya, Rakitin's social-biologic determinism entails a denial of first principles. Its relativism opens the way for an egocentric morality which precludes a meaningful human quest. To believe in God means to believe in man and his strivings, means the integration of individual freedom within the framework of a universally valid morality. Mitya passionately rejects Rakitin's mechanical order in which he is but a product of a biologic and social system. This imbues him with the feeling that a "new man" has risen in him, and he can now exclaim that *he exists*:

> And I seem to have such strength in me now, that I think I could stand anything, any suffering, only to be able to say and to repeat to myself every moment, "I exist." In thousand of agonies—I exist. I'm tormented on the rack —but I exist!

In this exultant feeling, Mitya is freer in prison than the "other-directed" characters in contemporary literature.[42]

Mitya's conception of freedom avoids becoming a mystic individualism due to his societal impulse. When Ivan discusses the sufferings of children, he is raising primarily a metaphysical-theologic problem. But, for Mitya, suffering is a concrete social phenomenon and he translates it into the suffering of the exploited Russian mother and her child. During the preliminary investigation, Mitya falls asleep and dreams:

> He was driving somewhere in the steppes . . . and a peasant was driving him in a cart with a pair of horses, through snow and sleet.

He sees the land desolate, the peasant women and their little children thin and wan. Mitya doesn't understand why they are so dark from misery and in his dream cries out: "Why don't they feed the babe?":

> And he felt that, though his questions were unreasonable and senseless, yet he wanted to ask just that, and he had to ask it just in that way. And he felt that a passion of pity, such as he had never known before, was rising in his heart, that he wanted to cry, that he wanted to do something for them all, so that the babe should weep no more, so that the dark-faced, dried-up mother should not weep, that no one should shed tears again from that moment, and he wanted to do it at once, at once, regardless of all obstacles, with all the recklessness of the Karamazovs.

Later, he tells Alyosha that it's "for the babe" that he is going to prison:

> Because we are all responsible for all. For all the "babes," for there are big children as well as little children. All are "babes." I go for all, because someone must go for all. I didn't kill father, but I've got to go. I accept it.

Here, Mitya moves from concern with himself to concern for others. He would step out of the Russian *troika* to save its big and little children from poverty and suffering, would rid the state of its social disease.

Mitya's development approximates the stages of the Rankian hero: His family claims to have an ancient and noble lineage; his conception may be said to have been difficult in that his mother "seems to have been the only woman who made no particular appeal" to his father's senses. When Mitya was three years old, he was abandoned by both his mother and father, later by parent-surrogates, and rescued by Grigory, the faithful servant. He then returns to challenge his father on the heritage his mother left him and on the woman for whom they compete. However, unlike Smerdyakov, he has a "guardian angel" who keeps him from murdering his father and he gradually develops into a kind of culture hero, thirsting for "reformation and renewal." Although he is condemned for an act which he did not commit, he accepts his ordeal for the sake of man, for the sake of "all the 'babes'."

Mitya is the hero of the book because he *learns* most from his trial. And he learns most because, more than the others, he descends to and goes through the Satanic depths. Where Ivan would meet the human situation by dialectic, Smerdyakov by the brute act, Alyosha by faith and submission, Mitya grapples with it by *Praxis*.[43] He experiences something of a catharsis by *emotionally living through* the Russian inferno and Purgatory. Mitya alone is not emasculated by his father-authorities and is the living hope that the Pan-Slavic values of communality and individual freedom might be re-created.

Epilogue: The Boys

The Brothers Karamazov ends with an account of the meeting between Alyosha and the boys. Here, the problem of the Karamazovs reappears on another level, with Kolya and Ilusha as possible future heroes. Mark Twain also saw the hope for America in her youth, the embodiment of America's native values of freedom and equality. Kolya exhibits the self-laceration and reckless daring of the Karamazovs, the passion of Mitya, the intellectualism of Ivan; he has his Smerdyakov (in the errand boy to whom he suggests killing the goose) and, at the end, reveals something of Alyosha's forgiving nature.

Yet, the boys are not intended to represent a repetition of the Karamazovs, for Ilusha reverses the trend. He loves his father who, in turn, is ready to sacrifice himself for his son. In reconciling Ilusha and Kolya, Alyosha would save the Russian Boys from Rakitin's Western materialistic "socialism," save them for the Slavic principle of *sobornost*. In his speech by the stone of Ilusha's grave, Alyosha calls on the twelve boys gathered there to "be generous and brave like Ilusha, clever, brave and generous like Kolya . . . as modest, as clever and sweet as Kartashov." He emphasizes the importance of good childhood memories:

> there is nothing higher and stronger and more wholesome and good for life in the future than some good memory, especially a memory of childhood, of home. People talk to you a great deal about education, but some good, sacred memory, preserved from childhood, is perhaps the best education.

However, in Dostoyevsky's Russia, children were abandoned or outraged. Following his dream of a happy age, Stavrogin notices a tiny red spider and sees Matrojosha, the little girl he violated,—sunken, feverish, her undeveloped body threatening him helplessly with her little fists. The final two chapters of *The Brothers Karamazov* likewise point to Dostoyevsky's reservations about the possibility of a human paradise. The first depicts the continuation of Mitya's plight; the second pictures the helpless little fists of the boys, helpless even in the case of Ilusha. For Ilusha is only a prayer on the part of Dostoyevsky—his dead body miraculously does *not* decompose.

Dostoyevsky saw no clear way for the resolution of the Russian trial. He transformed his criminals into saints with apocalyptic suddenness and Dionysian unrestraint precisely because the "natural" way was not available in his Russia. The country was ruled by an oppressive patriarchy and the Russian earth-mother was supplanted by a willful protectress. Dostoyevsky's Katya, along with Tolstoy's Anna Karenina, are analogous to the power-driven women, such as Strindberg's Laura and O'Neill's Lavinia. Hence, Dostoyevsky's heroes remain wildly rebellious. Raskolnikov continues to be a "dissenter" in Siberia—in his notes, the author has him planning a new crime—, and Mitya tells Alosha at the end: "I am not ready! I am not able to resign myself!"

Viewed as a whole, Dostoyevsky's work pictures the tension between the old Eastern myth of communal equality and the Western quest for individualism and freedom. The tension is expressed in the convulsive form of Dostoyevsky's novels, the precipitateness of the action, the wild swinging between extremes. Dostoyevsky finished none of his major novels and his characters never "finish" anything; when they reach the stage of betrothal, they run away from the altar, as Stefan Zweig observes. They plunge into the lowest depths in quest of the whole or of God. But this deity is never envisioned as in Job or Dante. Dostoyevsky's characters have no guide, act without "reason" in a bottomless underground in which the "first cause" remains unknown.

Yet, the widespread notion that Dostoyevsky found a value in suffering as such is misleading. He distinguished between characters, such as Father Ferapont and Lise for whom asceticism and torture are final values and those who suffer for an idea—the Zossimas and Mityas, the Raskolnikovs and Shatovs. Raskolnikov tells Sonya:

> They say it is necessary for me to suffer! What's the object of these senseless sufferings? Shall I know any better what they are for, when I am crushed by hardships and idiocy, and weak as an old man after twenty years' penal servitude?

Dostoyevsky did think that his hosanna had to come "through the great furnace of doubt," and that to transform the world, we must first "go through the period of isolation," as the mysterious visitor tells Father Zossima. Still despite its agonizing process, we feel the affirmative mood in Dostoyevsky's work because his people embrace the sensuousness of life. The Russia of his day was losing the memory of ancient Slavic values. *The Brothers Karamazov* would re-create their symbolic import and thus save them for all time.

NOTES

1. Russia's historic origins are obscure, since the records are oral. The patriarchal family developed later, as the Slavs moved north and the work of clearing woods, etc. fell to the men. Evidence pointing to the matriarchate as the earliest form can be found in M. Kovalevsky, *Modern Customs and Ancient Laws of Russia* (London, 1891), and in E. Elnett, *Historic Origin and Social Development of Family Life in Russia* (New York, 1926).

   The subsequent discussion draws on N. A. Berdyaev's *The Russian Idea* (New York, 1948), F. Fedotov's *The Russian Religious Mind* (2 vols.; Cambridge, Mass., 1946-1966), and Sir John Maynard's *Russia in Flux* (London, 1946). For related discussion, see L. Niederle, *Manuel de l'antiquité Slave* (2 vols.; Paris, 1923-26), F. Dvornik, *The Slavs: Their Early History and Civilization* (Boston, 1956), Adolph Stender-Petersen, *Russian Studies* (Copenhagen, 1956). Petersen emphasizes that Russia's pagan religion was that of "of the tillers of the soil." He refers to the concept in Russian folklore of "Mother moist earth" (*Mat' syra zeml'a*). Yet, he holds that the pre-historic Russian community was "essentially patriarchal."

2. Cf. V. Ivanov's *Freedom and the Tragic Life* (London, 1952). In the absence of a good *pater familias*, Dostoyevsky saw the Russian woman as "our only great hope, one of the pledges of our revival." ("The Pushkin Speech" in *The Diary of a Writer* [New York, 1954], pp. 959-1010.)

3. This "choric" mentality (Berdyaev's term) appears in the use of generic names: Strangers are addressed as "Mother," "Father," "Brother," "Uncle," etc.

4. See B. D. Grekov, *The Culture of Kiev Rūs* (Moscow, 1947) and N. K. Gudzy, *History of Early Russian Literature* (New York, 1949).

5. In his *Russian Folklore* (New York, 1950), Y. M. Sokolov notes the role of folklore and legend in Gorky's life, quoting from Gorky's essay on literature:

   ". . . by far the deepest and most vivid, the most artistically fashioned types of heroes are created by folklore, by the oral creations of the working people. . . . The better we come to know the past, the more easily, the more deeply and joyfully we shall understand the great significance of the present which we are creating."

   Sokolov's study also shows that Soviet ballads invoke ancient figures, such as Ilya Murom, Stepan Razin, leader of the peasants who revolted in the seventeenth century. See also T. V. Popova, *The Russian Folk Song* (Moscow, 1946).

6. In this old Slavic community, rights in land (although not the land itself) were held in common. According to B. H. Sumner (*A Short History of Russia* [New York, 1949]), the *mir* organized periodic redistribution of land "in accordance with either working strength . . . or the number of 'eaters' in the family," with the village meeting making all decisions with regard to cultivation of the land. Prior to the introduction of money-economy, there was economic equality among the members. Summing up, Maynard states that the *mir* was "an agent of equalization; and equality made a stronger appeal than freedom."

The *mir* persisted even after Peter the Great and his followers consolidated feudalism and was used by the centralized state as a convenient means for collecting taxes from the whole community.

The spirit of the *mir* penetrated pre-modern Russian life which was organized into "big families," or clans which encompassed several generations and included adopted children: "Each member of the household was not an individual but merely a component part of a collective individuality — the family to which he belonged." Even in its patriarchal stage, the clan was "monarchical in its form but democratic in its substance," with the Common Council at the head of all. The whole spelled "a sort of family communism." Cf. E. Elnett, *Origin and Social Development of Family Life*, pp. 4 ff. To Fedotov, the Russian nation "could once be thought of as an immense *gens* or *rod*, of whom the Tsar was the father." Where the Greek Eleusian mysteries promised immortality to the individual soul, primitive Russian paganism considered the individual only as a transient moment in the eternal life of the *rod*. *Russian Religious Mind*, pp. 16, 19. See also G. T. Robinson, *Rural Russia under the Old Regime* (New York, 1949).

7. *Russian Religious Mind*, pp. 33, 35, 55 ff. Aside from the "black" clergy which practiced celibacy, orthodox theology does not feature original sin and atonement. In Maynard's formulation, this prepared the way for the Communist "vision of the Kingdom of God *upon earth*," with communism stressing the service of Man. On the differences between Orthodoxy and Dostoyevsky's religious concepts, see N. Gorodetzky, *The Humiliated Christ in Modern Russian Thought* (London, 1938).

8. Translations are by Constance Garnett, the Modern Library Giant edition of *The Brothers Karamazov*.

As the official church became subservient to Tsarism, religion "became increasingly divorced from the organized panoply of the Orthodox Church." (Cf. B. H. Sumner, *Short History of Russia*, p. 164.) Yet, we should note democratic features: a collective synod, instead of a Pope, and the teaching that the Son is not separated from the Father and the Holy Ghost. Furthermore, the Bible was brought closer to the masses in that the liturgy came from Slavic Bulgaria and the common people were able to pray in an idiom near to their own. It should also be noted that the saints of old Russia were laymen. Fedotov stresses the social mindedness and the pagan-Christian symbiosis in their faith, in contrast to Byzantine self-mortification. See his Introduction to *A Treasury of Russian Spirituality* (London, 1950).

9. *The Russian Idea*, pp. 250 ff.

10. In early Russian history, woman was an economic-social partner of the man and the *Bylini* picture her as bold, strong and dauntless. While she often chooses and captures the groom, she is also a symbol of love and peace. With the development of the patriarchate and under the influence of Byzantine Christianity, the values of virginity, asceticism and passivity come to the fore. In the nineteenth century, the revolt against woman being treated as a chattel

expressed itself in George Sandism where the woman cried out for freedom, giving up the responsibility of educating her children.

11. Here is the context for Dostoyevsky's sympathy with the criminal. Father Zossima in *The Brothers Karamazov* is especially devoted to the greatest sinners.

12. To be sure, some, such as Khomiakov, thought that a form of monarchy was necessary to fulfill the Russian mission. They apotheosized the national past including the pre-Petrine social system. Here, they were at one with nineteenth century German Romanticism. However, they were opposed to both Catholicism which Khomiakov called "an unnatural tyranny" and to Protestantism which he called "an unprincipled revolt."

13. Turgenev's recollection of Belinsky is apropos: In the course of a heated debate, someone suggested that they eat. To this, Belinsky exclaimed: "We have not yet decided the question of the existence of God and you want to eat!"

14. This opposition was also manifested in the populist, terrorist and Marxist movements of the time. See Hans Kohn, *The Mind of Modern Russia* (New Brunswick, N. J., 1955), A. Yarmolinsky, *Road to Revolution* (London, 1957).

15. See Dostoyevsky's attack on the West in *Winter Notes of Summer Impressions* (New York, 1955). Dostoyevsky was particularly outraged by child labor in the West, and thought that its freedom was only for those who had the means and power to satisfy it. Western Europe, he wrote, lives on "the personal principle, the principle of separateness, intense self-preservation, selfish labor, self-determination of one's ego." Quoted in A. Yarmolinsky's *Dostoyevsky. A Study of his Ideology* (New York, 1921), p. 28. See also Ernest J. Simmons, *Dostoyevsky* (New York, 1940), pp. 289, 331-332. Even Turgenev who lived much of his life in the West was critical of Westernism. In his biography of Turgenev, Yarmolinsky refers to one of his tirades: "The Latins were *hommes de la loi*, in whose veins ran the milk of the Roman she-wolf, sticklers for the conventions, conformers to a code, martyrs to an artificial sense of honor. The Russians, on the contrary, were *hommes de l'humanite*, possessed of a warmer social consciousness, irreverent toward man-made rules, rooting for fundamentals, unafraid of the crude, the bare, the simple."

16. In his speech, Dostoyevsky idealized Pushkin as the incarnation of the common Russian folk. Indeed, Pushkin is regarded by many as the most typical Russian figure of the rootless "wanderer" who is to be redeemed by the Russian woman. On the Pushkin cult, see Marc Slonim, *The Epic of Russian Literature* (New York, 1950).

17. Dostoyevsky, *Letters from the Underworld*, trans., C. J. Hogarth (London and New York, 1913), pp. 27, 34.

18. Marc Slonim (*Three Loves of Dostoyevsky* [New York, Toronto, 1955]), suggests that his pedophelia may go back to the relationship with his younger sisters who were the only females he knew up to the age of sixteen. The two women Dostoyevsky loved most passionately, Polina and Anna, were some twenty years younger than he.

19. Dostoyevsky's sexual difficulties with Anna are dramatically indicated when on the bridal night, he suffered an epileptic attack. We should also note his strange attitude towards her former lover Vergunov. Following his marriage to

Anna, Vergunov became "dearer than a brother" to him and, despite his own financial straits, Dostoyevsky borrowed money to help him. There may be a connection here with his feeling towards his own brother Michael. While waiting to be executed, Dostoyevsky wrote him: "I thought of you, brother, and of yours; and at the last moment you alone were in my thoughts, and then I realized how much I loved you, beloved brother!" And from Siberia: "I dream of you every night." He asked Baron Wrangel to write what his brother thinks of him, adding: "He used to love me passionately. . . . Has his feeling towards me grown cold?"

For a portrait of Dostoyevsky as revealed in his letters, see Jessie Coulson, *Dostoyevsky. A Self-Portrait* (London, 1962).

20. In a letter (to S. D. Janofsky in 1872), Dostoyevsky wrote that he was *"sick in mind* (I realize it now) *before my journey to Siberia,* where I was cured." Freud argues that if this refers to his seizures, then that "would merely substantiate the view that his sezures were his punishment. He did not need them any longer when he was being punished in another way." Dostoyevsky writes from Siberia that he "had some epileptic fits." Cited in André Gide, *Dostoyevsky* (Norfolk, Connecticut, 1923), pp. 35, 62.

21. Quoted by Sir John Maynard, *Russia in Flux*, p. 96.

22. Mitya calls him Silenus and he is also referred to as Aesop. In his essay "Dreams and Myth" (*Clinical Papers*, Vol. II [New York, 1955]), Karl Abraham quotes from old Indian myths where the drink of the gods is considered equivalent to semen and to Creation (the birth of Dionysus, the God of wine, shows the same identification between drink and creation). He notes that wine is often used as a symbol of procreation or fertilization.

23. In the case of Lizaveta, Fyodor exhibits something akin to "grace": Had he not acted out his buffoonery, Lizaveta might never have gotten to know motherhood.

24. They may also be seen as approximating the four elements: the sub-soil in Smerdyakov, fire in Mitya, air-water in Ivan-Alyosha.

25. Ivan loosens Alyosha's faith in the divine order of things, and provides the logic for Smerdyakov's murder of the father.

26. According to the Inquisitor, the Western Church has reversed the Christ who rejected the devil's three temptations.

27. Cf. Simmons, *Dostoyevsky*, pp. 376, 377.

28. Dostoyevsky's position towards political radicalism is ambiguous, especially after his Siberian imprisonment. But, there is no ambiguity about Dostoyevsky's affirmation of rebellion as a *psychological* attitude. Simmons' comment is here relevant: "The more he strives to make Verkhovenski (*The Possessed*) the symbol of a hated doctrine, the more the character divests itself of the stuff of reality." He is "merely a caricature of a revolutionist."

29. Mark Kanzer: "The Vision of Father Zossima" (*American Imago*, VIII, No. 4 [1951]). Dr. Kanzer notes first that Fyodor and Zossima meet their ends on successive nights. He also points out that Alyosha's released impulses in the scene with Grushenka are predominantly oral—craving for food and drink. He next beholds Christ converting water into wine, "as though to say that food

may be obtained from the body of the father as well as the mother." And, as Alyosha clutches and kisses the earth, we find symbols of "bisexual gratification." The disgust aroused in Alyosha by the odor of the monk's corpse "is familiar to analysts as a defense against the desire of oral incorporation." Furthermore, "we find little difficulty in recognizing, in Alyosha's swoon, his falling to the ground, his writhing and his ecstasy, phenomena of epilepsy; his ambivalent religiosity, suppressed criminal impulses and hallucinatory experiences represent familiar psychic concomitants."

30. In his relation to Ivan, Smerdyakov is the submissive "female" partner, waiting for a "sign" from "the God Almighty." Smerdyakov is fond of cooking and fastidious in his dress. When Fyodor suggests getting him a wife, Smerdyakov becomes pale with anger. His epileptic discharge seems to be his sole sexual expression. After Fyodor learns of Smerdyakov's epilepsy, he begins to show some kindness towards him. Does Fyodor sense in Smerdyakov's fits a kinship to his own distorted sexuality?

31. Ivan's persistent questioning of the devil and of Smerdyakov (in his three interviews with each) is an ironic uncovering of his own function in the murder of his father, analogous to Oedipus' persistant questioning of the Herdsmen and of Tiresias. There is an analogy between Ivan's attitude towards Smerdyakov and the Grand Inquisitor's towards the people: Both have erected a rationalistic scheme to circumscribe the thoughts of others. The difference is that, for Dostoyevsky, Western Caesarism is a foreign drop of blood in the Russian Ivan. Where the cardinal wants the masses to remain subservient, Ivan unconsciously wants Smerdyakov to rebel.

32. Mitya, in particular can be likened to Oedipus and Hamlet. He too is more intent on uncovering the truth than is anyone else. In doing so, he likewise arouses suspicion against himself and contributes most to his condemnation. Father Zossima's kneeling before Mitya (seen by a member of his order as the elder's sensing that Mitya is contemplating the murder of his father) is a kind of warning, such as the oracle gives Sophocles' Oedipus. Mitya's celebration with Grushenka at Mokroe (it is their "wedding") takes place after his near-attempt to kill his father and after he thought he had killed his surrogate-father Grigory.

33. Dostoyevsky offers but scanty material for Katya's motivation. He does suggest some identification between Katya's father and Mitya. Both were lieutenants, are in disgrace and "gamble" away their honor and that of the family. Katya conceives her role to be that of saving both, first her father and later Mitya. Is her offering herself to Mitya a form of revenge, an acting out of a masochistic sexual fantasy?

34. A related "strategy" occurs in Thomas Mann's *Doctor Faustus* where Leverkühn sends a friend to woo Marie, whereupon the friend and Marie fall in love with each other.

35. Katya would also impose her will on Grushenka. She invites the rival to her house and would have her be "an angel" who will give up Mitya because that

is best for him. Alyosha feels that Katya has fastened on Mitya because "a character like Katerina Ivanovna's must dominate, and she could dominate some one like Dmitry, and never a man like Ivan."

36. In this sense, there is something to the point made in Komarowitsch's *Die Urgestalt der Brüder Karamasoff* (München, 1928) that Katya's love demands the same unlimited subservience as the Grand Inquisitor's. Komarowitsch refers to Dostoyevsky's comment in his Notebooks: "Katya: Rome, unique objet de mon ressentiment." The line is taken from Corneille's *Horace* and is spoken by a heroine who curses her native land. Incidentally, Grusha calls Katya "mother" (in a derogatory sense). Garnett regrettably translates the Russian word *matj* as "my girl."

37. The number three is a leading "motif" in *The Brothers Karamazov* as it is in other mythopoesis. In Dostoyevsky's novel, it also has a diabolic sign (the violence of the three brothers, the abandonment of Mitya when he was three years old, the 3000 rubles, the three blows with which Smerdyakov kills Fyodor, Ivan's three interviews with Smerdyakov and the devil's three visits with Ivan) and its resurrectory sign (Mitya's three ordeals, his arrest on the third day of his struggle to save himself).

38. As Fyodor would buy Grusha with 3000 rubles, so Mitya offers the Pole 3000 rubles if he would release her. Grusha herself is at first attracted to or binds herself to father-figures: Samsonov, the Pole and Fyodor, whom she does not discourage at first.

39. Mitya himself is not aware of his complex involvement with Katya. She is, indeed, the great "secret" of his life and of the novel. She comes to Mitya secretly, asks him to send off the 3000 rubles secretly; Mitya would keep the fact secret that he spent half of her money on Grushenka. Above all, the nature of his "debt" to Katya is Mitya's "great secret" and "disgrace."

40. Earlier Mitya declared that what he wants is "to have done with her and with father!" It seems to Mitya that he could be freed from Fyodor if his father returned the heritage his mother left him. Would Mitya be getting his "mother" back from father in this way and thus be liberated from the temptation to kill him? And would he be released from the "debt" to the surrogate mother by giving her his own mother's money?

41. For a note on Freud's Analysis of a Katya Figure in Zweig's Story, see Appendix VI.

42. The point of Dostoyevsky's long account of the trial seems to be this: Both lawyers argue "pro and contra," like Ivan, both missing Mitya's "angel." Their primary interest is not Mitya, or "the babe," but to get votes from the public.

43. In his notes on *Crime and Punishment* ("Idea of the Novel"), Dostoyevsky wrote: ". . . life's calling and consciousness (i.e., the immediately-felt in body and spirit, i.e., in the whole vital process) is acquired by experience *pro* and *contra* which must be felt in the process of living." (Quoted by Simmons, *Dostoyevsky*, p. 150.)

The Marxist Homage
to Creative Labor
Pelle the Conqueror

THE MOST PROMINENT argument in Marx's theory has an oppositional character. It would unmask metaphysical, religious and other absolutes as maneuvers by which ruling groups have veiled their ideologies. To reverse this strategy, Marx placed emphasis on change and historical process, on class-truths and class-values.

Marx did not face the problem of how his own system transcended such historical limits and escaped being another type of ideology. Yet, an examination of his work, especially his earlier writings, reveals that Marxism does contain certain universal categories, centering in the idea of man and of human labor. To be radical, Marx declared, means to go to the roots of things, and the root of things, he added, is man. This thought has implications for the place of history in man's development.

Marx regarded history as "a nightmare on the brain of the living." Yet, commenting on the seizure of power by Louis Bonaparte, Marx wrote that every revolution was accompanied by the "conjuring up of the dead." He realized that man does not make history by himself, but "in circumstances directly found, given and transmitted from the past." Here, Marx referred to those elements in history which persist as lasting values. This idea is specifically applied to art and culture.

Contrary to some interpretations, Marx and Engels did not identify culture with its passing social basis. Engels acknowledged in *Anti Dühring* that seminal thoughts arose in class societies. He stated that the broad outlines of the dialectic method were discovered by the early Greek physicists, were analyzed by Aristotle, and that Descartes, Spinoza, Diderot, Rousseau and Hegel were its brilliant exponents. Marx had high praise for Shakespeare, Goethe, Hegel, Balzac, and particu-

284

larly for Greek art and mythology. In his *The Critique of Political Economy* Marx notes that Greek art and mythology could not exist under modern technological conditions. Jupiter, he notes, could do nothing against the lightning rod and Hermes against the Crédit mobilier. But, Marx continues:

> the difficulty does not consist in understanding that Greek art and the epic are bound up with the well known forms of social development. The difficulty consists in understanding that they still continue to give us artistic pleasure, and in a certain sense preserve the value of a standard and an unattainable example.

Greece, he writes, is the most beautiful example of the childhood of human society, and possesses "an eternal charm." He likens them to children "who have the wisdom of old age," adding: "Many of the ancient peoples belong to this category. The Greeks were normal children."[1]

In the Marxist system proper, the mythic category is labor which it regards as "an eternal necessity imposed by nature itself," one that is independent of all forms of society.

In his discussion of Russian folklore, Sokolov traces the Marxist position on the interrelationship of work, rhythm and speech to Karl Bücher's *Arbeit und Rhythmus* (Leipzig, 1924). According to Bücher, the decisive factor in the rise and development of art was the rhythm of work which evoked the rhythm of bodily movement, melody and speech: "The sounds of speech . . . were, originally, an imitation of sounds, and reproduced the sounds of work and of rhythmicized emotional exclamations." In time, culture and language lost their direct connection with the laboring process; yet the origins of poetic creation still are evident "in so far as rhythm and melody play an important part in it; and in oral reproduction, where gesture and movement are also factors."[2]

Marxian anthropology centers in Engels' notion that labor is

> the primary basic condition for all human existence, and this to such an extent that, in a sense, we have to say that labour created man himself.

Similarly, according to Marx,

> labour is a necesary condition for the existence of the human race, and one that is independent of all forms of society; it is an eternal necessity imposed by nature itself, without which there can be no material exchanges between man and nature, and therefore no life.

The point is also made by Gorky:

> For the main hero of our books we must take labour, that is, the human be-
> ing organized by the labour process . . . the human being who in turn orga-
> nizes labour to be easier and more productive, elevating it to the degree of
> art. We must learn to think of labour as creative effort.[3]

Labor is Marx's universal constant and its process is the lever for the
changes and developments in man's biological nature. And, since labor
entails cooperation, it converts the animal herd into human society. By
virtue of the laborer's close and sensuous handling of materials, he has
the most direct relation to the material aspect of reality. Beyond this,
he molds and forms the raw material, that is, gives it an individual form.
Herein, the laborer is something of a creative artist who develops his
own "slumbering powers:"

> By thus acting on the external world and changing it, he at the same time
> changes his own nature. He develops his slumbering powers and compels
> them to act in obedience to his sway. . . . We presuppose labour in a form
> that stamps it as exclusively human. . . . What distinguishes the worst archi-
> tect from the best of bees is this, that the architect raises his structure in
> imagination before he erects it in reality.[4]

Viewed in terms of the structure of the myth, the first act in the
Marxist drama is the stage of primitive communism. But, it is primarily
concerned with Act Two in which private ownership and exploitation
have produced alienation in which man is estranged from his tool, his
work, his fellowmen, and finally from himself as a whole human being.
Class divisions and divisions of labor make the worker

> a cripple, a monster, by forcing him to develop some highly specialized dex-
> terity at the cost of a world of productive impulses and faculties . . . the in-
> dividual himself is split up, is transformed into the automatic motor of some
> partial operation. Thus is realized the foolish fable of Menenius Agrippa,
> which depicted a human being as nothing more than a fragment of his own
> body.

Even where the worker does not suffer economic servitude, he is still a
slave. For, in being used as a tool, he is determined by his external nature. The implication of Marx's argument in "The Fetishism of Commodities" in *Capital* is that the mystique of exchange value, particularly
money, converts qualities into quantities and man into a profit-pro-
ducing commodity. A man's value now consists not in what he is, but
in what he has, not in what he gives, but in what he acquires.

Although man is conditioned by his history, he can still become its
master and make it his own. Marx and Engels rejected the notion that
man is at the mercy of natural, divine or historical powers:

History does nothing. . . . It is rather man—real living man—who acts, possesses and fights in everything. It is by no means "History" which uses man as a means to carry out its ends as if it were a person apart; rather History is nothing but the activity of man in pursuit of his ends.[5]

The means for this transformation lie in social consciousness. The Spinozistic axiom "Man thinks" is transposed by way of the Hegelian logic into the social realm and becomes a philosophy of conscious activity leading to liberation from "external purposiveness." Control over economic and social determinants spells human freedom. The ultimate aim is not only economic, social and political emancipation. Freedom, for Marx, lies "beyond the sphere of purely material production," and begins with "that development of human power which is its own end."[6]

The working class is the lever for human freedom because it becomes conscious of the fact that class divisions dehumanize not only the oppressed but also the oppressor: "The owning class and the proletariat represent the same human self-alienation. . . . The former possesses through it the *illusion* of human existence." In *True Humanism*, Jacques Maritain pays tribute to Marx's moral indictment of capitalism. Marx, he says,

> had a profound intuition, an intuition which is to my eyes the great lightning flash of truth which traverses all his work, of the conditions of heteronomy and loss of freedom produced in the capitalist world by wage-slavery, and of the dehumanization with which the possessing classes and the proletariat alike are simultaneously stricken. (pp. 38, 39)

The working class aims not only for the abolition of the capitalist order, but of itself as a dictatorship, realizing that it can be redeemed only "through the redemption of the whole of humanity." Philosophy, Marx wrote, "cannot realize itself without abolishing the proletariat; the proletariat cannot abolish itself without realizing philosophy." In these formulations, Marx attempted to fuse class and classless values, the particular and the universal, existence and essence.

Is the classless society Marxism's third and final act? Does the revolutionary dialectic cease to function under communism? Will modern specialization which, as Marx charged, transformed the worker into an "automatic motor" no longer present the same threat? Will tragedy be eliminated when economic-social conflicts no longer exist?

Marx and Engels did not seem to rule out the need for stages beyond socialism. In *Ludwig Feuerbach* (New York, 1934), Engels stated that each historic stage must be succeeded by a higher form which, in turn, will also decay. And Maxim Gorky even paid tribute to the perennial revolutionary temper, saying that the task is to go beyond the existing to "the desirable, the potential," adding that thus:

> We arrive at that romanticism which is the basis of all myths and which is of great value because it favors the birth of a revolutionary attitude towards reality, i.e. of an attitude that wants to change the world. (*Literature and Life* [London, 1946], p. 138.)

There remains the wide realm of natural necessity, of decay and death, disappointments and frustrations which cannot be eliminated by "practically changing the world." Indeed, when man can no longer attribute human suffering to avoidable social maladjustments, then tragedy emerges pure and absolute.

PELLE AS MYTHIC HERO

The idea of the hero implies an exceptional status differentiating him from the mass. Yet, all our culture heroes are "democratic" in that their quest is in the interests of the others. All mythopoeic heroes from Prometheus, Oedipus and Aeneas to Hamlet, Faust and Mitya Karamazov rebel against a diseased state and would revitalize their society. Yet, with the exceptions of Don Quixote, Ahab and Huck Finn, they come from the upper social strata.

Martin Andersen Nexö's *Pelle the Conqueror* (New York, 1913) is the first major epic in which the hero arises from the ranks of labor. At the same time, the work pictures him as representing the universally human. Pelle is drawn neither as a pitiful victim nor as an invincible superman, neither as a class-angled automaton nor as a free existentialist, but as the bearer of human values which are worthy of being redeemed.

The novel interweaves Pelle's development with the history of labor—his childhood and adolescence with feudalism and the guild system, his early manhood with capitalism, his marriage and family life with the establishment of a socialist cooperative. Beneath the personal and the historic run mythic motifs: Pelle is the dangerous child who rebels against his rotten state and engages in a journey to find the answer to the problem of the social disease.[7] In his quest, Pelle becomes a sacrifice, with the promise that his idea will be carried forward by others. But in this myth of labor, evil authority is balanced by good authority, embodied in father Lasse and Marie. And Pelle's disciples, Dreyer and Morton, are not mere followers, but re-creators of his social idea.

Pelle's Boyhood is his Eden-state. He is at one with the world of nature and of man, drawing nourishment and strength from the earth and the sea which offer comfort and stability. To be sure, this Eden is set in nineteenth century Denmark, still governed by the vestiges of feudalism. Yet, the book is a joyous affirmation of life, of nature and man:

> It was so good to be here. . . . Every sound was like a mother's caress, and everything was a familiar toy, with which a bright world could be built. . . . Pelle's childhood had been happy by virtue of everything: it had been a song mingled with weeping. Weeping falls into tones as well as joy, and heard from a distance it becomes a song. And as Pelle gazed down upon his childhood's world, they were only pleasant memories that gleamed toward him through the bright air. . . . He had seen enough of hardship and misfortune, but had come well out of everything: nothing had harmed him. With a child's voracity he had found nourishment in it all; and now he stood here, healthy and strong—equipped with the Prophets, the Judges, the Apostles, the Ten Commandments and one hundred and twenty hymns! and turned an open, perspiring victor's brow toward the world.

The memory of this world remains the leading reference of the epic which is dominated by the seasonal metaphor. At the end, Pelle returns to the land, bringing with him knowledge of the social barriers which disturb this world and of the tragic surd in the human situation itself.[8]

NOTES

1. Quoted by Y. M. Sokolov in his *Russian Folklore*, pp. 30-31.
2. H. Werner, *Die Ursprünge der Lyrik* (München, 1924), cited in Sokolov, *Russian Folklore*.
3. See Engels, "Dialectics and Nature" in *Marx-Engels Archiv*, II (New York, 1940); Marx, *Capital*, Vol. I; (New York, 1929); Maxim Gorky, "New People" in *Soviet Literature*, VI (1949), 119.
4. *Capital*, section on "The Labour Process or the Production of Use-Values and the Capitalistic Character of Manufacture."
5. Engels, "Dialectics and Nature," p. 165.
6. This concept brings Marxism near to the classical tradition of Plato, Aristotle, Spinoza and Hegel. What differentiates Marxism from these thinkers is its stress on the social means for bringing this goal about. See Vernon Venable's *Human Nature: The Marxian View* (New York, 1945).
7. There are suggestions of parricide in Pelle's neglect of father Lasse and the little mother Marie.
8. For a detailed discussion of the novel, see the chapter, "Pelle the Conqueror" in my *Three Ways of Modern Man* (New York, 1937. Reprinted by Kraus Reprint Corporation, New York, 1969).

The French Myth of the
Living Social Chain
André Gide's *Theseus*

FRENCH LITERATURE has not produced a mythopoeic hero comparable
to the Greek Prometheus, the Roman Aeneas and the Italian Dante,
the Spanish Don Quixote, the German Faust or the American Ahab. Its
classical stature consists less in outstanding single works by individual
authors than in collective products of schools and academies. The myth
of the hero is not treated with the solemnity which the Teutonic tradition accords Faust and Siegfried, but—where the theme of the exceptional personality is projected, as in Gargantua—is approached in a comic mood. Aided by a fortunate historical development which allowed
for early consolidation of the nation and its language, French literature
has been molded by the values of tradition and continuity. The hero is
not so much a prophet and savior as part of a communal chain. In short,
the myth of the hero becomes *the myth of the living social chain.* However, this attachment to tradition has not resulted in idolatry of the existing society. As Romain Rolland indicated in *Jean Christophe*, it has
been constantly quickened by sensitiveness to innovation and revolution. Society does not become identical with the state or nation. *L'État*
never attains eulogistic overtones. Society, as a mythic category, is both
French and universal.

The work of Racine is the nearest French approximation of classic
mythopoesis. However, Racine labored under an extraordinary historic
burden. French seventeenth century society was true neither to French
nor to human tradition. It was not in continuity with the rich medieval
residue of French literature, but broke sharply with it. And its Palace
society encouraged only a formal and narrow identification. The Phèdre
of the court-dramatist is held down by an imprisoning *raison* and

gloire of an hierarchial order, and her *amour* can express itself only in underground revolt.[1] In Corneille and Racine, the Salon takes on the mythic form of a devouring parent. Both dramatists (Corneille quite indirectly) picture the false myth of the court suppressing the human myth of *coeur*. In accepting their fathers' values, Corneille's sons and daughters gain *honneur*, but surrender their individual will and human desires. Racine's characters react in near-primitive Bacchic revolt against the polished sterility of their society.

This critique became a major note in French literature from Molière to Voltaire, from Balzac to Zola, from Barbusse and Aragon to Sartre and the existentialists. It reaches its most organized and sustained form in André Gide.

The Secessionist Myth

The myth, as we have noted, rests on and finally reaches out towards a harmonious state. The secession of the hero is but a transitional moment in its total dialectic. From this angle, Gide appears to be at the other pole of the mythic perspective. His work has always seemed to be at war with all that which strains towards collective integration and the visionary projection of syntheses. However, his latest story on the myth of Theseus should correct this estimate of Gide. That a man of his dissident temper should come to affirm the myth is a striking testimony to its persistence. It is a further instance of the recurring phenomenon that mature and responsible artists experience an irresistible pull towards mythopoesis.

Gide's concern with the myth is not new.[2] But in his earlier work where he dealt with the myths of Narcissus, Philoctetus, Prometheus, and later with Oedipus and Persephone, the focus is largely on its narcissistic elements.[3] The hero is "the bastard," glad that he resembles no one but himself, and his heroism consists in carrying out the unmotivated "gratuitous" act. In this phase, Gide questions not only organized society, but the organized self as well.

This emphasis lent Gide's work the character of a secessionist Protestantism. The very titles of his works—"Counterfeiters," "Immoralist" —sounded this note. His central characters are the unattached and the illegitimate who defy convention either by indulgence (*The Immoralist*) or by asceticism (*Strait is the Gate*). Gide himself stated that the raison d'être of the artist is "to be at odds with the world," and that his own function is "to disturb." In *Le Prométhée*, man is defined as "the animal capable of the gratuitous act." Critique tends to become identical with morality. Individual non-conformity, such as practised by Nathanaël, takes on divine character ("Nathanaël" means "gift of God"). In *Les Nourritures terrestres*, he is told to adopt the motto: "Ne demeure jamais," for "nothing is more dangerous to you than your family, your room, and your own past." He is urged: "Throw away my book," for (as we hear in another work, *Un Esprit non prévenu*) "nothing is more inhibiting than disciples." Here, Gide approaches Nietzsche, the Nietzsche whose Zarathustra asks his followers to leave him. "It is all alone," Alissa tells Jerome in *Strait is the Gate*, "that each of us must go to God."

In this oppositional mood, Gide's characters may be said to have made a pact with the devil, a pact which does not allow final grace. Indeed, *L'Immoraliste* identifies art with *nouveauté* and with *vice*. The *Journal* (1916) transforms Descartes' *cogito ergo sum* into *cogito ergo Satanas*. The Evil One has been invited and is believed in as a positive, enterprising principle.

Gide carried this temper into his style. His writing took the form of a soliloquy (*L'Immoraliste* was conceived as a monologue) or as an internal debate (the *Journal*). *The Counterfeiters*, Gide's "only novel," would violate its traditional "fictional" form. It would include "everything," infringing on the esthetic requirement of selection; it would destroy the idea of illusion by introducing the author as one of the characters. In his zeal for "truth", Gide went so far as to aim at non-metaphoric writing (*Les Nourritures terrestres*).

Gide's life itself exhibits this apartness. His opposition to conformity (which Gide sometimes identified with "the bourgeois," not as a class, but as a level of thought) is carried forward in his later criticism of the Soviet Union. It is continued during the Second World War. When the Allies entered Tunis, Gide was asked to speak about the liberation of the city from the Fascists. But Gide refused. "I fail to see," he notes in *Imaginary Interviews*, "what 'declaration' I could make which, if it remained sincere, would not be of a nature to offend all parties."

Such individual intransigence brought Gide close to Nietzschean transvaluations, if not to existentialist freedom, and furthest removed from the mythic attitude which begins and ends with a "yes".

The Negation of Negativism

What militated against Gide's criticism becoming mere protest was his deep sense of moral and social responsibility. One of his favorite books was the Bible (particularly the New Testament),[4] and one of his recurrent themes has been social injustice (particularly in *Travels in the Congo*). Gide's rebelliousness has been in the Latin-Mediterranean tradition—realistic and social opposition. Gide realized that one cannot live in Cartesian doubt, that a society cannot function solely on the basis of individual morality. Sisyphus, the existentialist hero, is not an example of fortitude to Gide, but an instance of a sorry effort. *Se depasser* becomes one of his favorite terms.

Gide's critical dialectic is applied to criticism itself. The hero of *L'Immoraliste* realizes at the end that freedom must have an object. Bernard's rebelliousness in *The Counterfeiters* incites him "to rebel against his very rebellion." Above all, the novel distinguishes between genuine and "counterfeit" secessionism. Real freedom does not lie in the unscrupulous licentiousness of Passevent or Lady Griffith, not in the nihilism of Strouvilhou which leads to Vincent's madness, to the masturbatory dissipation and suicide of Boris. Such "freedom" is transcended in Olivier and Bernard. Boris' suicide is the traumatic event which shocks Olivier into rejecting Passeventism. Bernard rebels only against a counterfeit society, and in the end, he *returns* to his home. In his awareness that negation was but an interim phase which must be passed through and beyond towards affirmation, Gide must be distinguished from his nihilistic following.

THE LIVING CHAIN: THE MYTH OF THESEUS

In *Imaginary Interviews* (New York, 1944), Gide makes an important concession to tradition. He calls it "a living chain" and the basis for culture. For culture, he notes, "implied a continuity, and therefore it called for disciples, imitators, and followers to make a living chain: in other words, a tradition." This pull towards unity and affirmation makes itself felt throughout Gide's work. The *Journal* expresses sadness over the prevalent tragic need to hate. To be sure, critique is essential if we are not to be enchained by fossilized tradition, by the dead past and the dead myth. Yet, the self cannot operate responsibly without a communal reference and art cannot create an enduring hero, that is a myth, without it. Already Gide's *Oedipus* (1931) thinks not of defiance and thrills, but is set on the adventure of liberating men from the dead past. And the work ends on a humanistic note. But it is in *Theseus* that we find this note fully developed and sustained. "What happens, in the case of the hero," we read here,

is this: his mark endures. Poetry and the arts reanimate it and it becomes an enduring symbol. That is how it is that Orion the hunter is riding still,

293

across Elysian fields of asphodel. That is how Tantalus' throat is parched to all eternity, and how Sisyphus still rolls upward towards an unattainable summit the heavy and ever-rebounding weight of care which tormented him in the days when he was King of Corinth.[5]

Theseus makes it possible for us to view Gide's work as a whole. The theme had occupied the author for some three decades. It is not so much a reversal of Gide's earlier persuasions as their incorporation within a broader compass. It joins Gide's former anti-bourgeois esthetics with a communal ethic, the earlier fear of organization with the affirmation of the need for the Ariadne-thread linking beginnings and ends.

The style and mood of this story indicate the shift. Where Gide's work had been largely stern and unsmiling, *Theseus* is carried along by ease and relaxedness. It has a rhythm of play and a mood of high comedy. The multiple perspectivism of *The Counterfeiters* has given way to a focal mythic center. The new character begins as a Narcissus and an Absalom, but ends as an Oedipus, Aeneas and Faust, becoming the founding father of a people's city.

The mythic theme of identification and re-creation is stated in the opening sentence. Theseus says that he wanted to tell the story of his life "as a lesson for my son Hippolytus." Now Hippolytus is no more, but Theseus will tell it "all the same," as a lesson for us, his symbolic sons. The opening also speaks of a *good* heritage. Theseus' father Aegeus was "one of the best." Here, Gide affirms the living residue of mythic Creation which serves as a nodal reference in the labors of *re-creation*. From his father (Aegeus or Poseidon), Theseus also got his inconstancy and unsettledness of temper, that is, the urgency of the Quest. Finally, he learned from him to go beyond this state, "to rebel against myself." To this, "I owe all that I have achieved."

The body of the story deals with the second act of the mythic process: the Quest through apostasy, adventure and conquest.

Theseus begins his story with a playful reference to his half-conscious act of patricide. Theseus "forgot" to run up the white sails, the sign that was to announce to his father that he was returning alive and in triumph. This caused the father's death. It was not really forgetfulness for, as Theseus admits, "Aegeus was in my way," particularly since he formed "the exasperating idea that a second meridian of (marital) enjoyment was his for the asking—thus blocking my career. . . ." This act is necessary in the hero's battle with "the gods," if he is "to purge the earth once and for all of a host of tyrants, bandits and monsters." This impious attitude becomes an interim way of life for the young hero. He despises comfort, idleness, ease, crying out, "What have I to do with safety." He would break free, drawn to what lies ahead, never allowing the past to involve or detain him. Carrying out the pact with the devil, he will not love or marry, but enjoy an adventurous life.

His supreme adventure is with the Minotaur who was annually devouring seven young men and seven young girls from Attica. The Minotaur is the "herald," the summoner to the test. He initiates the ritual of the Journey, a journey by water and through the labyrinth, the passage through which the hero is to gain the maturity of manhood. At the end of the journey Theseus, the "savage," is socialized, marries and founds a city.

To vanquish the monster, Theseus needs the help of others. Assistance comes from Ariadne, Minos' older daughter, who provides him with the thread which leads him out of the labyrinthine maze in which the monster lives. This thread becomes the symbol of the binding chain between beginnings and endings, Creation and Re-creation. This thread, Theseus is told, "will be your link with the past. Go back to it. Go back to yourself. For nothing can begin from nothing, and it is from your past, and from what you are at this moment that what you are going to be must spring." The real difficulty in conquering the monster, he hears, is "to preserve unbroken, to the last inch of thread, the will to come back."

Ariadne and her thread are one of his guides. The other is Dedalus, his father-mentor, who explains to Theseus the nature of the labyrinth he built to house the Minotaur. This labyrinth points to a dual danger: the danger of sloth and the danger of pointless activity: "I thought that the best way of containing a prisoner in the labyrinth", Dedalus tells Theseus,

> was to make it of such a kind, not that he couldn't get out (try to grasp my meaning here) but that he wouldn't want to get out. I therefore assembled in this one place the means to satisfy every kind of appetite . . . The prime necessity was to fine down the visitor's will power to the point of extinction.

Dedalus burned plants in the stoves which distributed heavy gases, inducing

> a delicious intoxication, rich in flattering delusions, and provoke the mind, filled as this is with voluptuous mirages, to a certain pointless activity: "pointless," I say, because it has merely an imaginary outcome, in visions and speculations without order, logic or substance. The effect of these gases is not the same for all of those who breathe them; each is led on by the complexities implicit in his own mind to lose himself, if I may put it, in a labyrinth of his own devising.

The most surprising thing about these perfumes is that

when one has inhaled them for a certain time, they are already indispensable.
. . . And that, above all, is what keeps one inside the labyrinth.

In this adventure, Theseus experiences the demonic threat in which the hero is "possessed" by a "numinous dread" (R. Otto's term in *The Idea of the Holy* [London, 1950]), menacing him at once from without and from within. They are the threats to Aeneas in Dido's Carthage, to Dante in the dark woods, to Faust in Helen's Arcadian idyll, to Siegfried on Brunhilde's mountain top, to Mann's Joseph in Egypt. The threat lies in the two-fold temptation to deny Creation and the Quest, to invite the slavery of stagnation and the slavery of "pointless activity."

In Dedalus' admonition that Theseus may not linger in the labyrinth nor in the embrace of Ariadne, we recognize the characteristic stress of the Gide we have known. This stress is not discarded but transformed.[6] Having slain the monster, Theseus is now ready to assume the responsibility of organization: "Where I had sought to conquer, I now sought to rule . . . there is a time for conquest, a time for cleansing the earth of its monsters, and then a time for husbandry and the harvesting of well-cherished land." Only now is he fit for "great things," things "beside which these exploits will seem, in the future, to have been the amusements of a child." He is ready to marry and to found the city of Athens.

"This was not easy." Theseus finds an inherited mass of petty townships continuously quarreling for dominance. His father thought he could assure his own authority by perpetuating these quarrels. And, although he was "one of the best" fathers, Theseus finds another way. He traces the source of most evils to "the general inequality of wealth and the desire to increase one's own fortune." He sets about to do away with these social divisions by abolishing the unreal supremacy of wealth, but maintaining the supremacy derived from personal merit, "an aristocracy not of wealth, but of intellect." Thanks to Theseus, the Athenians thus came to deserve "the fine name of 'people'." And herein, he adds, "lies my fame."

The mythic epilogue is, of course, peculiarly suited to Gide's temperament. In *Theseus*, we meet it first in a comic view of the myth itself. Theseus calls some of the exploits which legend ascribes to him "imaginary," and admits that he even improved upon some of them, so as not to encourage irreverence. It appears especially in the final section where Oedipus is brought in as a contrasting mythic hero. Here, Gide's Oedipus accepts suffering as a means of redeeming man from his natively sinful taint. Where Oedipus failed in all which he undertook, Theseus succeeded. Yet, Theseus himself feels that, in comparison with Oedipus, his own triumph seems "merely human—inferior, I might say." However, Theseus' fate has not been an unmitigated triumph. He loses his wife Phedra and his son Hippolytus. He now admits that he feels lonely and that he is old.

Still, Theseus is content. He has played out his mythic role, fulfilled his destiny to build the city which is dearer to him "even than my wife and son." He is happy to think that "after me, and thanks to me, men will recognize themselves as being happier, better and more free." The story closes with this note: "I have worked always for the good of those who are to come. I have lived." The thought in the last lines is new. Yet, it has its precedent in the earlier Gide. The *Journal* speaks of a constant need for reconciliation, for marrying Heaven and Hell, à la Blake, for reconciling individualism and communism. Gide once expressed gratitude to Edmund Gosse for discerning under the new France the old France that has always been. His *Theseus* is at once a "remembrance" of his Huguenot-Catholic origins and beyond that a reaffirmation of his belief that man strives towards the good. In *Theseus*, the Gidean debate between dissidence and affirmation has moved from a split Protestant dialectic towards the fullness of mythic dramatism.

Still, the epilogue carries over into Gide's Theseus. His final years are in a sense more tragic than Oedipus' who is at least left with his two daughters. Theseus has lost his one son Hippolytus and, at the end, is all alone. Theseus states that Athens "has been dearer to me even than my wife and son." This may be the attitude of a God or demi-God. But Theseus is wholly human and his loneliness is the tragedy of *la condition humaine*.

NOTES

1. See M. Turnell, *The Classical Moment* (New York, 1949).
2. In 1919, Gide published *Considérations sur la mythologie grecque. Fragments du Traité des Dioscures*, in which he briefly discusses Greek mythic heroes (including Theseus) as exhibiting "un fatalité psychologique."
3. *Le Traité du Narcisse* (1891), *Philoctète* (1899), *Le Prométhée mal enchainé* (1899), *Oedipe* (1931), *Perséphone* (1934).
4. Characteristically, Gide interprets the Gospels in the manner of St. Paul, as emancipating men from false divinities. He finds the Gospel "more emancipated . . . more concerned about individual value" than Nietzsche did, and (with Dostoyevsky) sees them as standing in contrast to organized religion, especially Roman Catholicism.
5. Gide, *Two Legends: Oedipus, Theseus* (New York, 1950). All subsequent references are to this edition.
6. In this sense, Theseus' social act is prepared by his earlier role.

297

Contemporary Myth of the Impersonal Antagonist

Franz Kafka

THE WESTERN MYTH of Franz Kafka meets with the Eastern of Fyodor Dostoyevsky in the threat posed by modern coordination, conformity and the steamroller of the anonymous machine. Dostoyevsky's Underground Man does not want to become "the keyboard of a piano"; Kafka's characters do not want to be condemned by faceless committees. Dostoyevsky saw hope in countering Western technological collectivism by the sensuousness of Slavic impersonality, rooted in an agrarian people and its memory of the fertile, earthy Mother-Goddess. By the time of Kafka, man had come to be dominated by an impersonal, sexless Moloch, by the invisible and intangible dictatorship of trusts and documents. Yahweh, Moira and God had become anonymous secretaries.

The Hebrew Job, the Greek Prometheus and Oedipus, the Catholic Dante are never in doubt as to the authority behind their "arrest." The doubts begin with Hamlet and become "organized" in Kafka to the point where his figures have lost nearly all the passion with which earlier characters confront their accusers. That is, they too take on the quality of their antagonist, become shadowy epiphenomena.

Kafka's work centers in depicting the nature of the Quest for the illusive Lord and the illusive Devil. The High Court of *The Trial*, the Authorities of *The Castle* remain invisible and unreachable.

The theme of the impersonal enemy runs through much of modern literature. The individual is shown confronting communal ghosts, is diverted from basic quests by a busy-ness civilization which operates by intermediaries, delegates and by pushing buttons, driven and ridden by things.

The single-mindedness with which Kafka concentrated on presenting impersonality as the quality of our time has found a startling reception. His cult began during his own lifetime, before any of his major works had been published. In the forties, the Kafka-vogue took on something of a legendary character. W. H. Auden declared in 1941 that Kafka "bears the same kind of relation to our age that Dante, Shakespeare and Goethe bore to theirs." He has been hailed as one of our profoundest religious thinkers, on a level with Pascal, Kierkegaard and Karl Barth.

Kafka has also been called the most extraordinary *artist* of our day. Now, art is distinguished from religion in that its "insights" are not abstract propositions but are embodied in concrete, individual characters and situations. Given the specific nature of Kafka's task—to present deindividualized, de-personalized forces—he could "succeed" only by creating ill-defined, ghostly characters and scenes. From here follow the necessary limitations of Kafka's art. His work consists of spare modifications of a single theme: all of his characters are in search of Justice, Truth or Goodness, and all of them much in the same way. We read again and again that modern existence obstructs the human quest by a maze of hierarchies. This makes for a slender esthetic compass, severely limits its flexibility and manifoldness. In a sense, Kafka's theme is exhausted after the first chapters; thereafter, we get variations of the initial motif. There is no dramatic development of plot or character and little suspense. Edwin Muir, perhaps the staunchest admirer of Kafka's style, implicitly admits this limitation. He states that Kafka was concerned with religious *truth*. He was not concerned with religious *characters*, as were Dostoyevsky, Tolstoy, Undset or Claudel. In Zola, "evil" is embodied through Chaval, in Tolstoy through Anatol; in Shakespeare through Iago and Goneril; in Goethe through Mephisto. Herman Melville, also concerned with the elusiveness of the quest, finally *shows* us Moby Dick.

Absence of sensuousness also characterizes the non-dramatic character of Kafka's work. His novels are lacking in genuine dramatic conflict, and for this reason, there is no catharsis. The feeling of dread and anxiety is rarely lifted, and at the close the reader is still in the grip of the modern furies. It is not a question of an "unhappy ending." The great classical heritage is mainly that of tragedy; and the modern novel, from *Madame Bovary* and *The Possessed* to *Buddenbrooks* and *The American Tragedy*, also ends on a tragic note. But we are purged of pity and fear partly because the enemy appears in dramatic-sensuous form and can therefore be *met*. And defeat at its hands is rendered noble because it has been met. No such freedom issues from Kafka. His passionless dialectic does not resolve tension.

To be sure, these limitations of Kafka's art also contain its value. Its very restricted nucleus gives it compactness. While the First and Final Causes remain a secret in Kafka, he does suggest the regions which border on original and ultimate mysteries.

JOSEPH K'S MYTHIC CRIME

In *The Trial* (New York, 1937), Joseph K. is arrested and "tried" for a crime which is never stated by the authorities.[1] Yet, the novel suggests that Joseph K. is guilty. As in the case of Job, his crime is not in the nature of an overt act. It consists in his having been content with leading a routine life, according to the accepted conventions. In this sense, his arrest (as that of Job) constitutes his awakening to the fact that he had not lived. Although he states that he "cannot recall the slightest offence that might be charged against me," he admits that he is "by no means very surprised" at his arrest. It expels him from a false Eden towards a questioning of the values he had automatically accepted.

Now, it is characteristic of Kafka's dialectic that his figures seek their way through the labyrinth with the guidance of the very "court-" authorities which hem them in. This approach is reenforced by the priest's legend of the doorkeeper who stands on guard before the Law. The doorkeeper tells the man who begs for admittance that he cannot admit him "at the moment," but adds that if the man is strongly tempted, he might try "to get in without my permission." But the man continues to sit before the door "waiting for days and years" until he is nearly ready to die. At this point, the doorkeeper tells him: "No one but you could gain admittance through this door, since this door was intended only for you." The implication is that had the man not been a simpleton (suggested by the German *Mann vom Lande*), and had insisted on entering, he could have done so.

Franz Kafka had less ground for faith in his tradition than earlier mythmakers in theirs. Yet, he possessed enough faith to seek *Logos* within the Law, to discern the potential heroic qualities in his characters. Joseph in *The Trial* is not only a routinized bank official; he is also something of Joseph the Dreamer in his "insatiable" quest. His arrest catapults him towards something approximating rebirth:

> He felt as if he were seasick. He felt he was on a ship rolling in heavy seas. It was as if waters were dashing against the wooden walls, as if the roaring of breaking waves came from the end of the passage, as if the passage itself pitched and rolled and the waiting clients on either side rose and fell with it . . . Could his body possibly be meditating a revolution and preparing to spring something new on him, since he had borne with the old state of affairs so effortlessly?

In *The Castle*, Kafka moves towards the third act of his mythic drama, turns towards the people of the village, in the feeling that he was fighting "not only for himself, but clearly for other powers as well which he did not know." Such promise of salvation by alignment with selected "others" is faintly suggested in Joseph K's vision at the end of *The Trial*:

> His glance fell on the top storey of the house adjoining the quarry. With a flicker as of a light going up, the casements of a window there suddenly flew open; a human figure, faint and insubstantial at that distance and that height, leaned abruptly far forward and stretched both arms still farther. Who was it? A friend? A good man? Someone who sympathized? Someone who wanted to help? Was it one person only? Or were they all there?[2]

Kafka realized that the self needs to go beyond itself to find the full expression of its individuality. He did not penetrate far enough to distinguish between necessary and avoidable social-individual evil, to see the broader and deeper bearing of temporal pressures on *la condition humaine*. Nor did Kafka have enough of the hope which lies in converting submerged experience into consciousness—he was unable to communicate the identity of the enemy. Perhaps the enemy was too deeply submerged in him to become "known," and it was not possible for him to find the perspective and distance necessary for esthetic embodiment.[3]

NOTES

1. A comic-tragic form of this type of trial appears in Bert Andrews' story of "Mr. Blank" (*Washington Witch Hunt* [New York, 1938]). Mr. Blank was dismissed from the Department of State, without being informed of the charges against him. The committee before which he appeared would neither put nor answer any questions, but asked him to say anything he pleased which he believed relevant: "You might think back over your own career and perhaps in your own mind delve into some of the factors that have gone into your career which you think might have been subject to question." A distinction is made between "loyalty" as "a conscious proposition" and "security risk" which "might be conscious or unconscious." The situation is analogous to psychoanalytic procedure where the patient is asked to "talk" and thus discover his hidden guilt.
2. In Kafka's work, it is primarily the female figures who offer help without asking for any reward. Nearly all come from "the underground," especially Pepi in *The Castle*.
3. For fuller discussion of Kafka's work, see the chapter in my book, *No Voice is Wholly Lost*. See also my essay "The Vogue of Franz Kafka" in *Franz Kafka Miscellany* (2d ed; New York, 1946).

The Existentialist Myth
The Value of Homelessness
The Myth of Sisyphus and The Flies

IN SOME ANALYSES, existentialism is viewed as an expression of the historic dilemmas confronting man in the aftermath of the Second World War. To be sure, these have been the catalysts for the movement, have provided its mood and accent. Yet, existentialism is based on old principles with a renowned philosophical ancestry, reaching back to the "either-or" of Kierkegaard, the voluntarism of Nietzsche, the phenomenology of Husserl, up to the "anxiety" and "anguish" of Heidegger and the irresolvable antinomies of Karl Jaspers.

The supra-historical import of existentialism appears more directly in its reference to the myth. Camus, at one time closely related to the movement, wrote of the Sisyphus myth and Sartre has treated the Orestes myth in *The Flies*. Now, the differentiating character of the existentialist approach is that it is concerned exclusively with the second act of the mythic drama, that is, with the revolt of the individual. Its primary motive is to affirm the individual's unconditioned freedom from "systems," "essences," and any type of organized control, and to accept the resulting homelessness and anguish as final. It does not explore the question of the sources and bases out of which this homelessness arises. The individual is not born—he is "thrown" into existence. He has no parents and produces no offspring. For this reason, existentialism cannot and does not ask the question of rehabilitation. Existentialism does refer to "temporality" and the future. It even speaks of the past and of tradition. But this past is "freely" created, not discovered as an objective existence. Where the classic myth relates the ego's rebellion to the common ground of things, existentialism would relate it to the groundlessness of things, to "Nothing." It begins with "Nothing" and its goal, at least with some, is the nothingness of death.

SISYPHUS

The characteristic mythic hero of existentialism is not Prometheus, created by his mother Terra, and finally coming to terms with Father Zeus, but Sisyphus. Not Prometheus who would free mankind both *from* fear of nature and man as well as *for* control of physical and human nature, but Sisyphus, forever condemned to roll a rock to the top of a mountain, with the rock always falling back of its own weight. It is Sisyphus who absorbs the interest of Albert Camus at the moment when he descends to the plain "towards the torment the conclusion of which he will not know."[1] For this is "the hour of consciousness!" In these moments, Sisyphus transcends his destiny. Although powerless, he "knows that the entire extent of his clairvoyance which constitutes his torment contains at the same time his victory." In this moment, Sisyphus sees that his destiny belongs to him; the very succession of unconnected actions which is his destiny, has been created by him, "unified under the gaze of his memory, and soon broken off by his death." His is the superior loyalty "which denies the gods and lifts the rocks." And Camus imagines that in all this, Sisyphus experiences a silent joy. Sisyphus is happy in his useless labor, his labor of indifference, happy because it is *his* uselessness and *his* indifference, happy because he continues, even in his punishment, to rebel against the system. It is he, not someone else, who is being tormented; it is he, not some other, who continues to roll the rock up the mountain.

In its abstract formulation, existentialism may well be philosophically untenable. Spinozists, Kantians, Hegelians and Marxists, critics from Guido de Ruggiero to Günther Anders have attacked its notions of undetermined freedom and causeless action. They question the claim that a non-objective attitude can have an objective value, that you can derive a morality from non-moral action, and quote Marx's characterization of Stirner, (the "proud possessor of no possessions") as applicable to existentialism.

However, it is doubtful whether the heart of the doctrine is reached by this approach. Nor does its meaning necessarily emerge from the affiliations of the existentialists. In point of fact, various groups, from Catholics to atheists claim that their platforms derive from existentialism. Its art work, on the other hand, presents its philosophy in sensuous, dramatistic form. It can tell us what is meant by personality, freedom, involvement, action, and anguish, since it presents characters in concrete relations and inter-participation. Art is also the most favorable context for revealing the element of irony or self-criticism. Sartre's *The Flies*,[2] his most effective art work, deals most directly with a myth, that of Orestes.

THE MYTH OF ORESTES

The scene is Argos whose people (with the exception of Electra) have been enchained by a propaganda technique of fear and guilt. They fear the ghosts of the past and feel guilty in keeping silent about the murder of Agamemnon. The dead are used to rule the living. The people have been reduced to a cringing attitude of submission, are slaves to "the good old piety of yore, rooted in terror." The religious and secular "systems" of Zeus-Aegisthus have brought "the flies" to plague the city. Its people have indeed become "flies" themselves, humming and buzzing about without human communication. When Orestes appears with his tutor, they try to speak to someone. But no one opens the door or listens to them. Their very fear and guilt are officially regulated. Their piety is to dead mummery. The Greek Chorus has been converted to the people as a mob-swarm.

Orestes has come to restore to the people "their sense of human dignity." As a result of the liberal education given him by his tutor, he has become "free as air," free from prejudice and superstition. He has "no ties, no religion, and no calling . . . no home, no roots." However, this homelessness has created a void within him, and he wishes he could acquire the people's memories, their hopes and fears. He admits to his sister Electra that "of all the ghosts haunting this town today, none is ghostlier than I." And he confesses: "I want to be a man who belongs to some place, a man among comrades." Undecided as to whether he should stay and avenge his father, he calls on Zeus to point a way. Now Zeus, like Aegisthus, has but one passion, the passion for ritual and order. His sign counsels Orestes to live at peace. This at once makes for Orestes' resolution to do the very opposite—not to take orders from gods or men, but to follow his own path. He gives up his "aery lightness," and would take over the people's crime and remorse by killing Aegisthus and Clytemnestra. By thus "stealing" the burden of guilt from the people, he means to liberate them to act freely.

The play was purportedly written as an attack on the Nazi system and Vichy collaboration. Yet, it is more an indictment of the people than of the system which forged their chains. In fact, Zeus, Aegisthus, and Clytemnestra have some stature or evoke sympathy. Aegisthus has kept order, but at the sacrifice of hope, love, even of lust. "No man in Argos is sadder than I," he tells Clytemnestra. Nor is he unscrupulous: he does not resist Orestes and opposes Zeus's urgings to throw him into a dungeon. Clytemnestra is a resigned, almost pitiful figure, bearing "the heaviest load of guilt." Zeus is actually depicted as having dignity. He is a French Wotan without the Wagnerian metaphysical pretensions. He accepts his defeat gracefully with fore-knowledge that it had to come.

The most dramatic repudiation of Orestes' freedom is objectified in Electra. She begins in a challenging, though ineffective, fearlessness *before* the arrival of Orestes but after she is exposed to Orestes's teaching and behavior, Electra renounces his form of freedom. Although she loves her brother and offers the closest and most direct subject for Orestes's persuasions, she decides to stay behind with Zeus to be saved "from my brother, from myself." She is frightened by Orestes who shows no regret over having killed his mother. Electra is the warmest and most human character in the drama. It is she who offers the most telling critique of Orestes' freedom from all ties when she asks: "Can you undo what has been done? Something has happened and we are no longer free to blot it out." She is converted by Orestes—*in reverse*. Orestes helps no one, not the people whom he despises, not his sister whom he loves. He only helps himself to anguish.

Even as Orestes would reject biological and social determinants, he actually *does commit* himself, and does react to existing authorities. His acts are not causeless, as are those of Dostoyevsky's Kiriloff. "Man is nothing but what he makes of himself," writes Sartre. Orestes does not "make himself," but re-acts to Zeus in *precise reverse*. The sole act that might be said to have "nothing" as a motivation is the murder of his mother. In Aeschylus, and even in O'Neill, some attempt is made to explain matricide. There is none in Sartre's play. Orestes kills his mother for no "reason." Even his sister's pressure is absent—Sartre's Electra rather urges: "She can do us no more harm," now that Aegisthus is dead. Orestes himself thinks that his act is right. But this "knowledge" is his own mystery. He makes no attempt to *make* it known to others or even to himself. The sole basis for Orestes' murder is the traditional plot of the legend. That is, in this "free" existentialist act, Sartre's hero acts like an unfree man, enslaved by the mere ritual of the old myth.

At the end, Orestes leaves. He does not know or care where he is going. With Wagner's Siegfried, he might say: "In der Ferne bin ich heim."
He has rejected his origins (he has no "memories"), rejected the authorities of Zeus, Aegisthus, and his mother. For the people he has only contempt. With no base to start from, he has no lever to propel himself. His
"free" act consists of the cold, mechanical, and unmotivated murder of
his mother.

Now, Orestes presumably kills for the sake of the people. That is,
Sartre would reintroduce the social motif into existentialism. But the
play depicts the people in a manner which does not make them worthy
of being saved. They show no change in attitude which might be a
basis for their future self-liberation. On the contrary, Orestes' treatment
of them only tends to de-dignify them even more. His freedom-act remains a gesture.[3]

In Aeschylus' version, Orestes violates the tradition of tribal guilt
enacted by the Erinyes. But the turning-point of the Oresteia is the
transformation of the malign Erinyes into the benign Eumenides, not
their elimination. The old harbors elements which make possible its assimilation with the new, under the aegis of a rising Athenian democracy. Athena herself employs "social" means in her recourse to an Athenian jury, in her use of reason and persuasion on the Erinyes. And
Orestes, who begins with matricide, ends by accepting and being accepted by the surrogate mother, Athena.

The situation in Goethe's *Iphigenia in Tauris,* as in the Euripides
version, is that, following the murder of Clytemnestra, Iphigenia has
found refuge with King Thoas in Tauris. The king first appears as
primitive authority intent on exacting tribal vengeance on all Greeks
who enter his land. Orestes is in a related state and would oppose Thoas
by stealth and force. But he and Iphigenia tame their demon, and in
the end Thoas is persuaded by both, as Aeschylus's Erinyes are persuaded by Athena. To be sure, in Goethe's play, there is no chorus, no
jury of Athenian citizens to contribute to the redemption. Goethe is
writing in eighteenth century Germany, when the people's voice is
largely subdued, and when the inner, ethical approach of the individual
alone appears representative.

Thus, in Aeschylus and Goethe, the hero defies an old tradition, but
chooses an alternative high tradition. In Sartre, there appears to be no
room for any tradition, no room for persuasion, reason, or ethics to banish the Furies. His Orestes would carry the burden by himself without
reference to God, society, or family.

A more related approach to Sartre's Orestes appears in O'Neill's

Mourning Becomes Electra. Electra (Lavinia) is the central pivot. (Orestes is a weak, sickly figure.) Her form of freedom is acted out in satanic defiance and in a will to power. In pursuit of this power, O'Neill's characters defy their origins. But this does not free them, and his Electra remains in the grip of the Furies. In his earlier and later work (*The Hairy Ape* and *Days without End*), the dramatist suggests the need for communal reference. But in *Mourning Becomes Electra*, the self is freed only to be forever alone with itself, at home only in blank and black despair.

Temporal Involvements

The variations of the Orestes myth in Aeschylus, Goethe, and O'Neill are bound up with their varying historic and cultural demands. Existentialism too has received its accent in response to particular historic pressures.

Existentialism would annul the category of mediation. Its protest is against *mediators*, (the machine, documents, organization) which strip the person of his singularity and of his human warmth, dissolving him in a gray anonymity. Yet this protest against the reduction of the individual to the role of an intermediary is itself the expression of a midway position. It is the voice of those resisting a situation where they hover somewhere *between* upper and lower powers, are not *themselves*, but are manipulated to serve either group.

This midway status may be said to have received its impetus with the Renaissance and the rise of the middle classes. But the themes of homelessness and solitude are peculiarly relevant to the German bourgeoisie. Its late rise and retarded development long placed it at the mercy of the Junker strata, and later in fear of the proletariat. Existentialism is primarily a *German* import. Elements of it are to be found in Goethe's Faust, who would emancipate himself completely, first from his Gothic heritage, and later from the old pair, Philemon and Baucis. Yet in the end, Faust joins a social and religious communality. Wagner's Siegfried, on the other hand, would be born out of nothing. He does not know his father or mother, kills his surrogate parent Mime, bypasses Wotan, and falls victim to society, "the court" of Gunther, finally to end in "nothing," the pyre of the *Götterdämmerung*. He is not born *from* but *against* society (Fricka), free of tradition and of fear, existing in pure opposition to existing tables of value. And, as Sartre's Zeus cannot prevent the birth of the free man, so Wagner's Wotan is helpless against Siegfried.[4]

This note is continued by Nietzsche who warred simultaneously against German metaphysics and Wagner's aristocratic pretensions, and against "the many, all too many." In Nietzsche too, we find "leaps" and transcendence, which make for the restless and nervous pace of the Superman. Nietzsche could still attempt to limit freedom by the determinism in his theory of eternal recurrence. Kierkegaard countered the world of "clearance sales" by a leap of faith, and Strindberg approximated a similar leap in his last years. Ibsen launches his heroic men on their free path. But dramatically he shows that the Brands and Peer Gynts are in need of grace to be redeemed, that the Stockmanns cannot help the people by remaining their "enemy."

Twentieth-century Germany could be more "heroically" desperate. It sought consolation in Spengler's proud *Untergang*, in expressionistic freedoms, and in Heidegger's dignification of *Sorge*. As Günther Anders points out,[5] Heidegger's return from the First World War was a homecoming to no home. There arose the insistence "to be there," to be "themselves" (the basic existentialist vocabulary). He had faced "Death" and "Nothing" in the war and now wanted "to be" and to be "himself," to exist—not in general and for others—but to himself. In Anders' formulation, this expressed the bourgeois despair, the despair of those who are the victims of the abused bourgeois freedoms, who have never had real opportunities for freedom, but have lived for the objectives of more powerful groups. This also fitted in with the ideology of the Third Reich on the analogy of the German self coming to itself after being robbed by the "world" and the Versailles "system." In reality, this freedom is a desperate affirmation of boundedness.[6]

Sartre tells us that his studies in Heidegger immediately after Hitler's accession to power led to his theory of existentialism. This German product grew in the soil of the Vichy era among those who felt themselves caught midway between foreign and native systems both of which denied their individual existence. But this German phenomenon has been a drop of foreign blood in the French body. Irrationality, free individualism, metaphysical concern with "nothing," all this is indigenous to the historic curve of the German bourgeoisie. The roots of modern France lie in Cartesian rationalism, the critical tradition of Montaigne, the realism of its literature, in its sense of tradition, its concentration around "schools" and "academies," and finally, in the *reality* of its revolutionary tradition from 1789, 1830, 1848, 1871 to the self-liberation of Paris.

There are indeed some differentiations between Sartre and Heidegger. The latter supported the Nazis—half-heartedly; Sartre was a staunch supporter of the Resistance movement. We find a deviation in theory as well. Sartre recognizes that "individualism is impossible without collective responsibility," that "man must use his free will to establish a working basis for living collectively without destroying the dignity of the individual."[7] To be responsible for oneself means to be responsible for all men. This is the principle of "inter-subjectivity" which holds that "the man who becomes aware of himself through the *cogito* also perceives all others, and he perceives them as the condition of his own existence."[8] While Sartre denies that there is a universal human nature, he speaks of a universal human condition, the necessity to exist in the world with others, the duty of involving oneself in the problems of the day.[9]

However these qualifications remain sketchy and are not worked through towards linking freedom with tradition. Sartre says that primary reality is "being-in-the-world." Kenneth E. Douglas well points out that Sartre "forgets his hyphens and dwells exclusively on the conflict between man, with his inescapable freedom, and the external world which is in-itself but not for-itself."[10]

Are exisistentialists aware of the insufficiency in their individual stress? They argue that freedom spells anguish. Does anguish arise from their sensing that "collective responsibility" is not met by the individual free act? That the gratuitous act by the isolated individual is not effective in a world of private and public corporate powers? Have not the existentialists generalized existence so that it has itself become an essence, albeit a particularized essence?

The insufficiency of exclusive centering in the second act is dramatically illustrated in Sartre's account of the student who came to him for advice. The young man faced the choice of joining the Resistance movement or staying at home with his mother. Sartre told him that this must be his own choice. The young man then decided to stay with his mother; and Sartre adds that, in deciding to come to him, the young man had already made his choice. He had wanted to stay with his mother and knew that Sartre would not make any decision for him. This story presents an astoundingly naive attitude toward the problem of human choice. It assumes that what a person thinks he wants, on the basis of his immediate knowledge about himself, is equivalent to what he might want if he learned more about his motivation. Might not an analysis of an individual's choice reveal that his motives are based on an immediate desire which is contrary to his broader and long-range interests? In that existentialism discourages such analysis, it tends to encourage a freedom in terms of compulsive wish-fulfillments. Perhaps Ruggiero has this in mind when he charges that Existentialism corrupts the youth.

Still, the movement has a salutary function. It is a wholesome warning against the dead and false myth, against a sexless, mechanical collectivism. Writing about America, Sartre notes that there

> the myth of liberty co-exists with a dictatorship of public opinion; the myth of economic liberalism with monster corporations which embrace a continent, which finally belong to no one . . . 100 million Americans who try to satisfy their need for the marvellous by reading the incredible adventures of Superman or Mandrake the Magician.[11]

The cathartic value of the movement is to rouse the individual against surrender and submission to impersonality by placing in the center of its thought the idea that man continuously transcends himself.[12] In a time when the individual feels that he is a powerless thing, the existentialist's insistence that man is "nothing else but what he makes of himself" can contribute to a true human condition.

NOTES

1. Albert Camus, *The Myth of Sisyphus and Other Essays* (New York, 1957).
2. Jean-Paul Sartre, *No Exit and Three Other Plays* (New York, 1946). Subsequent references are to this edition.
3. Translated into forensic existentialist terminology, the people of Argos have "being" (*Dasein*), whereas Orestes is true "existence." The first are finite, temporal, and guilty; the latter is an emergent transcendence out of being. But existentialism does not make clear *how* emergence transpires. The antithesis between the two catetories (Orestes and the people) is drawn so sharply that it is difficult to see how existence can "emerge" from being. Ruggiero's comment on this point is relevant: "Existence springs like a fungus from the flat ground of the *Dasein*, or better, to twist a metaphor wrongly used by existentialists against idealism, emerges like Baron Münchhausen pulling himself by the hair out . . . with the strength of his own arm. . . . To make of existence the protagonist of becoming means to exchange the effect with the cause." *Existentialism* (London, 1947), pp. 48-49.
4. For elaboration of O'Neill's position and of the factors in German development discussed below, see chapters on O'Neill, Nietzsche, and Spengler in my *No Voice Is Wholly Lost.*
5. "Nihilismus und Existenz," *Neue Rundschau* (October, 1946). Hamlet has been wrongly interpreted as an existentialist character. His problem arises precisely from the circumstance that he *cannot* justify—morally or socially—complete severance from the Ghost, his mother, and even Claudius. Hamlet goes to Wittenberg and later to England, but each time returns to the court. The situation in the Scandinavian countries, placed in a non-heroic position in relation to European industrial development, is more relevant, as indicated by the problems in Kierkegaard, Strindberg, and Ibsen.

6. Karl Jaspers' doctrine of final "shipwreck" is a version of Heidegger's "Death." He also inveighs against the *unity* of opposites. But he is more aware of the dialectic relation between opposites. This moves him away from the camp of existentialism.

7. Interview with Dorothy Norman, *The New York Post* (April 9, 1946).

8. *Existentialism*, New York, 1947.

9. "We Write for Our Time," *The Virginia Quarterly Review*, XIII (Spring, 1947).

10. "The Nature of Sartre's Existentialism," *The Virginia Quarterly Review*, XIII (Spring, 1947).

11. Quoted in *The New York Times* (February 2, 1947).

12. Sartre, in his social stand, and Jaspers in his philosophy veer away from such extreme individualism. To Jaspers, philosophy is "a faith in communication," and an individual "cannot become human by himself."

Threat and Promise in
Germanic Insulation
The Magic Mountain and *Doctor Faustus*

THOMAS MANN introduces his *Doctor Faustus* by quoting from the second Canto of Dante's *Inferno*. In preparation for the terrifying and warlike journey he is about to undertake, Dante invokes the Muse and high Genius to help him in the task of giving expression to the true nobility of Memory.

For Mann, memory of tradition is preeminently incorporated and lived by the folk. In *The Beloved Returns*, (New York, 1940), Mann gives us Goethe's musings on its nature-wisdom:

> Ah, the folk! the folk-nature, part of nature, itself, elemental, earthy, pagan, full of folk- and nature-wisdom, fruitful soil of the unconscious, nourishing vale of renewed youth! How good to mingle with them at their immemorial feasts, fontanalia and maypole games. (p. 284)

But Mann warns that myth may mean the destruction of life when memory of tradition deteriorates into idolatry or is used to bolster a national *Blut und Boden* ideology.[1]

Awareness of man's mythic role constitutes for Mann "the lived myth," and choice of the *high* norms of a tradition signifies "the birth of the Ego out of his mythical collective." In a letter to Carl Kerenyi, Mann states that psychology is "the means by which the myth can be wrested from the Fascist obscurantists and be made into a function of the human. This connection seems to me to represent the world of the future." In the Joseph story, "the myth has been taken out of Fascist hands and humanized down to the last recess of language,—if posterity finds anything remarkable about it, it will be this." Mann regarded his work as having a mythic function and he himself went into exile, calling on Germany to recollect its human tradition to counteract the destructive tradition of Nazism.

The Germany with which Thomas Mann has always identified himself is that associated with Dürer, Bach, Luther and Goethe, that is, the period of Germany's first awakening to a national consciousness with a universal cultural mission. Mann's birthplace, Luebeck, exhibited some of these traits: Head of the Hanseatic League and a "free city" from the 12th century on, it retained the character of a bourgeois cultural tradition, relatively free of the Junker and industrial barons who dominated German history.

The work of Thomas Mann deals with four mythic levels: the Germanic in *Buddenbrooks* and *Death in Venice*, the European in *The Magic Mountain*, the international in the Joseph story and the Fascist transformation of primitive Teutonism in *Doctor Faustus*. In each, Mann counterposes the human to the inhuman myth. In the first, German memory of *Gemeinschaft*,—in the form of a philosophic and musical pantheism—is to correct Prussianism; in the second, the Latin-Mediterranean concept of "civilization" is to correct the German Kultur-cult; in the third, monster nationalism is to be counteracted by a human internationalism, based on the Judaic-Hellenic-Christian tradition; finally, the motif of musical "howling" in *Doctor Faustus* is seen as a possible "breakthrough" beyond the howling of Fascism.

Yet, these corrections are themselves affected by the very intractable situations in which they arise. The result is ambiguity or, to use Mann's favorite term, "irony."[2]

DER ZAUBERBERG

In his Foreword to *The Magic Mountain*, Thomas Mann tells us that the story of Hans Castorp has "something of the legend about it," that it "belongs to the long ago," and "comes out of the depth of the past."

Hans Castorp as Mythic Hero

Hans Castorp's "hermetic" seven years on the enchanted mountain hints at the association of his story with legends in which a character leaves the world for some forest-island-or mountain-retreat. Writing of Merlin's enchanted forest, Henrich Zimmer notes in *The King and the Corpse* that the forest

> has always been a place of initiation, for there the demonic presences, the
> ancestral spirits, and the forces of nature reveal themselves. . . . It holds

313

... secrets, terrors, which threaten the protected life of the ordered world of common day. (p. 182)

All lose their way in it except the chosen one who leaves it a changed man.

The author calls Castorp a "mediocre hero," quickly adding that he is such "in an entirely honorable sense." Castorp's apparent mediocrity is conditioned by the age in which he lives which induces "a certain laming of the personality":

> A man lives not only his personal life, as an individual, but also, consciously or unconsciously, the life of his epoch and his contemporaries. . . . Now, if the life about him, if his own time seem, however outwardly stimulating, to be at bottom . . . hopeless, viewless, helpless, opposing only a hollow silence to all the questions man puts, consciously or unconsciously, yet somehow puts, as to the final, absolute, and abstract meaning in all his efforts and activities; then, in such a case, a certain laming of the personality is bound to occur, the more inevitably, the more upright the character in question.[3]

Here, then, is the "honorable" aspect of Castorp's character: finding the deficiencies of his epoch "prejudicial to his own moral well-being," he unconsciously rejects the ruling symbols of a commercialized world where "one is rich—or else one isn't," as he later says to Settembrini. Castorp's revolt takes on the German, Romantic form of passive resistance. The unconscious nature of Castorp's rebellion appears in his anemic state which prevents him from going ahead with his engineering studies and sends him up to the Berghof sanatorium for a period of seven years.

Journey In The Labyrinth

Early in the story, Settembrini characterizes Castorp's arrival on the mountain as a descent into the inferno. Hell on the Berghof consists in time appearing to stand still. Now, Castorp's "flatland" was another form of hell. When Castorp has acquired sufficient "distance," he readily accepts Settembrini's designation of this world as both "phlegmatic and energetic,"—phlegmatic with respect to human values and energetic about business and pleasure. And, on this plane, the "round" mountain is the replica of the "flat" land. Castorp's mountain harbors the classical temptations faced by the mythic hero—the alternatives of insensibility and of directionless motion. Castorp has rejected "the tyranny of time," only to fall victim to the tyranny of timeless apathy, has rejected one labyrinth only to fall into another. The "utopia" of the Olympian mountain is the "ideology" of the commercial market rushing towards the First World War. Yet, even as the mountain is the counterpart of the valley, its symbolic life contains an element of transcendence through which Castorp's insulated existence saves his mythic role.

Castorp's mountain with its sharp and clear air is a twentieth century Olympus. It suggests a Platonic Republic, composed of the artisan (Castorp), the soldier (Joachim) and the philosopher (Settembrini and Naphta). But here, the Socratic truth is split into two ideologies which contradict each other. Castorp's philosophic guides are ambiguous "talkers," and the "Earthly Paradise" towards which Settembrini leads Castorp is as suspect as the City of God which the Augustinian Naphta would reveal to Castrop.

Settembrini: the Brother Guide

Ludovico Settembrini is Castorp's Virgilian guide through the shades of the enchanted mountain, instructing him in the Latin precepts of political and social virtue—a theme which the German un-political *Kultur-Mensch* has ignored. Settembrini is the Mediterranean critic of German musical romanticism as well as of all authoritarianisms. He is the herald of secession, opposes all traditional absolutes, championing the endless continuity of the quest. He urges change, work, action, and freedom without basing them on firm principles. Settembrini urges Castorp to go back to the world of work. But Castorp is only "half-listening," for Settembrini does not meet his reservations about this "cruel and ruthless" world where values consist of money and possessions. Indeed, Settembrini's guidance is ambiguous. This spokesman for Protestantism comes from Catholic Italy, the critic of bourgeois life maintains bourgeois forms, the social internationalist supports the nationalistic war of 1914. He who prompts Castorp to leave the Berghof for a life of action himself can only talk. Settembrini admits that he is "rather ill," that is, he too is "honorable," and cannot live in the world of "progress." On the first night on the mountain, Castorp dreams of Settembrini, calling him "a brother":

> he was unexpectedly vouchsafed a signal insight into the true nature of time; it proved to be nothing more or less than a "silent sister," a mercury column without degrees, to be used by those who wanted to cheat.

On Walpurgis-Night, Castorp thanks Settembrini for lecturing him about freedom and progress, individualism and work, thanks him at the very moment when he is about to dismiss this champion of Western values and approach the Eastern Mother. The thanks are deserved: the very logic of Settembrini's negative liberalism, which offers Castorp no replacements, only serve to lead Castorp *away* from his disciplined

315

world of labor. In this ironic way, Settembrini "frees" Castorp for indulging himself in the licenses and licentiousness of the Witches' Kitchen on Walpurgis-Night.[4]

Clavdia: The Mountain-Mother

The Mountain is Castorp's womb in which he finds protection, security, comfort. Its "invisible government" makes no demands, offers a surfeit of food and induces sleep. On Walpurgis-Night, Castorp, takes leave of his Virgilian guide to be enveloped by the mother-mistress in "Eden." Regressed to a child-like state, "blind," (his eyes closed,) "speechless," ("parler sans parler," in a language which is neutral to both), Hans Castorp kneels before Clavdia Chauchat, "swaying and quivering," begging for admission and recognition. Later that night, in a scene "wordless to our ears," engulfed in bliss,

> his twitching lips had stammered and babbled, in his own and foreign tongues, for the most part without his volition, the maddest things: pleas, prayers, proposals, frantic projects, to which all consent was denied.

Settembrini had issued warnings, had referred to Clavdia as Adam's first wife, Lillith, "a night-tripping fairy, . . . dangerous to young men especially." But on this night, Castorp has become a *ragazzo*, who cannot hear his mentor's foreign admonitions not to jeopardize his Western individualism.

In her careless *nichevo* manner, Clavdia is old Russia, in its ambiguous "French" form. In Castorp's associations, the ambiguity extends to her sex, reminding him of his schoolmate, the boy Hippe. The hours he spends in her room on Walpurgis-Night only produce a "spiritual" x-ray picture of the upper part of her body. Castorp's union with Clavdia, like Faust's with Helena, is in the nature of union with a shade.

Leo Naphta: The Distorted Christ

As an ironic guide, Settembrini also leads Castorp to his adversary, Leo Naphta. Where Settembrini views history as continuous progress by reason and individual freedom, Naphta teaches the values of Christian communality and sees history as split into dual warring forces. If Clavdia *lives* the decline of the West, Naphta *argues* the decline of Settembrini's "capitalistic world-republic." On the historical plane, he represents the variety of authoritarian systems, from Catholicism to Fascism and Communism which exert a special appeal to our 20th century Hans Castorps.

Naphta too is an ambiguous "talker," is sick and belongs on the mountain-sanatarium. His ambiguity arises from the fact that his precepts stem from a private burden. He was "set out" in the pogroms suffered by his family, with his father "nailed crucifix-wise on the door of his burning home." Later, Leo rebelled against the rabbi, his surrogate father, and was once again cast out. This event took place "precisely at the time when Rahel Naphta (his mother) lay dying."

At this point, Leo turned to Marx and then to Hegel. The latter (whom he called a "Catholic thinker") becomes the bridge to his Catholicism and Jesuitism. In joining the church, Naphta forgave, indeed, identified himself with those whose warped Christianity had been the instrument of his father's murder. Is this identification with his family's crucifiers the source of his deep guilt feeling, guilt over disloyalty to his personal father? Are his implacable dualism and his doctrine of "The Terror" an attempt to reach the very bottom of the Satanic abyss, to find and wrestle with the archdevil, seeking an absolute explanation for pain and suffering? So deep and exposed were Naphta's personal wounds that he was in desperate need of a physical home. And, since Marxism offered only a conceptual framework, a rational, socio-economic explanation for the pogroms, Naphta found it necessary to move within the "walls" of the Catholic-Jesuit enclosure. However, his reading of Marx led him to a revolutionary interpretation of Catholicism for which he saw a theological basis in St. Augustine. The world-proletariat, he declares, is

> today asserting the ideals of the *Civitas Dei* in opposition to the discredited and decadent standards of the capitalistic bourgeoisie. . . . The proletariat has taken up the task of Gregory the Great. . . . Its task is to . . . win back at length to freedom from law and from distinction of classes, to (man's) original status as child of God.

But Naphta's communistic Catholicism has a Fascist mode. He adopted not only the Augustinian castigation of the state and the Catholic critique of bourgeois commercialism, but also the Manichean heresy, of viewing the struggle between God and the devil as an eternal process which calls for the never-ending "Terror." But all this is also mainly "talk." He cannot practice what he preaches, develops his own "moist spot," rendering him unfit to apply his teachings in the practical realm. At the end, he turns the terror against himself. He did not want to be saved, but in his despair only hoped that his personal sacrifice might be the means of mankind's salvation.[5] In these distorted acts, Naphta reveals the "honorable" element by which Mann would save him as well.

317

Mynheer Pieter Peeperkorn: The Dionysian Corn-King

The most impressive character on the mountain, the only one who *is* a character, and who most visibly incorporates mythic traits is Mynheer Pieter Peeperkorn. With his mask-like face, he is a "persona," whose kingly features and majestic personality make him the father-guide of the mountain-community. In Mann's allusions, Peeperkorn becomes Jupiter (the eagle), Silenus (his royal drunkenness), Saturn-Pan (his celebrations and his homage to the nature water-fall). His name, Mynheer Peeperkorn, suggests the Corn-King whose arrival ushers in an apparent spring-like revival on the mountain. In his brief stay, he undergoes the ritual of the seasonal god, his spring and summer quickly turning to his fall and winter, with a faint promise that his death is not final, but that he only "went away."

Peeperkorn's role is that of the Dionysian god of wine and rapture on the Apollonian mountain. As in the case of Euripides' *The Bacchae*, his primitive force rouses the phlegmatic Western community towards a short-lived *Rausch*. He replaces Castorp's father-brother-authorities (Settembrini-Naphta, Behrens-Krokowski) and makes him his "son," who thereupon renounces his desire for the mother.

Yet, beneath Peeperkorn's pagan enjoyment of the "gifts of life," beneath "the heathen priest," one detects "the man of sorrows," whose talk consists of signs and portents. The evening repast takes on the character of a Last Supper at which Peeperkorn, surrounded by his twelve disciples, speaks of Gethsemane and the Last Judgment. The mixture of the pagan and the Christian is also evident at the water-fall, where "Peter" stands by "the rocks," and gives his "absolute" signs:

> They saw his head sink sideways, the broken bitterness of the lips, they saw the man of sorrows in his guise. But then quite suddenly flashed the dimple, the sybaritic roguishness, the garment snatched up dancewise, the ritual impropriety of the heathen priest.

Jesus' last request on earth was for something to drink. Peeperkorn's final gesture is to empty his beaker of wine in three gulps.[6] The scene at the waterfall combines Grecian *sparagmos* and Christian crucifixion. Where Naphta lives for the idea, Peeperkorn lives for passion. The extremes meet: Both commit suicide.

Peeperkorn is a sick Dionysus surrounded by a sick chorus. This corn-god is a watery figure, "prepotent," if not impotent, his "bread" turned to liquid which gives him a feverish fire. Outwardly dynamic and flourishing, he is inwardly static and tainted. Historically, Peeperkorn embodies the decline of the West. Yet, he too, is honorable in that he voluntarily abdicates his absolutism and is not a party to the Thunderbolt of 1914.

Return to the Folk

At the end of the novel, Hans Castorp returns to the world he had left behind. But his seven years' sojourn on the mountain has developed the "mediocre" into something of a mythic hero. From Settembrini he has learned the value of individual freedom and the need to join politics to poetry; from Naphta, the communal idea based on primary categories; from Peeperkorn, the "holy claims" of life. When Castorp returns, he does not join the "phlegmatic and energetic," but his "comrades," in his belief that they are fighting for love and peace. On the battlefield, he does not sing "Deutschland, Deutschland über alles," but Schubert's "Lindenbaum."[7] The *Lied* sums up Hans Castorp's *geniale Weg*, which leads to reconciliation with his folk.

Castorp's journey takes him through the several acts of the mythic drama. The first act is his nostalgic memory of his grandfather's "timelessness," the pre-technical, pre-bourgeois world which is later idealized in the first part of his dream in "Snow." The novel itself begins with the second act. The "orphan" leaves the flatland where he had lived a repressed existence, ascends the mountain-top in quest of another form of "timelessness," of a "free" life, similar to that sought by Joyce's Dedalus, Kafka's Joseph K, and other modern characters. Here, he would peer into the forbidden mysteries of the Mountain-Mother. These urges are partially held in check by the spokesman for Western patriarchal tradition, Ludovico Settembrini. For this "crime," Castorp is nearly "lost to life." But at the end, he returns "home", in an attempt to resolve the conflict of ideologies, not by philosophical dialectic, but by *Praxis*.

But only Castorp has changed. His society is fighting, not for Schubert's *Lied*, but for the firms of Tunder and Wilms which Castorp's "body" had rejected seven years before. At the end, our hero appears to be back in another Walpurgis-Night and Inferno, as he stumbles blindly in the murky chaos of the "shadow-land," with its "nude, branchless trunks of trees," in the "bemired woods," hearing "groans and shrieks" in the "fiery filth."

In his failure to recognize the historic reality, Castorp is as blind as Goethe's Faust was to the fact that his grave was being dug.[8] Yet, both Faust and Castorp are blind only in the manner of the man in Plato's cave who had gone forth to the sunny realm of the eternal Ideas and, on his return, is unable to distinguish between "the shadow" and "the substance." To be sure, from the historic platform, Castorp's "prospects are poor." Yet, as Joachim, Peeperkorn and Naphta are redeemed by their "honorable," supra-historical import, so hope remains for Castorp. For, he has not yielded to the pressures of his partisan guides, has witnessed the contradictions and disintegration of the authorities in their temporal guise: The Army (Joachim), the State (Peeperkorn), the various forms of authoritarianisms (Naphta). Castorp has rejected them and has returned to the authority of the Earth-Mother to participate in the agony of his people. Indeed, a Christ-motif is introduced when we see his bearded figure, "wet and glowing," singing "loving words" on his Golgotha-way. On the mountain, Castorp paid reverence to the sick and the *moribundi*, that is, he *invited* suffering, and following his purgatory, he came to the false paradise of Walpurgis-Night. At the end, the author allows a faint hope that "out of this extremity of fever. . . . Love one day shall mount."

This hope depends on the extent to which the Castorps recollect the high tradition inscribed in his "Christening Basin," and beyond it, the vision of the harmonious state he "remembered" in his dream in the snow. Castorp forsakes the realm of technics and rhetoric to "take stock" among the elements. In this dream, Hans Castorp reverses Walpurgis-Night. Then, he was nearly emasculated by the devouring mountain-mother. Here, he is saved from castration in the icy snow by his "anonymous and communal" dream which links him with the high points of his heritage: the promise of a polity in which work and play, life and art, the plastic and the musical coexist in harmony. To be sure, this harmony is only a wish and it is disturbed by the reality of the blood sacrifice which Hans *der Träumer* would rather not face. Still, the promise is there, imbedded in the deep recesses of Castorp's memory, and in the *Lied* which he "unconsciously" sings on the battlefield.[9]

Thomas Mann's work as a whole pictures the dissolution of the bourgeois world: In *Buddenbrooks*, through the decline of the family, in *Death in Venice*, through the decline of the artist in a pestilential city, in *The Magic Mountain*, through the war-convulsion of a continent, extended to nearly the entire world in *Doctor Faustus*. And the way in which Mann's sensitive artist-figures would escape the bourgeois world is by retreat to a *Kultur*-realm. *The Magic Mountain*, in particular, reverses the quest which began with Don Quixote, Hamlet and Faust. Where they leave their seclusion for a life of experience, Castorp leaves the world of experience for his insulated mountain.

Mann's subsequent work envisages two ways of transcending the bourgeois sphere. In the Joseph story, it leads upwards towards one human world. Here, Mann wrote, we leave the modern bourgeois sphere far behind to "pierce deep, deep into the human," in search "for man's essence, his origin, his goal." The pressures of Fascism forced Mann to seek another road, the way "downwards," in the hope that in the elemental, man find his common humanity.

The Magic Mountain ended on a hesitant and questioning tone. Castorp had moved from static insulation to dynamic, devouring "communication." His song of peace and love became a cacophony of music and strife, reestablishing the ancient Teutonic myth in which Wotan is at once God of war and music. The ambiguity of this union becomes deeper and more tragic in Thomas Mann's last major work, *Doctor Faustus*.

DOCTOR FAUSTUS:
THE MYTH OF BREAKTHROUGH

In his penetrating discussion of *Doctor Faustus*, Fritz Kaufmann connects the theme of isolation with Protestant freedom of the individual.[10] The German hero, in particular, would make solitude his home, and one is reminded of Nietzsche's "Oh Einsamkeit, du meine Heimat, Einsamkeit!" Goethe's Faust still attempted to break through his isolation by the social act. At the turn of our century, the artist passively distances himself from the insensitive world. Mann's Gustav Aschenbach would shun life and pay heed to artistic form. But the consequence is only that he falls victim to a life of formless disorder. In such phenomena, Thomas Mann saw Germany's pact with the devil, the "secret union of the German spirit with the Demonic." This pact appears, above all, in German music which he called "a demonic realm," a "Christian art with a negative prefix . . . such musicality of soul is paid for dearly in another sphere,—the political, the sphere of human companionship."[11]

Settembrini once urged that Castrop and his country will have to choose between East and West. And when Castorp maintains a stubborn silence, Settembrini movingly exclaims that one suspects Germany may break her silence with some deed. His surmise foreshadows Castorp's act at the end of his seven-year silence and sums up the pendular swing of the German hero between seclusion and expansion, between cultural autarchy and political coordination, between the *Lied* and *Schrecklichkeit*. Thus, Gustav Aschenbach moved from Prussian discipline to dissolute abandonment, Castorp from enchanted insulation to bewitched war-coordination, and Potiphar's wife from the chaste nun to the raving bitch. The same passage is taken by Adrian Leverkühn in *Doctor Faustus*.

Leverkühn's birthplace, Kaisersaschern, has somehow maintained the spirit of the older burgher life. But as Leverkühn experiences the Germany that is proceeding towards Hitler, he seals himself off to work on his musical compositions. But the "howling" which he would leave behind reenters his art and his music becomes an accompaniment of the wars in the world and of Nazi coordination.

Adrian's atonal technique replaces the diatonic system by an absolute order which does away with the central tone, is carried out in "total indifference to harmony and melody." Here, everything is mathematically organized and coordinated, with all twelve tones of the chromatic scale treated as equals. In Fritz Kaufmann's formulation, even the dissonant is put in uniform. (Earlier, Adrian had sought such absolute order in mathematics and theology). The compositions of Leverkühn, the *Tonsetzer*, are the tone for that steely *Gleichschaltung* which is being carried through in his social world. At the same time, his music is homeless, a breakdown of harmony and rhythm, with no fixed tone to which the music returns. This is the import of Mann's detailed analysis of Leverkühn's compositions: he would translate its technical forms into verbal meaning to show that music is not pure, but has realistic implications, that it may be "politically suspect," as Settembrini once said to Castorp.

Leverkühn's descent to the Bavarian valley repeats Castorp's ascent to the Swiss mountain. He maintains an even greater distance, distance from family, women, friends, people. The price for insisting on *noli me tangere* is that which the devil has demanded in the earliest forms of the Faust myth: "Thou maist not love."[12] One extreme is met by another: In the episode where Leverkühn insists on the love of the prostitute Esmeralda, the pure seeks the impure, the most solitary, the most promiscuous, the most individual, the most anonymous.[13] Adrian makes other attempts at "breakthrough," but they also take on a distorted form: his devotion to the friend has homoerotic overtones; his wooing of the woman is done from a distance and in a manner which invites betrayal by the friend.[14] In sum, insulation from human love results in Esmeralda love, lust of the brain in lust of the body, demonic spirituality in diabolic animality, romantic genius in romantic madness. In Adrian's German world, it manifests itself in autarchic nationalism attempting world domination by bestial methods.

Return to the Congregation

In his life, Adrian (like Faust) harmed or killed the people with whom he came in contact. At the close, he makes a final desperate effort to "communicate" in person and by the word to his "brethren and sisters." He confesses that his intoxication was born not of human warmth and love but of devilish cold and heat. It is Adrian's recognition-scene in which he becomes partially reconciled with his group. Here lie elements of hope in this stark, dreary and sombre story, the hope which comes from putting hopelessness into words. In his composition "Dr. Fausti Wehe-klag," the words stand above the choral and orchestral movements and "the final despair achieves a voice." The lament has no other consolation than "what lies in voicing it, in simply giving sorrow words." It is an echo of the consolation which Goethe's Tasso finds.

Hope is also embodied in Echo. The boy belongs to the mythic chain of the Heavenly Child, aspects of which were suggested in Mann's Hanno, Tadzio, young Joseph and Benjamin. As Fritz Kaufmann points out, Echo combines the features of the Christ-child (his prayers) and of a pagan Ariel who, at the end, returns to the elements. He dies for Adrian, helping him find the way to his congregation. In the final scene, Adrian himself appears as a pagan-Christian figure: Surrounded by a little troop of women, he speaks in a prophetic, anachronistic language of how one should *not* live. This sermon on hopelessness and his death are his sacrifice in the hope that the others might live.

Mythic Redemption

In the Joseph story, written during the ascendancy of Nazism, Thomas Mann said that he took the step from "the bourgeois and individual to the mythical and typical," and created a poem of world citizenship. In it, he looked back to the productive roots of the Western myth, and created a hero who combined sensitivity with health, art with politics. Likewise, he would redeem Adrian Leverkühn's music. And, it is characteristic of Mann's dialectic that the redemption arises out of the very material which produced the distortions. Hope resides in music which, by its very nature, is the language of international communication, above all, in Adrian's recognition that music can become this vehicle if it finds its way back to the people. In *The Magic Mountain*, this note is sounded in the *Volkslied* with its motif of communal love and peace which breaks through the fiendish cacophony of "The Thunder-

323

bolt." And, at the end of the secular hell in "Dr. Fausti Wehe-glag," the high G of a cello vibrates as an "echo" in the night:

> For listen to the end, listen with me: one group of instruments after another retires, and what remains, as the work fades on the air, is the high G of a cello, the last word, the last fainting sound, slowly dying in a pianissimo-fermata. Then nothing more: silence and night. But that tone which vibrates in the silence, which is no longer there, to which only the spirit hearkens, and which was the voice of mourning, is so no more. It changes its meaning; it abides as a light in the night.[15]

Like Goethe, Thomas Mann would redeem the living mythic values within the German *Innerlichkeit, Gemeinschaft* and *Maasslosigkeit,* which he sees in Bach's chorales and polyphony, Beethoven's chorus "Alle Menschen werden Brüder," in Faust's vision of a free people on a free soil. But this idea can be revitalized only if corrected by the European-Mediterranean tradition of society, an integration suggested in the unity of Hanno and Kai (*Buddenbrooks*), of Tadzio, Jaschu and Aschenbach (*Death in Venice*), of Castorp and his comrades. Together, they contain the promise in the union between Western freedom of the personality with Eastern equality and fraternity.

Thomas Mann once was fond of referring to Germany as "das Land der Mitte," as a country seeking balance and harmony. In *Germany and the Germans,* he stated that "wicked Germany is merely good Germany gone astray, good Germany in misfortune, in guilt and ruin." As in the case of Goethe, Mann's treatment of the Germanic myth is at once a warning against its diabolism and a tribute to its genius.

NOTES

1. Mann's entire work is oriented towards the mythic, the Joseph cycle and *Doctor Faustus* specifically treating mythic heroes and *The Beloved Returns* viewing Goethe as a mythic prototype of the genius. Mann has also devoted considerable critical discussion to the myth problem, especially in "Freud and the Future," "Goethe's Faust," "Richard Wagner and the Ring," "Voyage with Don Quixote" (all in *Essays of Three Decades* [New York, 1947]), *Pariser Rechenschaft* (Berlin, 1926), pp. 60 ff., *Nietzsche's Philosophy in the Light of Contemporary Events* (Washington, 1947), *The Theme of the Joseph Novels* (Washington, 1942), *Germany and the Germans* (Address delivered before the Library of Congress, May 29, 1941), and in his correspondence with Carl Kerenyi, (Carl Kerenyi, *Romandichtung und Mythologie. Ein Briefwechsel mit Thomas Mann,* Rhein Verlag [Zürich, 1945]).
2. I am restricting myself here to an analysis of *The Magic Mountain* and *Doctor Faustus.* The myth of Joseph is treated in my studies, *Thomas Mann's Joseph*

324

Story. An Interpretation (New York, 1938) and *No Voice is Wholly Lost.*

3. *The Magic Mountain* (New York, 1938). All subsequent references are to this edition.

4. Settembrini approximates the role of Faust's Mephistopheles: Both are critics of German idealism; for both, action is an absolute value. Following Settembrini's lecture on Western freedom, Castorp feels encouraged to approach Clavdia!

5. The inadequacy of Settembrini and Naphta as guides also appears in their apparent sexlessness, with Settembrini managing mild flirtations. Behrens also sublimates the loss of his wife by practicing medicine on the spot where she died and by his amateur paintings. Settembrini refers to him as Minos and Rhadamanthus. Minos is the judge in Dante's Second Circle of Hell who scrutinizes each sin, and "sees what place Hell holds for it fittest stall"; Rhadamanthus is the Judge in Virgil's Hell bringing to light crimes done in life which the perpetrator vainly thought were hidden (*Aeneid*, Book VI).

6. The number three is constantly associated with Peeperkorn. We should also note Mann's use of the number seven, representing a psychic-biologic cycle. Cf. the chapter on *The Magic Mountain* in my *Three Ways of Modern Man*, and the section on "The Seven Myth" in J. M. Robertson's *Christianity and Mythology* (London, 1936). For the sexual connotations of threefoldness and fourfoldness, see C. G. Jung and C. Kerenyi: *Essays on a Science of Mythology*, pp. 20 ff.

7. The linden tree belongs to the tradition of the German village, town and castle. Here, the elders held their counsels, the community gathered to hear sermons. In Goethe's *Faust*, the peasants gather under it ("Before the City Gate") and the home of Philemon and Baucis is identified by the old lindens.

8. Mann deliberately creates situations which are analogous to Goethe's *Faust*, at times employing actual quotations out of the poem. Both begin by turning against their tradition, and both end with war, and the theme of love and peace. Clavdia is Gretchen become dissolute in the twentieth century.

9. As Castorp's Walpurgis-Night corresponds to Faust's Witches' Kitchen and his German Walpurgis-Night, so the first part of his dream in snow approximates Faust's Classical Walpurgis-Night. In Goethe, Faust seeks Helena in a dreamlike state; in Mann, Castorp dreams of the harmony of classical culture. Faust's quest for Helena is followed by war and the Philemon-Baucis sacrifice; in the second part of his dream, Castorp sees the blood sacrifice foreshadowing the war which breaks out at the end of the novel.

10. "Dr. Fausti Weheklag," *Archiv fur Philosophie*, 3/1. See also the chapter on Doctor Faustus in Fritz Kaufmann's *Thomas Mann* (Boston, 1957).

11. *Germany and the Germans*, pp. 5, 6.

12. Mann's novel follows the Faust version of 1587, at times employing its precise wording, such as the formulation of the pact and Faustus' final speech. See my essay, "The Devil of Many Faces," *12th Street*, The New School for Social Research (Summer, 1949).

325

13. Adrian's Esmeralda episode corresponds to Faust's "Witches' Kitchen," where he hopes to be rejuvenated.

14. The woman has the features of his mother and the child Echo (the son of his sister), becomes his child by symbolic incest.

15. *Doctor Faustus* (New York, 1948). In his essay *Freud and the Future*, Mann speaks of Nietzsche's understanding of disease "as an instrument of knowledge." Nietzsche "well knew what he owed to his morbid state, and on every page he seems to instruct us that there is no deeper knowledge without experience of disease, and that all heightened healthiness must be achieved by the route of illness." Mann's description of Adrian's disease bears striking similarity to his account of Dostoyevsky's epilepsy (*The Short Novels of Dostoevsky with an Introduction by Thomas Mann* [New York, 1945]). He writes that Dostoyevsky's epilepsy entailed "the incomparable sense of rapture . . . and the state of horrible depression . . . that follows it." It was also similar to Nietsche's disease: "A typical symptom of paralysis, presumably due to hyperenia of the affected cerebral parts. . . . Before it clouds its victim's mind and kills him, the disease grants him illusory (in the sense of sane normality) experiences of power and sovereign facility, of enlightenment and blissful inspiration." In his address on *Nietzsche's Philosophy in the Light of Contemporary Events*, Mann speaks of "the susceptibility of the saint to sin," and notes that Nietzsche's illness "was intertwined and connected with his genius, that the latter unfolded with it."

Conclusion

AT THIS HISTORIC MOMENT, mythopoesis leads a precarious existence. The effort to communicate across national and cultural boundaries, to sound the theme of the human condition is in danger of being lamed by a thermonuclear Golem which our age has fashioned. With the discovery and application of nuclear fission, Robert Oppenheimer once declared, physicists had come to know "sin."[1] This sin carries the seeds for generating hosts of "Doctor Strangeloves" in the Pentagons of the world, foreboding a Spenglerian "Untergang" for all life everywhere. The spectre of the Damocles Bomb gives one the feeling that the notion of permanence, of a meaningful human journey and destiny is irrelevant. Some retreat into existential apartness or, like Nietzsche, see homelessness as a home. Some settle by paying homage to the faceless computer and pragmatic operationalism. Others embrace the Methistophelian moment or, like Arnold Toynbee, somehow place hope in a miraculous "Transformation." (See Appendix VII.)

In the nineteenth century, Karl Marx had argued that industrial capitalism gives primacy to the fetichism of commodities and Emerson complained that "things ride mankind." In our century, Franz Kafka symbolized and allegorized the *human* inefficiency of mechanical "efficiency."

Kafka wrote before automation developed the hydrogen and neutron bomb. The bomb introduced a new Moloch of archaic nature, perhaps unknowable and uncontrollable, threatening a Nirvana of universal death. Individual or even collective responsibility for such a cosmic Armageddon is reduced to insignificance: It needs but one finger pressing a button thousands of miles away.

The incalculable power of this monster has not only caught us up in a mechanical reflex reaction, but has also brought an uncanny fascination for the sudden, violent death which is its promise—the terrifying theme in the film *Doctor Strangelove*.

Current preoccupation with Thanatos has its counterpart in the ob-

327

session with an explosive "Eros", set to a "rock and roll" pace—a contemporary version of the Bacchantes. This tendency to "live it up" alternates with and results in a "living it down." The contemporary Eros assumes a Thanatos dress or, one could say that the Thanatos drive takes the form of a frenzied narcissistic Eros.[2]

In the arts, this situation has brought forth what Ihab Hassan calls "The Literature of Silence."[3] We have the vogue of Zen which, as one of its spokesmen puts it, offers a philosophy without words. Norman O. Brown's recent book calls language "the fall," and silence "the mother tongue."[4] For Marshall McLuhan, the logical step after electric computers which need no words would be to bypass language.

The difficulty in achieving desired communication has also given rise to "self-expression," now being practiced by some of our distinguished literary critics. In much of our art and literature, this "self" skips over traditional syntax and grammar, comes close to pre-verbal expression of private "oceanic" feelings. In many of our novels and dramas, we have the non-or anti-hero in a state of psychological paralysis. We are presented, not with individualized characters, but with anonymous figures who, like "Dumbwaiters," passively await being acted upon. In plays, such as those of Harold Pinter, Jean Genet, Eugene Ionesco Samuel Beckett and Edward Albee, dramatic dialogue is replaced by spasmodic utterances, jerky pronouncements and "profound" pauses. Plot consists of unrelated scenes and "the absurd" is raised to a first principle.

In classical literature, in Shakespeare and even in Chekhov, silence does have a communicative function, and sometimes "speaks" with awesome effect. One thinks of the lapidary words, spoken by Hamlet at the end: "The rest is silence," of Christ's dramatically eloquent silence in Ivan's Poem of The Grand Inquisitor, of Mynheer Peeperkorn's unheard "speech" by the roaring waterfall which holds those about him spell-bound.

Now, literature which has some artistic form, always says "yes." And, the contemporary voices of silence or of Dionysiac rage are also crying out *for* something— for the restoration of what makes man human. Even as its vocabulary is reminiscent of primitive mythology, it is saying, as does the little man in *Rhinoceros*: I refuse to capitulate. This literature is a protest against our Babylonic chaos and computerized happy ending, and it is saying that when the canons roar, we can make ourselves heard only by whispering or stammering.

Indeed, there are creative impulses here even when they take the form of Beatniks and Hippies and of psychedelic art. What they are saying is that the creatively new can come only if we bypass or break through the miasma of our institutionalized processes. They are saying, with Peer Gynt, that we must go "round" the Behemoths of the Establishment. They are saying that, if we are not to be ensnared by the chimera of a linear progress or be sucked in by the whirlpool of circular motion, we must go "underground." And there is imagination and poetry in the cinematic world created by the Bergmanns, the Antonionis and the Lelouchs.

Earlier, James Joyce sounded this need to penetrate the catacombs of language and customs to catch the sound of the elemental. Freud, too, had argued for this strategy, taking as a motto to his *Interpretation of Dreams* the line from Virgil's *Aeneid*: "Flectere, si nequeo superos, Acheronta movebo" (If I cannot bend the Higher Powers, I will move the Infernal Regions.).

The Ghost's words "Remember me" echo throughout Hamlet's journey, and we noted that in Greek mythology, Memory was the Mother of the Muses. One such memory issues from the Chthonic realm and it contains the springs of inspiration and creative vision. And, there is another which reminds us that, in the beginning, was the Word, the *Logos* and the Act, that is, the necessary condition for order, reason and harmony. Together, they remind us that man is the desiring and wishing, as well as the speaking, thinking and symbolical animal.

Nietzsche noted that the more a tree grows towards the sun, the deeper do its roots reach into the earth. And Freud reminded us that the Latin *altus* means both "high" and "low." The mythopoeic prototypes examined in this study move in a synergic rhythm between the dark pits and the sun-lit heights. To reach upwards, they lie on the heap of ashes with Job, stand on the Crossroads with Oedipus and Dante, go down into the Caves of the Mothers with Don Quixote and Faust, expose themselves to the ravages of primitive sensualism with Mitya Karamazov and the oceanic terrors with Captain Ahab, traverse the lonely regions with Joseph and Adrian Leverkühn. Transfiguration calls for going *through* the rites of passage—the recurrent motif in mythology and mythopoesis.

Much as we may place our faith in the continuity between the past and the present, and great as is the promise contained in our mythopoeic chain, we cannot rely on its power alone to meet the contemporary juggernaut which is threatening to burn up the fruits of Demeter. This is the awareness of our distinguished writers—Nexö, Gide, Camus, Malraux, Thomas Mann, and among our poets, Robert Lowell. They have urged that artists and writers cannot rest with symbolic depiction, but need to become involved in the social demands of the hour by the act as well as the word. Their voices are the counterpoints to the entropic currents of the day. Theirs is the quest for a re-creation of the human heritage towards an approximation of a world of unity in dynamic interplay. As a whole, mythopoesis from the Book of Job to Mann's Joseph story helps keep alive the memory of man's genius and nobility.

This quest depends on favorable social and historic conditions. And hence, the task of cleansing the Augean stables of society is never-ending. In this process, the hero is forever mangled and the inevitable sacrifice places mythopoesis on a tragic plane.

The present contains the possibility of approximating the Third Act of mythopoesis, the integration of fraternity and freedom. The first is in the center of Eastern, the second of Western mythopoesis. The living myth depends on the coalescence of equality and excellence, directed towards One World—the *Grundbass* of mythopoesis. It will not eliminate tragedy. Yet, it could transpose our trials into the plane where they arise, not from avoidable historic pressures, but from the nature of things and of man. It can temper tragedy by mobilizing our powers towards fulfilling ourselves within human limits.

NOTES

1. Cf. Jerome D. Frank, *Society and Survival. Psychological Aspects of War and Peace* (New York, 1967).
2. Cf. my article "Eros and the Trauma of Death," *American Imago*, Vol. XXI, Nos. 3-4 (1964).
3. Ihab Hassan, *The Literature of Silence* (New York, 1967). Hassan sees in its negation of art a necessary condition for an apocalyptic rebirth of art.
4. Norman O. Brown, *Love's Body* (New York, 1966).

Appendices

I. Primitive and Oriental Mythology

PRIMITIVE MYTHOLOGY

MODERN ANTHROPOLOGISTS recognize that primitive life was not devoid of individualistic expression. Still, in the food-gathering stage, land was held in common; tilling of the soil, fishing, and hunting were carried on by the group. The organization of primitive life approximated a large scale family in which men and gods, the animal and vegetable kingdom, as well as the elements, formed what Levy-Bruhl calls a "mist of unity."[1] This sense of belonging was organized by myth and its rituals. Ancestor worship and other rites supported the feeling of the individual that he was, first of all, part of his tribe or clan, that his function was to play *a* role, not *the* role.[2]

It is now established that in primitive culture the myth was not a Romantic hypothesis, but operated as a living principle. The research of scholars, from Frazer, Malinowski and Paul Radin to G. Thomson, Henri Frankfort and Margaret Mead, shows that, while the origin of myth is emotional, its function is practical. The point is summed up by Bronislaw Malinowski. His *Myth in Primitive Psychology* (New York, 1926) states that myth is not

> an idle rhapsody, not an aimless outpouring of vain imaginings, but a hardworking, extremely important cultural force . . . not merely a story told, but a reality lived.

In his studies of a typical Melanesian culture, Malinowski found that its myth was not a symbolic fiction, historical speculation, or mere amusement, but "a warrant, a charter, and often even a practical guide to the activities with which it is connected." Myth is regarded as sacred, expressing and justifying belief and action. It serves as a precedent which determines and shapes the practical day-by-day life and the fate of mankind. For the primitive, the myth is an

> everpresent, live actuality . . . a statement of a bigger reality still practically alive . . . in that its precedent, its law, its moral still rule the social life of the natives . . . a vital ingredient of human civilization.[3]

For the primitive, the myth shaped work, ritual and play into a single whole.

The Seasonal Ritual

Primitive man depended for his existence on the elements and the seasonal changes. He felt them to be divine powers which spelled drought or deluge, an arid or fertile soil—that is, death or life. They were not regarded as automatic events, but had to be adjured by elaborate ceremonies. The seasonal rituals were at once commemorations of what had happened and incantations that they happen again. The succession of the seasons represented a *crisis,* and the entire community was engaged to meet this crisis by rituals of propitiation.[4] The promise that such propitiation would be successful rested on the feeling that man stood in a *familial* relation to these powers. The primitive anthropomorphized the elements and the seasons, thinking of them as fathers, mothers and siblings.[5]

Of the four elements, the Earth was generally regarded as the Great Mother who gave birth to man, to whom he returned and from whom the cycle of birth began once more. Water often shared equal prominence as the source of creation and invigoration. It too was often a mother figure, standing for the mother-breast and cradle.[6] In some Hindu hymns, the waters gave birth to gods who were conceived as mothers or young wives. The Egyptian God Atum arose from the primeval waters, begot the first pair of gods and began the creation of the world. In Greek mythology, the River Ocean was the all-enveloping source of existence, and the philosopher Thales raised water to a primary substance. This idea was revived by the nineteenth century Romantic nature-philosopher Oken who declared that everything living came from the sea.[7]

In contrast to the passive nature of earth and water, fire was conceived as dynamic. In his chapter on "The Interpretation of the Fire-Festivals," (*The Golden Bough,* I [New York, 1929] 641 ff.), Frazer speaks of fire as a productive and reproductive energy. Hence, the widespread custom of kindling great bonfires and of processions with blazing torches. The ambivalent function of fire is particularly stressed in mythopoesis.[8]

Myth, Ritual and Initiation

Anthropologists and ethnologists are agreed that myth and ritual are intimately related.[9] In the case of primitive tribes who have no developed mythology, ritual ceremonies are the only means whereby we can study their mythic attitudes.

Modern pragmatism tends to belittle the function of ritual. But John Dewey's statement that rites are mere "embroidery," actions performed for fun, applies to ceremonies in our own era in which myth often degenerates into mimicry. However, when the myth is alive, rites are expressions by which man tries to secure and adapt to his world and in which the individual finds collective identification. Ritual performance is the group's formalized dramatization of an emotional state. And, through the identical repetition of the ceremony, a past event is commemorated as a permanent "It is."[10] Primitive initiation rituals had a more specific function. They were the way by which the individual moved into adulthood and the candidate gained magical control over the crops and over the welfare of the community.[11]

ORIENTAL MYTHOLOGY

The mythology of the primitive stemmed from his cooperative organization. On the other hand, that of the Oriental Kingdoms—around 3000 B.C.—derived from a hierarchical structure, dominated by a priestly caste. Beginning with the monarchic eras in the second half of the Iron Age, "ideology" enters, and the function of mythology was to preserve the social divisions among the king, the priest and the slave. The rulers were invested with *mana*-power, and existing power-relations were mythicized into sacred institutions. History was immobilized and fixed to the past, becoming a kind of eternal spatial present.[12]

In the *Poetics*, Aristotle stated that the ancient religious myths did not acquire *meaning* until Greek tragedy endowed them with form and structure by means of a unified plot and a "single action." The Hindu *Vedas*, epics, the Egyptian *Book of the Dead*, the Persian *Zend-Avesta* are the products of multiple authors, resulting in amorphous overgrowths of legends, maxims, liturgy and ritual. The Oriental Kingdoms did not produce mythopoesis, such as the Book of Job or *Prometheus* because their social structure did not sanction a rebellious hero. Except for Babylon, their mythology taught that things were to be brought back to the beginning. This ideal was symbolized in the Egyptian myth of the Phoenix who rearises in the identical form of its previous existence, in the Hindu notion of the Four Ages which begin and end with "Nirvana," and in Confucius' ancestor cult. Only in the relatively democratic conception of kingship in Babylon do we get an approximation of the mythopoeic hero in Marduk and Gilgamesh.

Egypt: The Permanence of Osiris

The center of the Egyptian myth was the idea of spatial permanence, with the annual rise and fall of the Nile serving as a paradigm for the eternal static order of things.

This idea shaped Egyptian art and religion. The geometric forms of its sculpture, pyramids, graves and embalmings expressed the lastingness of bodily existence, with the dead celebrated as forever alive. (Breasted notes that the word "death" does not occur in the Pyramid texts, except when referring to the enemy.) Egyptian wordly immanence stood in contrast to Hindu spiritual otherworldliness; its static optimism differentiated it from the sense of conflict and crisis in Mesopotamian and from the temporal futurism of Persian and Hebrew mythology.

At the head of the Egyptian hierarchy stood Amon-Re, who, Phoenix like, was "the half-begotten youth." Amon-Re was the sun-god who created dry land within the primeval waters and whose regular solar movements assured eternal order, justice, victory and immortality. Rebellion against his divine status, such as that by Hathor and Isis, constituted violation of the heavenly order.

This constellation was transposed into the myth of Osiris. The son of Nut (the sky) and of Geb (the earth), Osiris was the God of the Nile and of the grain. He was the dead ruler who was ever alive. Frankfort states that the vitality of the earth was one of the manifestations of Osiris. He dies when the Nile recedes and is "found" when the waters begin to rise and fertility returns.[13] The Osiris myth also introduced the motifs of patricide and incest: In some versions, Osiris castrated his father Sebk and is in turn killed or castrated by his brother, Seth, who throws the pieces of his corpse into the Nile. Isis, his sister-wife, retrieves the body, and, with Osiris' resurrection, nature and vegetation revive.

The oedipal theme appears in a thinly disguised form in the folklore version of the Egyptian *Two Brothers*. Bitiou is tempted by Anoupu, the wife of his older brother. Bitiou rejects her, saying that she and his brother are like mother and father to him. When she tells her husband that his brother had attempted to attack her, Bitiou castrates himself to prove his innocence. We have here an early form of mythic decomposition in which the father and mother appear in the guise of other figures.[14]

Hindu Mythology: From Maya to Nirvana

Of Oriental mythology, the Hindu is most "Eastern" in its derogation of action, individuality and striving, which are viewed as belonging to the illusory world of "Maya."[15] According to the *Gita*, only he attains peace "who lives devoid of longing, abandoning all craving, without the sense of 'I' and 'mine'."[16] Where Egyptian mythology stressed the prolongation of life in death, where the Confucian saw value in practical ethical acts, and the Iranian saw promise in the future, Hindu mythology held that the world of time and activity was chimerical and that the goal was withdrawal from the world.

In Hindu mythology, the world began with "nothing," and the aim was to return to "nothing" or "Nirvana." Between the two lies the three-fold cause of suffering: "thirst for existence, thirst for prosperity, thirst for pleasure." The Four Ages start with the Golden Age of Krta of which the Creation Hymn in the *Rig-Veda* says:

> Then was non-existent, nor existent . . .
> Death was not then, nor was there aught immortal . . .
> That one Thing, breathless, breathed by its own nature:
> apart from it was nothing whatsoever. . . . (X, 129)

Desire, individualism and action arise in the Ages of Treta and Dvapara, when virtue declines and ceremonials increase. In the Fourth Age of Kali, religion disappears, castes become confused, leading to universal destruction by fire and flood. This is followed by rebirth into the original Golden Age where the wheel of time is broken, its stream flows no longer and suffering comes to an end.[17] Here, action, history, striving are of no avail, in that the new Age is identical with the old.

Vishnu represents the creative principle of Brahma and battles against man's ancient adversary, the ten-headed evil spirit Ravana.[18] One of Vishnu's incarnations is Krishna, whose story follows the lines of the Rankian hero: King Kamsa orders all of his nephews killed after he is warned by a voice from heaven that one of them would put him to death. But Krishna is saved and reared by a shepherd in a cave. Later, he kills his uncle Kamsa, becomes king and clears the land of monsters.[19]

Krishna plays a decisive role in the *Mahabharata*. It tells of the war between the Kurava Brothers, who represent the evil principle, and their cousins, the Pandava Brothers, who stand for the good principle. The conflict is brought on when the old, blind Kurava king chooses a Pandava to be monarch, regarding him as superior to his own nephews. In this war, Prince Krishna sides with the Pandavas.[20] However, in the *Bhagavat Gita* Krishna tells one of the Pandava warriors that it was his *duty* to fight for his caste, even if that meant fighting against one's own cousins. The *Gita* thus contributed towards support of the Hindu caste system. On the other hand, it combated the derogation of worldly life, declaring that if one did his caste-duty, one could be saved and enjoy life. In Hindu mythology as a whole, reincarnation higher up was not possible for "outcasts," except for those who were *good* slaves. Later, Buddha (563-483 B.C.) attempted to counteract some of these elements, preaching the Middle Path and the avoidance of all extremes, both those of pleasure and of fleshly mortification. And he was unsympathetic to the caste-system. But is was his challenge to the ancient Indian social system which was successfully met and ritualized in the *Gita*.

336

Babylon: Legends of Marduk and Gilgamesh

Henri Frankfort distinguishes between the relative serenity of the Egyptian festivals and those of Mesopotamia which were never free of anxiety. He connects this phenomenon with the contrast between the protected isolation of the rich Nile valley and the exposed position of Mesopotamia, which was "periodically robbed and disrupted by the mountaineers on its east or the nomads on its west." He further contrasts the never-failing rise of the Nile with Mesopotamia's uncertain rainfall and its unaccountable, turbulent Tigris. Frankfort also relates these factors to the aristocratic conception of kingship in Egypt and the democratic in Mesopotamia. Thorkild Jacobsen's studies established that the oldest political institution in Mesopotamia showed traces of "primitive democracy," harking back to an age which knew no kings. The Mesopotamian king was not a god, as was the Pharaoh, but a member of the community. Even the gods Anu and Enlil made decisions only after a general council.

This social situation is the basis for the Babylonian myth of Creation and the Gilgamesh epic which approximate Western mythopoesis in which the hero's unrest and rebellion are legitimized. Marduk successfully turns against his parental authority; Gilgamesh dares reject the goddess Ishtar, and he would find the plant through which man might become immortal.

The Myth of Creation: Tiamat-Marduk

In contrast to the Egyptian myth of a creator who rules the world for all time, the Mesopotamian myth speaks of the world as beginning with chaos and with conflicting authorities. The Babylonian Creation myth (*Enuma Elish*) deals with Tiamat's war against her son Marduk (Tiamat is a prominent example of the "Devouring Mother" in mythology).[21] The oedipal theme is suggested in Marduk's motives for subduing his mother. Marduk sends word to her:

> "Thou hast exalted Kingu to thy spouse . . .
> Thou has followed after evil,
> And against the gods my fathers thou hast contrived
> Thy wicked plan
> Stand! I and thou, let us join in battle."[22]

The Gilgamesh legend (about 2000 B.C.) is the first major story which explicitly sounds the motif of unrest in the hero's quest. When Gilgamesh is about to set out on his mission to kill the monster Khumbaba, his mother prays to the sun-god Shamash:

"Why hast thou for my son Gilgamesh
Provided a heart
Whose stormy unrest findeth no peace?"[23]

The twelve tables tell how Gilgamesh frees the nation from the Elamites, and relates Ishtar's passion for the hero. Attracted by his beauty and achievements, Ishtar, the Babylonian goddess of love and vegetation, proposes marriage. But Gilgamesh declines, for he has heard of the fate which had overcome her previous lovers:

"Which of thy husbands didst thou love forever? . . .
For Tammuz, thy youthful husband, thou causest to weeping every year. . . ."

She appeals to her father, the mighty god Anu, who sends a bull to kill Gilgamesh; but the hero vanquishes the animal.

Ishtar's unrequited love is preceded by the story of the friendship between Gilgamesh and Enkidu. Enkidu eats grass, lives with cattle and seems to be the nature-complement to Gilgamesh. After Enkidu is humanized by contact with a harlot, Enkidu and Gilgamesh become close friends and together they overthrow the tyrant Khumbaba. When Enkidu dies, Gilgamesh descends to the underworld to find his friend.[24]

Langdon, Jack Finegan, Morris Jastrow, Henri Frankfort, Thorkild Jacobsen and others stress the conservative social factors involved in the Babylonian myth of Creation and in the Gilgamesh story. According to Finegan, the "one purpose of the creation epic is to show the prominence of Babylon over all other cities in the country. . . ." And Langdon states that the lesson taught by the Babylonian myths of plants and floods (the "plant of birth") was that kings are appointed by the gods, and are the source of all civilization. In Frankfort's formulation, "man's position in the state of the universe precisely paralleled that of the slave in the human city-state."[25]

NOTE ON CHINESE AND PERSIAN MYTHOLOGY

The central note in ancient Chinese writings is the heavenly origin of tradition which is to be accepted as an unchangeable order, thereby ensuring tranquillity of soul. Confucius regarded himself as a transmitter of the past. His maxim was to honor the spirits of one's ancestors and to "act as though they are ever-present witnesses of thine actions, but seek to know nothing further about them." Yet, the Chinese idea of the past was oriented towards its practical, moral bearing on the present. In this spirit, Confucius' *Analects* placed less emphasis on immortality.

338

It opposed the divinity of the caste system, held that the law was above the state, and that there was no place for priestly castes. However, in the later teachings of Buddhism (which entered China from India about 70 A.D.) and in the Taoism of Lao-tse, the stress is on faith, inactivity and tranquillity, which bring vision of the one immovable order.

Of Oriental mythology, only the Iranian points to a futurism, similar to that in the Hebrew myth. In it, the priestly order is not privileged, and salvation comes not only through god, but also through man. The older polytheism is reduced to the duality of Ormazd, the god of light and clarity, and Ahriman, the god of darkness and evil. At the end, the power of evil is broken.[26] In its humanistic concept of individual morality, Persian mythology forms a bridge to later mythopoesis. Iran also contributed the story of Sohrab and Rustum in the tenth century *Book of Kings* by Firdausi, a version of the Oedipus theme of Greek mythology and the Old High German legend of Hildebrand and Hadubrand.

II.   A Note on the Prometheus of Shelley and Goethe

Milton's Satan is an "Arch-Angel ruined" by his rebellion. Shelley's Prometheus becomes "the Champion." Echoes of Shelley's attitude towards the French Revolution are sounded in Prometheus' initial irreconcilable attitude towards "the Oppressor" Jupiter, whose tyrannical rule marks the end of the Saturnian golden age, brings suffering and strife into the world, "fear and self-contempt and barren hope" to man. Yet, although Shelley's Jupiter does not give up his tyranny, Prometheus renounces his rebellion, wishing "no living thing to suffer pain." Unbound by Hercules, he finds his gentle words "sweeter even than freedom long desired." He dethrones the tyrant by his spirit of love, which augurs the third age of an "unclassed" future when men are free, equal and fraternal:

> And behold, thrones were kingless, and men walked
> One with the other even as spirits do,
> None fawned, none trampled . . .
> The loathsome mask has fallen, the man remains
> Sceptreless, free, uncircumscribed, but man
> Equal, unclassed, tribeless, and nationless,
> Exempt from awe, worship, degree, the king
> Over himself: just, gentle, wise: but man

> Passionless?—no, yet free from guilt or pain,
> Which were, for his will made or suffered them,
> Nor yet exempt, though ruling them like slaves,
> From chance, and death, and mutability.

Shelley's Prometheus moves from absolute intransigence to absolute love, and his scene from absolute disharmony to absolute harmony. This lends the work (apart from the first act) a non-dramatic quality and makes it a lyrical pageant which familiarizes the reader, as Shelley himself put it, "with beautiful idealisms and moral excellence."

Yet, the poem contains traces of Shelley's hidden reservations about his idealized Prometheus. They appear in the charge of the Furies that he has weakened man by awakening desires in him which he can never still:

> Then was kindled within him a thirst which outran
> Those perishing waters; a thirst of fierce fever,
> Hope, love, doubt, desire, which consume him for ever.

These lines sound the Renaissance theme, found in *Hamlet, Faust, Moby Dick, The Brothers Karamazov*, that the very gift of an open, unlimited universe makes for a world in which man is incessantly driven from object to object:.

> The good want power . . .
> The powerful goodness want . . .
> The wise want love and those who love want wisdom;
> And all best things are thus confused to ill.

In contrast to Shelley's drama, Goethe's poem *Prometheus* remains impious to the end. If Shelley's work expresses both the rebellious mood of the French Revolution and its vision of harmony, Goethe's youthful poem is the voice of Germany's *theoretic* revolutionism claiming that he has created and maintained himself and the world—this at a time when the German "shopocracy" was a passive, obedient tool of the German state. The point is developed in the chapter on the Faustian myth.

III.   A Note on Virgil's Aeneid

In the Middle Ages, Virgil was regarded as a Christian poet and Dante makes him his guide in *The Divine Comedy*.

The central motif of *The Aeneid* is Piety. Aeneas' heroism lies in his obedience to the demands of his Roman authority. He is brave, fearless, persistent, but always within the framework of his public duty.

Aeneas falls in love with Dido. He tells her that he would rather stay with her and admits that he was going to Italy, not by his own volition ("Italiam non sponte sequor"), yet he leaves her. Aeneas is essentially "driven" by his duty to Rome, which he conceives as the bearer of the chosen people. *The Aeneid* is the first mythopoesis which apotheosizes a national idea in the guise of an international order.

The overt aim of the epic was to sanction the imperialism of Augustus by a myth of the divine Roman mission. Tribal Troy was to be replaced by an universal empire in peace (Pax Romana), with Aeneas as its prince. But we must note the reservations which are contained in Virgil's art. The poet pictures Aeneas as a man who never questions the mission with which he has been entrusted, and behaves somewhat like an unbending soldier. Virgil begins his epic with the word *arms* (*arma*) and ends it with the word *death* (*ombras*). These terms convey the mood of the poem and suggest Virgil's underlying feeling about the cruel war which was carried on in the interests of Augustus' imperialism.

IV. A Note on Eissler's Goethe

K. R. Eissler's monumental book, *Goethe: A Psychoanalytic Study 1775-1786* (2 vols.; Detroit, 1963), published after this chapter on *Faust* had been written, examines Goethe's life through his Italian journey and discusses *Wilhelm Meister, Iphigenia* and many poems and lesser known works which bear on the decade of Goethe's life centering in his relation to Charlotte von Stein.

Eissler regards Goethe as a genius and as "an ideal type of creativity" (p. 1353). The pivotal thesis of his book is that the necessary condition for such creativity is that the genius may not permit himself fully satisfying object-relationships. He must live under the condition of maximum tension combined with maximum frustration. However, Eissler adds that the creation of great art requires that the ego function remain uninjured even as there is an interplay between the ego and the repressed (p. 1165). His over-all view of Goethe is that he is an example of a "constructive or organizing" disease (p. xxxiii). For a discussion of the relationship between genius psychopathology and creativity, see *American Imago*, Vol. XXIV, Nos. 1-2 [1967].

In his examination of Goethe's biography, Eissler indicates that Goethe was able to circumvent the oedipal relationship to his father, partly by being nearer in years to his mother than she was to her husband. This made possible Goethe's near-identification with his mother.

Eissler sees Cornelia as focal for Goethe's problem. He shows that Goethe was incestuously fixated on his sister. Apart from an early love affair, Goethe could not fall in love so long as Cornelia remained unmarried. Her marriage to Schlosser brought Goethe close to suicide, an impulse partially sublimated in his *Werther*. Goethe's deepest guilt stemmed primarily from his relation to Cornelia. At the same time, this fixation helped save Goethe from a full-blown psychosis and from overt homosexuality (a tendency, evidenced in his relation to Behrisch, Merck, Karl August, Lavater) in that he was able to act out towards her the roles of both mother and father. She provided the condition which drove him from one achievement to another (both real and symbolical).

The most startling, ingenious—and, on the whole, persuasive—of Eissler's contributions to the understanding of Goethe's life-work is his painstakingly worked out thesis that Charlotte von Stein enacted the role of a proto-analyst in relation to Goethe for a crucial decade of his life, 1775-1786 (similar to that which Goethe himself attempted with F. Plessing). To begin with, she came to represent all his past love-objects, including those of the infantile period. She thus acquired "a unique and exclusive position comparable to that of the analyst" (p. 1091). Furthermore, she fulfilled the analyst's function by consistently holding up the reality principle. She made no demands on Goethe in love or marriage, and thus constituted no threat to him in his feeling of identity (p. 183). She stood for duty, adjustment to work, and her refusal to surrender to him helped stem his drive towards heedless acting out. Goethe's attraction to Charlotte is seen as the derivative of his past attachment to Cornelia (both were frigid) and thereby helped him overcome his fear of incest. Acceptance of resignation became the principle of Goethe's relationship to Charlotte. (Discharge of homosexual libido towards the Duke made it less difficult for Goethe to tolerate celibacy with respect to Charlotte.) Eissler believes that the ten years with her "preserved him from a catastrophe that would have severely interfered with his creativity" (p. 683). He also believes that this relationship led to the clinical removal of Goethe's sexual defect (p. 1091), resulting in his ability to have sexual intercourse for the first time in his life while in Rome. Summarily, she influenced him towards a change "from relying predominantly on the primary processes in artistic production to invoking increasingly secondary ones" (p. 1069).

To be sure, Eissler notes the unavoidable limitations in Charlotte's function as Goethe's analyst. In the transference, Charlotte could not become the target for his expression of hostility and aggression. Nor could she help him "dissolve the transference."

Christiane Vulpius, like Charlotte von Stein, is viewed as a sister image, even as Christiane was the antitype of Charlotte. He needed the latter's insistence on sexual renunciation in his pre-Italian period. In the post-Italian phase, Goethe found compensation in enjoying that which Charlotte had disallowed.

Eissler's study is a mine of original, highly stimulating observations (especially in the appendices of Volume II). It is based on most careful and minute consideration of voluminous data which should be the envy of the most scholarly "Goethe-Forscher."

V.   A Note on Mark Twain and Walt Whitman

Melville's *Moby Dick* appeared at a stage in our history when America was still economically and intellectually attached to its European heritage. Writing in a later and industrialized era, Mark Twain, Walt Whitman and Carl Sandburg have sought for a tradition rooted in America's own experience, created more indigenous American figures and situations, expressed in an idiom which is more characteristically American.

Mark Twain rejected the European feudal legacy which took form in Southern slavery with its primitive vendetta and fake chivalry. At the same time, he warred against the industrialism of the North, its gilded values, its splitting up of the personality and its exploitation of man.

Huckleberry Finn continues Melville's theme of the foundling's quest for his sources. Melville's Pacific Ocean becomes the Mississippi river and his primitive international crew is transposed into the American boy. In him, Mark Twain saw America's native qualities of fraternity and cooperation, coupled with the desire for freedom. His heroes are either boys, such as Tom Sawyer and Huck Finn or child-like grown-ups, such as the Negro Jim. All rebel—Tom in a romantic manner, creating an imagined world gleaned out of *Don Quixote*, Huck and Jim in a practical realistic way. Through their fantasy, daring and non-pragmatic outlook, the boys manage to outwit their adult-world. They repudiate the lords of the earth, their counterfeit idealism and their social-economic enslavement. They secede from their parental homes, go on a river journey which becomes their initiation by water.

Yet, Twain's American myth is an idyll, away and apart from the ruling centers of American society. In Huck and Jim, Mark Twain pictures America as a child adrift, without a guide or destination, seeing only omens and portents. They are the hunted and, at times, the haunted children, never reach sex-maturity, and experience no homecoming. This gives point to Twain's later pessimistic determinism where he spoke of the "damned mangy human race." In *The Mysterious Stranger* and *What is Man,* he saw the future in terms of more and bigger wars determined by small cliques leading men like sheep. Still, in Tom Sawyer and Huck Finn, Mark Twain pointed to the American promise in the union between bold imaginative adventurousness and its fraternal friendship.

Walt Whitman attempted to enlarge Mark Twain's brotherhood to encompass all men, races, nations and tongues in what he called an oceanic form. His poem "Great Are The Myths" evinces a child-like interest in and acceptance of everything.

> Great are the myths—I too delight in them;
> Great are Adam and Eve—I too look back and accept them;
> Great the risen and fallen nations, and their poets, women, sagas, inventors,
>   rulers, warriors, and priests . . .
> Great is Youth—equally great is Old Age—great are the Day and Night;
> Great is Wealth—great is Poverty—great is Expression—great is Silence.

Whitman's exuberant delight in life includes its terminus, death, which is viewed as continuous with it and passing over into a new creative existence.

Whitman's ideal goes back to what George Santayana called "the innocent style of Adam, when the animals filed before him one by one and he called each of them by its name." His world is a totalitarian pageant, an indiscriminate classlessness of people and their experiences. This vision of absolute democracy, of identical "leaves of grass," was "the song of the pioneer," who bypassed the complexities and fixities of modern America. Whitman's universe is Melville's world without its hero. In his fear that democracy has been "so retarded and jeopardized by powerful personalities," Whitman thought it necessary "to reduce everything to a dead level." It was his hope that this might be the preparatory stage "for grander individualities than ever."

Mark Twain and Walt Whitman celebrate the American mythic values of fraternity and freedom which Melville spoke of in his "Knights and Squires." In his Preface to the first edition of *Leaves of Grass* (1855),

344

Whitman declared that the genius of the United States is "always most in the common people. . . . Their deathless attachment to freedom . . . their good temper and open-handedness." He felt that differences do not make for classes "any more than one eyesight countervails another." He saw in the average American the virtues of the traditional aristocratic hero:

> The ranges of heroism and loftiness with which Greek and feudal poets endow'd their god-like or lordly born characters—indeed prouder and better based and with fuller ranges than these—I was to endow the democratic averages of America.

Contemporary writers, such as John Steinbeck, Carl Sandburg, Mark VanDoren, Alfred Kreymborg, William Carlos Williams and Benjamin Appel have refined this theme. In Carl Sandburg's lines from *The People, Yes*:

> The People sleep
> Ai! ai! The people sleep
> Yet the sleepers toss in sleep
> And the sleepers wake.
> Ai! ai! The sleepers wake.

VI.   Freud's Analysis of A Katya-Figure in Zweig's Story

In his essay "Dostoyevsky and Parricide" (St. Ed., Vol. XXI [London, 1961]), Freud does not mention Katya. And, he obviously refers to Grushenka when he writes that Mitya's motive of sexual rivalry with his father is openly admitted.

Careful scrutiny discloses, however, that Freud does sense Katya's role in the novel. This appears in Freud's discussion of Stefan Zweig's story "Four-and-Twenty Hours in a Woman's Life," which he includes in his essay on Dostoyevsky. His manifest purpose here is to illuminate Dostoyevsky's gambling mania and its connection with his onanistic burden. But what Freud says about the woman in Zweig's story applies—with allowance for digressive "free association"—to Dostoyevsky's Katya.

In his essay on Freud's "Study of Dostoyevsky," Theodor Reik pays tribute to it, making only some minor criticisms. One of these is that Freud's summary of Zweig's story is "an error in proportion" (*From Thirty Years with Freud* [New York, 1940]). In a letter (cited in Reik's essay), Freud grants "that the parenthetical Zweig analysis disturbs the balance." Yet,—as though Freud felt that this digression *was* somehow relevant—he continues: "If we look deeper, we can probably find what was the purpose for its addition." Freud's discussion is "an error in proportion," if we limit ourselves to his avowed intention. But, as Freud suggests, if we "look deeper," that is, if we examine it for clues to Freud's unconscious "purpose," it is not "parenthetical," but central.

Freud summarizes the Zweig story in the following way:

An elderly lady of distinction tells of an experience she had more than twenty years earlier. "She had been left a widow when still young and is the mother of two sons, who no longer need her." In the gambling rooms of Monte Carlo, into which she wanders aimlessly, she is attracted by the hands of an unlucky gambler, who evidently leaves the gambling rooms in the depths of despair, with the evident intention of ending his hopeless life.

> "An inexplicable feeling of sympathy compels her to follow him and make every effort to save him . . . she . . . finds herself obliged, in the most natural way possible, to join him in his apartment at the hotel, and finally to share his bed. She "exacts a most solemn vow from the young man . . . that he will never play again, provides him with money for his journey home . . . is ready to sacrifice all she has in order to keep him." But instead, "the faithless youth had gone back to his play. She reminds him of his promise, but, obsessed by his passion, he calls her a spoil-sport, tells her to go and flings back the money with which she had tried to rescue him. She hurries away in deep mortification and learns later that she has not succeeded in saving him from suicide." ("Dostoyevsky and Parricide," p. 192)

Transposed into the relationship between Katya and Dmitry:

Katya's father dies while she is still young. She tries to be a mother to two of Fyodor's sons, Mitya and Ivan. Katya learns that Mitya has been leading a "gambling" life and that he is in despair. After the death of her father (who is analogous to the woman's husband in the Zweig account), she comes to Mitya's room. She does not share his bed, except in Mitya's phantasy and perhaps also in her own. Katya attaches herself to him, gets his promise to reform and gives him money, expressing her readiness to sacrifice everything to save him. But, here too, the hero surmises the woman's actual motivation and goes back to his "play." He is now seized with the obsession to return the money to her, who would interfere with his gambling life. At the end, Katya learns that she did not succeed in saving Mitya.

In the course of his analysis of Zweig's story, Freud writes:

> The equation of the mother with the prostitute, which is made by the young man in the story . . . brings the unattainable within easy reach. The bad

346

conscience which accompanies the phantasy brings about the unhappy ending. (pp. 193)

The woman wants to save the young man's soul. But this is a disguised facade. To be sure,

> faithful to the memory of her husband, she has armed herself against all similar attractions; but—and here the son's fantasy is right—she did not, as a mother, escape her quite unconscious transference of love on to her son, and fate was able to catch her at this undefended spot. (pp. 193-194)

Earlier, Freud speaks of

> "Dostoevski's burden of guilt" which "had taken a tangible shape as a burden of debt, and he was able to take refuge behind the pretext that he was trying by his winnings at the tables to make it possible for him to return to Russia without being arrested by his creditors." (p. 190)

Most of this applies to Mitya's relation to Katya.[1]

Freud's Martha and the Matriarchy

The question arises: How to explain Freud's omission of a central figure in the oedipal situation? A thorough answer would entail a detailed analysis of Freud's life and work. But perhaps some light may be thrown on this problem by considering briefly one element in Freud's life.

As is well known, Freud's oedipal scheme centers in the patriarchal cycle of human history. It has little to say about the matriarchy beyond noting that "the maternal inheritance is older than the paternal one" (Footnote to "The Savage's Dread of Incest" in *Totem and Taboo*). In his essay, "The Heart of Freud" (Haldeman-Julius Publications, 1951), A. Bronson Feldman suggests that this may be connected with the fact that in his own life, Freud "had never experienced a mother's dictatorship." In his biography of Freud, Ernest Jones speaks of Freud's mother as "indulgent." Where "the father stood for the reality principle," Jones states, the mother stood for "the pleasure principle" (p.7). Freud's conception of what women and mothers are or should be corresponds roughly to the nineteenth century German conception: the soft, giving, noncompetitive figure.[2] He writes to his wife:

> Nature has determined woman's destiny through beauty, charm, and sweetness. Law and custom have much to give women that has been withheld from them, but the position of women will surely be what it is: in youth an adoring darling and in mature years a loved wife. (Jones, p. 176).

Ironically enough, we learn from Jones' account that Freud did experience some measure of a "mother's" dictatorship. The most prominent women in Freud's life were, aside from his mother (about whom Jones gives very little), Martha Bernays, who became his wife, and her mother. Martha's mother was the head of the family and, according to Jones, Freud found in her "too masculine an attitude." Freud himself says of her that she "exacts admiration" (Jones, p.116). Freud had some bitter quarrels with this strong-willed woman and even threatened to break with Martha unless she defied her mother. Later, however, Freud got on quite good terms with the mother.

Now, Freud wanted to think that Martha was not like her mother. "If, for instance," he writes to his wife

> I imagined my gentle sweet girl as a competitor it would only end in my telling her, as I did seventeen months ago, that I am fond of her and that I implore her to withdraw from the strife into the calm uncompetitive activity of my home (Jones, p. 176).

And again: "I seek similarities with you (and her mother), but hardly find any." (Jones, p. 116).

"Hardly any," yet some. For, referring to a photograph Martha sent him, Freud sees in her face "an almost masculine expression, so unmaidenly in its decisiveness." Jones adds that Freud was painfully to discover that "she was not at heart docile and she had a firmness of character that did not readily lend itself to being molded" (p. 102).

Actually, Freud's courtship was no simple idyll. There were years of separation; passion alternated with resentment and with torturing doubts about Martha's love for him of which Freud needed repeated reassurance. It, too, was at first a "secret" relationship, jeopardized by the displeasure of Martha's family. In his first letter to her, shortly before their betrothal, Freud would assure her "of a relationship which perhaps will have for long to be veiled in secrecy.—How much I venture in writing that!" (Jones. p.106). Only once did Freud allow himself to express some public resentment against his fiancée. This happened in connection with the Cocaine Episode in which Freud held her indirectly responsible for the delay in publishing his manuscript on cocaine. In his Autobiography, Freud would explain

> how it was the fault of my fiancée that I was not already famous at that early age . . . but I bore my fiancée no grudge for her interruption of my work.

Jones comments that Freud's excuse is "somewhat disingenuous," that "it does not tally very closely with the facts," and that it "must cover a deeper explanation" (p.79).

According to Jones, Freud thought of Martha as a truly noble character in whose presence one could not have a mean or common thought. He refers to Freud's feeling of being in "debt" to Martha:

> When he said he would be in her debt when he died he had more than one reason for his gratitude. She protected him from any kind of meanness, and he would do nothing improper or unworthy even in order to gain her in marriage (p. 125).

This feeling of "debt" should be considered along with what Jones calls Freud's "great dislike of helplessness and his love of independence." Yet, Jones observes that "in all major personal issues," Martha "proved stronger than Freud and held her ground." He speaks of "a remarkable concealment in Freud's love life," and that in his relation to Martha, Freud "often needed to express some hardness or adverse criticism before he could trust himself to release his feelings of affection" (pp. 129, 122, 124).[3]

However, Martha was not only "masculine." Jones notes that "Martha's tact and sweetness," again and again, "succeeded in smoothing things over." Thus, it was possible for Freud to see in Martha that which he wanted: "the gentle sweet girl." But the competitive, "masculine" strain was there, in Martha and more so, in her mother. It constituted a threat to Freud's ideal conception of woman, and he tried to keep it out of his sight. Here may be one of the roots for his failure to appreciate the historic function of the matriarchy. And here may be the explanation why Freud did not consciously recognize Katya's dominating personality as a mother-figure.

VII. Conclusion:
Related Philosophic Attitudes

Analogous to this outlook are those approaches which renounce the quest for certainty and for a firm tradition. Here belong the philosophies of Hans Reichenbach and John Dewey, of Logical Positivism and Existentialism, as well as Spengler's and Toynbee's philosophy of history.

In Hans Reichenbach's *Rise of Scientific Philosophy* (Berkeley and Los Angeles, 1951), the new scientific philosophy does not look to the past. "The glorification of the philosophy of the past . . . has undermined the philosophic potency of the present generation." (p. 325) Similarly, for John Dewey, "consequences, not antecedents, supply meaning and truth. . . . Change rather than fixity is now a measure of reality," and "the only *ultimate* result is the result that is attained today, tomorrow, the next day, and day after next." In this view, the world is open at both ends, firm principles are dissolved into liquid operations, and tradition becomes the ashcan of history. Morris Raphael Cohen (*American Thought* [Glencoe, Ill., 1954]) has characterized this approach as one in which one is concerned with being on the go.

> We in America are especially in need of realizing that perpetual motion is not the blessed life and that the hustlers may not be the only ones, nor perhaps even the first, to enter the kingdom of heaven. (p. 301)

The philosophies of history which correspond to this temper are the spherical *Untergang* of Oswald Spengler, the linear "shipwreck" of the existentialists, and with a mixture of both, Arnold Toynbee's "Transformation."

Spengler's philosophy may be termed the cartel-view of history in which the "Faustian" cartel is the final phrase. Existentialism counters by what may be termed the free enterprise view of history. Both are based on the idea of self-creation—the various autonomous cultures in the one and the undetermined individual in the other. In neither, is there a reference to a derived tradition, and hence, neither can find a basis for a recreated tradition.

Toynbee rejects Spengler's biologic analogy of final disintegration, Henry Adam's law of entropy, as well as the existentialist picture of man doomed to the free and useless Sisyphus labor. He would replace them with his theory of the anthropological process of growth issuing from successful response.

In the section "The Mythological Clue," in *A Study of History*, Toynbee makes the point that physical science by itself cannot explain the genesis of civilization and suggests that the language of mythology offers an alternative clue. The story begins with what he calls a perfect state of Yin. It is followed by "an adversary," who instils

> distress or discontent or fear or antipathy. This is the role of the Serpent in Genesis, of Satan in the Book of Job, of Mephistopheles in *Faust*, of Loki in the Scandinavian mythology, of the Divine Lovers in the Virgin myths. (p. 63)

The Yin-state passes over into Yang-activity or the "withdrawal" of the individual which makes it possible for him to realize his powers which might otherwise remain dormant.

The elemental rhythm in the alternating beat of Yin and Yang is "Victory by defeat, creation by destruction, birth by death." This movement is not vain repetition, for the Wheel of Existence is not just a devilish engine for inflicting everlasting torment on a damned Ixion. On this showing the music that the rhythm of Yin and Yang beats out is the song of creation. (p. 557)

Toynbee assigns the highest place in this process to the idea of the second coming of the historical Christ. Here, as in Dante, the symbolic nature of the mythic journey is fixed to a particular historical occurrence.

Toynbee does see the possibilities of growth for the personality. Here, growth depends on the hero having no organic tie with the social mass which is capable only of imitating the heroic person. Toynbee thinks that "the growths of civilizations are the work of creative individuals or creative minorities. . . . The superior personalities, geniuses, mystics or supermen. . . ." Ordinary humanity is the common clay which can learn something from the action of the genius through a mechanical social imitation.

It has been pointed out that on the basis of this sharp separation, Toynbee cannot account for the culture myth and epic in which the hero identifies himself with the higher levels of his social group. Toynbee states that our civilization need not die, provided "we have the grace to kindle the divine spark of creative power." This can come about if we reject "archaism" and "futurism" and adopt an Oriental "detachment" from wordly affairs. This is the method of "Transfiguration" which would produce the "Universal Church." As in the case of existentialism, the free creative act appears to spring full-headed from a miraculous agency. Both attempt to counteract the effects of the technological and political machine in which the gadget and the committee would replace the cult of the personality.

NOTES
APPENDIX I

1. In its earliest forms, there were no rulers or ruled, only the leadership of the most able, and relations were expressed in terms of kinship, not territory or possession. Whether the mode of reckoning kinship was patrilineal, matrilineal or bilateral, each sex contributed its respective share. In this stage, Frazer writes, "the world is viewed as a great democracy." To be sure, this was a limited democracy. The primitive had no concept of universal humanity and, with the growing scarcity of fishing and hunting grounds, conflicts developed among different tribes. This situation probably contributed to the rise of taboos and prohibitions, such as endogamy, incest and patricide. See the perceptive study by Joseph Campbell, *Masks of God: Primitive Mythology* (New York, 1959).

2. According to Elsdon Best (cited by Ernst Cassirer), when a primitive says "I defeated the enemy," the "I" may mean his tribe many generations earlier.

351

3. Malinowski calls attention to the fact that natives have no abstract word for Being, but instead words of action, such as to lie, to stand, etc.

4. According to Frazer, the ceremony told the story of a young and beautiful god who is beloved of a goddess. He suffers a tragic death and is then restored to life. In *Kingship and the Gods* (Chicago, 1948), Henri Frankfort argues against Frazer's formulation, pointing to important differences among the gods: Adonis is a youth who dies before his prime, whereas Tammuz was a mature and virile figure; in the cult of Adonis and Tammuz, royalty played no part. In any case, most of the gods were original vegetation deities (the title of Marduk was "Plougher of the Field"). In time, the physical and material advantages which the gods bring were extended to cultural benefits, and Jessie Weston indicates that, in the case of the Christian ritual, they were converted into spiritual and religious values: Christianity identified "the deity of vegetation, regarded as Life Principle, with the God of the Christian Faith." Weston's study also shows that the origin of the Grail legend lies in the vegetation ritual, treated from the esoteric point of view as a Life-cult. Jessie L. Weston, *From Ritual to Romance* (New York, 1957).

5. This idea was carried forward in the so-called "sacred marriages" of the Oriental fertility deities (Marduk and Sarpanitum in Babylon, Osiris and Isis in Egypt, Attis and Cybele in Asia, and, later, Zeus and Hera in Greece). They were a guarantee for the fertility and growth of nature and of the human community.

6. In the hierarchic thought of Egypt, the earth (Geb, Osiris) and the primeval ocean (Nun) have male character, but in Greek mythology, despite the reign of Zeus, creation came from a mother-goddess. In Hesiod (*Theogony*, 116), Gaia (Earth) came after primeval Chaos. In Aeschylus' *Prometheus* and *Oresteia*, the earth is the mother of Prometheus and the "primeval prophetess." The name "Delphi," the site of the Greek oracle, was connected with fish and means mother-body. Yet, Homer's Oceanus, Poseidon-Neptune, and the Tritons are male.

7. Water as nourisher and purgator appears in Hebrew mythology (Micah 7, 19) where we are told that God will cast our sins into the depths of the sea—a notion ritualized in the "Tashlich" ceremony, when, on the first day of the Hebrew year, sins are thrown into the water.

   In medieval literature, water stands for milk, the mother-milk by which the Virgin works the miracle. In the Eucharist, it appears as wine (combined with bread). Robert Greer Cohn has pointed out the ambivalence of water in the old French word "amer" (to love) which combines "mer" (the sea), "mere" (mother), "amere(e)" (bitter) and Marie (the bitter sea). See Robert Greer Cohn's *L'Oeuvre de Mallarme un coup de des.* (Paris, 1951).

8. In Aeschylus' *Prometheus*, fire is a useful and a dangerous tool; in Dante, it appears as hell-fire, but also as purging and heavenly; in Goethe's *Faust*, we have the fire in which the Earth-Spirit appears and the fire which consumes Philemon and Baucis; in Wagner a fire forges Siegfried's sword, protects Brunhilde, and consumes the world.

9. There is argument over which is temporally prior: The Boas school holds that ritual derives from myth; Robertson Smith thinks that myth is a later, artistic interpretation imposed on ritual. Similarly, Jane Harrison and the Cambridge anthropologists see myth as the spoken version of the ritual act. According to Clyde Kluckhon the issue over priority is largely spurious, something like "the hen or egg" question. Ritual centers in action; myth moves into meaning. The two are interdependent.

10. Theodor Gaster writes that the function of ritual within the scheme of the seasonal ritual is "to translate the punctual into terms of the durative. . . . What the king does on the punctual level, the god does on the durative." *Thespis* (New York, 1950), pp. 5-6. Cf. Mircea Eliade's concept that the ritual enacts primal time. See his *Birth and Rebirth* (New York, 1958), pp. 6-7 and passim.

11. According to George Thomson (*Aeschylus and Athens* [New York, 1950], pp. 97 ff.), the rites took various forms: The initiate was swallowed by a spirit, underwent a surgical operation, amputation or injury to a part of the body, scorching by fire, etc. Following a long period of seclusion, the candidate received a new name. Sometimes, he returned in a state of temporary insanity, possessed by his guardian spirit which had entered his body. The ritual was usually carried out by a secret fraternity and its mystery revealed to the uninitiated only in its outward form.

   The hero in mythopoesis reenacts some of these phases, particularly injury to a bodily organ: Job's skin, Prometheus' liver, Oedipus' ankles, Ahab's leg. More prominent is the inner injury, taking the form of "insanity": the frenzy of Io, Orestes, Medea and Pentheus, the "madness" of Don Quixote, Hamlet, Ahab and Mitya Karamazov. Their "madness" follows contact with a "guardian spirit" who possesses them: Io by Zeus, Don Quixote by his chivalric heroes, Hamlet by the Ghost, Ahab by Moby Dick. Some also receive a new name.

12. In Egyptian mythology, the archetypal waters of chaos from which life emerged were regarded as eternally present in the Nile waters which annually revived the fertility of the Nile valley. See H. and H. A. Frankfort *et al.*, *The Intellectual Adventure of Ancient Man* (Chicago, 1946).

13. *Kingship and the Gods*, pp. 185 ff. This discussion is based largely on Frankfort's studies.

   Osiris was identified with Seth and with his son Horus whom he had with his sister-wife Isis. Seth and Horus were perennial antagonists, yet both were embodied in Pharaoh, and in the end were reconciled. "Reconciliation, an unchanging order in which conflicting forces play their allotted part—that is the Egyptian's view of the world and also his conception of the state." The Egyptian community "sacrificed all liberty for the sake of a never changing integration of society and nature." (pp. 6, 22)

14. Oriental legends abound in the union between the mother-goddess and the husband-son: Ishtar-Tammuz, Astarte-Adonis, Isis-Osiris, Cybele-Attis, Maja-Agni, Iznani-Iznagi, etc.

15. The esoteric formulation of Hindu mythology is contained in the *Vedas* and its commentaries (*Brahmanas, Puranas, Sutras, Upanishads*), whereas the great

epics, the *Ramayana* and *Mahabharata*, present some of the myths through stories of battles and adventures.

16. Quoted in *Vedanta for the Western World*, ed., Christopher Isherwood (Hollywood, 1945), p. 216. Hindu thought was revived by Schopenhauer and Wagner in the nineteenth century and in our day by Aldous Huxley, Gerald Heard and Christopher Isherwood.

17. In Hesiod, the Four Ages account for all time; in the Hindu account, they recur eternally.

18. Here, too, the gods are associated with the elements and the seasons. It has been suggested that the victory of the storm-god Indra over Vrtra pictures the bursting forth of the rainy season.

19. A cosmological version of the oedipal theme appears in the story of the Vedic Dasyu, the night-demon, who is doomed to be destroyed by his solar offspring.

20. The conflict is over a woman, Krishna, who is married to five Pandava brothers.

21. The Babylonian myth begins with a dual principle—the male Apus (the primeval sweet water ocean) and Tiamat (the primeval salt water ocean). In his attempt to subdue the unruly and over-ambitious sons, Apsu is slain by the God Ea. Tiamat then spawns monster-serpents and asks one of them, Kingu, to revenge the parents. But Kingu is also killed and the gods fashion mankind from his blood. Cf. Alexander Heidel, *The Babylonian Genesis* (2d ed.; Chicago, 1951); also his *The Gilgamesh Epic and Old Testament Parallels* (2d ed.; Chicago, 1949).

    The Babylonian story of Creation was associated with the spring equinox, and the annual death of the Sumerian god at midsummer with the drought of the Mesopotamian valley. The battle between Marduk (who controls the wind) and Tiamat (who created the waters) was based on the annual storms and the spring floods which turn the plains into a watery chaos, until the winds dry up the waters (in the legend, the winds carry away Tiamat's blood). Cf. Morris Jastrow, "Babylonia and Assyria," in *The Sacred Books and Early Literature of the East*, Vol. I (New York and London, 1917); Thorkild Jacobsen, "Mesopotamia," in H. and H. A. Frankfort, *Ancient Man*, p. 180.

22. The point is reinforced by the manner in which Marduk subdues his mother: He catches her in a net, drives winds into her mouth and belly, pierces her belly with a spear, splits her in two halves, forcing "his way to the midst of Tiamat" becoming "the Seizer of the Midst."

23. One legend about Gilgamesh suggests features of the Rankian hero. Cf. S. H. Langdon in *Mythology of All Races*, V (Boston, 1931), 234.

24. Later, Gilgamesh goes to the land of Utnapishtim in quest of the plant of rejuvenation. Here, he is told the story of the Flood and learns that immortality is not for man. See the translation of the Creation epic *Enuma Elish* and of *Gilgamesh* by E. A. Speiser in *Ancient Near Eastern Texts*, ed., James B. Pritchard (Princeton, 1950 and 1955).

25. Morris Jastrow (*An Old Babylonian Version of the Gilgamesh Epic* [New Haven, 1920]), suggests that there may be some relationship between the twelve tablets of the Gilgamesh story and the twelve months of the year:

"Thus in the 6th tablet, the rejection by Gilgamesh of the advances made by the goddess Ishtar, the goddess of love and vegetation and general fertility, is probably a reflection of the decline of vegetation after the summer season had reached its height; and again the story of a destructive deluge, related in the 11th, is clearly associated with the 11th month, in which the rains and storms of the wintry season are at their height." (p. 187)

Cf. Langdon, in *Mythology of All Races*, p. 166; J. Finegan, *Light from the Ancient East* (Princeton, 1946), p. 51; Jastrow, *Gilgamesh Epic*, p. 187; Frankfort, *Ancient Man*, p. 149. There is also a rhythmic use of the numbers six and seven, suggesting the crisis which came to the valley towards the end of summer; Gilgamesh spurns Ishtar in tablet six, accusing her of instability; Engidu dies in the seventh tablet—the beginning of the rainy season. The crisis element in the numbers six and seven also appears in the following episodes: Engidu loves the priestess for six days and seven nights; Gilgamesh laments Enkidu's death for seven days and nights; he tells Ishtar of the "seven and again seven pitfalls" she dug for those she fell in love with; the deluge lasts six days and nights.

26. For specialized studies of Oriental mythology, see E. O. James, *The Cult of the Mother Goddess* (New York, 1959), and his *The Ancient Gods* (New York, 1960); Joseph Campbell, *The Masks of God: Oriental Mythology* (New York, 1962); R. T. Rundle Clark, *Myth and Symbol in Ancient Egypt* (New York, 1960).

APPENDIX VI

1. Freud's letter to Reik contains a sentence which is a kind of quick summation of the Katya-Mitya relation. Dostoyevsky, Freud notes, "really only understands either crude, instinctive desire or masochistic submission and love from pity."

2. Interestingly enough, in Teutonic mythology, women are distinguished not by their beauty or softness, but by their bravery and warrior-role, e.g., the Walküre.

3. Did Martha's firmness and nobility represent a concealed threat to Freud's love of independence (similar to that which Mitya felt in Katya)?—A possible clue may be contained in Freud's dream of the Botanical Monograph (*The Basic Writings of Sigmund Freud* [New York, 1938], pp. 241-46). In his analysis of the dream, Freud writes that he reproaches himself for remembering so seldom to bring his wife flowers, "as she would like me to do," and is reminded "that we often forget in obedience to a purpose of the unconscious." His next association is the monograph on the coca plant. (We know that he indirectly blamed Martha for interruption of his work on this subject). He further notes that the Genus Cyclamen which Freud remembers having seen next morning is "my wife's favorite flower." And he associates his dreaming of the "dried

specimen of the plant, as though from a herbarium" to his having become "a *book-worm* (cf. *herbarium*)." Erich Fromm would seem to be on the right track in commenting that "the monograph about the cyclamen stirs up his feeling that he fails in that aspect of life which is symbolized by love and tenderness" (*The Forgotten Language* [New York, 1951], p.92). Might one further suggest that Freud's desire for "independence" appears in the dreamer seeing a "dried specimen of the plant" instead of a "blooming" cyclamen? In his analysis of the dream, Freud twice mentions the fact that the cyclamen is "my wife's favourite flower."

Index

Abraham, Karl, 281
Albee, Edward, 328
Albright, William F., 63, 66
Anders, Günther, 308
Appel, Benjamin, 225, 242, 345
Aquinas, Saint Thomas, 104, 110, 129, 130
Aristophanes, 93
Aristotle, 40, 70 *Poetics*, 94, 97, 161, 334
Arlow, Jacob A., 34, 35, 44
Art, 35; form, 30; integrative function, 27-28
Asch, Sholem, 64
Aeschylus, 68-69, 72-73, 74, 75, 80, 97-99; Prometheia, 75-82, 99. *See also* Mythopoesis
Auden, W. H., 147, 153, 244, 245, 299
Auerbach, Erich, 110, 116, 117, 128
Augustine, Saint, 104, 109, 129, 185, 215

Babylonian Job, 47, 63
Bacchae, The. See Mythopoesis
Bacon, Francis, 35
Bacon, Helen, 101
Beckett, Samuel, 328
Benardete, M. J., 129
Berdyaev, N. A., 249
Bergler, Edmund, 26, 28-30, 43
Bergson, Henri, 42
Bergstraesser, Arnold, 221
Bickerman, J., 141, 150
Blake, William, 19, 42
Bloch, Ernst, 41
Boas, Franz, 19, 23, 42

Böhm, Wilhelm, 210
Bonaparte, Marie, 26
Borgese, G. A., 121
Bronislawski, J., 29
Brothers Karamazov. See Dostoyevsky. *See also* Mythology, Mythopoesis
Brown, Norman A., 328
Bunyan, Paul, 241
Butler, E. M., 185, 215
Buttenwieser, Moses, 63, 66
Byron, Lord, 150

Campbell, Joseph, 243, 245, 351
Cassirer, Ernst, 17, 20, 29, 31, 33, 43, 44, 64, 70, 105, 219
Castro, Americo, 147
Cather, Willa, 50
Catholic Vision, 103. *See* Dante, Mythopoesis, Cervantes. *See also* Don Quixote
Christianity and Myth, 103-105. *See* Mythology
Claudel, Paul, 168
Cohen, Morris Raphael, 350
Cohn, Robert Greer, 352
Corneille, Pierre, 155, 291
Creativity, 13-17
Croce, Benedetto, 105, 198
Culture Hero, 15, 24, 32
Curtius, Ernst, 129

Dante Alighieri, 103; Beatrice and sex-love, 111, 121; deviations in theology and art, 107; mythic crime, 113; pattern of the *Inferno*: Paolo and Francesca, 115; practical import, 116;

357

purgatory: visual recognition, 118; tragic residue in the *Paradiso*, 125.
Deutsch, Helene, 98
Dewey, John, 241, 334, 349
Di Fiore, Joachim, 104
Dodds, E. R., 69, 73, 97, 98, 102
Don Quixote: cave of Montesinos, 142; Cervantes and the Don, 134; chivalry and the chivalric myth, 132, 150; Don Quixote and Prince Myshkin, 153; Dulcinea: the poetic guide, 139; mythic function of the horse, 151; mythic tradition of the fool, 147, 152; Sancho Panza: the folk-guide, 140; social determinants, 133
Dostoyevsky, Fyodor: art-form, 253, 262, 277; epilepsy, 251, 265, 277; life, 250-253, 280-281; works, 246, 277, 280, 283; *Brothers Karamazov*, 248-283; Alyosha, 254, 262-264; boys (Kolya and Ilusha), 276; Devil, 266; Father Zossima, 248, 254, 260, 279; Four-fold quest, 256; Fyodor, 254; Grushenka, 270; Ivan, 254, 256, 282; the Jobian poem of the Grand Inquisitor, 257; Karamazovism, 256; Katya (latent incest figure), 267, 345; Mitya, 254, 273; Rakitin, 274; Smerdyakov, 254, 264-266, and Ivan 265, 282. *See also* Pan-Slavic Image of the Earth Mother, 247, 283.
Dreiser, Theodore, 224, 241
Driver, S. R., 66

Edwards, Jonathan, 224
Eissler, K. R., 26, 181, 214; On Goethe, 341-343
Eliade, Mircea, 61, 353
Eliot, T. S., 128, 159
Emerson, Raph Waldo, 225
Elnett, E., 279
Engels, Friedrich, 126
Entwistle, Wm. J., 142
Epistle of James, 47
Eros-Thanatos, 327
Euripides. *See* Mythology, Mythopoesis (Greek)
Existentialist myth, 230, 302, 307, 350; Camus, Albert (*Sisyphus*), 303;

Sartre, Jean Paul, comparison with Goethe and O'Neill, 306; comparison with Wagner's Siegfried, 307; *The Flies*, 304
Ezekiel, 47, 48

Fairley, Barker, 181, 214
Farrington, B., 99
Faulkner, William, 224
Faust: Germanic *Kultur*-freedom, 190; Faust I, 189-199; Gretchen, 179, 218; Mephistopheles, 193, 216, 217, 219, 220; sexual imagery, 217; wager, 195; Faust II, 199; Euphorion, 219; Helena, 219, 220; Homunculus, 201, 219; The Mothers, 201, 218; phallic-vaginal imagery, 218; Philemon and Baucis, 205; Sorge, 207, 220. *See* Goethe, Mythology, Mythopoesis, the Faust legend
Fedotov, F., 246, 248, 279
Feldman, A. Bronson, 347
Ferenczi, Sandor, 26, 30, 85
Fergusson, Francis, 82, 130
Finegan, Jack, 63, 338
Frank, Waldo, 148, 149
Frankfort, H. and H. A., 61, 62, 63, 64, 68, 337, 338, 352
Frazer, J. G., 20, 333, 351, 352
Freeman, Derek, 45
Freiligrath, Ferdinand, 188
French Myth, 290
Freud, Sigmund, 41, 54, 67, 88, 152, 329; his dramatic structure, 36; on Dostoyevsky, 345; on mythology, 20, 27, 28, 30, 32, 33, 99; on the Prometheus legend, 80
Fromm, Erich, 45, 356; on Oedipus, 82, 88-90, 101
Frye, Northrup, 65

Gaster, Theodor, 64, 353
Genet, Jean, 328
Gide, Andrè, 291-298; style, 292, 294; *Theseus*, 291-298
Glover, Edward, 44
Goethe, Johann Wolfgang, 16, 40, 178, 180, 223; mythic thinking, 187; social

and personal burden, 181-185, 341, 343
Gordon, Pierre, 131
Gorky, Maxim, 278, 286, 287
Gorodetzky, N., 279
Graves, Robert, 67, 152
Greek mythology and mythopoesis, 67. See Aeschylus, Sophocles, Euripides, Mythology
Greenacre, Phyllis, 26, 30, 42
Groddeck, G. W., 216
Gundolf, Friedrich, 172

Hamilton, Edith, 60
Hamlet, 155; The art of the dialectic paradox, 170, 173; confession in the closet, 166; Fortinbras-Horatio, 169; the Ghost, 156, 167; legendary background, 155, 173; mythic allusions, and residue, 156, 158, 169; Osric, 170; the playlet and the nephew, 165; the psychic burden, 159; the seasonal ritual, 171; The Tempest, 172, Interpretations: Bradley, A. C., 174-176; Gollancz, Sir Israel, 173, 177; Holland, Norman H., 175; Jones, Ernest, 158, 173, 175, 177; Smirnov, H. A., 159, 174; Walker, Roy, 174, 176; Wertham, Frederic, 176; Wilson, J. Dover, 162, 165, 175, 176; Zinzow, A., 177. See Shakespeare
Haroutunian, Joseph, 124, 128
Harrison, Jane, 72
Hartmann, Heinz, 44
Hassan, Ihab, 328, 330
Hawthorne, Nathaniel, 265
Hebrew Myth. See Book of Job, Mythology, Mythopoesis
Hegel, G. W. F., 116
Heidegger, Martin, 302, 308
Heine, Heinrich, 223
Heraclitus, 71, 75
Hesiod, 67, 75, 99
Hocking, William E., 14, 187
Homer, 87, 98
Hooke, S. H., 14
Hopper, Stanley Romaine, 105
Hosea, 49, 63

Howe, Irving, 43
Humboldt, Alexander, 180
Husserl, Edmund, 302

Ibsen, Henrik, 308
Identity, problem of, 12, 15
Ionescu, Eugene, 328
Irwin, William, 63

Jacobsen, Thorkild, 337
Jaeger, H., 220
Jaeger, Werner, 68
James, E. O., 129
James, Henry, 223
Jaspers, Karl, 302, 311
Jastrow, Morris, 48, 63-65, 354
Jeffers, Robinson, 224
Jeremiah, 47, 48, 50
Job, Book of, 47-66; Behemoth and Leviathan, 57; birth of Job's ego, 54; Elihu as herald, 55, 59; the friends, 52; Job as mythic hero, 50; psychic process, 58-60; traditional exegeses, 48; Yahweh, conceptions of, 50, 52, 56. See Mythology, Mythopoesis
Jones, Ernest, 26, 45, 347-349
Joseph, Miriam, Sister, 170
Joyce, James, 27, 329
Jung, C. G., 17, 26; on Job, 63

Kafka, Franz, 298, 327; The Castle, 301; his art, 298; The Trial, 300
Kahler, Erich, 44, 61
Kallen, Horace, 56, 65
Kant, Immanuel, 43, 180, 210
Kanzer, Mark, 26, 43, 100, 264, 281
Kaplan, Abraham, 32, 39, 44
Kaufmann, Fritz, 321, 323, 325
Kautsky, Karl, 103
Kepes, G., 44
Kerenyi, Carl, 17, 39, 98, 151
Kierkegaard, Søren, 302
Kissane, Edward D., on the Book of Job, 56, 64, 65
Kleist, Heinrich von, 216
Kluckhohn, Clyde, 45
Köhler, Wolfgang, 29
Korzybski, Alfred, 29
Kreymborg, Alfred, 225, 345

Kris, Ernst, 26, 27, 33, 43, 44
Kroeber, A. L., 46
Kubie, Lawrence S., 26, 29-30, 33, 43

Langdon, S. H., 62, 64
Langer, Susanne K., 20
Leigh, Gertrude, 121, 129, 130
Leonhard, Kurt, 129
Lessing, Gotthardt Ephraim, 185-187, 209, 215
Levin, A. J., 100
Lévy-Brühl, Lucien, 42
Lewis, Wyndham, 178
Lewisohn, Ludwig, 181, 214
Linton, Ralph, 46
London, Jack, 239, 244
Lovejoy, Arthur E., 128, 154
Lowell, Robert, 329
Lukacs, George, 110, 180, 222
Lunacharsky, A. V., 221

Machiavelli, Niccolo, 19
Madariaga, Salvador de, 136, 138
Malinowski, B., 45, 332, 352
Malone, Kemp, 173, 175
Malraux, Andre, 30
Manas (a journal), 17
Mann, Thomas, 13, 29, 36, 41, 42, 74, 146, 152, 312; Doctor Faustus, 194, 282, 312, 321-326; The Joseph Story, 39, 50, 62, 152, 312, 321; The Magic Mountain, 313-326. See Mythology, Mythopoesis
Mannheim, Karl, 180
Marcuse, Herbert, 38, 44, 45
Maritain, Jacques, 62, 107, 109, 129, 287
Marlowe, Christopher, 35, 145-187
Marrett, R. R., 42
Marshall, Roderick, 131
Marx, Karl, 284-290. See Nexö, M. A. and Pelle the Conqueror
Matthiessen, F. O., 238, 241, 244, 245
Maynard, Sir John, 278, 279
McLuhan, Marshall, 328
Medea, 94-96. See Mythopoesis, Greek
Melville, Herman, 223; American mythic tradition, 223; Moby Dick: Ahab, the maimed Satanic hero, 228, his psychic burden, 230; Ishmael, 238; quest for creation, 236; the savage elements, 226; whiteness: demonic ambiguity, 237; the white whale: parental sex-mystery, 232
Mendelssohn, Isaac, 58
Milton, John, 216
Muir, Edwin, 299
Müller, Max, 19
Mumford, Lewis, 21
Myth, and mythopoesis, 34-36, 14-17; practical function, 332-334; and religion, 21-22; and reality, 19; and science, 20-21; and ritual, 353
Mythology: American. See Melville, Moby Dick; Babylonian, 334, 354; Chivalric, See Don Quixote; Chinese (Confucius), 338; Egyptian, 333-335; Greek, 333, 352; Hebrew, See Book of Job; Hindu, 333-336; Pan-Slavic, See Brothers Karamazov; Persian (Iranian), 339; Primitive and Oriental, 332, 353; Teutonic, 178. See Goethe, Mann, Faust
Mythopoesis: drama in three acts with an epilogue, 23-26; and history, 39-41; and psychology, 26-39; revolutionary leaven, 25-26, 34; tragic residue, 23, 25-26. Aeschylus, 86, 72, 74, 75, 80, 97, Prometheia, 75-82, 99; American. See Melville; Catholic. See Dante; Chivalric. See Don Quixote; Euripides, 72, 93, Bacchae, 95, Medea, 94, 96, revival of Dionysian worship, 94, social changes, 93, 96; Existentialist. See Camus, Sartre; French. See Gide; Germanic. See Goethe, Mann; Greek, 67, Apollo and Dionysus, 69-74, 94-102; historic-social function, 68, Moira, 68, oracle, 71, Plato's myth of Er, 71, Erinyes and Eumenides, 99, 101, 306; Hebrew. See Book of Job; Modern. See Kafka, Marx, Nexö; Pan-Slavic. See Dostoyevsky, Brothers Karamazov; Renaissance. See Hamlet; Roman. See Virgil; Sophocles, 82, Oedipus Rex, Oedipus In Colonus, 82-93, 100

Nebel, Gerhard, 70, 82
Neumann, Erich, 244
Nexö, M. A. *See* Marx
Niebuhr, Reinhold, 105
Nietzsche, Friedrich, 23, 29, 69, 72, 75, 93, 97, 98, 178, 179, 302, 308, 329
Nilsson, M. P., 96
Northrop, F. S. C., 178
Novalis (Friedrich von Hardenberg), 112

Odets, Clifford, 225
Oedipus. *See* Mythopoesis, Mythology
Oesterley, W. O. E., 63
O'Neill, Eugene, 224
Oppenheimer, Robert, 327
Oresteia. *See* Aeschylus, Mythopoesis, Mythology
Oriental Mythology, 24. *See* Mythology
Orphism, 97
Otto, Walter F., 69, 97

Pan-Slavic myth, 247-283. *See Brothers Karamazov*, Dostoyevsky
Paracelsus, 186
Paul, Saint, 104
Pelle the Conqueror. *See* Nexö, Marx
Plato, 21, 41, 67, 68, 74
Pliny, 75
Poetic Edda (Voluspa), 179
Pre-Socratic philosophy, 98
Primitive Mythology, 24. *See* Mythology
Prometheus. *See* Mythology, Mythopoesis, Aeschylus
Protagoras, 70

Quest, The, 15

Rabelais, François, 155
Racine, Jean Baptiste, 155, 290
Raglan, Lord, 42
Rank, Otto, 25, 30, 41, 90, 99, 101, 152
Ransom, John Crowe, 31
Raphael, Max, 73
Rappaport, Angelo S., 62
Read, Herbert, 44
Reich, Hermann, 193
Reichenbach, Hans, 349
Reichert, Victor E., 63, 66

Reik, Theodor, 26, 33, 101, 183, 214, 218, 345
Renaissance mythopoesis, 154, 178. *See Hamlet*
Rickert, Heinrich, 213, 218
Ricklin, Franz, 41
Riesman, David, 170
Robertson, J. M., 128
Robinson, Th. H., 63
Rohde, Erwin, 69, 97
Rosenberg, Harold, 67
Ruggiero, Guido de, 309

Sachs, Hanns, 26, 30
Sandburg, Carl, 345
Santayana, George, 15, 125, 126, 130, 187, 210, 223, 344
Sapir, E., 33
Schachtel, Ernest G., 44
Schiller, Friedrich, 180
Schlegel, Wilhelm, 93, 98
Schneider, D. E., 26, 43
Schneider, Reinhold, 210
Schopenhauer, Arthur, 178, 179
Schorer, Max, 21
Sedgwick, William E., 243
Shakespeare, William, 153. *See Hamlet*
Sharpe, Ella, 26
Shelley, P. B., 215, 339. *See* Prometheus
Simmel, Georg, 221
Simmons, Ernest J., 252, 280, 281
Slonim, Marc, 251, 280
Socrates, 70
Sokolov, Y. M., 278, 285
Sorel, George, 19, 41
Spengler, Oswald, 178, 179, 350
Spiegel, Shalom, 63
Spinoza, Baruch, 21
Stender-Petersen, A., 278
Strauss, David Friedrich, 19
Strindberg, August, 100
Sumner, B. H., 278, 279
Symbols and symbolism, 20, 21, 29

Tarachow, Sidney, 45
Tate, Allen, 124, 125
Tauber, E. S. and Greene, M. R., 43
Theophrastus, 99

Theseus, 291. *See* Gide
Thomson, George, 68, 72, 97, 98, 353
Tillich, Paul, 105
Toller, Ernst, 13
Tolstoy, Leo, 116, 218, 254
Toynbee, Arnold, 105, 107, 178, 250, 350
Turgenev, I., 280
Twain, Mark, 243, 276, 343-344

Unamuno, Miguel de, 134
Underhill, Evelyn, 42

Van Doren, Mark, 113, 345
Veblen, Thorstein, 62
Verrall, A. W., 93
Viëtor, Karl, 210
Virgil (*Aeneid*), 340-341
Vossler, Karl, 106, 111, 112, 118, 126, 130, 188

Wagner, Richard, 26, 181, 216, 227
Walton, William H., 129
Watts, Alan W., 107, 128

Weber, Max, 180
Weiss, Paul, 52
Werfel, Franz, 64, 96
Wertheimer, Max, 29
Weston, Jessie L., 24, 240, 242, 243, 244, 352
Whitman, Walt, 344
Wicksteed, E. H., 130
Williams, Charles, 110, 116, 119, 124, 127
Williams, Tennessee, 220
Williams, William Carlos, 345
Winckelmann, Johann J., 69, 97
Wittgenstein, Ludwig, 40
Wolfe, Thomas, 225
Wundt, Wilhelm, 19

Yarmolinsky, A., 280
Yeats, William Butler, 31

Zimmer, Heinrich, 114, 151, 201, 217, 313
Zweig, Stefan, 277

Harry Slochower is Visiting Professor at Drew University, and Adjunct Professor at Syracuse University, 1969-70. Dr. Slochower is Editor-in-Chief of *American Imago* and also a psychoanalyst in private practice.

The manuscript was edited by Sandra Shapiro. The book was designed by Mary Jowski. The type face for the text is Caledonia linotype designed by Stanley Morison in 1931 and the display face is Weiss Roman designed by E. R. Weiss about 1928.

The book is printed on Bradford Book paper and bound in Holliston Mills' Roxite linen over binders board. Manufactured in the United States of America.

21st century skills

Rethinking How Students Learn

Solution Tree | Press

555 North Morton Street
Bloomington, IN 47404
800.733.6786 (toll free) / 812.336.7700
FAX: 812.336.7790

email: info@solution-tree.com
solution-tree.com

Visit **go.solution-tree.com/21stcenturyskills** to view chapter 6 and 11 graphics in full color and to access live links to tools and materials.

Printed in the United States of America
14 13 12 11 10   2 3 4 5

FSC
www.fsc.org
MIX
Paper from
responsible sources
FSC® C013483

Library of Congress Cataloging-in-Publication Data

21st century skills : rethinking how students learn / [edited by] James Bellanca, Ron Brandt.
    p. cm. -- (Leading edge)
  Includes bibliograpical references and index.
  ISBN 978-1-935249-90-0
  1. Learning ability. 2. Learning strategies. I. Bellanca, James A., 1937- II. Brandt, Ronald S. III. Title: Twenty-first century skills.
  LB1134.A22 2010
  370.15'23--dc22
                                    2010002492

Solution Tree
Jeffrey C. Jones, CEO & President
Solution Tree Press
President: Douglas M. Rife
Publisher: Robert D. Clouse
Vice President of Production: Gretchen Knapp
Managing Production Editor: Caroline Wise
Senior Production Editor: Suzanne Kraszewski
Copy Editor: Rachel Rosolina
Proofreader: Sarah Payne-Mills
Cover Designer: Orlando Angel
Text Designer: Amy Shock

Acknowledgments

Assembling a coherent book from the ideas of a group of highly individualistic and creative thinkers is never easy. Our efforts to develop this volume were facilitated by the cooperative spirit of the contributing authors and the editorial staff at Solution Tree Press. In fact, the book's development has been a model of the skills we seek to promote: collaboration, communication, creative and critical thinking, and lots of problem solving.

Special thanks go to Robb Clouse, Solution Tree Press publisher. Robb became the third musketeer in identifying potential authors, establishing criteria, selecting the articles, and making helpful suggestions. We also appreciate the support and attention to detail of Gretchen Knapp, vice president of production, and Suzanne Kraszewski, senior production editor.

Table of Contents

About the Editors vii

Preface   *Ron Brandt* ix

Foreword   21st Century Skills: Why They Matter, What
They Are, and How We Get There
Ken Kay xiii

Introduction *James Bellanca and Ron Brandt* 1

Chapter 1   Five Minds for the Future
Howard Gardner 9

Chapter 2   New Policies for 21st Century Demands
*Linda Darling-Hammond, Interviewed
by James Bellanca* 33

Chapter 3   Comparing Frameworks for 21st Century Skills
Chris Dede 51

Chapter 4   The Role of Professional Learning
Communities in Advancing 21st Century Skills
Richard DuFour and Rebecca DuFour 77

Chapter 5   The Singapore Vision: *Teach Less, Learn More*
Robin Fogarty and Brian M. Pete 97

Chapter 6   Designing New Learning Environments to
Support 21st Century Skills
Bob Pearlman 117

Chapter 7   An Implementation Framework to Support
21st Century Skills
Jay McTighe and Elliott Seif 149

Chapter 8 Problem-Based Learning: The Foundation
for 21st Century Skills
John Barell 175

Chapter 9 Cooperative Learning and Conflict Resolution:
Essential 21st Century Skills
David W. Johnson and Roger T. Johnson 201

Chapter 10 Preparing Students for Mastery of
21st Century Skills
Douglas Fisher and Nancy Frey 221

Chapter 11 Innovation Through Technology
Cheryl Lemke 243

Chapter 12 Technology Rich, Information Poor
Alan November 275

Chapter 13 Navigating Social Networks as Learning Tools
Will Richardson 285

Chapter 14 A Framework for Assessing 21st Century Skills
Douglas Reeves 305

Afterword Leadership, Change, and Beyond the 21st Century
Skills Agenda
Andy Hargreaves 327

Index 349

About the Editors

James Bellanca and Ron Brandt

James Bellanca, MA, is founder and CEO of International Renewal Institute, Inc., and acting director of the Illinois Consortium for 21st Century Skills. He founded SkyLight Professional Development in 1982. As its president, he mentored more than twenty author-consultants as he led SkyLight in pioneering the use of strategic teaching in comprehensive professional development. Bellanca coauthored more than twenty books that advocated the application of thinking and cooperating across the curriculum with the theme "not just for the test, but for a lifetime of learning." Currently, Bellanca is building on the theories of cognitive psychologist Reuven Feuerstein to develop more effective responses to the learning needs of students whose academic achievement continues to lag. A longtime proponent of teaching that is aligned with the advocated best practices of 21st century skills, Bellanca's most recent publications include *Designing Professional Development for Change: A Guide for Improving Classroom Instruction*; *Enriched Learning Projects: A Practical Pathway to 21st Century Skills*; *Collaboration and Cooperation in 21st Century Schools*; *200+ Active Learning Strategies and Projects for Engaging Students' Multiple Intelligences*; and *A Guide to Graphic Organizers: Helping Students Organize and Process Content for Deeper Learning.*

 Ron Brandt, Ed.D., was editor of publications for the Association for Supervision and Curriculum Development (ASCD), Alexandria, Virginia, for almost twenty years before his retirement in 1997. During his career at ASCD, he was best known as executive editor of *Educational Leadership* magazine. In the 1980s, he promoted the teaching of thinking in elementary and secondary schools, collaborating with Robert Marzano and a team of other educators in development of a book, *Dimensions of Thinking*, and a related teacher training program, *Dimensions of Learning*. He is also the author or editor of numerous other publications. Before joining the staff of ASCD, he was a teacher and principal in Racine, Wisconsin; director of staff development in Minneapolis, Minnesota; and for eight years was associate superintendent of the Lincoln Public Schools in Lincoln, Nebraska.

Preface

Ron Brandt

Educators are faced once again with a daunting challenge: this time, it is to equip students with 21st century skills. Critics oppose the idea on the grounds that emphasizing skills such as critical thinking and problem solving will erode the teaching of important content, including history and literature. Their concern may be valid, but their position that "skills can neither be taught nor applied effectively without prior knowledge of a wide array of subjects" (Common Core, 2009) is not. Both knowledge *and* skills are needed, and they are interdependent; advocates and critics agree about that. And the authors of this book know from experience that effective teaching involves students *using* skills to acquire knowledge.

No generation can escape the responsibility of deciding what students should learn by analyzing what adults are called upon to do. When the United States was young, citizens of New England were taught to do simple calculations, write letters, and read the Bible. In the 1900s, as farming grew in complexity, high schools in rural areas began teaching vocational agriculture. With the current blitz of fast-moving developments in technology, schools are beefing up their science and mathematics programs.

The obvious need for education to relate to society's demands was satirized in a delightful little book published seventy years ago that told how, in Paleolithic times, schools supposedly came to teach fish grabbing and saber-toothed tiger scaring (Benjamin, 1939). The book's purpose was not to belittle efforts to match curriculum to societal needs; rather, it used gentle humor to warn how difficult it can be to keep up these efforts. When Paleolithic educators finally decided to add a course in tiger scaring, for example, they could locate only two harmless, moth-eaten old tigers for students to scare.

So trying to foresee students' future needs is not being trendy; it is a necessity. But, of course, it is only the beginning. The hard parts are, first, determining how these new demands fit in relation to the existing curriculum; second, finding ways they can be taught *along with content*; and then, managing the complex process of implementation. This book is intended to help you with these momentous tasks. Like the fictitious Paleolithics in Benjamin's book, we may not be completely successful in these efforts, but we must accept the challenge.

References

Common Core. (2009). *A challenge to the Partnership for 21st Century Skills.* Accessed at www.commoncore.org/p21-challenge.php on November 5, 2009.

Benjamin, H. R. W. (1939). *The saber-tooth curriculum.* New York: McGraw-Hill.

Ken Kay

Ken Kay, JD, has spent the past twenty-five years bringing together the education, business, and policy communities to improve U.S. competitiveness. He is president of the Partnership for 21st Century Skills, the nation's leading advocacy organization focused on infusing 21st century skills into education and preparing every child to succeed in the new global economy. He also serves as the CEO and cofounder of e-Luminate Group, an education consulting firm.

Throughout his career, Kay has been a major voice and premier coalition builder on competitiveness issues in education and industry—particularly policies and practices that support innovation and technology leadership. As executive director of the CEO Forum on Education and Technology, he led the development of the StaR Chart (School Technology & Readiness Guide), used by schools across the country to make better use of technology in K–12 classrooms. A lawyer and nationally recognized coalition builder, Kay has also facilitated initiatives by universities and technology leaders to advance research and development policy and by computer industry CEOs to advance U.S. trade and technology policy.

In his foreword, Kay presents the Framework for 21st Century Learning advocated by his group. He responds to three key questions—(1) Why are the skills listed in the framework needed for learning in the future? (2) Which skills are most important? and (3) What can be done to help schools include these skills in their repertoire so that 21st century learning results?—and argues for realigning the teaching-learning relationship so that it focuses on outcomes.

Foreword

21st Century Skills: Why They Matter, What They Are, and How We Get There

Ken Kay, President, Partnership for 21st Century Skills

The writer Malcolm Gladwell (2000) astutely describes how and why social change happens when we arrive at a "tipping point," the moment when a critical mass of circumstances come together and sets us on a new and unstoppable course. Scientists, economists, and sociologists all use this term to describe moments when significant change occurs and results in a new reality that is markedly different from the old.

I believe we are on the threshold of a tipping point in public education. The moment is at hand for a 21st century model for education that will better prepare students for the demands of citizenship, college, and careers in this millennium.

I am honored that the editors have asked me to introduce this book and set the context with the overarching theme of 21st century skills, using the Framework for 21st Century Learning developed by the Partnership for 21st Century Skills (2009a). This book is a compilation of reflections on the possibilities for 21st century learning by some of the most thoughtful educational minds in the United States. It is gratifying that so many of them are engaged in envisioning and substantiating more robust approaches to educating young people, particularly since those of us in the Partnership have worked since 2001 on the same exciting project.

The vision for 21st Century Learning offers a holistic and systemic view of how we can reconceptualize and reinvigorate public education, bringing together all the elements—21st century student outcomes and 21st century education support systems—into a unified framework.

The vision for 21st century learning developed by the Partnership for 21st Century Skills (2009a), summarized in figure F.1, offers a compelling context for the chapters in this volume. This vision offers a holistic and systemic view of how we can reconceptualize and reinvigorate public education, bringing together all the elements—21st century student outcomes and 21st century education support systems—into a unified framework. For us, the starting point for this framework is actually the end result: the outcomes—in terms of mastery of core academic subjects, 21st century themes, and 21st century skills—that should be expected of students once they leave school to venture successfully into higher education, workplaces, and independent life. It's only when we understand these outcomes that we can then begin building the supporting infrastructure that will lift the education system to commanding heights. The raison d'être for the support systems—standards and assessments, curriculum and instruction, professional development, and learning environments—should be to achieve the results that truly matter for students.

Without a clear and thorough articulation of the outcomes that students need, reshaping the infrastructure is premature. Here's an analogy: if you are building a house, it doesn't make sense to order the plumbing fittings before the architect finishes the design specifications. In education, 21st century student outcomes *are* the design specs for the rest of the system.

The Partnership has crafted an all-encompassing vision for a 21st century education system. We don't have all the answers, however. As the contributions to this book make clear, there are many more wonderful ideas percolating that will strengthen the vision of 21st century learning and help transform every aspect of the system.

Core Subjects
- English, Reading, or Language Arts
- World Languages
- Arts
- Mathematics
- Economics
- Science
- Geography
- History
- Government and Civics

21st Century Themes
- Global Awareness
- Financial, Economic, Business, and Entrepreneurial Literacy
- Civic Literacy
- Health Literacy
- Environmental Literacy

Learning and Innovation Skills
- Creativity and Innovation
- Critical Thinking and Problem Solving
- Communication and Collaboration

Information, Media, and Technology Skills
- Information Literacy
- Media Literacy
- Information and Communications Technology (ICT) Literacy

Life and Career Skills
- Flexibility and Adaptability
- Initiative and Self-Direction
- Social and Cross-Cultural Skills
- Productivity and Accountability
- Leadership and Responsibility

21st Century Education Support Systems
- 21st Century Standards and Assessments
- 21st Century Curriculum and Instruction
- 21st Century Professional Development
- 21st Century Learning Environments

Source: Partnership for 21st Century Skills, 2009a. Reprinted with permission.

Figure F.1: The Partnership for 21st Century Skills Framework for 21st Century Learning.

We aren't rigid about the language used to describe 21st century skills, either. We say *adaptability*, for instance, while others prefer *resiliency*. We say *critical thinking*; others say *systems thinking*. No matter—we're all talking about the same concepts. On the other hand, the term *21st century skills* is not a vague and squishy catchword that can mean anything. Every element of our model has been defined, developed, and vetted by leading experts, scholars, educators, business people, parents, and community members.

We invite individuals and organizations to use our framework to spark a lively national dialogue about all of the elements required for enriching 21st century minds. It is particularly important to engage educators and representatives of the business community in this dialogue (Wagner, 2008). It's critical for states, districts, and schools to have these conversations and agree on the student outcomes they value—and then to create systems that can deliver.

Why Do We Need a New Model for Education in the 21st Century?

The forces instigating the inevitable changes on the horizon in education have been building for some time:

- **The world is changing**—The global economy, with its emerging industries and occupations, offers tremendous opportunities for everyone who has the skills to take advantage of it. There has been a dramatic acceleration in global competition and collaboration over the past thirty years, spurred by information and communications technology. The service economy, which is driven by information, knowledge, and innovation, has supplanted the industrial economy and reshaped businesses and workplaces. More than three-quarters of all jobs in the United States are now in the service sector. Manual labor and routine tasks have given way to interactive, nonroutine tasks—even in many traditionally blue-collar occupations. Technology has replaced workers who perform routine work, while it complements workers with higher-level skills and empowers them to be more productive and creative (Autor, Levy, & Murnane, 2003). Advanced economies, innovative industries and firms, and high-growth jobs increasingly reward people who can adapt and contribute to organizations, products, and processes with the communications, problem-solving, and critical-thinking skills that enable them to customize their work and respond to organizational expectations (Partnership for 21st Century Skills, 2008).

In this era of rapid change, the social contract prevalent for a good part of the last century doesn't exist anymore. Doing well in school no longer guarantees a lifelong job or career as it did for previous generations of Americans. Today, people can expect to have many jobs in multiple fields during their careers. The average person born in the later years of the baby boom held 10.8 jobs between the ages of eighteen and forty-two, according to the U.S. Bureau of Labor Statistics (Bureau of Labor Statistics, U.S. Department of Labor, 2009). The new social contract is different: only people who have the knowledge and skills to negotiate constant change and reinvent themselves for new situations will succeed. Competency in 21st century skills gives people the ability to keep learning and adjusting to change. Twenty-first-century skills are the ticket to moving up the economic ladder. Without 21st century skills, people are relegated to low-wage, low-skill jobs. Proficiency in 21st century skills is the new civil right for our times.

- **U.S. schools and students have not adapted to the changing world**—Our current public education system is not preparing all students for the economic, workforce, and citizenship opportunities—and demands—of the 21st century. Many students do not receive the family and societal support they need to stay in school. On top of that, many students are

> The forces instigating the inevitable changes on the horizon in education have been building for some time:
>
> - The world is changing.
> - U.S. schools and students have not adapted to the changing world.
> - The United States has no clear sense of purpose or direction for securing our future economic competitiveness.

not engaged or motivated in school learning that seems out of step with their lives and irrelevant to their futures. The high school dropout rate has reached crisis proportions, with only 70 percent of students—and only 50 percent of minorities—graduating from high school on time and with a regular diploma (Swanson, 2009).

Alarmingly, we now face two achievement gaps—one national and one international. Nationally, Black, Hispanic, and disadvantaged students perform worse than their peers on national assessments (see, for example, Grigg, Donahue, & Dion, 2007; Lee, Grigg, & Donahue, 2007; National Center for Education Statistics, 2009), dragging down the collective capacity of the future workforce. This is especially troubling as the demographics of the United States are shifting, with minority populations growing at a much faster pace than the rest of the population (U.S. Census Bureau, 2008).

Internationally, American students score lower than the average on the Programme for International Student Assessment (PISA), the benchmark assessment in reading, mathematics, and science for the developed countries of the world (see, for example, Organisation for Economic Co-operation and Development, 2009). PISA results are telling because these assessments measure the applied skills—what we call *21st century skills*—of critical thinking and problem solving. Even the best U.S. students cannot match their peers in other advanced economies on PISA.

Even if all students earned a high school diploma and mastered traditional academic subjects, they *still* would be ill prepared for the expectations of the new economy. Today, a different set of skills—21st century skills—increasingly powers the wealth of nations. Skills that support innovation, including creativity, critical thinking, and problem solving, are in great demand (Casner-Lotto & Barrington, 2006; Conference Board, 2007; Lichtenberg, Woock, & Wright, 2008), yet employers report substantial deficiencies in these and other applied skills among even college-educated entrants into the workforce.

Educational attainment is no longer a guarantee of either academic or skills proficiency (van Ark, Barrington, Fosler, Hulten, & Woock, 2009).

- **The United States has no clear sense of purpose or direction for securing our future economic competitiveness**—The United States remains the most competitive nation on the planet, but "creeping complacency" could erode this dominance (International Institute for Management Development, 2009; Scott, 2009). Science, technology, engineering, and mathematics (STEM) experts in industry and higher education have been warning for years that the United States is losing ground when it comes to preparing an adequate supply of workers for these critical fields. Competitor nations in Asia and Europe have gotten the message that skills matter, and they are catching up. Concerted international efforts—and marked success—at improving education and 21st century skills mean that the United States is no longer unrivaled in producing highly qualified, nimble, and ambitious workers for the new economy. In addition, the substantial economic growth fueled by information technology since the late 1980s and early 1990s is likely to max out without investment in intangible workforce assets, including ideas, knowledge, and talent (van Ark et al., 2009).

What Should a 21st Century Education Look Like?

Meeting the challenges we face requires a new model for education—one in which every aspect of our education system is aligned to prepare Americans to compete.

The Partnership for 21st Century Skills has spent the better part of a decade developing a robust Framework for 21st Century Learning (shown on page xv in figure F.1) that responds to the changing demands young people face today. Sustained and enthusiastic support from leading education organizations, the business community, and policymakers—and reality checks with parents, frontline K–12 and postsecondary educators, and community organizations—have shaped this framework into a comprehensive, intentional, and purposeful vision for 21st century education (Trilling & Fadel, 2009).

The graphic is powerful because it communicates at a glance the integration of core academic subjects, 21st century themes, and 21st century skills, with the educational support systems clearly aligned to these student outcomes. The Framework for 21st Century Learning offers a compelling, responsive, and viable direction for public education—starting now—for a number of reasons.

The Framework Focuses on Results That Matter

A 21st century education must be tied to *outcomes*, in terms of proficiency in core subject knowledge and 21st century skills that are expected and highly valued in school, work, and community settings. It is a national travesty that a majority of U.S. students leave high school without the core competencies that employers and postsecondary educators cite as the most critical for real-world performance and advanced learning. Critical thinking, problem solving, creativity, and the other 21st century skills are the tools people need to move up the economic ladder.

> A 21st century education must be tied to *outcomes*, in terms of proficiency in core subject knowledge and 21st century skills that are expected and highly valued in school, work, and community settings.

With 21st century skills, students will be prepared to think, learn, work, solve problems, communicate, collaborate, and contribute effectively throughout their lives. Some say these kinds of skills are not unique to the 21st century. This is true. We call them out for three reasons.

First, these skills are rarely incorporated deliberately throughout the curriculum, nor are they routinely assessed. This status quo relegates these skills into the "nice to have" rather than the "must have" domain in education, which means they are taught unevenly. It is more likely that young people pick up these skills by chance in everyday living and job experiences and, yes, sometimes in school—if they are lucky enough to have good mentors or are astute enough to recognize and build these skills on their own. We simply can no longer afford to continue this haphazard approach to developing the most critical skills if we are to remain a competitive nation.

Second, these skills are essential for *all* students today, not just an elite few. In bygone economies, Americans lived in a hierarchical world with an assembly-line mentality. Top managers and experts took on the lion's share of the thinking, problem solving, decision making, and communicating for their organizations. They gave orders, and most workers were expected simply to follow directions. This is not so today. Competitive organizations have flattened management structures, increased their use of technology, created more flexible work arrangements, and given greater responsibility to frontline workers and collaborative project teams. Such significant organizational and behavioral shifts have boosted productivity and innovation (Black & Lynch, 2004; Gera & Gu, 2004; Pilat, 2004; Zoghi, Mohr, & Meyer, 2007). With these realities, students who do not master 21st century skills will never fulfill their economic potentials.

In this flattened structure, every worker has more information and tools at his or her disposal—and much greater autonomy in using them. In exchange, workers are expected to be self-directed and responsible for managing their own work. As a manager at Apple told me, any employee who needs to be managed is no longer employable. The same shift of responsibility to individuals applies to personal life. There are fewer authority figures to take care of people or tell them what to do. Today, people have to manage their own health care, arming themselves with information, making choices about coverage, acting as their own advocates, and partnering with health-care providers to manage their health. Likewise, participating in civic life requires people to seek out information to understand issues on their own. The decline of print journalism, for example, means that the latest local news may not be delivered to the doorstep every day.

Third, the skills that employers and postsecondary educators say are required for success have converged. Even entry-level employees now are expected to use 21st century skills to accomplish their work (Casner-Lotto & Barrington, 2006; Conference Board, 2007; Lichtenberg, Woock, & Wright, 2008). Most jobs that pay a living wage today require at least some postsecondary education—and this is particularly the case for the 271 jobs with high-growth potential over the next ten years, according to the U.S. Department of Labor (Bureau of Labor Statistics, U.S. Department of Labor, 2008).

Most students aspire to college because they understand this. Indeed, there has been a significant increase in the proportion of the labor force with at least some level of higher education (Carnevale & Desrochers, 2002). Twenty-first-century skills are equally important for successful transitions to college and workforce training programs. Among the components of college readiness presented by the Bill & Melinda Gates Foundation are "academic behaviors" and "contextual skills and awareness" (Conley, 2005, 2007), which reflect the kinds of skills captured in the Framework for 21st Century Learning. All students should be prepared with the skills they need to do well, whatever route they decide to take in the future.

The Framework for 21st Century Learning also incorporates several new 21st century themes that might not seem familiar. Again, employers and educators—along with parents, policymakers, and community advocates—identified these themes and skills as crucial. Typically, though, they are not emphasized in public education. These themes are grounded in everyday life as people across the United States are living it now. They want schools to integrate these new themes, which blend content and skills, to better prepare young people to thrive in a complex world.

For example, global awareness is a new essential in the global economy. Americans need a secure understanding of global issues that affect them as citizens and workers. They need to be able to learn from and work collaboratively with people from a range of diverse cultures and lifestyles. They need to be able to communicate in languages other than English.

Likewise, financial, economic, business, and entrepreneurial literacy are new imperatives. Guaranteed pensions are a rarity today, so the responsibility for retirement planning, saving, and investment management falls on individuals. Recent crises in the banking, credit, and mortgage industries—and the severe recession—underscore the importance of understanding how economic forces impact people's lives. Failure to make responsible financial choices could adversely affect individuals' quality of life for years. At work, people need to know how they fit in and contribute to a larger organization, and they need to bring an entrepreneurial mindset to their lives. By recognizing opportunities, risks, and rewards, they can enhance their workplace productivity and career options and take changing circumstances in stride.

Finally, the Framework for 21st Century Learning articulates several skills that definitely break new ground, at least in education: creativity and innovation, flexibility and adaptability, leadership and cross-cultural skills—for *all* students. These are the kinds of skills that set people apart. Small leaps of imagination can result in tremendous personal and organizational advances. A willingness to respond positively to change leaves people open to new possibilities and more comfortable with the inevitable vagaries of life. Taking on leadership roles gives people more control over their lives, while cross-cultural skills strengthen their effectiveness in interacting with others they encounter in school, work, and the community.

These new skills also differentiate leading from lagging organizations and nations. They undergird every aspect of competitiveness: ingenuity, agility, and continuous improvement; the capacity to turn bold ideas into innovative products, services, and solutions; and the ability to champion worthwhile endeavors, overcome obstacles, and bridge cultural divides.

Taken together, the combination of core academic subjects, 21st century themes, and 21st century skills redefines rigor for our times. Many Americans have been advocating a more rigorous education to prepare students for college and career readiness—a position that we share.

However, *rigor* traditionally is equated with mastery of content (core subjects) alone, and that's simply not good enough anymore. Knowledge and information change constantly. Students need *both* content knowledge *and* skills to apply and transform their knowledge for useful and creative purposes and to keep learning as content and circumstances change.

I've heard John Bransford, a noted professor of education and psychology at the University of Washington and the coauthor of *How People Learn: Bridging Research and Practice* (2000) and *How Students Learn: Science in the Classroom* (2004), put it this way: In the United States, we tell students the same thing a hundred times.

On the 101st time, we ask them if they remember what we told them the first hundred times. However, in the 21st century, the true test of rigor is for students to be able to look at material they've never seen before and know what to do with it.

Infusing 21st century skills into core subjects actually ratchets up rigor. Recalling facts or terms from a textbook, or performing simple processes or procedures, places a low level of cognitive demand on students. Demonstrating deeper understanding through planning, using evidence, and abstract reasoning, for example, is more demanding. Making connections among related ideas within the content or among content areas, or devising an approach to solving a complex problem, requires extended thinking and even higher cognitive demand (Webb, 1997).

The connection between skills and rigor shows up on international assessments such as PISA. Students who can apply critical thinking and problem solving to math and science content perform better than those who cannot. In a 21st century education system, rigor must refer to mastery of content *and* skills.

As I see it, then, there are plenty of convincing indicators that proficiency in 21st century skills is the right result for our time. Enriching minds for the 21st century requires organizing the public education system around this goal.

The Framework Recognizes That Educational Support Systems—Especially Professional Learning Experiences—Are Vital

The vision for 21st century learning is situated in reality: producing the results that matter in terms of student outcomes in 21st century skills requires every aspect of the education system to be aligned toward this goal.

The vision for 21st century learning is situated in reality: producing the results that matter in terms of student outcomes in 21st century skills requires every aspect of the education system to be aligned toward this goal.

While this might seem to be a monumental aspiration, the evidence suggests that states are prepared—even very willing—to take on this work. By October of 2009, fourteen states (Arizona, Illinois, Iowa, Kansas, Louisiana, Maine, Massachusetts, Nevada, New Jersey, North

Carolina, Ohio, South Dakota, West Virginia, and Wisconsin) had committed to retooling their standards and assessments, curriculum and instruction, professional development, and learning environments to support 21st century skills outcomes. The states and districts that are making real progress are those that take a holistic and systemic approach, articulating the skills they value and aligning every other part of their systems to move in this direction.

Many of these states face daunting challenges. Major industries are restructuring and eliminating jobs. The recent economic downturn has exacerbated this problem, and seriously affected state budgets and schools. Nevertheless, these states have carefully examined the framework and endorsed it as their model for building a 21st century education system. They realize that they must reinvent their education systems to renew their workforces and their economies. West Virginia, for example, is revising and refocusing its standards, assessments, instruction, professional development, teacher preparation, preK, and technology programs around the Partnership's Framework for 21st Century Learning.

Professional development is far and away the most important part of the work. Steve Paine, superintendent of schools in West Virginia, tells me that 80 percent of his efforts are devoted to improving teacher effectiveness in delivering 21st century instruction. He has it right. Articulating the skills that matter is only the first step. States and districts cannot assume that teachers can break out of the 20th-century box without sustained professional development. The West Virginia Department of Education has put a full-court press on this mission, initially training every teacher in the state during in-depth summer sessions on 21st century skills and in follow-up web-based coaching during the school year. The state also has a dynamic, interactive website, Teach 21, with a wealth of resources to assist teachers in their everyday classroom practices.

At the Partnership, we've developed detailed content maps and online resources that add layers of specificity to 21st century learning for teachers. These resources promote the kinds of hands-on, inquiry-based learning and development of higher-level thinking skills that the most effective teachers employ (Darling-Hammond et al., 2008). Indeed, many classroom teachers and educators who work closely with students in schools are leading the way in delivering this kind of instruction. All of the teaching resources are available at a dedicated website: Route 21 (www.21stcenturyskills.org/route21/).

The entire supporting infrastructure of education must be modernized to establish the conditions for 21st century teaching, learning, and outcomes. And, as we have learned from previous standards-setting initiatives, ignoring the infrastructure puts an undue burden on students. It is unfair and unproductive to expect students to meet new and higher expectations if the supporting infrastructure does not exist. To help states, districts, and schools move forward, we have developed and updated our MILE guide with implementation guidance and self-assessment tools (Partnership for 21st Century Skills, 2009b).

All of the critical elements of an education system contribute to 21st century skills outcomes, and they cannot be left to chance.

The Framework Resonates With Policymakers, Educators, the Business Community, Community Organizations, and Parents

Plenty of organizations have developed models for improving education. Not many have had the courage to vet their models with thousands of people from every walk of life. Our model of core subjects, 21st century themes, and 21st century skills has been put to this test.

We developed the framework in concert with our nearly forty membership organizations, including the National Education Association and its 3.2 million members. We took the framework on road tours, reaching out to policymakers, educators, business people, community organizations, and parents. We listened to their comments and strengthened the themes and skill sets. We surveyed business people and parents, who strongly agree that 21st century skills are vital for success today (Casner-Lotto & Barrington, 2006; Partnership for 21st Century Skills, 2007). They also believe by overwhelming margins that schools should teach 21st century skills. Their beliefs are based in reality—the expectations of workplaces, the demands of citizenship, and the challenges of life that they face every day. We've been informed by the surveys and reports of other organizations, which confirm our findings.

This is not a small point. A major difference between 21st century skills advocacy and other improvement initiatives, such as the 1980s push to revamp education, is that the leaders of this movement include policymakers, educators, *and* the business community. We are speaking with a united voice. Together, we have taken the time to gauge the interest and attitudes of key stakeholders in public education. And we have strived to build broad-based support for our model from the top down and the bottom up. In many states, governors, leaders in state education agencies and state boards of education, local school boards, business people, community organizations, educators, parents, and the voting public are engaged and energized by our model.

> We are speaking with a united voice. Together, we have taken the time to gauge the interest and attitudes of key stakeholders in public education.

There is much more work to do to build public understanding nationwide—in every district, community, and family. Yet the support we already have, plus the accomplishments of our fourteen leadership states, gives us the opportunity to engage in a vigorous national conversation about new student outcomes for the 21st century—and to bring more supporters on board.

State, district, and school leaders and their communities will want to examine the changes their economies have experienced over the past twenty years. They'll want to think through the new skills students will need for the next twenty years and beyond. And once they articulate these new skills in their own words, they will be ready to align their education systems to make their vision a reality.

The Future of Learning

This book is another telltale sign that we've reached a tipping point in education. That so many notable minds are thinking hard about the future of learning is a signal that we just might be on the cusp of bold action.

At stake at this moment are the nation's competitiveness and all that goes along with it: a strong democracy, international leadership, lasting prosperity, and better prospects for generations to come. It is as true today as ever in our history that the American people are the engine of economic growth. In this time, for this era, however, they need to be equipped with knowledge and skills to compete in the 21st century.

In meeting rooms and classrooms across the country, I have met thousands of people who are ready to take on this challenge. The broad public support for the Framework for 21st Century Learning suggests the strong potential for building political will for a 21st century education system. It is exciting that the framework has generated this kind of interest, but it is far too early to proclaim victory.

> We need to move from consensus about the *vision* of 21st century learning to a thorough understanding of and commitment to the *outcomes* of 21st century learning.

We need to move from consensus about the *vision* of 21st century learning to a thorough understanding of and commitment to the *outcomes* of 21st century learning. There is a danger, in fact, that a "21st century education" or "21st century skills" could mean anything. Many people equate technology-rich classrooms or modern schools or rigorous core subjects with 21st century learning, regardless of whether students are mastering 21st century skills. In reality, the ability to use digital devices in no way means that students know anything about global awareness or health literacy, learning and innovation skills, life and career skills, or even media literacy skills. Similarly, many educators claim that they already teach 21st century skills, even though these skills are not systemically infused into standards and assessments, curriculum and instruction, or professional development and learning environments.

The most important next step is to agree on outcomes in terms of proficiency in 21st century skills. And it's not enough to want these outcomes—it's essential to plan the entire education system intentionally and transparently around them. A great place to start is to use the lens of 21st century outcomes to aggressively pursue the ideas in this book.

Acknowledgments

Special thanks to the former and current members of the Partnership for 21st Century Skills board and strategic council for their tremendous support of 21st century skills, and to Martha Vockley for her special contributions to the development of this foreword.

References

Autor, D. H., Levy, F., & Murnane, R. J. (2003, November). The skill content of recent technological change: An empirical exploration. *Quarterly Journal of Economics, 118*(4), 1279–1333.

Black, S. E., & Lynch, L. M. (2004, February). What's driving the new economy?: The benefits of workplace innovation. *The Economic Journal, 114,* 97–116.

Bureau of Labor Statistics, U.S. Department of Labor. (2008, June 27). *Number of jobs held, labor market activity, and earnings growth among the youngest baby boomers: Results from a longitudinal survey.* Washington, DC: Author. Accessed at www.bls.gov/news.release/pdf/nlsoy.pdf on December 8, 2009.

Bureau of Labor Statistics, U.S. Department of Labor. (2009). *Occupational projections and training data, 2008–09 edition.* Accessed at www.bls.gov/emp/optd/optdtabi_5.pdf on December 8, 2009.

Carnevale, A. P., & Desrochers, D. M. (2002, Fall). The missing middle: Aligning education and the knowledge economy. *Journal for Vocational and Special Needs Education, 25*(1), 3–23.

Casner-Lotto, J., & Barrington, L. (2006). *Are they really ready to work? Employers' perspectives on the basic knowledge and applied skills of new entrants to the 21st century U.S. workforce.* New York: The Conference Board. Accessed at www.21stcenturyskills.org/documents/FINAL_REPORT_PDF09-29-06 .pdf on June 18, 2009.

Conference Board. (2007). *CEO challenge 2007: Top 10 challenges* (Research Report 1406). New York: Author.

Conley, D. T. (2005). *College knowledge™: What it really takes for students to succeed and what we can do to get them ready.* San Francisco: Jossey-Bass.

Conley, D. T. (2007). *Toward a more comprehensive conception of college readiness.* Eugene, OR: Educational Policy Improvement Center. Accessed at www .gatesfoundation.org/learning/Documents/CollegeReadinessPaper.pdf on June 18, 2009.

Darling-Hammond, L., Barron, B., Pearson, P. D., Schoenfeld, A. H., Stage, E. K., & Zimmerman, T. D., et al. (2008). *Powerful learning: What we know about teaching for understanding.* San Francisco: Jossey-Bass.

Donovan, S., Bransford, J., & Pellegrino, J. W. (Eds.). (2000). *How people learn: Bridging research and practice.* Washington, DC: National Academies Press.

Donovan, S., & Bransford, J. (2004). *How students learn: Science in the classroom.* Washington, DC: National Academies Press.

Gera, S., & Gu, W. (2004, Fall). The effect of organizational innovation and information technology on firm performance. *International Productivity Monitor, 9,* 37–51. Accessed at www.csls.ca/ipm/9/gera_gu-e.pdf on June 18, 2009.

Gladwell, M. (2000). *The tipping point: How little things can make a big difference.* Boston: Little, Brown.

Grigg, W., Donahue, P., & Dion, G. (2007). *The nation's report card: 12th-grade reading and mathematics 2005* (NCES 2007-468). U.S. Department of Education, National Center for Education Statistics. Washington, DC: U.S. Government Printing Office. Accessed at http://nces.ed.gov/nationsreportcard/pdf/main2005/2007468.pdf on December 7, 2009.

International Institute for Management Development. (2009). *IMD world competitiveness yearbook.* Lausanne, Switzerland: Author.

Lee, J., Grigg, W., & Donahue, P. (2007). *The nation's report card: Reading 2007* (NCES 2007-496). Washington, DC: National Center for Education Statistics, Institute of Education Sciences, U.S. Department of Education. Accessed at http://nces.ed.gov/nationsreportcard/pdf/main2007/2007496.pdf on December 7, 2009.

Lichtenberg, J., Woock, C., & Wright, M. (2008). *Ready to innovate: Key findings.* New York: The Conference Board. Accessed at www.artsusa.org/pdf/information_services/research/policy_roundtable/ready_to_innovate.pdf on June 18, 2009.

National Center for Education Statistics (2009). *The nation's report card: Mathematics 2009* (NCES 2009-451). Washington, DC: Institute of Education Sciences, U.S. Department of Education. Accessed at http://nces.ed.gov/nationsreportcard/pdf/main2009/2010451.pdf on December 7, 2009.

Organisation for Economic Co-operation and Development (2009). *Top of the class: High performers in science in PISA 2006.* Paris: Author. Accessed at www.pisa.oecd.org/dataoecd/44/17/42645389.pdf on December 7, 2009.

Partnership for 21st Century Skills. (2007). *Beyond the three Rs: Voter attitudes toward 21st century skills.* Tucson, AZ: Author. Accessed at www.21stcenturyskills.org/documents/P21_pollreport_singlepg.pdf on June 18, 2009.

Partnership for 21st Century Skills. (2008). *21st century skills, education & competitiveness: A resource and policy guide.* Tucson, AZ: Author. Accessed at www.21stcenturyskills.org/documents/21st_century_skills_education_and_competitiveness_guide.pdf on June 18, 2009.

Partnership for 21st Century Skills. (2009a). *Framework for 21st century learning.* Tucson, AZ: Author. Accessed at www.21stcenturyskills.org/documents/framework_flyer_updated_april_2009.pdf on November 1, 2009.

Partnership for 21st Century Skills. (2009b). *The MILE guide: Milestones for improving learning & education.* Tucson, AZ: Author. Accessed at www.21stcenturyskills.org/documents/MILE_Guide_091101.pdf on December 8, 2009.

Pilat, D. (2004, December). *The economic impact of ICT: A European perspective* (IIR Working Paper 05–07). Paper presented to the Conference on IT Innovation, Tokyo. Accessed at www.iir.hit-u.ac.jp/iir-w3/event/WP05–07pilat.pdf on June 18, 2009.

Scott, M. (2009, May 19). Competitiveness: The U.S. and Europe are tops. *Business Week.* Accessed at www.businessweek.com/globalbiz/content/may2009/gb20090519_222765.htm on June 18, 2009.

Swanson, C. B. (2009, April). *Cities in crisis 2009: Closing the graduation gap.* Bethesda, MD: Editorial Projects in Education. Accessed at www.edweek.org/media/cities_in_crisis_2009.pdf on December 7, 2009.

Trilling, B., & Fadel, C. (2009). *21st century skills: Learning for life in our times.* San Francisco: Jossey-Bass.

U.S. Census Bureau. (2008, August 14). *An older and more diverse nation by midcentury.* Washington, DC: Author. Accessed at www.census.gov/Press-Release/www/releases/archives/population/012496.html on December 7, 2009.

van Ark, B., Barrington, L., Fosler, G., Hulten, C., & Woock, C. (2009). *Innovation and U.S. competitiveness: Reevaluating the contributors to growth.* New York: The Conference Board.

Wagner, T. (2008). *The global achievement gap: Why even our best schools don't teach the new survival skills our children need—and what we can do about it.* New York: Basic Books.

Webb, N. L. (1997, April). *Criteria for alignment of expectations and assessments in mathematics and science education* (Research Monograph 6). Madison, WI: National Institute for Science Education. Accessed at http://hub.mspnet.org/media/data/WebbCriteria.pdf?media_000000000924.pdf on June 18, 2009.

Zoghi, C., Mohr, R. D., & Meyer, P. B. (2007, May). *Workplace organization and innovation* (Working Paper No. 405). Washington, DC: U.S. Bureau of Labor Statistics.

Introduction

James Bellanca and Ron Brandt

Initiatives for significant change in an important sector of society often come mostly from outsiders. That is the case with the movement known as 21st century skills, spurred by the Partnership for 21st Century Skills. The Partnership includes large corporations, national professional organizations, and state offices of education. These agencies are concerned because they foresee a need for people with skills that go beyond those emphasized in today's schools. Elected leaders, including President Obama and many state governors, agree that this change is essential if U.S. students are to remain competitive in the global job market.

To accomplish its goals, the Partnership has delineated a Framework for 21st Century Learning that it would like to see each state adopt as the preeminent agenda for improving teaching and learning (see figure F.1 on page xv of the foreword by Ken Kay, president of the Partnership for 21st Century Skills). The redesign of policies in partner states is expected to begin with modification of current educational standards. Next, the Partnership wants to see practices aligned with the standards, with the result that students will show that they have developed the necessary skills.

In fact, desired practices that are intended to garner these outcomes are beginning to show. Early adopting teachers, principals, district leaders, and school boards have begun to put the framework into place. There are individual teachers who have changed their classrooms into technology-rich learning places. Their students experiment, do projects, take risks, and solve meaningful problems.

1

Although the number of whole schools that are attuned to the 21st century skills agenda falls short of those that continue to be mired in the practices and content of the 20th century, pockets of change are emerging. This is especially true in states that are members of the Partnership. In some states, the leaders of schoolwide change are charter schools organized to escape the "same old, same old" model of teaching and learning. In others, they are public schools that are redefining the teaching-learning connection.

At the district level, systemic reform for 21st century learning has a higher mountain to climb. In Tucson, Arizona, and Warrenville, Illinois, school leaders, starting with the school board and central administration, have gone public with a vision for 21st century learning and districtwide strategic plans. These plans are driving step-by-step actions that include new building designs, curriculum changes, long-term professional development for leaders and teachers, and the integration of technology in each school.

At the state level, West Virginia, an early 21st century skills partner, leads an increasing number of state offices of education in promoting 21st century skills. West Virginia has created a user-friendly website, Teach 21 (http://wvde.state.wv.us/teach21/), that offers 21st century *power standards*—instructional guides, unit plans, and sample project-based learning ideas—across content and special needs areas. West Virginia has also prepared a cadre of teacher leaders to facilitate teachers' use of project-based learning throughout the school year. Individual teachers and schools, such as tiny Washington District Elementary School in Buckhannon, are encouraged to revise instruction and assessment to align practice with this rich collection of resources and put project-based learning into daily practice.

Illinois has taken a different tack. When the Illinois State Board of Education formally signed on as a member of the Partnership, a group of education and business leaders formed an independent consortium to engage school districts in planning for implementation of the Partnership's Framework. The Illinois Consortium's vision includes plans to link multidistrict collaboratives that will provide long-term professional development and systemic change for member schools.

The Consortium's leadership, working closely with Illinois State Board of Education officials, is connecting its "bubble up" innovation process with the State Board's direction-setting initiative. The bubble-up process, named at New Trier East High School (Winnetka, Illinois) by then associate superintendent Mary Ida Maguire, encourages diverse constituent groups—teachers, parents, and administrators—to generate ideas for improvements to be funded for the next school year. The best ideas determined within each group rise to the top. A committee with members selected at random from each of the basic groups set criteria, agree on the best ideas, and make recommendations to the school board's budget committee. The Consortium's thirty member board of directors uses the bubble-up process to identify innovative projects for which it will pursue implementation funds.

On the national stage, a handful of professional organizations, most notably the National Council of Teachers of English, National Science Teachers Association, the National Council for Social Studies, and the American Library Association, have collaborated with the Partnership to develop online resource guides for integrating 21st century skills into content areas. Other organizations, such as the National Education Association and Association for Supervision and Curriculum Development, have taken steps to raise member awareness.

With the chapters in this volume, we begin the process of filling in the vision established by the Partnership. We know this collection will not be the last word on the subject, but we believe it is a valuable next step.

Our first task in envisioning this volume was to identify key issues that would contribute to the dialogue. We then identified a group of authors, each with the experience and farsightedness required to address these issues. We asked them to help answer three basic questions that would illuminate the theme of 21st century skills: (1) Why are the skills listed in the framework needed for learning in the future? (2) Which skills are most important? and (3) What can be done to help schools include these skills in their repertoire so that 21st century learning results?

Chapter Overviews

In his foreword, Ken Kay, president of the Partnership for 21st Century Skills, presents the Framework for 21st Century Learning advocated by his group. He responds to our three key questions and argues for realigning the teaching-learning relationship so that it focuses on outcomes.

In chapter 1, Howard Gardner identifies five types of minds society should encourage in future generations, three primarily cognitive and two in the human sphere. He outlines the major features of each type, the ways they can be shaped, and ways they could be distorted. He concludes by offering suggestions for how the five types might be integrated in a single, thriving human being.

In an interview for chapter 2, Linda Darling-Hammond calls for major policy changes to guide development of 21st century schools. She advocates deep alignment of standards, curriculum, instruction, and assessment; strengthening professionalism among teachers and school leaders; redesign of school time to allow for increased participation in professional decisions by teachers; and equitable distribution of resources among all schools. She insists that the United States must take a more balanced approach to school reform and that these changes are essential if the United States is to restore its lost leadership for educational excellence.

In chapter 3, Chris Dede compares several prominent lists of 21st century skills. He asks, "How diverse are these definitions for 21st century skills?" and notes that a lack of clarity about the nature of 21st century skills could be problematic. His examination illuminates what the various frameworks have in common and what each uniquely adds to the overarching concept.

In chapter 4, Richard and Rebecca DuFour discuss school settings for teaching 21st century skills. They observe that the most appropriate environment for teaching the life and career skills espoused by the Partnership for 21st Century Skills is a professional learning community (PLC) that models these skills. On this basis, they argue that the PLC is an essential tool for bringing about the changes that 21st century skills advocates envision.

In chapter 5, Robin Fogarty and Brian Pete carry the discussion to Singapore, where they have worked as educational consultants with the nation's ambitious "Teach Less, Learn More" initiative. Fogarty and Pete share the thoughts and feelings of teachers torn between the old ways of authoritarian, competitive schools and the new ways of shared decision making and collaborative study that encourage students to construct meaning rather than memorize facts.

In chapter 6, Bob Pearlman takes a walk through innovative school buildings designed for collaborative learning. He reminds us that the familiar box-based design of most current schools was suited for an outdated factory-model agenda. He shows us that form follows function in these innovative buildings as well—but the functions are now engagement, problem solving, and communication.

In chapter 7, Jay McTighe and Elliott Seif address the question of how to infuse 21st century outcomes into the overcrowded curriculum left over from the previous century with a systematic approach that takes advantage of the principles and practices of Understanding by Design. Using familiar concepts adapted from Schooling by Design, the authors outline five interrelated components: (1) the mission of schooling, (2) the principles of learning, (3) a curriculum and assessment system, (4) instructional programs and practices, and (5) systemic support factors. They examine how each of these components can help schools transform themselves to implement a viable approach to teaching and learning that ends in the acquisition of 21st century skills for all students.

In chapter 8, John Barell shows that problem-based learning is an ideal way to develop 21st century skills. He describes how teachers shift their standards-based curriculum from direct instruction of passive students to active engagement of problem solvers and question askers. His concrete examples illustrate ways problem-based inquiry can be adapted for meaningful use with students of all ages, talents, and challenges.

In chapter 9, David Johnson and Roger Johnson point out four important challenges of the 21st century: (1) greater global interdependence, (2) the increasing number of democracies throughout the world, (3) the need for creative entrepreneurs, and (4) the importance of interpersonal relationships that affect the development of personal identity. They discuss how cooperative learning, constructive controversy, and problem-solving negotiations will play a central role in teaching students the competencies and values they need to cope with these challenges and lead productive and fulfilling lives.

In chapter 10, Douglas Fisher and Nancy Frey describe three ways for teachers to respond to the extreme shifts in technological advancement and student needs for the 21st century: (1) considering functions rather than tools, (2) revising technology policies, and (3) developing students' minds through intentional instruction.

In chapter 11, Cheryl Lemke introduces three important innovations of 21st century learning: (1) visualization, (2) democratization of knowledge, and (3) participatory cultures for learning. She provides an impressive demonstration of ways technology permits greater balance between a visual approach and traditional language-based communication.

In chapter 12, Alan November reinforces Pearlman's rationale for redesigned schools. He cautions against using expensive technology to continue the trend of schools as managers of student learning. It's time, he says, to redesign not only the physical structure but the culture of schools. Technology makes it possible for students to become less dependent on schools and take more responsibility for managing their own learning.

In chapter 13, Will Richardson calls attention to the explosion of social network technologies. This powerful new landscape is fraught with danger, he says, but it is also rich with potential for learning. Richardson describes the rise of the virtual, global classroom, the challenge of this unrestricted learning, its potentials and pitfalls, and how educators can make the shift to network literacy in order to improve the quality of students' learning experiences.

In chapter 14, Douglas Reeves tackles the challenging problem of assessment. He argues that the new outcomes envisioned by advocates of 21st century skills can properly be measured only by abandoning standardized tests. He offers three criteria for determining how educators can know students are learning 21st century content and skills and shows how these might apply in practice.

In the afterword, Andy Hargreaves concludes the collection by asking tough questions about the 21st century skills movement. He uses metaphor to illuminate the historic ways that change has occurred in education and will occur in the future. He categorizes the emphasis on 21st century skills as the Third Way. He lists positive and negative results from each of the prior ways and looks ahead to an even more desirable Fourth Way.

Howard Gardner

Howard Gardner, Ph.D., is the John H. and Elisabeth A. Hobbs Professor of Cognition and Education at the Harvard Graduate School of Education. Among numerous honors, Gardner received a MacArthur Prize Fellowship in 1981. He has received honorary degrees from twenty-six colleges and universities. In 2005 and 2008, he was selected by *Foreign Policy* and *Prospect* magazines as one of the one hundred most influential public intellectuals in the world.

The author of over twenty books translated into twenty-eight languages, and several hundred articles, Gardner is best known in educational circles for his theory of multiple intelligences, a critique of the notion that there exists but a single human intelligence that can be assessed by standard psychometric instruments. Building on his studies of intelligence, Gardner has also authored *Leading Minds*, *Changing Minds*, and *Extraordinary Minds*. In 1994, in collaboration with psychologists Mihaly Csikszentmihalyi and William Damon, Gardner launched the GoodWork Project to study work that is excellent in quality, socially responsible, and personally meaningful. More recently, Gardner and collaborators at Harvard Project Zero have embarked on applications of good work insights in secondary schools and colleges, investigations of conceptions of trust and trustworthiness in young people, and studies of ethical issues associated with the new digital media.

In this chapter, Gardner identifies five types of minds society should encourage in future generations—three primarily cognitive and two in the human sphere. He outlines the major features of each type, the ways they can be shaped, and the ways they could be distorted. He concludes by offering suggestions for how the five types might be integrated in a single, thriving human being.

Chapter 1

Five Minds for the Future

Howard Gardner

Educational institutions change very slowly. In some ways, this conservatism is positive; it discourages faddism and encourages educators to build upon tried-and-true methods. Of course, such conservatism can go too far. I remember a revealing experience I had in China more than twenty years ago. I was invited to observe a college course in psychology and was dismayed to find that the class consisted entirely of students simply reciting the textbook content verbatim. Afterward, with the interpreter by my side, I engaged in a ten-minute debate with the instructor. I emphasized that the students all knew the rote material and suggested that it would be far more productive to raise provocative questions or ask the students to draw on the memorized material in order to illuminate a new phenomenon. The instructor was not the least bit convinced. Indeed, after we went back and forth, she finally cut off the discussion with the statement, "We've been doing things this way for so long, we *know* it is right."

With the benefit of historical insight, we can identify eras when education had to undergo fundamental changes. Probably the most dramatic changes occurred during classical times, when writing became common, and during the Renaissance, when print emerged. Within the United States, pivotal times included the rise of the American common school in the middle of the 19th century, and the commitment, in the middle of the 20th century, to educate all Americans, regardless of race, gender, social class, or ethnicity. At such times, we can no longer just carry on as before: we must consider whether fundamental changes may be in order.

I believe that, at the beginning of the 21st century, we live in such a time. The forces of globalization entail major changes in all of our lives: I refer here to the increasing power of and reliance on science and technology; the incredible connectivity that results; the enormous amount of information, often of dubious quality, that is at our fingertips; the convergence of cultures in economic, cultural, and social terms; and the incessant circulation, intermingling, and periodic clashing of human beings of diverse backgrounds and aspirations. Intimately and inextricably connected to others, we need to be able to communicate with one another, live with one another, and, where possible, make common cause.

In this chapter, I portray the kinds of minds that we should cultivate in the future. Three of these minds are primarily cognitive: the disciplined mind, the synthesizing mind, and the creating mind. Two minds deal with the human sphere: the respectful mind and the ethical mind. I indicate the major features of these forms of mind, the ways in which they can be shaped, and the ways in which they can be distorted. I describe some of the tensions among minds and offer suggestions of how to possibly integrate these minds within a single thriving human being.

Here are a few clarifying comments: First, in conceptualizing the future, I refer to trends whose existence is widely acknowledged; to be sure, none of the five minds is exclusive to the future: one could have called for them fifty or perhaps even five hundred years ago. Yet their individual and joint cultivation assumes particular urgency at the present time.

> To be sure, none of these five minds is exclusive to the future: one could have called for them fifty or perhaps even five hundred years ago.

My second point is that I intend to be both descriptive and prescriptive. I am descriptive in the sense that I seek to explain what these minds are; I am prescriptive in the sense that I believe we need to cultivate these kinds of minds. Certainly, thriving as individuals and as societies without a generous dosage of these five mental predispositions is not possible. Indeed, it is possible that the cultivation of the respectful and ethical mind will determine whether human beings survive as a species.

A third point concerns the scope of the enterprise. Increasingly, education will take place in all kinds of venues and continue throughout one's productive life. So, the minds under discussion here are as much the concern of the fifty-year-old executive or manager as of the teacher or mentor of the young. Moreover, throughout their life cycle, individuals must tend to the development of their own mind, as well as the minds of other individuals—their offspring, students, or employees—over whom they have responsibility.

Finally, as the individual who developed the concept of multiple intelligences, I should forestall a possible confusion. When I write as a psychologist investigating individual differences, I describe human beings as exhibiting different intellectual strengths and different intellectual profiles; thus, William excels in linguistic intelligence, while Pablo is strong in spatial intelligence (Gardner, 2006). But when I wear the mantle of an educator, in the broad sense just described, I call for each person to develop all five kinds of minds. Considerations of differences among individuals fade into the background.

The Disciplined Mind

In English, the word *discipline* has two distinct connotations. We speak of the mind as having mastered one or more disciplines: arts, crafts, professions, or scholarly pursuits. By rough estimate, an individual takes approximately one decade to learn a discipline well enough to be considered an expert or master. In most cases, individuals acquire such mastery through some kind of tutelage: either formally, in a school, or less formally, through some combination of apprenticeship and self-instruction.

Perhaps at one time, an individual could rest on his or her laurels after initially achieving such disciplinary mastery. No longer! Disciplines evolve and ambient conditions change, as do the demands on individuals who have achieved initial mastery. Over succeeding decades, an individual must continue to educate both himself or herself, and others. Such hewing of expertise can continue only if an individual possesses discipline—in the second sense of the word. That is, an individual needs continually to practice in a disciplined way to remain at the top of his or her game.

Once basic literacies have been mastered, the chief burden of educational systems is the acquisition of an ensemble of scholarly disciplines. In my own work on precollegiate education, I stress four disciplines: mathematics, science, history, and at least one art form. I make a sharp distinction between subject matter and discipline. The subject matter of history consists of learning detailed factual information about the past. Such television quiz-show knowledge is always welcome and sometimes lucrative. But this amassing of information differs qualitatively from disciplinary competence. For example, an individual who has acquired the discipline of history can think like a historian. That is, the student of history appreciates that he or she must work with textual, graphical, and other kinds of records; and those records must be reconstructed and sensitively interpreted. Unlike science, historical events occur only once and cannot be replicated exactly or interpreted unambiguously. Historians must impute motives to personages from the past; each generation will necessarily rewrite history. Yet historians are bound to respect the facts and to strive for as accurate and comprehensive a record as possible. Other major disciplines, ranging from genetics to economics, exhibit analogous regularities and constraints.

Individuals first acquire a disciplined mind in school. But relatively few go on to become academic disciplinarians. The rest master disciplines that are not, strictly speaking, scholarly. Yet the same need to master *a way of thinking* applies to the range of workers—whether one is dealing with professionals, such as lawyers or engineers, or with those in business, such as individuals in personnel, marketing, sales, or management. Such education may occur in formal classes or on the job, explicitly or implicitly. In the end, a form of mastery is achieved, one that must continue to be refined over the years.

Nowadays, the mastery of more than one discipline is at a premium. We value those individuals who are genuinely interdisciplinary, but the claim must be real. We would not acknowledge someone as bilingual unless he or she could speak more than one language. The claim of interdisciplinarity makes sense only if a person has genuinely mastered and can integrate two or more disciplines. For most individuals, the attainment of multiple perspectives is a more reasonable goal.

Nowadays, the mastery of more than one discipline is at a premium.

Pathological forms exist with respect to any kind of mind. Those related to the disciplined mind are, first, the individual who is overly disciplined, who approaches every issue, whether professional or personal, through the same set of beliefs and practices. Next is the individual who, at one time, had mastered the discipline but who no longer keeps up—exhibiting the patina of the disciplinarian but no longer possessing the requisite contents, skills, and understandings. Finally, there is the avowed interdisciplinarian, who may, in fact, be a jack-of-all-trades but the master of none.

Scholars of cognition generally believe it takes ten years to master a discipline. This leaves little time for multiple forms of mastery. But thanks to excellent computer pedagogy, forms of expertise are more rapidly attainable, perhaps in half the time. Also, because of shrewd scaffolding for those who have yet to attain mastery, hope remains that we will nonetheless be able to participate in a number of disciplines and to synthesize knowledge obtained therefrom.

Scholars of cognition generally believe it takes ten years to master a discipline.

The Synthesizing Mind

Murray Gell-Mann, Nobel laureate in physics and an avowed multidisciplinarian, made an intriguing claim about our time: in the 21st century, the most valued mind will be the synthesizing mind—the mind that can survey a wide range of sources; decide what is important and worth paying attention to; and then put this information together in ways that make sense to oneself and, ultimately, to other persons as well.

Gell-Mann is onto something important. Information has never been in short supply, but with the advent of new technologies and media, most notably the Internet, vast and often overwhelming amounts of information now deluge individuals around the clock. Shrewd triage becomes an imperative. Those who can synthesize well for themselves will rise to the top of the pack; those whose syntheses make sense to others will become invaluable teachers, communicators, and leaders.

Strangely, my own discipline of psychology seems to have fumbled with regard to explicating the skill of synthesizing. Compared to a half century ago, a great deal of knowledge exists about how individuals learn to read, calculate, and master basic concepts in history, science, economics, or philosophy; but I have been unable to locate comparable knowledge about how an individual synthesizes.

Nonetheless, identifying the basic constituents of the synthesizing process is possible. To begin, a person must decide on the area that he or she wishes to synthesize. Sometimes, the individual has time to reflect on this; sometimes the demand for synthesis is pressing.

Consider an example from business. Suppose that you are an executive, and your company is considering the acquisition of a new company in a sector that seems important but about which you and your immediate associates know little. Your goal is to acquire enough information so that you and your board can make a judicious decision within the next two months.

The place to begin is with the best existing synthesis: fetch it, devour it, and evaluate it. If none exists, you turn to the most knowledgeable individuals and ask them to provide the basic information requisite to synthesis. Given this initial input, you then decide what information seems adequate and which important additional data you need. At the same time, and of great moment, you need to decide on the form and format of the ultimate synthesis: a written narrative, an oral presentation, a set of scenarios, a set of charts and graphs, an equation, a mind map, or an ordered list of pros and cons leading to a final judgment.

Then the actual work of synthesis begins in earnest. New information must be acquired, probed, evaluated, followed up with, or sidelined. The new information needs to be fit, if possible, into the initial synthesis; and where fit is lacking, mutual adjustments must be made. There is constant reflection and regular tinkering.

At some point before the final synthesis is due, you need to develop a protosynthesis that should be tested with the most knowledgeable associates, preferably an audience that is critical and constructive. To the extent that time and resources are available, more than one trial run is desirable. But ultimately there arrives a moment of truth, at which point the best possible synthesis must suffice.

What kind of mind is needed to guide the synthesis? Clearly, although he or she should have a "home" area of expertise, the synthesizer cannot conceivably be up to speed on every relevant discipline. As compensation, the synthesizer must know enough about the requisite disciplines to be able to make judgments about whom and what to trust—or to identify individuals who can help make that determination. The synthesizer must also have a sense of the relevant forms and formats for the synthesis, being prepared to alter when possible but to make a final commitment as the deadline approaches. The synthesizer must always keep his or her eyes on the big picture, while making sure to secure adequate details and arrange them in useful ways. It is quite possible that certain individuals are blessed with a *searchlight intelligence*—the capacity to look widely and to monitor constantly, thus making sure that nothing vital is missing—and that such individuals also have the capacity to value the complementary *laser intelligence* that has fully mastered a specific discipline or problem area. Such broad-gauged thinkers should be identified and cherished. But it is crucial that we determine how to nurture synthesizing capacities more widely, because this facility is likely to remain at a premium in the coming era.

Anyone who has read a clutch of textbooks or attended a variety of weekend seminars knows that not all syntheses are equally effective. Some syntheses are too sprawling, attempting to cover too much material. Some syntheses are too focused, serving as briefings for specialists, not nutrients for generalists. Some are too technical; others are too popular. Different aesthetics can also be brought to bear. I favor literary syntheses that make judicious use of organizers, stories, metaphors, and analogies. Others may prefer syntheses that are devoid of linguistic artifice and that instead rely heavily on charts, graphs, and captionless cartoons. The good synthesizer must know what works both for him and for those who must make use of his synthesis.

The Creating Mind

Most artists, scientists, and scholars plow the same paths as their peers; most politicians and executives are substitutable for one another. In sharp contrast to those conventional experts, those who possess the creating mind forge new ground. In the current popular argot, creators think outside the box. In our society we have come to value those individuals who attempt new things, monitor whether they work, cast about continually for new ideas and practices, pick themselves up after an apparent failure, and so on. Society gives special honor to those rare individuals whose innovations actually change the ideas and practices of their peers—in my trade, we call these individuals *big C creators.*

> In our society we have come to value those individuals who attempt new things, monitor whether they work, cast about continually for new ideas and practices, pick themselves up after an apparent failure, and so on.

What is special about our time? Put succinctly, nearly every practice that is well understood will be automated. Mastery of existing disciplines will be necessary but not sufficient. Whether at the workplace or in the laboratory, on the political platform or the theatrical stage, individuals face pressure to go beyond the conventional wisdom or the habitual practice—to try to improve upon previous practices and current efforts by themselves or their competitors.

Of course, sheer innovation is much easier to accomplish than effective creation. I could write this essay in numerous original ways—for example, putting nonsensical phrases between every sentence. These insertions may well be an original act, but such a ploy serves no useful purpose and is unlikely ever to influence future essayists. Suppose, however, I devise a set of Web links to key points, and those links can be varied, based on questions raised by particular readers or on a shrewd assessment of the interests and sophistication of various audiences. Were such a practice desirable, and my pilot work proved successful, such an innovation might eventually be judged as creative.

Ascertaining the relationship among the three kinds of minds introduced thus far is important. Clearly, synthesizing is not possible without some mastery of constituent disciplines—and perhaps there is, or will be, a discipline of synthesizing, quite apart from such established disciplines as mathematics, music, or management. Creation is unlikely to emerge in the absence of some disciplinary mastery and, perhaps, some capacity to synthesize; it's not possible to think outside the box unless you have a box.

Nonetheless, we must bear in mind that the most imaginative instances of creating typically emerge with individuals who are young—perhaps twenty or thirty years old in science or mathematics, perhaps a decade or so later in other pursuits. Disciplinary acumen and synthesizing capacities continue to accrue throughout a lifetime. This fact suggests that too much discipline, or excessive synthesizing, may actually prove counterproductive for the aspiring creator. The challenge is to acquire enough discipline and sufficient synthesis early in life in order to take the confident leap—to go beyond what is known, and stretch in new and unexpected directions.

In comparing creating with synthesizing, we should not minimize the originality of synthesizing. A valued synthesis is not simply an algorithmic exercise; rather, it gains power when it provides that sense of meaning, significance, and connectedness that so many seek today.

Let me put it another way. If synthesis were simply the following of rules, a well-programmed machine could carry it out. But if synthesis is to respond to human concerns, to concerns not just of the moment but also concerns *sub specie aeternitatis*, then it becomes a distinctly human endeavor. And so, I offer the suggestion that powerful synthesizing builds on the candidate human intelligence that I have been studying most recently: *existential intelligence*, defined as the capacity to raise and address the largest questions. When these questions are new ones, synthesizing blends into creating.

As a student of creativity, I long assumed that creating was primarily a *cognitive feat*—having the requisite knowledge and the apposite cognitive processes—but I now believe that personality and temperament are equally important, and perhaps even more important, for the would-be creator. Many individuals know a great deal, and most can

As a student of creativity, I long assumed that creating was primarily a *cognitive feat*—having the requisite knowledge and the apposite cognitive processes—I now believe that personality and temperament are equally important, and perhaps even more important, for the would-be creator.

acquire knowledge and skills indefinitely. Those who would reach for the Promethean fire must possess a robust personality and temperament. More than willing, creators must be eager to take chances, to venture into the unknown, to fail, and then, perhaps smiling, to pick themselves up and once more throw themselves into the fray. Even when successful, creators do not rest on their laurels. They have motivation again to venture into the unknown and to risk failure, buoyed by the hope that another breakthrough may be in the offing, able to frame an apparent defect as a valuable learning opportunity.

In 1909, psychoanalyst Sigmund Freud and his close associate Carl Jung went to America. It was Freud's first and last trip—he did not like the New World. Jung remained longer; he was lionized by audiences. With great enthusiasm, Jung wired back to Freud: "Great news: psychoanalysis big success in the United States." According to legend, Freud immediately wired back: "What did you leave out?" Far from enjoying the acclaim, Freud was more intent on raising the tension, on venturing beyond anything suggestive of easy acceptance or conventional wisdom.

In the United States, people often ask me how to cultivate creativity. I give two responses, which are neither expected nor immediately popular. First, I talk about the need to pose challenges, obstacles, and boulders. An individual cannot achieve a robust temperament without taking chances, often failing, and learning that the world does not thereupon end. Of course, the frustrations must be manageable; they cannot be allowed to break a person's spirits. Second, and at the risk of being politically incorrect, I question whether it is important to cultivate creativity in American schools. That is because messages about the importance—the cash value—of creativity are ubiquitous in American society: on the streets, in the media, and in the marketplace. Probably more emphasis on disciplines and synthesis would yield greater dividends. But in other countries, where rote instruction is entrenched and innovations are greeted with suspicion, I would favor a curriculum and a pedagogy oriented toward the cultivation of the creative person and the discovery and exploration of the creative idea.

Until this point, I've reviewed the kinds of minds most familiar to me as a cognitive psychologist. If I had written this essay a decade ago, I would probably have stopped here. Indeed, I could summarize the three minds very crisply: the disciplined mind involves depth; the synthesizing mind entails breadth; and the creating mind features stretch.

More recent events, however, prompted me to postulate and ponder two additional kinds of minds: the respectful mind and the ethical mind. To begin, there is my fifteen-year collaborative study of good work—work that is excellent, engaging, and ethical. This line of research sensitized me to kinds of minds that I might otherwise have ignored. In addition, many social and political trends in the world disturbed me. Sheer cultivation of cognitive capacities, in the absence of the human dimension, seems a dubious undertaking. I agree with Ralph Waldo Emerson's assertion that "character is higher than intellect."

The Respectful Mind

Almost from the start, infants are alert to other human beings. Absent frank pathology, even neonates display keen interest in anything that resembles a human face or voice. The attachment between parent (typically the mother) and child is predisposed to develop throughout the early months of life; and the nature and strength of that bond determines the capacity of individuals to form relationships with others throughout life.

Of equal potency is the young human's capacity to distinguish among individuals and among groups of individuals. Within months, the infant can distinguish his mother from other young females; by the end of the first year of life, the infant recognizes, and can modulate his reaction to, a range of individuals in his environment. By the age of two approximately, the toddler is able to make all manner of group discriminations: male versus female, young versus old, familiar versus unfamiliar, and, most revealingly, classification of members of different racial and ethnic groups.

Human beings are wired to make such distinctions readily; indeed, survival depends upon the ability to distinguish among those who are likely to help and nourish, and those who might do harm. But the particular messages in an individual's own environment determine *how* that person labels specific individuals or groups. An individual's own experiences, and the attitudes of the peers and elders to whom he or she is closest, determine whether he or she likes, admires, or respects certain individuals and groups; or whether, on the contrary, that individual comes to shun, fear, or even hate these individuals.

In earlier eras, when human beings met only a few hundred people in the course of a lifetime, the nature of their interpersonal or intergroup attitudes was of less moment. Today, individuals live in an era when nearly every person is likely to encounter thousands of other individuals personally, and when billions of people have the option of traveling abroad or of encountering individuals from remote cultures through visual or digital media.

A person possessed of a respectful mind welcomes this exposure to diverse persons and groups. Such a person wants to meet, get to know, and come to like individuals from remote quarters. A truly cosmopolitan individual gives others the benefit of the doubt, displays initial trust, tries to form links, and avoids prejudicial judgments. To be sure, such a posture is not uncritical or automatic; it is possible for another individual to lose one's respect, even to merit one's distrust or hatred. The respectful mind, however, starts with an assumption that diversity is positive and that the world would be a better place if individuals sought to respect one another.

> The respectful mind starts with an assumption that diversity is positive and that the world would be a better place if individuals sought to respect one another.

The threats to respect are intolerance and prejudice. A prejudiced person has preconceived ideas about individuals and groups, and resists bracketing those preconceptions. For example, if I am a disrespectful straight, white American and you are German, African American, or homosexual, I will assume that you are no good, distance myself, and take every opportunity to put you down verbally or physically. An intolerant person has a very low threshold for unfamiliarity; the default assumption is that strange is bad. No matter what you look like or who you are, if I don't already have a reason to embrace you, I won't.

Sham forms of respect exist. For example, I might "kiss up and kick down." That is, as long as you have power over me, or can do me a favor, I will treat you well; but once I am in a more important position, I won't give you the time of day. Or I might respect you publicly, but once you have left the room, I will make fun of you or the group to which you belong.

To come to respect others once feared, distrusted, or disliked is not easy. Yet, in an interconnected world, such a potential for growth, for freshly forged or renewed respect, is crucial. In war-torn lands, commissions of truth and reconciliation have taken on deserved importance; and at least at times, they succeed in reconstituting badly frayed ties. When countries are at loggerheads, sporting events (such as ping-pong diplomacy between Chinese and Americans) or cultural events (such as orchestras made up of young Israelis and Palestinians) can sometimes pave the way for reconciliation with "the other." When it comes to the causes of terrorism, these are no quick fixes; only genuine respect, nurtured and earned over the decades, can reduce the appeal of terrorism.

The Ethical Mind

The road to respect is paved from the earliest age, one smile or frown at a time. An ethical stance is in no way antithetical to a respectful one, but it involves a much more sophisticated stance toward individuals and groups. A person possessed of an ethical mind is able to think of himself or herself abstractly, and is able to ask, "What kind of a worker do I want to be? What kind of a citizen do I want to be?" Going beyond the posing of such questions, the person is able to think about himself or herself in a universalistic manner: "What would the world be like if all workers in my profession took the stance that I have, if all citizens in my region or my world fulfilled their roles in the way that I do?" Such conceptualization involves a recognition of rights and responsibilities attendant to each role. Crucially, the ethical individual behaves in accordance with the answers that he or she has forged, even when such behaviors clash with self-interest.

My own insights into the ethical mind come largely from fifteen years of study of professionals who are seeking to do good work—work that is excellent, engaging, and ethical (Gardner, Csikszentmihalyi, & Damon, 2001). Most individuals admire good work and want to achieve it. That is, they would like to behave ethically, and they would like others to behave ethically. But this wish does not translate automatically or smoothly into reality. Determining what is ethical is not always easy, and such a determination can prove especially challenging during times like our own, when conditions change very quickly, and when market forces are powerful and often unmitigated. Even when an individual determines the proper course, behaving in an ethical manner is not always easy; that proves particularly so when one is highly ambitious, when others appear to be cutting corners, when different interest groups demand contradictory things from workers, when the ethical course is less clear than one might like, and when such a course runs against one's immediate self-interest.

> Most individuals admire good work and want to achieve it.

Although most children lack the capability to conceptualize the ethical course, the building blocks that form the basis of an ethical life are identifiable: the words and actions of respected elders at home, at school, and in the community. Developing an ethical mind is much easier, so much more natural, when an individual inhabits an ethical environment. When adults are reflective about their decisions, and explicitly cite moral concerns, young people get the message even when the details elude them. Such an environment is rarely sufficient, however. Crucial contributions are made by the atmosphere at a person's first places of work: how do the adults in positions of authority behave; what are the beliefs and behaviors of one's peers; and, above all, what happens when there are clear ethical deviations, and—more happily if less frequently—when an individual or a group behaves in an ethically exemplary fashion? Education in ethics may not begin as early as education for respect, but neither "curriculum" ever ends.

I've suggested that an ethical stance requires the abstract attitude that typically does not develop until adolescence. But even young children are parts of communities—home, school classroom, or church—and they can be acculturated into the ideals, attitudes, and behaviors appropriate to their roles within these communities. Indeed, sensitivity to *institutional culture*—the norms of a particular group as manifest in daily operation—is certainly within the ken of the child in the elementary school. (Alas, so is acculturation into unethical frames of mind.) Thus, society should infuse ethics into the sinews of all important institutions in which the child is involved. An important step will have been taken toward an ethical career and citizenship.

Given the high standards necessary for an ethical mind, examples of failures abound. It is not difficult to recognize behaviors that are strictly illegal, such as theft or fraud, or behaviors that are obviously unethical—for example, the journalist who publishes a story that he knows is untrue or the geneticist who overlooks data that run counter to her hypothesis. More subtle discrimination is needed to detect instances of compromised work—for example, the journalist who fails to confirm a tip before publishing or the geneticist who elects quick publication over running an indicated control group. Compromised work and bad work can undermine institutions and societies; the former may occur more slowly, but unless the trends are reversed, the undermining of the profession is equally decisive.

My examples of ethics are drawn from the professional world, the one that I've studied. But none of us are simply professionals; we are also family members, citizens of a community, and inhabitants of the world. In each case, the ethical mind must go through the exercise of identifying the kind of individual one wants to be. And when a person's own words and behaviors run counter to that idealization, that individual must take corrective action.

I would add that as one gets older, it does not suffice simply to keep one's own ethical house in order. One acquires a responsibility over broader realms of which one is a member. For example, an individual journalist or geneticist may behave ethically, but if his or her peers fail to do so, the senior worker should assume responsibility for the health of the domain. I deem such individuals *trustees*: veterans who are widely respected, deemed to be disinterested, and dedicated to the legitimacy of the domain. As the French playwright Jean-Baptiste Molière commented, "We are responsible not only for what we do but for what we do not do."

Tensions Between and Among the Minds

Of the five minds, the ones most likely to be confused with one another are the respectful mind and the ethical mind. In part, this is because of ordinary language: we consider respect and ethics to be virtues, and we assume that it is impossible to have one without the other. Moreover, very often they correlate; persons who are ethical are also respectful, and vice versa.

However, as indicated, I see these as developmentally discrete accomplishments. An individual can be respectful from early childhood, even without having a deep understanding of the reasons for respect. In contrast, ethical conceptions and behaviors presuppose an abstract, self-conscious attitude: a capacity to step away from the details of daily life and to think of oneself as a worker or as a citizen.

For example, even as a youth, Abraham Lincoln never liked slavery; he wanted to treat slaves as human beings with their own aspirations, not as mere property. Yet it took him many years to become a political opponent of slavery because as a citizen and as a political figure, Lincoln felt that it was his ethical obligation to obey the law, which protected slavery in much of the United States. As he put it, his own personal views—his own respect for Negroes—was irrelevant to his official role. Only after much soul-searching and many tumultuous political events did Lincoln reconceptualize his role as a political leader and begin to favor emancipation. In this particular case, he brought into closer alignment his respectful and ethical minds.

Whistle-blowers are another example. Many individuals observe wrongdoing at high levels in their company and remain silent. They may want to keep their jobs, and also to respect their leaders. It takes both courage and a mental leap to think of oneself not as an acquaintance—or even a friend—of one's supervisor but rather as a member of an institution or profession, with certain obligations attendant thereto. The whistle-blower assumes an ethical stance at the cost of a respectful relationship with his supervisor.

Economist Albert O. Hirschman (1970) wrote insightfully about such a sequence. Initially, he contends, one owes allegiance, or loyalty, to one's organization; this is a matter of respect. If, however, the offending situation remains or magnifies, then one has an obligation so speak up. At this point, voice trumps respect. Ultimately, if such an effort to alert and to change the organization is judged to be futile, then the individual should exit the organization; that is the only ethical course. Such a sequence is difficult to realize in a totalitarian society, where other options are few and the penalties for voice can be severe. Nor is it easy to realize if an individual has no other employment options.

Sometimes, respect trumps ethics. Initially, for example, I believed that the French government was correct in banning Muslim women from wearing scarves at school. By the same token, I defended the right of Danish newspapers to publish cartoons that poked fun at Islamic fundamentalism. In both cases, I took the American Bill of Rights at face value—no state religion, guaranteed freedom of expression. But I eventually came to the conclusion that this ethical stance needed to be weighed against the costs of disrespecting the sincere and strongly held religious beliefs of others. The costs of honoring the Islamic faith emerged as less than the costs of honoring an abstract principle. Of course, I make no claim that I came to the right conclusion—only that the tension between respect and ethics can be resolved in contrasting ways.

Here is another example: the creative mind often finds itself in conflict with other minds. In East Asia, an individual is expected to respect his or her mentor throughout life. This stance is difficult to maintain when that person engages in creative iconoclasm—more bluntly, when one's own work overthrows that of the mentor or, equally devastating, renders it irrelevant. For this reason, many aspiring creators from East Asia moved to the West in past decades so that they could avoid the appearance of disrespecting their teacher or mentor. By the same token, too much of an emphasis on discipline, or too much of a dedication to synthesis, also clashes with pursuit of creative breakthroughs. Some discipline and some synthesizing are necessary—but not too much.

The Minds and Multiple Intelligences

As the originator of the theory of multiple intelligences (MI theory), I am often asked about the various intelligences in the development of the five minds. The disciplined and creating minds can and do draw on any and all intelligences, depending on the area of work. Thus, whether disciplined or creative, a poet depends on linguistic intelligence, an architect on spatial intelligence, a therapist on interpersonal intelligence, and so on. Respect and ethics clearly draw on the personal intelligences. Ethics, reflecting an abstract way of thinking, draws as well on logical intelligence.

The synthesizing mind poses a problem for MI theory because synthesis often involves the operation of one, two, or even several intelligences. I suspect that gifted synthesizers achieve their goals in different ways. For example, as a synthesizer, I rely heavily on linguistic, logical, and naturalistic intelligences, but others may draw on spatial, artistic, or personal intelligences to achieve and convey their synthesis. And so, I offer the suggestion that powerful synthesizing may build on the candidate intelligence that I have been contemplating most recently: existential intelligence.

Assessment and the Five Minds

Once individuals hear about the five minds, they ask how to best assess their occurrence and their enhancement. In the United States, the assessment question almost always comes up soon. Assessing the minds is hardly a straightforward matter; and indeed, I worry about too rapid a move to the "test" for synthesizing or ethics. Nonetheless, a few preliminary thoughts are in order.

Assessing the minds is hardly a straight-forward matter.

We know the most about assessing the disciplined mind. Experts in nearly every discipline have developed both quantitative and more qualitative (or more subjective) ways of assessing individual attainment in the discipline. Indeed, educators could not legitimately teach the disciplines in the school, and award licenses or diplomas, without some reasonably consensual evaluation metrics.

As I formulate it, creativity can be assessed only after the fact. An individual work or product is creative if, and only if, it changes the ways in which others in the relevant field think and act. Sometimes this judgment about creativity can be made quite rapidly (as in the case of a riveting movie format), but this assessment can take years or even decades. And so, we can assess an individual's potential for achieving middle C or big C creativity only by looking at what small C creativities have already been achieved.

Syntheses are best judged by laying out beforehand the criteria for a successful synthesis and determining, by consensus, whether those criteria have been achieved. Chapter 3 of my book *Five Minds for the Future* (2007) provides an example of how to do this.

This leaves respect and ethics. If I have the opportunity of observing a person, a group, or an institution, particularly when no one is aware of my presence, I can readily determine whether an aura of respect pervades. In contrast, ethics can be assessed only if a set of explicit principles characterizes a role (professional, citizen). Those responsible for upholding the principles may then render judgments about who abides by the principles and who crosses the line into compromised or bad work.

Of course, even if it could not please a psychometrician, sometimes a general guideline can take an individual quite far. Hearing about the five minds, my friend and distinguished educator Patricia Graham commented, "We respect those who behave in an ethical manner." Indeed, although ethics might be judged in many ways, consensus that a person or institution in question is worthy of respect is an extremely persuasive indication.

Are There Other Minds?

When I wrote *Five Minds for the Future*, I was unaware of Daniel Pink's book *A Whole New Mind: Why Right-Brainers Will Rule the Future* (2006); and Daniel Pink does not mention my writings in his book. Ignorance is never to be preferred over knowledgeability; nonetheless, this state of affairs means that two writers could each put forth their own views independently, and readers could judge the extent to which these views were congruent or in conflict.

Pink is impressively alert to the softer sides of cognition, which he calls design, story, symphony, and play. Although much of my own research has probed the arts, I do not specify areas of discipline, synthesizing, and creating; a person can choose to work in architecture, dance, or film, as well as in business, finance, or management consultancies. However, I agree with Pink that those capacities that can be carried out automatically by machines, or far more cheaply in other parts of the world, will cease to be at a premium in the developed nations. Therefore, the so-called right-brain capacities will come increasingly to the fore.

My work brings out points that Pink ignores or minimizes. Even though mastery of a discipline seems old-fashioned and left-brained, mastery is still vital. Those who do not have a discipline, as well as a sense of discipline, will either be without work or will work for someone who does. Also, Pink leaves out how individuals behave toward others (respect) and how they carry out their roles as workers and citizens (ethics). He might respond that the new mind features "empathy," and that is true enough. Nonetheless, an empathetic person does not necessarily behave desirably. Empathy can be used to produce hurt—indeed, that is what sadism is, taking pleasure in the pain that others feel.

I endorse Pink's discussion of meaning. The thirst for significance has always existed in human beings. The faster the changes, the weaker the ambient religious and ideological systems, the more isolated the individual and the greater the thirst for meaning. I had considered the importance of meaning in my study of existential intelligence. The newly suggested link between synthesizing, on the one hand, and existential intelligence, on the other, resonates with Pink's interest in meaning.

As Pink reminds us, in a world that so honors the STEM disciplines (science, technology, engineering, and mathematics), we require extra efforts not to ignore the other fields of human knowledge and practice. I worry particularly about the arts and humanities. There is less demand for these topics, which were once seen as central to a liberal education. Parents, policymakers, and pupils are all pulled toward the professions, and particularly those that have the potential for making one wealthy (preferably quickly). Yet I believe that an individual cannot be a full person, let alone have a deep understanding of the world, unless he or she is rooted as well in art, literature, and philosophy. Moreover, these realms of knowledge should not be rewards for the harried middle-aged executive, but rather the cornerstone of education for all young persons. In the absence of a strong demand for these topics on the part of consumers, it is incumbent on those with the responsibility of trustee to make sure that humanistically oriented fields are protected. By the same token, those who would hope to continue teaching literature, music, philosophy, and history need to present these topics in ways that speak to new generations, while avoiding "inside baseball" curricula that speak only to those with a professional stake in the field.

Integrating Five Minds Into One Person

Even if one believes that all five of these minds ought to be cultivated, many questions remain about how best to accomplish this goal. One could, for example, randomly assign young persons to one of five classrooms or schools; or, more deliberately, one could attempt to assess mental affinities, and then place each child in the most congenial track (Johnny seems like he has a lot of potential to synthesize; let's put him in track two). I do not favor this alternative. I feel individuals will be better served if they have the opportunity to cultivate all five minds even if, in the end, some will emerge as stronger in one variety, while others exhibit a contrasting profile.

Among the minds is no strict hierarchy, such that one mind should be cultivated before the others, and yet a certain rhythm does exist. An individual needs a certain amount of discipline—in both senses of the term—before undertaking a reasonable synthesis; and if the synthesis involves more than one discipline, then each of the constituent disciplines must be cultivated. By the same token, any genuinely creative activity presupposes a certain disciplined mastery. Although prowess at synthesizing may be unnecessary, nearly all creative breakthroughs—whether in the arts, politics, scholarship, or corporate life—are to some extent dependent on provisional syntheses. Still, as argued previously, too much discipline clashes with creativity; those who excel at syntheses are less likely to effect the most radical creative breakthroughs.

> I feel individuals will be better served if they have the opportunity to cultivate all five minds even if, in the end, some will emerge as stronger in one variety, while others exhibit a contrasting profile.

Without question, the respectful mind can be cultivated well before an ethical stance is conceivable. Indeed, respect ought to be part of the atmosphere from the earliest moments of life. When it comes to the cultivation of creativity, it is important to underscore personality and temperament factors. The building of a robust temperament, and a personality that is unafraid of assuming reasonable risks—cognitive and physical—can begin early in life; these dispositions mark the future creator.

Whatever details of ordering may obtain, in the end it is desirable for each person to have achieved aspects of all five mental capacities, all five minds for the future. Such a personal integration is most likely to occur when individuals are raised in environments that exhibit and value all five kinds of minds. So much the better if role models—parents, teacher, masters, or supervisors—regularly display aspects of discipline, synthesis, creation, respect, *and* ethics. In addition to embodying these kinds of minds, the best educators at school or work can provide support, advice, and coaching that help to inculcate discipline, encourage synthesis, prod creativity, foster respect, and encourage an ethical stance.

In the end, however, no one can compel the cultivation and integration of the five minds. The individual must come to believe that the minds are important, that they merit the investment of significant amounts of time and resources, and that they are worthy of continuing nurturance even after external supports fade. The individual must reflect on the role of each of these minds at work, in a favored avocation, at home, in the community, and in the wider world. The individual must be aware that sometimes these minds will find themselves in tension with one another, and that any resolution will come at some cost. In the future, the mind that is likely to be at greatest premium is the synthesizing mind. And so, it is perhaps fitting that the melding of the minds within an individual's skin is the ultimate challenge of personal synthesis.

References

Gardner, H. (2006). *Multiple intelligences: New horizons in theory and practice.* New York: Basic Books.

Gardner, H. (2007). *Five minds for the future.* Boston: Harvard Business School Press.

Gardner, H., Csikszentmihalyi, M., & Damon, W. (2001). *Good work: When excellence and ethics meet.* New York: Basic Books.

Hirschman, A. O. (1970). *Exit, voice and loyalty: Responses to decline in firms, organizations, and states.* Cambridge, MA: Harvard University Press.

Pink, D. H. (2006). *A whole new mind: Why right-brainers will rule the future.* New York: Riverhead.

Linda Darling-Hammond

Linda Darling-Hammond, Ph.D., is Charles E. Ducommun Professor of Education at Stanford University, where she launched the Stanford Educational Leadership Institute and the School Redesign Network. She has also served as faculty sponsor for the Stanford Teacher Education Program. She is a former president of the American Educational Research Association and member of the National Academy of Education. Her research, teaching, and policy work focus on issues of school restructuring, teacher quality, and educational equity. Among Darling-Hammond's more than three hundred publications are *Preparing Teachers for a Changing World: What Teachers Should Learn and Be Able to Do* (with John Bransford, for the National Academy of Education, winner of the Edward C. Pomeroy Award for Outstanding Contributions to Teacher Education from the American Association of College Teachers for Education); *Teaching as the Learning Profession: A Handbook of Policy and Practice* (coedited with Gary Sykes, recipient of the National Staff Development Council's Outstanding Book Award for 2000); and *The Right to Learn: A Blueprint for Schools That Work* (recipient of the American Educational Research Association's Outstanding Book Award for 1998).

In this interview, Darling-Hammond calls for major policy changes to guide development of 21st century schools. She advocates deep alignment of standards, curriculum, instruction, and assessment; strengthening professionalism among teachers and school leaders; redesign of school time to allow for increased participation in professional decisions by teachers; and equitable distribution of resources among all schools. She insists that the United States must take a more balanced approach to school reform and that these changes are essential if the United States is to restore its lost leadership for educational excellence.

Chapter 2

New Policies for 21st Century Demands

Linda Darling-Hammond, Interviewed by James Bellanca

We badly need a national policy that enables schools to meet the intellectual demands of the twenty-first century.

—Linda Darling-Hammond (2007)

James Bellanca: *In your article for* The Nation *magazine (Darling-Hammond, 2007), you call for a national policy so that students can meet the intellectual demands of the 21st century. What are these demands?*

Linda Darling-Hammond: Our economy and our lives today are much more complex than many people understand. That complexity is exacerbated by the extraordinarily fast rate of knowledge growth in this century. Some people say that the amount of technological knowledge in the world is almost doubling every two years. Thus, the notion that we could take all of the facts that a person needs to know, divide them into twelve years of schooling, and learn those facts and be done does not clearly equip young people for the future. Twenty-first-century students need a deeper understanding of the core concepts in the disciplines than they receive now. In addition, students need to be able to design, evaluate, and manage their own work. Students need to be able to frame, investigate, and solve problems using a wide range of information resources and digital tools.

James Bellanca: *Does this mean that students have to get smarter?*

Linda Darling-Hammond: All students need to develop more complex cognitive abilities so that they can find, analyze, and use information for a range of purposes, including the development of new products and ideas. Students need to collaborate and communicate so that they can take advantage of each other's knowledge and expertise. Their communication abilities must include writing and speaking in world languages, as well as using mathematical symbols. These changes in student abilities and knowledge do not happen by accident; changes start at the top with national policy.

James Bellanca: *In the 1980s and 1990s, educators paid attention to the skills and understandings students were said to need to confront the 21st century work world. How is this different than our current perspective?*

Linda Darling-Hammond: I think we were on the right track in the early 1990s, especially in the efforts to create new content standards that incorporated the cognitive skills. However, pendulum swings in the conceptualization of what students need to learn and how they need to learn it have been very destructive. Back-and-forth swings between teaching for understanding and assessing authentic performances versus basic skills measured by multiple-choice and short-answer test items have cost the United States a lot of time and progress. The emphasis today on more complex skills is entirely different from what people were trying to pursue in the early 1990s. What is different today is the effort to correct from the extreme back-to-basics approach represented by the No Child Left Behind Act of 2001 and instead put cognitive skills into the context of what learners need to know for the work world of the 21st century.

I also think the impetus for the changes is different. In the last century, a handful of educators pushed to add "higher-order thinking skills" to instruction. Today, the move to change policy comes from multiple groups, including some groups from the business community, state education departments, and the president of the United States himself. And there is a new recognition that these skills cannot be taught in isolation. The only way to return the United States to a position of leadership in the international education community is with a comprehensive, systemic approach that reaches all children.

I also think the impetus for the changes is different. In the last century, a handful of educators pushed to add "higher-order thinking skills" to instruction. Today, the move to change policy comes from multiple groups, including some groups from the business community, state education departments, and the president of the United States himself.

James Bellanca: *What is the evidence that the United States has fallen behind?*

Linda Darling-Hammond: Let me focus on the most startling indicator—the data from the 2006 Programme for International Student Assessment (PISA). On that assessment of forty countries, the United States ranked thirty-fifth in mathematics and thirty-first in science. (No U.S. reading scores were reported because of editing problems.) Each assessment showed a glaring United States decline from the 2003 results. Furthermore, as I reported in a recent *Phi Delta Kappan* article (Darling-Hammond & McCloskey, 2008), in each disciplinary area tested, U.S. students scored lowest on the problem-solving items. I also noted that the United States had a much wider achievement gap than the most highly ranked jurisdictions, such as Finland, Canada, Australia, New Zealand, Hong Kong, Korea, and Japan.

James Bellanca: *What is it that separates the performances of the top-scoring nations from the United States?*

Linda Darling-Hammond: The competing nations do not experience the pendulum swings I spoke of. They do not zigzag back and forth every decade. These nations stay focused on developing a strong curriculum and a set of thoughtful assessments. Their assessments, most of which are open-ended performance assessments, require students to demonstrate what they can do with what they are learning. To prepare their students, these nations are steadily improving the quality of their instruction. In the meantime, the United States moves back and forth between polar extremes.

The competing nations do not experience the pendulum swings. . . . These nations stay focused on developing a strong curriculum and a set of thoughtful assessments.

James Bellanca: *How are these pendulum swings hurtful?*

Linda Darling-Hammond: The problem is the harm done to practitioners, teachers, and students. If you listen to great teachers, their answer about basic skills and thinking skills is always *both/and,* not *either/or.* These effective teachers balance how and what they teach. They prepare children *both* for decoding *and* for comprehending text. They ask students to build basic vocabulary *and* to understand literature, draw inferences, and use information for novel purposes. In math, these teachers teach students *both* how to compute math facts *and* how to reason, think, and communicate mathematically. In science, they prepare students *both* to understand key concepts in science *and* to engage in scientific investigation. These are the teachers who stay above the wars and reconcile the pendulum swings in daily practice.

James Bellanca: *Shouldn't this balanced practice be expected of all teachers?*

Linda Darling-Hammond: Many teachers are less sure of their own knowledge and abilities. They have had neither the preparation nor the support that enables them to stay out of the either/or trap. These teachers dutifully do what they are told. In one decade, it is back to basics; in the next, it is higher-order thinking. Although both practices are necessary, the every-decade administrative mandates to switch gears midstream confuse these teachers. To cope, many teachers respond by saying, "This, too, will pass."

James Bellanca: *What happens if we continue to have these pendulum swings?*

Linda Darling-Hammond: The United States has little chance to move ahead. Teachers will be unable to develop the foundation skills for thinking that their students need for real learning. Without that foundation, students will not know how to make sense of new information, apply knowledge in novel situations, or learn on their own. And if that happens, the United States will continue to compete poorly on international assessments.

James Bellanca: *Why are these international assessments important?*

Linda Darling-Hammond: Washington economic policy discussions often refer to international assessments rankings when emphasizing the need for the United States to benchmark expectations with those of the highest-performing nations. The aim is to make the school system more "internationally competitive." But analyses of results reveal other ways to approach teaching and learning than what occurs commonly in too many classrooms in the United States. For example, the analyses show that higher-achieving countries teach fewer topics more deeply each year; focus more on reasoning skills and applications of knowledge, rather than on mere coverage; and have a more thoughtful sequence of expectations based on developmental learning progressions within and across domains. This focus aligns closely with the many different frameworks for 21st century skills, including those from the Partnership for 21st Century Skills (see figure F.1 in the foreword on page xv).

James Bellanca: *So the assessment results can actually help us understand the cause of the differences?*

> The analyses show that higher-achieving countries teach fewer topics more deeply each year; focus more on reasoning skills and applications of knowledge, rather than on mere coverage; and have a more thoughtful sequence of expectations based on developmental learning progressions within and across domains.

Linda Darling-Hammond: Yes. To understand why students from other countries do so well, we must examine *how* those students are taught and assessed. European and Asian nations that have steeply improved student learning have focused explicitly on creating curriculum and assessments that emphasize the so-called 21st century skills.

James Bellanca: *What kinds of testing programs do these nations use?*

Linda Darling-Hammond: I have done analyses of assessment systems in the highest-achieving nations—Finland, Korea, Hong Kong, Singapore, The Netherlands, Sweden, Canada, and Australia. Unlike the continuous testing system required by the No Child Left Behind Act, which is accomplished primarily with externally provided multiple-choice tests, these top-performing countries have little external testing. These countries instead emphasize extensive school-based assessments driven by curriculum standards and teacher-developed syllabi that detail what is to be learned. In countries such as Finland, Hong Kong, and Singapore, only two grade levels have sample tests from the outside. The United Kingdom has a modest amount of external testing. And the external tests that are used include mostly open-ended items that require students to solve problems, show their work, write answers to questions, and sometimes actually demonstrate what they can do. Most importantly, teachers score and evaluate curriculum-based performance tasks that *they* developed. This approach is part of the accountability system that aligns the internal and external tests across the grade levels with the standards and with instruction.

James Bellanca: *How does this approach influence achievement?*

Linda Darling-Hammond: Several things are critically important here. When you have this alignment of standards, instruction, and assessments, teachers continually learn about what their students know. The teachers understand the standards deeply because they themselves are part of the assessment process around the standards. They learn how to refine curriculum so that they become increasingly more effective in teaching the standards. As a consequence, the school-based assessments result in greater curriculum equity for students. This method is the learning engine that drives all students to higher achievement.

James Bellanca: *How is this approach different from the approach in the United States?*

Linda Darling-Hammond: When I was in Australia learning about their assessment system, I talked about the American system. One of the Australian teachers asked me, "Do you mean that American teachers don't know what will be on the test?" I said, "They do *not* know. In the United States, testing is conceptualized as the measurement of factual recall. The tests are secret; they arrive in brown-paper wrappers. The completed scoring sheets go out in the same wrappers." She said, "How can they teach productively if they don't know what will be on the assessment?" This question shows how assessment is considered differently in other countries. For the most part, teachers in the United States teach facts, often covering every page of a textbook or a workbook; they have little idea about what facts will be tested. In the high-achieving countries, teachers are involved in designing tests that assess understanding and cognitive skills. Because these teachers also design and teach the lessons that lead students to these more rigorous outcomes, they align standards, instruction, and assessment. These educators know full well what they must do to ensure that every student achieves the intended results.

James Bellanca: *What are the implications for the United States?*

Linda Darling-Hammond: Abandoning the conception of assessment as a checkup on teachers whom we cannot trust to be involved in the assessment process is extremely important. It is also important that the United States move toward assessments in which teachers and students are intimately engaged in work that is intellectually ambitious, challenging, and worthwhile. Testing is not just what can be done in a couple of hours in April on a machine-scored instrument; it is also finding what students understand and can do cognitively as called for by rigorous standards. With this information, teachers can make real adjustments to how they instruct and assess so that every child really succeeds.

James Bellanca: *What kind of assessments should teachers use with their own students?*

Linda Darling-Hammond: True assessment does not limit students to quizzes and fact tests for grades. Effective assessment means assigning a piece of student work—whether it is an essay, a research project, a scientific inquiry, or a sculpture—and allowing a student to work on that selected task with support while scaffolding instruction and giving feedback that expands the student's understanding and skill. Teachers may combine peer assessment, student self-assessment, or their own assessment so that the students learn how to look at their work, learn strategies for framing and solving problems, and then understand how to continually revise their work so that they are getting closer and closer approximations to expert practice. This process produces

> Effective assessment means assigning a piece of student work—whether it is an essay, a research project, a scientific inquiry, or a sculpture—and allowing a student to work on that selected task with support while scaffolding instruction and giving feedback that expands the student's understanding and skill.

a substantially more thoughtful and rigorous outcome. In this way, grades, tests, and quizzes give way to the students' products, which show clearly what the students have come to know and understand.

James Bellanca: *The change from grades and quizzes to more authentic assessment sounds like a difficult challenge.*

Linda Darling-Hammond: Yes, but it's necessary. To use authentic assessment, teachers must rethink their understanding of the curriculum and the teaching process. Rather than expecting to just cover some information, give a test, and then assign a grade on whether students remember the information given, teachers need to think about what kind of skills and applications their students should develop. This assessment style requires that teachers develop a process that results in the learning of those skills and applications. Teachers must provide time for students to refine their work, receive feedback, revise their work, and gradually become more expert.

James Bellanca: *Why do you call this kind of assessment "authentic"?*

Linda Darling-Hammond: Because this type of assessment is like the development of expertise in the real—or authentic—world by real workers. How often do sculptors just sit down and knock off a new piece? Which authors don't write multiple drafts? How many scientists make a big break with the first experiment? In order for their students to develop expertise, teachers need a lot of professional development that is embedded in the content they teach; around the kinds of tests they want students to engage in; with colleagues trying strategies and debriefing them together, fine-tuning their plans, developing what I think of as a two-way pedagogy in which teachers learn to listen to students and look at student work, so that they get information about the learning process, as well as directly instruct students and provide information. That reciprocal kind of pedagogy is part of what gets refined in professional development with colleagues when teachers continually bring student work to the table and problem solve the teaching and learning process with colleagues.

James Bellanca: *How can we stop the pendulum swings you refer to and make progress toward a more aligned and balanced approach?*

Linda Darling-Hammond: Progress starts with respectful discourse. All must agree that both content and skills are important for serious schooling in the 21st century. For example, the American Enterprise Institute and others recently launched a set of volleys against the 21st century skills concept. These organizations fear that the "skills people" will lose sight of valuable content. They envision that the skills people will put an undisciplined emphasis on collaboration, teamwork, and project-based learning. They see students working with clay and toothpicks without actually mastering challenging intellectual content. On the other side, skills people are worried that the "content people" will try to reduce what is to be known and demonstrated to a list of dry, disconnected facts tested by multiple-choice items without attention to meaning or application.

A more respectful discourse can result in agreement about the value of both positions. With such an agreement, all could engage in serious conversation about rigorous content standards being paired with well-disciplined

> A more respectful discourse can result in agreement about the value of both positions.

ways to promote the important skills. With that agreement, everyone will have to acknowledge that we must develop and prepare teachers and school leaders much more deeply. All teachers need the ability to engage in high-quality instruction that adequately represents both the content and the cognitive skills that enhance all students' deep understanding of content. And all teachers need to be more disciplined in order to move toward an integrated vision that invests in what practitioners need to know and be able to do.

James Bellanca: *If leaders on both sides could reach that kind of agreement, what national policies would advance our schools in a way that is free of the extreme pendulum swings?*

Linda Darling-Hammond: There are four necessary policy changes, and they are interdependent. First, we need an aligned standards, instruction, and assessment system. This alignment will be most apt if it includes not only the thinking and learning skills I have described, but also is firmly rooted in a deep understanding of each content area. In this process, we cannot do what we have done in the past, which is jump from standards to tests while we ignore curriculum. The development of a lean, not overly prescribed, curriculum that outlines the expected learning progressions applicable to all students and is assessable by teachers in authentic ways is essential.

There are four necessary policy changes, and they are interdependent:

1. An aligned standards, instruction, and assessment system

2. An infrastructure that gives teachers and school leaders sufficient time to do the alignment work

3. Schools that are more supportive of in-depth teaching and learning

4. More equitable distribution of resources

James Bellanca: *And we don't have such an aligned system now?*

Linda Darling-Hammond: Not in a way or to the degree that provides the necessary help. Currently, we have a loose system in which teachers in each school must guess at what the mandated state tests will cover. Teachers may be left on their own to choose what to teach each day, or perhaps they are given scripts to read that ignore student differences. In the aligned vision I propose, teachers would participate in solid curriculum development. They would know how their curriculum aligns with the mandated standards.

We cannot expect individual teachers to develop all this curriculum on their own, but the opportunity to sequence, organize, and create strong learning units is essential. Each unit must be one that they can use productively with real children in very diverse classrooms to accomplish common standards. To be most effective, teachers need the opportunity to use their professional judgment to determine what is appropriate for their classrooms. Overly prescriptive scripts only continue to thwart increased learning.

James Bellanca: *If I were a teacher with my day-to-day workload, I might feel overloaded by your long list. I might be inclined to resist.*

Linda Darling-Hammond: I hear a lot about teacher resistance to change. I have been in the field for more than thirty years, working with people from all different parts of different school systems, and I have three observations about so-called teacher resistance.

First, to the extent that *sometimes* teachers are resistant to change, resistance is actually not an irrational response. We throw so many changes at teachers with such blistering speed that mandated changes come and go in the blink of an eye. And then the changes change—based on who the current superintendent is, which company came and sold the latest hot product, what the school board has decided to do now, what the state legislature has decided to do now, what money is coming into the system, and so on. So, for teachers who know that the latest change is only temporary, resistance is a rational response.

Second, I have seen many reform-minded school settings in which the school board, the parent leadership, or the administration is more resistant to a change than the teachers. Sometimes teachers are saying, "We really want to do this," or "We have a great idea for our students, and we are ready to get on it." Meanwhile, the principal or a central office administrator is not ready to move in that direction or does not want to rock the boat. I have found, more often than not, that teachers are more progressive in their interest to shape instruction in better ways than the policy and administrative forces that stand over them.

Third, the problem in making constructive change is not how to get around perceived teacher resistance. The problem is how to get everybody onto the same path—and sticking to that path—rather than indulging in these pendulum swings. In the long run, we must buffer education more effectively from the vicissitudes of politics. High-achieving nations typically have a highly professionalized ministry of education. They try to identify the core values of the system, the essential beliefs about teaching and learning, and then continually refine practice. There are changes always being made, but changes in this context are more in the direction of refining the system rather than throwing out the system every time a new fad pops up or the next administrator plays a personal card.

> The problem is how to get everybody onto the same path—and sticking to that path—rather than indulging in these pendulum swings.

James Bellanca: *How can American education be more like that?*

Linda Darling-Hammond: We need to strengthen professionalism in the American education enterprise. We need to be sure that capable teachers and administrators have access to a strong knowledge base and trust them to be responsible for teaching and learning.

James Bellanca: *In many schools, teachers have limited time to do the work you describe. What do you propose?*

Linda Darling-Hammond: That answer is not difficult. It leads to the second policy change I mentioned earlier: one that allows us to build an infrastructure so that teachers and school leaders have sufficient time to do the alignment work I described. Again, we can learn about this from high-performing nations.

> Build an infrastructure so that teachers and school leaders have sufficient time to do alignment work.

James Bellanca: *What sorts of things could we learn?*

Linda Darling-Hammond: To begin, you get what you pay for. These systems completely underwrite three to four years of high-quality teacher preparation during which teachers receive a full salary. Teachers do not have to teach full time at their regular job and pay out of their pockets for a step-and-scale salary increase for a degree that may have little to do with their classroom work. Instead, they engage in a strong clinical experience that readies them to work with the most struggling students who have a wide range of needs. They prepare to develop formative and summative performance assessments that align with the prescribed standards. They spend intense hours developing their content knowledge and pedagogy, learning to use research and how to conduct action research to improve their own practice. This preparation is done universally—for all teachers in all contexts.

James Bellanca: *You also mentioned significant changes in leadership preparation.*

Linda Darling-Hammond: Yes. I believe leadership preparation needs a similar—if not greater—emphasis. School leaders need an undistracted engagement in learning to lead a school. This must include an intense clinical experience that prepares potential leaders to work in the most diverse and difficult schools. Shadowing a few administrators for a few weeks will not suffice. Leader candidates must prove their success as effective teachers, including use of performance assessments aligned with standards, knowledge of high-quality instruction that is based firmly in research, and helping other teachers develop their expertise. Those selected should already display leadership potential. Once selected, they need to have multiple years of high-quality, purposeful preparation without worrying about where the money will come from.

James Bellanca: *What you want leaders to study doesn't seem to align with the standard certification requirements for school administrators.*

Linda Darling-Hammond: No, it doesn't. I believe that the school leader's major responsibility is to enable excellent teaching in every classroom. Although we have given lip service to instructional leadership, little has happened in the last decades to make it a common or significant reality. School leaders in the next decades need to engage in three practices that we haven't always seen as part of school administration. First is constructing time for teachers to work together on the development of curriculum and assessments. Second is designing and implementing comprehensive professional development programs. This includes formation of professional learning communities, providing coaching and mentoring for teachers who have been identified as needing additional assistance, and encouraging peer support teams that address the special needs of struggling students. Third is helping teachers to find another profession if they are unable to improve after having received purposeful support.

> The school leader's major responsibility is to enable excellent teaching in every classroom.

James Bellanca: *That is a strong statement.*

Linda Darling-Hammond: Yes, it is. We can no longer tolerate bad teaching in any school. If a leader recognizes that a teacher needs improvement and he or she provides the types of support that are part of a professional learning community but still sees no constructive change, then the leader must counsel that teacher into a more appropriate career.

James Bellanca: *Does a school leader need other skills in order to be an instructional leader?*

Linda Darling-Hammond: Yes, being an instructional leader in the type of school I have described requires organizational development knowledge and skill. When an individual takes charge of a school, it most likely will be organized in an assembly-line fashion, which is the factory model we inherited. Leaders will have to redesign their schools. This redesign often starts with the creation of more sustained, productive relationships between adults and children. At the high school level, for example, leaders can make sure that students have advisors who work with a small number of students and have time to reach out and work with the parents. They can form students into smaller houses with teacher teams and advisors to prevent students from getting left behind. Leaders can push for school rubrics and performance assessments that create shared norms about the intellectual work expected.

Finally, I would say good leaders must be able to manage constructive change. They must be able to engage all the stakeholders, manage distributed leadership so that teachers are part of the leadership cadre, and ensure that parents and students have a voice and are engaged. They must develop the faculty as a professional learning community ready and able to take on the many challenges for aligning curriculum, instruction, and assessment to match 21st century learning needs. The days in which principals are expected just to manage the school bells, make the buses run on time, order the textbooks, keep order in the cafeteria, quote the school manual, and ensure that everyone is in their place must soon end. Without the changes required to bring all schools to up 21st century standards, we cannot expect 21st century results.

James Bellanca: *As you said, the second policy change involves finding the time for the intense experiences you're describing.*

Linda Darling-Hammond: Again, we can look at the PISA high-performing nations. In most of those nations, teachers have fifteen to twenty-five hours each week in which they plan their lessons together. They may engage in lesson study and action research. They may observe each other in the classroom. They may meet with students or parents, evaluate student work together or alone, conference with their site leaders or mentors, build assessments aligned to the standards, investigate models of teaching, study best practice research, or develop deeper understanding of their course content. These professional, collegial learning experiences inform their practice in ways that allow for rich improvements in what and how they teach. It is a well-prepared leader who makes these events happen.

Jim Bellanca: *Are these changes possible without other more substantive changes?*

Linda Darling-Hammond: No. The recommendation for giving teachers time to work together on the improvement of practice gets us to the third policy I recommend: redesigning schools so that they become more supportive of in-depth teaching and learning. We continue to struggle with the factory model that we inherited one hundred years ago. That model neither values relationships between adults and children nor the time for in-depth study. To make the school factory model work, we adopted the age-grading system that sends elementary school students to a different teacher every year and middle and high school students to a different teacher every forty-five or fifty-five minutes. If students get to high school, their teachers may face 100–125 students a day; if they attend high school in an urban area, students may join 150–175 others in each teacher's stamp-and-pass-on day. The notion that anyone can get deep, rigorous, high-quality learning in a system that treats students as assembly-line widgets is implausible. If we are serious about the kind of learning needed in the 21st century, redesigning our schools is imperative.

> I recommend redesigning schools so that they become more supportive of in-depth teaching and learning.

James Bellanca: *What sorts of things need redesigning?*

Linda Darling-Hammond: Foremost among these changes is use of time. To accomplish the outcomes being discussed now, teachers need the opportunity to work with students over longer periods of time. It takes time to teach content deeply, to challenge students to apply what they know with projects, to investigate ideas in depth, to solve significant learning problems, and to assess what students can do.

James Bellanca: *I believe you said you are seeking four changes in policy.*

Linda Darling-Hammond: Yes. The fourth policy calls for more equitable distribution of resources. Currently, the United States has

> Currently, the United States has the most inequitable system of education of any leading industrialized country.

the most inequitable system of education of any leading industrialized country. Most countries fund schools centrally and equally; they may add additional funding for high-need students.

In the United States, huge funding differences exist between the highest- and lowest-spending schools. The ratio between the highest- and lowest-spending schools in the United States is 10:1. Within most states, the ratio is 3:1, exacerbated by differences among states. The education of some children is well supported, with every imaginable accoutrement. These students receive superior support in terms of teacher quality, curriculum offerings, specialists, technology, textbooks, athletic facilities, and so on. In contrast, other students attend schools in third-world conditions or worse.

James Bellanca: *How does the issue of resource inequity relate to your other policy points?*

Linda Darling-Hammond: The four policy changes I recommend are connected systemically. Each depends on the others. For any one policy to work effectively, all are needed. In our continued use of the factory model, we see the degree of inequity, the spread of outcomes that is related to the spread of input. We cannot expect to radically change the outcomes unless we also ensure adequate resources in every school, including time for teachers to work on the alignment issues, time for professional learning so that teachers can develop the knowledge and skills they need to do this development, and so on.

James Bellanca: *What would you like to see happen to put these policy changes in place?*

Linda Darling-Hammond: Policy implementation should be done in a systematic, sustained way, based on a set of reforms that allows teachers and administrators in every school to develop more thoughtful instruction. We have great schools in some places and great classrooms in some schools, but we need to be able to spread that greatness more uniformly across the national system, following a straighter path without those destructive pendulum swings.

> We have great schools in some places and great classrooms in some schools, but we need to be able to spread that greatness more uniformly across the national system.

References

Darling-Hammond, L. (2007, May 2). Evaluating No Child Left Behind. *The Nation*. Accessed at www.thenation.com/doc/20070521/darling-hammond on November 2, 2009.

Darling-Hammond, L., & McCloskey, L. (2007, December). Assessment for learning around the world: What would it mean to be internationally competitive? *Phi Delta Kappan, 90*(4), 263–272.

Chris Dede

Chris Dede, Ed.D., is the Timothy E. Wirth Professor in Learning Technologies at Harvard's Graduate School of Education. His fields of scholarship include emerging technologies, policy, and leadership. His funded research includes three grants from the National Science Foundation (NSF) and the U.S. Department of Education Institute of Education Sciences to explore immersive and semi-immersive simulations as a means of student engagement, learning, and assessment. In 2007, he was honored by Harvard University as an outstanding teacher. Dede has served as a member of the National Academy of Sciences Committee on Foundations of Educational and Psychological Assessment and a member of the 2010 National Educational Technology Plan working group. He serves on advisory boards and commissions for PBS TeacherLine, the Partnership for 21st Century Skills, the Pittsburgh Science of Learning Center, and several federal research grants. He is coeditor of *Scaling Up Success: Lessons Learned From Technology-Based Educational Improvement* (2005) and editor of *Online Professional Development for Teachers: Emerging Models and Methods* (2006).

In this chapter, Dede compares several prominent lists of 21st century skills. He asks, "How diverse are these definitions for 21st century skills?" and notes that a lack of clarity about the nature of 21st century skills could be problematic. His examination illuminates what the various frameworks have in common and what each uniquely adds to the overarching concept.

Chapter 3

Comparing Frameworks for 21st Century Skills

Chris Dede

Many groups have called for all students to learn 21st century skills. In response, some organizations have developed, as part of their institutional brand, frameworks for the new millennium that delineate content and processes teachers should convey as part of students' schooling. How diverse are these definitions for 21st century skills, and is the term becoming an umbrella phrase under which advocates from various groups can argue for almost any type of knowledge? Lack of clarity about the nature of 21st century skills could be problematic; many educational reforms have failed because people use the same terminology, but mean quite different things. What do the various frameworks for 21st century skills have in common? What can they add to the overarching concept of knowledge necessary for new graduates to be effective workers and citizens?

The Rationale for Formulating 21st Century Skills

The 21st century is quite different from the 20th in regard to the skills people now need for work, citizenship, and self-actualization. Proficiency in the 21st century differs primarily due to the emergence of very sophisticated information and communication technologies (ICTs). For example, the types of work done by people—as opposed to machines—are continually shifting as computers and telecom-munications expand their capabilities to accomplish human tasks. Economists Frank Levy and Richard Murnane (2004) highlight a crucial component of what constitutes 21st century knowledge and skills:

> Declining portions of the labor force are engaged in jobs that consist primarily of routine cognitive work and routine manual labor—the types of tasks that are easiest to program computers to do. Growing proportions of the nation's labor force are engaged in jobs that emphasize expert thinking or complex communication—tasks that computers cannot do. (pp. 53–54)

These economists go on to explain the "components of expert thinking: [1] effective pattern matching based on detailed knowledge; and [2] metacognition, the set of skills used by the stumped expert to decide when to give up on one strategy and what to try next" (Levy & Murnane, 2004, p. 75). Inventing new problem-solving heuristics when standard protocols have failed is an important skill; when all diagnostics are normal, but the patient is still feeling unwell, for instance, a skilled physician can think outside the box and become an expert decision maker. According to Levy and Murnane (2004), "complex communication requires the exchange of vast amounts of verbal and nonverbal information. The information flow is constantly adjusted as the communication evolves unpredictably" (p. 94). Therefore, a skilled teacher is an expert in complex communication, able to improvise answers and facilitate dialogue in the unpredictable, chaotic flow of classroom discussion.

Sophisticated ICTs are changing the nature of "perennial" skills valuable throughout history, as well as creating novel "contextual" skills unique to new millennium work and citizenship (Dede, in press). For example, collaboration is a perennial ability, valued as a trait in workplaces for centuries. Therefore, the fundamental worth of this suite of interpersonal skills is not unique to the 21st century economic context. However, the degree of importance for collaborative capacity is growing now that work in knowledge-based economies is increasingly accomplished by teams of people with complementary expertise and roles, as opposed to individuals doing isolated work in an industrial setting (Karoly & Panis, 2004).

Further, the nature of collaboration is shifting to a more sophisticated skillset. In addition to collaborating face-to-face with colleagues across a conference table, 21st century workers increasingly accomplish tasks through mediated interactions with peers halfway across the world whom they may never meet face-to-face. Thus, even though perennial in nature, collaboration is worthy of inclusion as a 21st century skill because the importance of cooperative interpersonal capabilities is higher and the skills involved are more sophisticated than in the prior industrial era.

In contrast, the ability to rapidly filter huge amounts of incoming data and extract information valuable for decision making is a contextual capability. Due to the prevalence of ICTs, people are—for the first time in human history—inundated by enormous amounts of data that they must access, manage, integrate, and evaluate. Rather than rummaging through library stacks to find a few pieces of knowledge, an activity characteristic of information access in the 20th century, users of modern search engines receive thousands or even millions of "hits." However, many of these resources are off-target, incomplete, inconsistent, and perhaps even biased. The ability to separate signal from noise in a potentially overwhelming flood of incoming data is a suite of 21st century skills not in *degree*, as with collaboration, but in *type*.

Weinberger (2007) describes the power of "digital disorder," which takes advantage of the fact that virtual information can transcend the limited properties of physical objects (like books or index cards). Rather than relying on a single method of organization with a fixed terminology (such as the Dewey Decimal System as a means of categorizing knowledge), modern information systems can respond to natural language queries and can instantly sort digital data into whatever category structure best suits a particular person's immediate needs. This approach creates a new set of contextual 21st century skills centered on "disorderly" knowledge co-creation and sharing.

Overall, the distinction between perennial and contextual skills is important because, unlike perennial capabilities, new, contextual types of human performances are typically not part of the legacy curriculum inherited from 20th century educational systems. Conventional, 20th century K–12 instruction emphasizes manipulating predigested information to build fluency in routine problem solving, rather than filtering data derived from experiences in complex settings to develop skills in sophisticated problem finding. Knowledge separated from skills and presented as revealed truth, rather than as an understanding that is discovered and constructed, results in students simply learning data about a topic instead of learning how to extend their understanding beyond information available for assimilation. In 20th century instruction, problem-solving skills are presented in an abstract form removed from their application to knowledge; this makes transfer to real-world situations difficult. The ultimate objective of that type of education is presented as learning a specific problem-solving routine to match every situation, rather than developing expert decision-making and metacognitive strategies that indicate how to proceed when no standard approach seems applicable.

> In 20th century instruction, problem-solving skills are presented in an abstract form removed from their application to knowledge; this makes transfer to real-world situations difficult.

In 20th century instruction, little time is spent on building capabilities in group interpretation, negotiation of shared meaning, or co-construction of problem resolutions. The communication skills it stresses are those of simple presentation, rather than the capacity to engage in richly structured interactions that articulate perspectives unfamiliar to the audience. Face-to-face communication is seen as the gold standard, so students develop few capabilities in mediated dialogue and in shared design within a common virtual workspace.

Given that the curriculum is already crowded, a major political challenge is articulating what to deemphasize in the curriculum—and why—in order to make room for students to deeply master core 21st century skills. This is not a situation in which an equivalent amount of current curriculum must be eliminated for each 21st century skill added, because better pedagogical methods can lead to faster mastery and improved retention, enabling less reteaching and more coverage within the same time frame (VanLehn, 2006). However, what education should emphasize as core is politically controversial even if substantial sections of the 20th century curriculum are not eliminated.

Beyond curricular issues, classrooms today typically lack 21st century learning and teaching, in part because high-stakes tests do not assess these competencies. Assessments and tests focus on measuring students' fluency in various abstract routine skills, but typically do not assess their strategies for expert decision making when no standard approach seems applicable. Essays emphasize simple

> Given that the curriculum is already crowded, a major political challenge is articulating what to deemphasize in the curriculum—and why— in order to make room for students to deeply master core 21st century skills.

presentation rather than sophisticated forms of rhetorical interaction. Students' abilities to transfer their understandings to real-world situations are not assessed, nor are capabilities related to various aspects of teamwork. The use of technological applications and representations is generally banned from testing, rather than providing an opportunity to measure students' capacities to use tools, applications, and media effectively. Abilities to successfully utilize various forms of mediated interaction are typically not assessed either. As discussed later, valid, reliable, practical assessments of 21st century skills are needed to improve this situation.

Lack of professional development is another reason 21st century skills are underemphasized in today's schooling. Providing educators with opportunities to learn about the ideas and strategies discussed in this volume is only part of the issue. A major, often unrecognized challenge in professional development is helping teachers, policymakers, and local communities unlearn the beliefs, values, assumptions, and cultures underlying schools' industrial-era operating practices, such as forty-five-minute class periods that allow insufficient time for all but superficial forms of active learning by students. Altering deeply ingrained and strongly reinforced rituals of schooling takes more than the superficial interchanges typical in "make and take" professional development or school board meetings. Intellectual, emotional, and social support is essential for "unlearning" and for transformational relearning that can lead to deeper behavioral changes that create next-generation educational practices. Educators, business executives, politicians, and the general public have much to unlearn if 21st century skills are to assume a central place in schooling.

Lack of professional development is another reason 21st century skills are underemphasized in today's schooling.

Current approaches to using technology in schooling largely reflect the 20th century pedagogy of applying information and communication technologies as a means of increasing the effectiveness of traditional instructional approaches: enhancing productivity through tools such as word processors, aiding communication by channels such as email and threaded asynchronous discussions, and expanding access to information via Web browsers and streaming video (Dede, 2009a). All these have proven worthy in conventional schooling, as they have in workplace settings; however, none draw on the full power of ICTs for individual and collective expression, experience, and interpretation—human capabilities emerging as key work and life skills for the first part of the 21st century. So how are various organizations that advocate for 21st century skills formulating these capabilities?

Current Major Frameworks for 21st Century Skills

Current conceptual frameworks for 21st century skills include the Partnership for 21st Century Skills (2006), the North Central Regional Education Laboratory (NCREL) and the Metiri Group (2003), the Organisation for Economic Co-operation and Development (OECD, 2005), and the National Leadership Council for Liberal Education and America's Promise (LEAP, 2007). In the particular area of information and communications technology—which, as mentioned previously, is richly interwoven with 21st century skills—these frameworks include the revised International Society for Technology in Education (ISTE) student standards for technology in the curriculum (2007), as well as digital literacy standards from the Educational Testing Service (ETS, 2007). Individual scholars such as Dede (2005) and Jenkins (2009) have also formulated lists of "digital literacies" that complement reading, writing, and mathematics as core capabilities for the 21st century. The figures that follow highlight each framework and are followed by an analysis of what each formulation adds to the Partnership for 21st Century Skills Framework for 21st Century Learning (2006).

The Partnership's Framework (2006) and the many ancillary publications produced since then serve as a baseline for this analysis because the Partnership's conceptualization of 21st century skills is more detailed and more widely adopted than any of the alternatives discussed later. For reasons of space, this chapter presents only a bare-bones outline of the Partnership's Framework (figure 3.1). The complete framework is available at www.21stcenturyskills.org, and an additional abridged version appears in the foreword on page xv of this volume.

Core subjects. The No Child Left Behind Act of 2001, which reauthorizes the Elementary and Secondary Education Act of 1965, identifies the core subjects as English, reading, or language arts; mathematics; science; foreign languages; civics; government; economics; arts; history; and geography.

21st century content. Several significant, emerging content areas are critical to success in communities and workplaces. These content areas typically are not emphasized in schools today: global awareness; financial, economic, business, and entrepreneurial literacy; civic literacy; and health and wellness awareness.

Learning and thinking skills. As much as students need to learn academic content, they also need to know how to keep learning—and make effective and innovative use of what they know—throughout their lives. Learning and thinking skills are comprised of critical-thinking and problem-solving skills, communication skills, creativity and innovation skills, collaboration skills, contextual learning skills, and information and media literacy skills.

ICT literacy. Information and communications technology literacy is the ability to use technology to develop 21st century content knowledge and skills, in the context of learning core subjects. Students must be able to use technology to learn content and skills—so that they know *how* to learn, think critically, solve problems, use information, communicate, innovate, and collaborate.

Life skills. Good teachers have always incorporated life skills into their pedagogy. The challenge today is to incorporate these essential skills into schools deliberately, strategically, and broadly. Life skills include leadership, ethics, accountability, adaptability, personal productivity, personal responsibility, people skills, self-direction, and social responsibility.

Figure 3.1: The Partnership for 21st Century Skills Framework for 21st Century Learning.

continued on next page →

21st century assessments. Authentic 21st century assessments are the essential foundation of a 21st century education. Assessments must measure all five results that matter: core subjects, 21st century content, learning and thinking skills, ICT literacy, and life skills. Assessment of 21st century skills should be integrated with assessments of core subjects. Separate assessments would defeat the purpose of infusing 21st century skills into core subjects. To be effective, sustainable, and affordable, assessments must use modern technologies to increase efficiency and timeliness. Standardized tests alone can measure only a few of the important skills and knowledge students should learn. A balance of assessments, including high-quality standardized testing along with effective classroom assessments, offers students and teachers a powerful tool to master the content and skills central to success.

Source: Partnership for 21st Century Skills, 2006. Reprinted with permission.

Figure 3.1: The Partnership for 21st Century Skills Framework for 21st Century Learning.

In contrast to the Partnership's Framework used as baseline in this analysis, NCREL and the Metiri Group produced a 21st century skills framework three years earlier, in 2003 (figure 3.2).

Digital-age literacy. Basic, scientific, economic, and technological literacies; visual and information literacies; multicultural literacy and global awareness

Inventive thinking. Adaptability, managing complexity, and self-direction; curiosity, creativity, and risk taking; higher-order thinking and sound reasoning

Effective communication. Teaming, collaboration, and interpersonal skills; personal, social, and civic responsibility; interactive communication

High productivity. Prioritizing, planning, and managing for results; effective use of real-world tools; ability to produce relevant, high-quality products

Source: North Central Regional Educational Laboratory & the Metiri Group, 2003.

Figure 3.2: enGauge Framework from the North Central Regional Education Laboratory and the Metiri Group.

The enGauge Framework adds "visual literacy" as related to information literacy. It includes "curiosity" and "risk taking" as core skills, as well as "managing complexity." It stresses "prioritizing, planning, and managing for results." "Multicultural literacy" is an explicit component. With the exception of the "effective communication" category, this shorter list focuses less on the overlap with 20th century curriculum than does the Partnership's Framework. More emphasis is placed on new contextual skills and knowledge.

In 2005, the OECD provided its conception of 21st century skills as shown in figure 3.3.

Competency category 1: Using tools interactively. Use language, symbols, and texts interactively; use knowledge and information interactively; use technology interactively.

Competency category 2: Interacting in heterogeneous groups. Relate well to others; cooperate and work in teams; manage and resolve conflicts.

Competency category 3: Acting autonomously. Act within the big picture; form and conduct life plans and personal projects; defend and assert rights, interests, limits, and needs.

Source: Organisation for Economic Co-operation and Development, 2005.

Figure 3.3: Organisation for Economic Co-operation and Development Competencies.

The OECD competencies highlight "using language, symbols, and texts," as well as "managing and resolving conflicts." "Acting autonomously" is a major category in this framework that includes "life plans" and "defending and asserting rights, interests, limits, and needs." Compared to the Partnership's Framework, this framework focuses less on overlaps with the 20th century curriculum and, like the NCREL/Metiri skillset, more on new contextual skills. Affective and psychosocial skills receive greater emphasis than in frameworks generated by U.S. organizations.

In 2007, LEAP developed a framework delineating the 21st century skills that graduates of higher education should attain (figure 3.4, page 60).

Beginning in school, and continuing at successively higher levels across their college studies, students should prepare for 21st century challenges by gaining:

Knowledge of human cultures and the physical and natural world, including study in
- Sciences and mathematics, social sciences, humanities, histories, languages, and the arts

Focused by engagement with big questions, both contemporary and enduring

Intellectual and practical skills, including
- Inquiry and analysis
- Critical and creative thinking
- Written and oral communication
- Quantitative literacy
- Information literacy
- Teamwork and problem solving

Practiced extensively across the curriculum in the context of progressively more challenging problems, projects, and standards for performance

Personal and social responsibility, including
- Civic knowledge and engagement—local and global
- Intercultural knowledge and competence
- Ethical reasoning and action
- Foundations and skills for lifelong learning

Anchored through active involvement with diverse communities and real-world challenges

Integrative learning, including
- Synthesis and advanced accomplishment across general and specialized studies

Demonstrated through the application of knowledge, skills, and responsibilities to new settings and complex problems

Source: National Leadership Council for Liberal Education and America's Promise, 2007.

Figure 3.4: National Leadership Council for Liberal Education and America's Promise Essential Learning Outcomes.

The LEAP college-level essential learning outcomes (presumably developed as a foundation in K–12 schooling) add "knowledge of human cultures" to the Partnership's Framework. This skillset stresses "engagement with big questions, both contemporary and enduring," an intellectual capability that higher education has long sought to inculcate. "Inquiry" and "quantitative analysis" are specifically cited as important analytic skills. Learning by doing, rather than by assimilation of information, is tacitly stressed in the language LEAP uses.

Current Conceptual Frameworks for Digital Literacies

In part to emphasize the ways in which ICT skills are central to the 21st century, in 2007 the ISTE revised its student standards for technology in the curriculum as shown in figure 3.5.

Creativity and innovation. Students demonstrate creative thinking, construct knowledge, and develop innovative products and processes using technology by:

- Applying existing knowledge to generate new ideas, products, or processes
- Creating original works as a means of personal or group expression
- Using models and simulations to explore complex systems and issues
- Identifying trends and forecasting possibilities

Communication and collaboration. Students use digital media and environments to communicate and work collaboratively—including at a distance, to support individual learning, and to contribute to the learning of others by:

- Interacting, collaborating, and publishing with peers, experts, or others employing a variety of digital environments and media
- Communicating information and ideas effectively to multiple audiences using a variety of media and formats
- Developing cultural understanding and global awareness by engaging with learners of other cultures
- Contributing to project teams to produce original works or solve problems

Figure 3.5: International Society for Technology in Education National Education Technology Standards for Students.

continued on next page →

Research and information fluency. Students employ digital tools to gather, evaluate, and use information by:

- Planning strategies to guide inquiry
- Locating, organizing, analyzing, evaluating, synthesizing, and ethically using information from a variety of sources and media
- Evaluating and selecting information sources and digital tools based on the appropriateness to specific tasks
- Processing data and reporting results

Critical thinking, problem solving, and decision making. Students draw on critical thinking skills to plan and conduct research, manage projects, solve problems, and make informed decisions using appropriate digital tools and resources by:

- Identifying and defining authentic problems and significant questions for investigation
- Planning and managing activities to develop a solution or complete a project
- Collecting and analyzing data to identify solutions and/or make informed decisions
- Using multiple processes and diverse perspectives to explore alternative solutions

Digital citizenship. Students show understanding of human, cultural, and societal issues related to technology and practice legal and ethical behavior by:

- Advocating and practicing safe, legal, and responsible use of information and technology
- Exhibiting a positive attitude toward using technology that supports collaboration, learning, and productivity
- Demonstrating personal responsibility for lifelong learning
- Exhibiting leadership for digital citizenship

Technology operations and concepts. Students demonstrate a sound understanding of technology concepts, systems, and operations by:

- Understanding and using technology systems
- Selecting and using applications effectively and productively
- Troubleshooting systems and applications
- Transferring current knowledge to learning of new technologies

Source: National Educational Technology Standards for Students, Second Edition, © 2007, ISTE® (International Society for Technology in Education), www.iste.org. All rights reserved.

Figure 3.5: International Society for Technology in Education National Education Technology Standards for Students.

Beyond the Partnership's Framework, the ISTE ICT skills stress "creating original works as a means of personal or group expression," "using models and simulations to explore complex systems and issues," and "identifying trends and forecasting possibilities." Other capabilities include "identifying and defining authentic problems and significant questions for investigation" and "using multiple processes and diverse perspectives to explore alternative solutions." It highlights "safe, legal" use of information and technology, as well as "digital citizenship." "Troubleshooting systems and applications" and "transferring current knowledge to learning of new technologies" are seen as key skills. As might be expected, the digital literacies this educational technology organization articulates are more detailed than those in the Partnership's overall framework.

In a similar vein, in 2007, the ETS released its ICT Digital Literacy Framework as shown in figure 3.6 (page 64). The framework delineates five levels of progressive mastery for each literacy.

The ETS Digital Literacy Framework adds "technical proficiency: a foundational knowledge of hardware, software applications, networks, and elements of digital technology." The example digital literacy activities provided in this framework seem less sophisticated than those implied by the other frameworks analyzed here; the illustration is closer in spirit to the ISTE framework for digital literacies developed in the late 1990s.

As the ISTE and ETS ICT frameworks suggest, much of what distinguishes 21st century skills from 20th century competencies is that a person and a tool, application, medium, or environment work in concert to accomplish an objective that is otherwise unobtainable (such as the remote collaboration of a team scattered across the globe via groupware). However, ICTs are not mere mechanisms for attaining the desired behavior; through distributed cognition, the understandings they enable are intrinsic to the fluent performance (such as a group co-constructing a sophisticated conceptual framework using the representational tools available in a wiki).

Frameworks that discuss new literacies based on the evolution of ICTs help to illuminate this aspect of 21st century learning. With funding from the Macarthur Foundation, Henry Jenkins and his colleagues (2009) produced a list of digital literacies as shown in figure 3.7 (page 65).

> **Cognitive proficiency.** The desired foundational skills of everyday life at school, at home, and at work. Literacy, numeracy, problem solving, and spatial/visual literacy demonstrate these proficiencies.
>
> **Technical proficiency.** The basic components of digital literacy. Includes a foundational knowledge of hardware, software applications, networks, and elements of digital technology.
>
> **ICT proficiency.** The integration and application of cognitive and technical skills. ICT proficiencies are seen as enablers; that is, they allow individuals to maximize the capabilities of technology. At the highest level, ICT proficiencies result in innovation, individual transformation, and societal change.
>
> An illustration of a five-level literacy in ICT proficiency follows:
>
> **Access**—Select and open appropriate emails from the inbox list.
>
> **Manage**—Identify and organize the relevant information in each email.
>
> **Integrate**—Summarize the interest in the courses provided by the company.
>
> **Evaluate**—Decide which courses should be continued next year, based on last year's attendance.
>
> **Create**—Write up your recommendation in the form of an email to the vice president of human resources.
>
> *Source: Educational Testing Service, 2007, pp. 18, 20.*

Figure 3.6: Educational Testing Service ICT Digital Literacy Framework.

These digital literacies have a different tone than the ISTE and ETS frameworks presented earlier. The emphasis is not on proficiency with the tool, but on types of intellectual activity performed by a person working with sophisticated ICTs. While some perennial capabilities—like judgment—are listed, other skills—such as performance—are contextual in their emphasis on new types of 21st century capacities.

These digital literacies not only represent skills students should master for effective 21st century work and citizenship, but also describe the learning strengths and preferences people who use technology now bring to educational settings. Dede (2005) presents a framework of neomillennial learning styles that are based on new digital literacies as shown in figure 3.8 (page 66).

Play. The capacity to experiment with one's surroundings as a form of problem solving

Performance. The ability to adopt alternative identities for the purpose of improvisation and discovery

Simulation. The ability to interpret and construct dynamic models of real-world processes

Appropriation. The ability to meaningfully sample and remix media content

Multitasking. The ability to scan one's environment and shift focus as needed to salient details

Distributed cognition. The ability to interact meaningfully with tools that expand mental capacities

Collective intelligence. The ability to pool knowledge and compare notes with others toward a common goal

Judgment. The ability to evaluate the reliability and credibility of different information sources

Transmedia navigation. The ability to follow the flow of stories and information across multiple modalities

Networking. The ability to search for, synthesize, and disseminate information

Negotiation. The ability to travel across diverse communities, discerning and respecting multiple perspectives, and grasping and following alternative norms

Source: Jenkins, 2009.

Figure 3.7: Jenkins' digital literacies based on new media.

Since the articulation of this framework, the emergence of Web 2.0 media has fueled a shift in online leading-edge applications that reinforces these learning strengths and preferences. The predominant learning activities on the Internet have changed from the presentation of material by website providers to the active co-construction of resources by communities of contributors. Whereas the 20th century Web centered on developer-created material (such as informational websites) generated primarily by a small fraction of the Internet's users, Web 2.0 tools (such as Wikipedia) help large numbers of people build online communities for creativity, collaboration, and sharing.

Fluency in multiple media. Valuing each medium for the types of communication, activities, experiences, and expressions it empowers

Active learning. Collectively seeking, sieving, and synthesizing experiences rather than individually locating and absorbing information from some single best source

Expression through nonlinear, associational webs of representations. Authoring a simulation and a webpage to express understanding, in contrast to writing a paper

Codesign by teachers and students. Personalizing learning experiences to individual needs and preferences

Source: Dede, 2005.

Figure 3.8: Dede's neomillennial learning styles.

Dede (2009b) delineates a category system for current Web 2.0 tools:

1. *Sharing*

   - Communal bookmarking
   - Photo/video sharing
   - Social networking
   - Writers' workshops/fan fiction

2. *Thinking*

   - Blogs
   - Podcasts
   - Online discussion forums

3. *Co-creating*

   - Wikis/collaborative file creation
   - Mashups/collective media creation
   - Collaborative social change communities

This framework shows a loose progression from top to bottom, with sharing leadership to thinking together to collective action in which sophisticated groups seeking change use subsets of the nine media listed before the last entry—collaborative social change communities—to accomplish their shared objectives. Overall, growing use of these Web 2.0 tools has led to an intensification of the learning styles and digital literacies described earlier.

Leu and his colleagues (2007) described four characteristics of the "new literacies" generated by ICTs. First, emerging ICT tools, applications, media, and environments require novel skills, strategies, and dispositions for their effective use. Second, new literacies are central to full economic, civic, and personal participation in a globalized society. Third, new literacies constantly evolve as their defining ICTs are continuously renewed through innovation. Fourth, new literacies are multiple, multimodel, and multifaceted. These characteristics are in accord with the media-based styles of learning presented in this section and with the 21st century capabilities this chapter discusses.

Comparing Alternative Frameworks for 21st Century Skills

In summary, these 21st century skills frameworks are generally consistent with each other. The additions to the Partnership's skillset that the alternative frameworks offer are of two types. First, other groups identify some subskills within Partnership categories as particularly important. As an illustration, the ISTE subskill "troubleshooting systems and applications" easily falls within the Partnership's overall category of ICT literacy; it also requires "technical proficiency: a foundational knowledge of hardware, software applications, networks, and elements of digital technology," which is a foundational subskill advocated by ETS. Highlighting this subskill may reflect an assessment of which 21st century skills teachers are likely to overlook given the current culture of schooling; for example, students seldom have opportunities to learn "troubleshooting" because teachers instinctively don't want problems to emerge in an instructional situation.

Second, groups other than the Partnership stress some areas they feel are underemphasized in its categories. As an illustration, "students acting autonomously" is a major category for OECD that, again, is contrary to the current culture of U.S. schooling. Similarly, the NCREL/Metiri framework stresses student "risk taking," but this is unlikely to be encouraged by many U.S.

These 21st century skills frameworks are generally consistent with each other.

teachers unless special emphasis is put on this skill as crucial to 21st century work and citizenship.

The stress on skills that may be underemphasized because they are inconsistent with current classroom culture highlights a substantial challenge to infusing these 21st century skills frameworks into educational practice and policy. At this point in history, the primary barriers to altering curricular, pedagogical, and assessment practices are not conceptual, technical, or economic, but instead psychological, political, and cultural. We now have all the means necessary to move beyond teaching 20th century knowledge in order to prepare all students for a future quite different from the immediate past. Whether society has the professional commitment and public will to actualize such a vision remains to be seen.

Advances in the Assessment of 21st Century Skills

The Education Sector's report, *Measuring Skills for the 21st Century* (Silva, 2008), discuses several metrics for assessing 21st century skills. Which parts of the synthesized 21st century skills framework do these assessments cover?

The College and Work Readiness Assessment

The College and Work Readiness Assessment (CWRA) measures how students perform on constructed-response tasks that require an integrated set of critical thinking, analytic reasoning, problem solving, and written communication skills. The CWRA is delivered entirely over the Internet in a proctored setting. Critical thinking, analytical reasoning, problem solving, and writing are "collective outcomes" that cannot fully be taught in any one class or year; so all teachers and faculty have a responsibility to teach for such skills within each subject area and discipline.

Performance tasks. Students must complete a real-life activity (such as preparing a memo or policy recommendation) that involves reviewing and evaluating a series of documents. Completion of these instruments does not require the recall of particular facts or formulas; instead, the measures assess the demonstrated ability to interpret, analyze, and synthesize information.

Analytic writing tasks. These tasks evaluate students' ability to articulate complex ideas, examine claims and evidence, support ideas with relevant reasons and examples, sustain a coherent discussion, and use standard written English.

The Programme for International Student Assessment

Several metrics for assessing 21st century skills are discussed in the Education Board's report *Measuring Skills for the 21st Century* (Silva, 2008).

The Programme for International Student Assessment (PISA) is based on the OECD Definition and Selection of Competencies project (DeSeCo). PISA seeks to measure how well fifteen-year-olds, approaching the end of compulsory schooling, are prepared to meet the challenges of today's knowledge societies—what PISA refers to as "literacy." The assessment is forward looking, focusing on young people's ability to use their knowledge and skills to meet real-life challenges, rather than merely on the extent to which they have mastered a specific school curriculum. This orientation reflects a change in the goals and objectives of curricula themselves, which increasingly address what students can do with what they learn at school and not merely whether they can reproduce what they have learned.

The assessment covers the domains of reading, mathematical, and scientific literacy not merely in terms of mastery of the school curriculum, but in terms of important knowledge and skills needed in adult life. Tests are pencil-and-paper, with the assessment lasting a total of two hours for each student. Test items are a mixture of multiple-choice items and questions requiring students to construct their own responses. The items are organized in groups based on a passage setting out a real-life situation. Assessment covers a total of about seven hours of test items, with different students taking different combinations of test items. Students also answer a background questionnaire, which takes twenty to thirty minutes to complete, providing information about themselves and their homes. School principals are given a twenty-minute questionnaire about their schools as well.

Key Stage 3 ICT Literacy Assessment

Also discussed in Silva (2008) is the Key Stage 3 ICT Literacy Assessment. This gauges students' ICT capabilities at the end of "Key Stage 3" (ages twelve to thirteen) in Great Britain's national curriculum. The test not only assesses students' ICT skills, but also their ability to use those skills to solve a set of complex problems involving research, communication, information management, and presentation. Test results provide both summative information—in the form of a national score for each student—and detailed formative feedback about student performance that could be used to inform future teaching and learning.

The ICT test is set in a complex virtual world, within which students carry out tasks using a "walled garden" of assets (such as text, pictures, data, and "canned" websites) without access to the Internet. Students are also provided with a toolkit of applications to enable them to complete the tasks; all of these assets are generic software programs developed by the Qualifications and Curriculum Authority to provide the same capabilities as familiar productivity software on the level playing field of a nonbrand-specific platform. As students work through the test session, their actions are tracked by the computer and mapped against expected capabilities for each level of the national curriculum; this includes both technical skills and learning skills, such as "finding things out," "developing ideas," and "exchanging and sharing information." The information collected about a student's performance allows a score to be awarded along with a profile of individual strengths and weaknesses.

All three assessments potentially could cover substantial amounts of the 21st century skills delineated in the frameworks presented in this chapter. However, CWRA and PISA are limited in their effectiveness by their formats: paper based and, at times, test-item focused. The Key Stage 3 has more potential to measure the full range of 21st century capabilities, including digital literacies, because it is conducted in a virtual world and based on activities more sophisticated than making forced-choice decisions among a limited number of alternatives.

Beyond these current assessments, many researchers are working on virtual performance assessments for specific higher-order intellectual performances, such as scientific inquiry, that soon may provide reliable, usable, and valid measures for many 21st century skills (Ketelhut, Dede, Clarke, Nelson, & Bowman, 2008). Research has documented that higher-order thinking skills related to sophisticated cognition (such as inquiry processes, formulating scientific explanations, communicating scientific understanding, and approaches to novel situations) are difficult to measure with multiple choice or even with constructed-response pencil-and-paper tests (Quellmalz & Haertel, 2004; Resnick & Resnick, 1992; Wilson & Bertenthal, 2006). In the late 1980s and 1990s, educators attempted to use performance assessments in accountability programs. However, the developers of both hands-on and virtual performance assessments encountered a number of technical, resource, and reliability problems in large-scale administration (Cronbach, Linn, Brennan, & Haertel, 1997; Shavelson, Ruiz-Primo, & Wiley, 1999). At that time, these problems were substantial enough to undercut the potentially greater construct validity for science inquiry that performance assessments can provide over pencil-and-paper tests. Now, however, teams of scholars are using modern technologies to develop virtual performance assessments of various types (such as http://virtualassessment.org) that may solve this problem of providing reliable, valid measurements for sophisticated intellectual and psychosocial skills (Quellmalz & Pellegrino, 2009).

Overall, the increasing availability of valid assessments for 21st century skills is leading to calls for all states to participate in "international benchmarking," or comparing their educational processes and outcomes to the best models around the world (National Governors Association, 2008). Widely used international assessments centered on curricular areas include the Trends in International Mathematics and Science Study for grades 4, 8, and 12, as well as

> The increasing availability of valid assessments for 21st century skills is leading to calls for all states to participate in "international benchmarking," or comparing their educational processes and outcomes to the best models around the world.

the Progress in International Reading Literacy Study of fourth-grade reading levels (Silva, 2008). *Benchmarking for Success: Ensuring U.S. Students Receive a World-Class Education* calls on states to implement five types of benchmarking:

- **Action 1**—Upgrade state standards by adopting a common core of internationally benchmarked standards in math and language arts for grades K–12 to ensure that students are equipped with the necessary knowledge and skills to be globally competitive.

- **Action 2**—Leverage states' collective influence to ensure that textbooks, digital media, curricula, and assessments are aligned to internationally benchmarked standards and draw on lessons from high-performing nations and states.

- **Action 3**—Revise state policies for recruiting, preparing, developing, and supporting teachers and school leaders to reflect the human capital practices of top-performing nations and states around the world.

- **Action 4**—Hold schools and systems accountable through monitoring, interventions, and support to ensure consistently high performance, drawing upon international best practices.

- **Action 5**—Measure state-level education performance globally by examining student achievement and attainment in an international context to ensure that, over time, students are receiving the education they need to compete in the 21st century economy. (Adapted from National Governors Association, 2008, p. 6)

Recent U.S. federal activities to promote coordination among states in developing comparable, high-quality curriculum standards are building momentum to generate and use assessments that can measure sophisticated intellectual and psychosocial skills needed for the 21st century.

Reconceptualizing for the 21st Century

Fortunately, groups developing conceptualizations of 21st century skills have built sufficiently on each other's ideas to avoid speaking a different language about the same topic. As this analysis shows, organizations that argue for 21st century skills have frameworks largely consistent in terms of what should be added to the curriculum. However, each group has different areas of emphasis within the overarching skillset. For instance, taking the Partnership's Framework as a baseline, groups focused on technical skills—such as ISTE, ETS, and those who advocate for digital literacies—emphasize that aspect of the Partnership's Framework and articulate in greater detail which fluencies in information and communications technologies are most important.

Each organization also introduces complementary ideas to the concept of 21st century skills. For example, as discussed earlier, additions to the Partnership's Framework from OECD and NCREL/Metiri incorporate autonomous actions by students that typically are not a part of conventional classroom culture. This highlights a metacognitive challenge for the 21st century skills movement: to systematically examine all the tacit beliefs and assumptions and values about schooling that are legacies from the 20th century and the industrial age. Compilations such as this volume are making important contributions in aiding this reconceptualization of education for the 21st century.

References

Cronbach, L. J., Linn, R. L., Brennan, R. L, & Haertel, E. H. (1997). Generalizability analysis for performance assessments of student achievement or school effectiveness. *Educational and Psychological Measurement, 57,* 373–399.

Dede, C. (2005). Planning for neomillennial learning styles: Implications for investments in technology and faculty. In D. G. Oblinger & J. L. Oblinger (Eds.), *Educating the net generation* (pp. 226–247). Boulder, CO: EDUCAUSE.

Dede, C. (2009a). Determining, developing and assessing the capabilities of North Carolina's future-ready students. *Friday Institute White Paper Series.* Raleigh: North Carolina State University.

Dede, C. (2009b, May). Comments on Greenhow, Robelia, and Hughes: Technologies that facilitate generating knowledge and possibly wisdom. *Educational Researcher, 38,* 260–263.

Dede, C. (in press). Technological supports for acquiring 21st century skills. In P. Peterson, E. Baker, & B. McGaw (Eds.), *International Encyclopedia of Education* (3rd ed.). Oxford, England: Elsevier.

Educational Testing Service. (2007). *Digital transformation: A framework for ICT literacy.* Princeton, NJ: Author. Accessed at www.etsliteracy.org/Media/

Tests/Information_and_Communication_Technology_Literacy/ictreport .pdf on December 13, 2009.

International Society for Technology in Education. (2007). *National educational technology standards for students* (2nd ed.). Eugene, OR: Author.

Jenkins, H. (with Purushotma, R., Weigel, M., Clinton, K., & Robison, A. J.). (2009). *Confronting the challenges of participatory culture: Media education for the 21st century.* Cambridge, MA: MIT Press.

Karoly, L. A., & Panis, C. W. A. (2004). *The 21st century at work: Forces shaping the future workforce and workplace in the United States.* Santa Monica, CA: RAND Corporation.

Ketelhut, D., Dede, C., Clarke, J., Nelson, B., & Bowman, C. (2008). Studying situated learning in a multi-user virtual environment. In E. Baker, J. Dickieson, W. Wulfeck, & H. F. O'Neil (Eds.), *Assessment of problem solving using simulations* (pp. 37–58). New York: Lawrence Erlbaum.

Leu, D. J., Zawilinski, L., Castek, J., Banerjee, M., Housand, B. C., Liu, Y., et al. (2007). What is new about the new literacies of online reading comprehension? In L. S. Rush, A. J. Eakle, & A. Berger (Eds.), *Secondary school literacy: What research reveals for classroom practice* (pp. 37–68). Urbana, IL: National Council of Teachers of English.

Levy, F., & Murnane, R. J. (2004). *The new division of labor: How computers are creating the next job market.* Princeton, NJ: Princeton University Press.

National Governors Association. (2008). *Benchmarking for success: Ensuring U.S. students receive a world-class education.* Washington, DC: Author.

National Leadership Council for Liberal Education and America's Promise. (2007). *College learning for the new global century.* Washington, DC: Association of American Colleges and Universities.

North Central Regional Educational Laboratory & the Metiri Group. (2003). *enGauge 21st century skills: Literacy in the digital age.* Chicago: North Central Regional Educational Laboratory.

Organisation for Economic Co-operation and Development. (2005). *The definition and selection of key competencies: Executive summary.* Paris: Author.

Partnership for 21st Century Skills. (2006, July). *A state leaders action guide to 21st century skills: A new vision for education.* Tucson, AZ: Author.

Quellmalz, E. S., & Haertel, G. (2004). *Technology supports for state science assessment systems.* Washington, DC: National Research Council.

Quellmalz, E. S., & Pellegrino, J. W. (2009, January). Technology and testing. *Science, 323,* 75–79.

Resnick, L. B., & Resnick, D. P. (1992). Assessing the thinking curriculum: New tools for educational reform. In B. R. Gifford & M. C. O'Connor (Eds.), *Changing assessments: Alternative views of aptitude, achievement, and instruction* (pp. 37–75). Boston: Kluwer Academic.

Shavelson, R. J., Ruiz-Primo, M. A., & Wiley, E. W. (1999). Note on sources of sampling variability in science performance assessments. *Journal of Educational Measurement, 36*, 61–71.

Silva, E. (2008, November). *Measuring skills for the 21st century*. Washington, DC: Education Sector.

VanLehn, K. (Ed.). (2006). *The Pittsburgh Science of Learning Center theoretical framework*. Pittsburgh, PA: Pittsburgh Science of Learning Center. Accessed at www.learnlab.org/clusters/PSLC_Theory_Frame_June_15_2006.pdf on December 13, 2009.

Weinberger, D. (2007). *Everything is miscellaneous: The power of the new digital disorder*. New York: Times Books.

Wilson, M. R., & Bertenthal, M. W. (Eds). (2006). *Systems for state science assessment: Committee on test design for K–12 science achievement*. Washington, DC: The National Academies Press.

Richard DuFour

Richard DuFour, Ed.D., was a public school educator for thirty-four years, serving as a teacher, principal, and superintendent at Adlai Stevenson High School in Lincolnshire, Illinois. During his tenure, Stevenson became what the United States Department of Education (USDE) described as "the most recognized and celebrated school in America." Stevenson is one of three schools in the United States to win the USDE Blue Ribbon award on four occasions and one of the first comprehensive schools designated a New America High School by the USDE as a model of successful school reform. DuFour has written multiple books on the theory and practice of professional learning communities (PLCs) emphasizing the model used at Stevenson.

Rebecca DuFour

Rebecca DuFour, M.Ed., has served as a teacher, school administrator, and central office coordinator. As a former elementary principal, DuFour helped her school earn state and national recognition as a model professional learning community. DuFour is coauthor of many books and video series on the topic of PLCs.

In this chapter, DuFour and DuFour discuss school settings for teaching 21st century skills. They observe that the most appropriate environment for teaching the life and career skills espoused by the Partnership for 21st Century Skills is a professional learning community that models these skills. On this basis, they argue that the PLC is an essential tool for bringing about the changes that 21st century skills advocates envision.

Chapter 4

The Role of Professional Learning Communities in Advancing 21st Century Skills

Richard DuFour and Rebecca DuFour

When the Partnership for 21st Century Skills articulated the knowledge and skills essential to the future success of students in the United States, it stressed that the traditional school culture was not designed to deliver those outcomes. To its credit, the Partnership recognized that if its initiative were to have a positive impact on student achievement, educators would need to transform their schools and districts into professional learning communities (PLCs).

The Partnership (2009) was emphatic on this point and stipulated that the environments best suited to teach 21st century skills "support professional learning communities that enable educators to collaborate, share best practices and integrate 21st century skills into classroom practice." The Partnership called for schools to be organized into "professional learning communities for teachers that model the kinds of classroom learning that best promote 21st century skills for students" and urged educators to encourage "knowledge sharing among communities of practitioners, using face-to-face, virtual and blended communications."

The Three Big Ideas of the PLC concept mirror this emphasis from the Partnership. These three ideas are as follows:

1. A commitment to high levels of learning for *all* students

2. The imperative of a collaborative and a collective effort to fulfill that commitment

3. The intense focus on results that enables a school to respond to the needs of each student, inform teacher practice, and fuel continuous improvement

We agree that the best environment for teaching the 21st century life and career skills espoused by the Partnership—setting goals, managing time, prioritizing work, engaging in ongoing learning, contributing to a team, being responsible to others, and focusing on and producing results—is one in which adults model those behaviors and skills. The PLC concept is designed to help educators develop their individual and collective capacity to utilize these precise skills. Thus, we fully concur with the conclusion by the Partnership that students are unlikely to acquire the skills and knowledge essential for the 21st century unless schools function as PLCs.

We hope that this national initiative to impact what and how students learn will be far more successful than its predecessors. We advocate this view precisely because this reform effort is grounded in the recognition that substantive and sustainable school improvement will require new school cultures. Successful implementation of 21st century skills will require more than the creation and adoption of new curriculum; it will require educators to embrace different assumptions, develop interdependent relationships, and, most importantly, act in new ways.

As John Kotter and Daniel Cohen (2002) conclude in their seminal study of the change process, the central challenge and core problem of all improvement initiatives is "*changing people's behavior* . . . [addressing] what people do, and the need for significant shifts in what people do" (p. 2).

In our past work (DuFour, DuFour, Eaker, & Many, 2006), we attempted to identify the nature of the cultural shifts necessary for schools and districts to function as PLCs. Those shifts are highlighted in table 4.1.

Table 4.1: The Cultural Shifts From Traditional Schools to Professional Learning Communities

From	To
The job of teachers is to teach; the job of students is to learn.	Teaching without learning isn't teaching at all; it's just presenting. The purpose of school is to ensure all students *learn*.
Professionals are free to use their own judgment and discretion regarding how they go about their work.	Professionals have an obligation to seek out best practices for those they serve.
Protecting individual teacher autonomy is more important than ensuring students have access to a guaranteed curriculum, are assessed according to the same criteria, or receive similar support and assistance when they struggle.	Professionals must address the crucial issues impacting student learning collectively rather than in isolation. Teachers must build a collaborative culture and systems that promote effectiveness and equity.
Teachers work best when they work alone.	Teachers who work in isolation will never help all students learn at high levels. Teachers must take collective responsibility for their students.
Schools work best when districts provide them with site-based autonomy.	Schools work best when they operate within clearly defined and clearly communicated parameters regarding their purpose and priorities, receive assistance in aligning their practices with the specified purpose and priorities, are held accountable for doing so, and have latitude regarding how to best achieve goals.
Teachers have no control over the factors that cause students to learn.	The individual and collective efforts of educators can have an enormous positive impact. The key factors that impact student learning are within their sphere of influence.

An abundance of research establishes that changes in behavior *precede* the changes in the assumptions, beliefs, expectations, and habits that constitute the culture of an organization.

Educators must begin to act in new ways in order for these cultural shifts to occur. An abundance of research establishes that changes in behavior *precede* the changes in the assumptions, beliefs, expectations, and habits that constitute the culture of an organization (Elmore, 2004; Fullan, 2007; Kotter & Cohen, 2002; Pfeffer & Sutton, 2006; Reeves, 2006). As Kotter and Cohen point out, "In a change effort, culture comes last, not first" (p. 175). Culture changes only when new behaviors become the norm—"the way we do things around here." Thus, educators must engage in behaviors that reflect the PLC culture, but recognize those behaviors "will not take hold until the very end of the process" (p. 176).

Changing Behavior

A study of the men and women who are extraordinarily effective in bringing about change reveals that they all focus on behavior (Patterson, Grenny, Maxfield, McMillan, & Switzler, 2008). These "influence geniuses" start the change process by asking, "In order to improve our existing situation, what must people actually *do*?" (p. 26). They identify and focus on a few high-leverage vital behaviors, create new structures and revise existing structures to align with the behaviors, coach the behaviors, provide resources and rewards to reinforce the behaviors, and confront those people who fail to act appropriately.

So what are the vital behaviors of a school seeking to become a PLC? People must work collaboratively rather than in isolation. They must engage in collective inquiry to address the issues most essential to student learning. They must resolve issues and answer questions by building shared knowledge about both their current reality and the most promising practices occurring both within and outside of the school and district. They must continuously monitor student learning and gather evidence of that learning in order to inform and improve their professional practice, respond to students who need additional support, and drive their continuous improvement process. When these behaviors become the norm in a school or district, educators are in a position to meet the challenge of providing students with the knowledge and skills essential to their future success.

To illustrate, imagine a staff is committed to implementing 21st century skills in their school. An abundance of evidence indicates that an essential step in helping students learn at high levels is to ensure that each teacher is clear on exactly what students are to learn and committed to providing the curriculum and instruction that ensures each student acquires the intended outcomes. Whether these outcomes are referred to as "essential curricular goals" (Lezotte, 1991), "power standards" (Reeves, 2002), a "guaranteed and viable curriculum" (Marzano, 2003), "a crystal clear curriculum that includes a compact list of learning intentions and success criteria" (Saphier, 2005), or "clear learning intentions" (Hattie, 2008), research and common sense indicate that educators improve their effectiveness when they are clear on and committed to the knowledge, skills, and dispositions each student is to acquire. This clarity and commitment require teachers to participate in collective inquiry and build shared knowledge on vital issues of curriculum, pacing, instruction, and assessment. In short, if schools are to teach students 21st century skills, educators must collaboratively engage in the process to clarify what those skills are, the indicators they will monitor to ensure each student has acquired the skills, and the best strategies they can employ in helping students develop the skills.

In districts still using traditional quick-fix inservice, educators receive a copy of the 21st century skills and perhaps attend a workshop or two to get an overview of the initiative. In contrast, educators in PLCs jointly study the resources with the members of their collaborative teams. They honor the 21st century skills framework that calls for schools to eschew shallow coverage of many topics and focus instead on helping students to acquire a deep understanding of the knowledge and skills necessary for success in work and in life. These educators engage in vertical dialogue with those who teach the course or grade level above theirs to enhance their understanding of the learning that is most essential to the success of their students. They seek clarification where there is confusion or disagreement. They

> In short, if schools are to teach students 21st century skills, educators must collaboratively engage in the process to clarify what those skills are, the indicators they will monitor to ensure each student has acquired the skills, and the best strategies they can employ in helping students develop the skills.

establish time frames for when to teach key concepts. Most importantly, at the end of the process, they commit to their colleagues that all students will have access to the same knowledge and skills regardless of the teacher to whom they are assigned.

> One of the most critical elements of successful implementation of 21st century skills involves assessing whether or not students are acquiring those skills.

One of the most critical elements of successful implementation of 21st century skills involves assessing whether or not students are acquiring those skills. Once again, a growing body of research supports the power of assessment to improve, rather than merely report, student achievement (Black & Wiliam, 1998; Hattie, 2008; Little, 2006; Marzano, 2006; National Commission on Teaching and America's Future, 2003; Popham, 2008; Stiggins, 2004; Wiliam & Thompson, 2008). In PLCs, collaborative teams of teachers work together to develop their assessment literacy. They explore the nature of effective assessments and apply their learning to establish effective formative assessments in their classrooms each day. They work together to create a balanced and varied *common* assessment process. They agree on the criteria they use in assessing the quality of student work and practice applying those criteria to authentic performance-based and project-based assessments until they can do so with great consistency. They help their students become active participants in monitoring the progress of their own learning. They make frequent and varied common formative assessments one of the most potent weapons of their assessment arsenal.

In PLCs, conversations regarding student achievement focus on evidence from ongoing assessments, the particular skill that a specific student has yet to master, and the precise prerequisite learning that the student needs in order to become proficient. It will not be enough to say, "Johnny failed the last test," or even "Johnny needs help in math." The team will be able to say, "Johnny struggles with this particular skill, and here are the specific steps we can take to bring him to mastery," because members are clear on the sequence of skills needed to close the gap between Johnny's current level of learning and the intended outcomes he must achieve. Generalities about groups give way to specificity about individuals, and precision in intervention replaces generic oversimplification about remedies.

Of course, in order for all students to acquire 21st century skills, some students need additional time and support. In a PLC, every educator, parent, and student knows that the school has a plan to *ensure* each student who struggles to acquire an essential skill will receive additional time and support for learning in a timely, directive, and systematic way that never removes the student from new direct instruction. Administrators develop schedules to reflect this priority, and educators have increased access to the students who need them most during the school day. Furthermore, the plan has multiple levels of intervention so that if the existing amount of time and support does not produce the desired results, additional steps built into the process provide even more time and more support. The *school* responds when a student struggles rather than leaving the issue to the individual classroom teacher.

This collaborative and collective effort requires educators to function not merely as groups, but as teams—people working *interdependently* to achieve a *common* goal for which members are *mutually accountable*. Therefore, teams must establish specific, measurable, attainable, results-oriented, timebound (SMART) goals directly tied to student learning and then work interdependently to achieve them. Students who are not learning are the concern of the entire team rather than their individually assigned teacher. The dialogue focuses on evidence of student learning and is specifically intended to impact instructional practice in ways that have a positive effect on student achievement.

Because student learning is the priority, evidence of student learning is easily accessible and openly shared among members of collaborative teams. Educators transform data into information by using common assessments that provide them with a basis of comparison. They seek out indicators of the strengths and weaknesses of their individual and collective efforts and put processes in place to ensure that they are able to learn from one another. Teachers who are struggling to help their students acquire a skill have timely and direct access to colleagues who are highly effective in teaching that skill. Schools and districts identify and study *positive deviants*—teachers and schools that are achieving exceptional results—so that others can benefit from their expertise. Teams are hungry for evidence of the most effective instructional practices, and members support one another as they implement those practices and assess their impact. This constant collective inquiry into effective practice fuels the continuous improvement process for the individual, the team, the school, and the district.

The Work of Professional Learning Communities in the Future

We believe that the future work of PLCs in implementing 21st century skills will continue to revolve around the same critical issues that drive the collaborative work of effective PLCs today: what do we want each student to learn, how will we know when each student is learning, how will we respond when a student is not learning, and how will we enrich and extend the learning for those who are proficient? We suggest, however, that the manner in which the work is conducted will differ in the following ways.

PLCs Will Have a Clearer Understanding of 21st Century Essential Skills

In the United States, the question of what is essential for students to learn is left to each of the fifty states. The commonality among all fifty states is that their attempt to answer the question has resulted in far too many standards. We anticipate that the future will bring greater consensus and clarity regarding the knowledge, skills, and dispositions all students should acquire as a result of their education, and greater recognition of the fact that all students—whether they live in Kansas or California—need these outcomes. The 21st century skills initiative is an important step in this direction. The Common Core State Standards project is another. This project—launched by the Council of Chief State School Officers; the National Governors Association Center for Best Practices; Achieve, Inc.; ACT, Inc.; and the College Board—intends to establish standards for grades K–12 that will be "fewer, clearer, and higher" and "internationally benchmarked and evidence- and research-based" (Council of Chief State School Officers, 2009, p. 2). Upon completion, individual states will be invited to adopt the standards. As of September 2009, forty-eight states had agreed to participate in the project, moving the United States closer to establishing a shared understanding regarding what students must learn.

As the specific elements of the essential learning come more sharply into focus, the conversations of teachers in collaborative teams will change. Teams not only will grapple with the challenge of how to develop curriculum, instruction, and assessments that lead students to deeper understanding of important concepts, but also will consider ways to engage students in work that fosters the collaboration, creativity, critical thinking, problem solving, and self-directed learning called for in the Partnership for 21st Century Skills Framework for 21st Century Learning. These skills, in turn, will call for much more varied and sophisticated methods of assessment. Once again, an abundant amount of research demonstrates that the best structure and strategy for providing educators with the skills needed to become more proficient in assessment is the collaborative team engaged in job-embedded professional development (Hattie, 2008; Little, 2006; Popham, 2008; Stiggins, 1999; Wiliam & Thompson, 2008). High-quality assessment has always been the linchpin of the PLC process, and it will be vital to the effort to provide students with 21st century skills.

PLCs Will Use Technology to Support and Accelerate the PLC Process and Expand the Concept of Community

Although technological innovation does not have the power to transform traditional school cultures into PLCs, technology can support educators who are determined to make that transformation. For example, imagine a team of algebra teachers that has identified a particular set of skills students must acquire to advance their ability in mathematical reasoning. The team accesses a national network of demonstration lessons to observe some of the most effective math educators in the country teaching the skills. The website provides lessons for every course, discipline, and grade level, and for all of the essential skills and concepts students are expected to acquire. The team not only observes and discusses how the lesson is taught, but also has free access to the lesson plans, handouts, informal and formal assessments, teaching tips, and frequently asked questions about the skills they will teach.

Although technological innovation does not have the power to transform traditional school cultures into PLCs, technology can support educators who are determined to make that transformation.

As team members introduce the unit in their respective classrooms, they use the available technology to gather instant feedback on each student's level of understanding of each new skill or concept. Because the classroom has been structured into collaborative learning teams, the instant a student experiences difficulty, that student receives immediate clarification and support from members of his or her team, as well as from the teacher.

When the team utilizes more formal assessments, such as quizzes and tests, members have access to national assessment banks that provide hundreds of sample items for each skill and indicators of how students across the United States performed on those items. Teams integrate some of those items into their assessments and create their own items as well. On the day of these more formal assessments, a student is able to pass a wand over his or her answer sheet and get immediate feedback regarding performance. Furthermore, the feedback points out the nature of any mistakes and provides clarification to address those mistakes. Meanwhile, the results for the entire class are available both to the individual teacher and the team the moment students complete the assessment. The team reviews the results and can pinpoint with precision the exact skill or concept a particular student has yet to acquire, and then returns to the national network of effective teaching to examine the scaffolding of learning that will be most powerful in helping bring that student to proficiency.

When the team uses projects or various forms of performance-based assessments, members have access to the clear and challenging recommended criteria they should use in assessing the quality of student work. Members practice applying the criteria to actual examples of student work until they establish consistency and inter-rater reliability, and then teach those criteria to their students.

This scenario is not a pipedream. The technology exists, and small steps have been taken to give educators greater and more instantaneous access to the quality materials, pedagogy, and feedback that can assist them in their important work. We remain hopeful that, at some point, educators will have free and open access to a powerful knowledge base that supports their profession.

Technology can also help educators redefine their concept of collaboration. We frequently hear the lament that "I am the only person who teaches my course or grade level in my school and, thus, I cannot collaborate." The assumption behind such a statement is that it is impossible to collaborate with anyone outside of the walls of one's own school. This notion is patently untrue. As Ken Blanchard (2007) writes, "There is no reason that time and distance should keep people from interacting as a team. With proper management and the help of technology, virtual teams can be every bit as productive and rewarding as face-to-face teams" (p. 173). The combination of agreed-upon standards and increased access to technology means teachers who are not in the same building or even the same state could, nevertheless, work interdependently to achieve common goals for their students. Teachers interested in working in collaborative teams can look to many websites and professional organizations that facilitate collaboration. We recommend Parry Graham and Bill Ferriter's (2010) persuasive and pragmatic insights regarding the use of technology to support powerful collaboration that contributes to the effectiveness of teams and the ongoing professional development of each member.

The PLC Concept and the Teaching Profession Will Align

We are hopeful that the profession will take meaningful steps to align all its practices with the PLC concept. Those who enter the teaching profession through university training will go through programs specifically designed to prepare them to work in a PLC. When student teaching, they will be placed in schools that have brought the concept to life and assigned to a team of teachers rather than an individual. Accreditation agencies will require universities to demonstrate that their graduates in education have training in such areas as effective instructional practice, group processes, assessment literacy, data analysis, working interdependently with team members to achieve common goals, implementing action research, and accessing the knowledge base on best practice.

As a teacher enters the profession, his or her collaborative team will play a role in the hiring process and will assume responsibility for providing a smooth transition. Instead of the traditional sink-or-swim introduction to teaching, neophytes will have the advantage of a guaranteed curriculum, agreed-upon pacing guidelines, common team assessments, and criteria for assessing the quality of student work—all of which contribute to the clarity essential to effective teaching. More importantly, each member of the team will have the benefit of ongoing evidence of the learning of his or her students compared to the learning of students taught by their colleagues. When members of the team discover problem areas, they will have multiple sources of support to help improve their instructional practices. Colleagues whose students demonstrated high achievement on a particular skill or concept will provide the initial support, and support will then expand beyond the team to others in the school. Support continues to expand beyond the school to educators in the district who have demonstrated particular expertise in that area. Finally, the team will have access to the national video bank of effective practice referenced previously. As John Hattie (2008) concludes in his exhaustive study of the factors that impact student learning, individual teachers who reflect on their practice in isolation are unlikely to improve their effectiveness. Reflection leads to improved practice only when it is based on actual evidence of student learning and when it is done collectively. When reflection includes not only the individual teacher, but also an entire team, and when the team has access both to expertise within the district and vivid national examples of proven effective practice, educators will be in a much better position to meet the challenges they face.

Teachers will abandon traditional practices and structures that reinforce working in isolation. Principals will spend less time trying to supervise individual teachers into better performance through formal evaluation and will spend more time working on building the capacity of collaborative teams. The practice of rewarding individual teachers for pursuing isolated courses and workshops through varied colleges and programs will give way to professional development that is ongoing rather than episodic, collective rather than individual, job-embedded rather than external, and systematically aligned with school and district priorities rather than random.

For example, at Adlai Stevenson High School in Lincolnshire, Illinois, a teacher's contribution to his or her team is a significant factor in his or her evaluation because the collaborative team is regarded as vital to the effectiveness of the school. The time for collaboration that is built into the school calendar each week provides teachers with the continuing professional development credits required for their ongoing certification. The school offers its own graduate courses, taught by its own staff, on topics that represent priorities for the district, and those who complete the courses receive credit on the salary schedule. The success stories of collaborative teams are told at every faculty meeting, and a team reports on its work at every meeting of the board of education. Everything the school does—hiring, evaluation, professional development, scheduling, rewards, and recognition—is designed to support the message that helping all students learn at high levels requires a collaborative and collective effort.

Can Professional Learning Communities Become the Norm in Education?

If, as the Partnership for 21st Century Skills has concluded, schools must function as PLCs in order for students to acquire the knowledge and skills essential to their future, then the ability of educators to develop PLCs is crucial. But in order for the concept to become the norm in schools and districts throughout North America, educators must assume a more realistic position regarding the complexity of substantive change. Although many school reform initiatives of the past engaged educators in superficial change at the margin of professional practice, the PLC concept calls upon them to engage in deep, substantive, real change. And real change is *really hard*! False starts, mistakes, and setbacks are inevitable, and how educators respond to those mistakes determines their success or failure in implementing the concept.

Although many school reform initiatives of the past engaged educators in superficial change at the margin of professional practice, the PLC concept calls upon them to engage in deep, substantive, real change. And real change is *really hard*!

To assume that educators can flawlessly execute the complex transformation that the PLC concept requires is naïve, unrealistic, and counterproductive. Niels Bohr, the Nobel Prize–winning physicist, once observed, "An expert is a person who has made all the mistakes that can be made in a very narrow field." The only way to develop expertise in the concept is to learn by doing, which, to a large extent, is learning through mistakes.

It is equally unrealistic to assume that the profound cultural changes required to move a traditional school to a PLC can occur without tension and conflict. In fact, the absence of tension and conflict suggests the changes being made are probably too superficial. Educators must learn to surface the conflict, acknowledge and honor the varying perspectives, build shared knowledge, identify the criteria to be used in making decisions, and search for common ground. Developing these skills in managing conflict will not occur until educators recognize and embrace the inevitability of conflict and see it as a problem to be solved rather than an issue to be glossed over or an indication of failure. The crucial differences between those who succeed and those who fail in implementing the PLC concept often come down to resilience, tenacity, and persistence in overcoming mistakes and resolving conflict.

Despite the magnitude of the challenge, there is reason for optimism. As Michael Fullan (2007), one of the leading authorities on the change process in schools concludes, "I believe we are closer than ever in knowing what must be done to engage all classrooms and schools in continuous reform" (p. 19). The reason for his optimism, he explains, is that "developing [PLCs] has turned out to be one of the leading strategies of reform," and "PLCs are becoming . . . more sharply defined" (p. 98). Moreover, "the press for PLCs and the resources to aid and abet them are becoming increasingly explicit" (p. 151).

Fullan is not alone. In *The Tipping Point*, Malcolm Gladwell describes that "magic moment when an idea, trend, or social behavior crosses a threshold, tips, and spreads like wildfire" (2002, back cover).

The tipping point is reached when a few key people in the organization who are highly regarded by and connected to others (the Law of the Few) present a compelling argument in a memorable way (the Stickiness Factor) that leads to subtle changes in the conditions of the organization (the Power of Context).

The Law of the Few seems to be at work as key influencers in the profession have lined up to support the PLC concept. Virtually every leading educational researcher and almost all professional organizations for educators have endorsed it.

The increasing number of schools and districts that have become high-performing PLCs contributes to the "stickiness" of the argument to support the concept. Today, model sites throughout North America help to persuade educators that the concept is not only desirable but also feasible. The fact that entire districts have implemented the concept in ways that have raised student achievement in all of their schools demonstrates that the PLC concept is not limited to isolated success stories of individual schools, but can instead represent the norm for larger organizations.

Finally, unlike most educational reforms, which have focused on structure, the specific intent of the PLC concept is to change the context and culture of the school and district. Furthermore, the contextual changes it creates align with the most powerful levers for changing people's behavior. Kerry Patterson (2008) and his colleagues found that the peer pressure of social networks was one of the most powerful and accessible tools for influencing the behavior of others. This tool is unavailable in organizations in which people work in isolation. So the PLC concept changes the context by breaking down the walls of isolation to ensure people are on meaningful teams that work interdependently to achieve common goals for which members are mutually accountable.

A second powerful lever for change, particularly for educators, is concrete evidence of irrefutably better results (Elmore, 2004; Fullan, 2008; Patterson et al., 2008). This tool is unavailable in schools and districts where teachers are buffered from sharing results and the analysis of assessment data is left to each individual teacher. So the PLC concept changes the context by using frequent *common* assessments and making results transparent so that educators can identify their individual and collective strengths and weaknesses and take action accordingly.

Finally, Patterson (2008) argues the "greatest persuader" and the "mother of all cognitive map changes" is "personal experience" (p. 51). Schools and districts that implement the concept successfully are very purposeful in their efforts to create new experiences for people throughout the organization. This concept is a new experience for educators who have worked in traditional schools—to work collaboratively rather than in isolation, to use common formative assessments to inform their professional practice rather than merely to assign grades, and to contribute to a system of intervention and enrichment rather than leaving these issues to the discretion of each individual. Thus, PLCs change the context of schooling, and as Fullan (2007) concludes, "improvement occurs only when you change context" (p. 302).

Perhaps we are approaching that moment in history described by the National Commission on Teaching and America's Future (2003) when PLCs will no longer "be considered utopian" but will in fact "become the building blocks that establish a new foundation for America's schools" (p. 17). Perhaps we are nearing "a tipping point—from reform to true collaboration—[that] could represent the most dramatic shift in the history of educational practice. . . . We will know we have succeeded when the absence of a 'strong professional learning community' in a school is an embarrassment" (Schmoker, 2004, p. 431).

Learning by Doing

Educators committed to helping students acquire the knowledge, skills, and dispositions essential to their future must operate from the assumption that improvement in student outcomes will require changes in adult behavior. Teachers, principals, and central office administrators must develop their own individual and collective capacity to function as members of a PLC, and the best strategy for developing that capacity is to learn by doing—that is, to engage in the behaviors that are vital to a PLC.

Assuming that the skills vital to student success will remain static for the foreseeable future is unrealistic. Students and those who teach them will confront formidable challenges that we cannot anticipate today. But the chances of overcoming those challenges dramatically increase in schools and districts where educators have learned to work collaboratively rather than in isolation; engage in collective inquiry to

> Educators committed to helping students acquire the knowledge, skills, and dispositions essential to their future must operate from the assumption that improvement in student outcomes will require changes in adult behavior.

address the issues most essential to student learning; resolve issues and answer questions by building shared knowledge regarding the most promising practices; and continuously gather evidence of student learning to inform and improve professional practice, respond to the learning needs of students, and drive continuous improvement. Those skilled in the PLC process are best positioned to prepare not only their students but also themselves for the challenges and opportunities of an uncertain future.

References

Black, P., & Wiliam, D. (1998). The formative purpose: Assessment must first promote learning. In M. Wilson (Ed.), *Towards coherence between classroom assessment and accountability* (pp. 20–50). Chicago: University of Chicago Press.

Blanchard, K. (2007). *Leading at a higher level: Blanchard on leadership and creating high performing organizations.* New York: Prentice Hall.

Council of Chief State School Officers. (2009). *Common core state standards initiative.* Accessed at www.CoreStandards.org/Files/CCSSIOne-Page.pdf on August 8, 2009.

DuFour, R., DuFour, R., Eaker, R., & Many, T. (2006). *Learning by doing: A handbook for professional learning communities at work.* Bloomington, IN: Solution Tree Press.

Elmore, R. F. (2004). *School reform from the inside out: Policy, practice, and performance.* Cambridge, MA: Harvard Educational Press.

Fullan, M. (2007). *The new meaning of educational change* (4th ed.). New York: Teachers College Press.

Fullan, M. (2008). *The six secrets of change: What the best leaders do to help their organizations survive and thrive.* San Francisco: Jossey-Bass.

Gladwell, M. (2002). *The tipping point: How little things can make a big difference.* Boston: Back Bay Books.

Graham, P., & Ferriter, W. M. (2010). *Building a professional learning community at work^TM: A guide to the first year.* Bloomington, IN: Solution Tree Press.

Hattie, J. A. C. (2008). *Visible learning: A synthesis of meta-analyses relating to achievement.* New York: Routledge.

Kotter, J. P., & Cohen, D. S. (2002). *The heart of change: Real-life stories of how people change their organizations.* Boston: Harvard Business School Press.

Lezotte, L. W. (1991). *Correlates of effective schools: The first and second generation.* Okemos, MI: Effective Schools Products.

Little, J. W. (2006, December). *Professional community and professional development in the learning-centered school.* Washington, DC: National Education Association. Accessed at www.nea.org/assets/docs/mf_pdreport.pdf on November 25, 2009.

Marzano, R. J. (2003). *What works in schools: Translating research into action.* Alexandria, VA: Association for Supervision and Curriculum Development.

Marzano, R. J. (2006). *Classroom assessment and grading that work.* Alexandria, VA: Association for Supervision and Curriculum Development.

The National Commission on Teaching and America's Future. (2003, January). *No dream denied: A pledge to America's children.* Washington, DC: Author.

Partnership for 21st Century Skills. (2009). *21st century support systems.* Accessed at www.21stcenturyskills.org/route21/index.php?option=com_content& view=article&id=58&Itemid=17 on July 1, 2009.

Patterson, K., Grenny, J., Maxfield, D., McMillan, R., & Switzler, A. (2008). *Influencer: The power to change anything.* New York: McGraw-Hill.

Pfeffer, J., & Sutton, R. I. (2006). *Hard facts, dangerous half-truths, and total nonsense: Profiting from evidence-based management.* Boston: Harvard Business School Press.

Popham, W. J. (2008). *Transformative assessment.* Alexandria, VA: Association for Supervision and Curriculum Development.

Reeves, D. B. (2002). *The leader's guide to standards: A blueprint for educational equity and excellence.* San Francisco: Jossey-Bass.

Reeves, D. B. (2006). *The learning leader: How to focus school improvement for better results.* Alexandria, VA: Association for Supervision and Curriculum Development.

Saphier, J. (2005). *John Adams' promise: How to have good schools for all our children, not just for some.* Acton, MA: Research for Better Teaching.

Schmoker, M. (2004, September). Learning communities at the crossroads: Toward the best schools we've ever had. *Phi Delta Kappan, 86*(1), 84–88.

Stiggins, R. (1999, November). Assessment, student confidence, and school success. *Phi Delta Kappan, 81*(3), 191–198.

Stiggins, R. (2004, September). New assessment beliefs for a new school mission. *Phi Delta Kappan, 86*(1), 22–27.

Wiliam, D., & Thompson, M. (2008). Integrating assessment and learning: What will it take to make it work? In C. A. Dwyer (Ed.), *The future of assessment: Shaping teaching and learning.* New York: Lawrence Erlbaum.

Robin Fogarty

Robin Fogarty, Ph.D., is president of Robin Fogarty and Associates, Ltd., a Chicago-based educational consulting and publishing company. A leading proponent of the thoughtful classroom, Fogarty has trained educators throughout the world in curriculum, instruction, and assessment strategies. She has taught at all levels, from kindergarten to college, served as an administrator, and consulted with state departments and ministries of education across the globe. She is the author of numerous articles and books.

Brian M. Pete

Brian M. Pete is cofounder of Robin Fogarty & Associates. He comes from a family of educators—college professors, school superintendents, teachers, and teachers of teachers—and has a rich background in professional development. Pete has observed and recorded class-room teachers and professional experts in schools throughout the world. Pete is the author of numerous educational videos.

In this chapter, Fogarty and Pete carry the discussion to Singapore where they have worked as educational consultants with the nation's ambitious "Teach Less, Learn More" initiative. Fogarty and Pete share the thoughts and feelings of teachers torn between the old ways of authoritarian, competitive schools and the new ways of shared decision making and collaborative study that encourage students to construct meaning rather than memorize facts.

Chapter 5

The Singapore Vision:
Teach Less, Learn More

Robin Fogarty and Brian M. Pete

Singapore's visionary education framework—*Teach Less, Learn More*—was created for the nation's entry into the 21st century (Singapore Ministry of Education, 2004). It is part of a larger framework consisting of four separate but interrelated components: (1) a vision for the whole nation, (2) a vision for Singaporean education, (3) a vision for implementing school change, and (4) a vision for the collaborative constructs—the professional learning communities—that are necessary to anchor the change in each school.

The synergy created by these four distinct, yet interdependent, visions provides the catalyst for significant change efforts in Singapore's schools. In fact, it is the blending of these components that makes the country's journey of change an educational exemplar. Together, these four visions propel substantive change to previously accepted practices, and they support the transformation of Singapore's education system to meet the challenges of the 21st century. The visions create a landscape for others to contemplate as they begin their own journeys of 21st century change. The framework is shown in table 5.1 (see page 98).

Table 5.1: Singapore's Framework

Vision One	The Vision for a Nation: *Thinking Schools, Learning Nation*
Vision Two	The Vision for Education: *Teach Less, Learn More*
Vision Three	The Vision for Implementation: *Tight, Loose, Tight*
Vision Four	The Vision for Collaboration: *Professional Learning Communities*

Vision One: The Vision for a Nation

Thinking Schools, Learning Nation is the first vision in the framework. This, the nation's overarching vision, is deeply embedded in the education philosophy for all of Singapore's schools. It defines the proud plan of an entire country committed to an educational system of prestige and excellence. Thinking Schools, Learning Nation is about building a core set of life skills (thinking, creating, problem solving), attitudes (collaboration, wonderment), and dispositions (tolerance for ambiguity, persistence) in students that will create a mindset of innovation and enterprise, which is integral to the prosperity and well-being of the individual and the country. The vision is a national signature that inspires and brings hope.

Singapore possesses a unique synchronicity of city, state, and country that allows the government to plan, implement, and support expansive change. With this synchronicity, they are able to coordinate planning, implementation, and institutionalization at all levels of the change process. They are able to develop support within the community, the schools, and the state. In essence, they are able to create the critical mass necessary for meaningful and lasting change.

Vision Two: The Vision for Education

Teach Less, Learn More is the second vision in the framework. It is integral to the first vision and speaks to the goal of "teaching in ways that help students learn without being taught" (Loong, 2004). The Teach Less, Learn More vision for education provides a strong and steady anchor for transformational bridging from 20th century education to 21st century skills.

The 21st century skills as defined by the Partnership for 21st Century Skills (2007) are the skills inherent in the Teach Less, Learn More vision. They include the global skills of learning and innovation; career skills; information, media, and technology skills; and practical life skills (family, school, community, state, and nation). These are juxtaposed with core subjects from the various and traditional disciplines, and laced with timely 21st century themes of global awareness, and financial, economic, business, entrepreneurial, civic, and health and wellness literacies. Teach Less, Learn More is manifested in the work of pilot schools, called Teach Less, Learn More (TLLM) Ignite Schools. The TLLM Ignite Schools are focused on promoting intrinsic interest in learning. They are primary and secondary schools of various sizes guided by carefully crafted missions. They seek admission to the pilot program through a competitive application process.

Vision Three: The Vision for Implementation

Tight, Loose, Tight is the third component in Singapore's framework for the 21st century. A school reform with a goal of Teach Less, Learn More has little sustainability if it is not flexible enough to address a variety of local school needs or able to accommodate immovable constraints. The Tight, Loose, Tight formula combines an adherence to central design principles (tight) with expected accommodations to the needs, resources, constraints, and particularities that occur in any school or district (loose), when these don't conflict with the theoretical framework (tight) and, ultimately, with the stated goals and desired results (tight). Singapore's leaders wisely encourage implementation that adheres to a tight, loose, tight philosophy (Wylie, 2008). While leadership does not provide specific models, they encourage inventiveness and far-reaching thinking through the theoretical underpinnings of the Tight, Loose, Tight model, and they advocate a framework for change shaped by the innovative thinking of the particular school staffs.

Vision Four: The Vision for Collaboration

Professional Learning Communities is the fourth component. Grounded in the seminal work on professional learning communities (PLCs) by Richard DuFour and Robert Eaker (DuFour & Eaker, 1998;

see also DuFour and DuFour on page 77 of this volume), it completes Singapore's framework for change. As part of the national reform initiative, schools receive professional development to function as PLCs with resources available through the Ministry of Education, the TLLM network of schools, and through their own professional-development planning teams. While every PLC is not yet expert at this process, PLCs are in place in every TLLM Ignite School, in varying stages of effectiveness.

The TLLM Ignite Schools are committed to the Professional Learning Communities vision. These schools are held accountable by the Ministry of Education to demonstrate results. They are expected to perform and to show evidence of their progress each year. Schools are made up of learning teams with members who work interdependently through structured collaboration to propel the implementation process. The collaborative work—the back-and-forth and imperfect process of articulation orchestrated within and across PLCs—distills the essence of each group's thinking. Believing that social discourse bears the fruit of creative thought (Vygotsky, 1978), educators embrace this as their instrument of change, and they welcome the collaborative spirit and the camaraderie that accompanies the teamwork. Team members are committed to implementing their PLC efforts with fidelity. And in the end, the proven PLC process yields insightful and inspired teaching and learning connections. This, in fact, is the hallmark of PLCs. They tend to emerge as the "think tanks" for differentiation, emergent creativity, and real innovation.

Teach Less, Learn More

Couched within the national mantra of Thinking Schools, Learning Nation, the concept of *Teach Less, Learn More* speaks to lifelong, life-fulfilling, and life-sustaining learning. For the Ministry of Education, this paradoxical statement—Teach Less, Learn More—calls for a subtle look at "remembering why we teach, reflecting on what we teach, and reconsidering how we teach" (Ministry of Education, Singapore, 2004). It is a story told quietly, through the collective voices of the PLCs, as they come to know and understand the meaning of teaching less and learning more.

At first glance, Teach Less, Learn More sounds contradictory. Why do teachers need to teach less? If they do, how do students learn more? When moved beyond the literal interpretation, Teach Less, Learn More naturally becomes a central topic of discussion in the PLCs. These professional discussions reveal answers, but subsequently move the teams along the endless stream of additional questions they generate in their journey. For example, as a team of teachers discusses the perceived need to develop more creative thinking and genuine risk taking from students, teachers question how they might foster that kind of thinking. That question leads to others about the impact of the traditional behaviors of competition and compliance on creative thinking and risk taking. The theory is clear, but the practical path to implementation is complex.

The PLCs undertake and embrace the dedicated process as they learn together and teach together. The change process is about evolutionary thinking, not revolutionary thinking, and it all begins with these critical collaborative conversations.

Teach Less

Teach Less is the first of the complex concepts teachers struggle to embrace within the structure of PLCs. The idea of teaching less is hard to comprehend in a country such as Singapore with an undeniable and well-known

> The change process is about evolutionary thinking, not revolutionary thinking, and it all begins with these critical collaborative conversations.

focus on traditional subject-matter content and ever-looming high-stakes examinations, with class sizes of forty or more, with traditional didactic teaching models firmly and at times fiercely in place, all in a world ripe with data, facts, figures, images, and in an endless flow of information.

The world of knowledge expands every day at a rate that is almost incomprehensible. Teachers are expected to absorb a growing body of work in their fields of study. The curricula balloons with information. Teachers are expected to be current and conversant in a wide array of subjects—from politics, economics, and ever-changing geographical data, to medicine, technology, and space exploration; from business, industry, and educational innovation, to literature, art, music, and the dramatic media.

In addition, the world of instant communication complicates the work of teachers. In the early lifetime of many of Singapore's teachers, the fax machine was an unknown tool. Now, it is already almost obsolete. School leaders, busy appropriating funds to create and wire computer labs, incredulously, had no real knowledge of or access to the Internet. Now, the simple cell phone debuts as the new laptop for ten to fifteen million schoolchildren. It presents just one of the impending technology challenges teachers struggle to keep pace with in this information-rich society. Within a brief span of time, entire newspapers, complete literary works, and classic dictionaries have become electronic, and interactive encyclopedias and global positioning devices have become everyday phenomena. The world is the world of high-speed connections, online communications, blogs, wikis, podcasts, and RSS feeds with Time Machine and Mozy backup systems. Search engines such as Google, Yahoo, and Bing locate targets in milliseconds. Visual media, film libraries, video inventories, YouTube, TeacherTube, Hulu, comedy hours, sportscasts, and online gaming are readily available all day, every day.

Today, the digital world of schooling is immersed in an era of anytime, anywhere learning with Blackboard and Moodle platforms and interactive whiteboards. There are web-based graduate courses, online master's and doctoral programs, webinars and video conferencing, Kindle and Wikipedia. In turn, social-networking tools, such as MySpace, Facebook, Linkedin, Twitter, and Skype, provide platforms for instant and immediate personal connections both near and far-reaching.

Hand-held PDAs, with hundreds of applications for the savvy user, permeate the environment both in and out of school. Phoning, texting, emailing, indexing, organizing, and crunching data merely scratch the surface of the sophisticated surfing functions savvy users can perform. The iPhone has over 135,000 applications on its open-source platform. Why, indeed, would a transformational education policy advocate teaching students *less* when there is so much *more* to know, as all of these new tools put even more information at our fingertips on a daily basis?

Professional learning communities must address the Teach Less question, even as they recognize that they could so easily teach more. Through conversations, Singapore's teachers come to understand that Teach Less does not mean that they should actually teach less—not less in terms of hours of teaching time, not less in terms of fundamental discipline-based knowledge, and not less in terms of a watered-down or minimalist curriculum. They know that Teach Less does not mean reduce the core curriculum and teach less essential material. Nor does it mean eliminate, omit, or slight parts of the basic curriculum. Over time, and with many meetings and conversations, they come to accept that Teach Less has a strikingly different connotation that is far removed from the literal translation.

The PLCs' deeper understanding of Teach Less often happens as the teams address two essential concerns: what to teach and how to teach it. *What to teach* involves the quantity/quality conundrum of a standards-based curriculum. *How to teach* refers directly to the delivery methods teachers employ. Members of the PLCs address the quantity and quality question. They know that there is a core curriculum for the various disciplines that has always reigned supreme in their schools. Yet while they are still tied to Singapore's traditional discipline-based curriculum, they are committed to its Teach Less, Learn More vision. They know they must find a way to manage the enormous quantity of content in the curriculum, and, at the same time, look at the issue of the quality of that content as it relates to 21st century skills.

One example of teaching less is the emergent focus on cooperative learning in the TLLM Ignite Schools. TLLM schools frequently incorporate student teamwork for uncovering what they know and think about the learning at hand—a major shift from the traditional Singaporean methods of covering the content in a didactic manner; however, these emergent methodologies can cause concern for teachers as they try to balance the new instructional strategies with the old. The feature box on page 104 shows an example of the kind of conversations that often take place.

Teacher 1: Let's use cooperative teams for our investigations of environmental issues. We can jigsaw the various aspects, and let student teams research and unpack the essential information.

Teacher 2: How will we guarantee students are addressing the key issues required for the examination? Students could get pretty freewheeling when the teams strike out on their own.

Teacher 3: I know exactly what you mean. I have the same concern, yet I know from past projects that even though the use of student teams does present content-management challenges, the student results are always worth it.

Teacher 1: What do you mean?

Teacher 3: I mean that the students often take the research in a direction of genuine interest that motivates them to go deeper and to really own the learning. It's in their hands, but we are always there to guide the process and to point them in the direction of the essential learnings.

Teacher 2: You're right. I have had that same feeling with authentic project learning. It's just tough to let go of the control. But I'm in agreement. Let's use the collaborative team approach.

Learn More

Through the articulation process inherent in the PLCs, teachers in the TLLM Ignite Schools begin to look at the quantity/quality issue through a different lens. While their system has traditionally compartmentalized the curriculum by disciplines that honor *quantity* of subject matter, they find that this structure can be deliberately shifted to focus on essential 21st century questions, conceptual themes, and life skills that honor the *quality* of student outcomes.

In addition to raising essential questions, PLCs in Singapore begin to examine conceptual themes—the 21st century themes of change, design, conflict, structure, and justice—that broaden the scope of learning beyond the traditional subject-matter content.

When PLCs explore the idea of essential questions—characterized by authentic inquiry learning models that require active, engaged learning—they discover these are universal questions that have many possible answers. For example, how is justice served? How literate must one be? What is the nature of conflict? How is balance achieved?

The "what" questions. In addition to raising essential questions, PLCs in Singapore begin to examine conceptual themes—the 21st century themes of change, design, conflict, structure, and justice—that broaden the scope of learning beyond the traditional subject-matter content. While the study of economics as a subject is a robust part of the core curriculum, teachers soon see how the concept has more lasting impact when it becomes a 21st century theme. For example, when the theme *entrepreneurship* is the pivot point for integrating core economics subject matter, students sense the excitement of a dynamic, modern-day theme. This theme adds a needed relevancy for students and produces opportunities ripe for rich projects in which students take on the simulated roles of entrepreneurs in authentic classroom projects.

Finally, discussions in the PLCs turn to the idea of life skills. Team members see how the skills of learning to learn, problem-based learning, decision making, and technology should be woven into the subject-matter content, not merely as implicit tools used to navigate a unit of study, but rather as a set of invaluable lifelong learning tools, explicitly taught and purposefully imbedded into meaningful core curriculum.

The "how" questions. Over the course of many PLC sessions, the teachers' focus moves to the second type of critical question: how? The team reflects on *how* they teach, *how* they deliver the information, and their options as they embrace 21st century skills as the basis for designing dynamic curriculum.

How can we teach less? In deep discussions peppered with personal stories of classroom experiences, teachers gradually come to understand that Teach Less does mean teaching less in the traditional didactic delivery of information—less teacher talk, less "pour and store," and less-frequent one-way broadcasts.

They discover that Teach Less means using a wider and deeper instructional repertoire: interactive methodologies, hands-on learning, collaborative interactions, and multimodal

> They discover that Teach Less means using a wider and deeper instructional repertoire: interactive methodologies, hands-on learning, collaborative interactions, and multimodal learning in the classroom.

learning in the classroom. As the PLCs examine models of authentic, engaged learning and learning-to-learn skills, members discover, uncover, view, and review the wide range of complex and powerful curricular models available. These include cooperative learning, brain-compatible learning, Habits of Mind, problem-based learning, multiple intelligences, integrated thematic instruction, integrated curriculum, Understanding by Design, mediated learning, case studies, creativity and innovation, differentiated instruction, assessment as learning, drama as pedagogy, use of the arts as a teaching and learning tool in mathematics and English, and art and teaching for understanding. The PLCs explore and investigate what makes these models worthy of their scrutiny. This is where the conversation of the vision for implementation—Tight, Loose, Tight—begins to surface. This is when teams begin to feel empowered in the freedom to choose widely and wisely within the established structure of the Teach Less, Learn More vision *how* they will teach *what* so that their 21st century students learn more, faster and deeper.

While the PLCs actively seek appropriate theoretical models for their students, the discussion often leads to other insights. They talk about how they *already know* about these authentic, hands-on, student-centered learning models and how they have never felt able to stray from the traditionally accepted, more didactic Singaporean classroom template. And they marvel at the fact that they are now being asked to radically reconceptualize the teaching and learning process. They realize that they are, in fact, being urged to honor the Teach Less initiative, with all of its potential power, and they begin to feel a sense of urgency about renewing their approach to the curriculum. Figure 5.1 tracks this shift in thinking as it often occurs in the journey of the PLCs.

As these critical conversations about what teachers teach and how they teach begin to surface, parallel conversations weave their way into the PLC sessions. The teachers subsequently attend to the idea of more student-centered models of learning and how those theoretical structures fuel the second part of the first vision—Learn More.

How can students learn more? From a student perspective, Learn More addresses two crucial foundational questions about the

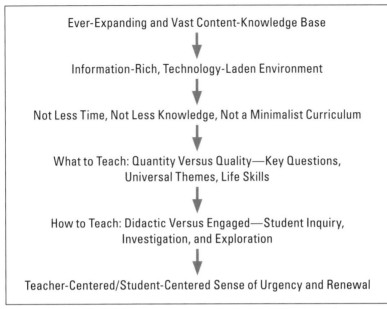

Ever-Expanding and Vast Content-Knowledge Base

↓

Information-Rich, Technology-Laden Environment

↓

Not Less Time, Not Less Knowledge, Not a Minimalist Curriculum

↓

What to Teach: Quantity Versus Quality—Key Questions, Universal Themes, Life Skills

↓

How to Teach: Didactic Versus Engaged—Student Inquiry, Investigation, and Exploration

↓

Teacher-Centered/Student-Centered Sense of Urgency and Renewal

Figure 5.1: Flow chart showing PLCs' thinking about the Teach Less concept.

teaching and learning process. Just as with the earlier questions: What do students learn? And how do they learn it?

As the PLCs explore what students learn, again, the core curriculum is front and center. Even when bridging learning to 21st century skills, these teachers understand that there is no argument about the basics. It is a given that students need core content knowledge. What is not a given—yet—is the urgent need to equip students with skills of life, skills of learning, and skills of an already-present future.

Teachers are aware that the students they are teaching are already immersed in a plethora of future skills. Teachers talk about how effortlessly students adapt to technology tools. They gobble up shiny new hardware, and they show no hesitation with the ever-expanding repertoire of software applications available. Teachers lament that students are omnivores when it comes to "playing around" with the technological tools that debut almost daily. Professional learning communities provide the perfect platform to discuss this well-known and often dismissed dilemma: students are ahead of the curve with technology in every way, shape, and manner. Students in today's schools have known no other way in their short lifetimes. Yet it is sometimes acknowledged, but rarely addressed with interest and integrity, how the school curriculum often lags far behind the students in the integration and blending of available technologies.

With this context in mind, conversations in the PLCs invariably lead to the idea that students do need more than a knowledge-based curriculum. Teachers realize that students need a curriculum that goes above and beyond the present state of affairs; that they need a dynamic, more relevant curriculum that is laced with cutting-edge technologies—one that truly does bridge to the 21st century of fast-paced, ever-changing, technology-rich living and learning.

> Conversations in the PLCs invariably lead to the idea that students do need more than a knowledge-based curriculum.

As the discussion unwinds, teachers begin listing the litany of life and learning skills: skills of reasoning, research, and resilience; skills of technology, team building, and teamwork; skills of communication, collaboration, and collegiality; and skills of innovation, invention, and industry. The PLCs talk about how students need to learn skills that develop attitudes, dispositions, and habits of mind; that students need rich, rigorous, and relevant learning experiences that bridge a core content-knowledge base with the unknown and unforeseen challenges of the 21st century and beyond. When discussing what students need to learn, the PLCs see that the list is long and full of new items. They realize that learning cannot be just about discipline-specific knowledge. What students learn must go much further than the status quo. This is an exciting breakthrough for PLCs, and the conversations continue.

In the natural course of events, these collegial conversations find their way into talks of how students learn the curriculum best. The team discusses teaching methods, what works for them as teachers, and what does not, what other teachers do, and what they have not yet tried. Within these coveted collegial conversations, a whole repertoire of teaching strategies is revealed. This beginning of authentic professional dialogue and articulation sparks changes in practice.

While most teachers agree that their primary mode of delivery is in a straightforward blast of facts, data, and reasons, they also know that in those all-too-rare moments when they diverge from the didactic—in those moments when they orchestrate a unit-driven project or a meaningful excursion—their students are engaged quite differently. They recall the intensity and the involvement of a classroom of eager learners. As the teachers exchange scenarios of these experiences that transform passive learners into lively, active, and engaged participants, they know they have struck a chord.

The teams have more breakthroughs. Realizing that Teach Less, Learn More calls for this kind of learner engagement, teacher teams are motivated to try new methods apart from the traditional class instruction. Of course, all this robust conversation occurs over time, over several or many meeting sessions, as the PLCs struggle to come to agreement on their theoretical model. They discuss the various models of student inquiry, investigations, discovery learning, hands-on experimentation, exploration, and problem solving. They consider team collaborations; a deeper, not wider curriculum focus; and a definite and aggressive technology thread. They weigh the pros and cons of each of the many models, narrowing the choices down as they unearth concerns and priorities.

And the PLCs address, again and again, the ever-present concern about the core curriculum, as they are always cognizant of Singapore's high-stakes examinations. Yet they now know that core curriculum can be presented not as inert knowledge to be "covered," but as a dynamic flow of information that incorporates life's challenges in ways that are structured yet experiential, and in ways that are authentic, relevant, and meaningful.

Some Teach Less, Learn More school applications are simple, yet they are eloquent in their mindfulness of what and how to teach differently. Other school implementations of Teach Less, Learn More are intricate and exquisite in their applied methodologies as they follow the Tight, Loose, Tight implementation vision. Note in figure 5.2 (page 110) the flow of thinking that occurs when school teams move toward their ultimate goal of implementing an innovative model of curriculum that bridges learning to the demands of the 21st century.

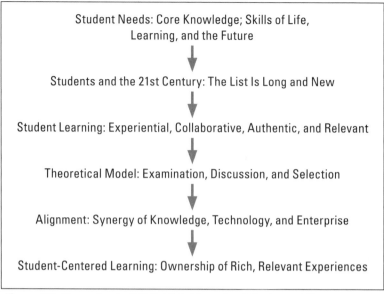

Student Needs: Core Knowledge; Skills of Life, Learning, and the Future

↓

Students and the 21st Century: The List Is Long and New

↓

Student Learning: Experiential, Collaborative, Authentic, and Relevant

↓

Theoretical Model: Examination, Discussion, and Selection

↓

Alignment: Synergy of Knowledge, Technology, and Enterprise

↓

Student-Centered Learning: Ownership of Rich, Relevant Experiences

Figure 5.2: Flow chart of PLCs' thinking about the Learn More concept.

What do the implementation results from a collegial conversation look like? The examples presented in the following sections show the results in two schools. One profile is a primary school implementation plan that marries traditional content with 21st century skillsets. The second depicts a secondary school curriculum plan that reaches rigorously into the rich technologies of the 21st century.

An Elementary School Example

Changkat Primary School's PLC chose to adopt a simple but eloquent model of instruction (Ministry of Education, Singapore, 2004). They use Costa and Kallick's (2000) *Integrating and Sustaining Habits of Mind* as a theoretical model for understanding narrative text. Teachers at Changkat know the weight comprehension skills carry in terms of continued student success, so they teach about metacognition and the learning-to-learn skills of awareness and control over one's learning. They emphasize student understanding of (1) knowing what they know, (2) knowing what they don't know, and (3) knowing what to do when they don't know. As students learn to take responsibility for reading with understanding, they focus on such habits of mind as managing impulsivity, persistence, continuous learning, and monitoring, and modifying and managing their own learning. These same students are taught how to systematically code narrative text for more explicit comprehension, using a set of specific symbols: (+) New; (rr) Reread; (?) Question; (_____) Connection; (!) WOW; (^) Empathy; (V) Visualize; (*) Research; (I) Infer; and (=) Clue.

This explicit coding provides concrete evidence of the students' understanding and use of specific strategies that deepen their comprehension. The coding engages complex thinking skills used in qualitative data analysis and interpretation of ethnographic studies. The coding process raises the bar significantly for student understanding of informational text.

This elementary school PLC decided that these are habits of mind and learning-to-learn skills that will serve their students for years to come. While this may appear at first glance to be a more traditionally focused application of Teach Less, Learn More, in truth, it establishes noble goals for these primary students.

The difference between a common and an uncommon application of Teach Less, Learn More lies in the subtle shift in teachers' understanding and execution of core content. The explicitness with which comprehension of a narrative is approached takes comprehension from a "phantom skill" that is often alluded to, but not often actually taught, to explicit skillsets for reading with comprehension (inference, visualization, empathy, and so on), enhanced by lifelong skills of learning to learn.

A Secondary School Example

The team at Jurong Secondary School collaborates with industry partners and uses a problem-based learning approach (Barrows & Tamblyn, 1980) with differentiated learning (Tomlinson, 1999), and a unique set of e-PBL tools (problem-based learning tools) tools that immerse students in information-communication technology (Ministry of Education, Singapore, 2004). As part of this unique experience, an engine with artificial intelligence capacity processes student data about learning dispositions. This media-literacy project in which students are evaluating sources of information, communicating ideas through various media tools, and making use of technology with responsibility and ethics is truly an intricate and eloquent adaptation of the 21st century vision.

The Challenge of Change

While significant change is happening in these pilot schools, teachers come to realize that what they are doing is not a perfect science. It is an imperfect, messy, human process. Ultimately, however, the PLCs understand the overriding benefits to students. Teachers come to realize that by moving toward student-centered curriculum models, students willingly and assertively take over the ownership of the learning experiences inherent in the innovative curriculum projects being planned and implemented.

These are the trials and tribulations, the tools and techniques of reflective practice that come to the surface as the PLCs mature—as team members adjust to other members, build a sense of community, and begin to feel empowered to move forward with their mission.

A sense of instructional renewal slowly emerges from the dual focus on the core curriculum and student-centered 21st century skills. With the Teach Less, Learn More dichotomy of ideas tediously, intensely, and thoroughly sorted and exposed through the collaborative conversations of PLCs, these school teams continue to dig into their theoretical models of choice and advance the process of alignment to their core curricular content.

As curriculum designs develop, the Learn More aspect of the vision takes shape. The teacher teams begin to grasp why Teach Less, Learn More is neither more nor less of the same. They begin to realize that the Teach Less, Learn More vision is about teaching with passion and foresight about what to teach along with relevancy and richness in how to teach. Teachers begin to look past the isolated subject area boundaries toward a richer, fuller, and more meaningful curriculum inter-twined with 21st century skills.

> Teachers begin to look past the isolated subject area boundaries toward a richer, fuller, and more meaningful curriculum intertwined with 21st century skills.

This examination of what students learn and how students learn lies at the center of the Learn More element of Singapore's educational vision. As these PLCs proceed with their dynamic discussions, they think more about student learning—learning that is relevant to the world students live in and the world they will live in. Teachers talk about students learning more when they are given responsibility for that learning and when they are given the tools needed to meet the challenges they encounter. Teachers discuss how students learn more when they "own" their learning, when they have choices and options, when they must struggle a little to complete the task, and when they feel the joy of accomplishment and achievement. There is no way to measure the power of these collegial conversations as the teachers shift from notions of traditional schooling to teaching for the 21st century. It shows, over and over again, that teachers, working as professional communities of learners, come to embrace the emerging philosophy of Teach Less, Learn More, and, in turn, evolve as more reflective practitioners who focus on the outcomes they have created.

A Bridge to the 21st Century

All is not perfect in this imperfect process of change, engineered by imperfect humans, functioning as imperfect PLCs. Yet as the process unfolds, as the school teams fight to keep their nation's global stature by producing the highest standardized test scores, they are striving at the same time to shift toward more engaged learning that may not herald the examination at the same priority level as in times past. Nevertheless, these schools continue to demonstrate success for students and are still among the most acclaimed and esteemed in the world's educational community for their willingness to accept the challenges involved in this dual task.

This is the story of how TLLM Ignite Schools conceptualize the 21st century core curriculum above and beyond the basic, foundational learning of traditional schooling. These schools are attempting to unlock the creative minds of teachers and students, set in motion the talents and abilities of the students in their care, and honor Singapore's mission of Thinking Schools, Learning Nation. This is the story of how Singapore's educators are preparing for the 21st century.

This story is not yet complete, and many questions about the future course of the journey still remain: What does Singapore's journey have to do with schools in other nations? What are the lessons

As the process unfolds, as the school teams fight to keep their nation's global stature by producing the highest standardized test scores, they are striving at the same time to shift toward more engaged learning that may not herald the examination at the same priority level as in times past.

learned that apply to different systems? What can our school leaders take away in their quest to bridge learning to 21st century skills? How does Singapore's journey relate to others leading the way to 21st century skills?"

What any educational community can take away from this visionary framework begins with the four visions within Singapore's framework. Singapore's visions can inspire, guide, and bridge; they can crystallize, teach, and empower. They can embrace, embody, transfer, and transform. They can begin conversations, spur debate, and provide a source for reflection.

Teach Less, Learn More! The mantra is simple. This vision is the frame and the fuel for the conversation within the school system's PLCs. What begin as ordinary conversations among colleagues evolve into practical missions for school teams. There are no miracles here. The lessons learned by these PLCs are the lessons of collaboration, communication, and celebration. These lessons translate to other schools and other teachers and other places around the world—the lessons of visionary journeys, creative thinking, authentic learning, and spirited collaborations, the universal lessons of challenge and change.

References

Barrows, H. S., & Tamblyn, R. M. (1980). *Problem-based learning: An approach to medical education.* New York: Springer.

Costa, A. L., & Kallick, B. (Eds.). (2000). *Integrating and sustaining habits of mind.* Alexandria, VA: Association for Supervision and Curriculum Development.

DuFour, R., & Eaker, R. (1998). *Professional learning communities at work: Best practices for enhancing student achievement.* Bloomington, IN: Solution Tree Press.

Loong, L. H. (2004, August 12). *Our future of opportunity and promise.* Speech presented at the Singapore National Day Rally, Singapore. Accessed at www.pmo.gov.sg/NR/rdonlyres/63C7AA0A-FC1B-45C8-9FC3 -3310E29E5057/0/2004NDR_English.doc on April 30, 2009.

Ministry of Education, Singapore. (2004). *Teach less, learn more: Reigniting passion and mission.* Singapore: Ministry of Education. Accessed at www.MOE.edu .sg/bluesky/tllm on May 30, 2009.

Partnership for 21st Century Skills. (2007). Framework for 21st century learning. Accessed at www.21stcenturyskills.org/index.php?Itemid=120&id=254& option=com_content&task=view on May 30, 2009.

Tomlinson, C. A. (1999). *The differentiated classroom: Responding to the needs of all learners.* Alexandria, VA: Association for Supervision and Curriculum Development.

Vygotsky, L. S. (1978). *Mind in society: The development of higher psychological processes.* Cambridge, MA: Harvard University Press.

Wylie, E. C. (Ed.). (2008). *Tight but loose: Scaling up teacher professional development in diverse contexts.* Accessed at www.ets.org/Media/Research/pdf/ RR-08-29.pdf on April 30, 2009.

Bob Pearlman

Bob Pearlman has been a key leader of national educational reform efforts in his unique thirty-year career as a teacher, codirector of computer education, teacher union leader and negotiator, foundation president, and director of education and workforce development. Pearlman's experience and expertise includes whole-district reform, new school development, business-education partnerships and coalitions, school-to-career and workforce development, union–school district negotiations, school restructuring and technology, project-based learning, professional development, educational finance, and school-site assessment and accountability. Pearlman is currently a strategy consultant for 21st century school and district development. He served as the director of strategic planning for the New Technology Foundation from 2002 to 2009. Pearlman consults in the United States and in the United Kingdom on 21st century learning, focusing on new school development and districtwide implementation of 21st century skills.

In this chapter, Pearlman takes a walk through innovative school buildings designed for collaborative learning. He reminds us that the familiar box-based design of most current schools was suited for an outdated factory-model agenda. He shows us that form follows function in these innovative buildings as well, but the functions are now engagement, problem solving, and communication.

Visit **go.solution-tree.com/21stcenturyskills** to view the graphics in this chapter in full color and to access live links to tools and materials.

Chapter 6

Designing New Learning Environments to Support 21st Century Skills

Bob Pearlman

Visit any number of new school buildings across the United States, and behind the beautiful, new (and sometimes green) facilities, you will still see the same old 700- to 900-square-foot classrooms, superbly designed for a teacher to stand in front of a class of thirty students set in neat rows, listening, taking notes, and doing worksheets. Yes, you might see wiring for computers and interactive whiteboards at the head of the classroom, but other than that, little has changed.

Go across the pond to England, where they are six years into the eighty-billion-dollar Building Schools of the Future (BSF) program to replace or renovate every secondary school in that country, and you will see some significant innovations beginning to emerge. The aspirations of many local education authorities are high: "BSF is being seen as the catalyst for transformation of education in [England]. BSF is not simply a buildings programme, and must not result in 'old wine in new bottles'" (Hertfordshire Grid for Learning, 2009). What you see, however, in the first wave of new builds and renovations, is still mostly the same "old wine"—traditional education. But because the United Kingdom's process is so much deeper, involving so many more institutions, companies, local education authorities, and student voices, some significant innovations are emerging.

The United States has always had pockets of innovation in schooling, and the first decade of the 21st century is no exception. But it is happening mostly through the work of not-for-profit school development groups. Little innovation has issued from the federal or state governments. Elliot Washor (2003), cofounder of Big Picture Learning, studied these trends and found little innovation in school facilities:

> Three themes emerge from a review of research and literature on school facilities design. First, facilities designs have been shown to have an impact on learning. Second, these designs have been shown to have an impact on students and others who work in the schools. Third, there have been few innovations in school facilities design. (p. 10)

Hasn't anything changed? Are students today different from their parents? Do they come to school with different capabilities and interests for learning than previous generations? Have new technology tools enabled more learner-centered approaches to education (Watson & Riegeluth, 2008)? Has the new flat world significantly expanded the knowledge and skills that students need to be successful workers and citizens?

If these changes are real, then schools are now enabled to move away from teacher-directed whole-group instruction to create learner-centered workplaces for a collaborative culture of students at work. Many new school designs in the United States and the United Kingdom have done this. A review of best practice illuminates these new 21st century learning environments and school facilities to help school designers and developers and education, civic, and business leaders launch the next generation of innovative schools.

The Digital Natives Are Restless

A torrent of publications are illuminating the new behaviors and capabilities of today's students, from Don Tapscott's *Growing Up Digital: The Rise of the Net Generation* (2001), to Marc Prensky's *Digital Natives, Digital Immigrants* (2001), to the more recent work of Frank S. Kelly, Ted McCain, and Ian Jukes, *Teaching the Digital Generation: No More Cookie-Cutter High Schools* (2008).

A key thesis in all of these publications is that students learn best when they are engaged and that students can now do most of the work. Prensky urges moving from "telling/lecturing" to the "'new' pedagogy of kids teaching themselves with the teacher's guidance" (Prensky, 2008).

Is this any surprise? These students are millenials—digital natives, social networkers, keen to work on their own or in collaboration with others. At home they are likely to be equipped with computers, Internet access, iPods, and smartphones. At school, they typically sit at small desks, push a pencil or pen, and do worksheets.

New Skills and Pedagogy for the 21st Century

There is a growing recognition in the United States and other countries that 21st century knowledge and skills not only build upon core content knowledge, but also include information and communication skills, thinking and problem-solving skills, interpersonal and self-directional skills, and the skills to utilize 21st century tools, such as information and communication technologies. The Partnership for 21st Century Skills (2003) has defined and articulated these 21st century skills. (See Ken Kay's foreword on page xiii of this volume.)

New standards in the United States, United Kingdom, and other countries often stress creativity, critical thinking, problem solving, communication, and so on; however, few curricula bring these standards to life as learning outcomes, and few countries assess them either in national or state tests or in classroom practice. Practitioners have made headway at the classroom level, however, by emphasizing projects, authentic assessment with rubrics that are transparent to students, products, presentations, and exhibitions.

We are now more than a decade into the standards and accountability movement in the United States and the United Kingdom, and already the limitations of a standards-based school accountability system that focuses on basic skills in a fast-changing, globalizing world have been revealed. Calls for change are coming from many places.

In the United Kingdom, the Innovation Unit, supported by the Paul Hamlyn Foundation, published *Learning Futures: Next Practice in Learning and Teaching* (2008), which "sets out the reasons why innovation in pedagogy is needed in order to inspire young people":

There is a new argument taking centre stage. It is no longer the usual debate over standards and structures but instead a discussion about how young people best learn in the 21st century, and how we can make schools (and those who work in them) catalysts for vibrant engagement, not simply achievement. By looking at how young people choose to learn, what motivation and love of learning mean in the context of school, and how we can give more emphasis to student engagement and voice, there is an almost inevitable sharpening of focus upon what goes on in and out of the classroom. This is a focus on new pedagogy, a domain which has not been prominent in recent secondary school initiatives, but forms the locus of a new programme of work. (Paul Hamlyn Foundation and the Innovation Unit, p. 3)

Innovators in the United States and abroad have adopted a new pedagogy—project-based learning (PBL), coupled with performance assessment—as the best way to engage and challenge students and provide them with the learning experiences that lead to 21st century knowledge and skills.

Project- and Problem-Based Learning—Keys to 21st Century Learning

How do schools move, as Marc Prensky urges, from "telling/ lecturing" to the "'new' pedagogy of kids teaching themselves with the teacher's guidance" (Prensky, 2008)? According to Paul Curtis, chief academic officer for the New Technology Foundation, what is needed is "a new type of instruction that better reflects the goals we want each student to achieve, demonstrate, and document" (Pearlman, 2006).

Since 2001, the New Technology Foundation (NTF), based in Napa, California, has helped fifty-one communities in ten states launch and implement 21st century high schools based on the model and practices of New Technology High School in Napa, California. The New Tech network's experience is that students best work, produce, and construct knowledge through project-based learning (PBL).

The Buck Institute of Education, which shares the same rigorous PBL methodology as NTF, defines standards-focused PBL as "a systematic teaching method that engages students in learning knowledge and skills through an extended inquiry process structured around complex, authentic questions and carefully designed products and tasks" (Buck Institute of Education, 2003).

Projects at New Tech schools are typically one to three weeks long. New Tech teachers start each unit by introducing students to a realistic, real-world project that both engages their interest and generates a list of information students need to know. Projects are designed to tackle complex problems, requiring critical thinking.

Innovators in the United States and abroad have adopted a new pedagogy—project-based learning (PBL), coupled with performance assessment—as the best way to engage and challenge students and provide them with the learning experiences that lead to 21st century knowledge and skills.

Some examples of projects include presenting a plan to Congress on solving the oil crisis, or inventing, under contract from NASA, new sports that astronauts can play on the moon so they can get exercise.

Through projects, New Tech teachers are able to embed all the learner outcomes (content and 21st century skills) and assess against them. Learner outcomes are the same across all subjects and interdisciplinary courses. Projects have associated rubrics for content, collaboration, written communication, oral communication, critical thinking, and so on, and are all posted online for students so they can decide on their own whether to achieve basic, proficient, or advanced work.

Assessment for Learning

Effective assessment for learning provides students with just-in-time information about their own learning and links it to information on the criteria needed to do better. At New Tech schools, students access an online grade portal. Grades on projects and all learner outcomes are updated whenever new assessment information is available. The usual composite course grades are also available per subject, and across courses for the skills of the learner outcomes. Students and their parents can look at their grades anytime, from anywhere.

Self-assessment is a critical element of assessment for learning. Students look at their grades on a daily basis and check the online rubrics for a project's criteria for basic, proficient, and advanced work. By making the assessment criteria transparent and understandable, students are then able to make their own decisions about what performance target or level they wish to accomplish. Such just-in-time feedback, coupled with the assessment criteria, provides students with the information needed to foster self-directed behaviors.

Self-assessment is a critical element of assessment for learning.

At the end of a project, student teams present to an external audience of community experts and parents. They are assessed on their product and on their communication skills (oral and written). New Tech students also assess their team members on their collaboration skills and get to see how their peers assessed them on their collaboration skills. They also write reflections on what they learned and how the project can be improved.

From Innovative Pedagogy to Innovative School Facilities

Schools must embrace a new pedagogy today that will engage 21st century students and enable them to acquire and master 21st century skills. Once they embrace the necessary changes in pedagogy, they realize the need for change in the physical learning environment. "Instead of starting from the physical, you need to start with the program you know you need to have," says Betty Despenza-Green, former principal of the Chicago Vocational Career Academy. "Then you can see how your existing structure won't let you do that. And then you do the work of making physical changes" (Davidson, 2001).

Elliot Washor (2003) urges school developers to "translate pedagogical designs into facilities" (p. 22). Kenn Fisher, director of learning environments at Rubida Research, links pedagogy and space for the design of new learning environments (Fisher, 2005). Fisher further divides pedagogy into five distinct aspects: delivering, applying, creating, communicating, and decision making, all of which inform the new environments.

Designing 21st century schools and new learning environments starts with defining the outcomes. We must ask, "What knowledge and skills do students need for the 21st century?" But real design needs to go much further and address the following questions as well:

- What pedagogy, curricula, activities, and experiences foster 21st century learning?

- What assessments for learning, both school-based and national, foster student learning of the outcomes, student engagement, and self-direction?

- How can technology support the pedagogy, curricula, and assessments of a 21st century collaborative learning environment?

- What physical learning environments (classroom, school, and real world) foster 21st century student learning?

After defining these outcomes, the key design issues might be illustrated as depicted in Figure 6.1.

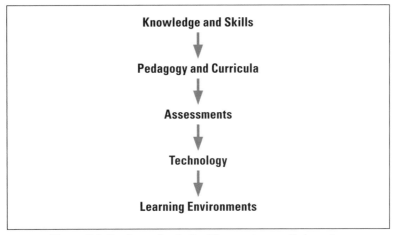

Knowledge and Skills

Pedagogy and Curricula

Assessments

Technology

Learning Environments

Figure 6.1: Design criteria for 21st century collaborative learning environments.

What Does 21st Century Learning Look Like?

Walk into a classroom in any school in any country today and what you will mainly see is teacher-directed whole-group instruction. Walk into a classroom at a New Technology High School and you will see *students at work* on their own learning—students writing journals online, doing research on the Internet, meeting in groups to plan and make their websites and their digital media presentations, and evaluating their peers for collaboration and presentation skills.

Walk into a classroom in any school in any country today and what you will mainly see is teacher-directed whole-group instruction.

Another teacher's students are also there, in a team-taught interdisciplinary course.

This classroom learning environment looks a lot different. It's double the size with a double group of students, two teachers, and a double-block period for an interdisciplinary course. The classroom is populated by worktables and rolling chairs, not individual student desks. Every student has access to a desktop or a laptop. The tables can be put together as needed for collaborative student project groups, or for teachers-led workshops or seminars constructed around student "need to knows." The classroom, or student workroom, can also serve as a design workshop or even as a space for end-of-project student presentations. The classroom can be set up to accommodate project teams, seminars, or workshops for some of the students while others continue working.

There is also a lot of glass. Glass walls or large glass windows make visible to the students and to visiting adults that this is a school where all students are at work.

Gareth Long (n.d.), a U.K.-based senior consultant on new secondary schools and school learning environments, writes on his work developing new secondary campuses in the Cayman Islands:

> The new learning environments being built are designed to promote total agilty [sic] and be capable of continuously reconfiguring themselves. They will allow project based learning rather than discipline based learning and will able teachers to respond to the "blurring" between phases and specific subjects. The ongoing trend towards longer lessons and interdisciplinary coursework reduces the need for student movement and increased effective use of spaces to allow for a variety of teaching and learning styles. They are also being designed for 24/7/360 use.

What Do Students Say?

In the United Kingdom, much work has been done to solicit student input into the design process for new or renovated secondary schools.[1] This student input has been inspired by "The school I'd like" (Birket,

---

[1] U.K. secondary schools go from year 7 to year 11 and sometimes include years 12 and 13.

2001), a national essay competition by *The Guardian*, for students across the United Kingdom (done in 1967 and 2001), followed by the books of the same name (Blishen, 1969; Burke & Grosvenor, 2003).

In the Knowsley Metropolitan Borough Council near Liverpool in North West England, during April to June 2005, School Works managed a participatory project involving local school communities in the design of eight new learning centers. Student participants identified key ways in which they learn:

- Looking
- Concentrating
- Thinking ahead
- Matching/comparing
- Creativity

- Listening
- Searching
- Negotiating
- Teamwork
- Learning

Knowsley's conclusion from student input and also from teacher and parent input was that pedagogy had to change to enable these learning modes, and that new learning environments and facilities should support these new modes (School Works, 2005).

Kids who have experienced the new pedagogy are even more emphatic in understanding their learning functions and the form that their learning environments need to take. Students from New Technology High School in Napa, California, commented on the design of a classroom of the future as participants with SHW Group architects in the 2009 Open Architecture Challenge (Open Architecture Network, 2008):

Colin: To really be engaged, I need to have an interactive environment where I feel connected to others but can find a place to get away and think, too. I need easy access to all of the tools I might want to use for learning. I need to be able to adjust the space to be more comfortable and to fit the activities we are doing.

Zaira: During project-based learning, we move through a variety of activities. We start with forming our teams and analyzing the problem. Then, we determine what we need to know and how to get the information. We have the research phases, problem-solving phases, and presentation phases. For all of these activities, we need specific tools and need to be able to arrange the space accordingly. In addition, different teams are in different phases at different times, so we need the flexibility to have a variety of options in the same classroom.

"No More Classrooms!": The Language of School Design

"Classrooms are out! No more classrooms! Don't build them," says Roger Schank, founder of the Institute for Learning Sciences at Northwestern University (Fielding, 1999). Schank sees three key student work modes: computer work, talk with others, and making something. These modes, he argues, require three distinct environments for learning: focused work environments, collaborative work environments, and hands-on project work environment.

Innovators no longer speak of classrooms. Instead they have changed the language in order to change the mental model, as urged by Elliot Washor and also Randall Fielding and Prakash Nair of DesignShare and Fielding Nair International. Fielding and Nair are coauthors with Jeffrey Lackney of *The Language of School Design: Design Patterns for 21st Century Schools* (2005), a book that has strongly influenced new design in many countries. Students now work in learning studios, learning plazas, and home bases. They shift as needed into many varied extended learning areas and collaboration zones. These include project-planning rooms, workrooms, and other breakout areas.

Kenn Fisher (2005) translates pedagogy into many learning spaces: the student home base, the collaboration incubator, storage space, specialized and focused labs, project space and wet areas, outdoor learning space, display space, breakout space, the individual pod, group learning space, presentation space, and teacher meeting space. Most innovative schools still feature specialized classrooms for making things, including art, engineering, media, and design labs.

Classrooms, libraries, and labs used to be the only spaces where students spent their school hours. Wireless, laptops, and project learning have changed that. Until a few years ago, laptops were not powerful enough to handle high-level applications. Likewise, wireless was not powerful enough to handle continuous Internet access by even a small school of four hundred students in a one-to-one environment. Now it is. This has transformed all school spaces into potential extended learning areas, even the corridors and alcoves.

Technology in 21st Century Schools

The signature characteristic of 21st century schools is *students at work*. Pedagogy—a project-based curriculum and companion performance assessment—enables this new shape of schooling. But it is technology and new learning environments that support this new collaborative culture.

Students utilize new technology tools as investigators and producers of knowledge. The best 21st century schools provide every student with a computer, which increasingly means a laptop in a wireless environment. But personal computing by itself without the new pedagogy and learning environments, even when it is one computer for each student, is no solution at all. It doesn't work. Instead it often reinforces the old teacher-directed whole-group instruction.

> The signature characteristic of 21st century schools is *students at work.*

Students in 21st century schools first use computers and Internet access to research their projects. They find the information they need through Internet research, but also through email communication and Skype video interviews of experts. Then, working individually or in a collaborative team, they construct products—models, booklets, videos, podcasts, websites, PowerPoints, digital portfolios, and so on. Finally, they utilize technology to present their findings, often to an authentic audience of community experts.

Computers, cameras, and interactive whiteboards all come to life as student tools in a 21st century PBL classroom. Newer Web 2.0 tools—including blogs, wikis, and social networking sites—add greatly to the student toolset for individual and collaborative work. Students utilize all these tools to be investigators and producers of knowledge.

However, equipping students with appropriate technology and tools is the beginning, not the end. They also need 24/7 access to their project information, project calendar, assessment rubrics, and their just-in-time assessments. If

> Equipping students with appropriate technology and tools is the beginning, not the end.

they work in collaborative teams, they also need discussion boards, journals, email, and special evaluation tools.

The original New Tech High School in Napa, begun in 1996, built all these special technology tools and implemented them on a Lotus Notes platform. The New Technology Foundation took these tools and professionalized them into the New Tech High Learning System, a learning management system or learning platform specially designed for PBL schools. Since 2008, New Tech has developed that platform into a Web portal called PeBL. PeBL includes the online grade portal. The PeBL learning platform also provides teachers with the tools to design projects, assessments, and calendars and post them online for student access.

The New Learning Environments

New learning environments are needed to support technology-equipped students at work both individually and in collaborative teams, and to provide environments for what Roger Schank calls "focused work, collaborative work, hands-on project work," and for presentation and exhibition (Fielding, 1999).

There has been significant work on these issues by DesignShare and architects Randall Fielding, Prakash Nair, and Bruce Jilk in the United States, and by many parties in the United Kingdom, including the Partnership for Schools (PfS), the British Council on the School Environment (BCSE), the Specialist Trust, the Innovation Unit, and many individual architects and educators.

Five schools in the United States and the United Kingdom exemplify the best of the new learning environments. Each is original in its design and features:

- Columbus Signature Academy, Columbus, Indiana
- New Tech High @ Coppell, Coppell, Texas
- The Metropolitan Regional Career and Technical Center, Providence, Rhode Island
- High Tech High, San Diego, California
- New Line Learning Academy, South Maidstone Federation, Maidstone, Kent, England

Columbus Signature Academy

Columbus, Indiana, a small city forty-six miles south of Indianapolis, boasts the third-greatest assemblage of public and private architecture in the United States, behind New York City and Chicago. Years ago the CEO of Cummins Engine established a fund to support the architecture fees for all buildings built in the city, as long as the commissions went to a list of the ten top architects in the country.

The Bartholomew Consolidated School Corporation (BCSC) has benefited from this funding and the concomitant community spirit. BCSC hired CSO Architects, based in Indianapolis, to work with local educators to develop the new Columbus Signature Academy, launched in 2008 and built in two phases. The academy's program was to be modeled on that of New Tech High School, featuring project-based learning, collaborative teams, authentic assessment, and one-to-one computing. The story of the design process is captured by CSO in three videos available at www.csoinc.net/?q=node/172 (CSO Architects, 2008; for live links and to view graphics from this chapter in full color, visit go.solution-tree.com/21stcenturyskills).

Representatives from CSO visited four sites in California to see the actual implementation of the New Tech curriculum. The original New Tech High School in Napa has two distinct design characteristics that have been emulated in some form by all New Tech schools across the country. The first is the classroom footprint: it is typically double-sized, housing a double group of students in a two-teacher, team-taught interdisciplinary class in a double-block period (see the feature box on page 130 for examples of these interdisciplinary courses). Figure 6.2 (page 130) shows students in a learning studio at Columbus Signature Academy.

The second signature design characteristic is either no walls or glass walls separating classrooms from corridors and breakout spaces. This means that students and adult visitors walking the corridors can see what is going on everywhere. What they see are students at work on their projects. Recent projects have included projects on volcanoes, mitosis videos, electronic games, and motorized toys. This helps establish the collaborative culture of the school. (See figure 6.3, page 131, a 3-D floor plan of Columbus Signature Academy.)

**Examples of Team-Taught Interdisiplinary
Classes at New Tech High Schools**

Global Issues: English and Geography

World Studies: English and World History

American Studies: English and U.S. History

Political Studies: English, U.S. Government, Economics

Scientific Studies: Physics and Algebra 2

BioLit: Biology and Literature

Environmental Studies: Environmental Science and Environmental Issues

Biotechnology Ethics: Biology and Psychology

The CSO team, which included John Rigsbee and Rosemary Rehak, was especially inspired by a dinner meeting with Ted Fujimoto, who as a young business leader in Napa was one of the founders of New Tech High. "We asked Ted what should be done differently," recounted Rigsbee. "His response: 'Fewer barriers. Like a corporate office. Collaborative office space. Teachers as project managers'" (personal communication, June 8, 2009).

Rigsbee continued, "We saw students work as a project team, then break loose and work as individuals. This describes our architect's office, our design studios. That's why we decided not to use the word *classroom* anymore. Instead we now call all these spaces *studios*."

Figure 6.2: A learning studio for an integrated interdisciplinary class at Columbus Signature Academy. Reprinted with permission.

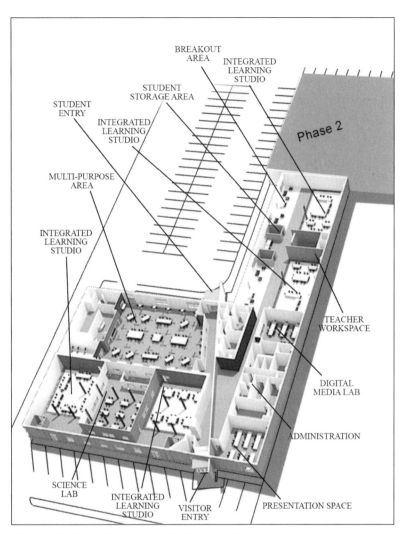

Figure 6.3: A 3-D floor plan of Columbus Signature Academy showing a double-sized integrated learning studio, presentation room, and multipurpose commons area. Drawing by CSO Architects. Reprinted with permission.

On their return, they brainstormed with BCSC personnel to plan the transformation of an auto parts warehouse into a model New Tech High campus. At 44,812 square feet, the academy is designed for four hundred students.

CSO designed these unique learning environments with integrated learning studios, breakout areas, distance learning and presentation rooms, and project conference rooms for preparing presentations. There are specialty labs for science and graphic media. They also designed a large multipurpose room to serve as a cafeteria and commons area, and to house large-group meetings and presentations, science fairs, and student exhibitions.

CSO wanted as few walls as possible in the new building, so learning studios do not have a fourth wall and instead are open on one end with breakout spaces, which are used for informal individual and small-group work.

Phase two will add more integrated learning studios and more specialty labs, including for engineering. "We know so much more now," says Rigsbee. "Our original plan was that students would go back to regular high schools for art, music, and physical education/ fitness. Now students want their own specialty rooms, which we hope to provide in the phase two development."

Furniture is also unique to allow studios to be arranged flexibly for large-group, small-group, or individual work as needed. Studios feature rolling tables and chairs. Tables flip up for post-its and other displays.

New Tech High @ Coppell

At New Tech High @ Coppell, Coppell, Texas, a new small high school launched in 2008, there are no students and no teachers. Instead, *learners* fill the classrooms and project rooms and are supported in their work by *facilitators*. The school has adopted a new language to describe the new roles of both students and teachers. Students are now learners responsible for their own learning; teachers are now facilitators, responsible for designing projects and assessments and guiding and coaching learners and learner teams on their project work.

Learners at New Tech High @ Coppell have a vast array of technology tools and learning spaces in which to do their work. (See figure 6.4, a student project team at work in the open space media library at New Tech High @ Coppell; to view images in full color, visit go.solution-tree.com/21stcenturyskills.) Learners say it is "more professional here" and "we have a big advantage over students at other schools" (personal communication, June 1, 2009). Other learners made the following comments:

Figure 6.4: A student project team at work in the open space media library at New Tech High @ Coppell. Reprinted with permission.

Courtney: We have a big advantage going into the professional world.

Morgan: My brother-in-law does the same stuff at work.

Claire: My Dad really got into giving me ideas on my project on the green revolution and hybrid cars.

Coppell Independent School District worked with SHW Group architects to renovate an old elementary school into the New Tech High @ Coppell. The following text describes these renovations:

In order to maximize the potential of the learners in the project-based model, the design had to accommodate a radical shift from the classroom layout in the existing elementary school, while recognizing a very modest budget. By strategically removing walls in some locations and opening up others with glass, the spaces transformed from stand-and-deliver classrooms, to energized multi-use spaces for collaboration and teaming that allowed the learners to engage in a variety of activities using wireless internet and moveable furniture.

To build on the educational initiatives of collaboration and transparency in the learning process, certain rooms open out to hallways and, in some cases, glass was inserted into existing walls so that visitors, learners, and facilitators can see the processes at work. Visitors to New Tech High @

Coppell might feel more like they are in an art gallery or a high-end book store or café than a typical classroom building.[2]

SHW Group developed spaces throughout the building to provide settings for individual, small-group, and large-group interations. SHW called these settings small-group collaboration zones, project rooms, facilitator collaboration zones, single subject-matter learning environments, dual subject-matter learning environments, a digital media library, and large multigroup collaboration zones. (See figure 6.5, distinct activity zones at New Tech High @ Coppell.)

The designers took advantage of the planned robust wireless environment (both inside and outside) and the plan to issue every student a laptop for school and home use and made every space in the building external to the "classrooms" an extended learning area:

- Corridors—Learners and learner teams sit in the corridors to do their work.

- Alcoves—Student work groups use these little corner areas with soft furniture.

- Project planning rooms—Project teams plan their work and presentations in these small conference rooms with whiteboards. Learners call these spaces *workrooms*. New Tech High @ Coppell was the first New Tech High in the country to have small project planning rooms. Phase two of the construction added additional and bigger project planning rooms.

- Media library—Learners and learner teams do their work in this large area of open space with lots of comfortable furniture and some high-end equipment. (See figure 6.6, page 136, a picture of the digital media library at New Tech High @ Coppell.)

The single or dual subject-matter learning environments, which are characteristic of the New Tech model, provide spaces for large group, small group, or individual work, and can be repurposed for any working modality, or "interaction type," using flexible tables and

---

[2] From SHW Group's project narrative submission to the Council of Educational Facility Planners International for the 2009 James D. MacConnell Award.

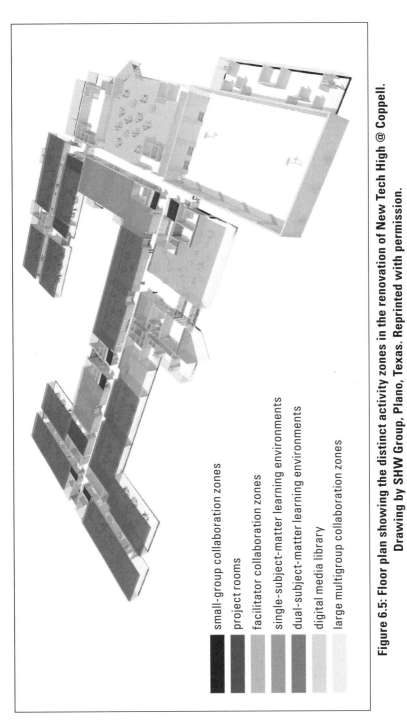

small-group collaboration zones

project rooms

facilitator collaboration zones

single-subject-matter learning environments

dual-subject-matter learning environments

digital media library

large multigroup collaboration zones

Figure 6.5: Floor plan showing the distinct activity zones in the renovation of New Tech High @ Coppell. Drawing by SHW Group, Plano, Texas. Reprinted with permission.

Figure 6.6: Student collaborative project teams working in the digital media library at New Tech High @ Coppell. Reprinted with permission.

chairs. Because New Tech High @ Coppell is fully wireless, with 100 percent laptop and battery bays in every room, the rooms have few dangling power cords or other obstructions.

The Metropolitan Regional Career and Technical Center

The Metropolitan Regional Career and Technical Center (The Met) was founded in 1996 in Providence, Rhode Island, by Dennis Littky and Elliot Washor. The initial school site for one hundred students was housed in a downtown building. A second small Met of one hundred students opened in 1999 in a remarkable facility that includes classroom workrooms, project rooms, advisory rooms, and a large common room. Four additional small schools opened in 2002 on a common campus using a similar facility design for each small school.

Each one-hundred-student site (small school) at the Met has eight teachers in four learning groups and eight advisory groups. The small size is aimed at personalizing student learning. A key slogan and practice at the Met is "One kid at a time." Students are organized into advisories of fifteen individuals at the same grade level, led by an advisor who stays with them through their four years.

At the Met, the curriculum is Learning Through Interests/ Internships (LTIs). Students work with expert mentors in the real world, two days a week, in internships that are based on the students' interests, and come to school the other days to reflect on what they are learning on the job and work on their projects. Students work with their parents, teacher/advisor, and workplace mentor to develop their own personal learning plan. Popular LTI sites include the Audubon Society, New England Aquarium, hospitals, theater companies, law firms, architecture firms, multimedia companies, and more. To the Met, LTI sites are part of their facilities. The school site is designed to support students working on their LTIs.

Classrooms/workrooms have state-of-the-art computers, peripherals, and presentation technologies for students to do their work and exhibit it. Workrooms also have tools for making scale models, structures, and products for exhibition. Students do projects related to their LTIs. One student worked on a team to develop a 2,400-square-foot museum exhibit, another developed a brochure for new mothers in the neonatal unit at a hospital, and another student did a video project that documented the work of the radiology department at a local hospital.

There are now more than sixty Met schools across the United States and many more internationally. Big Picture cofounder Elliot Washor has been the conceptual architect of the Met design. He identified key elements and functions of the school building: "We needed spaces for individual work, one-on-one, small group, advisory, large space, to make stuff, and to display student work," Washor recalled (personal communication, June 8, 2009). The second Met building was then designed to include a commons, advisory rooms, project rooms shared by two advisories, conference rooms, meeting rooms, and wet lab space for art and science.

At the Public Street Met Campus, four distinct Met schools, each in their own distinct two-story building, share facilities (theater performance center and fitness center) across a campus. In the separate two-story buildings, the commons resides on the first floor and doubles as a cafeteria and an informal workspace. The advisory rooms are larger, now incorporating much of what the separate project rooms served in the past (see figure 6.7, a Met advisory room, on page 138). In addition, the second-story commons serves as an informal and purposeful workspace. (See figure 6.8, a floor plan of the Public Street Met buildings, on page 139.)

Learning environments are characterized by demountable walls, advisory rooms, project rooms, commons, meeting rooms, and more storage space for student projects. These spaces are intended to provide a variety of options for students: quiet space, meeting space, commons space, and advisory space.

Furniture also supports individual and group work. Soft, cushioned seats are dispersed throughout. Chairs move up and down, conform to the contours of the body, and feature sled bottoms or gliders.

Future Met schools, says Washor, will likely include garage-door openings to workrooms and rooms for artists in residence in blacksmithing, metallurgy, pottery making, and other arts, crafts, and specialized technologies. Currently, Met schools find comfortable settings for these activities in the community.

Figure 6.7: Advisory room at the Met doubles as project room for Met students. Reprinted with permission.

High Tech High

High Tech High, San Diego, California, is a public charter high school launched in 2000 with a diverse student population of four hundred students that mirrors the San Diego Unified School District. High Tech High brings to life its design principles of personalization, intellectual mission, adult world immersion, and performance-based student work and assessment through its size and school organization, facilities, program, and technology.

High Tech High is now nine schools in the San Diego region, six in a family of schools (elementary, middle, and high school) in San

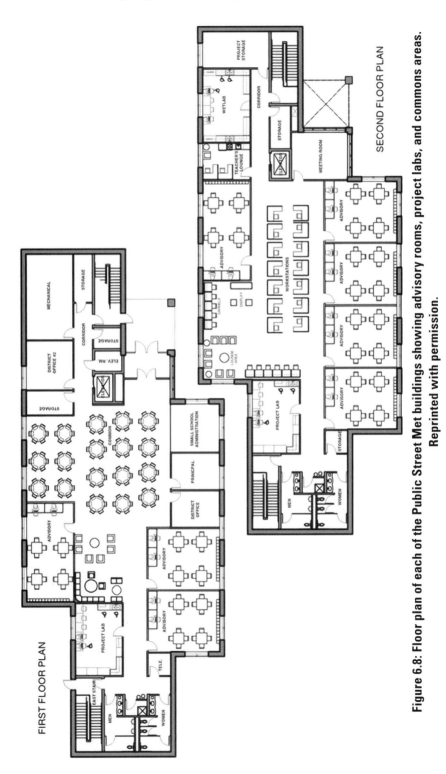

Figure 6.8: Floor plan of each of the Public Street Met buildings showing advisory rooms, project labs, and commons areas. Reprinted with permission.

Diego, a high school and middle school in North County, California, and a new high school in Chula Vista, California.

David Stephen, the conceptual architect for High Tech High, San Diego, working with the Stickler Group and Carrier Johnson, notes that "the original design sought to provide students with personal and small-group workspaces, use of technology, and a high-performance workspace. Key functions were inquiry-based learning, content delivery plus independent investigation, and building and fabricating things" (personal communication, June 8, 2009).

High Tech High originally featured seminar rooms, labs, project studios, small and large conference rooms, a commons area, and a great room. The great room had workstations and collaborative spaces for students. Stephen notes that "we moved away from the great room concept very quickly" because:

We needed the student workstations and workspaces to be much nearer the classrooms. Now our basic model is a set of four to six classrooms with glass walls clustered around a centralized studio work area for multipurpose activities, including presentations, student project work, fabrications, and so on. (personal communication, June 8, 2009)

In the middle school, says Stephen, classrooms are clustered in a neighborhood concept (see figure 6.9, a cluster area studio surrounded by four flexible classrooms at High Tech Middle).

Figure 6.9: Cluster area studio surrounded by four flexible classrooms at High Tech Middle, San Diego, California. Photo by Bill Robinson. Reprinted with permission.

Wireless technologies and laptops have made a difference. In the new High Tech High in Chula Vista, four classrooms are clustered around a common studio work area (see the video of the new Chula Vista campus at www.hightechhigh.org/dc/index.php). Each classroom is separated by a removable wall to another classroom to enable team teaching by two teachers. (See figure 6.10, a floor plan of High Tech Middle, which is now common in High Tech High buildings as well.) Each classroom has thirteen laptops for student use, and students can bring their own laptops to school.

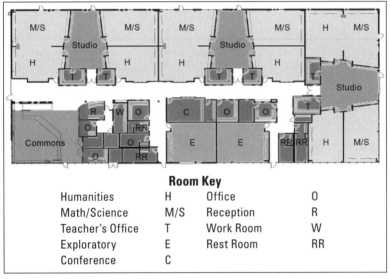

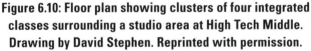

Room Key

Humanities	H	Office	O
Math/Science	M/S	Reception	R
Teacher's Office	T	Work Room	W
Exploratory	E	Rest Room	RR
Conference	C		

Figure 6.10: Floor plan showing clusters of four integrated classes surrounding a studio area at High Tech Middle. Drawing by David Stephen. Reprinted with permission.

"It's all about ownership," says Stephen. "Kids and teachers need a sense of place . . . where everyone knows one another." The commons provides a place for whole-school gatherings, student presentations, and an informal student work area.

Project studios have also evolved over the years. Originally these were separate from the seminar rooms; now every classroom includes the functionality of a project room. Specialized labs, what High Tech High calls "exploratories," include biotechnology, engineering or "fabrication," art, music, multimedia, and digital arts. "Furniture is really key," says Stephen. "It helps to turn atriums, corridors, and alcoves into work areas for individual students and for project teams."

New Line Learning Academy

One of the most interesting new learning environments comes from school innovator Chris Gerry, executive principal of the South Maidstone Federation in Maidstone, Kent, England. The county of Kent, which lies east of London and runs all the way to the English Channel, is the largest local authority in the country, with over six hundred schools. Gerry was formerly principal at Hugh Christie Technology College, where he first grouped ninety students engaged in project-based learning in a large open space, which he now calls a learning plaza.

Gerry is opening new buildings for New Line Learning (NLL) Academy and Cornwallis Academy in 2010 and refining his ideas in a pilot site developed by architect Philip Gillard of Gensler, a global architecture, design, planning, and consulting firm. The heart of the design is a learning plaza large enough to house ninety or 120 students. (See the animated plaza video at www.newlinelearning .com/new-builds/view/146/New-build-at-NLL-Academy or visit go.solution-tree.com/21stcenturyskills for direct links and full-color graphics.) Modular and mobile lecture-style seating is used to accommodate larger groups and divide plaza space. Each academy will house eight learning plazas. (See figure 6.11, the learning plaza prototype at New Line Learning Academy.) According to Gensler (2009):

> The "Plaza" concept was devised with the Academy to provide a higher degree of collaboration between teachers and pupils through an IT rich, flexible environment that promotes and enables a variety of static and fluid learning settings to occur simultaneously within the physical fabric—from individual personalised learning, to group based activities and a whole plaza scenario of 120 pupils—whilst providing a safe and secure home base. [The concept utilizes] technology such as 360° projection and large display areas, biometric lighting techniques to control and vary the ambience of individual spaces, and flexible and adaptable furniture to allow a variety of work mode settings orientated around sizes of user groups and activities being undertaken.

Figure 6.11: The learning plaza prototype at New Line Learning Academy shows the plaza divided in multiple ways for large-group, small-group, and individual learning. Reprinted with permission.

Gensler adopted a new language, adapted from Nair, Fielding, and Lackney (2005), to describe the different activity modes that take place in each environment and the degree of collaboration involved:

- Multiple intelligence—Allows for different work modes

- Studio—Allows for a mix of different work modes

- Campfire—Allows for class work

- Watering hole—Allows for small-group work

- Cave—Allows for self-study

Due to the pervasive technology and the flexible furniture, the plaza can be set up in many different configurations to aid the learning process. Furniture includes modular tables and mobile lecture-style amphitheater seating to accommodate larger groups and divide plaza space. The learning plaza incorporates a ground floor, a mezzanine, and an outdoor area. The plaza ground floor provides spaces for project-based learning, group work, lectures, and has breakout areas and a vestibule. The plaza mezzanine provides spaces for independent learning, small-group work, a balcony for spectators of project-based learning, and an outdoor classroom. In addition to the learning plaza, there are specialist plazas that contain specialty equipment for art, technology, and science.

New Learning Environments for Students at Work

What do all have these new learning environments have in common? There is much in common among the physical designs discussed here. All these schools do PBL, though the practice is different in all. Each design seeks to provide spaces for individual work, small-group work, large-group work, lectures, presentations, breakouts, and whole-school or cluster meetings. Table 6.1 summarizes the main features of each school.

Linking Pedagogy and Space

Most new school building construction in the United States and the United Kingdom today is still pouring "old wine into new bottles," replicating the 30-student, 900-square-foot classrooms that both support and often dictate teacher-directed whole-group instruction. These environments will not support student learning of 21st century skills and will be seen in the coming years as outmoded learning spaces requiring a building retrofit.

As school planners look to implement 21st century skills, they will increasingly link pedagogy and space and look to exemplars like Columbus Signature Academy, New Tech High @ Coppell, the Met, High Tech High, and New Line Learning Academy. These designs will be widely emulated and the experience of students, or learners, in these environments will inform the next generation of 21st century learning environment design.

Table 6.1: New Learning Environments in U.S. and U.K. Innovative Schools

	Columbus Signature Academy	New Tech High @ Coppell	The Met	High Tech High	New Line Learning Academy
Primary Student Work Area	Learning studio	Dual subject-matter learning environment	Advisory/project room	Clustered classroom/common studio	Learning plaza
Presentation Space	Presentation room	Large multigroup collaboration zones	Commons	Commons	Learning plaza
Large-Group Space	Multipurpose room	Large multigroup collaboration zones	Commons	Commons	Learning plaza
Extended Learning Spaces	Breakout area and project conference room	Corridor alcoves, project planning rooms, media library, and outdoor benches	Conference rooms, meeting rooms, and commons	Small and large conference rooms, common studios, and commons	Learning plaza, watering holes, and caves
Specialty Labs	Graphic, media, and science labs	Science	Fabrication	Biotech, engineering, art, music, multimedia, and digital arts	Art, technology, and science
Furniture	Rolling tables and chairs, and flip-up tables	Mix-and-match tables, office chairs, lounge chairs, and sofas in extended learning spaces	Cushioned seats, contour chairs, and flexible tables	Benches in extended learning spaces	Modular tables and mobile lecture-style amphitheater seating

References

Birkett, D. (2001, January 16). The school I'd like. *The Guardian*. Accessed at www.guardian.co.uk/guardianeducation/story/0,3605,422486,00.html on January 3, 2009.

Blishen, E. (Ed.). (1969). *The school that I'd like*. Baltimore: Penguin.

Buck Institute of Education. (2003). *Project based learning handbook*. Accessed at http://www.bie.org/index.php/site/PBL/pbl_handbook_introduction/ #standards on January 3, 2009.

Burke, C., & Grosvenor, I. (2003). *School I'd like: Children and young people's reflections on an education for the 21st century*. London: RoutledgeFalmer.

CSO Architects. (2008). *K–12 Education: Columbus Signature Academy New Tech High. Episode one, two, and three*. Accessed at www.csoinc.net/?q=node/172 on December 18, 2009.

Davidson, J. (2001). Innovative school design for small learning communities. *Horace, 18*(1). Accessed at www.essentialschools.org/cs/resources/view/ ces_res/208 on January 3, 2009.

Fielding, R. (1999). The death of the classroom, learning cycles, and Roger Schank. Accessed at www.designshare.com/index.php/articles/death-of -the-classroom/ on January 3, 2009.

Fisher, K. (2005). *Linking pedagogy and space*. Melbourne, Victoria, Australia: Department of Education and Training. Accessed at www.eduweb.vic.gov .au/edulibrary/public/assetman/bf/Linking_Pedagogy_and_Space.pdf on January 3, 2009.

Gensler design firm. (2009). *Brief, design, and prototype: South Maidstone Academies, Kent, UK*. London: Author.

Hertfordshire Grid for Learning. (2009). *Building schools for the future— Introduction*. Accessed at www.thegrid.org.uk/leadership/bsf/intro.shtml on January 3, 2009.

Kelly, F. S., McCain, T., & Jukes, I. (2009). *Teaching the digital generation: No more cookie-cutter high schools*. Thousand Oaks, CA: Corwin Press.

Long, G. (n.d.). Schools of the future. *Gareth Long—Education blog*. Accessed at http://garethl.com/29501.html on January 3, 2009.

Long, G. (2009, February 14). Student voice—thinking about learning environments. *Gareth Long—Education blog*. Accessed at http://blog.garethl.com/2009/02/ student-voice-thinking-about-learning.html on December 18, 2009.

Nair, P., Fielding, R., & Lackney, J. (2005). *The language of school design: Design patterns for 21st century schools* (2nd ed.). Minneapolis, MN: DesignShare. Accessed at www.designshare.com/index.php/language-school-design on May 1, 2005.

Open Architecture Challenge. (2008). 2009 open architecture challenge: Classroom. Accessed at www.openarchitecturenetwork.org/competitions/challenge/2009 on December 18, 2009.

Partnership for 21st Century Skills. (2003). *Learning for the 21st century.* Tuscon, AZ: Author.

Paul Hamlyn Foundation and the Innovation Unit. (2008). *Learning futures: Next practice in learning and teaching.* London: Authors. Accessed at www .innovation-unit.co.uk/images/stories/files/pdf/learningfutures_booklet .pdf on January 3, 2009.

Pearlman, B. (2006). 21st century learning in schools: A case study of New Technology High School. *New Directions for Youth Development, 110.* Accessed at www.bobpearlman.org/Articles/21stCenturyLearning.htm on January 3, 2009.

Prensky, M. (2001, October). Digital natives, digital immigrants. *On the Horizon,* 9(5), 1–6. Accessed at www.marcprensky.com/writing/Prensky - Digital Natives, Digital Immigrants - Part1.pdf on January 3, 2009.

Prensky, M. (2008, November/December). The role of technology in teaching and the classroom. *Educational Technology,* 48(6), 64.

Secretary's Commission on Achieving Necessary Skills. (1991, June). *What work requires of schools: A SCANS report for America 2000.* Washington, DC: U.S. Department of Labor.

School Works. (2005). *Knowsley school design festival: Learning centres for the future—Final report.* Accessed at www.knowsley.gov.uk/PDF/Design _Festival_Report.pdf on January 3, 2009.

Tapscott, D. (1998). *Growing up digital: The rise of the net generation.* New York: Mcgraw-Hill.

Wagner, T. (2008). *The global achievement gap: Why even our best schools don't teach the new survival skills our children need—and what we can do about it.* New York: Basic Books.

Washor, E. (2003). *Innovative pedagogy and school facilities.* Minneapolis, MN: DesignShare.

Watson, S. L., & Reigeluth, C. M. (2008, September/October). The learner-centered paradigm of education. *Educational Technology,* 38(5), 42–48.

Jay McTighe

Jay McTighe, Ed.D., is the coauthor of ten books, including the best-selling *Understanding by Design* series with Grant Wiggins. He has written more than thirty articles and book chapters and published in a number of leading journals, including *Educational Leadership* and *The Developer*. He served as director of the Maryland Assessment Consortium, a state collaboration of school districts developing formative performance assessments. McTighe is well known for his work with thinking skills, having coordinated statewide efforts to develop instructional strategies, curriculum models, and assessment procedures for improving the quality of student thinking.

Elliott Seif

Elliott Seif, Ph.D., is currently an educational consultant, a member of the ASCD faculty and the Understanding by Design (UbD) cadre, and a UbD trainer. He also conducts program reviews for school districts. He has an MA in social science education from Harvard University and a Ph.D. in curriculum research from Washington University in Saint Louis. Seif was a social studies teacher, a professor of education at Temple University, and a director of curriculum and instruction services for the Bucks County (PA) Intermediate Unit. He is well known for his books, book chapters, articles, and studies on effective school practices, curriculum renewal, thinking skills development, standards-based education, and understanding-based approaches to teaching and learning.

In this chapter, McTighe and Seif examine how to infuse 21st century outcomes into the curriculum with an approach that takes advantage of the principles and practices of Understanding by Design.

Chapter 7

An Implementation Framework to Support 21st Century Skills

Jay McTighe and Elliott Seif

A growing number of voices within and outside the educational establishment are calling for an enhanced emphasis on "21st century outcomes"[1] that include "the knowledge, skill and expertise students should master to succeed in work and life in the 21st century" (Partnership for 21st Century Skills, 2009, p. 2). This call for a comprehensive focus on 21st century outcomes raises two important and practical questions for educators to ask:

1. How might we effectively infuse these outcomes into an already over-crowded curriculum?

2. Which current educational practices and school structures are likely to support the attainment of 21st century outcomes, and which may inhibit it?

To answer, we propose a framework for supporting 21st century learning that presents a systemic approach to educational reform, adapted from one found in *Schooling by Design* (Wiggins & McTighe, 2007). Figure 7.1 (page 150) shows a graphic representation of this

---

[1] For clarification of 21st century outcomes, see Kay (page xiii in this volume) and Dede (page 51 in this volume). These outcomes are also examined in some detail in *The Intellectual and Policy Foundations of the 21st Century Skills Framework* (n.d.), developed by the Partnership for 21st Century Skills (www.21stcenturypartnership.com).

framework, with essential questions linked to its five major, interrelated components: (1) the mission of schooling, (2) principles of learning, (3) a curriculum and assessment system, (4) instructional programs and practices, and (5) systemic support factors. We will examine each of these components and suggest ways that schools and districts can transform themselves to implement a viable approach to teaching and learning that results in 21st century skills acquisition for all students.

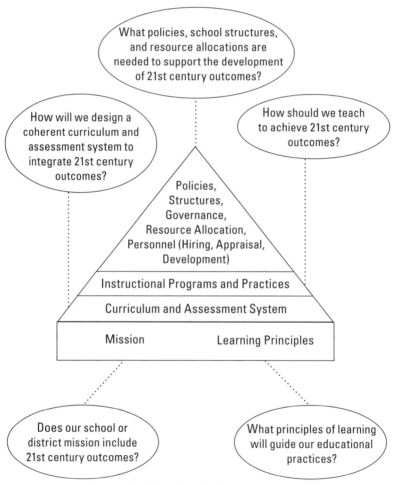

Figure 7.1: Schooling by Design organizer.

The Mission of Schooling

Does the school or district mission include 21st century outcomes?

A mission statement identifies the overall purpose of schooling and the kinds of graduates a school strives to develop. The best mission statements describe educational goals that are outcome—not input—oriented. Rather than specifying what the curriculum, learning environment, or extracurriculars will offer, a school or district mission should *overtly* articulate the 21st century knowledge, skills, habits of mind, and personal qualities to be cultivated in its learners.

In addition to their lack of focus on key learner outcomes, many district and school mission statements were crafted long ago and remain dormant, residing in a binder, on a website, or displayed through wall art. Such statements are empty words that have little or no impact on the daily operations of schooling. Even in cases where the educational mission is alive and influential, it may not identify a full range of 21st century outcomes. Given the centrality of a mission for an educational organization, we recommend that schools and districts, with the involvement of major constituencies, carefully examine and infuse key 21st century outcomes into their mission. These targeted capabilities and skills (for example, entrepreneurial literacy and global awareness) should be operationally defined, since precise outcomes will be needed to guide the development of appropriate curricula, assessments, and instructional practices to achieve them.

Principles of Learning

What principles of learning should guide educational practices in the 21st century?

Education is an enterprise devoted to learning. Thus, our work as educators should be guided by the most current understandings about the learning process. Since the last decade of the 20th century, research in cognitive psychology and neuroscience has significantly expanded our understanding of how people learn (see Bransford, Brown, & Cocking, 2000; Willis, 2006). Yet educational practice has not always kept pace with this new knowledge.

As a means of better aligning theory and practice, we recommend that schools and districts develop or adopt a set of learning principles based on research and best practices. Once in place, these principles provide a conceptual foundation for all school reform initiatives. As educators move to incorporate 21st century outcomes, learning principles will guide the development of the curriculum/assessment system and inform instructional practice and the selection of learning resources (such as textbooks and technology).

Figure 7.2 describes our own view of research-based learning principles, along with some of the implications of each principle for sound educational practice. We will use these learning principles to guide further discussion of the changes in curriculum, assessment, and instructional practices necessary to accommodate 21st century outcomes.

These first two components of the framework are foundational and linked. The mission defines the *what* of schooling, while the learning principles inform the *how.*

A Curriculum and Assessment System

How will we design a coherent curriculum and assessment system to integrate 21st century outcomes?

In a meta-analysis of the many factors that influence learning, noted educational researcher Robert Marzano (2003) found that the most important school-level factor impacting student achievement is a "guaranteed and viable curriculum." Marzano highlights the importance of building a curriculum that organizes a coordinated learning pathway *across* classrooms. This is especially important for the infusion of 21st century outcomes. Without an orchestrated design, the incorporation of designated skills, processes, and habits of mind will be predictably haphazard and unlikely to lead to the desired results. In other words, well-intentioned teachers working behind closed doors won't be able to guarantee a coherent curriculum of 21st century learning.

1. Learning is purposeful and contextual. *Therefore, students should be helped to see the purpose in what they are asked to learn. Learning should be framed by relevant questions, meaningful challenges, and authentic applications.*

2. Experts organize or chunk their knowledge around transferable core concepts ("big ideas") that guide their thinking about the domain and help them integrate new knowledge. *Therefore, content instruction should be framed in terms of core ideas and transferable processes, not as discrete facts and skills.*

3. Different types of thinking, such as classification and categorization, inferential reasoning, analysis, synthesis, and metacognition, mediate and enhance learning. *Therefore, learning events should engage students in complex thinking to deepen and apply their learning.*

4. Learners reveal and demonstrate their understanding when they can apply, transfer, and adapt their learning to new and novel situations and problems. *Therefore, teachers should teach for transfer, and students should have multiple opportunities to apply their learning in meaningful and varied contexts.*

5. New learning is built on prior knowledge. Learners use their experiences and background knowledge to actively construct meaning about themselves and the world around them. *Therefore, students must be helped to actively connect new information and ideas to what they already know.*

6. Learning is social. *Therefore, teachers should provide opportunities for interactive learning in a supportive environment.*

7. Attitudes and values mediate learning by filtering experiences and perceptions. *Therefore, teachers should help students make their attitudes and values explicit and understand how they influence learning.*

8. Learning is nonlinear; it develops and deepens over time. *Therefore, students should be involved in revisiting core ideas and processes so as to develop deeper and more sophisticated learning over time.*

9. Models of excellence and ongoing feedback enhance learning and performance. *Therefore, learners need to see models of excellent work and be provided with regular, timely, and user-friendly feedback in order to practice, retry, rethink, and revise their work.*

10. Effectively accommodating a learner's preferred learning style, prior knowledge, and interests enhances learning. *Therefore, teachers should pre-assess to find out students' prior knowledge, learning preference, and interests. They should differentiate their instruction to address the significant differences they discover.*

Figure 7.2: The principles of learning.

We believe that we need a different curriculum and assessment paradigm if 21st century outcomes are to be effectively integrated into the education system. This new curriculum and assessment system is built upon three operational guidelines:

1. Focus on the "big ideas" in core subjects and 21st century skills.

2. Assess valued outcomes in appropriate ways.

3. Map the curriculum backward from targeted transfer abilities.

Guideline One: Focus on "Big Ideas" in Core Subjects and 21st Century Skills

Nearly every teacher from preK to university level confronts the same challenge: too much content and not enough time to teach it all. The plethora of knowledge and skills identified in state and provincial standards documents can seem overwhelming, and the problem of content overload is exacerbated in many subject areas by "mile wide, inch deep" textbooks chock full of information.

The perceived expectation to teach to all of the standards and march through designated textbooks leads to superficial "coverage" of instructional content. Numerous studies have documented that coverage is the rule rather than the exception in American education. Many of these studies have noted the ill effects of coverage. For example, the Trends in International Mathematics and Science Study (TIMSS) International research studies document the fact that U.S. eighth-grade mathematics and science teachers cover far more content topics in mathematics and science than teachers in several other high-achieving countries (Schmidt, McKnight, & Raizen, 1997). TIMSS research also reveals that eighth-grade mathematics teachers in the United States focus more on applying algorithmic procedures to solving problems than on helping learners understand underlying mathematical principles (National Center for Education Statistics, 2003).

Similarly, a large-scale study by Pianta et al. (2007) revealed that much of elementary school instruction revolves around learning discrete skills taught through specific lessons and/or worksheets. In his study, approximately one thousand fifth graders in 737 science classrooms were observed across the United States. The study found that these fifth graders spend 91 percent of their time listening to the teacher or working alone, usually on low-level worksheets. Three out of four classrooms are "dull, bleak" places, the researchers report, devoid of any emphasis on critical reasoning or problem-solving skills.

We have observed similar circumstances in other core academic subjects. Why are these patterns so prevalent? The TIMSS research (Schmidt, McKnight, & Raizen, 1997) points out that it is not that teachers are disinterested in engaging student thinking and in-depth learning. Rather, the problem lies in what is to be taught. The current curriculum simply contains too many topics and is too fragmented, often without clear connections from one topic or one level to the next.

The costs of continuing with the current system are particularly germane when considering 21st century outcomes. The pressures of content coverage come at the expense of learner engagement and in-depth exploration of concepts and investigation of important questions. Thus, many of the very skills and processes needed to succeed in the modern world are blocked out of the curriculum.

> The current curriculum simply contains too many topics and is too fragmented, often without clear connections from one topic or one level to the next.

How then can we possibly add 21st century outcomes to an already overcrowded curriculum? Our proposal is straightforward: focus the curriculum around a core set of big ideas and essential questions within each subject area and across disciplines. Consider the popular 2003 film *Mona Lisa Smile*. The movie contains two scenes that illustrate the difference between a typical information-based learning experience in America's schools and an experience built around a less-crowded curriculum focused on big ideas and questions. In the first scene, Katherine Ann Watson, a beginning art teacher, uses a traditional art text and slide set to open an introductory art class with a lesson built around covering information about artists. She quickly discovers that her students have already read the text and have little to learn from her when she uses this approach. After agonizing over the situation, she comes to class with a different method. She begins with two essential questions that focus her teaching: "What is art?" and "What is the difference between 'good' and 'bad' art?" Next, she shows a new set of slides (including slides of her own artwork as a child) with these questions in mind, and begins to get thoughtful debate, discussion, disagreements, and even passion from her students. Her focus on differing perspectives of excellence in art causes her jaded students to become engaged and curious about the nature and meaning of art. As her students explore the questions, "What is art?" and "What is good art?" they think critically and creatively. They analyze and interpret paintings, communicate opinions, support their views, and develop creative ways of thinking about art. With time to think about and discuss provocative questions, her students realize deeper and more meaningful learning.

This example illustrates a key feature of the curriculum shift we advocate: a change in curriculum goals from broad surveys of too much academic knowledge and too many discrete skills to a focus on a few big ideas and essential questions, such as those illustrated in table 7.1. These are chosen because they are fundamental to the discipline, thought provoking, and support transfer of learning to new situations. Because the curriculum is more focused, there is greater opportunity for in-depth learning and infusion of 21st century skills.

Curriculum goals change from broad surveys of too much academic knowledge and too many discrete skills to a focus on a few big ideas and essential questions, chosen because they are fundamental to the discipline, thought provoking, and support transfer of learning to new situations.

In summary, the key to unclogging a crowded content-driven curriculum is to create a clear conception of a few really important ideas and essential questions in order to focus on understanding and integrate 21st century skills. With a pared-down set of learning goals devoted to in-depth exploration and reflection, 21st century skills can be integrated into the curriculum and interdisciplinary themes can be developed over time within and among subject areas. Because the curriculum is more focused, teachers have time to "uncover" it by engaging students in analyzing issues, applying critical and creative thinking to complex problems, working collaboratively on inquiry and research investigations, accessing and evaluating information, applying technology effectively, and developing initiative and self-direction through authentic, long-term projects.

Table 7.1: Examples of Big Ideas and Essential Questions

Big Ideas	Essential Questions
History involves interpretation, and individuals may interpret the same events differently.	Whose story is this? How do we know what really happened in the past?
We can measure and represent the same thing in different ways.	How can we best show _____ (distance, quantity, size, rate of change, and so on)?
Scientists attempt to replicate experimental findings to verify claims.	How do we know what to believe about scientific claims?
Great literature explores common human themes and issues.	How are stories from other times and places about us? What truths can fiction reveal?

Guideline Two: Assess Valued Outcomes in Appropriate Ways

Educational assessments have a huge impact on teaching and learning, wherever they originate—be it in the classroom or at state and national agencies. Professional educators, parents, and students are well aware of the axiom that what is assessed signals what is valued. Students frequently ask, "Will this be on the test?" and allocate their attention accordingly. Schools and districts tend to emphasize those subjects that are assessed on high-stakes accountability tests, often at the expense of those that are not.

Moreover, how something is assessed signals how it should be learned. The increasing use of large-scale standardized assessments tied to the requirements of No Child Left Behind has influenced instructional practice. Most standardized tests used in the United States rely on selected-response and brief constructed-response items to assess knowledge and basic skills. These formats can become seductive, leading to multiple-choice/short-answer teaching and the belief that learning equals the ability to recall and recognize information and make low-level inferences. Even those standardized tests that include constructed-response items have encouraged the teaching of formulaic responses, such as the five-paragraph essay. Indeed, test preparation focused on the short-answer assessment format has assumed an increasing presence in many schools, displacing more meaningful learning that utilizes 21st century thinking skills.

If we genuinely value the infusion of 21st century skills with core academic goals, then assessments at all levels—classroom, district, and state—should be aligned accordingly. We do not deny that the traditional assessment formats have a place in determining whether students know vocabulary terms, procedures, algorithms, and basic facts. But we also believe that a balanced approach to assessments is critical if 21st century learning goals are to be appropriately assessed. The majority of assessments should be more open-ended and performance-based—designed to reveal whether students meet 21st century learning goals such as demonstrating an understanding of big ideas, formulating responses to essential questions, reflecting on and analyzing important issues, solving genuine problems, conducting research and inquiry, working collaboratively, and using technology. Assessments should also reveal whether students are able to transfer and adapt their learning to novel situations, since a fundamental goal of 21st century outcomes is to prepare students for a complex and rapidly changing world with unpredictable challenges. The use of assessments that measure student understanding of big ideas and promote thoughtful application, research and investigation, creativity, and the like will encourage concomitant curricular and instructional changes that support the attainment of 21st century skills.

> The use of assessments that measure student understanding of big ideas and promote thoughtful application, research and investigation, creativity, and the like will encourage concomitant curricular and instructional changes that support the attainment of 21st century skills.

Cornerstone assessment tasks. Cornerstone tasks, as characterized by Wiggins and McTighe (2007), represent a natural fusion of 21st century skills with the big ideas of academic content:

> The most basic flaw in the writing of conventional school curriculum is that it is too often divorced from the ultimate accomplishments desired. Thus, when we advise educators

to design the assessment system first, we are not referring to typical tests of mere content mastery. We are speaking of worthy authentic performances that embody the mission and program goals. Think of them as "cornerstone" performances—merit badge requirements—reflective of the key challenges in the subject, the essence of "doing" the subject with core content. Here are some examples of such challenges in a number of disciplines:

In science, the design and debugging of significant experiments

In history, the construction of a valid and insightful narrative of evidence and argument

In mathematics, the quantifying and solving of perplexing or messy real-world problems

In communication, the successful writing for specific and demanding audiences and purposes

In the arts, the composing/performing/critiquing of a sophisticated piece

Like the game in sports or the play in drama, these cornerstone performance demands are meant to embody key learning goals by requiring meaning making and transfer of prior learning. (pp. 42–43)

Cornerstone tasks have the following distinguishing qualities:

- They reflect genuine, real-world accomplishments and are set in authentic contexts. Unlike the majority of items found on standardized tests and textbook or worksheet drills, cornerstone tasks are contextualized. This means they establish a real or realistic situation to which students apply their knowledge and skill. Such tasks provide meaningful learning targets, while bringing rigor and relevance to the classroom. Accordingly, they help teachers answer those familiar student queries: "Why do we have to learn this?" "Who ever uses this stuff?"

- They require students to apply (in other words, transfer) their learning. If students truly understand a concept, they can apply their knowledge and skills to new situations. Cornerstone tasks require transfer, and thus provide a measure of understanding. They also signal to learners that a major goal of education is to enable them to *use* their learning in ways valued in the wider world beyond the classroom.

- They naturally integrate 21st century skills with the big ideas of academic content. Rather than simply requiring recall or recognition, such tasks call for the thoughtful use of knowledge and skills naturally integrated within authentic contexts. Thus, they call for genuine applications of thinking (such as creative problem solving), technology (such as information access), communication (written, oral, or graphic), collaborative teamwork, and habits of mind (such as persistence)—just like in the real world. By their very nature, cornerstone tasks require 21st century outcomes.

> Cornerstone tasks require transfer, and thus provide a measure of understanding. They also signal to learners that a major goal of education is to enable them to *use* their learning in ways valued in the wider world beyond the classroom.

- They recur across the grades, in increasingly sophisticated forms. Think of athletics and the arts. Six-year-olds play the same soccer game as high school, college, and professional players. Similarly, young children use crayons to draw pictures depicting their observations, thoughts, and feelings; professional artists do the same, although with more varied and sophisticated media. In both cases, the tasks (soccer and artistic creation) are recurring, with the students' performance becoming more skilled and mature over the years. We propose that cornerstone tasks should also recur *throughout* the curriculum, moving toward more sophisticated performances within and across the disciplines. As we systematically apply 21st century skills in recurring cornerstone tasks, we concurrently develop more sophisticated applications of critical and creative thinking, technology, communication, and collaboration.

What does a recurring task look like and sound like? Figure 7.3 first presents a cornerstone task frame (figure 7.3a) and then two recurring versions of the same basic task (figure 7.3b and c), one at the elementary level and one at the secondary level. Both of these tasks share common elements from the task frame. Notice that each task establishes a relevant context for actively involving students in gathering, analyzing, and displaying data. Both tasks call for some forecasting or prediction based on observed patterns. Both call for communication of findings to a target audience.

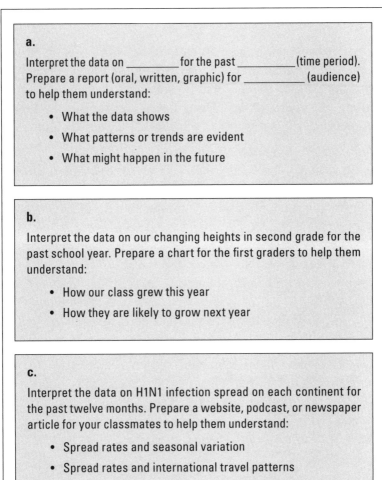

a.

Interpret the data on _____ for the past _____ (time period). Prepare a report (oral, written, graphic) for _____ (audience) to help them understand:

- What the data shows
- What patterns or trends are evident
- What might happen in the future

b.

Interpret the data on our changing heights in second grade for the past school year. Prepare a chart for the first graders to help them understand:

- How our class grew this year
- How they are likely to grow next year

c.

Interpret the data on H1N1 infection spread on each continent for the past twelve months. Prepare a website, podcast, or newspaper article for your classmates to help them understand:

- Spread rates and seasonal variation
- Spread rates and international travel patterns
- Spread rates and government policies

Figure 7.3: Cornerstone tasks: (a) sample task frame, (b) elementary example, and (c) high school example.

Elementary version. Second-grade students in three separate classes work in teams of four and take turns measuring the height of each member using tape measures affixed to the classroom walls. The height measurements are taken at the beginning of the school year and every seven weeks thereafter. When they begin, the second-grade teachers and classroom aides model the process and assist students with their measures and their recordings. As the year progresses, students require less help with the task, and by year end, many groups are working completely independently.

By mid-May, each second-grade class has obtained six height measures. The teachers demonstrate how to create a simple graph with height in inches plotted against the months of the school year, and the students plot their own data. Using rulers, they connect the dots to see "rise over run" (a visual representation of their growth over time).

The chart papers are posted throughout the room, and the students circulate in a gallery walk to view the changes in heights of the various groups. The teachers then ask the students to analyze the data by posing guiding questions: "In what months did we grow the most this year?" "Is there a difference between how boys and girls have grown in second grade?" "How does our class growth compare to that in the other second-grade classrooms?" (The teachers create an average class growth chart that they show to all second graders.) "What can we predict for next year's second graders about how they will grow based on our data?" Students are then asked to work in their groups to develop a presentation for the current first graders.

Secondary version. High school students use several Internet search engines to locate data from the World Health Organization, the National Institutes of Health, and at least two other sources on documented H1N1 (aka swine flu) cases. Working in teams, the students engage in the following task activities:

- Collect and record data from at least four sources on the spread of H1N1 virus in various countries.

- Compare and evaluate the four sources. (Which sources were the most thorough? Which were the most understandable? Which were the most credible?)

- Analyze the data. (What patterns did you notice with age and gender? What geographic patterns emerged? What about associated deaths? What was the impact of governmental policies, such as travel restrictions or quarantine, on the spread of infections? Do you have any predictions for future spread of the virus?)

- Prepare a summary report to effectively communicate the data and your analysis to a target audience (for example, a congressional committee, the general public, or teenagers) using an appropriate communications medium (such as a newspaper article, blog, website, podcast, or television news special). Include recommendations (such as for government policy or individual precautions) in the event of a future outbreak of a different flu strain.

Note that the secondary version of the task also incorporates the 21st century themes of global awareness and health/wellness, as well as critical thinking, information technology, and communication skills. All of the skills and processes in both tasks are transferable; they apply in mathematics, science, history, and a variety of real-world contexts.

Now imagine a recurring set of such tasks across the grades, emanating from the same task frame, but involving more sophisticated data from increasingly authentic situations. And imagine similar task frames established within and across all academic areas to guide other sets of recurring tasks. This is the type of *system* we advocate.

With such a system in place, students will become increasingly proficient and autonomous in their ability to apply core academic learning and 21st century skills, just as youth soccer or basketball players hone their knowledge and skills over the years. Cornerstone assessments have an added virtue—they become the source of documented accomplishments saved in a student's digital portfolio. The portfolio becomes a significant component of the curriculum/assessment system, since it creates a shift from an emphasis on Carnegie units and seat time to one favoring demonstrated achievement

> With such a system in place, students will become increasingly proficient and autonomous in their ability to apply core academic learning and 21st century skills, just as youth soccer or basketball players hone their knowledge and skills over the years.

on worthy tasks that incorporate 21st century outcomes. With this approach, students graduate from high school with a resume of authentic accomplishments that demonstrate their understanding of key ideas and their ability to apply 21st century skills, instead of merely a transcript of courses taken and a grade point average.

Guideline Three: Map the Curriculum Backward

Curriculum mapping offers a well-established process for orchestrating the scope and sequence of a curriculum to establish a coherent flow across grade levels, avoid unnecessary redundancies, and ensure that important knowledge and skills are not falling through the cracks. A more coherent and results-focused curriculum emerges when the curriculum is mapped according to the elements recommended in guidelines one and two (big ideas, essential questions, 21st century skills, and cornerstone assessment tasks) from grade 12 backward to kindergarten. By keeping the desired performances in mind (via the spiraling cornerstone assessment tasks), the curriculum maps remind teachers that their job is to uncover important ideas, explore critical questions, focus on learning and using 21st century skills, and prepare students to apply their learning to new situations.

> A more coherent and results-focused curriculum emerges when the curriculum is mapped according to big ideas, essential questions, 21st century skills, and cornerstone assessment tasks from grade 12 backward to kindergarten.

We encourage educators, as they map out a 21st century outcomes-based curriculum, to consider the fundamental concepts of the core disciplines along with the key, naturally recurring 21st century skills that grow out of the disciplines. We refer to subject areas as *disciplines* because they require disciplined ways of thinking and acting:

> Many people erroneously think of academic disciplines as the "content," but that is not what a discipline is. . . . Science is a "discipline" because the habit of jumping to conclusions based on prior beliefs runs deep in human beings (and novice scientists), and is overcome only through the "discipline" of trying to isolate key variables, and methodically testing for them. You have to learn the discipline of carefully observing, gathering apt evidence, and weighing its limited implications while remaining skeptical. The so-called scientific

method is not a "skill" but a set of dispositions, skills, and transfer abilities in the use of content, learnable only by doing. Similarly, the goal in learning to "do" history is to avoid present-centeredness and simplistic causal reasoning. One must learn to think and act like a journalist/curator/ historian to learn the "discipline" of history. Learning only the factual "content" or highly-scripted "skills" is as little likely to make you "disciplined" as merely practicing discrete moves in basketball will equip you to be a successful game player. (Wiggins & McTighe, 2007, pp. 47–48)

Instructional Programs and Practices

How should we teach to achieve 21st century outcomes?

The ideas suggested so far—the development of a 21st century mission statement; the adoption of learning principles that emphasize deep understanding of subject matter and transfer of learning; and the "backward design" of a curriculum and assessment system focused around big ideas, essential questions, and open-ended, performance, and cornerstone assessments at all school levels—imply the need for major changes in day-to-day teaching behaviors. We have synthesized our instructional recommendations into a set of five indicators that suggest what students should experience as they achieve 21st century outcomes.

Indicator One: Interactive Strategies Actively Engage Students in Developing Understanding of Big Ideas and the Application of 21st Century Skills

Making sense of key ideas is central to the learning process as the teacher helps students make connections to prior knowledge, explore essential questions, and explain key ideas. The teacher uses engaging, interactive strategies to guide learners in developing and deepening their understanding and developing and applying critical 21st century skills, such as the following:

- Problem-based learning

- Science experimentation and historical investigation

- Socratic seminars

- Collaborative projects and communications
- Creative problem-solving strategies
- Visual learning tools that help students make connections (such as graphic organizers)
- Interactive notebooks
- Essential questions, with probes and wait time

The teacher and student work is conceptually rigorous, and learners are intellectually challenged; for example, students are often asked to conceptualize and make connections among information and ideas, summarize their learning, write cogent and coherent analyses, and/ or support their ideas with substantive arguments.

Indicator Two: 21st Century Skills Are Explicitly Taught and Applied in the Academic Areas

Twenty-first-century skills and cornerstone tasks are integrated into academic learning areas and taught *explicitly* across the grades. As these skills are introduced in the younger grades, teachers break down the skills into critical components, and give students regular opportunities to practice and apply the skills while supported with coaching and feedback. Over time, we see students developing increased proficiency and the capacity to autonomously transfer these skills to new situations.

Indicator Three: Students Have Multiple Opportunities to Transfer Learning to New Situations

Students clearly understand that transfer is a major goal of their learning, and they are provided with many opportunities to apply their learning and understanding to novel situations. Students are regularly involved in relevant, real-life activities and assessments, such as writing letters to an editor, conducting research on problems of interest to students, examining current issues and controversies, and creating genuine products and performances. The teacher continually helps students to see the connections of ideas and skills to authentic experiences.

Indicator Four: Teachers Use Ongoing Assessments to Monitor Students' Level of Understanding of Ideas and Skills, and Adjust the Pace and Level of Instruction Accordingly

The teacher routinely uses pre-assessments to find out students' prior knowledge, interests, and preferred learning styles. As learning progresses, the teacher continually monitors the level of learning and understanding of targeted big ideas and 21st century skills for each student, and adjusts instruction as needed. Formative assessments, such as five-minute summaries at the end of a period, exit cards, no-fault quizzes, and informal observations are used to determine the level of learning and the needs of learners. The teacher provides timely and understandable feedback, along with opportunities for students to practice, rethink, and revise.

Indicator Five: Teachers Establish a Classroom Culture and Climate That Values Student Participation; Respects Student Ideas, Questions, and Contributions; and Encourages Students to Generate Ideas, Questions, and Conjectures

The climate of classrooms devoted to 21st century outcomes encourages intellectual risk taking and active meaning making. Mistakes are seen as growth opportunities, rather than failures. Students engage in the learning process in order to construct meaning, individually and collectively. They are encouraged to ask questions, offer their ideas, discuss their understanding of a principle, give feedback to each other, and create and share their thoughts and opinions. They are invited to regularly reflect on their learning, and their teachers are models of reflective practice.

Instructional Resources

Instructional resources have always had a significant influence on teaching practices. We believe this factor must be taken into account as we give greater attention to 21st century outcomes. Consequently, educators will need to carefully select instructional resources, including published programs and textbooks, technology, and software that are aligned with the recommended curriculum, assessment, and instructional practices we describe. To that end, we offer a set of review criteria (see table 7.2), built around the learning principles in figure 7.2 (page 153), that can be used to determine whether various resources will support 21st century learning.

Systemic Supports

> *What policies, school structures, and resource alloca-tions are needed to support the development of 21st century outcomes?*

Our suggestions for revamping mission, learning principles, curriculum, assessment, and instruction will only be put into place in districts, schools, and classrooms where the system policies and structures support their implementation. While we cannot address all the various systemic factors required for educational reform toward 21st century outcomes, we wish to emphasize the importance of *alignment* among all the elements of a system. These questions will help secure that alignment:

- To what extent do current district and school policies, proce-dures, operations, and practices support or hinder efforts to achieve 21st century outcomes?

- To what extent do staff, parents, and students know that the district/school mission includes 21st century outcomes?

- To what extent does the district curriculum and assessment system emphasize 21st century outcomes?

- To what extent do classroom instructional and assessment practices reflect principles of learning and support achieve-ment of 21st century outcomes?

- To what extent do job descriptions and staff appraisal processes reference 21st century outcomes?

- To what extent do the grading and reporting systems include 21st century outcomes?

- To what extent do curriculum, assessment, and staff develop-ment consistently promote the development and use of 21st century outcomes?

Table 7.2: Review Criteria for Instructional Resources

Learning Principle	Review Criteria To what extent does this resource . . .
1	Support contextualized learning experiences (for example, frame learning with relevant questions, meaningful challenges, and authentic applications)? Incorporate 21st century interdisciplinary themes (such as global awareness and entrepreneurial literacy)?
2	Identify a limited number of big ideas—concepts, principles, themes, issues—and/or include provocative essential questions around which knowledge is examined?
3	Engage students in higher-order thinking and related 21st century skills and processes (such as problem solving, critical and creative thinking, issues analysis, and research investigation)?
4	Include opportunities for students to apply their learning in meaningful and varied contexts? Include performance-based assessments aligned with 21st century outcomes?
5	Contain effective and engaging activities to help students make connections and construct meaning? Include pre-assessments to help teachers check for prior knowledge and students' readiness for new learning?
6	Support collaborative and interactive learning?
7	Support opportunities for students to discuss attitudes toward learning? Develop self-directed attitudes and values?
8	Continually revisit and refine big ideas and 21st century skills? Spiral to develop and deepen student understanding and transfer ability?
9	Support teachers in providing students with models of excellence and timely feedback, along with the opportunity to use them to improve learning and performance?
10	Cater to the diverse abilities, interests, and needs of students? Support teaching to students' varied learning styles or intelligences?

Table 7.3: Framework for 21st Century Learning: Summary of Key Points

Mission Statement	• Outcome oriented • Specific focus on 21st century outcomes and teaching for understanding and transfer • Known by key stakeholders • Regularly reviewed and used to guide educational policy and practice
Learning Principles	• Explicit conception of learning based on latest research and best practice • Cognitive/constructivist view of learning
Curriculum	• Focus on fewer topics and transferable big ideas and essential questions in academic areas • Greater emphasis on in-depth learning, thinking, and understanding • Emphasis on infusing 21st century outcomes into the curriculum • Use of multiple resources including technology
Assessment	• Inclusion of more performance tasks involving the integration of big ideas of content areas with 21st century skills • Recurring cornerstone performance assessments anchor the curriculum around authentic transfer tasks • Use of ongoing assessments provide feedback to teachers and learners
Instruction	• Actions guided by a set of agreed-upon learning principles • Emphasis on active learning and the use of constructivist-based strategies • Emphasis of teaching and coaching on understanding and transfer
Systemic Factors	• Long-term commitment to the implementation of 21st century outcomes • Robust use of the backward design model for curriculum planning and school improvement • All major elements of the educational system (mission, learning principles, policies, procedures, resource allocation, curriculum and staff development practices, and so on) aligned in support of 21st century outcomes • Supportive federal and state guidelines, financial incentives, and content standards for implementation of 21st century outcomes and a teaching-for-understanding approach

- To what extent do the allocation of resources (including money and time) signal that 21st century outcomes are a priority?

- To what extent do agendas for staff meetings and professional development signal that 21st century outcomes are a priority?

A 21st Century Learning Framework

The changes to the current educational system proposed by this framework for 21st century learning are summarized in table 7.3. While the changes we advocate are not a quick fix, nor will they be easy to implement, such changes to educational missions and methods are necessary if schooling is to remain relevant and will adequately prepare our children to live and work in the 21st century.

References

Bransford, J. D., Brown, A., & Cocking, R. (Eds.). (2000). *How people learn: Brain, mind, experience, and school.* Washington, DC: National Academy Press.

Covey, S. R. (1989). *The seven habits of highly effective people: Restoring the character ethic.* New York: Simon & Schuster.

Marzano, R. J. (2003). *What works in schools: Translating research into action.* Alexandria, VA: Association for Supervision and Curriculum Development.

National Center for Education Statistics. (2003, March). *Teaching mathematics in seven countries: Results from the TIMSS 1999 video study.* Washington, DC: U.S. Department of Education. Accessed at http://nces.ed.gov/pubs2003/2003013 .pdf on October 12, 2008.

Partnership for 21st Century Skills. (2009). *P21 framework definitions document.* Washington, DC: Author. Accessed at www.21stcenturyskills.org/documents/ p21_framework_definitions_052909.pdf on August 14, 2009.

Partnership for 21st Century Skills. (n.d.). *The intellectual and policy foundations of the 21st century skills framework.* Washington, DC: Author.

Pianta, R. C., Belsky, J., Houts, R., Morrison, F., & the National Institute of Child Health and Human Development. (2007, March). Teaching: Opportunities to learn in America's elementary classrooms. *Science, 315,* 1795–1796.

Schmidt, W. H., McKnight, C. C., & Raizen, S. A. (with Jakwerth, P. M., Valverde, G. A., Wolfe, R. G., Britton, E. D., Bianchi, L. J., & Houang, R. T.). (1997). *A splintered vision: An investigation of U.S. science and mathematics education.* Boston: Kluwer Academic.

Weiss, I. R., & Pasley, J. D. (2004, February). What is high quality instruction? *Educational Leadership, 61*(5), 24–28.

Wiggins, G., & McTighe, J. (2007). *Schooling by design: Mission, action, and achievement*. Alexandria, VA: Association for Supervision and Curriculum Development.

Willis, J. (2006). *Research-based strategies to ignite student learning: Insights from a neurologist and classroom teacher*. Alexandria, VA: Association for Supervision and Curriculum Development.

John Barell

John Barell, Ed.D., is professor emeritus of Curriculum and Teaching at Montclair State University, Montclair, New Jersey, and a former public school teacher in New York City. Since 2000, he has been a consultant for inquiry-based instruction and creation of science/social studies networks at the American Museum of Natural History in New York City in collaboration with the International Baccalaureate Organization. For most of his educational career, he has worked with schools nationally to foster inquiry, problem-based learning, critical thinking, and reflection. He is the author of several books, including *Teaching for Thoughtfulness: Strategies to Enhance Intellectual Development, Developing More Curious Minds, Problem-Based Learning—An Inquiry Approach,* and *Why Are School Buses Always Yellow?*

In this chapter, Barell shows that problem-based learning is an ideal way to develop 21st century skills. He describes how teachers shift their standards-based curriculum from direct instruction of passive students to active engagement of problem solvers and question askers. His concrete examples illustrate ways problem-based inquiry can be adapted for meaningful use with students of all ages, talents, and challenges.

Chapter 8

Problem-Based Learning: The Foundation for 21st Century Skills

John Barell

Recently, I noticed several magazine advertisements that summarized for me why it is so important to challenge today's students to become skillful problem solvers. The first advertisement depicted a serene Antarctic scene: an iceberg looking like a tall ship, high bowsprit facing into the winds, with surrounding ice in wonderful shades of blues and whites. The ad was by Kohler, a manufacturer of plumbing supplies, telling readers that if they substitute their usual shower head spraying 2.75 gallons of water per minute for one using only 1.75 gallons per minute, they can save 7,700 gallons of water per year (Kohler ad, 2009).

This advertisement led me to consider some current issues and critical problems that need solving in the wider world, such as conservation of natural resources, the United States' overreliance on foreign fossil fuels, and the need to develop alternative sources of clean, renewable energy.

In more ads for U.S. manufacturers, I noticed the following headlines:

- The word "inoperable" now applies to far fewer brain tumors. (Cleveland Clinic ad, 2008, p. 19)

- The world is growing by more than 70 million people a year. So is that a problem, or a solution? (Chevron ad, 2008, p. 36)

- How can we squeeze more food from a raindrop? (Monsanto ad, 2009, p. 3)

Obviously, these companies want us to purchase their products and services and may just be manipulating our concerns for profit. But they do urge us to recognize the significant challenges we all face in today's world, challenges requiring us to innovate, change, take risks, recognize problems, and imagine alternative futures.

In the 21st century, we need all of the skills that have marked humankind as the creators and sustainers of cultures, the innovators of technologies, and the designers of ways of living and governing. These skills, which are more crucial now than ever before, include "critical thinking, problem-solving, collaboration, creativity, self-direction, leadership, adaptability, responsibility [and] global awareness" (Walser, 2008, p. 2). To this list, I add the significant skill of inquiry.

But What Makes the 21st Century Special?

Yes, it is true; humans have always engaged in problem solving and critical and creative thinking. History is replete with examples:

- Early hominids figuring out how to capture, kill, and consume prey much larger than themselves while using only stone tools

- Socrates confronting the youth of Athens with what he called "perplexities" to challenge their thinking

- Leonardo da Vinci and Michelangelo creating masterworks that revolutionized the old, medieval ways of seeing

- Rosa Parks challenging segregationist practices by refusing to move to the rear of the bus in Montgomery, Alabama, on December 1, 1955

- Sally K. Ride, America's first woman astronaut, determining what failed during the *Columbia* shuttle flight on February 1, 2003

But what makes the 21st century special? What are the new and threatening problems we face, both domestic and foreign, that necessitate more attention to how we think and solve problems? In addition to the complexities of energy production and conservation, preserving the planet, and fighting terrorism, we face almost intractable situations when it comes to providing health care, ensuring equity within all of our educational and judicial systems, and figuring out how to preserve our financial markets after the worst economic meltdown since the Great Depression.

The increased complexity of these challenges makes it all the more important that we do a better job preparing our students as problem solvers. We must provide students with improved strategies to help them deal with problems—this is what holds the most promise in our education system. Problem-based learning (PBL) is one such strategy.

The PBL approach often raises serious questions among those who are first exploring this option:

1. What is PBL?
2. What are the key elements of PBL?
3. What does PBL look like in the classroom?
4. Why start with a problematic scenario?
5. Why is inquiry important within PBL?
6. How do we develop curricula for PBL?
7. How do we enhance PBL with 21st century technology?
8. What do we know about the effectiveness of PBL?

What Is PBL?

When discussing problem-based learning, we must first explore the meanings of the word *problem*. Problem-based learning is something different, but not wildly so, from what many students are experiencing today when they answer short-term "problems" at the end of textbook chapters. In math and science, students work on individual problems, often with answers in the back of the book. On a larger instructional scale, students sometimes contend with "problems" that call for them to find solutions, such as how to improve the school playground or the water quality of a neighborhood pond or stream.

Some teachers use problematic situations in literature and history to organize the curriculum. For example, in one third-grade classroom, I witnessed two excellent teachers read *Franklin in the Dark* by Paulette Bourgeois (1986). This is the story of a little turtle, Franklin, who is afraid of "small, dark places" like his shell. So he goes on a quest searching for solutions. Before the end of the story, the teachers asked the students, "What do you think Franklin's problem is?" and "How would you solve it?" These "problem" questions engaged the students in thinking about Franklin's solutions as well as their own.

Problem-based learning goes well beyond these short-term instructional instances or simple questions. It encompasses a rethinking of the entire curriculum so that teachers design whole units around complex, "ill-structured" problematic scenarios that embody the major concepts to be mastered and understood. By "ill-structured" or "ill-defined" I mean the realistic, authentic problems—such as pollution of the planet and feeding the hungry—that are so complex, messy, and intriguing that they do not lend themselves to a right or wrong answer approach; on the other hand, "How far does an automobile travel in 3.5 hours going 60 mph?" would be an example of "well-defined" problem because there is a right answer.

Problem-based learning goes well beyond these short-term instructional instances or simple questions. It encompasses a rethinking of the entire curriculum so that teachers design whole units around complex, "ill-structured" problematic scenarios that embody the major concepts to be mastered and understood.

While engaged in the unit, students will ask good questions, conduct purposeful investigations, think critically, draw conclusions, and reflect until they arrive at a meaningful solution. In addition, such units no longer are limited in use to children with high aptitudes, but are used with students of all ages and abilities, including those with special needs.

From this perspective, PBL challenges teachers to reconstruct their understanding of problem solving. It takes them from solving homework problems in a single lesson to using advanced thinking skills throughout a unit designed around in-depth problem solving. To accomplish this, PBL requires a complete rethinking of the roles of teachers and students, as well as the goals of educational programs. PBL teachers not only present information, but they also learn along with students and help them become more skillful problem solvers. In this capacity, students are no longer passive recipients of knowledge; they are decision makers about the nature and structure of their own learning as they work their way through the problem-based unit.

What Are the Key Elements of PBL?

Cheryl Hopper—a former ninth-grade teacher in Paramus, New Jersey, who will be discussed in more detail in the following section—designed a sample unit that includes ten key elements of problem-based learning:

1. Real-world problems that foster inquiry and embody key concepts like change, equality, and environment

2. Choices about content as well as ways to learn and share understandings

3. Objectives reflecting the highest of intellectual challenges, including the need to pose questions, conduct purposeful research, think critically, make decisions, and draw reasonable conclusions supported with evidence

4. Experiences in small-group collaboration such as listening, reasoning together, and building upon each others' ideas

5. Feedback students receive from classmates and teachers during rehearsals of final findings; such feedback—"What we liked and our questions"—is most helpful and reflects what occurs in actual life experiences

6. Occasions to revise, modify, and elaborate on findings

7. Engagement in planning of, monitoring of, and self-reflection on work, progress, and results

8. Opportunities to obtain pre-, formative, and summative assessment information

9. A clear and easy-to-follow curricular structure centered on authentic problems and inquiry

10. Teachers and students sharing control of decision making, teaching, and learning

What Does PBL Look Like in the Classroom?

Cheryl Hopper's ninth-grade classroom was no ordinary experience for her students. Cheryl was the kind of teacher who announced on the first day, "There are no rules here. There are very high expectations." Students knew immediately that they were in for an exciting and challenging journey through world history and geography. What they didn't know was that they would soon experience the key elements of problem-based learning, especially real-world problems, inquiry, and assessment feedback—elements that would fully engage them in their learning.

The Problem Scenario

At the beginning of an interdisciplinary unit exploring the geography, politics, economics, history, art, and religion of Africa, Cheryl put her students into the roles of problem solvers. She used this scenario:

> You are an African nation that desires a substantial loan from the World Bank. Your goal is to convince the World Bank that your country's needs are great and you deserve a loan. The World Bank has a limited amount to lend and many other countries are asking for loans. Therefore, you must prepare a strong case for receiving a loan and be able to defend your need for the money. (Barell, 2003, p. 145)

Imagine being a student confronted with this challenge of not only learning about an African nation of your choosing, but also conducting extensive research about the nation's natural resources, history, and culture. Imagine having to identify a country's most pressing economic, political, and health needs; devise a plan to meet them; and then present your plan to the World Bank—in this case, Mrs. Hopper herself. This is not passive learning.

Cheryl's Guided Inquiry

For this unit, Cheryl used a variation of the structured approach to inquiry known as KWHLAQ (figure 8.1). This organizing framework provides a tool to guide student-generated questions within the unit.

K   What do we think we already *know*? Explore prior knowledge.

W   What do we *want* and need to find out?

H   *How* will we proceed to investigate our questions? *How* will we organize time, access to resources and reporting? *How* will we self-assess our progress (such as with a scoring rubric)?

L   What are we *learning* (daily)? And what have we *learned* at the end of our investigations?

A   How and where can we *apply* the results of our investigations—to this and other subjects/to our daily lives?

Q   What new *questions* do we have now? How might we pursue them in our next units?

Source: Barell, 2007a, p. 85.

Figure 8.1: The KWHLAQ approach to inquiry.

After two days of showing students slides featuring different aspects of African culture, geography, and government, Cheryl asked them to identify what they thought they already knew about Africa. They made a graphic web of the comments that reflected their prior knowledge as well as what they saw in the slide show. For example, the graphic organizer students created ("What do we *think* we already know?") included concepts such as "language (linked to diversity), apartheid (Nelson Mandela), deserts (Kalahari), art (music), poaching, and second largest continent." Cheryl used the slides to awaken their background knowledge about Africa and, most likely, to create new knowledge and a heightened sense of curiosity and awareness.

After the students webbed out what they *thought* they knew, Cheryl challenged them to identify what they needed to know if they were to understand the continent, its countries, and the varied cultures.

Here are some of Cheryl's students' questions:

- How and why did powerful kingdoms emerge in Africa, especially West Africa?

- How do geographical features account for the cultural diversity of the continent?

- What were the effects of European rule? Of apartheid?

- How have traditional patterns of life stayed the same and how have they changed?

- How does the art of Africa reflect its cultural diversity?

- What is imperialism?

- Why did Europe carve up Africa into colonies?

- What were the effects of European rule? (Barell, 2003, p. 139)

When we afford students opportunities to respond to "What do we want and *need* to find out?" we are challenging them to think of themselves as young professionals, in this case historians, cultural anthropologists, linguists, artists, social scientists, geographers, and economists. Casting students in these roles lends more authenticity to the problematic scenario. It is possible, as one teacher mentioned to me, that "some students don't *want* to know very much!" Thus, we challenge them to think of themselves as professionals in a situation requiring solutions.

Cheryl then helped students analyze and collate these questions, searching for commonalities and ways to connect one to another. One result of this process was that students' specific questions now more closely resembled some of the unit's general essential questions that focused on the history of colonialism ("How do colonial empires develop?"), the growth of different cultures ("What factors influence the growth of various and different cultures?"), and influences of geography ("How does geography affect the history and culture of a continent or country?"). When students finished these tasks, Cheryl used their responses to guide the development of the unit. Using questions from the KWHLAQ approach, she asked, "How will we go about finding answers to our questions?" and "How will we structure and manage our class time and access to resources to solve the problem?" (see figure 8.1, page 181).

Once they classified and organized their questions, they selected questions to work on and formed themselves into different investigative groups. Working in teams, they conducted research, planned out daily lessons to teach the class, and involved the teacher in appropriate roles. Each team taught a lesson and designed a role within the lesson for Cheryl. She was still in charge of the entire unit, but her students assumed more ownership of the process. Through a variety of activities, like becoming docents at a local African art museum, the students gained more control of their own learning while discovering answers to their own—and to the unit's—essential questions.

When watching Cheryl interact with her students during the planning of their lessons, I saw another major benefit of the PBL inquiry approach: students collaborate as they decide how to best share their new knowledge with their peers. They learn what it takes to make knowledge meaningful. And one of the major positive effects of this approach is students' taking on more responsibility for their own learning. They are not merely sitting back and soaking up lots of factual knowledge to be repeated on a summative assessment at the end of the unit. Rather, they are collaborating, conducting research, analyzing findings critically, and drawing individual and group conclusions—all requisite life experiences.

Final Assessment

With a well-written problematic scenario like Cheryl's, teachers have the potential for a final assessment that provides students with multiple opportunities and ways to demonstrate their understanding of key ideas and concepts. Cheryl's unit culminated in small groups of "international developers" making their cases for setting up a hospital or constructing other needed buildings. They used written and oral reports, PowerPoint presentations, interviews, newspaper articles, and various art forms (pictures, maps, creative writings, and the like)—not merely five-paragraph expository essays.

After the students presented their initial group requests, Cheryl provided an opportunity for questions and direct feedback, which is an essential element in authentic assessment (Wiggins, 1998). Cheryl also facilitated needed adjustments and improvements before final presentations. To guide her feedback, Cheryl used a rubric created with the students that stressed solving problems; making sound

> With a well-written problematic scenario like Cheryl's, teachers have the potential for a final assessment that provides students with opportunities and ways to demonstrate their understanding of key ideas and concepts.

decisions; organizing and presenting cases in a logical, convincing fashion; and responding to questions.

The feedback Cheryl provided did not coddle the students. For instance, after a student presentation about building a health facility, fellow students commented, "I think you're being rather unrealistic. I don't think you can build a hospital for the amount of money you're asking for. Have you considered other variables, such as the costs of cutting through the forest with the needed energy, supplies, and staffing?" These comments and responses reflected the deepening of their knowledge and understanding. As such, they served as assessments on what students did and did not understand during the entire process. And, again, this penultimate form of feedback provided the young urban planners with information and points of view they needed to culminate a final presentation.

After the final presentations, Cheryl asked all students to reflect on their learning processes (the Q of the KWHLAQ). Here are some of their responses:

- [When] I compared my country to a state in the U.S. or another developed country about the same size, it was easier for the World Bank to understand our problems.

- The information was easy to get, but we had to focus on the problems, and that was hard.

- I ended up with the question of why people continue to reproduce if their lives are so hard. (Barell, 2003, p. 146)

These examples show students completing the last two elements of the KWHLAQ approach (see figure 8.1, page 181). Here students are applying what they've learned as well as continuing on with questions about the future. In a well-designed PBL unit, further questions about such complex issues are always expected.

Cheryl's African unit presents the highest level of intellectual challenge. In six weeks, her students not only gathered significant information, but also made critical choices as they figured out the needs of a country and how best to resolve its problems. As she subsequently told me, "Their questions met all of my unit goals (in the form of essential questions)."

Imagine how different this unit would have been with the "Open your textbook and let's start reading and remembering" approach!

Why Start With a Problematic Scenario?

A well-designed problem scenario includes two important ingredients that ensure students learn from the PBL unit. The first is delineation of a complex problem embedding the core concepts the students will be studying. The second is an outline of the authentic assessment parameters that stipulate what students are to understand about the concept. Remember that the problems designed by the teacher (perhaps with students) will be clear but will also reflect the complex, ill-defined, and messy nature of real-world dilemmas.

> A well-designed problem scenario includes two important ingredients that ensure students learn from the PBL unit. The first is delineation of a complex problem embedding the core concepts the students will be studying. The second is an outline of the authentic assessment parameters that stipulate what students are to understand about the concept.

A problematic scenario embodies the essential elements of the unit so that as students inquire and discern, they encounter the ideas and concepts the teacher wants them to think deeply about; this process introduces the core content of the scenario. Here are several other examples of problematic scenarios, each from a different grade level, that reflect these design principles.

Ocean Life: Grade 3

You are responsible for finding a way (or ways) to stop the destruction of the ocean so that the animal or plant life that you have chosen and researched can remain a part of the ocean community. You must find a way to show that your method of saving the ocean will help not only the species that you have chosen, but will also help to preserve all of the living and non-living things that the species is dependent on, and all of the things that are a part of the ocean community that depend on it (interdependence). (Catrupi, as cited in Barell, 2007b, p. 46)

This scenario could start several different units on ocean life, ecology, human actions, or the environment. Notice the charge in the first sentence: identify the core problem and figure out how to solve it. Students first become familiar with current conditions in the ocean—that life forms such as coral reefs are whitening and dying. Then they identify which problems to focus on and work toward resolving those problems.

In the second sentence of the scenario, the teacher challenges her students to present information that demonstrates their understanding of how all living things are interdependent. She sets the demands of authentic, summative assessment with reporting criteria that tell students from day one what she expects them to do and to learn.

Community Building: Grades 6–8, Special Needs

A major widget factory has announced that they are breaking ground within an undeveloped area. The factory will bring in a diverse population. You are a committee member that has the responsibility of determining and developing the community and the necessary facilities needed to make [the factory] functional . . . e.g. law enforcement . . . education . . . health . . . and emergency services. (Desotelle & Lierman, 2000, p. 2)

This community-building project for middle school students with special needs requires extensive research on what a community is, what services it provides, and what long-range planning is required. These students must develop their plans within a strict budget. After their presentations, their teacher and peers question the conclusions and provide feedback. How different is this from the usual special needs experience full of repetitious, boring worksheets?

High School: Literature

You are authors for a new publication on contributions of 19th century women authors. Readers are interested in the importance of the ideas of Anthony, Woolf, Austen, Chapin, the Brontës, Stanton, Stowe, and knowing what they might say about issues today. Readers will highly value your ability to state these 19th century authors' views clearly, analyze their importance, and make reasonable applications to and comparisons with one major current issue. Reasonable comparisons will be judged by logic, appropriateness, extensiveness of relationships, and drawing your own conclusions. (Adapted from Royer, 2000)

In this scenario, the teacher challenges students to conduct extensive research on one author, analyze her work, and predict (based on contextual evidence) what her stand on a contemporary issue might be. In the final sentence of the scenario, the student authors receive a set of criteria for reviewing each article. As in all well-formed scenarios, these criteria outline clear expectations for the treatment of the content.

Each of these problematic scenarios presents a significant and well-defined challenge requiring students to familiarize themselves with the subject, pose meaningful questions, think critically, and draw reasonable conclusions. According to Kim Nordin, these scenarios add "focus, drive and excitement to the unit" (personal communication, January 15, 2007).

Why Is Inquiry Important Within PBL?

We can have students solving problems, but to do so without a strong emphasis on inquiry as a curricular priority is a less than sound practice. As stated previously, inquiry is the driver of the complex thinking processes we have been engaged in since the dawn of consciousness: What lies beyond the hill? How will we feed, clothe, and protect ourselves? What do those lights in the sky mean? Today, with all the challenges we face in terms of providing equal access to education, employment, health, energy, security, nutrition, and growth opportunities, it seems logical that we highlight the role of inquiry.

The school board in Greenwich, Connecticut, has done just that. Their "Vision of the Graduate" proclaims that the following are the competencies students must have (assuming acquisition of content knowledge):

- Pose and pursue substantive questions
- Critically interpret, evaluate, and synthesize information
- Explore, define, and solve complex problems
- Communicate effectively for a given purpose

- Advocate for ideas, causes, and actions

- Generate innovative, creative ideas and products

- Collaborate with others to produce a unified work and/or heightened understanding. (Greenwich Public Schools, 2006)

If students graduate from this school system and others, they should be ready for college and life as responsible citizens.

Speaking on the nature of college education, Leon Botstein, president of Bard College in New York, made this statement about the importance of problem-solving skills for college students:

The primary skills [learned in college] should be analytical skills of interpretation and inquiry. In other words, know how to frame a question. . . . You should not be dependent on the sources of information, either provided by the government or by the media, but have an independent capacity to ask questions and evaluate answers. (as cited in Flaherty, 2002, p. 4A27)

Botstein sees higher learning institutions focused on a single, clear goal: to empower their students to be thoughtfully inquisitive. He concluded by saying, "A college education has to engender a lifelong habit of curiosity, as opposed to becoming more convinced that you are an authority" (as cited in Flaherty, 2002, p. 4A27).

What Is the Role of Inquiry in PBL?

One of the benefits of a PBL approach using the kinds of scenarios outlined here is the opportunity for students to ask a starter question that checks their prior knowledge for accuracy: "What do I *think* I know about this situation?" The use of *think* calls for students to recognize that what they "know" might also include some information they aren't quite certain of. It is, therefore, important to acknowledge what is accurate as well as what is in doubt.

Author Arthur Costa, when discussing the importance of asking what we *think* we know, said, "It is my belief that what we have in our memories is a mixture of fact and fiction, of understandings in accordance with facts and down-right misunderstandings" (personal communication, June 25, 1998).

A second benefit comes with the *W* of KWHLAQ: "What do we want and need to find out?" This question asks students to identify gaps in their knowledge and understanding and taps into what they are genuinely curious about. It tells what they will need to know and find out in order to meet the challenge of the problematic scenario. Again, when asking our own questions, we are acting as young professionals, as scientists, literary critics, artists, historians, mathematicians, nutritionists, and physical educators.

Inquiry and Critical Thinking

The question "What do we need to determine?" demands that students step back, take a deep breath, and ask questions that give them important information as well as lead them toward generating viable solutions for their problematic scenarios. It is even more beneficial when PBL teachers generate lists of key questions and post them around the room for everybody to reference if they encounter a problematic scenario in other classes, in the news, or in their personal lives.

For example, consider these claims:

- We will have deficits as far as the eye can see.

- It is very likely that humans have largely caused global warming.

- "The artificial sweetener aspartame has been proved responsible for an epidemic of cancer, brain tumors and multiple sclerosis" (Mikkelson & Mikkelson, 2007).

What fundamental questions should we ask? What do we need to know about each in order to accept or believe it?

We should ask about sources, evidence, assumptions, definitions, and slant or bias. As students encounter more of these kinds of claims and judgments, they ask questions to learn more before drawing their own conclusions (Barell, 2009). In this way, PBL not only strengthens the students' question-asking skills, but also encourages the transfer of those skills beyond the immediate unit.

The question framework (figure 8.2) presents another question-ing model used to promote inquiry skills with students from grade 4 upwards. The framework, similar to KWHLAQ, also provides a generic set of questions to pose about complex, perplexing situations. It allows the teacher to ask questions that help students examine a strange or puzzling situation. At the top, basic information is assessed; on the left, students search for causation; at the bottom, they compare; and on the right, they project into the future. To close, they clarify their tentative conclusions.

How Do We Develop Curricula for PBL?

Teachers often ask, "How can we prepare and plan for students' questions?" This question led me back to my own curriculum devel-opment roots. I formulated this step-by-step process to help clarify how teachers should organize units for problem solving and inquiry.

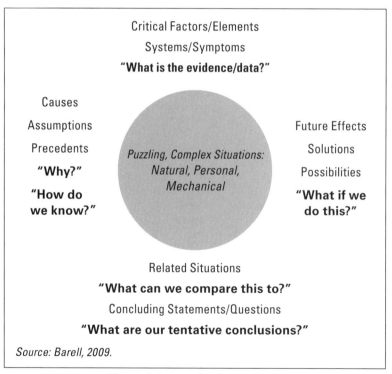

Critical Factors/Elements
Systems/Symptoms
"What is the evidence/data?"

Causes
Assumptions
Precedents
"Why?"
"How do we know?"

Puzzling, Complex Situations:
Natural, Personal,
Mechanical

Future Effects
Solutions
Possibilities
"What if we do this?"

Related Situations
"What can we compare this to?"
Concluding Statements/Questions
"What are our tentative conclusions?"

Source: Barell, 2009.

Figure 8.2: Question framework.

The following can be completed during planning time, alone, or with colleagues:

1. Identify a topic. Here teachers should refer to their district's curriculum as well as the state or provincial standards for what concepts and ideas they wish to present to their students.

2. Map out the concept. For example, if the topic is the U.S. Constitution, the teacher might map it as seen in figure 8.3.

3. Consult state and local standards to determine which of these subtopics you need and/or must include. Here in New York at the middle school level, students are expected to know and understand the origins and reasons for developing the Constitution; the forms and functions of three branches of the U.S. government; the Bill of Rights; and the concept of the Constitution as a "living document" (New York State Standards, n.d.).

4. Generate a set of intended outcomes or objectives for your unit, and specify essential questions. For instance, New York State considers the following to be essential questions for seventh and eighth graders engaged in the U.S. Constitution unit:

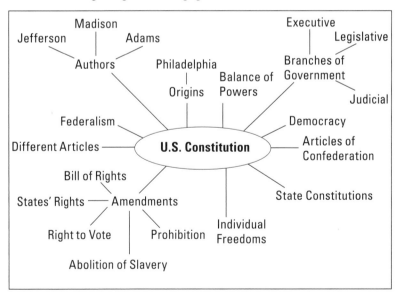

Figure 8.3: Concept map of the U.S. Constitution.

Why was the Constitution necessary? How does it embody the principles of the Declaration of Independence? How do federalism and the separation of powers promote the ideals within the Constitution and its various amendments? (New York State Standards, n.d.).

Specific outcomes that show how students understand the unit's content and can exercise their thinking include the ability to:

- *Define and explain* all major articles, the separation of powers, and similar concepts

- *Explain* reasons for the development of the Constitution

- *Compare* democracy with a republic/parliamentary system

- *Compare* our constitution with that of another country

- *Develop* a new constitution for your class/school/state and/or a fictitious country and be able to *compare/contrast* similarities and differences and *draw reasonable conclusions*

Having essential questions is splendid, but without specifically identifying what they expect students to be able to know and to do, teachers might not be able to determine the extent and quality of student understanding. These outcomes need to demand that students engage in the 21st century skills of questioning, problem solving, critical/creative thinking, hypothesizing, and reflecting. Note the emphasis on complex thinking with such phrases as "explain reasons," "compare," and "draw conclusions."

5. Design a problematic scenario that will spark students' interests and provide a structure for the entire unit. When creating such a scenario, teachers must incorporate knowledge and understanding of the essential concepts of the unit (in this case the U.S. Constitution) into the intended outcomes.

Here is one possible scenario:

You are a member of a delegation representing a new country in [name the geographical area]. You need to create your own constitution, but not copy the U.S. model. The constitutional committee of your home country wishes for you to present an explanation of the U.S. model, along with a critique and suggestions for modifications and improvements for your own country. You are not bound by the structure of the U.S. Constitution, but you need to demonstrate an understanding of key concepts such as federalism, balance/separation of powers, decision making, rights of states and citizens, and amendment powers. Furthermore, in your presentation to the constitutional committee in your home country you will need to justify the modifications and improvements you propose.

This scenario is designed to challenge students to not only learn as much as possible about the U.S. Constitution, but also to apply this new knowledge to crafting their own constitution. Of course, to do this properly they will need to know a good deal about U.S. history. Therefore, teachers could modify the scenario by challenging students to serve on a constitutional amendment committee charged with analyzing this "living document"—our U.S. Constitution—and make recommendations for altering it.

6. Formulate strategies that include inquiry approaches like KWHLAQ for observing artifacts and generating good questions. Students can help organize these questions in accordance with their needs, priorities, and ability level. In PBL, students conduct research and critically examine their findings for reliability, bias, verifiable assumptions, and so on. Then teachers collaborate with students on how to share the findings.

7. Use the problematic scenario as a summative assessment. There are many different ways for students to share what they know and understand about constitutions. They can engage in presentations as Cheryl's students did; share their ideas before a group of citizens; create videos and PowerPoints; engage in debates; write creatively; and, of course, reflect on their progress.

During the unit, the teacher should assess the quality of students' understandings using short-answer quizzes; essays; brief reports on research; and most importantly, writings in their inquiry journals. These journals will contain students' initial questions; research; subsequent questions; and daily, weekly, and/or final reflections on the important ideas they have learned, the process of inquiry, the application of ideas to other subjects, any new questions they have, and how these ideas correspond to their own lives.

How Do We Enhance PBL With 21st Century Technology?

We can enhance the problematic scenarios by using a wide array of 21st century technologies. Moreover, having students create their own connections among a variety of international points of view serves to enhance the significance of content as well as their understanding of what it means to live, survive, and prosper in a globalized world. Consider these examples:

> We can enhance the problematic scenarios by using a wide array of 21st century technologies.

- Daniel, the teacher of a Rosewood Elementary second-grade class in Rock-Hill, South Carolina, used a Promethean Activ-Board to help students understand concepts such as *climate* and *climate change*. The result was, in his own words, "a deluge of questions." As students became involved with the topic, Daniel was not only able to show Internet images of cold and warm fronts, but could also display several pages of a book he had previously scanned of polar ice floes (personal communication, January 15, 2009).

- Fifth-grade students in Charlotte, North Carolina, were planning their research questions for a final exhibit in an International Baccalaureate school. As they generated questions, the teacher was able not only to record them on the Promethean ActivBoard but also to save their jottings and discussions on their topics as well (personal communication, March 30, 2009).

- Middle school students in Van Nuys, California, and Winnipeg, Manitoba, Canada, communicated with each other across more than 1,500 miles "almost daily through blogs, wikis, Skype, instant messaging and other tools to share ideas about literature and current events" (Richardson, 2008, p. 37).

- Students in Webster, New York, used web-based social networking tools (blogs, wikis, Skype, and other tools) to "create their own networks" as they investigated the health of local streams around their schools (Richardson, 2008, p. 37). Through their efforts they learned about "global collaboration and communication," key elements for survival in the highly interdependent and competitive world of the 21st century (p. 37).

- At High Tech High in San Diego, California, students engaged in multidisciplinary projects that allowed them to communicate with experts within the community. For example, students in art, media, and biology came together to produce DVDs to solve problems on blood-related health issues. In a humanities, chemistry, and mathematics collaboration, students researched "African political struggles caused by a scarcity of natural resources," created documentary films, and modeled water-purification plants, which they then exhibited "before peers, teachers, parents and members of the community" (Rubenstein, 2008, p. 44).

What Do We Know About the Effectiveness of PBL?

Some researchers caution that we need to strengthen the conceptual foundations of PBL research (Belland, French, & Ertmer, 2009). There are others who tell us that challenging students to think through problematic situations can be "superior when it comes to long-term retention, skill development and satisfaction of students and teachers" (Strobel & van Barneveld, 2009, p. 44).

In terms of the efficacy of inquiry, however, we hear stronger support. A 2009 study concluded that "developmental research confirms the idea that curiosity drives intellectual development. . . . When a situation is designed to arouse curiosity, children display improved academic performance" (Engel & Randall, 2009, p. 184). Other studies indicate that when all students are challenged to "organize, synthesize, and explain" a complex problem or issue using the methods of inquiry and research, there is a positive impact on learning (Newmann & Associates, 1996, p. 29).

"Developmental research confirms the idea that curiosity drives intellectual development." (Engel & Randall, 2009, p. 184)

Other evidence of efficacy comes directly from teachers who have used these kinds of problematic scenarios with an emphasis on inquiry. Teacher Kim Nordin, for instance, tells us that this structure gave her students "focus, drive and excitement . . . allowing them to be inquirers . . . [who] felt like they had ownership of their projects" (personal communication, January 15, 2009). Suzy O'Hara, the International Baccalaureate coordinator, notes that the use of PBL "has provided our teachers with authentic and engaging ways to promote students' information gathering. It serves as the bridge connecting basic skills, with [the] problem solving and creative thinking needed to be successful in our ever changing world" (personal communication, July 16, 2009).

Enthusiasm for PBL is not limited to the lower grades. Ed Jernigan, the director of the Centre for Knowledge Integration at the University of Waterloo, Ontario, was focused on students solving authentic problems when he said:

> We have built our first-year curriculum around a sequence of real-world design challenges asking students to solve meaningful, open problems of societal and environmental concern. Their level of engagement and retention as assessed by case studies, their actual design presentations and their in-depth reflections is unique in my thirty-three years experience at Waterloo. (personal communication, July 20, 2009)

Obviously, more time and study of this real-world approach to teaching and learning is needed to provide deeper insight into its efficacy. As teachers develop expertise with PBL, however, I expect that the formal and informal results will give not only a clearer picture of its impact, but a positive one as well, showing that within such programs we liberate students' curiosity and imaginations to think boldly, innovate, and implement solutions to 21st century problems.

Final Thoughts

At this writing, the United States is struggling through the aftermath of the worst economic crisis since the Great Depression. With a warming planet, it is also striving to reach energy independence. Within this context, President Barack Obama laid out an educational challenge:

> I'm calling on our nation's governors and state education chiefs to develop standards and assessments that don't simply measure whether students can fill in a bubble on a test, but whether they possess 21st century skills like problem solving and critical thinking and entrepreneurship and creativity. (as cited in Henderson, 2009, p. 4)

To meet these intense and immediate challenges, we need educators like Kerry Faber in Edmonton, Alberta, Canada, whose sixth-grade students realize the importance of asking good questions to solve authentic problems. Some eagerly said, "When I ask good questions, I learn more. . . . Your mind will get stronger, sharper and prepare you for the real world. . . . You start thinking critically. . . . If you ask better questions, you get people thinking" (personal communication, March 15, 2009).

Our challenge in this new century is to help our students build upon their intrinsic curiosities about nature and our living, working, playing, creating and surviving therein. Posing and pursuing substantive questions is what we should all be doing, in schools and as good citizens of this republic. When asked what he and others had wrought at the Constitutional Convention in Philadelphia in 1787, Ben Franklin replied, "A republic. If you can keep it" (as cited in Platt, 1992).

To keep our republic, we need to educate for thoughtful engagement with all of its many challenges.

References

Barell, J. (2003). *Developing more curious minds.* Alexandria, VA: Association for Supervision and Curriculum Development.

Barell, J. (2007a). *Problem-based learning—An inquiry approach* (2nd ed.). Thousand Oaks, CA: Corwin Press.

Barell, J. (2007b). *Why are school buses always yellow? Teaching for inquiry, preK–5.* Thousand Oaks, CA: Corwin Press.

Barell, J. (2009). [Professional development materials]. Unpublished raw data.

Belland, B. R., French, B. F., & Ertmer, P. A. (2009). Validity and problem-based learning research: A review of instruments used to assess intended learning outcomes. *Interdisciplinary Journal of Problem-Based Learning, 3*(1), 59–89.

Bourgeois, P. (1986). *Franklin in the dark.* New York: Scholastic Press.

Chevron advertisement. (2008, September). *The Atlantic Monthly, 302*(2), 36.

Cleveland Clinic advertisement. (2009, November). *The Atlantic Monthly, 304*(4), 19.

Desotelle, J., & Lierman, L. (2000, Summer). *The lego community.* Paper submitted at the Facilitating the Future professional development workshop, Ashland, WI.

Engel, S., & Randall, K. (2009, March). How teachers respond to children's inquiry. *American Educational Research Journal, 46,* 183–202.

Flaherty, J. (2002, August 4). What should you get out of college? *The New York Times,* p. 4A27.

Greenwich Public Schools. (2006). *Vision of the graduate.* Accessed at www.greenwichschools.org/page.cfm?p=61 on December 4, 2009.

Henderson, J. (2009, June). Educating emerging entrepreneurs. *Education Update, 51*(6). Accessed at www.ascd.org/publications/newsletters/education_update/jun09/vol51/num06/Educating_Emerging_Entrepreneurs.aspx on December 30, 2009.

Kohler advertisement. (2009, May). *Vanity Fair, 585,* 20.

Mikkelson, B., & Mikkelson, D. P. (2007). *Kiss my aspartame.* Accessed at www.snopes.com/medical/toxins/aspartame.asp on December 5, 2009.

Monsanto advertisement. (2009, November 9). *The New Yorker,* 3.

Newmann, F. M., & Associates. (1996). *Authentic achievement: Restructuring schools for intellectual quality.* San Francisco: Jossey-Bass.

New York State Standards. (n.d.). *Social studies core curriculum.* Accessed at www.emsc.nysed.gov/ciai/socst/pub/sscore1.pdf on July 7, 2009.

Platt, S. (1992). *Respectfully quoted: A dictionary of quotations.* Accessed at www.bartleby.com/73/1593.htmlpn December 5, 2009.

Richardson, W. (2008, December). World without walls: Learning well with others. *Edutopia, 4*(6), 36–38.

Royer, C. (2000, Fall). *Undaunted—19th/early 20th century women writers, the need to be heard.* Paper submitted for Principles of Curriculum Development course, Montclair State University, Montclair, NJ.

Rubenstein, G. (2008, December). Real world, San Diego: Hands-on learning at High Tech High. *Edutopia, 4*(6), 40–44.

Strobel, J., & van Barneveld, A. (2009, Spring). When is PBL more effective? A meta-synthesis of meta-analyses comparing PBL to conventional classrooms. *Interdisciplinary Journal of Problem-Based Learning, 3*(1), 44–58.

Walser, N. (2008, September/October). Teaching 21st century skills: What does it look like in practice? *Harvard Education Letter, 24*(5), 2.

Wiggins, G. (1998). *Educative assessment: Designing assessments to inform and improve student performance.* San Francisco: Jossey-Bass.

David W. Johnson

David W. Johnson, Ed.D., is codirector of the Cooperative Learning Center at the University of Minnesota. In 2008, he received the Distinguished Contributions to Research in Education Award from the American Educational Research Association. He has coauthored more than five hundred research articles and book chapters, and more than fifty books. He is a former editor of the *American Educational Research Journal.* Johnson has also served as an organizational consultant to schools and businesses throughout the world.

Roger T. Johnson

Roger T. Johnson, Ed.D., is a professor in the Department of Curriculum and Instruction with an emphasis in Science Education at the University of Minnesota. Johnson has received several national awards, including the Exemplary Research in the Social Studies Award presented by the National Council for the Social Studies, the Helen Plants Award from the American Society for Engineering Education, and the Gordon Allport Intergroup Relations Award from the Society for the Psychological Study of Social Issues. He is codirector of the Cooperative Learning Center. In addition to numerous articles, he has coauthored more than fifty books on cooperative learning, conflict resolution, and positive negotiations.

In this chapter, Johnson and Johnson point out four important challenges of the 21st century and discuss how cooperative learning, constructive controversy, and problem-solving negotiations will play a central role in teaching students the competencies and values they need to cope with these challenges.

Chapter 9

Cooperative Learning and Conflict Resolution: Essential 21st Century Skills

David W. Johnson and Roger T. Johnson

When preparing to live in the tumultuous 21st century, it is essential that students learn how to function effectively in cooperative efforts and resolve conflicts constructively. Intentionally facilitating and teaching the skills of cooperation and constructive conflict resolution will raise the quality of collaboration students experience and deepen their learning, not only in face-to-face interactions in school, but also in their online relationships.

This chapter discusses four important challenges of the 21st century and how cooperation and constructively managed conflicts (constructive controversy and integrative negotiations) are at the heart of meeting these challenges.

The Tools for Meeting Four Important Challenges of the 21st Century

The 21st century brings four important challenges in which cooperation and constructive conflict resolution play a central role: (1) a rapidly increasing global interdependence that will result in increasing local diversity as well as more frequent and intense conflicts, (2) the increasing number of democracies throughout the world, (3) the need for creative entrepreneurs, and (4) the growing importance of interpersonal relationships that affect the development of personal identity. The tools for meeting these challenges include cooperative learning, constructive controversy, and problem-solving (integrative) negotiations.

Cooperative Learning

Cooperative learning is the instructional use of small groups so that students work together to maximize their own and each other's learning (Johnson, Johnson, & Holubec, 2008). Any assignment in any curriculum for any age student can be done cooperatively. When individuals cooperate, they work together to accomplish shared goals, and there is a mutual responsibility to work for one's own success. Three types of cooperative learning distinguish this type of learning from mere collaboration: formal, informal, and base groups.

Formal cooperative learning consists of students collaborating or working together, for one class period to several weeks, to achieve shared learning goals and complete jointly specific tasks and assignments. *Informal cooperative learning* consists of students working together to achieve a joint learning goal in temporary, ad hoc groups that last from a few minutes to one class period. *Cooperative base groups* are long-term, heterogeneous cooperative learning groups with stable membership in which students provide one another with support, encouragement, and assistance to make academic progress. They also help one another develop cognitively and socially in healthy ways, as well as hold one another accountable for striving to learn. Research since the early 1900s strongly indicates that cooperation (compared with competitive and individualistic efforts) results in the following (Johnson & Johnson, 1989, 2005):

- Greater effort exerted to achieve (for example, higher achievement and productivity, more frequent use of higher-level reasoning, more frequent generation of new ideas and solutions, greater motivation, greater long-term retention, more on-task behavior, and greater transfer of what is learned within one situation to another)

- Higher-quality relationships among participants (for example, greater interpersonal attraction, valuing of heterogeneity, and task-oriented and personal support)

- Greater psychological adjustment (for example, greater psychological health, social competencies, self-esteem, shared identity, and ability to cope with stress and adversity)

Because of the amount and consistency of research supporting its use, cooperative learning will always be present in 21st century educational practice. Any teacher who does *not* use cooperative learning or relies solely on telling students to "collaborate" may be considered not fully competent. As the research grows even stronger, the use of cooperative learning becomes more and more inevitable and foundational so that student achievement of content outcomes increases.

With cooperative learning comes conflict. The two types of conflict promoted most by positive interdependence are constructive controversy and integrative negotiations.

> Any teacher who does *not* use cooperative learning or relies solely on telling students to "collaborate" may be considered not fully competent.

Constructive Controversy

One of the central aspects of individuals promoting each other's success is disagreement and augmentation—that is, constructive controversy—among members of cooperative groups when they have to make a decision or come to an agreement. A controversy exists when one person's ideas, opinions, information, theories, or conclusions are incompatible with those of another, and the two seek to reach an agreement (Johnson & Johnson, 2007, 2009b). Constructive controversy involves what Aristotle called *deliberate discourse* (that is, the discussion of the advantages and disadvantages of proposed actions) aimed at synthesizing novel solutions (that is, creative problem solving).

With constructive controversy, teachers intentionally take time to enable students to become more efficient at resolving disagreements that threaten to waste students' time or to cause classroom disruptions. Teaching students how to engage in the controversy-resolution process begins with randomly assigning students to heterogeneous cooperative learning groups of four members (Johnson & Johnson, 1989, 2007,

2009b). Each group receives an issue on which to write a report and pass a test. Each cooperative group is divided into two pairs. One pair takes the con position on the issue; the other pair takes the pro position. Each pair receives the instructional materials necessary to define their position and point them toward supporting information. The materials highlight the cooperative goal of reaching a consensus on the issue (by synthesizing the best reasoning from both sides) and writing a quality group report. Students then (1) research, learn about, and prepare their assigned position; (2) present a persuasive case that their position is correct; (3) engage in an open discussion in which there is spirited disagreement; (4) reverse perspectives and present the best case for the opposing position; (5) agree on a synthesis or integration of the best reasoning from both sides; and (6) reflect on the process so that they may learn from the experience.

Overall, the research indicates that constructive controversies (compared with concurrence seeking, debate, and individualistic efforts) create higher achievement, greater retention, more creative problem solving, more frequent use of higher-level reasoning and metacognitive thought, more perspective taking, greater continuous motivation to learn, more positive attitudes toward learning, more positive interpersonal relationships, greater social support, and higher self-esteem (Johnson & Johnson, 1989, 2007, 2009b). Engaging in constructive controversy can also be fun, enjoyable, and exciting. The theory of constructive controversy, the supporting research, and the controversy procedure provide an empirical base for political discourse and collective decision making that can enhance student collaborations in a variety of situations both in and out of the classroom.

Integrative Negotiations

In order to function effectively in the 21st century, individuals must know how to negotiate constructive resolutions to conflicts of interest. A conflict of interest exists when the actions of one person attempting to maximize his or her wants and benefits prevents or interferes with another person maximizing his or her wants and benefits. Conflicts of interest occur frequently when people work together cooperatively. How conflicts are resolved has considerable influence on the quality of the cooperation and the long-term survival and health of the cooperative system. Twenty-first-century teachers can prepare students to mediate and to negotiate disagreements so that students resolve issues in a quality manner.

For example, teachers may use the program *Teaching Students to Be Peacemakers* (Johnson & Johnson, 2005b) to prepare students to solve problems. Students learn the following steps in their preparation to solve problems and mediate conflicts:

1. Recognize what is and is not a conflict, and the potential positive outcomes of conflicts.

2. Understand the basic strategies for managing conflicts (for example, withdrawal, forcing, smoothing, compromising, and engaging in problem solving and integrative negotiations).

3. Engage in problem solving and integrative negotiations by (a) describing what they want, (b) describing how they feel, (c) describing the reasons for their wants and feeling, (d) taking the other's perspective, (e) inventing three optional plans to resolve the conflict that maximize joint benefits, and (f) choosing one plan and formalizing the agreement with a handshake.

4. Mediate schoolmates' conflicts by (a) ending hostilities by breaking up hostile encounters and cooling off students, (b) ensuring disputants are committed to the mediation process, (c) helping disputants successfully use problem-solving negotiations with each other, and (d) formalizing the agreement into a contract.

5. Implement the Peacemaker Peer-Mediation Program. (Each day the teacher selects two class members to serve as official mediators. The role of mediator rotates so that all students serve as mediators for an equal amount of time.)

The outcomes of this program are manifold. The benefits of teaching students the problem-solving negotiation and the peer-mediation procedures include mastery of the negotiation and mediation procedures, retention of that mastery throughout the school year and into the following year, application of the procedures to their and other students' conflicts, and transference of the procedures to nonclassroom settings (such as the playground and lunchroom) and nonschool settings (such as the home). Trained students tend to use more constructive strategies, such as integrative negotiations, than do untrained students. Students' attitudes toward conflict tend to become more positive. Finally, when integrated into academic units, the conflict-resolution training tends to increase academic achievement and long-term retention of the academic material.

Four Crucial Challenges of the 21st Century

Cooperative learning, constructive controversy, and integrative negotiations are three essential approaches for meeting the four crucial challenges unique to the 21st century. These strategies provide students with the essential skills necessary to address each of these challenges in the more collaborative school and work environment.

> Cooperative learning, constructive controversy, and integrative negotiations provide students with the essential skills necessary to address 21st century challenges in the more collaborative school and work environment.

Challenge 1: Global Interdependence

The 21st century is characterized by increasing technological, economic, ecological, and political interdependence among individuals, communities, countries, and regions of the world. Thomas Friedman, in his book *The World Is Flat* (2005), argues that the world has to "connect and collaborate." British Prime Minister Gordon Brown stated that the nations and regions of the world urgently need to step out of the mindset of competing interests and instead find common interests and launch cooperative efforts to build new international rules and institutions for the new global era. Schools are the setting in which individuals will learn how to do so.

In a 2002 *Los Angeles Times* editorial, former U.S. President Bill Clinton asked whether this increasing world interdependence would be good or bad for humanity. Global interdependence accelerates the development of countries and increases incomes and living standards through heightened world trade. In contrast, global interdependence increases vulnerability of each country to all other countries. The economies of these countries are no longer autonomous. Internal economic disruptions in one country can affect the economy of many other countries. Inflation can spread across national borders. Drastic actions by one country can quickly translate into hardships for another. Thus, while interdependence creates greater worldwide prosperity and productivity, it also increases the capability of each country to influence the events within all other countries. The result is larger, more numerous conflicts that must be managed. Understanding the nature of interdependent systems, how to operate effectively within them, and how to manage conflicts are essential qualities of future citizens and leaders.

Global interdependence also means that the solution to most major problems individual countries face (for example, eradicating disease, world hunger, contamination of the environment, global warming, international terrorism, or nuclear proliferation) are increasingly ones that cannot be solved by actions taken only at the national level. This internationalization of problems blurs the lines between domestic and international problems. The international affairs of one country are the internal affairs of other nations. Countries are far more vulnerable to outside economic disruptions. Therefore, future citizens and world leaders must understand the nature of interdependent systems and how to operate effectively within them.

Diversity and pluralism. More intense global interdependence is increasing diversity and pluralism on the local level, due to advances in transportation and ease of moving from one country to another. Working cooperatively and resolving conflicts among diverse individuals will become a more commonplace need. Cooperative learning is especially helpful for capitalizing on the benefits of diversity (Johnson & Johnson, 1989) and ensures that all students are meaningfully and actively involved in learning. Active, involved students tend not to engage in rejecting, bullying, or prejudiced behavior. Cooperative learning ensures that students achieve their potential and experience psychological success so that they are motivated to continue to invest energy and effort in learning. Those who experience academic failure are at risk for paying no attention and acting up, which often leads to physical or verbal aggression against stereotyped classmates. Cooperative learning promotes the development of caring and committed relationships among

> Cooperative learning is especially helpful for capitalizing on the benefits of diversity.

students, including between majority and minority students. Students who are isolated or alienated from their peers and who have no friends are at risk for being targets or sources of physical or verbal aggression. The negative impact of isolation may be even more severe on minority students.

Cooperative learning groups provide an arena in which students develop the interpersonal and small-group skills needed to work effectively with diverse schoolmates. These interpersonal skills enable students to engage in discussions in which they share and solve personal problems. As a result, students' resilience and ability to cope with adversity and stress tend to increase. Children who do not share their problems and who do not have caring, supportive help in solving them are at more risk for physical or verbal aggression toward stereotyped classmates. Students in cooperative learning groups academically help and assist diverse groupmates and contribute to their well-being and quality of life. This behavior promotes a sense of meaning, pride, and self-esteem. Finally, the systematic use of cooperative learning provides the context for resolving conflicts in constructive ways, which is essential for positive relationships among diverse individuals.

International, national, intergroup, and interpersonal conflict resolution. As interdependence increases at the international, national, intergroup, and interpersonal level, so does the frequency and intensity of conflicts at all of these levels. These conflicts involve conflicts in collective decision making and conflicts of interest. *Destructive conflicts* tend to be competitive, where one party tries to win over another. *Constructive conflicts* tend to be cooperative, in which involved parties seek an agreement that benefits all. Conflict results when nations and organizations work together to solve mutual and/or global problems. Opposing groups can disagree about the nature and cause of the problems, have different values and goals related to outcomes and means, and disagree about how much each should contribute to the problem-solving efforts. How constructively such conflicts are resolved becomes a central issue in how effectively global interdependence is managed.

Disagreement about the care of the environment is one example of the need for understanding interdependence and applying that knowledge to resolving global conflicts constructively. Population estimates predict more than nine billion humans will inhabit the planet by 2050, and the ecosystems of the Earth will likely be unable to sustain such large numbers, especially if humans continue to deplete natural resources, pollute the environment, and reduce biodiversity. With increased population will come economic and social conflicts that could devastate the health and well-being of current and future human populations. The World Commission on Environment and Development recognized these difficulties in 1987 when it stated, "The Earth is one, but the world is not." The competencies students need to learn to effectively deal with such disagreement and conflict are those contained in constructive controversy and integrative negotiations. Teachers can help students learn from conflicts that arise in collective decision making and with conflicts of interest; rather than end these conflicts with punitive measures, teachers can teach the competencies and apply them to the higher-level conflicts students will experience outside the classroom.

Challenge 2: Increasing Number of Democracies

Due to increasing global interdependence, the spread of technology and information, and the increasing power of international organizations such as the United Nations, the number of democracies will increase throughout the world in the 21st century. In 1748, Charles de Secondat, Baron de Montesquieu, published *The Spirit of Laws* in which he explored the relationship between people and different forms of government. He concluded that while dictatorship survives on the fear of the people and monarchy survives on the loyalty of the people, a free republic (the most fragile of the three political systems) survives on the virtue of the people. Virtue is reflected in the way a person balances his or her own needs with the needs of the society as a whole. Motivation to be virtuous comes from a sense of belonging, a concern for the whole, and a moral bond with the community. The moral bond is cultivated by deliberating with fellow citizens about the common good and helping shape the destiny of the political community.

A number of important parallels exist between being an effective member of a cooperative learning group and being an effective citizen in a democracy (Johnson & Johnson, 2010). A cooperative learning group is a microcosm of a democracy. A *democracy* is, after all, first and foremost a cooperative system in which citizens work together to reach goals and determine their future. Similarly, in cooperative learning groups, individuals work to achieve mutual goals, are responsible for contributing to the work of the group, have the right and obligation to express their ideas, and are under obligation to provide leadership and ensure effective decisions. All group members are considered equal. Decisions result from careful consideration of all points of view. Group members adopt a set of values that include contributing to the well-being of their groupmates and the common good. All of these characteristics are also true of democracies.

Thomas Jefferson, James Madison, and the other founders of the United States of America considered the heart of democracy to be *political discourse*: the formal exchange of reasoned views on which several alternative courses of action could be taken to solve a societal problem. Political discourse is a method of decision making in a democracy. The intent of political discourse is to involve all citizens in the making of the decision, persuade others (through valid information and logic), and clarify what course of action would be most effective in solving the problem, such as poverty, crime, drug abuse, poor economic health, or racism. The expectation is for citizens to prepare the best case possible for their position, advocate it strongly, critically analyze the opposing positions, step back and review the issue from all perspectives, and then come to a reasoned judgment about the course of action the society should take. The clash of opposing positions is expected to increase citizens' understanding of the issue and the quality of decision making, given that citizens would keep an open mind and change their opinions when logically persuaded to do so. Engaging in political discourse involves both short-term and long-term positive interdependence. The short-term positive interdependence is the immediate creation of consensus among citizens as to which course of action will best solve the problem. The long-term interdependence is the improvement of the political process and the maintenance of the health of the democracy. Cooperative learning and constructive controversy have been used to teach elementary and secondary students how to be citizens in a democracy in such countries as Armenia, Azerbaijan, the Czech Republic, and Lithuania (Avery, Freeman, Greenwalt, & Trout, 2006; Hovhannisyan, Varrella, Johnson, & Johnson, 2005).

Digital citizenship skills. In addition to the citizenship skills needed to be productive and responsible citizens of a democracy, individuals need to develop digital citizenship skills. Digital citizenship skills enable individuals to use technology in safe and responsible ways. Like all skills, digital citizenship has corresponding attitudes about the responsible and productive use of technology, such as cooperativeness and the avoidance of competitiveness. In many ways, being a good citizen on the Internet is the same as being a good collaborator. Most technology is used to achieve mutual goals and is, therefore, a cooperative endeavor. Technology is aimed primarily at enabling members of a team, organization, society, or multinational entities to achieve mutual goals more effectively. Technology allows research teams from all over the world to coordinate their activities almost instantly. Members of the same organization in many different locations can receive simultaneously instructions on completing a joint task. It is technology that makes resources available to complete cooperative enterprises such as massively multiplayer online games. Technology also provides access to multitudes of potential collaborators and shared spaces in which to complete cooperative tasks. Furthermore, people's behavior online can define their identity in their online relationships. The next wave of social networking will move technology systems away from restricting users to walled-off membership in a few sites, such as Facebook, toward a more open and flexible sharing among numerous niche communities. This will help individuals to make visible their *social graph*, or the network of people they know, are related to, or work with, independent of any given address book or networking system. Digital citizenship skills will thus become an essential aspect of individuals' lives in the 21st century.

Challenge 3: The Need for Creative Entrepreneurs

The economic future of societies depends on their capability to grow, attract, and support talented, innovative, and creative entrepreneurs (Florida, 2007). Because creative entrepreneurs are highly mobile, countries with the highest quality of life will attract the highest number of creative entrepreneurs. The challenge for educational systems in each country is to produce creative entrepreneurs who will then contribute to the future economic health of the country.

Nations must first ensure their educational system is socializing students into being creative, productive people who believe that they can better their life through being entrepreneurs. Nations must also ensure that their quality of life is sufficient to attract and keep creative entrepreneurs. Two factors that largely determine quality of life are the absence of poverty and its resulting social problems and the ability of individuals to potentially better their lives through becoming entrepreneurs. Education is the key mechanism for individuals to rise from one social class to another. Thus, schools have the responsibilities to teach students how to be creative problem solvers and especially to maximize the achievement for students from lower socioeconomic groups, ensuring that they go on to universities and graduate programs.

Teaching students to be creative is not something many schools achieved in past eras. Creativity is the capability to create or invent something original or to generate unique approaches and solutions to issues or problems (Johnson & Johnson, 1989, 2005a, 2009a). Creativity is a social product advanced through mutual consideration of diverse ideas in a cooperative context; it does not emerge well in a competitive or individualistic context. Cooperative learning and constructive controversy (that is, students disagreeing with each other and challenging each other's conclusions and theories) tend to increase the number of ideas, quality of ideas, feelings of stimulation and enjoyment, and originality of expression in problem-solving tasks.

Research shows that cooperative learning, compared with competitive and individualistic learning, increases the number of novel solutions, results in the use of more varied reasoning strategies, generates more original ideas, and results in more creative solutions to problems. In addition, cooperative learning and constructive controversy encourage group members to dig into a problem, raise issues, and settle them in ways that show the benefits in a wide range of ideas and result in a high degree of emotional involvement in and commitment to solving the problems (Johnson & Johnson, 2005a).

In constructive controversies, participants tend to invent more creative solutions to problems, be more original in their thinking, generate and utilize a greater number of ideas, generate more high-quality ideas, analyze problems at a deeper level, raise more issues, experience greater feelings of stimulation and enjoyment, become more emotionally involved in and committed to solving the problem, and experience more satisfaction with the resulting decision (Johnson & Johnson, 2005a).

High-quality reasoning skills. In addition to creativity, more frequent discovery and development of high-quality cognitive reasoning strategies occurs in cooperative environments than in competitive or individualistic situations (Johnson & Johnson, 1989, 2005a). Studies from Jean Piaget's cognitive development theory and Lawrence Kohlberg's moral development theory indicate that cooperative experiences promote the transition to higher-level cognitive and moral reasoning more frequently than competitive or individualistic experiences. Furthermore, when members of a cooperative group express differences of opinion, according to Piaget as well as controversy theory, they enhance the level and quality of their cognitive and moral reasoning. Finally, in cooperative situations, students tend to engage in more frequent and accurate perspective taking than they do in competitive or individualistic situations. This accurate perspective taking enhances members' ability to respond to others' needs with empathy, compassion, and support.

Challenge 4: Changes in Interpersonal Relationships

In the 21st century, the emphasis on friendship formation and positive interpersonal interactions is increasing, as the rise in popularity of social networks already shows. These relationships will take place with increasing intensity in two settings: face-to-face interactions and online. Cooperation and constructive conflict resolution will play a vital role in building positive relationships in each setting, whereas competition and individualism will tend to result in negative relationships in each setting. Cooperative efforts promote considerably more positive regard among individuals. This is also true for relationships between majority and minority individuals, and for relationships between students with special needs and those without.

In the 21st century, the emphasis on friendship formation and positive interpersonal interactions is increasing, as the rise in popularity of social networks already shows.

Online relationships. Current trends seem to indicate that in the 21st century, relationships may start and/or develop online with increasing frequency. Relationships developed and maintained through such avenues as email, websites such as Facebook and MySpace, blogging, texting, tweeting, and online multiplayer games facilitate connections among peers. Online interaction can supplement face-to-face relationships, maintain previous face-to-face relationships as people move to different geographic locations, or be the setting in which new relationships form.

Online relationships are usually built around mutual goals and a common purpose; they tend not to be random. People read a blog for a purpose, find people with similar interests for a reason, and engage in games to have fun and test their skills. The fact that online relationships are built on a common purpose makes them by definition cooperative. The more people know about cooperative efforts and the more skilled they are in cooperating, the more successful their online relationships will be.

It is important to realize that online relationships are real relationships. Actual people read email messages, respond to comments on a blog, receive and send Twitter messages, post messages on Facebook, and so on. Not only are they real, but they are important. Relationships are based on the time individuals spend interacting with one another. More and more relationship time may be spent online. More and more people are spending as much or more of their relationship time online compared to face-to-face.

Electronic media offer the opportunity to expand the number of relationships a person has very quickly and very easily. There are few barriers for entry into online relationships, and the opportunity to do so is high. A person can use the Internet to easily find other people who have similar interests and beliefs. Entering one website may provide access to dozens of people with whom to interact about an area of mutual interest. Having such immediate access to large numbers of potential friends is difficult if not impossible in face-to-face situations. The ease of creating relationships online enhances individuals' ability to find collaborators and identify people who have resources essential for completing cooperative projects.

In Internet relationships, personal geography tends not to be relevant. No matter where an individual lives, it is possible to find friends all over the world. Thus, diversity of community may be unimportant to many people because, regardless of who their neighbors are, they can find a community of like-minded people on the Internet. Or, if a neighborhood is too homogeneous for an individual's tastes, he or she can use the Internet to find diverse friends and a wide variety of perspectives. Because diverse perspectives and resources enhance cooperation and constructive conflict, Internet relationships can enhance the quality of cooperation and constructive conflict considerably.

It is easy to interact with lots of people simultaneously on the Internet. The same email can be sent to dozens, even hundreds, of people. What a person posts on a Facebook page can be accessed by friends from all over the world who can then respond. In contrast, most face-to-face relationships are one-on-one. The speed at which communication takes place online enhances cooperation and coordination of efforts in most cases as long as messages are phrased cooperatively. If competitive messages are sent, the speed of communication may alienate more people more quickly.

In online relationships, people primarily know others through what they disclose about themselves. There can understandably be much skepticism about what people say about themselves online. In cooperative situations, trust may be higher, as individuals tend to be open, accurate, and honest in their communications and disclosures. Generally, however, the 21st century will no doubt see the development of new ways for assessing individual's online personas and honesty, such as assessing speed of keyboarding and responding, cleverness in phrasing responses, patterns of wording in messages, sense of humor, creativity in writing, and so on.

Online relationships can be highly positive and fulfilling. The arrival of email can bring joy. The honest disclosure of thoughts and feelings can be liberating. Support from online friends can be quite powerful. Not all online relationships, however, are positive. Cyberbullying and other negative interactions occur online. Nonetheless, the vast majority of online relationships seem to be quite positive, resulting in laughter, good humor, cheerfulness, joy, and fun. Such behaviors reflect positive relationships.

Material posted on the Internet spreads rapidly and widely and may be available to interested parties for decades. That means people must concern themselves more with what they post on the Internet and its impact on their privacy in public and face-to-face relationships. For example, behavior with a friend can be recorded on a cell phone and sent to dozens of people, and even end up posted on YouTube. Pictures of a teenager at a party can show up on a company website twenty years later.

Finally, online relationships focus attention on ethics, manners, and values. When people develop online relationships, they develop new systems of ethics and manners due to the nature of the technology. What is polite and what is rude, for example, may be different online than in face-to-face relationships. Online relationships can also affect individuals' value systems. A recent study found that in the United States, Japan, Singapore, and Malaysia, the more people played a prosocial online game, the more they tended to engage in prosocial behavior afterward, and when they played a violent online game, they were more likely to behave in competitive, obstructive ways afterward.

The Impact of Online Interaction on Face-to-Face Relationships

The increasing ease of building and maintaining online relationships in the 21st century will have considerable impact on face-to-face relationships. First, the majority of face-to-face interaction individuals may experience will take place in school. Second, as the amount of time spent in face-to-face relationships declines, the face-to-face interactions that do occur will increasingly include touch. Online relationships developed through voice chat and video provide additional cues such as tone of voice and facial expressions, but they do not provide touch (although touch-technology is under development). Touch is central to human social life. At birth, touch is the most developed sensory modality, and it contributes to cognitive, brain, and socioemotional development through infancy and childhood. Individuals deprived of human touch may develop serious psychological and developmental problems. Touch is essential to the emotional experiences in a relationship, because it communicates and intensifies emotions. Touch is especially important in communicating positive emotions, such as love, affection, caring, gratitude, empathy, and sympathy. As a person has fewer face-to-face relationships, the amount of touch in each relationship may tend to increase. Touch is especially important in cooperative relationships and when conflicts have been resolved constructively.

Identity Formation

A person's *identity* is a consistent set of attitudes that defines "who I am" (Johnson & Johnson, 1989). It is a generalization about the self derived from a person's interactions and relationships with other people, and from memberships in certain groups, communities, and cultures. Identity is made up of the multiple views we have of ourselves, including our physical characteristics, social roles, the activities we engage in, our attitudes and interests, gender, culture, ethnicity, and age. In addition, our identity includes ideals we would like to attain and standards we want to meet. All of these aspects of identity are arranged in a hierarchy that is dynamic, not static. Each aspect of a person's identity has positive or negative connotations. The sum of a person's approval or disapproval of his or her behavior and characteristics is referred to as *self-esteem*.

Forming an identity involves seeing oneself as a member of a moral community that shares a joint identity and engages in prosocial actions. Moral communities tend to reflect egalitarianism (that is, a belief in the equal worth of all members) and mutual respect. Identity in a competitive context, in contrast, defines a person as a separate individual striving to win. A competitor may have a moral identity involving the virtues of inequality, being a winner, and disdaining losers.

Cooperative experiences tend to increase the frequency with which participants engage in prosocial behaviors, whereas competitive experiences tend to increase the frequency with which individuals engage in antisocial behavior such as bullying and aggression with the intent of harm. Being prosocial has its benefits. Prosocial children tend to build positive relationships and enjoy positive well-being. Engaging in prosocial behavior influences a person's identity.

> Forming an identity involves seeing oneself as a member of a moral community that shares a joint identity and engages in prosocial actions.

The identities of people who rescued Jews during the Holocaust, for example, were still enhanced more than fifty years later by their good deeds. Elementary school students who privately agreed to give up their recess time to work for hospitalized children saw themselves as more altruistic immediately and a month later (Cialdini, Eisenberg, Shell, & McCreath, 1987).

Online Identity

In the 21st century, people's identities will be tied to the way they are perceived by the people with whom they have online relationships. Online identities are different from the identities people develop in face-to-face situations. Online, physical appearance is usually arbitrary, and identity comes more from a person's cleverness in phrasing messages, how he or she writes, the quickness and insightfulness of his or her responses, and what is unique about his or her insights, views, and contributions. For the identities to be positive, however, the online interaction needs to be within cooperative efforts in which conflicts are managed constructively. It is under those conditions that positive, strong identities tend to develop.

Coping With the Challenges

The challenges facing citizens of the 21st century begin with the increasing economic, technological, and environmental global interdependence. With global interdependence will come increased diversity at the local level, and frequency and intensity of conflicts among nations and regions, as well as individuals and groups. More and more countries will become democracies. In order for a country to prosper economically, it must develop, attract, and hold onto creative entrepreneurs. High-quality relationships will continue to hold considerable importance, but online relationships formed around cooperative endeavors will become more and more dominant. The Internet will also affect individuals' formation of personal identities. In all of these challenges, cooperative learning, constructive controversy, and problem-solving negotiations will play a central role in teaching children, adolescents, and young adults the competencies and values they need to cope with challenges and lead productive and fulfilling lives during the 21st century.

References

Avery, P., Freeman, C., Greenwalt, K., & Trout, M. (2006, April). *The "deliberating in a democracy project."* Paper presented at the annual meeting of the American Educational Research Association, San Francisco.

Cialdini, R. B., Eisenberg, N., Shell, R., & McCreath, H. (1987). Commitments to help by children: Effects on subsequent prosocial self-attributions. *British Journal of Social Psychology, 26,* 237–245.

Florida, R. L. (2007). *The flight of the creative class: The new global competition for talent.* New York: Collins Business.

Friedman. T. (2005). *The world is flat.* New York: Farrar, Straus and Giroux.

Hovhannisyan, A., Varrella, G., Johnson, D. W., & Johnson, R. (2005). Cooperative learning and building democracies. *The Cooperative Link, 20*(1), 1–3.

Johnson, D. W., & Johnson, R. T. (1989). *Cooperation and competition: Theory and research.* Edina, MN: Interaction Book Company.

Johnson, D. W., & Johnson, R. T. (2005a). New developments in social interdependence theory. *Genetic, Social, and General Psychology Monographs, 131*(4), 285–358.

Johnson, D. W., & Johnson, R. T. (2005b). *Teaching students to be peacemakers* (4th ed.). Edina, MN: Interaction Book Company.

Johnson, D. W., & Johnson, R. T. (2007). *Creative controversy: Intellectual challenge in the classroom* (4th ed.). Edina, MN: Interaction Book Company.

Johnson, D. W., & Johnson, R. T. (2009a). An educational psychology success story: Social interdependence theory and cooperative learning. *Educational Researcher, 38*(5), 365–379.

Johnson, D. W., & Johnson, R. T. (2009b). Energizing learning: The instructional power of conflict. *Educational Researcher, 38*(1), 37–51.

Johnson, D. W., & Johnson, R. T. (2010). Teaching students how to live in a democracy. In F. Salidi & R. Hoosain (Eds.), Democracy and multicultural education (pp. 201–234). Charlotte, NC: Information Age Publishing.

Johnson, D. W., Johnson, R. T., & Holubec, E. (2008). *Cooperation in the classroom* (7th ed.). Edina, MN: Interaction Book Company.

de Montesquieu, C. (1748/2004). *The spirit of laws.* New York: Kessinger.

World Commission on Environment and Development. (1987). *Report of the World Commission on Environment and Development: Our common future.* New York: United Nations Documents.

Douglas Fisher

Douglas Fisher, Ph.D., is a professor of language and literacy education in the Department of Teacher Education at San Diego State University and a teacher leader at Health Sciences High & Middle College. He is the recipient of an International Reading Association Celebrate Literacy Award, the Farmer award for excellence in writing from the National Council of Teachers of English, and a Christa McAuliffe award for excellence in teacher education from the American Association of State Colleges and Universities. He has published numerous articles and books on reading and literacy, differentiated instruction, and curriculum design.

Nancy Frey

Nancy Frey, Ph.D., is a professor of literacy in the School of Teacher Education at San Diego State University and a teacher leader at Health Sciences High & Middle College. Frey was previously a teacher at the elementary and middle school levels in the Broward County (Florida) Public Schools. She later worked for the Florida Department of Education on a statewide project for supporting students with diverse learning needs in general education curriculum. She is a recipient of the Christa McAuliffe award for excellence in teacher education from the American Association of State Colleges and Universities. She has coauthored books on literacy.

In this chapter, Fisher and Frey describe three ways for teachers to respond to the extreme shifts in technological advancement and student needs for the 21st century: (1) considering functions rather than tools, (2) revising technology policies, and (3) developing students' minds through intentional instruction.

Chapter 10

Preparing Students for Mastery of 21st Century Skills

Douglas Fisher and Nancy Frey

"Does it work?" asked a curious adolescent as she stared at the chalkboard at the front of the classroom.

We don't like to think of ourselves as getting older, but the bewildered question of a teen who is flummoxed by the sight of an object "us old people" take for granted, a common blackboard, certainly makes us feel old. What led up to this question requires a bit of explanation.

Nancy was scheduled to speak to a group of school principals in a nearby community during a professional development meeting on quality instruction for all learners. It has become our practice to include students from the high school where we work in our presentations, whenever possible, to bring the audience a student's perspective. Three tenth-grade students, Coraima, Susana, and Mariana, accompanied Nancy to this presentation. As the four of them entered the room where the meeting would take place, the girls stopped and let out an audible gasp.

"Does it work?" asked Coraima.

Nancy looked to the front of the room to see what Coraima was referring to, and then silently contemplated her own mortality. Coraima was referring to the chalkboard.

Given that there was a piece of chalk in the tray, Nancy was able to answer in the affirmative. She watched as the three teenagers approached the board and took turns making tentative marks with the chalk. "It's soft," said Mariana.

Nancy realized at that moment that the girls had never had a chalkboard in their classrooms, only whiteboards and dry-erase markers. More recently, they have become acquainted with interactive Smart Boards and document cameras. Their only experiences with chalk were with the sidewalk variety, where the rough surface requires more pressure and a firmer stroke. And as members of a digital generation, their syntax reflected a worldview of communication tools as active, not passive.

We're not saying that whiteboards or Smart Boards represent the cutting edge of technology, but rather that these students have a scope of experiences that differs from that of their teachers. This in itself is nothing new, but it does serve as a reminder that educational technologies can prompt a sea change in teaching. For instance, the invention of chalkboards more than two hundred years ago revolutionized schooling because it made it possible to move from individual study to large-group instruction (Krause, 2000).

These students have a scope of experiences that differs from that of their teachers.

The girls' use of technology throughout the day with Nancy illustrated how ubiquitous new forms of technology have become. They took photographs of themselves with their cell phones and sent them to one of their teachers to document their adventure. One of the girls also had a digital camera, and while Nancy finished her presentation, the girls recorded themselves lip-synching to popular songs, which they later uploaded to YouTube. They sent text messages to friends and parents and tweeted throughout the day to update them on their status and collected a few photos for possible use on their MySpace pages. What was most notable, however, was how ever-present these communication tools were in the hands of the girls. The point was not to use technology for its own sake. To these adolescents, these were tools to fulfill an ancient need to communicate, share, collaborate, and express. This evolution has even been captured in political cartoons. In figure 10.1, the artist and public commentator captures the fact that the need to communicate has remained consistent, yet the form has changed. At the same time, he raises a concern about the newer forms of communication and their potential limitations.

Figure 10.1: One person's view of the changing landscape of communication. Reprinted with permission from Mike Keefe, *The Denver Post*, and InToon.com.

Like the chalkboards of our school days, the best technologies fade into the background—they "weave themselves into the fabric of everyday life until they are indistinguishable from it" (Weiser, 1991, p. 94). The tools themselves evolve; our task as educators is to foreground communication while keeping abreast of the technologies that support it. If we focus on the tool but lose sight of the purpose, we are forever condemned to playing catch-up in a landscape of rapidly changing technology. Remember beepers? They enjoyed a brief popularity in the 1990s but became obsolete with the widespread use of cell phones. Few people use paging devices anymore because a new technology can fulfill a similar function more efficiently. Focusing on the tool at the expense of the purpose means that we shortchange our students. We risk failing to prepare our students to be 21st century learners who can adapt to new technology because they understand the collaborative, cooperative, and communicative purposes that underlie the tool. As architect Frank Lloyd Wright noted, "Form follows function."

When we keep the function in mind, the forms assume a "natural technology" so that they become a tool for our teaching repertoire (Krause, 2000, p. 6).

As urban educators, we are also concerned about the access students have to technology. The elementary school that the girls attended was a Title I school, with 100 percent of the students qualifying for free or reduced-price lunch. In addition, 72 percent of the students, including the three girls, were identified as English language learners. Yet even among students who come from low-income households, cell phones and cameras are ubiquitous. As well, they knew how to gain access to the Internet, even though none of them had laptops. What they did have going for them was a series of school experiences that ensured digital learning.

> As urban educators, we are also concerned about the access students have to technology.

Form and Function in the 21st Century

Others in this volume have noted that a major challenge facing educators is in preparing students for economies and technologies that do not currently exist. However, it is likely that they will be required to participate on an increasingly diverse and global playing field made possible by communication tools that allow them to respond to societal changes. A growing number of professional organizations have crafted position papers stating as much. For instance, the National Council of Teachers of English (NCTE) suggests that 21st century readers and writers will be able to:

Develop proficiency with the tools of technology;

Build relationships with others to pose and solve problems collaboratively and cross-culturally;

Design and share information for global communities to meet a variety of purposes;

Manage, analyze, and synthesize multiple streams of simultaneous information;

Create, critique, analyze, and evaluate multi-media texts; and

Attend to the ethical responsibilities required by these complex environments. (NCTE, 2009, p. 15)

We stated earlier that we try to include student perspectives in our work. Therefore, it seems only fair that we do so now. Consider the recommendations gathered in a survey (Project Tomorrow, 2009) of more than 280,000 students for how students would use stimulus package money to improve their schools:

- 52 percent recommended a laptop for each student.
- 51 percent asked for more games and simulations for teaching concepts.
- 44 percent requested use of digital media tools.
- 43 percent said they would like interactive whiteboards installed.
- 42 percent wanted online textbooks.
- 40 percent stated that email, instant messaging, and text-messaging tools would enhance their learning.

A superficial analysis of their feedback might conclude that it is no more than a shopping list of gadgets, but that would do a disservice to the student participants. They can't name the function, but they can name the form. It is our responsibility as educators to detect the functions that underlie the forms or tools. The students' requests connote a deep-seated need to communicate and collaborate, to access information at any time of the day or night, and to have the tools they need to synthesize, evaluate, and create information. Therefore, in our instruction, we must provide access to technology at the same time we are teaching the functions related to communication.

How Can Teachers Respond?

There are a number of ways we can join our students in their 21st century mindset. Thankfully, we are not the first group of educators who have had to make conceptual shifts in our approaches. Yes, it is true that these shifts are accelerating and technology is advancing at an alarming rate. Having said that, there are ways for teachers to respond. We focus on three here: (1) considering functions rather than tools, (2) revising technology policies, and (3) developing students' minds through intentional instruction.

Considering Functions, Not Tools

It's time for a confession: we feel stressed trying to keep up with the innovations of the 21st century. Not too long ago, we were asked to join a Ning, and we didn't know what it was. More recently, we were introduced to Twitter when a student wanted to tweet us. Our stress was reduced when we heard Marc Prensky, in his 2008 keynote at the National Council of Teachers of English conference, suggest that we have to stop thinking of technology in terms of nouns (PowerPoint, YouTube, or Twitter) and instead think in terms of verbs (presenting, sharing, and communicating). In other words, as teachers, we should focus on the functions of the technology rather than the tools or forms of technology. Thankfully, the functions are familiar to us. We'll never keep up with all of the tools (forms). We just need to understand the functions for which the tools are developed so that we can be smart consumers and pick and choose the tools that serve our instructional needs. This was a liberating realization.

Our list of functions, and some current tools associated with those functions, can be found in table 10.1. It is difficult to write this knowing that by the time this is printed, the tools will have likely changed. Think of the list, then, as a historical reminder, and feel free to add new tools to the functions on the list as you discover them. Hopefully, the acknowledgment that tools change yet functions remain will reduce stress and allow educators to select new tools for teaching that engage learners. Increasingly, these tools are moving away from an emphasis on the device and toward a sustained focus on the purpose.

Revising Technology Policies

Once we realized that the technology our students had could be used for good (learning) and not evil (distraction), we had to confront the technology policy. Like most schools, we initially banned technology. At this moment, most schools still ban technology. The week this chapter was written, Doug was in a school in which there were posters in every hallway that read, "If we see it, you lose it!" with pictures of

Table 10.1: Technology Functions With Current Tools

Functions	Tools
Communicating	Text messaging, Twitter, Digg, video conferencing
Listening	Podcasts, iTunes, streaming media, RSS feeds
Networking	MySpace, Facebook, Ning
Presenting	PowerPoint, Keynote, Wimba
Producing	GarageBand, iMovie
Searching	Google, Yahoo, Lycos
Sharing	YouTube, blogs, vlogs, Flickr, collaborating, wikis, VoiceThread, Google Docs
Storing	MP3 players, flash drives, servers, CD/DVD

MP3 players and cell phones. Of course, most of the teachers walking in the hallway had cell phones on their belts, but that's another story.

As we considered the impact of our technology prohibition, we realized that we were doing a disservice to students. They were not developing as global citizens who understood the power and responsibility that came with the technology. A common mobile phone today has more power than most computers a decade ago, yet most students do not know how to use one as a learning tool. In addition, people are routinely rude to one another with their technology. They talk during movies, interrupt dinner to take calls, text while driving, and engage in all kinds of other dangerous or inappropriate behavior. We asked ourselves what we were doing to combat this problem and teach young people to be courteous with their technology. After all, they are going to enter a world of work that is very different from ours—one in which technology is used to solve problems and locate information.

The result of our deliberation was an end to prohibition and a focus on courtesy. We now actively teach students how to use their technology in ways that are appropriate for the environment. A copy of our courtesy policy is shown in table 10.2 (page 229). After several years with this policy, we are pleased to say that technology is no longer an issue for us. We don't confiscate phones, and we don't spend valuable instructional minutes enforcing a policy that worked in the 20th century when few students carried these types of devices. Of course there are minor infractions from time to time, but they are addressed. Students understand that they will have a chance to use their technology in a time and place that is appropriate and that it is discourteous to listen to music or text friends while the teacher is talking or during productive group work.

Courtesy is a code that governs the expectations of social behavior. Each community or culture defines courtesy and the expectations for members of that community or culture. As a learning community, it is our responsibility to define courtesy and to live up to that definition. As a school community, we must hold one another and ourselves accountable for interactions that foster respect and trust. Discourteous behaviors destroy the community and can result in hurt feelings, anger, and additional poor choices.

In general, courtesy means that we interact with one another in positive, respectful ways. Consider the examples of courteous and discourteous behavior shown in table 10.2.

At our school, it is expected that students treat one another, the faculty, staff, and administration—indeed any adult—with respect, courtesy, and cooperation. Further, teachers are expected to treat one another, the students and their families, and the administration in courteous ways.

Discourteous behavior is recognized as an opportunity for learning. In general, students receive feedback, counseling, and guidance when they make mistakes and engage in discourteous behaviors. Repeated failure to engage in courteous behavior results in increasingly punitive consequences, including reparations, restoring the environment, meetings with faculty or staff, meetings with administrators, the development of a behavioral contract, removal of privileges, and/or suspension or expulsion from the school.

Today, students are routinely invited to use their technology to find information. For example, an English teacher we were visiting said to her students, "Who has unlimited service? Can you look up *progeny* for Andrew and talk about what it means?" This two-sentence exchange demonstrates the conceptual shift schools can make in the

Table 10.2: Courtesy Policy

Courteous	Discourteous
Saying please and thank you	Using vulgar, foul, abusive, or offensive language
Paying attention in class	
Socializing with friends during passing periods and lunch	Listening to an iPod during a formal learning situation such as during a lecture or while completing group work
Asking questions and interacting with peers and teachers	
Asking for, accepting, offering, or declining help graciously	Text messaging or talking on a cell phone during class time
	Bullying, teasing, or harassing others
Allowing teachers and peers to complete statements without interruptions	Hogging bandwidth and/or computer time
Throwing away trash after lunch	
Cleaning your own workspace	Not showing up for your scheduled appointments or not completing tasks
Reporting safety concerns or other issues that require attention to a staff member	Failing to communicate when you're not coming to school

21st century. First, technology can be used at school. Second, technology can be used for learning and finding information. And third, we should help each other be productive and learn.

Of course, the school technology policy is not the only thing that needs to change. We need to change Internet-access policies as well. Consider the greatest collection of free video content ever created—YouTube—and the fact that it is banned in most schools. In our school, we use YouTube on a daily basis. In fact, we're not sure that we could plan a lesson that doesn't involve a video clip. And we have yet to look for something and not find it—the collection is simply amazing. For example, we wanted to talk with students about memory formation and how they could use current understandings of the human brain to learn more efficiently. We searched YouTube and found several great sources of information to include.

But we can't get hung up on the tool. YouTube is great, but there will be other tools that eventually come along to meet this need. Our issue is the fact that most teachers can't access this treasure trove of information. We believe that this will change as educators become increasingly savvy in terms of both advocacy and use.

Developing Students' Minds Through Intentional Instruction

A significant part of our work has focused on developing students' thinking skills through intentional instruction (Fisher & Frey, 2008b). Our goal is to release responsibility for learning to students, yet still provide them with the support required to be successful. We have found the *gradual release of responsibility model* most appropriate to accomplish this goal. The gradual release of responsibility model suggests that teachers move purposefully from providing extensive support to using peer support and then no support. Or as Duke and Pearson (2002) suggest, teachers have to move from assuming "all the responsibility for performing a task . . . to a situation in which the students assume all of the responsibility" (p. 211).

The role of instruction in providing access to technology is vital in this regard. Many of our students don't have laptops or other expensive tools, but nearly everyone has a mobile phone, camera, or MP3 player. However, they may lack the opportunity at home to perfect their skills in using Web 2.0 features. That means that they need instruction and opportunities for using these tools to fulfill the functions of literacy learning during their school day. A gradual release model allows for students to gain expertise in the company of teachers and peers who can model, guide, and collaborate.

Unfortunately, in too many classrooms, releasing responsibility is too sudden and unplanned and results in misunderstandings and failure. Consider the classroom in which students hear a lecture and are then expected to pass a test. Or the classroom in which students are told to read texts at home and come to class prepared to discuss them. Or the classroom in which students are assigned a problem set twenty minutes after the teacher has demonstrated how to do the problems. In each of these cases, students are expected to perform independently but are not well prepared for the task. In addition, in each of these classrooms, modern technology tools are not mobilized to develop students' thinking.

Our interpretation of the gradual release of responsibility model includes four components: focus lessons, guided instruction, collaborative tasks, and independent learning (Fisher & Frey, 2008a). Our work, in terms of both teaching and research, suggests that implementation of this instructional framework leads to significant improvement in student engagement and achievement. However, we also want to emphasize that this is not a linear process and that teachers can implement the components in ways that are effective for their outcomes. Our criteria, however, are that all four are present each time students and teachers meet. Let's explore each of the components. Note that table 10.3 (page 232) contains a list of things to look for in a classroom using this framework.

Focus lessons. A typical focus lesson lasts from ten to fifteen minutes. It is designed to do two things: (1) establish a purpose and (2) provide students with a model. Often the purpose is written on the board and briefly discussed with students. Some teachers require that students include the purpose in their notes. Others make a verbal reference to the purpose several times during the class meeting. We aren't too concerned with where and how the purpose is listed, but rather that the students know what is expected of them and why they're learning what they're learning.

The second part of the focus lesson is the model. While volumes can and have been written on modeling, it's rarely done in the secondary classroom. Instead, middle and high school teachers tend to provide procedural explanations, emphasizing the *how*, but not the *why*. Modeling, on the other hand, is metacognitive and includes the thinking behind the thinking. When students get a glimpse inside the thinking of an expert, they begin to approximate that behavior. Imagine the science student who gets to hear her teacher's understanding of an atom or the history student who witnesses the internal debate his history teacher has about sources of information, including the search for corroborating evidence via the Internet. The models we provide students allow them access to academic language and academic thinking as well as information about expert problem

Table 10.3: Elements of a Gradual Release of Responsibility Lesson

Focus Lessons
The teacher uses "I" statements to model thinking.
The teacher uses questioning to scaffold instruction, not to interrogate students.
The lesson includes a decision frame for when to use the skill or strategy.
The lesson builds metacognitive awareness, especially indicators of success.
Focus lessons move to guided instruction, not immediately to independent learning.

Guided Instruction
The teacher uses small-group arrangements.
Grouping changes throughout the semester.
The teacher has an active role in guided instruction; he or she does not just circulate and assist individual students.
There is a dialogue between learners and the teacher as they begin to apply the skill or strategy.
The teacher uses cues and prompts to scaffold understanding when a student makes an error, and he or she does not immediately tell the student the correct answer.

Collaborative Tasks
The teacher uses small-group arrangements.
Grouping changes throughout the semester.
The concepts students need to complete collaborative tasks have been modeled by the teacher.
Students have received guided instruction of the concepts needed to complete collaborative tasks.
Students are individually accountable for their contributions to the group.
The task provides students with an opportunity for interaction.

Independent Learning
Students have received modeled, guided, and collaborative learning experiences related to concepts needed to complete independent tasks.
Independent tasks extend beyond practice to application and extension of new knowledge.
The teacher meets with individual students for conferencing about the independent learning tasks.

Source: Adapted from Better Learning Through Structured Teaching: A Framework for the Gradual Release of Responsibility, *Fisher & Frey, 2008a, pp. 127–128. Reprinted with permission. Learn more about ASCD at www.ascd.org.*

solving and understanding. Daily modeling is critical if students are going to understand complex content.

We have witnessed amazing examples of teacher modeling using technology to address functions and needs. For example, we observed a history teacher modeling his thinking about word solving. When he got to the word *ratify*, he took out his cell phone and sent a text message to a friend to clarify the meaning of the term. We observed a science teacher modeling her thinking about chemical reactions using an interactive website in which variables can be manipulated with different outcomes. We saw an art teacher model his understanding of light and perspective using a digital camera and computer, and we observed an English teacher modeling questions she had for an author by using iChat to send her questions directly to the author. In each of these cases, the teacher modeled his or her *thinking*, and that thinking provided an authentic reason to access 21st century technology, the technology our students use on a daily basis.

Guided instruction. Having a purpose and a model is not enough to ensure enduring understanding. Learners also need to be guided in their thinking. We define guided instruction as the strategic use of cues, prompts, or questions to encourage students to do some of the cognitive work. The latter part of the definition is critical—guided instruction is intended to result in greater student understanding and is not simply a restatement of the information provided during a focus lesson. Guided instructional events, whether with the whole class or small groups of students, are planned strategically such that teachers understand student thinking and can provide a precise scaffold.

We have been very impressed with our teaching colleagues who have used technology to support their guided instruction. We regularly see a biology teacher send instant messages and text messages to students who need scaffolding. We know a history teacher who uses Twitter to send messages to his students, providing them with cues about the tasks at hand. And we have a colleague in English who digitally records her writing conferences with students and then loads them on a course website (password

> Guided instruction is intended to result in greater student understanding and is not simply a restatement of the information provided during a focus lesson.

protected for each student) so that students can use the content from their individual interviews while writing their essays. Again, the technology tools are serving a specific instructional purpose; they are facilitating the transfer of responsibility from teacher to student and are providing the scaffolding necessary for students to develop their thinking skills.

Collaborative tasks. In order to learn—to really learn—students must be engaged in productive group tasks that require interaction. They have to use the language and thinking of the discipline with their peers to really grasp it. And they have to be accountable for their individual contributions to the group task so that the teacher knows which students understand the content and which need additional instruction. There are any number of collaborative tasks that are effective, including the following.

Collaborative writing tasks. We have an English colleague who uses Google Docs to provide students with opportunities to write and receive feedback from peers. We have another English teacher colleague who uses wiki technology (www.writingwiki.org) to provide students with a public outlet for their work. In both of these forums, students learn to collaborate with others, to share feedback in constructive ways, and to think critically about what they read because the writing has not been verified, censored, or edited in any formal way.

Internet reciprocal teaching. During Internet reciprocal teaching (for example, Castek, 2006), each member of the group is responsible for an aspect of comprehension (predicting, questioning, summarizing, or clarifying) and reads from websites while evaluating the information located on the site. A science teacher we know provides topics, and students find articles to read related to the topic. Donald Leu and his colleagues in the New Literacies Research Team at the University of Connecticut (n.d.) have developed a rubric (see table 10.4) for evaluating the quality of the discussions students have while in Internet reciprocal teaching groups.

Graphics production. Our history colleague invites students to create iMovies or digital comic books to demonstrate their understanding of differing perspectives in history. We were most impressed with a twenty-page graphic novel created using Comic Life that

Table 10.4: Internet Reciprocal Teaching Dialogue Rubric

Reciprocal Teaching Strategy	Beginning (1 Point)	Developing (2 Points)	Accomplished (3 Points)	Exemplary (4 Points)	Score
Questioning	Generates simple recall questions that can be answered directly from facts or information found within the website's home page.	Generates main idea questions that can be answered based on information gathered by accessing one or more links to the website's content.	Generates questions requiring inference. Facts and information must be synthesized from one or more links to the website's content and combined with prior knowledge.	Generates questions flexibly that vary in type, based on the content read and the direction of the dialogue.	
Clarifying	Identifies clarification as a tool to enhance understanding and initiates clarification dialogue when appropriate.	Identifies appropriate words for clarification with the dialogue's context.	Assists group in clarifying identified words based on context clues.	Uses strategies for word clarification that can be applied generally across reading contexts.	

continued on next page →

Reciprocal Teaching Strategy	Beginning (1 Point)	Developing (2 Points)	Accomplished (3 Points)	Exemplary (4 Points)	Score
Summarizing	Summary consists of loosely related ideas.	Summary consists of several main ideas but also many details.	Summary synthesizes main ideas, is complete, accurate, and concise.	Summary is accurate, complete, and concise and incorporates content vocabulary contained in the text.	
Predicting	Demonstrates knowledge of predictions as an active reading strategy.	Directs group predictions to set a clear purpose for reading.	Articulates predictions that build logically from context.	Provides justification for prediction and initiates confirmation or redirection based on information located in the text.	

Source: Reprinted with permission. Jill Castek, New Literacies Research Team, Protocol for Internet Reciprocal Teaching (IRT), n.d., pp. 6–7.

depicted life during the French Revolution. The students who created this included a blog on each page, which served a narration function as well as providing historically accurate information describing these events of the time. A sample page can be found in figure 10.2.

Regardless of the instructional routine used for collaborative tasks, there are two keys to making this component effective. First, it must provide students an opportunity to interact with one another using the language and content of the discipline. Second, students must be individually accountable for their contributions to the group. Together, these factors increase engagement and provide teachers with formative assessment information useful in planning future instruction.

Independent learning. As part of instruction, students have to apply what they have been taught. Ideally, this occurs under the guidance of the teacher as part of class time before homework is ever assigned. There are a number of in-class independent tasks that help

Figure 10.2: Graphic novel page created using Comic Life.
By Marina Bautista. Reprinted with permission.

students master content. For example, quickwrites allow students to clarify their thinking on a subject. Of course, students can complete these on their laptops. Quickwrites also provide teachers a glimpse into student understanding. Out-of-class independent learning—homework—should be saved until students have a firm grasp of the content. Simply said, students need practice before being asked to complete tasks on their own. But in many classrooms, students are assigned tasks for homework that have not yet been taught. As the MetLife (2008) survey documented, secondary teachers confessed that they "very often or often" assigned homework because they ran out of time in class. The practice of assigning homework for missed class content will not result in student understanding. In fact, it is more likely to reinforce misunderstanding because in many cases students are practicing ineffectively and incorrectly.

In terms of technology-enhanced independent learning tasks, we regularly see podcasts used to facilitate understanding. For example, English teachers can use the Classic Tales podcast (www .theclassictales.com), which makes narrated classic works of fiction available free of charge. There are thousands of free podcasts available online that can extend students' understanding of content, such as those from the History Channel, National Geographic, 60 Second Science, Scientific American, the Museum of Modern Art, and the Smithsonian, to name a few. In addition, discussion boards provide students an opportunity to independently engage in content. For example, a discussion board on *Romeo and Juliet* allows students in different English classes at the same school, or across many schools, to share their thinking and questions about the play.

We witnessed one student's learning using "old" and "new" literacies in a project for her tenth-grade English class. Edith is an English language learner and does not have a computer in her home. However, she has access to technology and instruction at school. Our students address a schoolwide essential question each quarter, and the one that focused Edith's study asked, "Does age matter?" Her English teacher modeled her thinking each day as she read aloud portions of J. M. Barrie's *Peter Pan* (2003). In addition, Edith met with other students to discuss and write about the related text she selected to read, *A Long Way Gone: Memoirs of a Boy Soldier* (Beah, 2007). The author's moving account of a childhood spent as an unwilling recruit in a rebel army in Sierra Leone prompted her to learn more about the plight of child soldiers and victims throughout the world. In addition to writing a traditional essay addressing the essential question, she completed an alternative assignment to represent similar ideas. Edith collaborated with another student to learn GarageBand in order to compose an original piece of instrumental music. Her English teacher showed her how to search Flickr for photographic images licensed under Creative Commons that would allow her to legally use them in an iMovie she made with the help of the technology coordinator at the school. She asked another faculty member to proof her draft presentation and gathered feedback from several trusted peers. The result was a four-minute video that addressed war, child soldiers, and corruption across nearly one hundred years and examined the heavy cost paid by children in the Middle East, Central America, Africa, and Asia when war is waged on civilians. What was most remarkable to us was the way Edith took leadership of completing this project. She gathered resources, both human and digital, to craft a very personal and individual response to an issue of global importance. Simply making technology available to her would have been insufficient. She needed the instruction that comes from a talented teacher, as well as access to peers and adults with whom she could collaborate. The technology became the tool for her to fulfill the timeless need to create and express her viewpoint about a complex topic.

An Invitation

Given that our attempts to ban technology have failed and technological innovation is accelerating, it's time that we consider the use of 21st century tools that serve long-standing functions. Humans need to communicate, share, store, and create. As a species, we've engaged in these functions for centuries. There's really nothing new about them. What is new are the forms, or tools, that students use to meet these needs. As their teachers, it is our responsibility to meet them halfway. We have been entrusted to guide the next generation, and doing so requires that we apprentice them in the functions they will need to be successful. And this success will involve tools that we haven't yet imagined. We're no longer stressed about this; we're excited to learn alongside students as they teach us tools and we help them understand functions.

References

Barrie, J. M. (2003). *Peter Pan* (100th anniversary ed.). New York: Henry Holt.

Beah, I. (2007). *A long way gone: Memoirs of a boy soldier.* New York: Farrar, Straus and Giroux.

Castek, J. (2006, April). *Adapting reciprocal teaching to the Internet using telecollaborative projects.* Symposium presented at the annual meeting of the American Educational Research Association (AERA), San Francisco.

Duke, N. K., & Pearson, P. D. (2002). Effective practices for developing reading comprehension. In A. E. Farstrup & S. J. Samuels (Eds.), *What research has to say about reading instruction* (3rd ed., pp. 205–242). Newark, DE: International Reading Association.

Fisher, D., & Frey, N. (2008a). *Better learning through structured teaching: A framework for the gradual release of responsibility.* Alexandria, VA: Association for Supervision and Curriculum Development.

Fisher, D., & Frey, N. (2008b, November). Releasing responsibility. *Educational Leadership, 66*(3), 32–37.

Krause, S. D. (2000, Spring). Among the greatest benefactors of mankind: What the success of chalkboards tells us about the future of computers in the classroom. *The Journal of the Midwest Modern Language Association, 33*(2), 6–16.

Leu, D., & the University of Connecticut New Literacies Research Team. (n.d.). *Protocol for Internet reciprocal teaching (IRT).* Accessed at www.newliteracies .uconn.edu/carnegie/documents/IRT.pdf on November 10, 2009.

MetLife. (2008). *The MetLife survey of the American teacher: The homework experience.* Accessed at www.ced.org/docs/report/report_metlife2008.pdf on August 29, 2008.

National Council of Teachers of English. (2009, March). Literacy learning in the 21st century: A policy brief produced by the National Council of Teachers of English. *Council Chronicle, 18*(3), 15–16.

Prensky, M. (2008, November). *Homo sapiens digital: Technology is their birthright.* Keynote presentation at the annual meeting of the National Council of Teachers of English, San Antonio, TX.

Project Tomorrow. (2009). *Speak up 2008 congressional briefing.* Accessed at www .tomorrow.org/speakup/speakup_congress.html on April 5, 2009.

Weiser, M. (1991, September). The computer for the 21st century. *Scientific American, 265*(3), 94–104.

Cheryl Lemke

Cheryl Lemke, M.Ed., is president and CEO of the Metiri Group, a consulting firm dedicated to advancing effective uses of technology in schools. Under her leadership, school districts across North America are using Metiri's innovative Dimensions21 system to benchmark their progress with 21st century learning. Prior to launching the firm, she was the executive director of the Milken Exchange on Education Technology for the Milken Family Foundation. Lemke specializes in public policy for K–12 learning technology, working at many levels with governors, legislators, superintendents, business leaders, and teachers. As an associate superintendent for the Illinois State Board of Education, Lemke managed a center for learning technology with over one hundred staff members, translating the fifty-million-dollar annual budget into a new statewide network, professional development centers, community-based technology planning processes for Illinois schools, and online curriculum projects designed to help students learn. She also oversaw the development of state learning technology plans in both Illinois and Washington. Recognized nationally as a proactive leader in learning technology, and sought after as a consultant, speaker, and writer, Lemke has designed policy in the state house that translates into sound educational practice in the schoolhouse.

In this chapter, Lemke introduces three important innovations of 21st century learning: visualization, democratization of knowledge, and participatory cultures for learning. She provides an impressive demonstration of ways technology permits greater balance between a visual approach and traditional language-based communication.

Visit **go.solution-tree.com/21stcenturyskills** to view the graphics in this chapter in full color and to access live links to tools and materials.

Chapter 11

Innovation Through Technology

Cheryl Lemke

There is no turning back. The Internet has become integral to life in the 21st century—a place for work, play, communication, and learning. It is easy to lose sight of just how integral it has become, and how knowledge-based the world economy has become. The combination of human ingenuity and digital tools has led to innovations that have, in some cases, become viral (Foray & Lundvall, 1998). The statistics are staggering: in 2009, the mobile world celebrated its four billionth connection (Global System for Mobile Communications, 2009); over one trillion unique URLs have been registered in Google's index (The Official Google Blog, 2008); there have been nearly sixty-one million views to date of the YouTube most-watched video, *Guitar* (Jeonghyun, n.d.; Shah, 2005); on average, nine hundred thousand blogs are posted every twenty-four hours (Singer, 2009); over 2.5 billion tweets have been sent (Reed, 2008); YouTube was sold to Google in 2006 for $1.65 billion (Associated Press, 2006); over one hundred million users are logging onto Facebook every day; and approximately 2.6 billion minutes globally are dedicated to using Facebook daily, in thirty-five different languages (Singer, 2009).

Regardless of whether you find these statistics energizing or overwhelming, there is no question that the line between our digital and physical lives is blurring.

Outside of school, 96 percent of nine- to seventeen-year-olds embrace the Web 2.0 culture of social networking, blogging, twittering, GPS mapping, or interactive gaming at some level (National School Board Association, 2007). These youth communicate in real time through texting, instant messaging, and sharing of media files. According to the National School Board Association (2007), they typically spend about nine hours per week outside of school using social networking and ten hours watching television. But the reality is that there are significant variations among youth across the country with respect to the type and frequency of such digital media use (Jenkins, 2007). That holds true in schools as well, with significant differences in the type and frequency of technology use across states (*Education Week* and the Editorial Projects in Education Research Center, 2009b). A June 2009 Nielsen publication reported that, while children and youth do use electronic media in excess of six hours per day, using more than one medium simultaneously 23 percent of that time, they also enjoy reading books, magazines, and newspapers. Nielsen found that 77 percent of U.S. teens have their own mobile phone, 83 percent text message, and 56 percent use picture messaging. Teens average 2,899 text messages per month, which is fifteen times the average number of voice calls (191) they log each month. It would seem that email and phone calls are now considered their "father's mode of digital communication," not theirs (Nielsen Company, 2009).

The responsibility of educators is to ensure that today's students are ready to live, learn, work, and thrive in this high-tech, global, highly participatory world. To that end, U.S. school systems are conspicuously out of sync with the culture of today's society (U.S. Department of Education, 2009).

> The responsibility of educators is to ensure that today's students are ready to live, learn, work, and thrive in this high-tech, global, highly participatory world. To that end, U.S. school systems are conspicuously out of sync with the culture of today's society.

While the more progressive educators are seizing this moment in history to launch a quiet Web 2.0 revolution in preK–12 education, the majority have yet to act. A 2009 national survey conducted by the Consortium on School Networking (CoSN) suggests that the majority of American school districts are at a crossroads with Web 2.0. While school district administrators clearly acknowledge the potential of Web 2.0

tools for learning, the majority of school districts have yet to turn that potential to their students' advantage. According to administrators who responded to the CoSN survey, the top three reasons for using Web 2.0 in school are to (1) keep students interested and engaged in school, (2) meet the needs of different kinds of learners, and (3) develop the critical-thinking skills of students. To date, that potential remains untapped. Instead, many school districts are checking student technologies (such as smartphones, cell phones, iPods, and iTouches) at the schoolhouse door (Lemke, Coughlin, Garcia, Reifsneider, & Baas, 2009).

At the same time, U.S. Secretary of Education Arne Duncan is calling for school districts to innovate using technology. At a national institute in 2009, he said, "Technology presents a huge opportunity . . . good teachers can utilize new technology to accelerate learning and provide extended learning opportunities for students." He went on to say, "We must take advantage of this historic opportunity to use American Recovery and Reinvestment Act funds to bring broadband access and online learning to more communities" (U.S. Department of Education, 2009).

Nationally, there is a call to action for smart, innovative, and informed leadership in 21st century learning in preK–12 education. The combination of crisis and vision has served America well more than once in its two-hundred-year history as it has evolved as a nation. A crisis is now before the United States in the form of the global economic downturn. The question is whether policy leaders will create an informed, collective vision for 21st century learning to turn that crisis into opportunity, and thus turn a new page in American education.

Innovation: The Fuel for a Knowledge-Based Economy

Economists claim that innovation is the fuel for today's global, knowledge-based economy and for its recovery. As such, innovation must play a dual role in America's preK–12 education system: as a foundational principle to the new educational system, and as a 21st century skill acquired by professionals and students alike. *Innovation* is defined here as a creative idea that has achieved sufficient social and/ or professional acceptance so as to become the impetus for ongoing ripples of creativity and change (Drucker, 2002). To build upon the ideas of author Malcolm Gladwell (2000), an innovation is an idea that has tipped and is viral, influencing the system within which it spreads.

21st Century Learning and Student Engagement

In a significant turn of events, business and government leaders are now acknowledging the critical importance of preK–12 education to the economic future of the United States. To that end, policy leaders are advocating for the transformation of preK–12 schools into 21st century learning environments. For the purposes of this chapter, *21st century learning* is defined as the combination of a set of discrete 21st century skills (for example, critical thinking, collaboration, information literacy, and so on), and academic standards to be implemented through digital innovations in the context of emergent research from the cognitive sciences on how people best learn.

> In a significant turn of events, business and government leaders are now acknowledging the critical importance of preK–12 education to the economic future of the United States.

The intent of this chapter is to discuss three of the innovations rippling through our society that must inform America's bold new vision for 21st century learning. A key driver for this new vision is the current lack of student engagement in American schools that has contributed to an extremely high dropout rate nationally; nearly 30 percent of students who begin their ninth-grade year of high school do not graduate (*Education Week* and the Editorial Projects in Education Research Center, 2009a). Some of the disconnect to learning is explained through the concept of *flow*, which is defined as learning with the intensity cranked up—when the learner is at the top of his or her game (Csikszentmihalyi, 1990). Teachers create opportunities for students to get into that flow by balancing the complexity of the task with the students' current repertoire of learning strategies. Too much complexity without the requisite strategies results in frustrated students unable to do the work. On the other hand, if highly capable students with strong learning strategies are given too simple a task, they rapidly become bored. Figure 11.1 depicts the concept of flow (adapted from Csikszentmihalyi, 1990; Schwartz, Bransford, & Sears, 2006).

The research by Csikszentmihalyi (1990, 2002) shows that when that balance is perfected, students enter a flow experience in which

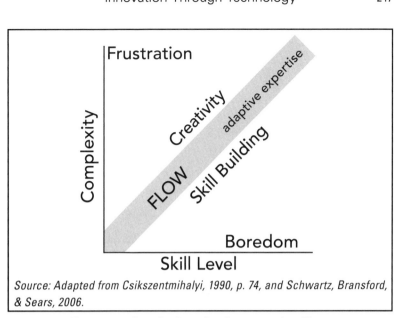

Figure 11.1: Developing adaptive expertise: Flow.

they are fully engaged, intrinsically motivated, and 110 percent invested in their learning. During flow experiences, many students report the sensation of time seeming to stand still as they engage in the experience. Leading cognitive science researchers suggest that the optimal flow experience balances skill level (that leads to efficiency in learning) with the level of task complexity (that leads to creativity and innovation). They contend that a balance between the two will lead to adaptive expertise in learners, which is necessary in dealing with the complexities of life in the 21st century.

The diagram in figure 11.2 (page 248) represents a framework for engaging students deeply in learning (Fredricks, Blumenfeld, & Paris, 2004; Lemke & Coughlin, 2008; Schlechty, 2002). In order to engage students fully in deep learning, they need to be motivated, curious learners who are in classrooms that scaffold that engagement through visualization, democratization of knowledge, and participatory learning.

Innovation One: Visualization

The link between visualization and learning can best be described as sense making. Physiologically, we are wired to swiftly process visuals, albeit differently than we process sound and text. Recent

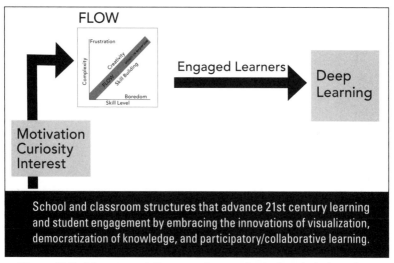

Figure 11.2: A framework for engaging students deeply in learning. Reprinted with permission from Metiri Group.

technological advances through functional magnetic resonance imaging (fMRI) scans confirm a dual coding system through which visuals and text/auditory input are processed in separate channels, presenting the potential for simultaneous augmentation of learning. Our working memory, which is where we do all our thinking, processes visuals and text/sound differently. Both of these channels are extremely limited in their capacity.

The implications of this for education are many. First and foremost, it is important to acknowledge that people learn better from combining visuals with text and sound than through using either process alone, provided the design of learning resources follows certain multimedia principles (Mayer & Moreno, 2003).

This set of seven principles related to multimedia and modality is based on the work of Richard Mayer, Roxanne Moreno, and other prominent researchers (Chan & Black, 2006; Ginns, 2005; Mayer, 2001; Mayer & Moreno, 2003).

1. **Multimedia Principle:** Student retention is improved through a combination of words (verbal or text) and visuals, rather than through words alone, provided it doesn't introduce redundancy of content.

2. **Spatial Contiguity Principle:** Students learn better when corresponding text and visuals are physically integrated rather than separated.

3. **Temporal Contiguity Principle:** Students learn better when corresponding text and visuals are temporally synchronized rather than separated in time.

4. **Split-Attention Principle:** Students learn better when extraneous words, pictures, and sounds are excluded rather than included.

5. **Modality Principle:** Students learn better when text is presented auditorily as speech rather than as on-screen text.

6. **Individual Differences Principle:** Design effects from these principles are higher for low-knowledge learners than for high-knowledge learners, and they are higher for high-spatial learners than for low-spatial learners.

7. **Direct Manipulation Principle:** As the complexity of the materials increases the impact of direct manipulation of the learning materials (animation, pacing) on transfer also increases.

Students engaged in learning that incorporates high-quality multimodal designs outperform, on average, students who learn using traditional approaches with single modes. This was borne out by a recent meta-analysis that revealed multimodality (the use of text or sound and visuals together) can positively shift achievement—provided the multimedia principles are followed. The meta-analysis found that, with noninteractive multimodal learning, such as text with illustrations or lectures with graphics, a student performing at the 50th percentile would, on average, increase performance to the 71st percentile (a gain of 21 percentiles). With interactive multimodal activities, such as simulations, modeling, and real-world experiences, a student at the 50th percentile would, on average, increase performance to the 82nd percentile (a gain of 32 percentiles) (Lemke, 2008).

> Students engaged in learning that incorporates high-quality multimodal designs outperform, on average, students who learn using traditional approaches with single modes.

Outside the classroom, the 21st century brings us a myriad of visual images in multimedia through a host of technology devices, at a rapid pace unparalleled in the history of mankind. Examples abound (for live links to the following examples, and to see a full-color version of this chapter, visit go.solution-tree.com/21stcenturyskills).

- *The New York Times* provides interactive media on the economic crisis that enables users to explore the recessions of past years and compare them to that of 2009 (Quealy, Roth, & Schneiderman, 2009).

- *The New York Times* also provided an interactive graphic during the 2008 presidential debates that innovatively displayed the candidate names mentioned by other presidential candidates during the series of debates leading up to the Iowa caucuses (Corum & Hossain, 2007).

Another interactive venue for learning through visualization is online gaming. It enables participants to join multiuser groups from around the world to interact competitively and cooperatively in games, such as *Civilization* and *World of Warcraft*, or interact via an avatar in *Second Life*. Visual media also enables us to exercise with interactive videos on the Wii; link up with friends via GPS mappings; capture and post visuals and video on YouTube; and access news in real time across the globe. A prime example of this last use was the coverage of recent protests and governmental reactions following the 2009 Iraqi elections. Real-time access occurred through Twitter posts, CNN news, and YouTube video and visuals from the smartphones of those present at the scene.

Every day, student users are exposed to visuals, videos, and animations embedded in television commercials and programming, multimedia sites, communications, interactive games, Web 2.0 tools, and presentations. Contrary to popular belief, students are not born with the full range of abilities required to interpret, think with, and build simple or complex multimedia communications that involve visuals, text, and/or voice and sound. They need to learn to become informed viewers, critics, thinkers, and producers of multimedia. Just as there is a grammar and syntax for text literacy, so there is for visual/multimodal literacy. The use of visualization is yet another way in which teachers can scaffold their students' learning.

Three strategies teachers might consider in using technology to capitalize on the power of visualization and build students' visual literacy are as follows:

1. Develop students as informed consumers of information.

2. Engage students in thinking critically and creatively using visuals.

3. Engage students in communicating using visuals.

Develop Students as Informed Consumers of Information

Students need to be informed consumers of visuals. One of the ways to achieve this is to help students analyze how advertisers manipulate images. KCTS Channel 9 in Seattle has produced a website that provides middle school students with opportunities to see the process in action. One of the offerings on the Don't Buy It: Get Media Smart site—Secrets of a Magazine Cover Model Revealed!—offers glimpses into the making of a "girl next door" into a fashion model (KCTS Television, 2004; http://pbskids.org/dontbuyit/entertainment/covermodel_1.html). Figure 11.3 shows screen captures from the process. These and other programs provide teens with an understanding of the digital manipulations routinely done in advertising. This is especially important given the pervasiveness of the idealization of models' bodies by consumers, which can lead to low self-esteem and

Source: KCTS Television, 2004, and PBS Kids. Reprinted with permission from Stephanie Malone, Drew Ringo, and KCTS Television.

Figure 11.3: From "girl next door" to fashion model.

eating disorders among children, teens, and adults. This recognition of the potential for manipulation of media is an important first step in media literacy. An informed consumer recognizes that people are impacted emotionally, psychologically, physiologically, and cognitively by visuals and, thus, interpret media accordingly.

Engage Students in Thinking Critically and Creatively Using Visuals

Visualization can also be an extraordinary tool in a student's repertoire for critical and creative thinking. The more authentic the work, the better. Teachers and students alike can use readily accessible public datasets to engage in authentic investigations of open-ended questions concerning a range of topics. Examples abound. One digital tool that is particularly compelling for schools is free of charge on a website called Gapminder (www.gapminder.org). This visualization tool is built around a dataset from the United Nations. The dataset includes worldwide demographics, health, energy, politics, security, and other key elements (Gapminder Foundation, 2009). Each country is represented by a dot on the screen. Each continent has a unique color. The user determines the dataset to be charted on each of the axes and then watches as the tool shows the shifts in countries' positions across the years. For example, the two charts in figure 11.4 display the percentage of adults with HIV charted against the income per person for the countries of the world in 1983 and then in 2007. Students can use the visualization tool to track HIV infection in specific countries, with options for looking at specific demographics and/or income brackets within those countries. The full datasets are available for export to further analyze the data (Gapminder Foundation, 2009; visit go.solution-tree.com/21stcenturyskills for live links and to see full-color versions of the graphics in this chapter).

The teachable moments that can be created with this tool are unlimited. Take a look at our second example in figure 11.5 (page 254). It is three screen shots of a data run in which the average life expectancy of citizens in South Africa is charted in relationship to the average income per person over time. This chart shows a strong, steady increase for income and life expectancy in South Africa from 1932 to 1980. Then, in 1980, the income began slipping backward,

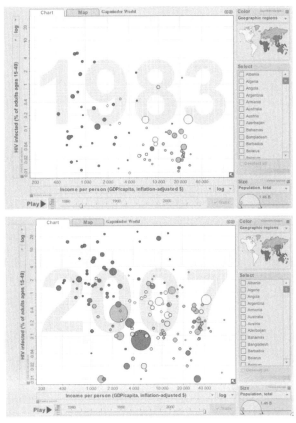

Source: Visualization from Gapminder World, powered by Trendalyzer from www.gapminder.org.

Figure 11.4: Charting the relationship over time between the percentage of adults with HIV in countries throughout the world in relation to the average income per person.

but the life expectancy continued to climb. In 1991, the upward trend in life expectancy reversed and began slowly decreasing; while at the same point in time, the income per person began slowly increasing. Those trends continued through 2007. Students exploring this data visualization quickly begin asking why the reversals happened in those specific years, and what factors caused the reversals. They might speculate that it was caused by a war, a natural disaster such as a famine or a tsunami, or perhaps industrialization. Students can rerun the scenario adding neighboring countries, zeroing in on

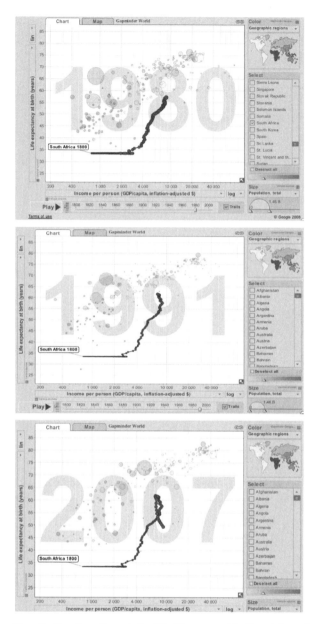

Figure 11.5: Life expectancy at birth by income in South Africa, 1800–2007.

particular years, charting new data elements, and, of course contextualizing their search through the use of other Web, print, and expert resources. This represents an extremely rich opportunity for critical thinking and problem solving with students.

Engage Students in Communicating Using Visuals

In addition to interpreting visuals, students should also understand how to create original visuals to communicate their ideas, represent their data, and tell their stories. Teachers can tap into websites that provide insight into which types of charts are most effective in displaying various types of datasets (see www.juiceanalytics.com/chartchooser/; visit go.solution-tree.com/21stcenturyskills for live links and to see a full-color version of the graphics in this chapter). As with any visual product, students need to adhere to the principles of multimodal design as described on pages 248–249. For example, in following the Spatial Contiguity Principle, charts should, where possible, integrate text into the design rather than using legends. In figure 11.6 (page 256), the cognitive load on working memory is higher for the nonintegrated example because the viewer has to look back and forth between the circle chart and the legend. In the integrated example, the load is reduced because the text is inside the chart.

A key strategy for scaffolding learning through visualization is the establishment and use of a set of guidelines that set high standards for the visual quality of student work. Many designers use a minimum of four key standards for design: contrast, repetition, alignment, and proximity (Williams, 2003) in concert with the multimedia principles listed previously. The visual design of digital products can increase or decrease the effectiveness of the communication:

- **Contrast**—The idea behind contrast is to ensure that each element of the visual design is *significantly different* from the others. The eye is attracted to differences; it is the element that attracts the reader to the work. For example, if two or more different sizes of fonts are used, use two that are very different, such as these:

9 point 18 point

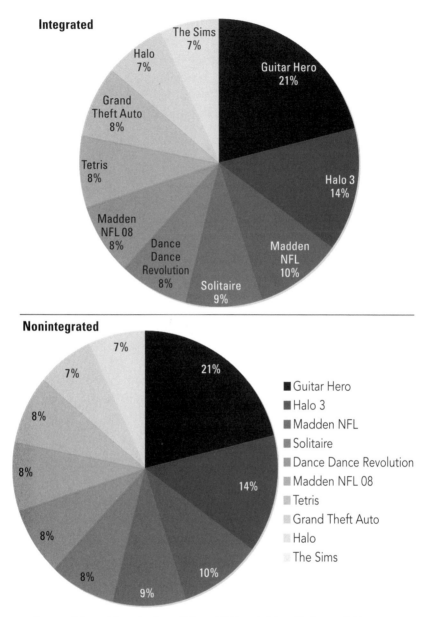

Integrated

- The Sims 7%
- Halo 7%
- Grand Theft Auto 8%
- Tetris 8%
- Madden NFL 08 8%
- Dance Dance Revolution 8%
- Solitaire 9%
- Madden NFL 10%
- Halo 3 14%
- Guitar Hero 21%

Nonintegrated

- 7%
- 7%
- 8%
- 8%
- 8%
- 8%
- 9%
- 10%
- 14%
- 21%

Legend:
- ■ Guitar Hero
- ■ Halo 3
- ■ Madden NFL
- ■ Solitaire
- ■ Dance Dance Revolution
- ■ Madden NFL 08
- ■ Tetris
- ■ Grand Theft Auto
- ■ Halo
- ■ The Sims

Source: Adapted from Lenhart, Kahne, Middaugh, Macgill, Evans, & Vitak, 2008. Data is from the Gaming and Civic Engagement Survey of Teens and Parents, November 2007–February 2008. Margin of error is ±3%.

Figure 11.6: The ten games most frequently played by teens.

- **Repetition**—Repeating elements of the design strengthens the unity of the piece. Repetition can be used with fonts, shapes, colors, thicknesses, spatial relationships, and so on. An example is shown in figure 11.7 (page 258) from the Technology Entertainment Design (TED) webpage (www.ted.com/talks/list), where each entry has the same style heading and format.

- **Alignment**—The way each element is placed on the page directs the order in which the reader's eye will move through the page. Thus, each element should have a visual connection with another element. In the example in figure 11.7, the eye is immediately drawn to the top headline and then drops to the visuals representing the six talks. For each talk, the proximity of the visual and text to its right causes the eye to flow to that text next, following the natural habit (in reading English) to move across the page, left to right. The natural inclination of the eye is to return to the visual but because the eye moves left to right, it returns to the text, and may repeat that eye movement several times. (The design thus creates eye movement that ensures all of the information in the text and visual will be processed.)

- **Proximity**—The eye prefers simple landscapes. Where possible, items that are related should be grouped close enough together to suggest to the eye that they are one visual element. This provides a clean structure, organizes information for the reader, and reduces visual noise. In the case of the Education Commission of the States Web heading in figure 11.8, there are four main elements, as outlined in the gray shading in the bottom portion of the graphic.

Visual literacy is a critical component of what it means to be literate in the 21st century. It can augment and extend students' critical thinking; deepen their understanding in science, math, social studies, and other core subjects; establish strong ties between the arts and sciences; provide a range of opportunities for expressions of what they know and are able to do; and help to ensure that they will be informed consumers of media.

Source: Technology Entertainment Design, n.d., www.ted.com. Reprinted with permission.

Figure 11.7: Example of repetition and alignment.

Source: Education Commission of the States, 2010, http://www.ecs.org.
Reprinted with permission.

Figure 11.8: Example of proximity.

Innovation Two: Democratization of Knowledge

The Internet has opened up a new opportunity for people to learn throughout their lives in both formal and informal environments, individually and in groups. Low-cost access to technology devices connected to high-speed broadband is now available to the majority of the population. Many communities are seeking broadband solutions to ensure equitable access for all members of the community. Despite this rapid growth of broadband in communities and homes, schools continue to play a role in ensuring that all students have robust access—at least within the school day.

The very ecology of learning is evolving. People are informally learning based on personal, professional, family, work, and community needs, interests, or responsibilities. Bridget Barron, a researcher from Stanford, has suggested that adolescent learning should be reconsidered in light of the informal learning opportunities now available to students (Barron, 2006). The diagram in figure 11.9 (page 260), based on Barron's work, identifies a host of formal and informal learning situations in which preK–12 students may be involved.

The implications for schools are significant. School is just one node among the learning contexts available to students; educators should be actively considering how to extend the formal learning launched in schools into other nodes. In addition, educators should seek to

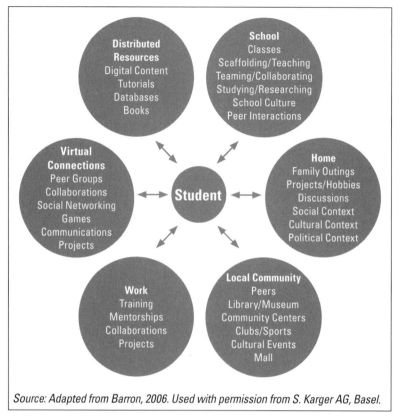

Source: Adapted from Barron, 2006. Used with permission from S. Karger AG, Basel.

Figure 11.9: Contexts for 21st century learning.

become sufficiently familiar with the informal learning students are actively engaged in outside of school in order to integrate student interests with formal learning experiences. The intent would be to bring added relevancy and student interest to the formal work within the classroom and to integrate, to some degree, students' formal and informal learning. Another responsibility of schools is to ensure that students gain knowledge and expertise in navigating, interacting, and learning within digital environments. The taxonomy that one might consider in thinking about the democratization of knowledge includes:

- **Browsing the Net**—The universal adoption of *google* as a verb says it all. Information is truly at the fingertips of the informed Internet navigator. The key word is *informed*. While information is available, it is critical that schools provide intensive work with students on informed searching, navigating the visible and invisible Web, critiquing websites to check for reliable sources, and persevering to ensure comprehensive, balanced searches.

- **Learning objects**—A learning object is a self-contained resource, usually digital and/or web-based, that can be used and reused to support learning. Many of the first learning objects were in the form of virtual manipulatives—dynamic objects through which students could explore properties to further their knowledge (Utah State University, 2007). Today, learning objects take the form of YouTube videos, iPod audio and/or video files, interactive websites, scripted slide shows, and so on. That means that twenty-four hours a day, seven days a week, these objects are available to interested learners. Learning objects can be used to supplement face-to-face classrooms, can be embedded in virtual classes, and can easily be accessed by students who are studying, but have not yet mastered the topic. For example, the National Council of Teachers of Mathematics Illuminations website provides many virtual manipulatives, including one that enables students to manipulate the areas that represent each element of the equation $(a + b)^2 = a^2 + 2ab + b^2$ (National Council of Teachers of Mathematics, 2009; visit http://illuminations.nctm.org/Activity/Detail.aspx?ID=127 to view this manipulative). A second example is a calculator students can use to determine the emissions of their homes. The program enables them to manipulate entries to see the results on carbon emissions (U.S. Environmental Protection Agency, n.d.; visit http://www.epa.gov/CHP/basic/calculator.html to view this manipulative).

- **Simulations**—The depth of student learning increases when students are able to experiment with the parameters behind a visual simulation. For example, in a new generation of tools called Yenka, a U.K. firm enables students to learn some rudimentary steps in programming by controlling a dancer's onscreen actions through their creation and running of a flowchart. These resources are available, free of charge, for use by individuals in their homes, and can also be licensed for a fee by schools (Crocodile Clips, 2009; visit www.yenka.com/en/Yenka_Programming/ to view the simulation). A free-of-charge simulation, SimCalcMathWorlds, enables students to experiment with rate, linear functions, and proportionality through graphing calculators and computers that generate math functions. For example, students are able to determine speed and rate of acceleration of two fish along a linear path while simultaneously watching the functions charted on a grid (see www.kaputcenter.umassd.edu/projects/simcalc/).

- **University courses available to the public**—In the first decade of the 21st century, many universities in the United States have made their courses available online. Currently, MIT Courseware (Massachusetts Institute of Technology, 2009) and Rice Connexions (Rice University, n.d.) have made thousands of courses available. Another digital access point for thousands of free university courses, lectures, and interviews is iTunes University.

- **Online courses for K–12 students and teachers**—According to a meta-analysis on online learning released by the U.S. Department of Education in May of 2009, online learning for both K–12 students and teachers is one of the fastest growing trends in educational technology (Means, Toyama, Murphy, Bakia, & Jones, 2009). The report indicated that the number of K–12 students enrolled in technology-based distance learning courses had increased by 65 percent from the 2002–2003 school year to the 2004–2005 school year. A recent report by the Sloan Consortium (Picciano & Seaman, 2009) estimated that more than one million U.S. K–12 students were engaged in online courses in 2007–2008, which represents a 47 percent increase since 2005–2006. The authors of that study reported a wide range of needs that were fulfilled through online courses, from those seeking advanced placement and college-level courses, to those needing credit recovery or remediation. This access provides a tremendous opportunity for students who are seeking an alternative to the local offerings in terms of courses available, timing of courses, and mode of learning.

The Florida Virtual High School (FVHS) is an example of one of the largest virtual high schools. In the 2007–2008 school year, FVHS enrolled approximately one hundred thousand students nationally (diplomas are granted by the student's local community school). FVHS announced in the summer of 2009 a new American History, full-credit high school course to be conducted completely within the gaming environment Conspiracy Code (Nagel, 2009).

- **Online course units**—Many school districts and individual teachers are leveraging online learning as a supplement to classroom work. In some cases, teachers are using online units as an integral component of their courses. One example of online units is from the federally funded web-based Inquiry Science site hosted at the University of California, Berkeley (http://wise.berkeley.edu). The science inquiry units offered on this site are free of charge to participating schools. Four of the self-contained units are as follows: Airbags: Too Fast, Too Furious? (Grades 11–12); Global Climate Change: Who's to Blame? (Grades 6–9); TELS: Mitosis and Meiosis (Grades 9–12); and Wolf Ecology and Population Management (Grades 7–12). The units are typically four to five days (one class period) in length, are aligned to standards, include lesson plans, and are highly interactive for student teams through the website.

The democratization of knowledge provides the opportunity for lifelong individual and group learning. For students to leverage that opportunity fully requires critical thinking, information literacy, and a measure of self-direction, all of which need to be developed in part by our school systems. The democratization of knowledge also provides tremendous opportunities for educators to begin transforming their schools into physical and virtual places of 21st century learning. One of the critical differences from conventional education is a solid foundation in inquiry learning that is student-centered and authentic. Educators are at a crossroads. They can embrace this democratization of knowledge by authentically connecting their students' formal and informal learning. Or they can ignore it and run the risk of obsolescence, becoming certification mills for the interactive learning that takes place out of school.

Innovation Three: Participatory Learning

Today's schools are focused on individual acquisition of knowledge, student by student, despite the fact that, increasingly, society, community, and work emphasize teaming, collaboration, and participatory learning.

While the Internet of the 1990s gave previously underrepresented groups a public voice, the Web 2.0 tools of the 21st century have given rise to a participatory culture. The advent of Facebook, YouTube, Flickr, Twitter, RSS feeds, GPS tracking, smart mobile devices, and robust international broadband networks have enabled millions to interact in real time twenty-four hours a day, seven days a week. Web 2.0 tools have enabled everyone with sufficiently robust Internet access to post, exchange, and comment on video, audio, and text files; share tagging perspectives through sites such as Delicious.com; interact on social networking sites; participate in live chats; interact and share perspectives within communities of interest/practice; use GPS tracking and texting to connect in real time; participate in interactive, online games and gaming communities; and stay connected and informed through RSS feeds, Flickr, and Twitter.

New social patterns are emerging at unprecedented rates. People now expect to be active participants in theses virtual communities, not just passive observers. At the heart of these communities is the evolutionary nature of community norms, content, discourse, and life cycle. Yes, someone establishes the foundational tools, but the community is seldom carefully and strategically planned. Rather, it evolves over time, shaped by dialogue, discussion, shared resources, responses to inquiries, commentary and critique, and levels of participation based on perceived value. An innovative example is the use of Facebook by a teacher to engage students in learning about the periodic table. (Visit go.solution-tree.com/21stcenturyskills for live links and to see full-color versions of the graphics in this chapter.)

At High Tech Middle School in San Diego, students used social networking to personally identify with the elements in the periodic table (see figure 11.10; http://staff.hthcv.hightechhigh.org/~jmorris/period%20table%20page.html). Students were asked to list personal characteristics, identify the attributes of elements, and then select which elements' attributes most closely aligned to their personal

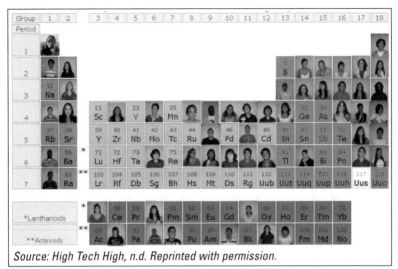

Source: High Tech High, n.d. Reprinted with permission.

Figure 11.10: The Periodic Table: Students' Facebook pages on the elements.

characteristics. Once their Facebook page was established for their element, they proceeded to "friend" other elements in alignment with their elements' attributes.

By clicking on the live site, each student's Facebook page reveals the characteristics of attributes they share with the element they believe aligns most closely to him or her. See figure 11.11 (page 266) for an excerpt.

That participatory culture is reflected in today's economic globalization. Multinational corporations in particular epitomize this participatory culture, where the success of an individual is directly tied to the success of the teams within which they work. Often the effectiveness of the teams lies in the social and emotional maturity of the members, the diversity of members' expertise, and members' leadership and commitment. This is indicative of Web 2.0 participatory cultures where the power lies in the quality, frequency, expertise, backgrounds, and commitment of the participants.

From an educational perspective, it is important to note that participation is not synonymous to collaboration. A participatory culture can range from the harmonious to the acrimonious. The topic of interest that brings a community together may range from social justice to the intellectual, the political, the social, the economic,

---

Student Entry: What I have in common with Hydrogen.

Gets Along Well With Others: I have an easy-going nature about me and would consider myself to have a go-with-the-flow personality. Just like Hydrogen, I like to be near others and hanging out with friends any chance I get. In this fast-paced world we live in, sometimes it's nice to just spend some time relaxing with friends.

Low Boiling Point (-252.87 C): Generally, I am a calm and collected individual. As is true of anyone, I have my moments of high stress and low patience, but for the most part I am a calm and caring individual. I share my cool nature with Hydrogen.

Just like Hydrogen, I am little but powerful. I have always thought of myself as someone who is small but mighty. I am a strong individual who can take care of herself and others. I am someone you can depend on for strength and dependability. I share this strength and usefulness with Hydrogen.

Source: High Tech High, n.d. Reprinted with permission.

Figure 11.11: Student's Facebook page on Hydrogen.

a community perspective, or simply entertainment and personal interest. The size of the community, its purposes, its longevity, and the norms within those communities vary considerably.

As the three innovations (visualization, democratization of knowledge, and participatory learning) introduced in this chapter ripple through society, people are using their ingenuity to use those innovations for their own purposes. In doing so, they continually influence and redefine the very ecology of the society—hence the ripple effect. This same phenomenon is true of learning. Researcher Kai Hakkarainen and his colleagues discuss how educators think about learning in three distinct ways (Hakkarainen, Palonen, Paavola, & Lehtinen, 2004). The first is an acquisition model, which emphasizes what the individual knows and is individually able to learn. The second model is participation. In this case, the educator goes beyond the acquisition model to acknowledge the social aspect of learning. While students in this model might engage in collaborative work, the measure of success is still largely focused on how much the individual is able to learn, accompanied perhaps by a measure of the student's ability to work within a group, community, network, or culture. The third model is knowledge creation. In this model, the output of the group or community is a valued asset, complemented by a measure of the individual's contributions to the team and acquisition of knowledge. The reality is that educators should be encompassing all three perspectives on learning.

Today's schools are out of sync with society—they are still operating on the acquisition model. They do register some forays into the participation model through collaborative learning, but they neither regularly establish structures that measure and value the group or community's collective knowledge construction, nor document the contributions of the student to that work. This translates into a need to restructure learning, teaching, and assessment to increasingly emphasize and value the participation in groups and the group's knowledge creation, in addition to the individual's acquisition of knowledge. This is necessary if schools are to graduate students who are ready to thrive in this new participatory culture.

Implications of the Three Innovations

Students who are learning in schools influenced by the innovations of visualization, democratization of knowledge, and participatory cultures need different skills than prior generations. Tremendously important to these students are the skills discussed throughout this book, including critical and creative thinking, self-direction, collaboration, multimodal learning, and adaptability. The ecology of learning will itself evolve over time, with students taking stronger, more active roles in shaping their learning trajectories, often blending informal and formal learning in face-to-face, virtual, and hybrid learning never before possible. One of the immediate ways in which schools can immerse students in such learning is through authentic learning. Such learning is defined by Fred Newmann as learning that has three key elements: (1) deep inquiry (Higher Education Academy, 2009) into the subject matter (as opposed to surface learning), (2) relevancy beyond the school day (students are working with teams outside of the school on projects that matter), and (3) knowledge construction (students are producing and constructing actual products to contribute to the community of interest as they demonstrate what their team now understands and what they individually understand).

Getting There From Here

To ensure U.S. students are ready to thrive in today's global, knowledge-based society, our schools need to embrace the innovations of visualization, democratization of knowledge, and participatory cultures for learning. This begins through leadership's creation of a culture of openness, risk taking, and adaptability within schools, where learners, teachers, and their communities can investigate how these innovations will change, grow, and adapt learning inside and outside of school. A first step is to gauge your school's readiness for 21st century learning. Metiri Group's Dimensions of 21st Century Learning (D21) provide a framework for gauging such readiness (Metiri Group, 2008):

- **Vision**—Does your school system have a forward-thinking, common vision for 21st century learning that represents societal innovations to serve as a unifying and energizing force of change?

- **Systems thinking/leadership**—Are all educators and staff thinking and acting systemically to embrace innovation in ways that advance the vision?

- **21st century skills/learning**—Has your school system adopted 21st century skills in the context of research-informed learning strategies?

- **21st century learning environments**—Is the vision of 21st century learning coming to life in your schools?

- **Professional competencies**—Are your teachers, administrators, and other staff ready to facilitate, lead, and assess 21st century learning among students, the community, and parents?

- **Access and infrastructure**—Is the access to technology devices and the infrastructure sufficiently robust to support 21st century learning?

- **Accountability**—Are learners, educators, and the system held accountable for making progress, while also provided with the data and support for achieving results?

For educators, this framework translates into a need for leadership that (1) establishes a culture of openness to new ideas in and outside of education, (2) encourages calculated risk taking, and (3) is sufficiently insightful to establish a process that accelerates the spread of powerful, creative ideas that have the potential to "tip and ripple." Authors from the *Harvard Business Review* suggest such leaders should be strategists, those who generate organization change in highly collaborative ways that, at times, challenge and change current assumptions (Rooke & Torbert, 2005).

It is time to challenge assumptions in today's preK–12 school systems and embrace the ripple effects of these three innovations: visualization, democratization of knowledge, and participatory learning.

References

Associated Press. (2006, October 10). Google buys YouTube for $1.65 billion. *MSNBC online*. Accessed at www.msnbc.msn.com/id/15196982 on July 1, 2009.

Barron, B. (2006). Interest and self-sustained learning as catalysts of development: A learning ecology perspective. *Human Development, 49*(4), 193–224.

Chan, M. S., & Black, J. B. (2006, April). *Learning Newtonian mechanics with an animation game: The role of presentation format on mental model acquisition.* Paper presented at the American Education Research Association Annual Conference, San Francisco.

Corum, J., & Hossain, F. (2007, December 15). Naming names. *The New York Times*. Accessed at www.nytimes.com/interactive/2007/12/15/us/politics/DEBATE.html on October 10, 2008.

Csikszentmihalyi, M. (1990). *Flow: The psychology of optimal experience.* New York: Harper and Row.

Crocodile Clips. (2009). *Yenka programming.* Accessed at www.yenka.com/en/Yenka_Programming/ on July 7, 2009.

Education Week and the Editorial Projects in Education (EPE) Research Center. (2009a, June 11). *Diplomas count 2009: Broader horizons: The challenge of college readiness for all students.* Bethesda, MD: Authors.

Education Week and the Editorial Projects in Education (EPE) Research Center. (2009b). *National technology report: Breaking away from tradition.* Bethesda, MD: Authors.

Drucker, P. F. (2002, August). The discipline of innovation. *Harvard Business Review, 80*(8), 95–103.

Foray, D., & Lundvall, B. D. (1998). *The knowledge-based economy: From the economics of knowledge to the learning economy.* In D. Need, G. Siesfeld, & J. Cefola, *The economic impact of knowledge* (pp. 115–122). New York: Butterworth-Heinemann.

Fredricks, J. A., Blumenfeld, P. C., & Paris, A. H. (2004). School engagement: Potential of the concept, state of the evidence. *Review of Educational Research, 74*(1), 59–109.

Gapminder Foundation. (2009). *Gapminder: Unveiling the beauty of statistics for a fact based world view.* Accessed at www.gapminder.org on June 5, 2009.

Ginns, P. (2005). Meta-analysis of the modality effect. *Learning and Instruction, 15*(4), 313–331.

Gladwell, M. (2000). *The tipping point: How little things can make a big difference.* Boston: Little, Brown.

Global System for Mobile Communication. (2009, February 11). *Mobile world celebrates four billion connections. GSM Association press release.* Accessed at www.gsmworld.com/newsroom/press-releases/2009/2521.htm on June 20, 2009.

Hakkarainen, K., Palonen, T., Paavola, S., & Lehtinen, E. (2004). *Communities of networked expertise: Professional and educational perspectives.* Amsterdam: Elsevier Science.

High Tech High. (n.d.). *We are the periodic table of elements.* Accessed at http://staff.hthcv.hightechhigh.org/~jmorris/period%20table%20page.html on January 28, 2010.

The Higher Education Academy. (2009). *Deep and surface approaches to learning.* Accessed at www.engsc.ac.uk/er/theory/learning.asp on October 1, 2008.

Jenkins, H. (2007, December 5). *Reconsidering digital immigrants. Confessions of an aca-fan: The official weblog of Henry Jenkins.* Accessed at www.henryjenkins.org/2007/12/reconsidering_digital_immigran.html on June 8, 2009.

Jeong-hyun, L. (n.d.). In *Wikipedia, the free encyclopedia.* Accessed at http://en.wikipedia.org/wiki/Jeong-Hyun_Lim on July 5, 2009.

KCTS Television. (2004). *Don't buy it: Get media smart.* Accessed at http://pbskids.org/dontbuyit/entertainment/covermodel_1.html on May 20, 2009.

Lemke, C. (2008). *Multimodal learning through media: What the research says.* Accessed at www.cisco.com/web/strategy/docs/education/Multimodal-Learning-Through-Media.pdf on June 6, 2008.

Lemke, C., & Coughlin, E. (2008). *Student engagement.* Culver City, CA: Metiri Group.

Lemke, C., Coughlin, E., Garcia, L., Reifsneider, D., & Baas, J. (2009, March). *Leadership for Web 2.0 in education: Promise and reality.* Culver City, CA: Metiri Group.

Lenhart, A., Kahne, J., Middaugh, E., Macgill, A. R., Evans, C., & Vitak, J. (2008). *Teens, video games, and civics*. Washington, DC: Pew Internet & American Life Project.

Massachusetts Institute of Technology. (2009). *MIT OpenCourseWare*. Accessed at http://ocw.mit.edu on June 9, 2009.

Mayer, R. (2001). *Multi-media learning*. Cambridge, UK: Cambridge University Press.

Mayer, R. E., & Moreno, R. (2003). Nine ways to reduce cognitive load in multimedia learning. In R. Bruning, C. A. Horn, & L. M. PytlikZillig (Eds.), *Web-based learning: What do we know? Where do we go?* (pp. 23–44). Greenwich, CT: Information Age Publishing.

Moreno, R., & Mayer, R. E. (2005). *A learner-centered approach to multimedia explanations: Deriving instructional design principles from cognitive theory*. Accessed at http://imej.wfu.edu/articles/2000/2/05/index.asp on October 8, 2008.

Means, B., Toyama, Y., Murphy, R., Bakia, M., & Jones, K. (2009, May). *Evaluation of evidence-based practices in online learning: A meta-analysis and review of online learning studies* (Report No. ED-04-CO-0040 Task 0006). Washington, DC: U.S. Department of Education. Accessed at www.ed.gov/rschstat/eval/tech/evidence-based-practices/finalreport.doc on June 30, 2009.

Metiri Group. (2008). *Dimensions of 21st century learning*. Accessed at http://D21.metiri.com on July 7, 2009.

Nagel, D. (2009, June 2). Virtual school begins rolling out game-based courses. *THE Journal*. Accessed at http://thejournal.com/Articles/2009/06/02/Virtual-School-Begins-Rolling-Out-GameBased-Courses.aspx on June 8, 2009.

National Council of Teachers of Mathematics. (2009). *A geometric investigation of (a + b)²*. Illuminations. Accessed at http://illuminations.nctm.org/ActivityDetail.aspx?ID=127 on July 7, 2009.

National School Board Association. (2007). *Creating and connecting: Research and guidelines on online social—and educational—networking*. Alexandria, VA: Author.

Nielsen Company. (2009). *How teens use media: A Nielsen report on the myths and realities of teen media trends*. New York: Author. Accessed at http://blog.nielsen.com/nielsenwire/reports/nielsen_howteensusemedia_june09.pdf on July 6, 2009.

Official Google Blog. (2008, July 25). *We knew the Web was big*. Accessed at http://googleblog.blogspot.com/2008/07/we-knew-web-was-big.html on June 20, 2009.

Picciano, A. G., & Seaman, J. (2009). *K–12 online learning: A 2008 follow-up of the survey of U.S. school district administrators*. Newburyport, MA: The Sloan Consortium. Accessed at www.sloanconsortium.org/publications/survey/pdf/k-12_online_learning_2008.pdf on April 4, 2009.

Quealy, K., Roth, G., & Schneiderman, R. M. (2009, January 26). How the government dealt with past recessions. *The New York Times.* Accessed at www.nytimes.com/interactive/2009/01/26/business/economy/20090126 -recessions-graphic.html on May 10, 2009.

Reed, N. (2008). *GigaTweet.* Accessed at http://popacular.com/gigatweet on July 7, 2009.

Rice University. (n.d.). *Connexions.* Accessed at http://cnx.org/ on June 6, 2009.

Rooke, D., & Torbert, W. R. (2005, April). Seven transformations of leadership. *Harvard Business Review, 83*(4), 67–76.

Schlechty, P. C. (2002). *Working on the work: An action plan for teachers, principals, and superintendents.* San Francisco: Jossey-Bass.

Schwartz, D. L., Bransford, J. D., & Sears, D. (2006). Innovation and efficiency in learning and transfer. In J. P. Mestre (Ed.), *Transfer of Learning from a Modern Multidisciplinary Perspective* (pp. 40–59).

Shah, J. A. (2005, December 20). *Guitar* [YouTube video]. Accessed at www .youtube.com/watch?v=QjA5faZF1A8 on July 5, 2009.

Singer, A. (2009, January 12). Social media, Web 2.0 and Internet stats. *The Future Buzz.* Accessed at http://thefuturebuzz.com/2009/01/12/social-media-web -20-internet-numbers-stats on July 2, 2009.

Technology Entertainment Design. (n.d.). *TED: Ideas worth spreading—Talks page.* Accessed at www.ted.com/talks/list on February 18, 2010.

U.S. Department of Education. (2009, June 8). *Robust data gives us the roadmap to reform.* [Speech Secretary Arne Duncan gave at the Fourth Annual IES Research Conference]. Accessed at www.ed.gov/news/speeches/2009/06/06082009 .html on June 19, 2009.

U.S. Department of Education. (2009, June 26). *U.S. Department of Education study finds that good teaching can be enhanced with new technology.* U.S. Department of Education Press Release. Accessed at www.ed.gov/news/ pressreleases/2009/06/06262009.html on May 10, 2009.

U.S. Environmental Protection Agency. (n.d.). *Household emissions calculator.* Accessed at http://epa.gov/climatechange/emissions/ind_calculator2.html #c=transportation&p=reduceOnTheRoad&m=calc_WYCD on July 7, 2009.

Utah State University. (2007). *National Library of Virtual Manipulatives.* Accessed at http://nlvm.usu.edu/en/nav/grade_g_2.html on May 20, 2009.

Williams, R. (2003). *The non-designers design book.* Berkeley, CA: Peachpit Press.

Alan November

Alan November, M.Ed., is recognized internationally as a leader in education technology. He began his career as an oceanography teacher and dorm counselor at an island reform school for boys in Boston Harbor. He has been a director of an alternative high school, computer coordinator, technology consultant, and university lecturer. As practitioner, designer, and author, Alan has guided schools, government organizations, and industry leaders as they plan to improve quality with technology. His writing includes dozens of articles and the best-selling book, *Empowering Students With Technology* (2001). November was cofounder of the Stanford Institute for Educational Leadership Through Technology and is most proud of being selected as one of the original five national Christa McAuliffe Educators.

In this chapter, November reinforces Pearlman's rationale for redesigned schools. He cautions against using expensive technology to continue the trend of schools as managers of student learning. It's time, he says, to redesign not only the physical structure but the culture of schools. Technology makes it possible for students to become less dependent on schools and take more responsibility for managing their own learning.

Chapter 12

Technology Rich, Information Poor

Alan November

Yesterday, I was in one of the most beautiful and caring independent schools I have ever visited. It had resources that took my breath away. When I addressed the combined junior and senior class, many of whom would be attending top-ranked universities upon graduation, I asked them if they knew why my website was ranked third out of more than seven hundred million results when I typed the word *November* into Google. Their responses were immediate and confident:

- "You have the most important content."

- "You paid Google."

- "Your site has the most visits."

All of these answers are incorrect. The students were so overly confident that they knew what they actually did not know—it was frightening. The teachers were shocked at what their students did not know. The Web has become the dominant media of our society, yet we are not teaching our children critical-thinking skills in this media. Calculate how easy it would be to manipulate people who believe the most important information is at the top of their search results. Also consider how many students (and adults) only look at the top page of results when they do a search. Or, how many only use one search engine when they are doing research. Why do we teach students to use PowerPoint and build wikis before we teach them to be literate in the most powerful information media ever invented by society?

"Houston, we have a problem."

Most educators agree that we need 21st century schools and that we need to prepare students for the information economy. However, what does this really mean, and what are the essential questions and planning processes needed to prepare our students to have a global work ethic?

> Most educators agree that we need 21st century schools and that we need to prepare students for the information economy. However, what does this really mean, and what are the essential questions and planning processes needed to prepare our students to have a global work ethic?

What it does not mean is giving every student a laptop without fundamentally changing our concept of curriculum, assessment, and the role of the teacher and learner. This chapter will focus on designing a planning process to help us manage the transition from paper as the dominant technology for storing and retrieving information (a static technology) to digital (a dynamic technology).

From Static to Digital Technology

Up until now, due largely to an initial lack of digital technology in our schools, the traditional planning paradigm has been to launch a technology planning committee. The driving questions in this approach are as follows: How much technology do we need? Where do we need it? And, what technical skills do our teachers and students need? However, technology is only the digital plumbing. Of course we have to ask how many computers/interactive boards/PDAs we need, where to put them, and how to train teachers and students to use them. But simply doing a really good job with the technology planning paradigm is not sufficient. What will distinguish our use of technology in our education system is preparing children to have a global work ethic. Technical skills are necessary, but they are not enough.

One of my clients, an executive in a high-tech company, calls what schools do with technology planning akin to "spray and pray" planning. The spray-and-pray model invests in a technocentric process that leads to bolting technology on top of traditional work instead of rethinking the work. In other words, students are usually given the same kinds of assignments and roles they had before the technology was implemented. For example, I have walked into many laptop schools and watched every student in a classroom taking notes with what amounts to a $2,000 pencil. As the famous quote goes, "The process whereby the lecture notes of the instructor get transferred to the notebooks of the students without passing through the brains of either" does not describe a 21st century practice, regardless of the tool used for the transfer. When I ask students to describe the most useful application of their laptops, the standard answer is "taking notes."

The saddest outcome of the spray-and-pray model of planning is that, in some cases, we have actually lowered the quality of student work in our rush to add technology. Plagiarism has significantly increased. Many students are looking for the easiest way to finish an assignment, and there has been a loss of deep understanding of concepts as students whip together their homework and projects. Students are using Web 2.0 tools (often blocked by filters in schools) to collaborate over social-networking sites to "share" homework. As more handheld devices, such as smartphones, come to school, the potential for distraction escalates. Read *The Dumbest Generation: How the Digital Age Stupefies Young Americans and Jeopardizes Our Future (Or, Don't Trust Anyone Under 30)* by Mark Bauerlein (2008) to learn more.

We are now in a cycle of constant change and innovation. We are approaching the handle curve of the hockey-stick pattern of change—straight up. There will be an explosion of new technologies (have you seen the Smartpen?), and we will continue to see the price of the hardware plummet and a plethora of new software tools emerge. We will see the end of textbooks and the explosion of online learning. It is up to us to take this historic time of change and to think

We have a chance to redesign the culture of teaching and learning to a more empowering authentic model of learning. This is the time to think big and to expand our boundaries of what we believe our children can achieve.

deeply about the implications of these powerful new learning and teaching tools and global connectivity. We have a chance to redesign the culture of teaching and learning to a more empowering authentic model of learning. This is the time to think big and to expand our boundaries of what we believe our children can achieve.

Big Idea Assumptions

While nearly impossible to predict, in the middle of this explosion of innovation, educators have to sort out what skills we teach today that will have a chance of outlasting the changes in the technology. Currently, schools are not designed for constant adaptation to innovations from society.

Let's start with the big picture trends that should guide our thinking about preparing our students to have a global work ethic:

- Immediate access to an over-abundance of information—How do we make sense of it all? YouTube serves up one billion videos per day. As of November 2009, there were 27.3 million tweets on Twitter per day.

- Essentially free global communications—We already have a range of tools such as Skype that provide essentially free global communication. Every one of our classrooms can become a global communications center.

- Job markets flowing to the people who can provide the highest quality at the lowest price wherever they happen to live—In his book *The World Is Flat,* Thomas Friedman (2005) explains that the Web creates opportunities for people around the world to earn a living without the need to immigrate. Are we preparing our children to have a global work ethic?

In direct response to the big picture trends are these specific skills, our students must learn:

- How to make meaning with overwhelming amounts of information

- How to work with people around the world (empathy)

- How to be self-directed, interdependent, and a superb lifelong learner

Our students must learn:

- How to make meaning with overwhelming amounts of information
- How to work with people around the world (empathy)
- How to be self-directed, interdependent, and a superb lifelong learner

If we wanted to prepare our students for the global economy, we would immediately turn every classroom into a global communications center linking students to authentic audiences around the world. We would be providing professional development for teachers to redesign their assignments to be more rigorous and authentic. We would be laser-beam focused on redefining what it means to be literate. Learning to read from books is essential but no longer sufficient. Where we now teach the grammar of paper, we will need to teach the grammar of the Internet as well. Too many adults read the Internet as if it were paper shoved down a wire. The Internet has its own grammar and syntax and architecture of information. It is amazing how many people are being manipulated by a media they mistakenly believe they understand.

Most importantly, we would be redefining the role of the learner, the teacher, and even the family.

When my work takes me overseas to developing countries such as China or Singapore, there is a clear sense of urgency by educators to connect their students to people around the world and to empower students to take more ownership of their own learning. For example, Singapore has crafted a national vision called "Thinking Schools, Learning Nation." One of the basic design elements is to "teach less, learn more." There is a clear understanding that the role of the teacher and the learner must fundamentally change if the country wants to prepare students to have a global work ethic. Students who are taught to be dependent upon the teacher managing learning for them will not necessarily develop the lifelong learning and problem-solving skills that are required in the global economy.

Re-engineering our planning process from technology planning to global work-ethic planning requires that we ask questions

Re-engineering our planning process from technology planning to global work-ethic planning requires that we ask questions that focus on the results of our investment.

that focus on the results of our investment. The real revolution is not the laptops and the wiring. The laptops we buy today will soon be replaced. What will not go away is access to the overwhelming amounts of shifting (and growing) information and global communications. Our planning focus must shift to clearly define what it means to be Web literate and to link our students to authentic audiences around the world and across the curriculum.

Currently, how many of our students graduate from school with a global work ethic? How many students have the discipline to manage their own learning? How many students understand how to organize teams of people from around the world to solve increasingly complex problems? Questions like these should be driving our planning.

Once we have the infrastructure (network, hardware, software) in place, we should be asking what information does everyone need in order to be the most effective teacher, learner, administrator, or parent. For example, with a computational knowledge engine such as Wolframalpha (www.wolframalpha.com), students can take responsibility for correcting their own math homework as they generate the graph and the solution set for any equation. While it may sound counterintuitive to ask students to correct their own homework, research suggests that immediate feedback while learning is very important. In his book *Flow: The Psychology of Optimal Experience*, Mihaly Csikszentmihalyi (1990) lists immediate *feedback* as critical to optimal learning. Again, while the technology is essential, a computational knowledge engine basically provides students with access to information they have never had before. It also places the learner in a more powerful position of managing his or her own learning.

With access to dynamic tools such as Wolframalpha, we can raise our expectations that our students can design their own homework. Further, if we add another free tool such as Jing (www.jingproject .com), our students can create screencast (video screen capture) tutorials for their classmates with their solutions. I have talked to students in Eric Marcos' classroom in Santa Monica, where he maintains a library of tutorials on a class website (www.mathtrain

.tv). One of Eric's young tutorial designers, age twelve, explained to me that she felt much more responsibility when she was challenged to design tutorials for her classmates. She said, "This is real work instead of homework." You can listen to her at www.mathtrain.tv. Take a look at her tutorial on factoring with prime numbers. More than five hundred people already have.

In too many classrooms, teachers do not have the right information at the right time to be their best. For example, I have watched classrooms where students take notes with a laptop, but the teacher has no way of knowing if everyone's notes in class are accurate. What generally happens is the bell rings, the students walk out, and many of them will be reinforcing incorrect concepts from inaccurate or incomplete notes (with or without a laptop).

What we could be doing in our classrooms is using free collaborative writing tools such as Google Docs where a team of official scribes can be writing together. In this way, it would be easy for the teacher to upload the collaborative notes for the whole class to review before the end of the period. This enables a group review for accuracy and completeness.

This process also provides instant feedback to the teacher about how well the class has organized the ideas and content. In my own work, I have gained immediate insight into the quality of my teaching with this tool after reading the notes from the official scribes with the class and listened to their classmates responses. There is nothing like real-time daily feedback for improvement. It is a humbling experience, but at the same time, a very exciting experience for me.

It is possible that collaboration is one of the most important 21st century skills. We need to prepare students who know how to manage their own work within a team setting and how to organize and manage global communications. In an interconnected world, our students will need to learn how to understand various points of view and how to work with people in different cultures. In this regard we need to globalize the curriculum.

It is possible that collaboration is one of the most important 21st century skills. We need to prepare students who know how to manage their own work within a team setting and how to organize and manage global communications.

For example, if I ever returned to teaching high school American history, I would connect my students to a live debate about the origins of the American Revolution with students in England. We would probably use Skype, a free global communications tool that is blocked in too many U.S. school districts. I believe many of my students would be more motivated to prepare for the live debate than for a written test I correct. We know that teens and preteens are social by nature. As soon as many students wake up in the morning and come home from school in the afternoon, they jump on Facebook and MySpace. They have a basic need to connect with other people. We should take advantage of this natural communications need and channel it toward rigorous academic work.

An authentic debate (as opposed to dividing the class into the British and the colonists) would also lead to more understanding. My students would learn why the British do not celebrate July 4 and why busloads of English tourists visit Lexington, Massachusetts, and ask to see Buckman's Tavern. Empathy might be one of the most important skills in a globally linked planet.

A Culture of Learning

We are within reach of creating a culture of learning where our students own more of their own learning and where they are creating content that benefits their classmates, and even students around the world. This redefines the role of the learner and the teacher. While the teacher's knowledge remains essential, the traditional transfer method from the teacher to the students now evolves to the whole class working as a team. It becomes the teacher's role to build capacity for the students to be self-directed and interdependent.

If we are applying very expensive technology to continue the dependency of our students upon the structure of school to manage their learning for them, we are making a terrible strategic mistake. The opportunity before us is to redesign the culture of our schools to empower students to take more responsibility for managing their own learning and to work collaboratively with classmates and people around the world. Asking the right questions about the design of an empowering culture of teaching and learning is more important than bolting technology onto our industrial model of education. This is a once in a lifetime opportunity. Think big. We can do it.

References

Bauerlein, M. (2008). *The dumbest generation: How the digital age stupefies young Americans and jeopardizes our future (or, don't trust anyone under 30).* New York: Tarcher/Penguin.

Csikszentmihalyi, M. (1990). *Flow: The psychology of optimal experience.* New York: Harper and Row.

Friedman, T. (2005). *The world is flat.* New York: Farrar, Straus and Giroux.

Will Richardson

Will Richardson, MA, is known internationally for his work with educators and students to understand and implement instructional technologies—and, more specifically, the tools of the read/write Web—into schools, classrooms, and communities. A former public school educator for twenty-two years, Richardson's own blog (Weblogg-ed.com) is a leading resource for the creation and implementation of Web 2.0 technologies on the K–12 level. He is a leading voice for re-envisioning learning and teaching in the context of the fundamental changes these new technologies are bringing to all aspects of life. His critically acclaimed, best-selling book *Blogs, Wikis, Podcasts, and Other Powerful Web Tools for Classrooms* (2010), now in its third edition, has sold more than fifty thousand copies.

In this chapter, Richardson calls attention to the explosion of social network technologies. This powerful new landscape offers its share of problems, he says, but it is also rich with potential for learning. Richardson describes the rise of the virtual, global classroom; the challenge of the unrestricted learning it brings; its potentials and pitfalls; and how educators can make the shift to network literacy in order to improve the quality of students' learning experiences.

Chapter 13

Navigating Social Networks as Learning Tools

Will Richardson

Nelson Smith could not start a fire, even if his life depended on it. In fact, he could not even produce smoke. He had the perfect piece of yellow pine, a nice blob of lint from his clothes dryer, a sturdy spindle, and a perfectly strung bow to make it spin. But thirty minutes of pulling and pushing the bow back and forth produced little heat where the wood pieces ground together. The wood stayed cool even as his skin turned hot.

However, Nelson, a twelve-year-old from Victoria, British Columbia, Canada, with a passion for outdoor survival skills, had a plan. He wanted to master this crucial, yet basic, part of bushcraft, and he knew the perfect tool to make it happen: his mom's video camera.

"Hello," Nelson says in the opening frame of his video as viewers see one of his grass-stained bare feet holding down the block of yellow pine and his hands clutching the pieces of his set. "I'm trying my hardest here to make a bow-drill set . . ."

The next three minutes and forty-six seconds chronicle Nelson's frustration, breathing heavily as he shows his spindle technique, close-ups of the lukewarm wood after the attempt, and detailed descriptions of the assembly of the kit and the aggravation that ensued.

But here is the best part: at one point, in the middle of his demonstration, Nelson speaks directly to his audience. "I'm doing it wrong; I know I am," he says. "Please comment down below so you can teach me how to do it."

And his audience did just that.

"Shorten the spindle to be the distance from your pinky to your thumb when your hand is fully spread," said HedgeHogLeatherworks one day after Nelson posted his video plea to YouTube (Smith, 2009).

"First your drill needs to be on the outside of your bowstring, not on the inside as you show here," added BCNW1. "Also, the notch needs to be cut like a slice of pie [that] stops just short of the center (yours is off to the side)."

Finally, came a comment from hobbexp, a Swedish gentleman with his own YouTube video channel on bushcraft: "Make the [drill] a little shorter so you can hang over it more, to get more down force, don't forget to breathe!"

You guessed it; Nelson was creating fire in no time.

The Rise of the Virtual Global Classroom

We now officially live in a world where even twelve-year-olds can create their own global classrooms around the things about which they are most passionate. And even better, grown-ups can, too. This is a world of learning built on the connections that individuals create with one another, the personal networks that people build with far-flung, like-minded students and teachers, and the anytime, anywhere communities of practice that grow from them.

But this world is also filled with complexity and pitfalls that pose huge challenges for all educators. The safety of children's interactions online is paramount, to be sure, but the greater challenges get to the heart of teaching and learning in general: What should classrooms be when we can connect with other teachers and learners around the world? What is the best role for teachers when knowledge is distributed widely in these networks? And, most importantly, how

> We now officially live in a world where even twelve-year-olds can create their own global classrooms around the things about which they are most passionate.

do we reframe our own personal learning experiences as educators and as people in light of these shifts?

How we as a society answer those questions may bring about a long-discussed transformation to a school system that, while now operating in the 21st century, still looks decidedly 20th (or even 19th) century in its form and structure. Or, it may not. One thing is certain: although schools may continue to fundamentally look and act as they have for more than one hundred years, the way individuals learn has already been forever changed. Instead of learning from others who have the credentials to "teach" in this new networked world, we learn with others whom we seek (and who seek us) on our own and with whom we often share nothing more than a passion for knowing. In this global community, we are at once all teachers and learners—changing roles as required, contributing, collaborating, and maybe even working together to re-create the world, regardless of where we are at any given moment.

These learning transactions require a shifted understanding of traditional literacies and the skills they employ, as well as new literacies and practices that learning in networks and online social communities demands. For educators, acquiring these *network literacies* is a crucial first step in developing new pedagogies and, in turn, new classrooms and curricula that prepare students for the future.

But at this moment, when the vast majority of connected kids are already flinging themselves headlong into the socially networked connections they can make online, the sobering reality is that most of them have no adults, neither teachers nor parents, in their lives who can help them see and employ the learning potential at hand. By and large, kids navigate these spaces on their own, with only their peers to guide them or an occasional warning from the old folks. They do not see these learning connections being modeled, nor are they being taught how to create, navigate, and grow these powerful, personal learning networks in safe, effective, and ethical ways.

Some kids are starting to figure it out on their own, and in that regard, Nelson's story is instructive on many levels. Take a moment to think of what he needed to understand about this new global classroom and the skills required to navigate it effectively. First, he knew that the Web is no longer a "read only" technology, that we now have a read/write relationship with other users that changes everything. Second, he knew that although there might not be anyone in his physical space who could provide answers about bushcraft, there were dozens (if not thousands) of others "out there" in cyberspace to answer questions about even the most esoteric subjects. Third, he knew enough of the basics of multimedia and Web technology to create the video and upload it for consumption. Finally, he did it all in a way that protected his privacy and identity—other than his bare feet and hands, and his screen name on YouTube, he revealed nothing about his identity. Captured in this movie of less than four minutes is a sophistication with the online world that most adults (and the vast majority of his peers) have not yet begun to come close to mastering.

What most of Nelson's peers are good at is staying connected to the friends and family that they see on a regular basis or those they have known in their physical lives for long periods of time. A 2008 MacArthur Foundation report found that kids are prolific at using online and mobile technologies in "friendship based" ways via texting or using MySpace or Facebook (Ito et al., 2008). But some young people are also beginning to use these tools and the vast array of other social technologies now available to develop "interest based" connections with other students—or even adults—whom they do not know offline yet but with whom they pursue real learning and collaborative creation around their passions. Those young people are, in effect, creating their own virtual classrooms, ones that look nothing like the spaces they inhabit during the school day where all of the desks are in rows.

In this way, the challenges these technologies present to traditional schooling are similar to the challenges the business, politics, music, and media industries face. The use of social networking technologies by political campaigns such as Barack Obama's changed the way Americans think about organizing and fundraising in campaigns both national and local. Businesses now put an emphasis on following and participating in the many conversations that take place online about their products. And in no other arena are the effects of these networks being felt more than in the media. Traditional newspaper models cannot survive in a world where readers are now writers (and photographers and videographers) and where people are able to share what they own easily with others. In almost every aspect of life, the ability to connect and communicate via the Web is changing long-held beliefs and habits, changes that education is finally beginning to feel as well.

The Challenge of Unrestricted Learning

In his book *Here Comes Everybody: The Power of Organizing Without Organizations* (2008), New York University professor and author Clay Shirky characterizes the moment of such change as a "tectonic shift," one that may be unprecedented in human history. And education cannot escape this moment of change:

> For any given organization, the important questions are "When will the change happen?" and "What will change?" The only two answers we can rule out are never and nothing. The ways in which any given institution will find its situation transformed will vary, but the various local changes are manifestations of a single deep source: newly capable groups are forming, and they are working without the managerial imperative and outside the previous strictures that bounded their effectiveness. These changes will transform the world everywhere groups of people come together to accomplish something, which is to say everywhere. (pp. 23–24)

As Nelson knows, learning—formal or informal—is no longer restricted to a particular place at a particular time. Individuals can learn anytime, anywhere, as long as they have access to the Web and, in turn, to other people with whom they can form groups. Learning is creative and collaborative, cross-cultural and conspicuous, and products are shared widely for others to learn with and from. No longer happening behind closed doors mainly for contrived purposes, the fruits of learning are now writ large, made transparent on the Web, for real audiences and real purposes. Learning networks bloom in the process.

No longer happening behind closed doors mainly for contrived purposes, the fruits of learning are now writ large, made transparent on the Web, for real audiences and real purposes. Learning networks bloom in the process.

All of this creates an interesting tipping point, according to Howard Gardner and his colleagues:

> Going forward, learning may be far more individualized, far more in the hands (and the minds) of the learner, and far more interactive than ever before. This constitutes a paradox: As the digital era progresses, learning may be at once more individual (contoured to a person's own style, proclivities, and interests) yet more social (involving networking, group work, the wisdom of crowds, etc.). How these seemingly contradictory directions are addressed impacts the future complexion of learning. (Weigel, James, & Gardner, 2009)

Those contradictions are at the heart of becoming a socially networked online learner, one who is able to follow his or her own personal passions in the context of diverse, global groups of people who share his or her interests. And from those contradictions rise a slew of important questions that are incumbent upon educators to answer for themselves and for their students: How do we find these people with whom we can learn? How do we make ourselves "findable" to them? How do we assess the people with whom we choose to interact? What roles do we as individuals play in our collaborative efforts to learn? How do we most effectively share the work we create? How do we maintain a healthy balance in our online and offline relationships? How do we make effective choices about our own privacy and that of the people to whom we are connected?

None of these questions are easily answered, and together they suggest a 21st century skillset, if not a new literacy altogether. The creation of and our participation in these learning networks requires a sophistication beyond the ability to find high school friends on Facebook. Teachers and their students must be well-versed in the process of sharing what they know, of finding others with whom to learn, of making sense of the huge stores of information and knowledge online, and of the operation of networks themselves.

The Potentials and Pitfalls of Sharing

Fundamental to this new skillset is fully understanding the potentials and pitfalls of sharing pieces of our work and pieces of ourselves online. Currently, approximately 80 percent of high school students in the United States engage in the act of publishing online, most of them through social networking sites such as Facebook and MySpace (Bernoff, 2009). These sites and others like them make easy work of publishing text, photos, and even audio and video to be shared with private groups or with the Internet public at large. At its heart, the read/write Web (or Web 2.0) is about the ease with which individuals can now publish. As a case in point, at this writing it would take more than four years of nonstop viewing to watch all of the videos uploaded to YouTube in one twenty-four-hour period (Lardinois, 2009). People are sharing at a pace and scale that literally boggles the mind. From a learning standpoint, the true power of this new Web comes in the second act, in the connections individuals create after they publish.

In this digital environment, a key characteristic of sharing is that the content is linkable, meaning others can take it and distribute it widely through hypertext. Every published artifact—be it a blog post, a YouTube video, or a wiki entry—has its own unique Web address. And it is that linkability that complicates the transaction and turns it into an exercise in participation. Linkability is the connective tissue upon which learning networks are built. Although the process of sharing is easy, the purposes and outcomes of that sharing are much more nuanced and complex. We write on blogs or post to YouTube not simply to communicate, but also to connect with an intention that others will interact, discuss, and perhaps collaborate with us. We do this writing transparently, in many cases under our real names, because we want to be part of a community of learners who we know and recognize and who know and recognize us. Although the bulk of what we share is relevant to our passions, we also share tidbits of our personal lives, creating a human face in a virtual world, all the while straddling the fence of privacy for ourselves and for our families. We are, in essence, creating our digital footprints, in many ways writing a new type of professional resume online, one that can be pulled together through a Google search. And we do this all knowing full well that we can never anticipate all of the audiences and readers that our work may find.

Without question, young people will be the subject of Google searches over and over again in their lives, and the results to those searches will play an integral role in their success. More importantly, however, is that future searchers, whether they are college admissions officers, potential employers, or future mates, will have an expectation of finding creative, collaborative, thoughtful, and ethical results to peruse. An empty Google search will beg the question, "What have you been doing with your life?" How well-prepared students are to answer that question will in large measure be determined by how well educators teach them to prepare for it.

Sharing in this way places an emphasis on the quality and consistency of the contribution. That is part of the way in which online reputations grow. If published content contains misinformation, shoddy research, illogical thinking, or if interactions lack empathy and respect, the writer's credibility suffers. The community of learners of which we become a part sets the expectations, and in education-related online networks, those standards are high. To reap the full learning benefits in these spaces, we must give as much as we take, and we must comport ourselves with a balanced dose of professionalism and personality.

Not to share means to cede the creation of this online reputation to others, and that could be devastating in students' lives. Part of this network literacy is a form of reputation management, the ability to monitor the conversation around online work. Knowing when others are writing or linking to the work that we share has multiple purposes; we can correct or clarify when others misread, and, most importantly, we can connect with those who find our work of interest. Becoming "findable" online by sharing is easy; recognizing those who find us and ensuring that they are appropriate and relevant takes a sophistication that must become an integral part of the K–12 curriculum. We must learn to "read" people, to regularly look for cues as to who they are, what their traditional credentials are, what connections they may have to others already in our networks, what their biases are, what the quality of their own sharing and contributions is, and much more. At the end of the process, we look for those with whom we can learn and trust in the virtual sense absent the typical physical space cues and interactions to which we are accustomed.

This process of sharing is all an integral part of what the National Council of Teachers of English (NCTE, 2008) describes as being able to "build relationships with others to pose and solve problems collaboratively and cross-culturally," one of the six skillsets that the organization articulated as requirements for 21st century readers and writers. In recognition of the massive amounts and forms of knowledge currently stored online, NCTE also suggests that students must be able to "manage, analyze and synthesize multiple streams of simultaneous information." This work, too, now occurs primarily in the context of networks.

Indeed, there is far too much information available for any one person to know. In the recent past, it was difficult to tap into the collective wisdom and knowledge of those who shared a passion or intelligence for any particular subject, but today those people are becoming more and more findable through their willingness to share their expertise on the Web. Through their blogs, their Twitter posts, the videos they share, or the podcasts they publish, we can begin to access and make sense of others' collective experiences and compare them with our own.

Managing all of that information is wholly different from managing the information streams most of us grew up with in the paper world. As the print world gives way to the digital age, the complexity of information increases. How do we find the most current reliable information? In many cases, we get that information not by mining Google but by mining our networks, perhaps by posting a question to Twitter when we need a resource or answer—thereby tapping into the wisdom of the community that many times provides more relevant and useful responses than the typical search engine—or writing a blog entry, or, as Nelson did, creating a video plea to his community. Our networks respond with answers and research, acting as a powerful human filter, raising the ratio of signal to noise in the information we access and process.

As suggested, what is new about this landscape of information is not only the people who inhabit it, but also the forms of information available. Consider Nelson's post as an example. At this moment, there are more than three thousand videos about bushcraft on YouTube, more than five thousand photos on Flickr, and more than ten thousand mentions of the word in blog posts. There is the Jack Mountain Bushcraft Podcast, among others, a handful of live-streamed amateur television shows on the topic at Ustream.tv, as well as bushcraft discussion groups, artwork, and even scholarly treatises on the subject. With acute editing skills, Nelson has access to more than enough material to create his own learning text around his passion. But here is the difference: whereas just a few years ago all of those materials could be looked upon as pieces of content, today Nelson can view all of them as potential connections, as entry points to new conversations, new teachers, and new learning.

This brings to bear important decisions we now must make when we find relevant learning online supplied by someone we can trust: Should we engage with the author of that content (or the one who supplied it)? If so, what is the most appropriate way to do so? For example, do we leave a comment on the author's blog, or do we write a post on our own blog regarding what we found? When do we email someone instead of comment? Do we create a video response? How do we disagree in appropriate ways? Unlike the paper days in which readers took a more passive stance toward consuming information, these communications require the reader to take on a much more active role, one who is capable of interactions in a variety of ways.

Even the way we organize the information we find takes on a dual role in light of participation with other learners. Accumulating handwritten notes in notebooks, on index cards, or in file folders may have seemed an adequate way of organizing thoughts not so long ago, but they pale in comparison to the digital tools now available. Online notes and captures are searchable, copyable, and, most importantly, shareable in ways that paper cannot be. We collect and save our research and artifacts online not only for ourselves, but also for others—if I find something that helps me understand the world more completely, I want you to find it as well. So I might save the best of those bushcraft artifacts to a social bookmarking site such as Delicious.com, where I can retrieve them with any device that allows me access to the Web, and, more importantly, where you can retrieve them as well. I organize these notes by assigning keywords, or *tags*, as I save them, using words that will help me find and retrieve the artifacts as needed, and using words that I think will allow you to find them too. We are participants in the process, constructing our personal, social taxonomies with one another in an effort to organize our information worlds more completely.

Similarly, because knowledge is now so widely distributed and accessible, we must participate more fully in making sense of it all. We are now the ones who must find and take disparate, related bits of knowledge and synthesize them into a greater understanding for ourselves; and in doing so, we create our own texts in the world. This knowledge work makes authors of all of us as we combine the most current, most relevant information we can for ourselves and, once again, for others. There is no better example than Wikipedia, which aspires to be "the sum of human knowledge online" (Wikimedia Foundation, 2006). Although the idea that anyone can contribute and edit anything on the pages of Wikipedia certainly lends itself to potential problems, the amazing resource that it has become is a testament to the potentials of this co-creation process on a large scale. Wikipedia makes clear the ways in which networks of connected, passionate souls can transform the knowledge world.

The Shift to Network Literacy

Becoming an online networked learner, however, requires more than the ability to navigate both people and information. The process takes a nuanced understanding of networks themselves, something that is difficult for young people (and some adults as well) to master. These online interactions we engage in must not simply affirm what we already know or support our current worldview. We must seek and embrace diversity in the connections, not in race, gender, or location so much as in including voices and viewpoints that are different from our own, people who are willing to respectfully challenge our opinions and assessments and be open for continuing debate or conversation (Downes, 2009). Not doing so could easily land us in an online echo chamber, which, although it may be a pleasant place to be, is not the most fertile learning environment. Similarly, we must ensure our networks are open to all, and at the same time, we must be able to discern those who may carry an agenda that may belie their sincerity to learn with us. In other words, to fully take advantage of what the Web makes possible, we must be network literate on many different levels.

For educators, the current challenge is how best to bring this new literacy to students so that every one of them can begin to leverage the amazing learning opportunities that the moment affords. Without question, that challenge is not so much about schools, curricula, or systems as it is about ourselves and our own abilities to connect and learn in these ways. At this crucial moment, we must be able to model for students our own connections outside of the physical spaces we inhabit, and we also must demonstrate our passion for learning transparently in our practice. We must become, in essence, network literate.

Unfortunately, many teachers find the path to network literacy a huge shift to undertake, for a wide variety of reasons. First, for many adults in general, the Web is an acquired taste, not simply a fundamental communication tool as many of our students see it. Many educators still live paper-based learning lives, and transitioning to digital technologies online or offline represents a huge shift in practice. Second, many schools have little or no access to technology in general, and a significant number of individuals are still without broadband access to the Web. Third, teachers complain of a lack of time not only to learn the tools, but also to create sound pedagogy around them. And the professional development opportunities they receive are primarily tool based, not based on connections or network building. Fourth, current assessment regimes make it difficult to integrate technology into the curriculum for fear of a lack of relevance. Finally, when it comes to social networking in general, most schools filter or completely block the tools out of fear, justified or not.

Because of these obstacles, the majority of schools are not rethinking their models in any significant way, and the stark differences between the ways we approach the learning process inside the walls as compared to online are pushing schools and classrooms toward a sense of irrelevance. These obstacles present a moment of huge disruption for the traditional model of education. As Tom Carroll, the president of the National Commission on Teaching and America's Future, suggests, in a networked world, schools can no longer see themselves as the "central learning hubs that they have been in the past." Instead, he says, "we must recognize that schools and classrooms are becoming nodes in networked learning communities" (Carroll, 2000).

How, then, do we begin to make this shift? Most simply, by becoming nodes ourselves. For anyone who has not experienced these passion-based learning connections, it is difficult to fully understand the pedagogical implications for curricula and classrooms. To be sure, at this moment, tens of thousands of teachers and no doubt hundreds of thousands of students around the world are employing social networking tools such as blogs and wikis in their classrooms. But close inspection of those implementations shows that the vast majority are little more than taking what has been done for years and years in the paper, analog curriculum and repurposing it into a digital format. In essence, we replaced a pen with a blog, and very rarely did the pedagogies change in the process. Why? Because the teachers leading those efforts are not networked learners themselves, ones who understand that the full potential of these tools is found not in the publishing of information, but rather in the resulting connections.

To change this disparity, we must look at adults in our classrooms as learners first and teachers second, and we must find ways to support rather than obstruct the creation and growth of global, personal learning networks among educators. These changes will require an investment in infrastructure and technology, a change in our learning worldview, and all sorts of other hugely complex shifts that will take many years to complete. From an individual teacher/learner standpoint, however, this work can and must begin now. At this moment, we as educators have a higher responsibility to understand these shifts and make them a part of our own practice so that we can more effectively model them and prepare our students for the technology-filled and network-driven future that we all will live in. For many of us, this will

> At this moment, we as educators have a higher responsibility to understand these shifts and make them a part of our own practice so that we can more effectively model them and prepare our students for the technology-filled and network-driven future that we all will live in.

require fundamentally changing what we do, not simply adding a layer of technology to it.

Make Technology a Part of Daily Practice

First, in a general sense, we must make technology a part of daily practice. We need to find comfort in digital environments, eschew paper when possible, and read and write online with fluency. We must move toward more mobile technologies, get comfortable with texting and instant messaging, and dabble in gaming environments online. In essence, we need to experience a steep "unlearning curve" that allows us to replace old habits of practice with newer, more interactive and collaborative ones. This may mean canceling the daily paper subscription and reading stories online (and participating in the conversations) or using cloud computing services such as Google Docs where we can create documents, presentations, and spreadsheets online securely for free and access them from any Internet connection. Or, it may mean treating the phone as a creation device, not simply a communication device, and experimenting with the capture of audio, video, and text. In whatever method we choose, we must embrace and become comfortable with the continuous changes that the Internet brings.

From a networked learning standpoint, however, the changes in our comfort zone may be even more difficult. First and foremost, we must be willing to accept, if not embrace, the ever-increasing "hypertransparent and hyperconnected" world in which we live (Seidman, 2007). Moving forward, the reality is that more and more of our lives and those of our students will be shared online, and we will be "econnected" ever more ubiquitously. That means that we must engage in the sharing process rather than avoid it, so that we can best understand the accompanying potentials and pitfalls. But we do so understanding, again, that sharing is not simply done to publish snippets of our personal or professional lives to communicate but to connect with others who may find those pieces interesting or relevant in their own learning. Long described as an isolated profession, teaching now has transparency: sharing lessons, reflections, or questions can move us into a real community of learners with others from far outside our physical spaces. And we do all of this in the context of our passions, whether it be bushcraft, mountain biking on a unicycle, or teaching Shakespeare. Grounding this work around the things we are most motivated to learn is a fundamental requirement for understanding it fully.

This sharing process can begin in small ways, perhaps by commenting on a blog post or contributing to a wiki. Sharing may grow into creating one's own blog, or publishing photos or videos online. All of this, however, we do with the knowledge that once we publish, we cannot take it back. And we do it using our real names, for if we truly want our networks to grow, we must be willing for others to find us online; the balance between network identity and privacy is struck by weighing the risk versus the reward. We want, in essence, to be googled well, so that we can become a part of other networks and grow our own, and so that we can model the creation of an appropriate online persona for our students. To that end, as we share, we monitor the effects of our sharing. With the distributed nature of the conversations on the Web, part of our own network literacy must be the ability to track the responses, citations, references, and links that are generated when others interact. We might use RSS (Real Simple Syndication), for example, to digitally subscribe to certain search results, bringing new conversations and reactions to us almost as they occur.

Further, we need to find comfort in co-creating content with others. The opportunities for collaboration online are almost endless, and we again need to understand the complexities of these interactions before we can fully prepare our students for a highly collaborative workplace. Whether the interactions are unit plans with other teachers or instructional videos with other bushcrafters, and whether the interactions are synchronous or time shifted, the process of identifying safe collaborators, negotiating the scope and pace, creating the products, and sharing those products widely is much more complex than it may seem.

Just as we look to others in our networks to help us filter information, give us feedback, and point us to the best, most interesting and relevant information, we must see ourselves as editors who contribute in this process as well. That means, as Donald Leu from the University of Connecticut suggests, that we must reframe the way we think about reading and writing: "Online reading and writing are so closely connected that it is not possible to separate them; we read online as authors and we write online as readers" (Leu, O'Byrne, Zawilinski, McVerry, & Everett-Cacopardo, 2009). Because of the expectation for active, participatory reading within our online networks, we must experience what it is like to read with the intent to share and to publish not as an end point but as a beginning to a continuing, distributed conversation. In other words, in networks, even the most basic of literacies shifts in important ways, ways that we must help students understand and leverage.

Model Balance

We must also find and model balance. With everything there is to know, and with the myriad of ways in which we can now engage others in learning around our passions, the pull of the Web can be powerful for young and old alike. Unfortunately, for many students, the Web has replaced the television as a babysitting tool, one that because of its interactive nature has a potentially addictive allure. Our own understanding of how best to balance online and offline relationships will speak volumes to students who have little context for what all of this means. It's important that we make transparent our own efforts to strike that balance by feeling free to discuss our own struggles and successes with our students, and encourage them to reflect on their own practice as well.

Schools need to support the efforts of educators to understand how online, virtual, social environments change personal learning practice, because good pedagogy around teaching with these technologies depends on it. Preparing students for a 21st century workplace cannot be done in an information literacy unit in the second half of eighth grade, nor can it be effective without getting technology into kids' hands. These new network literacies require a K–12 re-envisioning of curriculum where we teach even the youngest students in age-appropriate ways to assess information more carefully, collaborate with others, and share their work safely. Teachers must be able to do that for themselves first. Then, beginning in the earliest grades, they can make sound choices to include activities like creating podcasts, collaborating on wikis, even blogging with the intent of providing measured, appropriate ways that students can begin to understand the participatory and connective nature of the Web.

Make Network Literacy a Community Effort

Traditional professional development models are ineffective in these contexts because, again, this is not about tools. The mechanics of blogging, using a wiki, or creating a podcast are skills that can be learned in a two-hour workshop; in fact, the ease of the tools is one reason for the explosion of online publishing. Building networks around the work that we publish and share cannot be learned in "sit and git" trainings. As research from Stanford University and the National Staff Development Council suggests, effective professional development now "must be sustained, focused on important content, and embedded in the work of collaborative professional learning teams that support ongoing improvements in teachers' practice and student achievement" (Wei, Darling-Hammond, Andree, Richardson, & Orphanos, 2009). In other words, to make this shift, teachers and learners must immerse themselves in these networked environments over the long term, and they need educational leaders to be in there with them, participating, publishing, and collaborating with them.

These changes also require that schools bring parents and community members deeply into the conversation, helping them understand the ways in which our times look drastically different from recent history and explaining the new challenges of preparing students for the 21st century. A first step for schools is to become a node in the parents' learning network, modeling transparency and sharing, asking for input, and acting as a filter for reading and viewing that parents might find informative or provocative.

A New Landscape of Learning

This evolution to an anytime, anywhere networked landscape of learning will not be easy, for individuals or for schools. This "tectonic shift," as Shirky (2008, p. 21) describes it, is both vast and fast, and we are only at the beginning part of what promises to be a tumultuous process of change. It is change, however, that has significant implications for our students' futures. The 2009 *Horizon Report* (New

Medium Consortium, 2009), a collaboration between the New Media Consortium and the EDUCAUSE Learning Initiative, contextualizes the moment clearly:

> Increasingly, those who use technology in ways that expand their global connections are more likely to advance, while those who do not will find themselves on the sidelines. With the growing availability of tools to connect learners and scholars all over the world—online collaborative workspaces, social networking tools, mobiles, voice-over-IP, and more—teaching and scholarship are transcending traditional borders more and more all the time.

In the end, network literacy is all about our own ability to reach out to others to start our own fires, to attend to our own learning needs, and to navigate these new spaces with the same type of aplomb as Nelson Smith. This new networked space where we all can connect, create, and collaborate is one that is filled with amazing potentials for learning, many that promise to reshape the way we go about our lives both in and outside of school. How quickly we begin to understand those potentials, first for ourselves and then for our classrooms, will in no small way determine the preparedness of students to compete successfully in the world they will soon inherit.

References

Bernoff, J. (2009, August 25). *Social technology growth marches on in 2009, led by social network sites.* Accessed at http://blogs.forrester.com/ground-swell/2009/08/social-technology-growth-marches-on-in-2009-led-by-social-network-sites.html on December 17, 2009.

Carroll, T. G. (2000). If we didn't have the schools we have today, would we create the schools we have today? *Contemporary Issues in Technology and Teacher Education, 1*(1). Accessed at www.citejournal.org/vol1/iss1/currentissues/general/article1.htm on December 17, 2009.

Downes, S. (2009, February 24). *Connectivist dynamics in communities.* Accessed at http://halfanhour.blogspot.com/2009/02/connectivist-dynamics-in-communities.html on December 17, 2009.

Ito, M., Horst, H., Bittanti, M., Boyd, D., Herr-Stephenson, B., Lange, P. G., et al. (with Baumer, S., Cody, R., Mahendran, D., Martinez, K., Perkel, D., Sims, C., et al.). (2008, November). *Living and learning with new media: Summary of findings from the digital youth project.* Accessed at http://digitalyouth.ischool.berkeley.edu/files/report/digitalyouth-WhitePaper.pdf on December 17, 2009.

Lardinois, F. (2009, December 9). *Chad Hurley: YouTube needs to improve search—More live programming coming soon.* Accessed at www.readwriteweb.com/archives/chad_hurley_youtubes_revenue_is_up_-_operating_cost_down.php on December, 17, 2009.

Leu, D. J., O'Byrne, W. I., Zawilinski, L., McVerry, J. G., & Everett-Cacopardo, H. (2009). Comments on Greenhow, Robelia, and Hughes: Expanding the new literacies conversation. *Educational Researcher, 38*(4), 264–269. Accessed at www.aera.net/uploadedFiles/Publications/Journals/Educational_Researcher/3804/264-269_05EDR09.pdf on December 17, 2009.

National Council of Teachers of English. (2008, February 15). *The definition of 21st century literacies.* Accessed at www.ncte.org/governance/literacies on December 17, 2009.

New Media Consortium. (2009). *Horizon report.* Accessed at http://wp.nmc.org/horizon2009/chapters/trends/#00 on December 17, 2009.

Seidman, D. (2007). *How: Why how we do anything means everything—in business (and in life).* Hoboken, NJ: John Wiley & Sons.

Shirky, C. (2008). *Here comes everybody: The power of organizing without organizations.* New York: Penguin.

Smith, N. (2009, February 21). *Help with bowdrill set* [YouTube video]. Accessed at www.youtube.com/watch?v=JuFsDN8dsJU on December 17, 2009.

Wei, R. C., Darling-Hammond, L., Andree, A., Richardson, N., & Orphanos, S. (2009, February). *Professional learning in the learning profession: A status report on teacher development in the U.S. and abroad.* Dallas, TX: National Staff Development Council. Accessed at www.srnleads.org/resources/publications/pdf/nsdc_profdev_tech_report.pdf on December 17, 2009.

Weigel, M., James, C., & Gardner, H. (2009, March 3). Learning: Peering backward and looking forward in the digital era. *International Journal of Learning and Media, 1*(1), 1–18. Accessed at www.mitpressjournals.org/doi/full/10.1162/ijlm.2009.0005 on December 17, 2009.

Wikimedia Foundation. (2006, March 1). *English Wikipedia publishes millionth article.* Accessed at http://wikimediafoundation.org/wiki/Press_releases/English_Wikipedia_Publishes_Millionth_Article on December 17, 2009.

Douglas Reeves

Douglas Reeves, Ph.D., is founder of The Leadership and Learning Center. He has worked with education, business, non-profit, and government organizations throughout the world. Reeves is a frequent keynote speaker in the United States and abroad. The author of more than twenty books and many articles on leadership and organizational effectiveness, he has twice been selected for the Harvard Distinguished Authors Series. Reeves was named the 2006 Brock International Laureate for his contributions to education. He also received the Distinguished Service Award from the National Association of Secondary School Principals and the Parent's Choice Award for his writing for children and parents.

Reeves edited and contributed to the Solution Tree anthology *Ahead of the Curve* and contributed to the anthologies *On Common Ground* and *Change Wars.*

In this chapter, Reeves tackles the challenging problem of assessment. He argues that the new outcomes envisioned by advocates of 21st century skills can properly be measured only by abandoning standardized tests. He offers three criteria for determining how educators can know students are learning 21st century content and skills and shows how these might apply in practice.

Chapter 14

A Framework for Assessing 21st Century Skills

Douglas Reeves

How do we know students are learning? For most of the 20th century, the answer to that question was an idiosyncratic combination of subjective grades from classroom teachers and scores on standardized norm-referenced tests. From 1990 to 2010, norm-referenced tests were supplanted in elementary and secondary schools by standards-referenced tests, as their use exploded from twelve states in the early 1990s to fifty states in 2010. The use of tests linked to academic standards has also increased throughout Canada, the United Kingdom, Australia, and many other nations. Today, when someone asks, "How do we know students are learning?" the most common response is a test score that purports to show that students are "proficient" in meeting academic standards. Whereas in the previous era of norm-referenced tests, fewer than half the students could, by definition, be "above average," in the era of standards-referenced exams, all students can aspire to a combination of the knowledge, skills, and critical-thinking processes that combine to form the essential skills for 21st century learners.

Many thoughtful writers, such as Hargreaves and Shirley (2009), have suggested that standardized tests provide an insufficient answer to the question, "What is the evidence of student learning?" This chapter suggests that the question itself is flawed. Developing better tests of student learning in the 21st century is as futile as attempting to find a faster horse and buggy would have been in the 20th century. No amount of training or discipline would make the horse competitive with the automobile, airplane, or space shuttle. The nature of the horse makes such competition impossible. Similarly, the nature of testing—with its standardized conditions, secrecy, and individual results—is antithetical to the understanding, exploration, creativity, and sharing that are the hallmarks of a new framework for assessment.

Thus, teachers and school leaders need a different set of tools to determine whether or not students are learning in light of 21st century essential skills. In particular, we need practical ways to assess students in the following three ways:

1. In variable rather than standardized conditions

2. As teams rather than as individuals

3. With assessments that are public rather than secret

What Makes 21st Century Assessment Different?

The science of assessing human learning has a troubled history. In the classic *Mismeasure of Man* (1981), Stephen Jay Gould exposed the frauds of the 19th century, from the phrenologists who claimed to be able to infer intelligence from the shape of the head to the brain researchers of the day who claimed to measure cranial capacity with statistical precision and thus explained with scientific certainty the superiority of northern European males over the rest of the species. Equipped with another century of sophistication and social aware-ness, Richard Herrnstein and Charles Murray (1994) pleaded with readers of *The Bell Curve* not to shoot the messengers—they were simply interpreting the data, and, sadly enough, they reported that there were deeply ingrained differences in intelligence separating the races, which were reflected in educational and economic performance over the long term. Other scholars (Fraser, 1995; Gardner, 1995) have vigorously challenged both the statistical methodology and the conclusions of *The Bell Curve*.

Today, the terms *results* and *achievement* are almost invariably equated with the average performance of individual students on standardized tests. Some tests claim to assess 21st century skills because the instruments include constructed-response items (that is, students must write something rather than select a single response from four or five alternatives) and "authentic tasks" (that is, a context that might have applicability to the life and environment of the test taker). But it is not possible to reconcile the demands of 21st century skills with the realities of the traditional testing environment. Consider the contrast between what we expect of students and how we test them. The Partnership for 21st Century Skills offers both a compelling rationale and a useful framework for skills that are essential for students if they wish to enjoy lives that are free from want and fear, reminiscent of the clarion call enunciated by Franklin Roosevelt in his State of the Union message of 1941. The Partnership represents broad consensus among many stakeholders, including teachers, parents, employers, and policymakers. They note that while content knowledge remains a part of any education, the essentials also include global awareness, creativity and innovation, communication and collaboration, initiative and self-direction, and leadership and responsibility (see figure F.1 on page xv of the foreword of this volume for a complete list of the skills identified by the Partnership in their Framework for 21st Century Learning). But while the need for 21st century skills is clear, assessment practices lag far behind because they are bound by three destructive traditions: standardized conditions, secrecy of content, and individual results. Table 14.1 (page 308) contrasts these assessment parameters and the assumptions behind them.

Nonstandardized Instead of Standardized Conditions

The 20th century requirement for standardized conditions is based on the assumption that the purpose of the test is to compare one student to another. Therefore, all conditions—time, room environment, and the lead in the pencil (neither no. 1 nor no. 3 will do)—must all be the same. When we scientifically control the environment, then the only variation must be in the performance of the individual student. Under these conditions, students are rewarded for memorization and following established rules. Write within the lines, work within the

Table 14.1: Test Parameters and Assumptions

20th Century Test Parameter	20th Century Assumption	21st Century Test Parameter	21st Century Assumption
Standardized Conditions	The purpose of the test is to compare one student to another, so the only variation must be in the student, not in the conditions of the test. Students are rewarded for memorization and for following established rules.	Nonstandardized Conditions	The purpose of the test is to reflect the real world, so there is always variation and volatility. Students are rewarded for creativity and their reactions to the unexpected.
Secrecy of Content	Fairness means that no student knows in advance what is expected. Therefore, the more knowledge students acquire and recall, the less likely they will be surprised by anything on the test.	Openness of Content	Fairness means that students are partners in the assessment process. They not only are aware of the broad array of possible challenges on the test, but they have contributed some of these challenges themselves.
Individual Results	Success means beating other students. The leader is the one who is the boss and who knows the most. Teamwork sounds nice, but once students are taking the test, it's every person for him- or herself.	Combination of Individual and Team Results	Success is a reflection of individual and collaborative effort. The former without the latter is insufficient. The leader is the one who influences others with insight and support, not with authority.

time limits, and neither offer nor accept help from a classmate. Even if we assess something with a 21st century label, such as a constructed-response test item or a real-world task, every student will respond to the same item, and every scorer will use the same scoring guide. We will not let a contemporary label hinder us from our antiquated assumptions of stability, normality, and control. Therefore, even on these apparently new tasks, students are rewarded for following the formula: the same essay, the same graph, the same reasoning, and the same vocabulary. After all, the evaluation of the scorers rests upon their inter-rater reliability; that is, their agreement with one another. Consideration of creativity risks an inconsistent score, so it is better if the adults, like the students, stay within the lines.

Assessments with 21st century assumptions, however, are quite different. A standardized environment does not exist, and change and volatility are typical. Variation is neither good nor bad, but merely reflective of the complexity of the tasks and processes entailed in authentic assessment of 21st century skills. For example, some teams require more time for successful collaboration just as some individuals require more time for analysis of alternatives. The more challenging a task and the more variable the assessment environment, the less appropriate it is for time to be a standardized testing condition. Scorers of these assessments must be sufficiently sophisticated that they can recognize and reward creativity, critical thinking, and problem solving. Accordingly, they must be entrusted with the judgment to allow variability in the time, context, and processes for the assessment tasks.

Openness of Content Instead of Secrecy

The 20th century demand for secrecy is the result of a deep-seated sense of fairness. If one student knows the content of a test in advance and the other does not, then the former is cheating and has an unfair advantage. Secrecy is enshrined in test procedures and codified into law, making it a felony in some states for students or teachers to violate this sacred tenet of testing. In an environment of test secrecy, students are rewarded for maximum memorization.

The 21st century assessment, by contrast, values openness. Not only are test items openly available for study and consideration, but students themselves contribute to the creation of assessments. It is not cheating to know the questions in advance of the test; rather, it's the only thoughtful and responsible thing to do. Consider this the next time you board a commercial aircraft: the pilot in command of your aircraft had access to the Federal Aviation Administration's pilot test questions before he or she took the exam (Federal Aviation Administration, 2009). In one of the most high-stakes tests of the 21st century, we value openness, not secrecy. Applying this principle to student assessments, teachers who intend to pose two essay questions on a test should publish twenty or more such questions, giving students the opportunity for comprehensive study and preparation. Teachers should pool their potential test questions, making them widely available to all students. In fact, they should welcome contributions of test items from students, so that the test is no longer a mental fencing match between teacher and students, but a collaborative endeavor in which every student has a fair opportunity for academic success.

Both Individual and Team Results

The third characteristic of 20th century assessments, and the one most deeply ingrained in our educational tradition, is individual scores. Teamwork sounds fine in principle, but unfortunately, many people believe the most important purpose of assessment is to rank individuals and single out the best of the best. In my work with parents around the globe, this commitment to individualism appears to be strongly reinforced at home. When teachers attempt to support teamwork and collaborative effort, parents do not always express appreciation for the teacher's emphasis on this essential 21st century skill; they often express frustration that their own child's efforts were insufficiently recognized as superior when he or she was required to work in a team.

When these students enter the world of work, society, and life in the 21st century, their hyper-competitive habits of mind will be sadly out of place. Leadership will stem not from rank but from influence and service. Performance will be measured not by the success of the individual, but by the success of the team, perhaps a multinational team with members spanning the globe. The arrogance and individuality that brought early success will lead to a life that is professionally and personally unsatisfying. Because a preponderance of evidence has exposed the folly of the short-sighted and self-righteous pursuit of rewards based on individual merit, new reward structures will focus on teamwork and collaboration (Pfeffer & Sutton, 2006).

A Better Way: A New Framework for Assessing 21st Century Skills

Learning was the end goal in the 20th century. In the parlance of researchers, it was the dependent variable. Dependent variables are effects—test scores, for example; independent variables are causes— teaching, leadership, curriculum, demographic factors, and many other factors that influence the effects. Analyses of these variables can offer useful insights into a new framework for assessing 21st century skills. Think of this assessment framework as a constellation of stars. Individually, the stars may be bright and powerful, but they are only among the billions that illuminate the night sky. But stars in constellations have meaning because of their relationship to other stars and the interpretive framework that the viewer attaches to them. Similarly, 21st century skills will grow in complexity and number over time, but we can nevertheless put them into perspective with a framework that lends coherence to the skills.

Figure 14.1 (page 312) includes five essential core realms for the assessment of 21st century skills: learn, understand, create, explore, and share. This is not a comprehensive list of skills. In his foreword to this volume, Ken Kay has provided a much more extensive listing of 21st century skills. He also makes the point that these skills are not an alternative to academic content, but rather are integrally related to the need for students to learn and demonstrate proficiency in core academic standards. My framework is limited to these five core areas because they are adaptable to every academic level and subject. Moreover, the practical reality of the classroom is that teachers have ever-multiplying demands and fixed amounts of time. This framework offers a clear and consistent focus for every lesson that balances the need for learning and understanding of academic content with the need to create, explore, and share.

The circles surrounding the core of 21st century skills suggest the nonlinear, nonsequential nature of this new framework. They

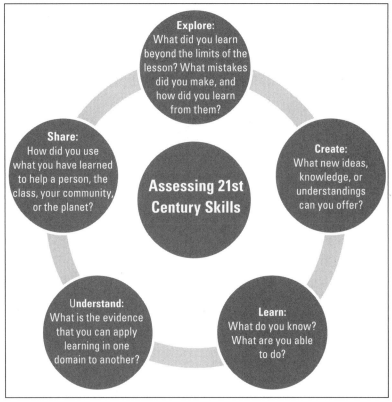

**Figure 14.1: A new framework for assessing 21st century skills—
a constellation of learning.**

also provide a sense of context: however elegant individual tests of learning may be, they are but a single star in the constellation. Teachers and school leaders can apply this framework to consider the gap between traditional assessments and the opportunities to create new challenges for students that respond to the demands of a new century. For example, most tests focus on the "learning" skill in the lower right of the framework. They typically consider the questions, "What do you know?" and "What are you able to do?" That assessment could be enhanced significantly by including the other elements of the framework and their associated questions:

- **Explore**—What did you learn beyond the limits of the lesson? What mistakes did you make, and how did you learn from them?

- **Create**—What new ideas, knowledge, or understandings can you offer?

- **Understand**—What is the evidence that you can apply learning in one domain to another?

- **Share**—How did you use what you have learned to help a person, the class, your community, or the planet?

Consider a brief example to illustrate how teachers apply the framework to transform a traditional test-based unit to one based on assessment that is far more engaging. Let's imagine a group of middle school social studies teachers who use this framework to create new assessments for a history lesson on the years before the Civil War. Their original three-week unit included readings, presentations, and test questions on the Underground Railroad, the rebellion by John Brown, and the presidential campaign of 1860. Because these specific historical facts are included in their state academic content standards, the teachers are obliged to address them in class. They use the framework to come up with assessments that go beyond traditional test questions to engage students in 21st century skills and to assess these skills.

First, the teachers decide to begin with a pre-assessment, challenging students to work first alone, then in pairs, and finally in groups to identify what they already know about the three historical events. Students then create a table displaying what they know as "historical fact," what they judge to be "conclusions based on facts," and "opinions and beliefs." For example, it is a historical fact that John Brown killed people at Harpers Ferry, but whether he was a freedom fighter or a terrorist is an opinion that must be subjected to critical review. From this activity, students would observe that collaboration quickly expands their knowledge base and personal insights.

In their next grade-level team meeting, the social studies teachers ask their colleagues in music, English, art, science, math, and technology what connections they might offer to deepen student understanding of these events. The music teacher suggests songs sung by slaves and slave owners, which offer starkly different descriptions of plantation life. The art teacher provides a searing image of John Brown that hangs in the Kansas State Capitol today. The technology teacher shares an electronic game based on the Underground Railroad that was created by a student for fun during the previous year. The English teacher suggests that U.S. Supreme Court decisions of the era, such as the Dred Scott decision confirming that slaves were property, are rich with literary and poetic allusions. By the end of the discussion, the social studies teachers have compiled an enrichment menu from which each student can choose a project to demonstrate his or her deeper understanding. For example, some students might explore the contrasts between art, music, and poetry created by slaves, abolitionists, and those sympathetic to slaveholders. Other students might explore the speeches of Abraham Lincoln and trace the development of his attitudes toward slaves and black people living in the north. Others might write a short play to speculate on what it might have meant for the country had Stephen Douglas been victorious over Abraham Lincoln in the presidential election of 1860.

Finally, the teachers consider other elements of the framework: creating, exploring, and sharing. Students and teachers collaborate to create new and challenging tasks. For example, one group of students might ask, "What would happen if the Lincoln-Douglas debates were broadcast today?" Their presentation might include the two debaters attempting to make their serious arguments, with interruptions and objections from other students mimicking various contemporary broadcasters. Another group might write and perform a spiritual, using the minor keys, rhythms, and language that members learned from studying the genre. Another group might expand on the interactive game mentioned previously by creating a much more complex web-based version that engages students in other schools who are studying the same topic.

Assessments that focus exclusively on what students know and do are worse than incomplete; omission of the other essential elements of the framework sends the clear message to teachers that 21st century skills don't count. Without a combination of critical thinking, problem solving, effective teamwork, and creativity, learning remains stagnant, more useful for passing a test than solving a real-world challenge. Sharing requires the deliberate application of learning to help others, a commitment that constrains the impulse to erect boundaries around knowledge. Later in this chapter, I will apply this framework to a real assessment—one that I thought was quite well designed. By exposing even well-designed assessments to the questions in this framework, teachers can take good assessments and make them more engaging, relevant, and responsive to the requirements of 21st century learning.

Consider the role that each element of this framework plays in the assessment of 21st century skills. I emphasize these not because other 21st century skills are unimportant, but because these particular skills have been identified by a variety of sources as particularly important for economic opportunity and social justice in the 21st century (Csikszentmihalyi, 2003; Hamel, 2009; Quelch & Jocz, 2007). I will first consider the deficiencies in even the best assessments, and then offer five essential realms for the assessment of 21st century skills.

Assessing Assessments

One of the more frequent criticisms of the 21st century skills movement is that it diminishes the importance of factual knowledge (Matthews, 2009), an allegation undone by any careful reading of the Partnership for 21st Century Skills' framework, which clearly places value on learning and testing for content knowledge and literacy skills. Students must continue to acquire knowledge, practice skills, and apply those skills at an expert level. Information acquisition, however, is a necessary but insufficient condition for assessing 21st century skills. Assessing learning provides us with important insights, not only about student progress, but also about the role of teaching (Darling-Hammond et al., 2008; Hattie, 2009; Schmoker, 2006) and leadership (Marzano, Waters, & McNulty, 2005; Reeves, 2008; White, 2009). Despite the depth and breadth of these inquiries—Hattie's tour de force includes data on more than eighty-three million students from more than eight hundred meta-analyses—this research fails to inform our judgment on four of the five realms of 21st century skills on which this chapter focuses, and this list is not close to a complete replication of the Partnership's framework.

It is easy to snipe at poorly worded test questions that are ambiguous, too easy, culturally distinctive, or otherwise ineptly phrased.

But what about thoughtfully constructed assessments that aspire to be relevant and require authentic performance? The argument about the limitations of learning assessment might be best made by using an example I created. Guided by insightful assessment advice from Wiggins (1998), Wiggins and McTighe (2005), Ainsworth and Viegut (2006), Stiggins (2007), and years of practical experience, I created a multipart performance assessment designed to engage students in a relevant task, require performance of multiple skills, and require work that was far beyond simply meeting standards or passing a multiple-choice test. I have personally used the assessment with middle school math students, and it has been distributed to more than fifty thousand teachers around the world, many of whom have also used it in their classrooms. In brief, the assessment, titled "Design Your Ideal School," includes the following performance tasks:

- Describe the ideal school. This task includes a written description and digital visual images.

- Create a plan for the ideal school. This task includes an accurate scale drawing using computer-assisted design (CAD) software and the calculation of area and perimeter of the structures and the land. Students use actual zoning and facility standards so that the footprint of the building conforms to requirements for outdoor recreational space and setbacks from other properties.

- Evaluate the model. This task requires the student to consider the physical space requirements of students and faculty and compare the ideal model to these actual needs.

- Estimate the cost. This task requires students to create a mathematical model to estimate the cost of their school using publicly available data on school construction.

- Modify and improve the plan. This task requires students to modify their plan, improving the description, scale model, and financial model based on feedback from fellow students, teachers, administrators, and policymakers (the typical challenge here is reducing the cost of the project while maintaining the quality of the building).

Each task is accompanied by a scoring guide in student-accessible language. Over the course of two weeks, students are able to demonstrate proficiency in many different standards that include mathematics, literacy, and social science. I took a good deal of satisfaction in the fact that this assessment was superior to so many worksheets, quizzes, and multiple-choice tests. I had never seen a state or system-level assessment with tasks that were this complex, relevant, and demanding. But does it meet the needs of my students in the 21st century? This assessment, as with other well-designed tasks, will determine the extent to which students have mastered essential content knowledge in writing and math. It's possible that some of the tasks move the depth of assessment from learning to understanding. While most students have been taught that the area of a rectangle is the product of length and width ($A = L \times W$), a better understanding of the concept is demonstrated when students combine the area of many different polygons (the rooms and hallways in the school) and compare that area to the available land (calculating the perimeter of the school requires students to create another series of invisible polygons to calculate the total land area). Moreover, students have a relevant reason for thinking about area: required recreation space for students and legally required distance from surrounding buildings.

What about creativity, exploration, and sharing? This assessment, which is better than many I have seen in middle school math classrooms, falls sadly short of the mark. The assessment provided only constricted focus on some math, writing, and social studies standards and only appeared to encourage creativity as a result of the differences in design. If a student had said, "Wait—I don't want to build a school, but I'm going to create a virtual learning community without any buildings at all," then my response to this creativity would probably have been a notation that the student failed to demonstrate proficiency in scale, area, and ratio by omitting the required accurate scale drawing of the school. What about exploration? While the assessment permits some limited exploration in tangential fields of inquiry—zoning requirements and school finance in particular—the boundaries of exploration are limited. What if a student wishes to change the venue from the local neighborhood to Bangladesh, and rather than build an impossibly expensive new school, the student wants to convert an abandoned warehouse into a school? The thought never occurred to me, nor did I model such intellectual leaps for my students. What about sharing? When Hargreaves (2009) talks about sharing, he refers to an inspiring vision and compelling moral purpose. But when students "shared" their results from this assessment, too often the objective was simply showing off. In sum, this is not a bad assessment—it is far more engaging, relevant, and challenging than the average worksheet in a middle school math class and dramatically more pedagogically sound than the typical standardized test. Nevertheless, that is damning with faint praise. Even this relatively good assessment falls far short of the mark for assessing 21st century skills. By publicly criticizing my own classroom assessment and teaching, I hope that I can encourage other veteran educators and leaders to examine their practice with the same critical eye.

Educational leaders cannot talk about the need for collaboration, problem solving, critical thinking, and creativity and at the same time leave teachers and school administrators fenced in by obsolete assessment mechanisms, policies, and assumptions. Consider the five essential realms of the new framework in light of the essential shifts that must be made in the design and administration of assessments. For each essential realm (learning, understanding, exploration, creativity, and sharing), I will explore the transformations required of assessments: from standardized to fluid conditions, from secrecy to openness, and from individual to collaborative assessments.

Learning

At the risk of redundancy, let us be clear: assessment of 21st century skills requires content knowledge. Students will continue to learn vocabulary, be able to perform calculations without electronic assistance, speak in complete sentences, and support their assertions with evidence. As Kay has made clear in his foreword to this volume, a commitment to content knowledge is not mutually exclusive with an expectation of 21st century skills. Rather, learning is the first step, not the end goal. But if we stop with learning, we have produced no more than a generation of *Jeopardy!* champions who can display their learning a fraction of a second faster than a competitor. We can and must do better. Typical demonstrations of learning depend upon the 20th century assessment parameters of standardization, secrecy, and individual scores. Progressing beyond learning requires a significant change in orientation, as table 14.2 (pages 320–321) illustrates. We change from standardized to fluid assessment conditions, from secret to open assessment protocols, and from individual scores to a combination of individual and team scores.

Understanding

While there are certainly some elements of assessment where secrecy will always be legally necessary (for example, patient privacy in the assessment of psychiatric diagnostics), most assessments of 21st century skills have a bias for openness. Students not only know the tasks in advance of the assessment, but they help to create them. Indeed, their ability to create relevant tasks and design challenging rubrics is an excellent way for teachers to assess their level of understanding. One of our best assessments of student understanding is their ability to explain their learning to others, an inherently collaborative act of learning.

Exploration

Colvin (2008), Hattie (2009), and Ericsson, Charness, Feltovich and Hoffman (2006) all converge in an understanding of the notion of "deliberate practice." Students do not achieve performance break-throughs through another week of perfect scores on spelling tests or by reciting "the square of the hypotenuse is equal to the sum of the square of the other two sides," a statement that the brainless Scarecrow said after he earned his diploma in *The Wizard of Oz*. Rather, students gain most when they explore. We venture from learning and understanding to exploration when we ask more challenging questions: "When was Pythagoras wrong?" "Why was he wrong?" "What does my understanding of correct spelling on last week's word list tell us about language development and political conquest?" While I confess that for many years I failed to ask these questions, I can attest as someone who continues to teach students from a broad range of economic and educational backgrounds that they are eager to explore these questions and many more like them. Nelson (2009) makes clear that while society reveres the individual explorers (who, for example, remembers the name of the third person to walk on the surface of the moon), veneration of the individual is based on the inaccurate mythology of the solitary hero. Exploration is an inherently collaborative endeavor.

Table 14.2: Practical Implications for Assessing 21st Century Skills

21st Century Skill Dimension	Standardized ⇨ Fluid Conditions	Secrecy ⇨ Openness	Individual ⇨ Group Scores
Learning	Use of standardized tests to check for knowledge of isolated skills is limited. Conditions are deliberately varied to reflect real-world application.	Secrets are kept only when essential for legal protection (for example, names of patients in psychiatric case studies). In general, there is a strong bias for openness, including the use of student-generated assessments.	Use of individual tests for "survival skills" such as literacy; use of group assessments for application. Individual assessment records include both individual and group assessment results.
Understanding	Flexible assessment menus help students achieve both competence and understanding.	Complete transparency is the norm; questions and tasks are readily available to students, parents, and teachers.	Evidence of individual understanding is only part of the assessment. Using that understanding to help others learn is also an essential process, and therefore collaboration is imperative.
Exploration	Teachers help open the door to the zone of exploration that is beyond the comfort of standardized conditions.	The goal of exploration is unlocking secrets, not maintaining them.	Exploration requires partnership, support, feedback, and inspiration by the paths of other explorers.

21st Century Skill Dimension	Standardized ⇨ Fluid Conditions	Secrecy ⇨ Openness	Individual ⇨ Group Scores
Creativity	Deliberately nonstandard conditions, with variations in place, time, and conditions, are all part of the expectation of students.	There are no secrets. Students are coauthors of assessments, not recipients of them.	While some creative processes are solitary, creative pursuits take place in a context that requires communication, feedback, and hyperlinked applications, all of which require collaboration.
Sharing	The attitude changes from "don't share your work" to "how have you shared your work recently?"	Students are not merely consumers of education, but share their new insights, processes, and ideas with students and teachers in their classroom and around the globe.	Interactions between student and teacher change from two-way exchanges to contributions by the student to a learning network. The goal is not simply for the student to prove his or her value to the teacher, but for the student to make a contribution to the learning community.

Creativity

In 1913, Igor Stravinsky conducted the premiere of *La Sacre du Printemps (The Rite of Spring),* a ballet with orchestral accompaniment that is now part of the standard repertoire of every major orchestra. But what is now regarded as a major creative stroke was, at the time, received with virulent insults and shouts of disapproval. Stravinsky and Schoenberg, along with almost every one of their iconoclastic successors, used the same twelve-tone scale that Bach used in the 16th century. While Stravinsky was profoundly creative, he accepted the basic boundaries of classical music upon which he had been trained. A few late-20th century and 21st century composers trained in the traditional classical twelve-tone scale have asked, "Why twelve tones?" Some South American and African musicians use quarter tones, giving them a palette that is four times larger than that used by Western artists. Jazz composer Maria Schneider goes further, incorporating the almost infinite range of Brazilian rain-forest bird songs into her music.

In the context of assessment, the idea of a standardized test of creativity is preposterous. Indeed, teachers must pursue precisely the opposite by challenging students to consider the boundaries of what they are already doing and then imaging a response to the challenge that violates all of those boundaries. I asked students to design a school so that they could demonstrate proficiency in math scale, area, perimeter, measurement, calculation, and other academic standards. But what are the scale, area, and perimeter of Web 3.0, where my next group of students may design their school? In fact, there are some mathematical responses to such a question (Barabási, 2003), but I simply never considered them for a middle school class. Creativity also requires collaboration, despite the stereotype of the lonely artist dancing to the tune of a different drummer. Vasily Kandinsky, one of the founders of abstract painting, was influenced by other ground-breaking musicians, from Richard Wagner in the 19th century to Arnold Schoenberg in the 20th (Messer, 1997). Creativity, therefore, does not imply alienation from learning and understanding, but is founded upon those essential elements. Wagner (2008) reminds us to be wary of our enthusiasm for new frameworks of knowledge lest we forget our debt to Aristotle, who presciently suggested that observation was one of only five means of conceptual understanding.

How do teachers translate the imperative for creativity into practical action in the classroom?

First, our assessments must support rather than punish errors. Errors are evidence that the students are taking risks and engaging difficult material in a creative manner, not evidence of failure. Second, we must encourage rather than punish collaboration. Collaboration encourages multiple perspectives, alternative points of view, and feedback, all vital to the creative process. Third, we must transform the assessment relationship so that students are not merely the recipients of piecework, but the co-creators of assessments and reflective feedback.

Sharing

The final star in the assessment constellation—sharing—requires a shift in student perspective. Students are not merely consumers of education laboring for the next reward. Their success is measured not just in terms of tests passed, but by the ways in which they apply their learning to help others. They measure their significance not by how they have distinguished themselves, but by the impact that they had on their communities and the world. When I first conducted my school assessment, students thought success meant completing the assignment and earning good grades. Today, I have students heading to Madagascar, and they are very impatient to build that school.

Meeting the Opportunities and Demands

The challenges of 21st century assessment can be overwhelming, requiring time, risk taking, and political courage. Political leaders, including school board members, are often those who achieved their present success by virtue of their performance on 20th century assessments. Standardization, secrecy, and individual assessment served them well, and many of them expect their own children to succeed within that same framework. Therefore, it will require explicit changes in assessment policy and practice if we are to meet the opportunities and demands of the 21st century.

References

Ainsworth, L., & Viegut, D. (2006). *Common formative assessments: How to connect standards-based instruction and assessment.* Thousand Oaks, CA: Corwin Press.

Barabási, A.-L. (2003). *Linked: How everything is connected to everything else and what it means.* New York: Plume.

Colvin, G. (2008). *Talent is overrated: What really separates world-class performers from everybody else.* New York: Portfolio.

Csikszentmihalyi, M. (2003). *Good business: Leadership, flow, and the making of meaning.* New York: Viking.

Darling-Hammond, L., Barron, B., Pearson, P. D., Schoenfeld, A. H., Stage, E. K., Zimmerman, T. D., et al. (2008). *Powerful learning: What we know about teaching for understanding.* San Francisco: Jossey-Bass.

Ericsson, K. A., Charness, N., Feltovich, P. J., & Hoffman, R. R. (Eds.). (2006). *The Cambridge handbook of expertise and expert performance.* New York: Cambridge University Press.

Federal Aviation Administration. (2009). *Sample airmen knowledge test questions.* Accessed at www.faa.gov/training_testing/testing/airmen/test_questions/ on December 11, 2009.

Fraser, S. (1995). *The bell curve wars: Race, intelligence, and the future of America.* New York: Basic Books.

Gardner, H. (1995, Winter). Cracking open the IQ box. *The American Prospect, 6*(20), 71–80.

Gould, S. J. (1981). *The mismeasure of man.* New York: Norton.

Hamel, G. (2009, February). Moon shots for management. *Harvard Business Review, 87*(2), 91–98.

Hargreaves, A. (2009). The fourth way of change: Towards an age of inspiration and sustainability. In A. Hargreaves & M. Fullan (Eds.), *Change Wars* (pp. 11–43). Bloomington, IN: Solution Tree Press.

Hargreaves, A., & Shirley, D. (2009). *The fourth way: The inspiring future for educational change.* Thousand Oaks, CA: Corwin Press.

Hattie, J. (2009). *Visible learning: A synthesis of over 800 meta-analyses relating to achievement.* New York: Routledge.

Herrnstein, R. J., & Murray, C. (1994). *The bell curve: Intelligence and class structure in American life.* New York: Free Press.

Marzano, R. J., Waters, T., & McNulty, B. A. (2005). *School leadership that works: From research to results.* Alexandria, VA: Association for Supervision and Curriculum Development.

Matthews, J. (2009, January 5). The latest doomed pedagogical fad: 21st-century skills. *The Washington Post,* p. B2.

Messer, T. M. (1997). *Kandinsky.* New York: Harry N. Abrams.

Nelson, C. (2009). *Rocket men: The epic story of the first men on the moon.* New York: Viking Adult.

Pfeffer, J., & Sutton, R. I. (2006). *Hard facts, dangerous half-truths and total nonsense: Profiting from evidence-based management.* Boston: Harvard Business School Press.

Quelch, J. A., & Jocz, K. E. (2007). *Greater good: How good marketing makes for better democracy.* Boston: Harvard Business Press.

Reeves, D. B. (2008). *Reframing teacher leadership to improve your school.* Alexandria, VA: Association for Supervision and Curriculum Development.

Schmoker, M. (2006). *Results now: How we can achieve unprecedented improvements in teaching and learning.* Alexandria, VA: Association for Supervision and Curriculum Development.

Stiggins, R. J. (2007). *Introduction to student-involved assessment for learning* (5th ed.). Upper Saddle River, NJ: Prentice Hall.

Wagner, T. (2008). *The global achievement gap: Why even our best schools don't teach the new survival skills our children need—and what we can do about it.* New York: Basic Books.

Wiggins, G. (1998). *Educative assessment: Designing assessments to inform and improve student performance.* San Francisco: Jossey-Bass.

Wiggins, G. P., & McTighe, J. (2005). *Understanding by design.* Alexandria, VA: Association for Supervision and Curriculum Development.

White, S. (2009). *Leadership maps.* Englewood, CO: Lead + Learn Press.

Andy Hargreaves

Andy Hargreaves, Ph.D., is the Thomas More Brennan Chair in Education at the Lynch School of Education at Boston College. He has authored or edited more than twenty-five books, which have been translated into a dozen languages. His book *Teaching in the Knowledge Society: Education in the Age of Insecurity* (2003) received the Choice Outstanding Book Award from the American Libraries Association for Teaching and the American Educational Research Association Division B Outstanding Book Award. Hargreaves' current research is funded by the United Kingdom's Specialist Schools and Academies Trust and the National College for School Leadership and is concerned with organizations that perform beyond expectations in education, sport, business, and health. He edited *Change Wars* (2009), a volume in Solution Tree Press' Leading Edge™ series, with Michael Fullan, which received the 2009 National Staff Development Council (NSDC) Book of the Year award. His latest book *The Fourth Way* (2009) discusses the inspiring future of educational change.

Hargreaves concludes this volume by asking tough questions about the 21st century skills movement. He uses metaphor to illuminate the historic ways that change has occurred in education and will occur in the future. He categorizes the emphasis on 21st century skills as the Third Way. He lists positive and negative results from each of the prior ways and looks ahead to an even more desirable Fourth Way.

Leadership, Change, and Beyond the 21st Century Skills Agenda

Andy Hargreaves

Whether men are from Mars or women from Venus is a matter of argument and assumption. One thing is clear, though: the 21st century skills agenda may be moving us all to another planet. Whether it will be swift Mercury or sustainable Earth, or a combination of the two, is the challenge before us.

In the 21st century, we are faced with four major change imperatives:

1. The aftermath of a global economic collapse has created the economic necessity of developing 21st century skills for an innovative and creative economy.

2. The spread of excessive affluence and economic inequality has reduced the quality of most people's lives and put the United States and the United Kingdom at the bottom of the developed world on international indicators of child well-being. This has given rise to a social justice imperative of developing better lives for those all over the world that extends beyond economically relevant skills alone to reduce inequalities (United Nations Children's Fund, 2007; Wilkinson & Pickett, 2009).

3. The impact of climate change threatens the very survival of our species and raises the necessity of producing both innovative technological solutions as well as changes in education about sustainable living in a world where there are now clear limits to growth (Giddens, 2009).

4. The generational renewal of the workforce—the replacement of the baby-boomer generation with Generations X and Y, whose approaches to life and leadership are swift, assertive, direct, team based, task centered, and technologically savvy, but also at risk of being hyperactively superficial—raises the imperative of producing a new cohort of skilled and responsible leaders who will be the stewards of the future (Howe & Strauss, 2000).

Before examining how these imperatives can be addressed in educational leadership and change, it is important to get some sense of the strengths and limitations of the direction of past reform efforts. These past efforts and their proposed solutions have not yet materialized as leaders face the challenges of the future.

Two Old Ways of Change: Venus and Mars

There have been four stages or "ways of change" in many developed countries since the 1960s (Hargreaves & Shirley, 2009). The characteristics of these stages can be likened to the mythical properties commonly attributed to the four planets of the inner solar system: Venus, Mars, Mercury, and Earth.

The First Way of Venus

The *First Way of Venus* has been described as the First Way of social reform (Giddens, 1999; Goodson, Moore, & Hargreaves, 2006). The welfare state defined the status quo from the end of World War II to the mid-1970s. Economist John Maynard Keynes and his followers presented investment in state services and welfare safety nets not just as a social good, but also as a benefit for the economy, as it developed the pools of talent that would fuel future prosperity. There was enormous confidence in the state's ability to solve social problems, fueled by a booming economy and spurred by the rising baby-boomer population.

In the latter years of this age, a rebellious and creative spirit entered public schools in the form of experimentation, innovation, and child-centered or progressive teaching. Teachers and other state professionals had great autonomy in the First Way of Venus. They enjoyed high levels of passive trust from an increasingly prosperous public and were left alone to get on with the job.

Teachers today are sometimes nostalgic for the freedom to develop curricula to meet the varying needs of their students as part of a mission to change the world. Others bemoan the loss of the same professional autonomy because they could teach their subjects just as they chose—irrespective of how much students benefited (Goodson, Moore, & Hargreaves, 2006). The First Way of Venus therefore suffered from huge variations in focus and quality. Teaching was improved largely intuitively and individually, through improvisation while on the job.

The First Way brought innovation, but it also brought inconsistency. Teachers from this period remember their principals as larger-than-life characters who left their stamp on the school, but not always in a good way. There was no leadership development or professional development to create widespread consistency of impact or effort. The profession was unregulated, and what little accountability existed was local only. Figure A.1 (page 330) depicts the First Way of Venus.

> The First Way brought innovation, but it also brought inconsistency.

The First Way of Venus has left a legacy of the importance of innovation—a legacy that needs to be recovered. Within and between schools, this innovation occurred only in islands—a danger that is present within the current concept of charter schools. Leadership made the biggest difference to the success of innovation, but investing in good leadership was not a focus, as it should now be. It was a matter of luck or chance. We also need to recapture the First Way's trust in educators as professionals; at the same time, however, we need to bear in mind that this trust was often blind. In the 21st century, we cannot presume trust; it has to be earned. The First Way might have expressed some of the love and passion of Venus, but with all the inconsistency that resulted, love was obviously not enough.

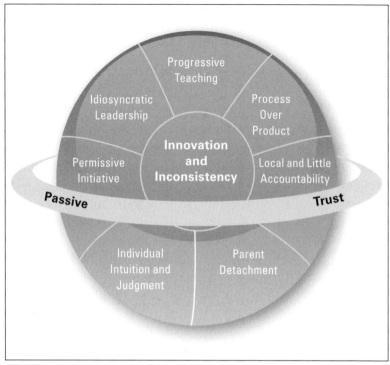

Figure A.1: The First Way of Venus.

The Second Way of Mars

A *Second Way of Mars*—more strident, aggressive, and competitive in nature, with an emphasis on markets and standardization—followed the First Way. With rising oil prices, long gas lines, and an economic recession, coupled with a maturing labor force in teaching that was becoming more expensive, people began to question whether the state was still the answer. During this time period, many Anglo-American nations placed schools in competitive systems of market choice for students and parents. The currency of this market was increasingly detailed standards linked to high-stakes tests that were widely publicized in league tables of performance and often combined with weakened levels of resourcing and accelerated timelines for implementation. This political strategy of educational change was subsequently adopted within the No Child Left Behind legislation in the United States.

Some benefits of this Mars-like way of force, competition, and conflict were evident in the emergence of clearer focus, greater consistency, and attention to all students, all with a stronger sense of urgency. But while achievement gains often occurred for a year or two, they soon reached a plateau. Parents had more choice, but only the affluent ones knew how to work the system to advance their interests and protect their privileges. The passive trust of the First Way of Venus was replaced by active mistrust between teachers and the public in the Second Way of Mars. Standards raised the bar, but shortfalls of professional support did not help students reach it. The costs were considerable to the quality, depth, and breadth of children's learning. The number of dropouts increased. Innovation declined, as did the caliber of teachers and leaders the profession could recruit and retain (New Commission on the Skills of the American Workforce, 2007; Nichols & Berliner, 2007; Oakes & Lipton, 2002).

In this Second Way, teachers bemoaned the "taking away of professional judgment and autonomy." They felt that "so much focus on meeting the standards set from the outside" meant they didn't "get to spend as much time thinking" about what was done in the classroom and enjoying it. Though some teachers were "still excited about teaching," they confessed that they couldn't "deal with the system . . . and [were] tired of fighting it" (Hargreaves, 2003, p. 91). Professional judgment was replaced by fidelity to prescribed methods. The Second Way of Mars precipitated a crisis of sinking professional motivation and lost classroom creativity.

Early in 2007, the prestigious New Commission on the Skills of the American Workforce pointed to America's declining educational performance compared to other nations. This was due to the relatively poor quality of the nation's teaching force, and to excesses of narrowly tested standardization that restricted the creativity and innovation necessary for a high-skill, high-wage workforce in a rapidly changing global economy.

In the Second Way, leadership was seen as overloaded, unattractive, and excessively exposed in the context of punitive accountability. Leadership had turned into line management. Teachers saw their leaders as managers who had forgotten how to lead. Their principals rotated in and out of schools with increasing frequency and seemed to have more attachment to implementing the district priorities or advancing their own careers than serving their own schools (Hargreaves, 2003). Figure A.2 depicts the Second Way of Mars.

A New Way of Change

A new way was needed that would focus on coherence and consistency, and retain the sense of urgency about learning and achievement for all students, but that would also restore professional energy and teacher quality, as well as develop the higher levels of creative learning and skill development essential for competitive economies and cohesive societies. In this *Third Way of Mercury*, 21st century skills would quickly gain prominence.

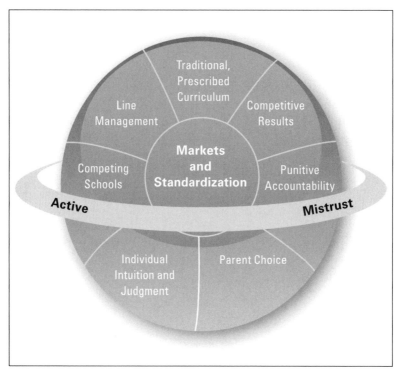

Figure A.2: The Second Way of Mars.

The Third Way of Mercury

The origins of the 21st century skills agenda stretch back to the late 1970s. In 1976, Daniel Bell invented the term *knowledge society* to describe a post-industrial world that would require an educated workforce capable of working in services, ideas, and communication. By the early 1990s, management guru Peter Drucker (1993) was anticipating a post-capitalist society where the basic economic resource of society would no longer be capital or labor, but instead knowledge, and where the leading groups of society would be "knowledge workers." In education, Phillip Schlechty (1990) was among the first to proclaim that the business of public education should shift to developing knowledge workers who would perform knowledge work. Meanwhile, former U.S. Secretary of Labor Robert Reich (2000) argued that, in a world of spiralling consumer choice, competitive companies needed the skills that could advance speed, novelty, cleverness, creation, invention, communication, and empathy with customer desires.

In the early years of the 21st century, leading international organizations began to take up the knowledge-economy cause. The Organisation for Economic Co-operation and Development (OECD) linked knowledge management to the challenges created by acceleration of change. This raised "profound questions for the knowledge students are being equipped with and ought to be equipped with" in the schools of tomorrow (OECD, 2001, p. 29). A world of just-in-time production and instant global communication requires people with ingenuity who can innovate and solve unanticipated problems swiftly and efficiently together (Homer-Dixon, 2000).

By 2003, I had discovered the pervasive negative effects of excessive competition and standardization in U.S. and Canadian schools, and was comparing these to a vision of a knowledge society that gave priority to the following:

- Deep cognitive learning, creativity, and ingenuity among students

- Research, inquiry, working in networks, and teams and pursuing continuous professional learning as teachers

- Problem solving, risk taking, trust in fellow professionals, the ability to cope with change, and commitment to continuous improvement as organizations

Teaching for the knowledge society, in other words, would promote creativity, flexibility, problem solving, ingenuity, collective (shared) intelligence, professional trust, risk taking, and continuous improvement (Hargreaves, 2003).

> Teaching for the knowledge society would promote creativity, flexibility, problem solving, ingenuity, collective (shared) intelligence, professional trust, risk taking, and continuous improvement.

The New Commission on the Skills of the American Workforce (2007) argues that America should have "a deep vein of creativity that is constantly renewing itself" (p. xvii). This requires "much more than a conventionally and unimaginatively tested curriculum focusing on basic skills and factual memorization." Instead, as well as strong skills in literacy and mathematics and core subjects, 21st century students must be comfortable with ideas and abstractions, good at both analysis and synthesis, creative and innovative, self-disciplined and well organized, able to learn very quickly, work well as a member of a team, and have the flexibility to adapt quickly to frequent changes in the labor market (pp. xviii–xix).

Tony Wagner (2008) identifies seven essential skills for adolescents and the modern economy that are rather reminiscent of the knowledge-economy skills listed earlier: critical thinking and problem solving, collaboration and leadership across networks, agility and adaptability, initiative and entrepreneurialism, effective communication, the ability to access and analyze information, and curiosity and imagination. Yong Zhao (2009) points out that many Asian competitors are already moving far faster in these directions than the United States.

The strategically influential Partnership for 21st Century Skills (2009) supports the work of these other organizations by emphasizing the essential skills that should be infused throughout the 21st curriculum: creativity and innovation; critical thinking and problem solving; communication and collaboration; information, media, and technological literacy; flexibility and adaptability; initiative and self direction; social and cross-cultural skills; productivity and accountability; and leadership and responsibility.

Twenty-first-century skills are part of a sort of Third Way of educational reform that is neither child centered and permissive, nor basic and standardized. Instead they are like the winged messenger of Mercury—characterized by speed and communication that suits a world of profit, trade, and commerce. This Third Way of Mercury promotes economically useful cross-curricular skills in learning; new patterns of professionalism, as well as professional interaction and networking among teachers; and more rapid and flexible ways of managing change in organizations. Figure A.3 depicts the Third Way of Mercury.

> Twenty-first-century skills are part of a sort of Third Way of educational reform that is neither child centered and permissive, nor basic and standardized.

The Third Way directly addresses three of the four 21st century imperatives outlined on pp. 327–328: (1) Its capacity to develop the

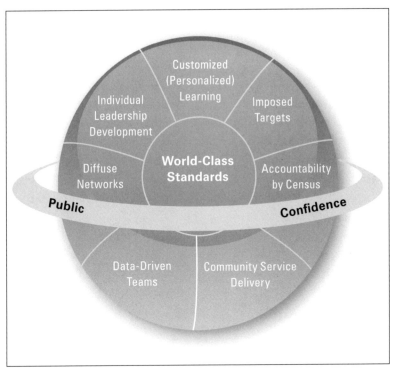

Figure A.3: The Third Way of Mercury.

skills and processes that accelerate innovation and knowledge circulation are vital for regenerating a floundering economy, (2) This culture of innovation and ingenuity may also be indispensible in dealing with the environmental challenges of climate change, (3) Engaging with the technical realities of the 21st century also appeals to students and their young teachers who have been born into this digital world. Economically, environmentally, and demographically, the 21st century skills agenda makes a good deal of sense. These developments are important and welcome; however, they are not without risk. In particular, the agenda harbors the following dangers:

1. It may overstate the advanced nature of the skills required in the new economy.

2. It does not really address the imperatives of social justice and increased equality.

3. In practice, it sometimes compromises 21st century ideals by maintaining Mars-like time-pressured performance goals related to standardized testing.

4. Its emphasis on speed and flexibility can lead to superficial engagements and interactions.

The dangers of the Third Way of Mercury. First, not all the work skills of the 21st century are 21st century skills. Matthew Crawford (2009) argues that many of today's middle-class workers are not dealing with complex problems at work using their judgment and discretion together. Instead, a great deal of white-collar work has been reduced to standardized operations. This is routine cubicle work, not advanced knowledge work. In other words, there are a lot more jobs like we see on NBC's *The Office* than those we see on the network's series *The Apprentice*. Brown and Lauder (2001) have pointed out that not all knowledge economies are like Finland with its high-skill, high-wage structure. Preparing cubicle workers to think critically and deal with complexity may sow the seeds of white-collar disaffection. It's not just people and their skills that need to change in the 21st century economy. The meaning of work has to be transformed as well.

Second, the 21st century skills agenda often (though not always) omits the knowledge, skills, and qualities that are beyond the world of business and sometimes directly opposed to it. Where in the 21st century skills agenda do we make sure that future business leaders will practice corporate integrity? How can we be sure that our teachers will teach that torture is always wrong, even in the name of democracy? Will attending to diversity just mean learning to get along with a range of others in the workplace, or will it also address the right of and necessity for different ethnic and religious groups to learn to live together? And where is the attention to ecological and organizational sustainability—to being prudent and thrifty in our lifestyles, buying smaller rather than bigger homes and vehicles, repairing rather than discarding broken items, sharing resources with our neighbours instead of guzzling greedily alone, avoiding working people to death, and so on? How can we be sure that 21st century skills will equip young people to fight for environmental sustainability, the eradication of poverty, and greater quality of life and social equality?

Interestingly, the OECD's (2008) international advocacy for 21st century skills addresses this second shortcoming of excluding the social agenda. It takes on much of this wider agenda compared to the Anglo-American nations when it describes the "core competencies and knowledge that OECD education systems aim to develop in students for the 21st century" (p. 11) as including ones that contribute to a happy life as well as to economic productivity. The question before all of us is whether we will define 21st century skills only as those skills relevant to the Third Way of Mercury's concern with speed, communication, and commerce, or whether it can and will also encompass the even broader and deeper concerns of quality of life, social justice, and sustainability.

For example, in 1996, the leadership of the U.S. Democratic Party signed a new declaration arguing for a political approach that could engage with a globalized economy, the end of the Cold War, and the collapse of the big institutions of industry and the state. They referred to this approach as the Third Way. Though Americans did not succeed in pushing this Third Way agenda forward—instead, the nation sank right back into the Second Way under No Child

Left Behind—Britain's new Labour Party government successfully broadened its base beyond the old working class and the unions. It sought to govern between and beyond the state and the market (Blair & Schröder, 1999; Giddens, 1999). England's Third Way emphasized responsibilities as well as rights, being tough on crime as well as the causes of it, maintaining social cohesion while stimulating a dynamic economy, and providing stronger support for state professionals at the same time as demanding more accountability from them. The Third Way was about developing the economy, but it was also about renewing the community and the social fabric of society. In the end, though, this larger Third Way went awry. The third and fourth dangers of the 21st century skills agenda illustrate why.

Third, in social policy and in education, the Third Way was undermined by persistence with too many negative aspects of the Second Way of Mars. In public education, a rebranded version of large-scale reform (LSR 2.0) has been even tighter in its imposition of ends than its Second Way predecessors, yet considerably more flexible in its orchestration of means (Barber, 2008; Fullan, 2006).

In LSR 2.0, government establishes a small number of specific goals, such as systemwide literacy and mathematics targets, and provides greater oversight in their prescription and pacing. Professional learning communities of inquiry in schools focus on test-score data, as do districts that then identify gaps and inconsistencies and design swift interventions accordingly. Collegial coaching and leadership supervision provide technical support to teachers while also ensuring they demonstrate fidelity to the reforms. League tables and school comparisons printed in newspapers and digital media inform the public about student achievement results, and parents in underperforming schools are given opportunities to transfer their children to schools with better results. Educators are encouraged to build lateral learning networks to generate professional motivation and drive change, and the public has access to information about teacher quality and student achievement levels. The government sponsors semiprivate alternatives such as charter schools or supplementary programs for students who are struggling in school. Politically imposed timelines for improvement are linked to short-term election cycles, and the failure of schools to meet these timelines leads to escalating amounts of intervention, so that, in general, intervention is inversely related to success.

Advocates of LSR 2.0 claim increased standards in measurable improvement, narrowed achievement gaps, enhanced professional quality and motivation, systemwide impact, and increased confidence in public education and the capacity of political leaders to manage it. Critics are more circumspect (see Hartley, 2007; Hargreaves & Shirley, 2009). They argue that the continuing overemphasis on tested and targeted basics marginalizes attention to arts, social studies, innovation, and creativity, which are essential for 21st century knowledge economies. There is also an inverse relationship between narrowly tested achievement and the development of the whole child and his or her overall well-being (Honoré, 2008; United Nations Children's Fund, 2007). The persistence of Second Way standardization both limits the economically relevant skills that schools can develop and ignores the other socially beneficial outcomes that exist beyond the economy. The intention to infuse 21st century skills into the curriculum is admirable, but if the skills are infused into an unchanged, Mars-like curriculum, then the aims of the new agenda will likely be thwarted.

This raises a challenge related to the fourth danger: speed. In 2005, Dennis Shirley and I inquired into and reported on a large school improvement network that had been established as a response to the plateau England's achievement results had reached under its LSR 2.0 strategy—the Raising Achievement Transforming Learning (RATL) project, initiated by the Specialist Schools and Academies Trust. The network was comprised of more than three hundred secondary schools that experienced a dip in student achievement scores over one or two years. Its approach was to promote improvement by schools, with schools, and for schools in peer-driven networks of lateral pressure and support, where participating schools were connected with each other and with self-chosen mentor schools, and then invited to conferences that supplied them with inspiration and technical support in analyzing achievement data, as well as a menu of short-, medium-, and long-term strategies for improving teaching, learning, and achievement results. The network's architecture emphasized transparency of participation and results, and most of its momentum and cohesion was basically lateral, rather than top-down (Hargreaves & Shirley, 2009).

The network was astonishingly innovative and, in terms of conventional outcomes, also highly successful. Two-thirds of network schools improved at double the rate of the national secondary school average in just two years. Pushing beyond and against the surrounding context of England's Third Way, the network elicited immense enthusiasm from educators. They were grateful for assistance in converting mountains of data into practical knowledge that they could act upon to improve student achievement, and they were appreciative of the concrete strategies they had gathered through conferences, visits with mentor schools, and on the Web portal. Here was a change network where energized educators could find and apply solutions in their own settings that produced demonstrable success.

Yet the network still had to allow for the pressing accountability processes of Third Way England, with its relentless pressure for ever-increasing and publicly displayed scores in examination results and standardized achievement tests. The consequence was what we call *addictive presentism* (Hargreaves & Shirley, 2009). This is when teachers' effervescent interactions often created a kind of hyperactive professionalism where they hurriedly and excitedly rushed around swapping successful short-term strategies with their mentors and each other in order to deliver the government's narrowly defined targets and purposes. The vast majority of strategies that teachers adopted were simple and short term, or "gimmicky and great" ones, as they put it, such as paying former students to mentor existing ones, establishing ways for students to access study strategies online from peers in other schools, and supplying bananas and water to hydrate the brain and raise potassium levels on test days. At conferences, school leaders engaged in interactions akin to speed dating in which they rotated in brief interactions of two or so minutes, swapped a successful strategy, and then exchanged business cards as they left. The ironic result was a new conservatism where collaborative interactions were pleasurable, but also hurried, uncritical, and narrow.

This kind of preoccupation with data-driven improvement too easily distracts teachers from deeper engagements with teaching and learning. An overwhelmingly short-term orientation leads to opportunistic strategies to improve results that secure only temporary success. What is missing here is a process by which educators can also develop and realize inspiring purposes of their own, or engage in deeper professional conversations about transforming teaching and learning. These consequences are not inevitable. As we continued our relationship with RATL and the network, it responded to our feedback, shifted its focus to longer-term transformations in teaching and learning, and developed specific strategies that still produced short-term improvements—but of the kind that supported and connected to these transformational goals, rather than diverting attention from them.

The risk of the Third Way of Mercury is that the age of instant information may combine with the political pressures of short-term election cycles to create a mercurial educational system of superficiality and unpredictability. But these risks are avoidable. It is not surprising that some of the most forward-looking educational systems in the world—like Singapore, Alberta, and Finland—have high degrees of political stability. Moreover, RATL demonstrated that it is possible to extend 21st century skills in learning, teaching, and change into the domain of broader transformation. Indeed, OECD's definition of such skills extends beyond economically related areas alone into the broader arena of personal development and public life.

We need an educational reform and leadership strategy that attends to the long term as well as the short term. This strategy must recognize that many business environments require not just speed and agility, but also the craft skills of cooking, carpentry, or even software development that take ten thousand hours or more of practice and persistence to hone to an expert level (Sennett, 2008). It must regard personalization of learning not only as a way of customizing existing learning in terms of how it is accessed (quicker or slower; online or offline; in school or at home; one pathway or another) but also as a way of transforming learning to connect it to personal interests, family and cultural knowledge, and future life projects. The Third Way of Mercury should be quick and agile and enable us to make urgent interventions when problems and needs are exposed, but it should avoid being driven by imposed targets and hurried meetings to make just-in-time adjustments to continuous flows of achievement statistics. And it can and should let go more readily of some of the controlling legacies of

> The risk of the Third Way of Mercury is that the age of instant information may combine with the political pressures of short-term election cycles to create a mercurial educational system of superficiality and unpredictability.

tested standardization that it has inherited. Alberta voted in 2009 to abandon one of its key standardized tests; and in its embrace of increasing innovation, England has not only abolished all but one of its standardized tests, but it has terminated its prescribed literacy strategy as well.

The Third Way of Mercury has part of the answer to the four imperatives, but not all of it. It offers immense promise compared to the preceding curriculum of excessive standardization and professional demoralization that characterized the Second Way of Mars. And it embraces creativity and professionalism without regressing to the incoherence and inconsistency of Venus. The 21st century skills agenda can be pushed harder into long-term transformation, like RATL; into a wider social agenda, like OECD; and into a creative and innovative world beyond the restrictions of standardized testing, like Alberta or England. Some of this can take place within the existing Third Way of Mercury, and some of it pushes into a Fourth Way beyond Mercury—the sustainable *Fourth Way of Earth*.

The Fourth Way of Earth

It's time to think about the future as well as the present, to care about our world as well as our work, to push for sustainability as well as success, and to commit ourselves to the common good of others as well as producing and consuming things for ourselves. Let's look at three examples of a Fourth Way of educational leadership and change that I have studied in partnership with colleagues.

> It's time to think about the future as well as the present, to care about our world as well as our work, to push for sustainability as well as success, and to commit ourselves to the common good of others as well as producing and consuming things for ourselves.

First is a report for OECD on the relationship between leadership and school improvement in Finland (Hargreaves, Halász, & Pont, 2008). Rebounding from an unemployment rate of almost 19 percent in 1992, Finland now tops the world on economic competitiveness and on the international PISA tests of pupil achievement. The secret of its astonishing recovery is Finland's inspiring mission of creativity and inclusiveness. This attracts and keeps highly qualified and publicly respected teachers on whom the country's future depends. In cultures of trust, cooperation, and responsibility, these teachers design curricula together in each municipality within broad national guidelines, and care for all the children in their schools—not just those in their own grades and classes. Schools also collaborate together for the benefit of the cities and communities they serve.

Second is a study with Alan Boyle and Alma Harris of the London Borough of Tower Hamlets. Unlike racially homogeneous Finland, Tower Hamlets serves an immigrant population from poor parts of the world like Bangladesh. In 1997, it was the worst school district in England. Now, it performs at or above the national average on primary school test scores and secondary school examination results. Refusing to apply the punitive interventions or develop the market-like academies that characterize England's Third Way reform strategy, Tower Hamlets' inspiring district leaders have communicated high expectations to and developed collaborative and trusting relationships with leaders in their schools. District administrators are very present in the schools. Relationships with people precede spreadsheets of performance. Schools set ambitious performance targets together. If one school falls behind, others rally round to help. Better teachers are cultivated and kept as a result of positive partnerships with local providers of teacher training. And droves of paid teaching assistants, hired from the local community, work alongside classroom teachers, easing the workload and developing active trust and committed engagement with parents and the community (Hargreaves & Shirley, 2009).

Third is a review of the Alberta Initiative for School Improvement (AISI). AISI contributes significantly to the strong educational performance of its province that almost matches that of Finland. Created by the teachers' union and other partners with the government, AISI involves 90 percent of schools in self-initiated changes, such as innovative teaching strategies, assessment for learning, and engaging aboriginal parents in their children's schooling. Schools select or design their own measures that extend far beyond test scores to monitor progress. They are also being increasingly networked with each other to promote peer learning, assistance, and success (Hargreaves et al., 2009).

What do we learn from these examples that push us even further into a Fourth Way of educational change, and what does this mean for 21st century skills?

The Fourth Way of Earth begins with an inspiring and inclusive mission, not a vague embracing of "world-class standards" or a limiting of our sights to merely increasing test scores. The teaching and learning of the Fourth Way is deep and mindful, and so is the learning of professionals. This learning is often slow, not speedy; reflective and ruminative, not just fast and quick. Indeed, says psychologist Guy Claxton (1999), this kind of learning is essential for developing creative thought. Reflecting, slowing down, stopping—these are the mindful elements that foster creativity and breakthroughs (Honoré, 2004; MacDonald & Shirley, 2010).

Fourth Way schools act urgently in the present in order to protect and sustain the future. Their short-term targets are connected to long-term commitments, and schools share and own those targets— they are not politically imposed from elsewhere. As with the Finns, responsibility precedes accountability. Accountability remains, but not through a census of everyone. Effective industries test samples of their products—they don't test every last one. Exactly the same should be true of educators. While samples prudently elicit accurate quality controls, high-stakes and profligate censuses exert pressure, overfocus on what is tested, and often lead to opportunism and cheating.

The Fourth Way of Earth doesn't only build public confidence in education through improved results; it builds community with parents and others in relationships of active and engaged trust through extended school days, paid community appointments, and the kind of robust community organizing that President Obama has made famous (Obama, 2004).

In the Fourth Way, as in the Third, teachers and schools work together, but teachers work in thoughtful, evidence-informed communities that value both hard data and soft judgment, applied to deep and compelling questions of professional practice and innovation. They do not just hurry through meetings to produce just-in-time reactions to spreadsheets of test-score data. And schools do not only network with distant partners, as in charter networks, though that is an extremely valuable direction in itself. They also collaborate rather than compete with immediate neighbors, within and across district boundaries, in pursuit of a higher common good in a community where the strong help the weak.

Leadership here is not individual but systemic (Hopkins, 2007). Effective leaders help other schools. The system provides resources to replace their time when they and their key leaders assist their peers in this way. This distributes leadership around them and develops successors behind them. In the Fourth Way, leadership is sustainable as well as successful. Figure A.4 (page 346) depicts the Fourth Way of Earth.

Will 21st century skills stay only on Mercury, or can they also make it back to Earth? The Fourth Way of Earth meets all four of the change imperatives outlined earlier: economic, social, ecological, and generational. Like all reforms, the 21st century skills agenda will do best if it learns from the reforms that came before it and those that exist in systems elsewhere in the world. From the First Way of Venus, we can rekindle innovation and professional respect, but leave behind inconsistency. From the Second Way of Mars, it is important to retain the urgent and focused emphasis on achievement for all students, but to leave behind the narrowing of knowledge and loss of professional motivation that the excesses of tested standardization created.

> The Fourth Way of Earth meets all four of the change imperatives outlined earlier: economic, social, ecological, and generational.

The Third Way of Mercury contributes a focus on creativity, flexibility, lifelong learning, teamwork, and diversity to the 21st century skills agenda. Embracing the wider international definitions of 21st century skills from organizations like OECD, rather than being restricted to economically beneficial ones alone, will further expand these focuses. Turning to the Fourth Way of Earth and its concerns with inspiration and sustainability will help bring people together as leaders work together across schools, where the strong help the weak to serve a higher and sustainable purpose and to set and address short-term targets together that are directly connected to these inspiring long-term purposes. Outside the United States,

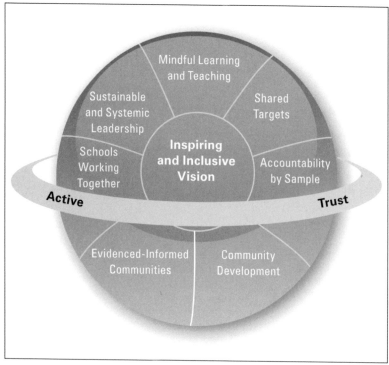

Figure A.4: The Fourth Way of Earth.

other nations have already attempted the Third Way, and we have much to learn from their findings of strengths and limitations. In other countries, we already have a sense of a wider agenda of 21st century skills that will not only enhance economic competitiveness (as in Finland), but also contribute to the social justice and quality of life that complement that competitiveness.

Twenty-first-century skills require 21st century schools. Mindful teaching and learning; increased innovation and curriculum flexibility; learning that is personally customized and also connected to students' wider life projects; evidence-informed rather than data-driven improvement; shared improvement targets; prudent accountability by samples on measures that match knowledge society objectives; energizing networks that connect schools to each other; and systemic leadership through which leaders assist weaker neighbors in the service of a greater common good—these are just some of the strategies that will give us the best 21st century schools that will develop the most challenging set of 21st century skills.

Twenty-first-century skills require 21st century schools.

References

Barber, M. (2008). *Instruction to deliver: Fighting to transform Britain's public services*. London: Methuen.

Bell, D. (1976). *The coming of post-industrial society: A venture in social forecasting*. New York: Basic Books.

Blair, T., & Schröder, G. (1999). *The third way/die neue mitte*. London: Labor Party and SPD.

Brown, P., & Lauder, H. (2001). *Capitalism and social progress: The future of society in a global economy*. New York: Palgrave.

Claxton, G. (1999). *Hare brain, tortoise mind: How intelligence increases when you think less*. Hopewell, NJ: Ecco Press.

Crawford, M. (2009). *Shop class as soulcraft: An inquiry into the value of work*. New York: Penguin.

Drucker, P. F. (1993). *Post-capitalist society*. New York: HarperBusiness.

Fullan, M. (2006). *Turnaround leadership*. San Francisco: Jossey-Bass.

Giddens, A. (1999). *The third way: The renewal of social democracy*. Malden, MA: Polity Press.

Giddens, A. (2009). *The politics of climate change*. Malden, MA: Polity Press.

Goodson, I., Moore, S., & Hargreaves, A. (2006, February). Teacher nostalgia and the sustainability of reform: The generation and degeneration of teachers' missions, memory and meaning. *Educational Administration Quarterly, 42*(1), 42–61.

Hargreaves, A. (2003). *Teaching in the knowledge society: Education in the age of insecurity*. New York: Teachers College Press.

Hargreaves, A., Crocker, R., Davies, B., McEwen, L., Shirley, D., & Sumara, D. (2009). *The learning mosaic: A multiple perspective review of the Alberta Initiative for School Improvement*. Alberta Education, Edmonton, Alberta, Canada.

Hargreaves, A., Halász, G., & Pont, B. (2008). The Finnish approach to system leadership. In B. Pont, D. Nusche, & D. Hopkins (Eds.), *Improving school leadership: Case studies on system leadership* (Vol. 2; pp. 69–109). Paris: Organisation for Co-operation and Development.

Hargreaves, A., & Shirley, D. (2009). *The fourth way: The inspiring future for educational change*. Thousand Oaks, CA: Corwin Press.

Hartley, D. (2007, June). The emergence of distributed leadership in education: Why now? *British Journal of Educational Studies, 55*(2), 202–214.

Homer-Dixon, T. (2000). *The ingenuity gap: Facing the economic, environmental, and other challenges of an increasingly complex and unpredictable future*. New York: Knopf.

Honoré, C. (2008). *Under pressure: Rescuing childhood from the culture of hyperparenting*. Canada: Knopf.

Honoré, C. (2004). *In praise of slowness: How a worldwide movement is challenging the cult of speed*. San Francisco: HarperSanFrancisco.

Hopkins, D. (2007). *Every school a great school: Realizing the potential of system leadership*. Columbus, OH: McGraw-Hill.

Howe, N., & Strauss, B. (2000). *Millennials rising: the next great generation*. New York: Vintage Books.

MacDonald, E., & Shirley, D. (2010). *The mindful teacher*. New York: Teachers College Press.

New Commission on the Skills of the American Workforce. (2007). *Tough choices or tough times: The report of the New Commission on the Skills of the American Workforce*. Washington, DC: National Center on Education and the Economy.

Nichols, S. L., & Berliner, D. C. (2007). *Collateral damage: How high-stakes testing corrupts America's schools*. Cambridge, MA: Harvard Education Publishing Group.

Oakes, J., & Lipton, M. (2002, December). Struggling for educational equity in diverse communities: School reform as social movement. *Journal of Educational Change, 3*(3–4), 383–406.

Obama, B. (2004). *Dreams from my father: A story of race and inheritance*. New York: Three Rivers Press.

Organisation for Co-operation and Development. (2001). *Schooling for tomorrow: What schools for the future?* Paris: Author.

Organisation for Co-operation and Development. (2008). *Innovating to learn, learning to innovate*. Paris: Author.

Partnership for 21st Century Skills. (2009). *Official website*. Accessed at www.21stcenturyskills.org/index.php on November 30, 2009.

Reich, R. B. (2000). *The future of success*. New York: Alfred A. Knopf.

Schlechty, P. C. (1990). *Schools for the 21st century: Leadership imperatives for educational reform*. San Francisco: Jossey-Bass.

Sennett, R. (2008). *The craftsman*. New Haven: Yale University Press.

Wagner, T. (2008). *The global achievement gap: Why even our best schools don't teach the new survival skills our children need—and what we can do about it*. New York: Basic Books.

United Nations Children's Fund. (2007). *Child poverty in perspective: An overview of child well-being in rich countries*. Florence, Italy: UNICEF Innocenti Research Centre.

Wilkinson, R., & Pickett, K. (2009). *The spirit level: Why more equal societies almost always do better*. London: Allen Lane.

Zhao, Y. (2009). *Catching up or leading the way: American education in the age of globalization*. Alexandria, VA: Association for Supervision and Curriculum Development.

Index

A

abstract thinking, ethical mind type and, 21, 22, 24, 26
academic standards. *See* standards
access to information
    rationale for formulating skills, 53, 56
    sharing online, potentials and pitfalls of, 293–295
    technology and culture of schooling, 276–278, 280–281
access to technology
    democratization of knowledge and, 259, 262
    elementary school data, 224
    intentional instruction and, 230
    network literacy and, 296
    online relationships and, 214–216
    participatory learning and, 264–265
    policy and, 229–230
    student feedback and, 225
accountability
    advances in assessment, 71
    First Way of Venus and, 329
    Fourth Way of Earth and, 344
    international benchmarking and, 72
    policies for 21st century demands, 38
    professional learning communities and, 83
    school building design and, 119
    Second Way of Mars and, 331
    Teach Less, Learn More and, 100
    Third Way of Mercury and, 338, 340
accreditation, professional learning communities and, 87–88
achievement. *See* student achievement
acquisition model, 266–267
adaptive expertise, flow and, 247

addictive allure of the Web, 300
addictive presentism, 340
Adlai Stevenson High School, 89
advertisements
    problem-based learning and, 175–176
    visualization and, 251–252
Africa
    Gapminder tool example, 252–254
    problem-based learning example, 180–185
age. *See also* child development
    age-grading system, 47
    mind types and, 17, 24
aggression
    global interdependence and, 207–208
    in online relationships, 215, 217
Alberta Initiative for School Improvement, 343
alignment standard for design, 257, 258
allocation of resources. *See* funding issues
American Enterprise Institute, 41
American Recovery and Reinvestment Act, 245
antisocial behavior. *See also* aggression; bullying
    identity formation and, 217, 218
    online games and, 216
architectural design of schools. *See* school buildings
art education
    cornerstone tasks and, 160
    disciplined mind type, 12
    implementation framework and, 155–156
    modeling and, 233
    right brain capacities and, 27–29
artificial intelligence, Teach Less, Learn More and, 111–112

artistic intelligence, mind types and, 26
Asia. *See also specific countries*
  competitiveness issues, xix, 334
  curriculum and assessments, 37
assembly-line mentality, xxi. *See also*
  factory model for schools
assessments. *See also* testing; *specific
  instruments and aspects*
  assessing assessments, 315–318, 322
  collaborative tasks and, 237
  create element of, 311–313, 317–318,
    322–323
  explore element of, 311–312, 317–318, 319
  framework for assessment, 305–323
  frameworks comparison, 55, 57–58,
    68–72
  history of, 305, 306
  implementation framework and, 150,
    152–165, 167–170
  individual and team results, 310–311,
    318–321
  learn element of, 311–312, 318–319,
    320–321
  mind types and, 26–27
  network literacy and, 296
  nonstandardized versus standardized
    conditions, 307–309, 318–322
  openness of content versus secrecy,
    309–310, 318–321
  opportunities and demands, 323
  overview of book, 6–7
  policies for 21st century demands,
    34–42, 44, 46
  problem-based learning and, 183–186,
    193–194, 197
  professional learning communities
    and, 82–83, 85, 86–87, 91–92
  school building design and, 119–120,
    121–123, 127
  share element of, 311–315, 318, 323
  understand element of, 311–314, 319
athletics, implementation framework
  and, 160, 163, 165
Australia
  framework for assessments, 305
  policies for 21st century demands, 38
authentic assessment. *See also*
  assessments
  definition of, 40

problem-based learning and, 183–185
authentic learning, definition of, 267
autonomy
  First Way of Venus and, 329
  Framework for 21st Century Learning
    and, xxi
  Second Way of Mars and, 331

B

backward mapping of curriculum,
  164–165
bad work, ethical mind type and, 24
bans on technology
  network literacy and, 296
  policy revisions, 226–228
  technology and culture of school-
    ing, 282
  technology use statistics, 245
Barell (2003), 180, 182, 184
Barell (2007b), 185
Barrie (2003), 238
Barron (2006), 259
Bartholomew Consolidated School
  Corporation, 129, 131
Bauerlein (2008), 277
Beah (2007), 239
beepers, technology changes and, 223
behavioral changes, professional learning communities and, 78, 80–84, 92
Bell (1976), 333
benchmarking, international. *See* international benchmarking
Benjamin (1939), ix–x
big C creators, 16
Bill & Melinda Gates Foundation, xxii
biology education. *See* science education
Blackboard platform, 102
Blanchard (2007), 87
blogs
  collaborative tasks and, 237
  network literacy and, 297
  online relationships and, 214
  social networks and, 291, 293–294
  technology in daily practice, 299
  technology use statistics, 243
Bohr, Niels, 90
Botstein, Leon, 188
Bourgeois (1986), 178

bow-drill set video, 285–288, 293–294
Boyle, Alan, 343
Bransford, John, xxiii–xxiv
broadband access. *See* access to technology
Brown, Gordon, 206
Brown, John, 313–314
Brown and Lauder (2001), 336
BSF. *See* Building Schools of the Future
bubble up innovation process, 3
Buck Institute of Education (2003), 120–121
budget issues. *See* funding issues
building design. *See* school buildings
Building Schools of the Future, 117–118
bullying
    global interdependence and, 207–208
    online relationships and, 215, 217
bushcraft video, 285–288, 293–294

C

calculators, virtual manipulation of,
    261–262
California
    participatory learning, 264–265, 266
    problem-based learning, 195
    school building design in, 120–122,
        125–126, 128–130, 138–142
cameras. *See also* photos; videos
    access to technology, 224, 230
    modeling and, 233
    technology changes and, 222
Canada
    Fourth Way of Earth and, 343
    framework for assessments, 305
    problem-based learning, 195, 196
    Third Way of Mercury and, 333–334,
        341, 342
career counseling, policies for 21st
    century demands, 45
Carrier Johnson, 140
Carroll (2000), 297
categorization of knowledge, rationale
    for formulating skills, 53
Cayman Islands, school building design
    in, 124
cell phones. *See* phones
certification
    policies for 21st century demands, 45
    professional learning communities
        and, 89

chalkboards, as novelty to students,
    221–222
Changkat Primary School, 110–111
charter networks, 344–345
charter schools
    First Way of Venus and, 329
    Framework for 21st Century Learning
        and, 2
    Third Way of Mercury and, 338
charts. *See* graphics
cheating
    openness of content versus secrecy,
        309–310
    "sharing" of homework, 277
Chevron ad (2008), 176
child-centered teaching
    First Way of Venus and, 329
    Third Way of Mercury and, 335
child development
    ethical mind type and, 22–23, 24
    respectful mind type and, 19, 24
China, educational conservatism in, 9
citizenship skills, digital, 211
citizen's role in democracy, 209–211
classical times, educational change in, 9
Classic Tales podcast, 238
classroom culture. *See* culture of
    schooling
classroom facilities. *See* school buildings
Claxton (1999), 344
climate change
    change imperatives and, 328
    Third Way of Mercury and, 336, 337
coding system, visualization and, 248
coding text, 111
cognition, softer sides of, 27–28
cognitive demand, redefinition of rigor,
    xxiv
cognitive development theory, 213
cognitive mind types. *See* mind types
cognitive skills
    advances in assessment, 71
    creative entrepreneurship and, 213
    policies for 21st century demands,
        34–36, 39, 41
Collaboration, Vision for, 97, 99–100
collaboration among teachers. *See*
    professional learning communities;
    teacher collaboration

collaboration compared to participation, 265
collaborative creation, social networks and, 288, 295, 299. *See also* cooperative learning; *specific aspects*
collaborative skills. *See also* cooperative learning
framework comparisons, 52–53
policies for 21st century demands, 41
technology and culture of schooling, 281, 282
collaborative tasks. *See also* cooperative learning
framework for assessments and, 310–311, 318–321, 323
gradual release of responsibility model, 231–232, 234, 237
participation model and, 266, 267
College and Work Readiness Assessment, 68–69, 70
college education. *See* postsecondary education
Columbus Signature Academy, school building design, 128, 129–132, 144
Comic Life, graphic novel using, 234, 237
common assessments, professional learning communities and, 82–83, 91–92. *See also* assessments
Common Core (2009), ix
Common Core State Standards project, 84–85
common purpose in online relationships, 214–215
communication skills. *See also specific aspects*
framework comparisons, 54
New Tech schools, 122
policies for 21st century demands, 34
visualization and, 252–254
communication technology. *See* technology
communities, online. *See* online communities; social networks
community-building example, 186
community organizing, 344
community role in ethical mind development, 23–24
competition in interpersonal relationships, 213, 215, 217
competitiveness

creative entrepreneurship and, 211–212
Fourth Way of Earth and, 342–343, 346
Framework for 21st Century Learning and, xvi–xix, xxiii, xxvii–xxviii
policies for 21st century demands, 35–37
Second Way of Mars and, 330–331
Third Way of Mercury and, 332, 333–334
complex communication, rationale for formulating skills, 52
comprehension skills. *See* reading education
compromised work, ethical mind type and, 24
computational knowledge engines, 280
computer-based testing, advances in assessment, 68–69, 70. *See also* assessments; testing
computer games. *See* online games
computer technology. *See* technology; *specific aspects*
concept map example, 191
conflict, cultural changes and, 90
conflict resolution. *See also specific aspects*
cooperative learning and, 201–218
global interdependence and, 207–209
integrative negotiations and, 204–206
overview of book, 5–6
conflicts of interest
definition of, 204
global interdependence and, 208, 209
Connecticut, problem-based learning, 187–188
consensus
in assessment of mind types, 27
constructive controversy and, 204
Consortium on Social Networking survey, 244–245
constituencies. *See* stakeholders
constructive controversy
creative entrepreneurs and, 212–213
democracies and, 210
global interdependence and, 208–209
relationship changes and, 213, 215, 217
role of, 203–204, 218
consumers of visuals, students as, 250, 251–252

content-driven curriculum. *See* curriculum

content standards. *See* standards

contextual skills, rationale for formulating skills, 52–54, 53

controversy resolution. *See* constructive controversy

cooperation in online relationships, 214–215, 217–218

cooperative base groups, description of, 202. *See also* cooperative learning

cooperative learning
challenges of 21st century and, 201–218
constructive controversy role and, 203–204
creative entrepreneurs and, 202, 211–213, 218
definition and types of, 202
democracies and, 201–202, 209–211, 218
global interdependence and, 201, 206–209, 218
identity formation and, 217–218
integrative negotiations role and, 204–206
problem-based learning and, 182–183
relationship changes and, 202, 213–218
role of, 202–203, 218
school building design and, 118–119, 122–145
Teach Less, Learn More and, 103–104

Coppell Independent School District, 133

core subjects. *See also* curriculum; *specific subjects*
framework comparisons, 57–58
implementation framework and, 154–157, 159, 164–165
policies for 21st century demands, 33
redefinition of rigor, xxiii–xxiv
Teach Less, Learn More and, 99, 103, 105–107, 109, 111–113
visualization and, 259

cornerstone assessment tasks, 158–164

Cornwallis Academy, school building design, 142

Costa (1998), 188–189

Costa and Kallick (2000), 110

courtesy policy, 227–229

Crawford (2009), 336

create element of assessments, 311–313, 317, 322–323

creating mind type
assessment of, 26–27
description of, 10, 16–19
integration of mind types, 29–30
multiple intelligences and, 26
relationships among mind types, 17
right brain capacities and, 27
tensions between mind types, 25

Creative Commons, independent learning and, 239

creative entrepreneurs, need for as challenge, 202, 211–213, 218

creativity. *See also* collaborative creation
Fourth Way of Earth and, 342, 344
Framework for 21st Century Learning and, xviii, xx
Third Way of Mercury and, 334, 342, 345

critical thinking
Framework for 21st Century Learning and, xviii, xx, xxiv
search result interpretation, 275–276
visualization and, 252–254, 259

Csikszentmihalyi (1990), 246–247, 280

CSO Architects, 129–132

cues, online interactions and, 216

culture of schooling. *See also specific aspects*
framework comparisons, 67–68, 73
implementation framework and, 167
innovation and, 268–269
network literacy and, 296–298
professional learning communities and, 77–80, 85, 90–91
student empowerment as goal, 282–283
technology and, 275–283

Cummins Engine, 129

curriculum. *See also* core subjects; *specific aspects*
backward mapping, 164–165
First Way of Venus and, 329
Fourth Way of Earth and, 343
Great Britain's national curriculum, 70
implementation framework and, 149–171
international benchmarking and, 71–72
legacy from 20th century, 54–55, 59

modeling balance, 300–301
network literacy and, 296–297
outcomes as framework focus, xx
PISA focus and, 69
policies for 21st century demands,
    34–35, 37–38, 40–42, 46
problem-based learning and, 175–197
professional learning communities
    and, 81–82
right brain capacities and, 29
school building design and, 119,
    122–123, 127, 136–137
Teach Less, Learn More and, 101–113
technology and culture of schooling,
    280–282
Third Way of Mercury and, 334–335,
    339, 342
U.S. background, ix
virtual global classrooms and, 287
curriculum and assessment system
    (implementation framework)
    guideline one, 154–157
    guideline two, 157–164
    guideline three, 164–165
curriculum standards. See standards
Curtis, Paul, 120
CWRA. See College and Work Readiness
    Assessment
cyberbullying, 215

D

D21 framework, 268–269
debates, live, technology and culture of
    schooling, 282
Dede (2005), 56, 64–66
Dede (2009b), 66–67
deliberate practice, notion of, 319
deliberative discourse, constructive
    controversy and, 203
Delicious site, 264, 294
democracies. See also specific aspects
    and entities
    number of as challenge, 201–202,
        209–211, 218
    torture and, 337
Democratic party, Third Way agenda,
    337–338

democratization of knowledge, as inno-
    vation, 259–263, 267–269
demographics. See also specific aspects
    achievement gaps and, xviii
    creative entrepreneurship and, 212
    Gapminder tool applications, 252–254
    global interdependence and popula-
        tion, 209
design of school buildings. See school
    buildings
design of visuals, 255–258
DesignShare, 126, 128
design side of cognition, 27
Desotelle and Lierman (2000), 186
Despenza-Green, Betty, 122
destructive conflicts, description of, 208
digital cameras. See cameras
digital citizenship skills, need for, 211
digital disorder, power of, 53
digital footprints, creation of, 291–292
digital generation. See also specific
    aspects
    chalkboards and, 222
    school buildings and, 118–119
    Third Way of Mercury and, 336
digital literacy frameworks, frameworks
    comparison, 56, 61–67, 73
digital literacy projects, Teach Less,
    Learn More and, 111–112
digital technology. See technology
Dimensions of 21st Century Learning
    framework, 268–269
Direct Manipulation Principle, 249
discipline, connotations of, 11–12, 164–165
disciplined mind type
    assessment of, 26
    description of, 10, 11–13, 19
    integration of mind types, 29–30
    multiple intelligences and, 26
    relationships among mind types, 17
    right brain capacities and, 27, 28
    tensions between mind types, 25
discussion boards, independent learn-
    ing and, 238
distance learning, democratization of
    knowledge, 262–263
distinguishing among individuals,
    respectful mind type and, 19–20

district-level reforms. *See also specific aspects*
  Fourth Way of Earth and, 343
  Framework for 21st Century Learning and, 2
diversity. *See also specific aspects*
  global interdependence and, 207–208, 218
  network literacy and, 295–296
  online relationships and, 215
  Third Way of Mercury and, 337, 345
Don't Buy It: Get Media Smart website, 251
Douglas, Stephen, 314
dropout rate
  Framework for 21st Century Learning and, xviii
  innovation and, 246
  Second Way of Mars and, 331
Drucker (1993), 333
DuFour, DuFour, Eaker, and Many (2006), 78–79
Duke and Pearson (2002), 230
Duncan, Arne, 245

E

Earth, Fourth Way of, 342–347
eating disorders, idealization of fashion models and, 252
ecology of learning, innovation and, 259, 267
ecology of society, innovation and, 266
economic competitiveness. *See* competitiveness
economic inequality as issue. *See* inequality as issue
economic issues. *See also* funding; workforce issues
  access to technology and, 224
  change imperatives and, 327
  creative entrepreneurship and, 211–212
  creativity's cash value, 18
  First Way of Venus and, 328–329
  Fourth Way of Earth and, 343
  Framework for 21st Century Learning and, xvi–xvii, xix–xxiii, xxv, xxviii
  Gapminder tool applications, 252–254
  global interdependence and, 206–207, 218

global work ethic as goal, 276, 278–282
innovation and, 243, 245–246, 265, 268
policies for 21st century demands, 33, 37
problem-based learning and, 177, 197
rationale for formulating skills, 52–53
Second Way of Mars and, 330–331
teacher pay, 44, 89
Third Way of Mercury and, 333–339, 341, 345
economics (subject matter), Teach Less, Learn More and, 105
editors, online participants as, 295, 299–300
Education, Vision for, 97, 98–99
educational assessments. *See* assessments
educational mission statements, implementation framework and, 151
educational reform, solar system metaphor for. *See* solar system reform metaphor
educational standards. *See* standards
educational support systems. *See also specific aspects*
  Framework for 21st Century Learning and, xiv, xx, xxiv–xxvi
  implementation framework and, 168, 171
Educational Testing Service (2007), 56, 63, 64, 67, 73
Education Commission of the States, 258
effectiveness of problem-based learning, 195–196
effectiveness of teachers. *See* teacher effectiveness
electronic mail and messaging. *See* email and messaging
electronic technology. *See* technology
Elementary and Secondary Education Act, 57
elementary schools
  citizenship skills, 210
  cornerstone assessment tasks, 162
  Framework for 21st Century Learning, 2
  policies for 21st century demands, 47
  problem-based learning, 185–186, 194, 197

Teach Less, Learn More, 99, 110–111
technology access data, 224
email and messaging
   modeling and, 233
   online relationships and, 214, 215
   school building design and, 127
   sharing, potentials and pitfalls of, 294
   student survey, 225
   technology bans and, 227, 228
   technology changes and, 222
   technology in daily practice, 298
   technology use statistics, 244
   virtual global classrooms and, 288
Emerson, Ralph Waldo, 19
emissions calculator, 261
empathy, right brain capacities and, 28
employment issues. See workforce issues
enGauge framework. See North Central
   Regional Education Laboratory and
   Metiri Group (2003)
Engel and Randall (2009), 195
engineering as discipline. See STEM
   disciplines
England. See United Kingdom
English education (subject). See also
   reading education; writing tasks
   independent learning, 238–239
   modeling and, 233–234
entrepreneurs, need for as challenge,
   202, 211–213, 218
environmental issues
   change imperatives and, 328
   emissions calculator, 261
   global interdependence and, 208–209
   Third Way of Mercury and, 336, 337
equality issues. See inequality as issue;
   social justice
equitable distribution of resources. See
   funding issues
ethical mind type
   assessment of, 26, 27
   description of, 10, 21–23
   integration of mind types, 30
   multiple intelligences and, 26
   research background, 19
   right brain capacities and, 28
   survival of species and, 11
   tensions between mind types, 24–25
ethics. See also cheating

global work ethic, 276, 278–282
   in online relationships, 216
   Third Way of Mercury and, 337
   virtual global classrooms and, 287
ETS digital literacy standards. See
   Educational Testing Service (2007)
Europe. See also specific countries
   competitiveness issues, xix
   curriculum and assessments, 37
   examinations. See assessments; testing
existential intelligence, synthesizing
   mind type and, 17, 26, 28
expert, definition of, 90
explore element of assessments, 311–312,
   317–318, 319

F

Faber (2009), 197
Facebook. See also social networks
   participatory learning and, 264–265, 266
   sharing online, potentials and pitfalls
      of, 291
   technology and culture of schooling, 278
   technology use statistics, 243
   virtual global classrooms and, 288
face-to-face relationships. See also interpersonal relationships
   changes in relationships, 213–218
   modeling balance, 300–301
facilities. See school buildings
factory model for schools, policies for
   21st century demands, 46, 47, 48
fashion models, idealization of, 251–252
Fielding (1999), 126, 128
Fielding Nair International, 126
financial issues. See economic issues;
   funding issues
findability of individuals via Internet,
   292, 293
Finland
   Fourth Way of Earth and, 342–343, 346
   as knowledge economy, 336
   Third Way of Mercury and, 341
First Way of Venus, 328–329, 330, 331, 345
Fisher (2005), 122, 126
Flaherty (2002), 188

flattened workplace structures,
Framework for 21st Century Learning
and, xxi
Flickr
independent learning and, 239
sharing online, potentials and pitfalls
of, 294
Florida Virtual High School, 262
flow concept, 246–247, 280
focus lessons, gradual release of responsibility model, 231–233
formal cooperative learning, description
of, 202. *See also* cooperative learning
Fourth Way of Earth, 342–347
Framework for 21st Century Learning
assessing assessments, 315
background of, xiii–xix, xxvi–xxvii,
1, 119
digital literacy frameworks and, 63
educational support systems and, xiv,
xx, xxiv–xxvi
framework for assessments and, 307
future of learning and, xxvii–xxviii
major frameworks and, 56–61
need for new model, xvi–xix
outcomes as focus, xiv, xx–xxvi
outline of, 57–58
overview of book, 4
professional learning communities
and, 85
reconceptualization as challenge, 73
stakeholders and, xvi, xxvi–xxvii
summary of, xiv, xv, xix–xx, 57
tipping point and, xiii
vision of, xix–xxvii
frameworks for 21st century skills. *See
also specific frameworks*
alternative frameworks, 67–68
assessment advances, 68–72
assessment framework, 305–323
comparison of, 51–73
competitiveness and, 37
digital literacy frameworks, 61–67, 73
major frameworks, 56–61
overview of book, 4
policies for 21st century demands, 37
rationale for formulating, 51–56
reconceptualization as challenge, 72–73
Franklin, Ben, 197

free republics, virtue in, 209
Friedman (2005), 206, 278
friendship formation. *See* interpersonal
relationships
Fujimoto, Ted, 130
Fullan (2007), 90, 92
function, as technology consideration,
223–227, 239–240
functional magnetic resonance imaging
scans, 247–248
funding issues. *See also* economic issues
bubble up innovation process, 3
policies for 21st century demands,
47–48

G

games, online. *See* online games
Gapminder tool, 252–254
GarageBand, independent learning and,
239
Gell-Mann, Murray, 13
generational renewal of workforce,
change imperatives and, 328
Gensler (2009), 142–143
geography education, problem-based
learning and, 180–185
Gerry, Chris, 142
Gillard, Philip, 142
Gladwell (2000), xiii, 246
Gladwell (2002), 90–91
global classrooms. *See* virtual global
classrooms
global connections and technology, 302
global economy. *See also* economic
issues
change imperatives, 327
Framework for 21st Century Learning
and, xvi–xix, xxii
global interdependence as challenge,
206–207
innovation and, 243, 245–246, 265, 268
Second Way of Mars and, 331
Third Way of Mercury and, 337–338
global interdependence as challenge,
201, 206–209, 218
globalization
major changes entailed in, 10
problem-based learning and, 194

global work ethic, technology and culture of schooling, 276, 278–282
good work, ethical mind type and, 19, 22
Google
  social networks and, 291–292, 293
  technology in daily practice, 299
  technology use statistics, 243
  as verb, 260
Google Docs
  collaborative tasks and, 234, 281
  technology in daily practice, 298
Gould (1981), 306
grading. *See also* testing
  framework for assessments, 305
  individual versus team results, 310–311
  New Tech schools, 121
  policies for 21st century demands, 40
gradual release of responsibility model, 231–239
Graham, Patricia, 27
Graham and Ferriter (2010), 87
graphics. *See also* visualization, as innovation
  graphic novel creation, 234, 237
  innovation and, 250
  syntheses and, 16
Great Britain, Key Stage 3 ICT Literacy Assessment, 70. *See also* United Kingdom
Greenwich Public Schools (2006), 187–188
group discriminations, respectful mind type and, 19–20
group reports, constructive controversy and, 204
guided instruction, gradual release of responsibility model, 231–234
Guitar video, viewing statistics, 243

H

H1N1 virus, task example, 162–163
habits of mind
  competitive habits, 310–311
  elementary school example, 110–111
Hakkarainen, Palonen, Paavola, and Lehtinen (2004), 266
Hargreaves (2003), 333–334
Hargreaves (2009), 318

Hargreaves, Halász, and Pont (2008), 342–343
Hargreaves and Shirley (2005), 339
Hargreaves and Shirley (2009), 339
Harris, Alma, 343
Hattie (2008), 88
Hattie (2009), 315
Henderson (2009), 197
Herbert et al. (2003), 154
Herrnstein and Murray (1994), 306
hierarchical workplace structures, Framework for 21st Century Learning and, xx–xxi
higher education. *See* postsecondary education
Higher Education Academy (2009), 267
higher-order thinking skills
  advances in assessment, 71
  policies for 21st century demands, 34–35, 36
high-quality reasoning skills, need for creative entrepreneurs, 213
high schools
  cornerstone assessment tasks, 162–163
  democratization of knowledge, 262
  dropout rate, xviii, 246
  Framework for 21st Century Learning, xviii, 3
  modeling and, 231
  policies for 21st century demands, 46, 47
  problem-based learning, 179–187
  professional learning communities, 89
  school building design, 128, 129, 132–136, 138–142, 144–145
  sharing online, potentials and pitfalls of, 291
  technology and culture of schooling, 282
High Tech High
  building design, 128, 138–142, 144
  problem-based learning, 195
High Tech Middle
  participatory learning, 264–265, 266
  school building design, 140, 141
Hirschman (1970), 24–25
history education. *See also* social studies education
  disciplined mind type, 12

graphic novel example, 234, 237
implementation framework and, 163,
    165
modeling and, 233
online courses, 262
problem-based learning and, 178,
    180–185
technology and culture of school-
    ing, 282
HIV infection, tracking of, 252, 253
hockey-stick pattern of change, 277
homework
    computational knowledge engines
        and, 280
    independent learning and, 237–239
    "sharing" of, 277
honesty in online relationships. See trust
Hopper, Cheryl, 179–185
Hugh Christie Technology College, 142
humanities as discipline, right brain
    capacities and, 28–29

I

iChat, 233
ICT (information and communication
    technology). See technology
idealization of models, 251–252
identity formation, 211, 217–218. See
    also online identities
ideological systems, thirst for meaning
    and, 28
Illinois
    Framework for 21st Century Learning
        and, 2–3
    professional learning communities, 89
Illuminations website, 261
illustrations. See graphics
iMovie, 239
implementation. See also implementa-
    tion framework; specific aspects
    Illinois Consortium and, 2–3
    policies for 21st century demands, 48
    professional learning communities
        and, 78, 82
    Teach Less, Learn More and, 97, 99,
        100, 106, 109
Implementation, Vision for, 97, 99, 106, 109
implementation framework

background of, 149–150
components overview, 150
curriculum and assessment system,
    152–165
instructional programs and practices,
    165–168, 169
mission of schooling, 151
overview of book, 5
principles of learning, 151–152, 153
summary of changes, 170, 171
systemic supports, 169, 171
income. See also economic issues;
    inequality as issue
    in South Africa, 252–254
    of teachers, 44, 89
independent learning, technology and,
    231–232, 237–239
Indiana, school building design in, 128,
    129–132
Individual Differences Principle, 249
individualism, interpersonal relation-
    ships and, 213, 217
individual versus team results, 310–311,
    318–321
inequality as issue. See also economic
    issues; social justice
    First Way of Venus and, 328
    Third Way of Mercury and, 336, 337
infants, respectful mind type and, 19
influence geniuses, study of, 80
informal cooperative learning, descrip-
    tion of, 202. See also cooperative
    learning
information, access to. See access to
    information
information and communication tech-
    nology. See technology
information management. See manage-
    ment of information
infrastructure of education. See educa-
    tional support systems
innovation. See also technology; specific
    aspects
    creating mind type and, 16
    D21 framework, 268–269
    definition of, 245–246
    democratization of knowledge as,
        259–263, 267–269
    First Way of Venus and, 329, 345

Fourth Way of Earth and, 345
knowledge-based economy and, 243,
    245–246, 268
overview of book, 6
participatory learning as, 263–267,
    267–269
in school building design, 117–145
Second Way of Mars and, 331
student engagement as goal, 245,
    246–248, 263
Teach Less, Learn More and, 99, 100
technology and culture of schooling,
    277–278
technology use statistics, 243–245
Third Way of Mercury and, 336
visualization as, 247–259, 267–269
Innovation Unit, 119
inquiry in problem-based learning, 176,
    180–183, 187–190, 193–196
inquiry learning, Web-based Science
    website, 263
instant messaging. *See* email and
    messaging
institutional culture, ethical mind type
    and, 23. *See also* culture of schooling
instructional process. *See also specific
    aspects*
    policies for 21st century demands,
        36–42
    professional learning communities
        and, 82–89
    rationale for formulating skills, 56
    Teach Less, Learn More and, 97–114
    Third Way of Mercury and, 339–342
instructional programs and practices
    (implementation framework)
    indicator one, 165–166
    indicator two, 166
    indicator three, 166
    indicator four, 167
    indicator five, 167
    instructional resources, 167–168, 169
instructional resources. *See also specific
    aspects*
    implementation framework and,
        167–168, 169
    Route 21 website, xxvi
integration of mind types, 10, 29–30
integrative negotiations
    global interdependence and, 209

role of, 204–206, 218
intellectual demands, policies for 21st
    century demands, 33–48
intentional instruction, technology and,
    230–239
interdisciplinarity, value of, 13
interest-based learning connections. *See*
    passion-based learning connections
intergroup attitudes, respectful mind
    type and, 20–21
international assessments. *See also*
    assessments; Programme for
    International Student Assessment
    advances in assessments, 71–72
    policies for 21st century demands,
        36–39
International Baccalaureate schools,
    194, 196
international benchmarking
    advances in assessment, 71–72
    professional learning communities
        and, 85
international relations. *See also*
    globalization
    global interdependence as challenge,
        201, 206–209, 218
    respectful mind type and, 21
International Society for Technology in
    Education (2007), 56, 61–63, 67, 73
Internet, access to. *See* access to
    technology
Internet communities. *See* online
    communities; social networks
Internet reciprocal teaching, 234, 235–236
Internet technology. *See* technology
interpersonal attitudes, respectful mind
    type and, 20–21
interpersonal intelligence, mind types
    and, 26
interpersonal relationships. *See also
    specific aspects*
    changes in, 202, 213–216, 218
    Fourth Way of Earth and, 343
    global interdependence and, 207–208
    modeling balance, 300–301
    online interaction and face-to-face
        relationships, 216–218
    virtual global classrooms and, 288
interpersonal skills, global interdepen-
    dence and, 208

intolerance, respectful mind type and,
    20–21. *See also* prejudicial judgments
iPhone, 102
Iraqi elections, coverage of reactions to, 250
isolation
    global interdependence and, 208
    professional learning communities
        and, 91, 92, 93
    technology in daily practice, 298
ISTE technology standards. *See*
    International Society for Technology
    in Education (2007)
Ito et al. (2008), 288
iTunes University, 262

J

Jack Mountain Bushcraft Podcast, 294
Japan, online behavior, 216
Jefferson, Thomas, 210
Jenkins (2009), 56, 63–64, 65
Jernigan (2009), 196
Jilk, Bruce, 128
Jing tool, 280
Johnson and Johnson (1989), 202–203
Johnson and Johnson (2005b), 205
Jung, Carl, 18
Jurong Secondary School, 111–112

K

Kadinsky, Vasily, 322
KCTS Television (2004), 251
Keynes, John Maynard, 328
Key Stage 3 ICT Literacy Assessment, 70
keywords, use of, 294–295
knowledge-based economy, 245–246,
    268. *See also* economic issues
knowledge creation model, 266–267
knowledge society, 333–334
Knowsley Metropolitan Borough
    Council, 125
Kohlberg, Lawrence, 213
Kohler ad (2009), 175
Kotter and Cohen (2002), 78, 80
KWHLAQ approach to inquiry, 180–185

L

labor force issues. *See* workforce issues

Labour Party, Third Way agenda and, 338
laptops
    access to technology, 224, 225, 230
    cell phones and, 102
    independent learning and, 238
    school building design and, 124,
        126–127, 134, 136, 141
    technology and culture of schooling,
        276, 277, 280, 281
large-scale reform (LSR 2.0), 338–339
laser intelligence, synthesizing mind
    type and, 15
Law of the Few, 91
leadership and change imperatives. *See*
    solar system reform metaphor
leadership as line management, 331–332
leadership development, First Way of
    Venus and, 329
leadership networking, in RATL, 340
leadership preparation, policies for 21st
    century demands, 41, 44–46
leadership quality, Second Way of Mars
    and, 331
leadership sustainability, Fourth Way of
    Earth and, 345
league tables
    Second Way of Mars and, 330
    Third Way of Mercury and, 338
LEAP framework. *See* National
    Leadership Council for Liberal
    Education and America's Promise
    (2007)
learn element of assessments, 311–312,
    318–319, 320–321
learning networks. *See* social networks
learning objects, description of, 260–261
learning principles, adoption of,
    151–152, 153
Learning Through Interests/Internships,
    136–137
Learn More concept, 104–110, 112–113
left brain capacities, mind types and, 28
Leu, O'Byrne, Zawilinski, McVerry, and
    Everett-Cacopardo (2009), 299–300
Leu, Zawilinski, Castek, Banerjee,
    Housand, Liu, et al. (2007), 67
Leu and the University of Connecticut
    New Literacy Research Team (n.d.), 234
Levy and Murnane (2004), 52

lifelong learning, online courses and, 263

life skills, Teach Less, Learn More and, 105, 108. *See also specific skill areas*

Lincoln, Abraham, 24, 314

linguistic intelligence, mind types and, 26

linkability, sharing and, 291

literary syntheses, 15–16

literature. *See* reading

Littky, Dennis, 136

live debates, technology and culture of schooling, 282

logical intelligence, mind types and, 26

Long (n.d.), 124

Lotus Notes platform, 128

LSR 2.0, 338–339

M

Madison, James, 210

magnetic resonance imaging scans, 247–248

Maguire, Mary Ida, 3

Malaysia, online behavior, 216

management of information. *See also* access to information

rationale for formulating skills, 53–54

sharing online, potentials and pitfalls of, 293–295

manners

online relationships and, 216

technology policy and, 227–229

mapping

concept map, 191

of curriculum, 164–165

Marcos, Eric, 280–281

market choice systems, Second Way of Mars and, 330–331

Mars, Second Way of, 330–332

Marzano (2003), 152

Massachusetts Institute of Technology (2009), 262

mathematics education. *See also* STEM disciplines

assessing assessments, 316–318, 322

computational knowledge engines, 280

creating mind type, 17

disciplined mind type, 12

Framework for 21st Century Learning and, xxiv

implementation framework and, 154, 162–163

international benchmarking and, 71

PISA focus and, 69

policies for 21st century demands, 35, 36

problem-based learning and, 177

professional learning communities and, 85–86

screencast tutorials, 281

U.S. curriculum background, ix

virtual manipulatives and, 261

meaning, thirst for, 28

Means, Toyama, Murphy, Bakia, and Jones (2009), 262

media literacy. *See* digital literacy frameworks; digital literacy projects

mediation of conflicts, 205–206. *See also* conflict resolution

mentors

Learning Through Interests/ Internships, 136–137

Third Way of Mercury and, 339–342

Mercury, Third Way of, 332–342

messaging, electronic. *See* email and messaging

Metiri Group (2008), 268

MetLife (2008), 238

Metropolitan Regional Career and Technical Center, 128, 136–138, 139, 144

middle schools

framework for assessments, 313–314, 316–318, 322

modeling and, 231

participatory learning, 264–265

policies for 21st century demands, 47

problem-based learning, 186, 191–194, 195

school building design, 140, 141, 316–318, 322, 323

visualization and, 251–252

Mikkelson and Mikkelson (2007), 189

mind types

assessment and, 26–27

changes in education and, 9–10

clarifying comments, 10–11

cognitive types/human sphere, 10, 19

creating mind overview, 16–19

disciplined mind overview, 11–13

ethical mind overview, 21–23
integrating into one person, 10, 29–30
multiple intelligences and, 11, 25–26
overview of book, 4
Pink's work and, 27–28
relationships among, 17
respectful mind overview, 19–21
synthesizing mind overview, 13–16
tensions between, 10, 24–25
mining of networks, 293
ministries of education
policies for 21st century demands, 43
Teach Less, Learn More and, 100
minority students. *See also* diversity
achievement gaps and, xviii
cooperative efforts and, 213
global interdependence and, 207–208
mission statements, implementation
framework and, 151, 152
MI theory. *See* multiple intelligences
theory
mobile phones. *See* phones
Modality Principle, 249
modeling
of balance, 300–301
as focus lesson element, 231, 233
independent learning and, 238–239
network literacy and, 296, 299
virtual global classrooms and, 287
Molière, Jean-Baptiste, 23
monarchies, loyalty in, 209
Monsanto ad (2009), 176
Moodle platform, 102
moral bond, in democracies, 209
moral communities, identity formation
and, 217
moral development theory, 213
MP3 players
access to technology, 230
bans on technology, 227
MRI scans, 247–248
Multimedia Principle, 248
multimodality, visualization and,
248–251, 255
multinational corporations, participatory culture of, 265
multiple intelligences theory, 11, 25–26.
See also specific intelligences
MySpace. *See also* social networks

digital generation and, 222
sharing online, potentials and pitfalls
of, 291
technology and culture of schooling, 278
virtual global classrooms and, 288

N

Nair, Fielding, and Lackney (2005), 126,
143
Nair, Prakash, 126, 128
Nation, Vision for, 97, 98
national assessment banks, professional
learning communities and, 86, 88
National Commission on Teaching and
America's Future, 92
National Council of Teachers of English
(2008), 293
National Council of Teachers of English
(2009), 224–225
National Council of Teachers of
Mathematics (2009), 261
National Leadership Council for Liberal
Education and America's Promise
(2007), 56, 59–61
naturalistic intelligence, mind types
and, 26
natural language queries, rationale for
formulating skills, 53
NCREL/Metiri framework. *See*
North Central Regional Education
Laboratory and Metiri Group (2003)
Nelson (2009), 319
network literacy, shift to, 287, 295–302
networks, online. *See* online communities; social networks
New Commission on the Skills of the
American Workforce (2007), 331, 334
New Line Learning Academy, school
building design, 128, 142–144
Newmann, Fred, 267
Newmann and Associates (1996), 196
new media, Jenkins' digital literacies
and, 65. *See also* technology; *specific
aspects*
New Media Consortium (2009), 301–302
newspapers
league tables in, 338

technology and, 244, 288–289, 298
tensions between mind types, 25
New Tech High @ Coppell, school building design, 128, 132–136, 144
New Tech High Learning System, school building design, 128
New Technology Foundation, school building design, 120–122, 128
New Technology High School system, school building design, 120, 123–125, 128, 129–131
New Trier East High School, 3
New York, problem-based learning, 191–192, 195
New York State Standards (n.d.), 191–192
New York Times, 250
Nielsen Company (2009), 244
19th century education, virtual global classrooms and, 287
Ning, technology functions, 226
No Child Left Behind Act
    framework comparisons, 57
    implementation framework and, 157
    policies for 21st century demands, 34
    Second Way of Mars and, 330, 337–338
nonstandardized versus standardized conditions, 307–309, 318–322
Nordin (2007), 187
Nordin (2009), 196
North Carolina, problem-based learning, 194
North Central Regional Education Laboratory and Metiri Group (2003), 56, 58–60, 67–68, 73
note taking, 277, 281, 294–295
NTF. *See* New Technology Foundation

O

Obama, Barack
    community organizing and, 344
    Framework for 21st Century Learning and, 1
    problem-based learning and, 197
    social networks and campaigns, 288
ocean life example, 185–186
OECD. *See* Organisation for Economic Co-operation and Development *headings*
O'Hara (2009), 196

online communities. *See also* social networks
    digital literacy frameworks and, 65–67
    identity formation and, 211, 217
    participatory learning and, 264–267
    relationships in, 215
online courses. *See also* virtual global classrooms
    democratization of knowledge, 262–263
    technology and culture of schooling, 277
online games
    chart example, 256
    digital citizenship skills and, 211
    relationships and, 216
    technology in daily practice, 298
    virtual high school course, 262
    visualization and, 250
online identities
    assessment of, 215, 218
    digital footprints and, 291–292
    technology in daily practice, 299
    virtual global classrooms and, 288
online networks. *See* online communities; social networks
online relationships. *See also* interpersonal relationships
    changes in relationships, 214–218
    modeling balance, 300–301
    network literacy and, 295–296
    sharing online, potentials and pitfalls of, 292–294
    technology in daily practice, 298–299
online reputations, 292. *See also* online identities
online resumes, 291
online testing. *See* computer-based testing; testing
Open Architecture Network (2008), 125–126
openness of content versus secrecy, 309–310, 318–321
Organisation for Economic Co-operation and Development (2001), 333
Organisation for Economic Co-operation and Development (2005), 56, 59, 67, 69, 73
Organisation for Economic Co-operation and Development (2008), 337, 341

organization of information, rationale for formulating skills, 53. *See also* management of information
originality of synthesizing, 17
outcomes. *See* student outcomes

P

pagers, technology changes and, 223
Paine, Steve, xxv
Paleolithic times, curriculum satire, ix–x
paper-based information storage. *See also specific aspects*
    framework comparisons, 53
    sharing online, potentials and pitfalls of, 294
    from static to digital technology, 276–278
paper-based testing, advances in assessment, 69, 70, 71. *See also* assessments; testing
parents. *See also* stakeholders
    Fourth Way of Earth and, 343–344
    network literacy and, 301
    policies for 21st century demands, 46
    respectful mind type and, 19
    Second Way of Mars and, 330–331
participation model, 266–267
participatory learning, as innovation, 263–267, 267–269. *See also specific aspects*
Partnership for 21st Century Skills (2003), 119. *See also* Framework for 21st Century Learning
Partnership for 21st Century Skills (2006), 56–61, 63, 67, 73. *See also* Framework for 21st Century Learning
Partnership for 21st Century Skills (2007), 99. *See also* Framework for 21st Century Learning
Partnership for 21st Century Skills (2009). *See also* Framework for 21st Century Learning
    framework definitions document, 149
    framework flyer, xiii–xix
    official website, 334–335
    support systems document, 77–78, 85, 89
passion-based learning connections

bow-drill set video example, 285–288, 293–294
modeling balance, 300
network literacy and, 296–297
sharing, potentials and pitfalls of, 291, 293–295, 299
unrestricted learning as challenge, 290
virtual global classroom's rise, 286–288
pathological forms, of disciplined mind type, 13
Patterson et al. (2008), 91, 92
Paul Hamlyn Foundation and the Innovation Unit (2008), 119–120
pay for teachers, 44, 89
PBL. *See* problem-based learning; project-based learning
PDAs, 102
Peacemaker Peer-Mediation Program, 205
PeBL Web portal, 128
peer-driven networks, 339–342
peer-mediation procedures, 205–206
peer pressure, social networks and, 91
peer support, intentional instruction and, 230
pencil-and-paper test. *See* paper-based testing
perennial skills, rationale for formulating skills, 52–54
performance assessments. *See* assessments
periodic table, Facebook example, 264–265, 266
personal experience as persuader, 92
personal intelligences, mind types and, 26
personality, creating mind type and, 17–18, 30
perspective taking, cooperative learning and, 213
phones
    access to technology, 224, 230
    culture of schooling and, 277
    Iraqi elections and, 250
    modeling and, 233
    privacy issues, 216
    Teach Less, Learn More and, 102
    technology bans and, 227
    technology changes and, 222, 223
    technology in daily practice, 298

technology use statistics, 244

photos. *See also* cameras
  independent learning and, 239
  online relationships and, 216
  social networks and, 289, 291, 294, 299
  technology changes and, 222
  technology use statistics, 244

physical aggression. *See* aggression;
  bullying

physical learning facilities. *See* school
  buildings

Piaget, Jean, 213

Pianta et al. (2007), 154–155

Picciano and Seaman (2009), 262

pictures. *See* graphics; photos

pilot schools, Teach Less, Learn More
  and, 99, 112. *See also* Teach Less,
  Learn More Ignite Schools

Pink (2006), 27–28

PISA. *See* Programme for International
  Student Assessment

plagiarism, technology and, 277

planets as reform metaphor. *See* solar
  system reform metaphor

play side of cognition, 27

PLCs. *See* professional learning
  communities

pluralism, global interdependence and,
  207–208

podcasts, independent learning and, 238

policy changes. *See also specific aspects*
  Framework for 21st Century Learning
    and, 1
  international benchmarking and, 72
  overview of book, 4
  policies for 21st century demands,
    33–48
  technology policy, 226–230

political discourse, democracy and, 210

political issues. *See also specific aspects*
  framework for assessments and, 323
  policies for 21st century demands, 43
  rationale for formulating skills, 54–55
  social networks and campaigns, 288
  Third Way of Mercury and, 337–339,
    341

population increase, global interdependence and, 209

postsecondary education

creative entrepreneurship and, 212
  CWRA and, 68–69
  democratization of knowledge, 262
  Framework for 21st Century Learning
    and, xviii, xxi–xxiii
  LEAP framework and, 59–61
  problem-based learning and, 188, 196

Power of Context, 91

prejudicial judgments
  global interdependence and, 207
  respectful mind type and, 20–21

Prensky (2008), 119, 120, 226

primary schools. *See* elementary schools

principals. *See also* leadership *headings*
  First Way of Venus and, 329
  PISA overview, 69
  policies for 21st century demands, 46
  professional learning communities
    and, 88–89
  Second Way of Mars and, 331–332

principles of learning, adoption of,
  151–152, 153

privacy issues. *See also* safety issues
  framework for assessments and, 319
  online relationships and, 216
  social networks and, 288–289, 291, 299

problem-based learning
  advertisements and, 175–176
  challenges of 21st century, 176–177, 197
  community building example, 186
  curriculum development for, 190–194
  definition of, 177–179
  effectiveness of, 195–196
  inquiry's role in, 176, 180–183,
    187–190, 193–196
  key elements of, 179
  KWHLAQ example, 180–185
  literature example, 186–187
  ocean life example, 185–186
  overview of book, 5
  school building design and, 120–121
  Teach Less, Learn More and, 111–112
  technology use and, 194–195

problem solving. *See also* problem-based
  learning
  constructive controversy and, 203,
    212–213
  Framework for 21st Century Learning
    and, xviii, xx, xxiv

integrative negotiations and, 204–206
policies for 21st century demands, 35
rationale for formulating skills, 54
technology planning and, 279
visualization and, 253
productivity software, 70
professional development
    First Way of Venus and, 329
    Fourth Way of Earth and, 344
    Framework for 21st Century Learning
        and, xxv
    network literacy and, 296–298, 301
    policies for 21st century demands, 40,
        43, 44, 46, 48
    professional learning communities
        and, 89
    rationale for formulating skills, 55–56
    Teach Less, Learn More and, 100
    technology and culture of school-
        ing, 279
professional learning communities
    behavioral changes and, 78, 80–84, 92
    cultural shifts and, 77–80, 85, 90–91
    future work of, 84–89
    learning by doing, 92–93
    need for, 77–78, 89
    network literacy and, 301
    as norm, 89–92
    overview of book, 4
    policies for 21st century demands, 45
    Teach Less, Learn More and, 99–114
    Third Way of Mercury and, 338
    Three Big Ideas of, 78
Professional Learning Communities
    vision, 99–100
Programme for International Student
    Assessment
    Fourth Way of Earth and, 342
    framework comparisons, 69
    Framework for 21st Century Learning
        and, xviii, xxiv
    policies for 21st century demands,
        35, 46
Progress in International Reading
    Literacy Study, 72
progressive teaching. See child-centered
    teaching
project-based learning, school building
    design and, 120–145

Project Tomorrow (2009), 225
Promethean ActivBoard, 194
prosocial behavior
    identity formation and, 217–218
    online games and, 216
protosynthesis, testing of, 15
proximity standard for design, 258
Public Street Met Campus, 137
purpose, establishing for focus models,
    231

Q

Qualifications and Curriculum
    Authority, 70
quality of teachers. See teacher effective-
    ness; teacher quality
question framework, problem-based
    learning and, 190
quickwrites, independent learning and,
    238
quizzes. See also testing
    implementation framework and, 167
    policies for 21st century demands,
        39–40
    professional learning communities
        and, 86

R

Raising Achievement Transforming
    Learning project, 339–342
reading education
    collaborative tasks and, 234
    independent learning and, 238–239
    international benchmarking and, 72
    PISA focus and, 69
    policies for 21st century demands, 36
    problem-based learning and, 178, 186
    reframing online reading and writ-
        ing, 299–300
    Teach Less, Learn More and, 110–111
    technology and culture of school-
        ing, 279
read/write Web. See Web 2.0 media
real names, use of online, 291, 299
Real Simple Syndication, 299
real-world accomplishments, corner-
    stone tasks and, 159–164

real-world approach to learning. *See* problem-based learning

reciprocal teaching, Internet, 234, 235–236

reform, solar system metaphor for. *See* solar system reform metaphor

Rehak, Rosemary, 130

Reich (2000), 333

relationships, interpersonal. *See* interpersonal relationships

religious issues
tensions between mind types, 25
thirst for meaning and, 28

Renaissance, educational change in, 9

repetition standard for design, 255, 257

reputations, online, 292. *See also* online identities

resource allocation. *See* funding issues

respectful mind type
assessment of, 27
description of, 10, 19–21
integration of mind types, 30
multiple intelligences and, 26
right brain capacities and, 28
survival of species and, 11
tensions between mind types, 24–25

responsibility, gradual release model for, 231–239

results as term, 307

resumes, online, 291

Rhode Island, school building design in, 128, 136–138, 139

Rice University (n.d.), 262

Richardson (2008), 195

right brain capacities, mind types and, 27–28

rigor, redefinition of, xxiii–xxiv

Rigsbee (2009), 130, 132

Romeo and Juliet discussion board, 238

Rooke and Torbert (2005), 269

Roosevelt, Franklin, 307

Rosewood Elementary School, 194

Route 21 website, xxvi

Royer (2000), 187

RSS (Real Simple Syndication), 299

Rubenstein (2008), 195

rudeness. *See also* aggression
online relationships and, 216
technology policy and, 227–229

S

saber-toothed tiger scaring, curriculum satire, ix–x

sadism, empathy and, 28

safety issues. *See also* privacy issues
technology in daily practice, 299
virtual global classrooms and, 286–288

salaries for teachers, 44, 89

San Diego Unified School District, 138

scaffolding
in gradual release of responsibility model, 233–234
innovation and, 247, 255
policies for 21st century demands, 39

Schank, Roger, 126, 128

scheduling. *See also* time management
policies for 21st century demands, 47
professional learning communities and, 83, 89
rationale for formulating skills, 55

Schlechty (1990), 333

Schmidt, McKnight, and Raizen (1997), 154, 155

Schneider, Maria, 322

Schoenberg, Arnold, 322

scholarly disciplines, disciplined mind type and, 12

school buildings
"Design Your Ideal School" assessment, 316–318, 322, 323
digital generation and, 118–119
emergence of changes, 117–118
from innovative pedagogy to innovative facilities, 122–123
language of school design, 126–127, 130, 143
learning environment appearance, 123–124
learning environment examples, 128–145
new skills and pedagogy, 119–122
overview of book, 5
student input regarding, 124–126

school culture. *See* culture of schooling

school improvement network (RATL), 339–342

Schooling by Design framework, 5, 149–150. *See also* implementation framework

school leader preparation. *See* leadership preparation

school principals. *See* principals

school reform, solar system metaphor for. *See* solar system reform metaphor

School Works (2005), 125

science education. *See also* STEM disciplines

advances in assessments, 69, 71

collaborative tasks and, 234

creating mind type, 17

democratization of knowledge, 261, 263

disciplined mind type, 12

Framework for 21st Century Learning and, xxiv

implementation framework and, 154–155, 162–165

international benchmarking and, 71

modeling and, 231, 233

participatory learning and, 264–265, 266

policies for 21st century demands, 35, 36

problem-based learning and, 177, 185–186, 194, 195

U.S. curriculum background, ix

scientific method, elements of, 164–165

Scott, Dred, 314

screencast tutorials, 280–281

searchlight intelligence, synthesizing mind type and, 15

secondary schools. *See also* high schools; middle schools

citizenship skills, 210

modeling and, 231

school building design, 117–118, 120, 124

Teach Less, Learn More, 110, 111–112

Third Way of Mercury and, 339–342

Secondat, Charles de, 209

Second Way of Mars, 330–332, 337–338, 339, 345

self-esteem

idealization of fashion models and, 252

identity formation and, 217

self-interest, ethical mind and, 21, 22

service economy, Framework for 21st Century Learning and, xvi–xvii

share element of assessments, 311–315, 318, 323

sharing on social networks. *See* social networks

Shirky (2008), 289, 301

SHW Group architects, 125, 133–135

Silva (2008), 68–70, 72

SimCalcMathWorlds, 261–262

simulations, visual, democratization of knowledge, 261–262

sincerity in online relationships. *See* trust

Singapore

online behavior, 216

Third Way of Mercury and, 341

visionary education framework. *See* Teach Less, Learn More framework

"sit and git" trainings, 301

Skype

school building design and, 127

technology and culture of schooling, 278, 282

small-group skills, global interdependence and, 208

Smart Boards, 222

SMART goals, professional learning communities and, 83

smartphones. *See* phones

Smith (2009), 285–288, 293–294, 302

social contract, Framework for 21st Century Learning and, xvii

social graph, description of, 211

social issues. *See also specific issues*

change imperatives and, 327

First Way of Venus and, 328

Fourth Way of Earth and, 342

Third Way of Mercury and, 336–339

social justice. *See also* inequality as issue

change imperatives and, 327

Fourth Way of Earth and, 346

Third Way of Mercury and, 336, 337

social networks. *See also* online communities; Web 2.0 media; *specific aspects*

bow-drill set video and, 285–288, 293–294

digital citizenship skills and, 211

homework "sharing" via, 277

as learning tools, 285–302

network literacy, 287, 295–302
overview of book, 6
problem-based learning and, 195
professional learning communities
    and, 91
relationship changes and, 213
sharing, potentials and pitfalls of, 215,
    216, 290–295, 298–299
shift to network literacy, 295–302
Teach Less, Learn More and, 102
technology and culture of school-
    ing, 282
technology use statistics, 244–245
unrestricted learning as challenge,
    289–295
virtual global classroom's rise, 286–289
social studies education. *See also* history
    education
curriculum development example,
    191–193
framework for assessments, 313–314
solar system reform metaphor
change imperatives for 21st century,
    327–328
First Way of Venus, 328–329, 330, 331,
    345
Fourth Way of Earth, 342–347
overview of book, 7
Second Way of Mars, 330–332,
    337–338, 339, 345
Third Way of Mercury, 332–342, 343,
    345–346
sound, processing of, 247–249
South Africa, Gapminder tool example,
    252–254
South Carolina, problem-based learn-
    ing, 194
South Maidstone Federation, 142
Spatial Contiguity Principle, 248, 255
spatial intelligence, mind types and, 26
Specialist Schools and Academies Trust,
    339
special needs students
cooperative efforts and, 213
Framework for 21st Century Learning
    and, 2
problem-based learning and, 177, 186
professional development and, 45
Split Attention Principle, 249

spray-and-pray planning model, 276–277
stakeholders. *See also specific types*
Framework for 21st Century Learning
    and, xvi, xxvi–xxvii, 307
mission statement and, 151
policies for 21st century demands, 46
standardized assessments. *See* assess-
    ments; testing
standards
Common Core State Standards proj-
    ect, 84–85
ETS standards, 56, 67
Fourth Way of Earth and, 344
Framework for 21st Century Learning
    and, 1
framework for assessments, 305
implementation framework and, 154
international benchmarking and,
    72, 85
ISTE standards, 56, 61–63, 67
policies for 21st century demands, 34,
    37–39, 41–42, 44
problem-based learning and, 191–192,
    197
professional learning communities
    and, 85, 87
school building design and, 119–120
Second Way of Mars and, 330–331, 339
Teach Less, Learn More and, 103
state governments. *See also specific
    states*
Common Core State Standards proj-
    ect, 84–85
equity issues in education, 48
Framework for 21st Century Learning
    and, xxiv–xxv, xxvii, 1–3
international benchmarking and,
    71–72, 85
New York State Standards, 191–192
STEM disciplines. *See also* mathematics
    education; science education
Framework for 21st Century Learning
    and, xix
right brain capacities and, 28
Stephen (2009), 140–142
Stickiness Factor, 91
Stickler Group, 140
story side of cognition, 27
Stravinsky, Igor, 322

Strobel and van Barneveld (2009), 195
student achievement. *See also*
  assessments
  cooperative learning and, 202–203
  creative entrepreneurship and, 212
  as equated with tests, 307
  Fourth Way of Earth and, 342–343, 345
  Framework for 21st Century Learning
    and, xviii
  implementation framework and,
    163–164
  international benchmarking and, 72
  multimodality and, 249
  policies for 21st century demands, 35,
    38–39
  professional learning communities
    and, 77, 82–83, 88, 91
  Second Way of Mars and, 331, 345
  Teach Less, Learn More and, 113
  Third Way of Mercury and, 332,
    338–341
student advisors, policies for 21st
  century demands, 46
student assessments. *See* assessments
student input
  on school buildings, 124–126
  on technology purchases, 225
student outcomes. *See also* assessments
  cooperative learning and, 203
  Framework for 21st Century Learning
    and, xiv, xx–xxviii, 1
  implementation framework and,
    149–171
  policies for 21st century demands,
    39–40, 48
  problem-based learning and, 191–192
  professional learning communities
    and, 81–82, 84, 92
  results as term, 307
  school building design and, 119,
    121–123
  Teach Less, Learn More and, 104, 113
  Third Way of Mercury and, 339–340
student teaching, professional learning
  communities and, 87
student teamwork. *See* cooperative
  learning
subject matter, discipline distinguished
  from, 12

support systems, educational. *See* educational support systems
sustainability
  Fourth Way of Earth and, 344, 345
  Third Way of Mercury and, 337
symphony side of cognition, 27
synthesizing mind type
  assessment of, 26, 27
  description of, 10, 13–16, 19
  integration of mind types, 29–30
  multiple intelligences and, 26
  relationships among mind types, 17
  right brain capacities and, 27, 28
  tensions between mind types, 25
systemic supports, educational. *See*
  educational support systems

T

tags, use of, 264, 294–295
Teach 21 website, xxv, 2
teacher assistants, Fourth Way of Earth
  and, 343
teacher collaboration. *See also* professional learning communities
  network literacy and, 301
  policies for 21st century demands, 45
  Teach Less, Learn More and, 100–101
teacher education, accreditation and,
  87–88. *See also* professional development; professional learning
  communities
teacher effectiveness
  Framework for 21st Century Learning
    and, xxv–xxvi
  policies for 21st century demands, 36,
    42, 44–45
  professional learning communities
    and, 81, 84, 88
teacher modeling, as focus lesson
  element, 231, 233
teacher pay, 44, 89
teacher preparation, policies for 21st
  century demands, 36, 41, 44–45. *See
  also* professional development
teacher quality. *See also* teacher
  effectiveness
  First Way of Venus and, 329
  Fourth Way of Earth and, 342–343

policies for 21st century demands, 41
Second Way of Mars and, 331
technology and culture of schooling, 281
Third Way of Mercury and, 332,
338–339
teacher resources. *See* instructional
resources
teaching-learning connection,
Framework for 21st Century Learning
and, 2
teaching process. *See* instructional
process
Teach Less, Learn More concept,
100–110, 279
Teach Less, Learn More framework
background of, 97
bridge to 21st century, 113–114
challenge of change, 112–113
elementary school example, 110–111
Learn More concept, 104–110, 112–113
overview of book, 5
secondary school example, 111–112
Teach Less concept, 101–104, 107
technology planning and, 279
vision for collaboration, 97, 99–100
vision for education, 97, 98–99
vision for implementation, 97, 99,
106, 109
vision for nation, 97, 98
Teach Less, Learn More Ignite Schools
bridge to 21st century, 113
Learn More concept and, 103
Vision for Collaboration and, 100
Vision for Education and, 99
Teach Less, Learn More vision, 98–99
Teach Less concept, 101–104, 107
teaming, innovation and, 263, 265, 266,
267. *See also* collaboration *headings;*
cooperative learning
team versus individual results, 310–311
technology. *See also* STEM disciplines;
specific aspects
alternative frameworks and, 67–68
bans on, 226–228, 245, 282, 296
critical thinking and search results,
275–276
culture of schooling and, 282
digital citizenship skills and, 211

digital literacy frameworks and,
61–67, 73
function as consideration, 223–227,
239–240
global connections and, 302
global economy and, xvi
independent learning and, 231–232,
237–239
innovation through, 243–269
intentional instruction and, 230–239
Key Stage 3 ICT Literacy Assessment, 70
major frameworks and, 56–60, 73
national policy and, 33–34
network literacy and, 296–298
overview of book, 6
as part of daily practice, 298–300
planning and culture of schooling,
275–283
policy revisions for, 226–230
problem-based learning and, 194–195
professional learning communities
and, 85–87
rationale for formulating skills, 51–53,
55–56
relationship changes and, 213–218
school building design and, 118–119,
123–145
scope of student experience with,
221–224
statistics on use of, 243–245, 278, 291
Teach Less, Learn More and, 101–103,
107–108, 110–112
Third Way of Mercury and, 336
"unlearning curve" and, 298
U.S. curriculum background, ix
virtual global classrooms and,
288–289
Technology Entertainment Design
website, 255, 257
tectonic shift, organizational change as,
289, 301
telecommunications technology. *See*
technology
temperament, creating mind type and,
17–18, 30
Temporal Contiguity Principle, 249
terminology (in general)
for 21st century skills, xvi, 51
for digital environments, 260–263

testing. *See also* assessments
  assessing assessments, 315–318
  Fourth Way of Earth and, 342–345
  framework comparisons, 55, 58, 68–72
  framework for assessments, 305–323
  history of, 305, 306
  implementation framework and, 157–158
  nonstandardized versus standardized conditions, 307–309, 318–322
  openness of content versus secrecy, 309–310, 318–321
  policies for 21st century demands, 37–42
  professional learning communities and, 86
  Second Way of Mars and, 330, 331
  Teach Less, Learn More and, 101, 109, 113
  Third Way of Mercury and, 336, 338–342
Texas, school building design in, 128, 132–136
text, coding, 111
text, processing of, 247–249
text messaging. *See* email and messaging
Thinking Schools, Learning Nation vision, 98, 113, 279
thinking skills. *See* cognitive skills
Third Way of Mercury, 332–342, 343, 345–346
Three Big Ideas, 78
Tight, Loose, Tight vision, 99, 106, 109
time management. *See also* scheduling
  network literacy and, 296
  policies for 21st century demands, 45, 46–47
TIMSS. *See* Trends in International Mathematics and Science Study
tipping point
  innovation and, 246
  professional learning communities and, 90–92
  social change and, xiii, xxvii
  social networks and, 290
TLLM. *See* Teach Less, Learn More *headings*
torture, democracy and, 337

touch, relationships and, 216–217
Tower Hamlets, 343
transfer of learning
  framework comparisons, 54–55
  implementation framework and, 156, 158–166
  school building design and, 133–134
  social networks and, 289, 291, 296, 298, 300–301
transparency
  assessments and, 119, 121
  Framework for 21st Century Learning and, xxviii
  professional learning communities and, 92
  Third Way of Mercury and, 339
Trends in International Mathematics and Science Study, 71, 154–155
trust. *See also* safety issues
  First Way of Venus and, 329
  network literacy and, 296
  Second Way of Mars and, 331
  sharing online, potentials and pitfalls of, 215, 292, 294
trustees of ethics, 23
Tucson, AZ, Framework for 21st Century Learning and, 2
tutorial screencasts, 280–281
20th century education
  curriculum changes, ix
  curriculum legacy, 54–55, 59
  definition of "learning," 246
  digital literacy frameworks and, 63, 66
  information access comparison, 53
  nonstandardized versus standardized conditions, 307–309
  openness of content versus secrecy, 309
  reconceptualization as challenge, 72
  Teach Less, Learn More and, 98
  technology policy and, 228
  virtual global classrooms and, 287
Twitter
  guided instruction and, 233
  Iraqi elections and, 250
  social networks and, 293
  technology functions, 226
  technology use statistics, 278
two-way pedagogy, policies for 21st century demands, 40

U

understand element of assessments, 311–314, 319

Understanding by Design principles, 5

United Kingdom. *See also* Great Britain
　framework for assessments, 305
　policies for 21st century demands, 38
　school building design in, 117–120, 124–125, 128, 142–145
　Third Way of Mercury and, 338–342, 343

United Nations, Gapminder tool and, 252

United States. *See also specific entities and locations*
　change imperatives, 327
　competitiveness of. *See* competitiveness
　curriculum background, ix
　curriculum standards coordination, 72
　equity issues in education, 47–48
　Fourth Way of Earth and, 345–346
　Framework for 21st Century Learning and, xvi–xix, xxi, xxvii–xxviii
　implementation framework and, 154, 157
　mind types, 18–19, 24–25
　online behavior, 216
　online courses, 262
　pivotal periods of change, 9–10
　policies for 21st century demands, 4, 33–48
　problem-based learning, 175–176, 197
　professional learning communities, 84–85, 86
　school building design in, 117–120, 128–142, 144–145
　technology use statistics, 244–245
　Third Way of Mercury and, 333–334, 337–338

units for online courses, 263

universalistic thinking, ethical mind and, 21

university education. *See* postsecondary education

University of Waterloo, 196

U.S. Bill of Rights, 25

U.S. Constitution, curriculum development example, 191–193

U.S. Department of Education (2009), 245

U.S. Environmental Protection Agency (n.d.), 261

Ustream website, 294

V

value systems, online communities and, 216, 264. *See also* ethics

Venus, First Way of, 328–329

verbal aggression. *See* aggression; bullying

videos. *See also* YouTube
　bow-drill set video, 285–288, 293–294
　independent learning and, 239
　Iraqi elections and, 250
　online relationships and, 216
　privacy issues, 216
　screencast tutorials, 280–281
　social networks and, 291, 294, 299
　technology changes and, 222
　technology policy and, 229–230
　technology use statistics, 243, 291
　virtual global classrooms and, 289

violence in online games, 216

virtual communities. *See* online communities

virtual global classrooms. *See also* online courses
　bow-drill set video, 285–288
　rise of, 286–289

virtual manipulatives, as learning objects, 261

virtual performance assessments, 70, 71. *See also* assessments; computer-based testing

virtue, in democracies, 209

Vision for a Nation, 97, 98

Vision for Collaboration, 97, 99–100

Vision for Education, 97, 98–99

Vision for Implementation, 97, 99, 106, 109

Vision of the Graduate program, 187–188

visualization, as innovation, 247–259, 267–269

visual simulations, democratization of knowledge, 259–262

voice chat, 216, 233

W

Wagner (2008), 322, 334

Wagner, Richard, 322
Walser (2008), 176
Warrenville, IL, Framework for 21st Century Learning and, 2
Washington District Elementary School, 2
Washor (2003), 118, 122, 126
Washor, Elliot, 136, 137–138
Web 2.0 media. *See also* social networks; *specific aspects*
  access to technology and, 230
  digital literacy frameworks and, 65–67
  homework "sharing" via, 277
  participatory learning and, 264–265
  school building design and, 127
  sharing online, potentials and pitfalls of, 291
  technology use statistics, 244–245
Web 3.0 media, 322
Web-based Inquiry Science website, 263
Web logs. *See* blogs
Web searches. *See also* Google
  contextual capability and, 53
  critical-thinking skills and, 275–276
  democratization of knowledge, 260
  RSS and, 299
  sharing, potentials and pitfalls of, 291–292
Web technology. *See* technology
Weigel, James, and Gardner (2009), 290
Weinberger (2007), 53
welfare state, First Way of Venus and, 328
West Virginia, Framework for 21st Century Learning and, xxv, 2
whiteboards, interactive, 102, 117, 134, 222, 225
Wiggins and McTighe (2007), 149–150, 158–159, 164–165
Wikipedia, 65, 295
wiki technology
  collaborative tasks and, 234
  culture of schooling and, 276
  framework comparisons, 63
wireless technology. *See* technology; *specific aspects*
Wolframalpha knowledge engine, 280
workforce issues
  career counseling, 45
  change imperatives, 328
  digital footprints and, 291–292

  disciplined mind type and, 12
  ethical mind type and, 22, 23
  First Way of Venus and, 328
  Framework for 21st Century Learning and, xvi–xxiii
  framework for assessments and, 310–311
  global work ethic as goal, 276, 278–282
  rationale for formulating skills, 52–53
  Second Way of Mars and, 331
  tensions between mind types, 24–25
  Third Way of Mercury and, 333–336, 341
working memory, visualization and, 248, 255
World Bank, 180
World Commission on Environment and Development (1987), 209
world economy. *See* global economy
writing conferences, recording of, 233–234
writing tasks. *See also* blogs
  analytic, assessment of, 69
  collaborative, 234, 281
  group reports, 204
  reframing online reading and writing, 299–300

Y

Yenka programming tools, 261
YouTube
  bow-drill set video, 285–288, 293–294
  Iraqi elections and, 250
  privacy issues, 216
  sharing online, potentials and pitfalls of, 291
  technology changes and, 222
  technology policy and, 229–230
  technology use statistics, 243, 278

Z

Zhao (2009), 334